TAKING

PAYSHENCE

**A FATHER'S QUEST AGAINST THE STATE
TO GET HIS LITTLE GIRL BACK**

by DeOne Ehlers-Rhorer

ISBN: 978-1-7239-6709-2
WGA Registration #1926967

Forward

This book is divided into two parts;

Life before Payshence was Taken

and Life After

NAMES OF THE CHARACTERS
HAVE BEEN CHANGED

To contact the author, email TakingPayshence@gmail.com
For updates, see author's blog on Amazon.com

Dedication

This book is dedicated to all those who have loved a child with the entirety or their soul and then had that child removed from their life by no act on their part.

To the grandmas and grandpas, the brothers and sisters, the step and half siblings, aunts and uncles, friends…anyone who grew to love a precious child but, for one reason or another, found themselves without options, without rights, without a way to continue that priceless relationship.

But most of all, this book is for Payshence because whatever the outcome, she needs to know her Daddy was always thinking of her, always fighting for her, always praying for Angels to surround and preserve her long enough for her to be in his protective arms again.

TABLE OF CONTENTS

CHAPTER 1
THE LITTLE TEXAN FIGHTER

He was the new kid. A sixth-grader with something to prove. Fresh from a Texas ranch where there was nothing but bluebonnet fields and long horn cattle as far as the eye could see; thrown into civilization at its finest - Chesterfield, Utah - the *west side* of Salt Lake City.

She was on the swing set. Several boys already had a claim to Her so He knew He had to earn Her. He did it the Texas way - a physical challenge of strength. He won Her quickly with the first boy going yellow belly and the two others meeting after school at the river bottoms, along with their older brothers for back up. He took the two boys quickly. But the brothers, impressed by His speed and strength, offered to give Him a ride home. He was quite sure if He got in their car, they would take Him somewhere without witnesses, but He went anyway. To His surprise, one brother turned to Him, nervous and ready in the rear seat, and asked his name.

"Jody," He responded. "Jody Rhorer."

"Well Jody Rhorer, you just beat up my brother. Congratulations." He handed Jody a beer. "Where you live bro? We'll take you home."

That day Jody gained some new friends and Teri, his first love. From then on, Jody pledged to be Teri's protector. He moved on to junior high, while she, one year younger, stayed back in elementary school. When class was out, he would take the bus to the overpass near her school, to see her home safely.

But home was *not* a safe place for Teri. She was not a desired or expected child. Mother was an alcoholic, irresponsible and reckless individual who provided booze to the boys that Teri brought home and in turn, required sexual favors from these underaged and willing young men.

Jody partook in the drinking, but wanted no part of Mother's games. He wanted Teri to be safe *and* he also wanted to be in the Olympics for gymnastics. When he was nine, another boy in school would do back hand springs during recess. Jody became obsessed with this trick and wanted to be better than the boy. When he got home, he took the mattress off his bed and placed it on the floor of the basement where he spent countless hours practicing. He perfected his hand spring and added other tricks to show his friends.

His formal training began shortly after moving to Chesterfield. His parents enrolled him in gymnastic classes. He was a natural and his lean and muscular build was perfect for the sport. His drive to be and do his best propelled him and soon he had a coach that recognized his potential and introduced him to another coach from Oregon State University. When the coach saw Jody's abilities the Olympic training began.

Jody also had a love for the water and desired to be a marine biologist. He spent much of his time swimming at the Chesterfield Recreational Center. The diving board became a way to show off his gymnastic moves and it wasn't long before he was spotted by a high school diving coach. The coach desired for Jody to compete at the high school level for diving, even though he was much younger.

In spite of the busy sports schedule, Jody still made Teri his priority and, thanks to her mother, there was always a party happening at her house. This went on for about three years. Jody had also added high school football to his regime and was winning awards in all three sports. He was doing so well in school and sports that his father rewarded him with his first dirt bike.

The golden boy was destined for greatness, scholarships, and hopefully, a medal honoring the USA for his number one love - gymnastics. He excelled in every aspect; vault, pummel horse, rings, uneven bars and floor routine, with vault being his favorite.

Funny how life has its own plans though; how destiny takes you places you never thought, hoped, wished, or conjured up on your own. Funny how talents and dreams can shatter in the matter of seconds. Funny is the only way to look at life if you don't want to fall into severe depression about what should have been, was inevitable, where all the planets in all the universes had aligned to ensure one's greatness. All it takes is one little slip, the slightest veer to the left of the target, to miss the mark entirely - to end up completely off the map of your life. One small, and seemingly natural moment. Just one.

"I'm *pregnant*," Teri announced.

Their relationship had gotten rocky over the three years. Teri had strayed. They broke up. They got together now and again. Now she was expecting. Jody was 16, Teri was barely 15. His dad, a solitary man of honor, promptly announced that Jody would *act* as a man since he was acting like a man. So, Jody was on his own. Life as he knew it and planned it ended abruptly with two words. He quit school, got a job as a stucco apprentice and a little apartment to prepare for the baby.

Things were *not* good. There was constant fighting between the couple but Jody was committed to the baby as he committed to all things in his life. One night, when they were asleep, Mother showed up at their apartment with a guy she met at a bar. Mother turned the music on in the living room, waking the sleeping pair. Teri went down to tell her mom to quiet down and saw her snorting cocaine off the coffee table. Rightfully angry, Teri whooshed the coke off the table with a brush of her hand and it disappeared into the carpet.

Now Teri was close to the end of her pregnancy at this time but Mother was so loaded that she unleashed on her daughter anyway. Tackling her, she sat on her pregnant belly and punched her repeatedly in the face. Jody ran downstairs and attempted to restrain Mother. She grabbed Jody by the hair, which he wore long at the time, and jumped on his back. Jody pulled her off and slammed her into the ceiling and then on to the floor, but she still had a strong hold on his hair. He asked her repeatedly to let go, but she would not.

"I'm warning you, if you don't let go of my hair, I'm going to break that arm of yours," he yelled.

She just laughed her psycho, echoing laugh.

"I mean it!" Jody warned.

Mother pulled harder.

Snap! Jody broke Mother's forearm without much effort. She released his hair, screaming at the top of her lungs.

Of course, the police came next, but the evidence of the cocaine exonerated Jody and Mother was taken away.

CHAPTER 2
FOR THE LOVE OF FAMILY

When Mona was born, it was true love. Being a daddy was as natural as a back handspring for Jody and even more rewarding. He took Mo, as he called her, everywhere with him. Jody changed diapers, made bottles, worked long shifts at his job, and provided for his little family. He became an artist at plastering and picked up stone work as well. He had plans of opening his own company.

Teri, on the other hand, didn't take to being a mother the way Jody took to being a dad. She continued seeing other men and when Mo was two, there was a terrible fight. This is when the revelation came that Mo's daddy was not Jody. There were three other potential fathers, but looking at the little face that he had given his heart and his future to, he knew which of the guys she belonged to. It was too late though. The little girl had his love and he realized that no one else would care for her and love her the way he did. But Jody and Teri split up. The infidelity was more than he could take.

It was at the 39th Street Galleria when Jody met Kelly for the first time. Jody was 18, she was 16. The spark was instant and they saw each other regularly, but Jody's heart was with his baby girl and he wanted to raise her so he reconciled with Teri and moved back in. Within months he found out she was pregnant again. He was more committed to his family now than ever. Baby girl number two was born, Tina, or Tiny as they liked to call her.

By this time, Jody had his own stucco company and was running a very profitable business. Teri's Mother, however, was still struggling and had moved in with the family after Tina was born. She had been evicted with nowhere to go so what was Jody to do? She was his girl's grandma after all.

To add to it all, Mother had taken up the practice of Wick-a and was teaching Teri witchcraft too. This added a huge strain and drama to the already touchy relationship. Mother also was using cocaine regularly and needed to support her habit and the grandchildren would be a perfect way to do so. She concocted a plan to claim Mo as her own baby and applied for welfare for the two of them.

One day, Jody got a garnishment in his paycheck from the Office of Recovery Services. When he discovered Teri's mother was behind it, he went directly to the ORS. He was given the option of pressing charges and putting Mother in jail but Teri was against it so Jody dropped it, but the State didn't return the money they garnished from him. However, Teri agreed mother had to leave.

Mother, a slender blond in her late 30's, had no problem attracting men and needed a place to go now that Jody's home wasn't an option. Mark, a co-worker of Jody's, was a respectable and good man with a house and a stable environment and this was the exact situation Mother was looking for. She set her sights on Mark and it wasn't long before they married and she moved to his home in Vernal, Utah.

In the meantime, Jody moved his family to a nice home in Kearns with a perfect yard for his growing girls. Work was going ok in Salt Lake but Mark persuaded Jody to come to Vernal and take advantage of the housing boom caused by the oil industry there. Jody began the 3-hour commute back and forth between Kearns and Vernal plastering the new homes as they were built.

This opened the door for Teri to get back with her party buddy, Mother. She didn't like Jody working in Vernal while she was stuck home taking care of the girls. Her desire to live the party life still ran deep in her veins. She was young, after all. Motherhood was difficult for a girl whose own mother had never grown up and was still a girl herself.

Teri decided to throw another dagger. She announced that Tina was most likely Jody's best friend Travis's baby. Betrayed again, a heated fight ensued followed by the police. The only thing Jody could think of to do was run. He ran to the creek behind his house and ran and ran while he got his mind around what he had just been told. How could she do this to him not once, but twice? This was his family. The thing he had dropped his entire future for was just a facade. He loved those baby girls with all his heart. He was the only daddy they knew and if he left them, chances were, no one decent would show up to take his place.

Teri's grandmother picked up her and the girls and took them to Vernal to be with Mother. Jody stayed in their new house in Kearns, alone and heart broken, continuing his long commute. Taking advantage of every opportunity he had to see the girls, he decided to take things slow and try to work it out for the sake of the family. Teri got her first job cleaning houses and things seemed to be gradually improving.

Jody planned activities for the family to do on the weekends and it was on one of these activities that he nearly gave his life to save that of his little daughter. The family was to go swimming in the Green River. Mother and Mark, Teri and the girls were all there having a picnic. Tiny was on Jody's shoulders and he was walking with her in waste deep water. The current was swift so the water was murky. He had no idea that a sand ledge lay so close to the river bank. As he stepped forward, the underwater sandbar broke under his feet, sending him and Tiny into the rough current. The current quickly swept them away from the family and rapidly down the river.

Jody was holding Tina's little legs, struggling to keep her head above the water. His mind flashed back to the night before. He had dreamed that he was swimming and demons were pulling him under the water, their black arms swirling with the strength of the tide. He awoke right before his lungs breathed their last breath of air and took in the dingy river. Was this going to be his fate? One thing he knew, it would not be Tina's.

Mother, Teri, and Mark had formed a human chain to reach the baby. Jody's head had gone under when they reached the family, but Tina's stayed above and she reached her little arms out. With a big stretch, Mother was able to grab her little hand. Jody felt the tug and loosened his grip from his baby's legs. She was safe but Jody continued down the river.

He was not sure how fate spared his life that day, but somehow, Jody found himself on the river bank, alone and coughing up water. Tina was safe and that was all that mattered to him. There were bruises on her legs from him holding on so tight and as the weeks and grip marks faded away, he was reminded how much he loved these girls.

CHAPTER 3
THE INLAW OUTLAWS

Teri got a one-bedroom apartment with the help of housing assistance and welfare in Vernal in addition to her housekeeping job. Jody continued his long commutes and spent all his spare time with the girls.

One weekend while he was in Vernal with his cousin, Jody went to visit his daughters. It was a Friday night and Teri was having a big party. It was clear she was following in Mom's ways. She was carrying on a sexual relationship with a minor named Miles, as well as providing alcohol for all the minor party goers. Jody, concerned about the girls, confronted Teri in front of her guest and kicked everyone out of the apartment. Angry, Teri took off down the road with a beer in her hand. Keep in mind, Teri is old enough to go to jail for sex with a minor, but not old enough to have a beer in her hand. When the cops found her stumbling along the street in the dark, she was arrested for public intoxication and that's when the trouble really began.

Broke, as usual, due to her ongoing alcohol and substance habits, Mother asked Jody to pay to bail Teri out. Reluctantly, Jody gave Mother the bail money and she and Teri hid the girls from him in fear he would take them with him back to Salt Lake.

Jody had had it. That would be his last trip. He got a smaller home with his cousin in West Valley City. Work was going well and he enjoyed a short amount of peace for a time. He would just work in Salt Lake and not go to Vernal any more. Trying to be a family wasn't going to work - Teri just wasn't interested. She was a cheater. She wasn't going to change.

Things in Vernal, however, were heating up. Like Teri, Mother just couldn't control herself either. She began an affair with the neighbor. Poor Mark. Good old solid-as-a-rock Mark just got his own dose of heartbreak. There was something about this crazy little alcoholic blond lady that kept life exciting - brought something interesting to the doldrum world he had existed in prior to becoming her target.

He decided to confront her about what was going on, but unbeknownst to Mark, Mother didn't like being confronted. She reacted much in the way a rabid dog in a corner would react - she attacked! Fortunately for Mark, there's not a whole lot of action for the cops in Vernal and they welcomed the opportunity to put Mother in jail for domestic violence. You gotta hand it to old Mark, he learned quick and divorced her soon thereafter. He would be one of the lucky ones that got away.

It wasn't going much better for Teri either. She lost her driver's license, her job and her housing voucher after the public intoxication arrest and had to moved back in with Mother and Mark. Of course, with the affair, the attack on his life and the divorce pending, Mark wanted Teri and the girls out. Having nowhere to go, she pleaded with Jody to move in with him. While this was an opportunity to be with his girls again, he recognized that he didn't have to be a couple with Teri to still be the girl's dad.

But deep down he longed for a stable family and the type of marriage his parents had. So, Teri and the little darlings returned again to Salt Lake.

About this time, Teri's father, a meth junkie living the hobo lifestyle, re-entered her life. Nothing like substituting one dysfunctional parent for another! During his absence from Teri, Jody's business had expanded and he was running a large crew. He was a subcontractor for a bigger company that had lent him tools and equipment for one of the jobs he was working on. Father was coming over daily while Jody was at work and bumming the $20.00 Jody was giving to Teri for her to get stuff for the kids. Eventually she got fed up with her dad and told Jody.

Father, financially cut off, had to come up with a new way to support his habit. The $20.00 got him the daily fix he needed, so without that, he became more and more listless and desperate. Father knew Jody had a lot of tools and tools are easy to pawn so he waited for nightfall when he was sure Jody was sleeping before he made his move. Not only did he steal all the tools Jody needed for his business, he also took the ones that had been leant to him by the larger company he was subcontracting for.

The ripple effects of one person's actions can run deep. This wound pierced all the way to the financial bone. Without tools Jody and his crew couldn't work. He lacked insurance to cover the loss. At the time, he didn't know who had stolen them and where to begin to look for them. And worst of all, he had to tell the contractor that the tools he borrowed were gone. The contractor, while understanding, withheld the value of the tools from Jody's check so he didn't get paid, which meant he couldn't pay his crew - which is a perfect example of the old adage "adding insult to injury".

Not one to sit around and mope, Jody hit the street to see if he could recover the tools and also find some sort of work to feed the family. They were doing well as long as he was working, but life was pretty much paycheck-to-paycheck. That evening, Jody returned home to a dark and quiet house. He had no clue where Teri had gone until later that night when she and Mother showed up after an evening out at the bar drinking. Just Jody's luck! Father disappears - Mother gets out of jail and fills the void. The cycle continues. Teri begged Jody to let Mother move in again.

Jody and Teri, obviously, got into a fight over Mother. While that was going on, Mother wandered into Jody's cousin's room, who Jody had rented the house with, and interrupted Cousin and his new girlfriend. To complicate things, Mother had been sleeping with Jody's Cousin prior to her residency at the Vernal County Jail and prior to her marriage to Mark. Now why an older woman with many men before and after Cousin would think that an eligible bachelor would be faithfully sitting there waiting for a spouse-abusing-alcoholic-cokehead to get out of jail, who knows. But she did. And she took one look at the Cousin's sweet young thing and tore into her.

So you have a visual of what will continue to be a reoccurring character in this story, Mother is about five feet five inches and one hundred fifteen pounds when she has been jail-fed, but the weight fluctuates to much lower when she is pursuing her habits. She was a teenage mom, so technically, she's not a normal age or maturity level of most mothers. And since Teri was a mother at 15, Mother became a grandma in her early 30's. But don't let the physique fool you. Mother had strength and power that was fueled by alcohol and cocaine. One can't be entirely sure, but there was a good chance she believed the Wick-a powers possessed her as well.

This poor little hood-rat girl from down the street didn't know what she was dealing with. When confronted about Cousin, by Mother, she barked right back. Mother snapped, which never took much, and began wailing on the unsuspecting girl. Cousin, of course, stepped in to defend his mate and Mother took right to his face, scratching it bloody.

Teri and Jody abandoned their fight to join this one. Jody, now a pro at dealing with the wild witch, picked her up and forced her out the front door. Mother went to the neighbor and phoned the police and her brother. Jody immediately left and went to his friends, knowing his girls were safe at their Great Grandma Irma's - one of the few stable forces in their lives at this point.

The police came, but no one suspected that the Cousin would be the one hauled away. Teri and Mother concocted a story about Mother being a resident in the home and being attacked by the Cousin. The police bought it. He was arrested for domestic violence and extradited to Missouri for outstanding child support warrants. Cousin sent his girlfriend to go find Jody.

When Jody returned, the police tried to arrest him for domestic violence as well. He had to reason with the cops by explaining that he was the only sober one and that both women were in violation of their probation and parole. Teri and Mother kept insisting Jody be arrested as they wanted to take over the house. With Jody and Cousin out of the picture, Mother could move right in and Teri and her party partner could resume their good times.

With much coaxing from Cousin, the police were finally convinced to let Jody off the hook. They never checked the claim of probation and parole violations, why should they after all? These women had no money to feed into the system. They would be a drain financially. Jody and Cousin, on the other hand, would be able to pay fines, or so they thought.

Now Jody had no job, no money, no business partner, and no roommate to help pay the bills. Jody made it clear Mother was not welcome to stay with them, so she had her brother come pick her up. He was so tired of the chaos he began packing his things into his Cousin's truck.

"Where are you going?" Teri asked.

"I'm done with this." Jody responded. "I'm going back to Texas. You can either pack up and come or you can stay here."

CHAPTER 4
COMING HOME

Teri packed what she could into her car and in the morning, they planned to get the girls and head to Dallas where Jody's parents and brother were living. Teri called Mother to fill her in on the plan. Mother, in turn called the police and claimed, once again, that Jody had beat her up. This time she was too late, he was already on the road; Teri reluctantly following behind in her car.

After the long trip and finally at Jody's parent's home, Teri called Great Grandma Irma to report in. Great Grandma had been carrying a burden she needed to unload. She had to snitch on her own son, Teri's bum dad. She knew he had stolen the tools and where he had disposed of them. They were at a pawn shop in Magna, Utah.

Jody called the police and the contractor he had subbed for. The contractor retrieved his tools and Jody's, but Jody never heard a word or saw a penny from that contractor again. Another hard lesson of trust learned.

But there was a new life to look forward to in Texas. Within two days of arriving, Jody began work with his brother as a finish carpenter making decent money and within a month, he and his brother rented a house together.

Some side notes about Brother. He's possibly a half-brother or possibly not a blood brother at all. The facts are that Jody's father, a very astute man of German descent and three times Mr. Corpus Christi, had been married prior to Jody's mother, to a very wealthy woman. During the marriage, there was a girl and a boy born. Whether these are actually Dad's children has not been fully established but they were born within the confinement of the marriage.

One day, when Jody was in third grade, his father announced that he had to go to the airport to pick up Jody's older brother.

"I have a brother?" Jody mused.

Yes, he had a brother of sorts. One that was barely 18 months older than him and never mentioned. One who's name was just one letter off of his own name.

Jody, after being in business for himself and now accustomed to making more money than the finish work was providing, was tired of having to fight every week to get his paycheck from the employer Brother had hooked him up with, so he came up with a plan to open another stucco company. He taught his brother about bidding and they purchased some scaffold. Their first break came with a small house, but when it was completed, their craftsmanship was so impressive the work began to flow in and they landed a whole subdivision. Now the company was grossing $20,000 to $30,000 a week and they were running a whole crew once again. Business was good. Life had stabilized but for a brief moment.

Re-enter Mother. She got a plane ticket and showed up in Texas. She was "just visiting" - supposedly - so let the party begin! Mother was there for several days before returning to Salt Lake. Teri was now drinking a lot and consuming Brother's liquor while he was at work, causing arguments.

News of sorts came. Cousin had been released from jail and needed a place to stay. Jody and Teri drove to Booneville, Missouri to pick him up. He moved into the small house that was already holding two families. But with the house, now too crowded, and money, now more abundant, Jody concluded it was time to get his family their own place. Jody, Teri and the girls moved to a house in Coffman County, Texas. Cousin tagged along and and went to work for Jody.

Business was great but the work was hard and it was due time for some hard play. The brothers and Cousin got three new dirt bikes and every weekend was consumed by motocross racing. A new truck and trailer soon followed with happy times, for a change. Every Sunday Jody took the family to his favorite BBQ restaurant. Teri seemed to have settled down without her extended family to throw her off track and it was time for a bigger house in a nicer neighborhood.

Poetry, Texas, here comes the Rhorer clan. They found a home on five acres with plenty of storage for the business equipment and built a motocross track on the property and bought some goats. Every weekend was good food and great memories with a lot of Jody's family nearby.

It was at this time that a contractor that the brothers were not familiar with contacted the stucco company to do the work on a new home for one of the members of a famous 80's rock band. The brothers were excited to team up with a high-end builder and started work on a custom mansion for him right away. There were some unexpected delays and the job took a bit longer than anticipated, but the finished product was sublime.

Next the contractor sent them to a home that had been started by another stucco company to finish up work that they hadn't completed. The contractor said as soon as that work was done, they could start on the Rocker's house. Still waiting for payment for the first job and getting excuses on why the Rock Star's house couldn't be started, they began work on another high-end home for a new contractor.

Abundance was showing up in many ways in Jody's life and he found out that Teri was expecting baby number three. All seemed to be going well, but still no money from the contractor. The company was owed nearly $50,000. The brother's phone calls were not being returned and any promises made were not kept. The company didn't have the money to pay their crew or supply company. Jody and Brother decided it was time to pay the contractor a personal visit. Apparently, he had the equivalent of a stucco Ponzi scheme going on. He would get everything he could out of a sub-contractor without paying them and when they walked off the job, he would hire another to come in and finish. This didn't sit well with the Rhorer's. Let's just say there was a physical confrontation and leave it at that. The Rhorer's were told they could not enter that town again by the authorities.

Jody and Cousin were working on a house when Brother came to the job site with $10,000.

"We are broke Jody," Brother said. "We have no money to pay our suppliers and I wrote a bunch of bad checks. Here's enough money to get you out of town."

Jody had suspected his brother had partied away much of the money. His parents had already relocated to Missouri so Jody packed up that night to leave with a pregnant Teri, Mo and Tina in tow. On the way out of town, he stopped by Brother's only to find him lounging in the house with no intentions of leaving. Jody was suspect that he had kept a nice sum of money for himself. Jody shook his head, got in the truck and left for Missouri.

Within days of arriving, Jody had lined up a job at Fucal Homes as a roofer, but when he was only paid $9.00 an hour, he quit. Brother had not been making payments on his truck and it was repossessed which left him in a bind, so after concocting a plan with BM, Brother called to inform Jody.

"Bro! Are y'all settled with the family?"

"Gettin there," Jody responded. "How you doin?"

"We're okay. So," Brother started, "been meaning to tell ya that your truck is actually in the name of the company which technically makes it not yours."

"Waddaya mean?" Jody started moving towards the window to get a view of the front driveway.

"Ya, well, my mom - she, she sent a repo man to get it."

"My truck? Your mom sent a repo man to get MY TRUCK?" Jody could now see the empty spot in the drive where the truck had been. He slammed down the phone and called the police.

The highway patrol found the man driving Jody's truck on the freeway but he said he had a valid claim and BM was well known in the area and was heir to a large estate so they let him go.

Let's talk about Brother's Mother, or BM as we will refer to her. In Jody's words, "She has more money than Texas." She comes from money but that wasn't enough for her. Her children were sent away to boarding school as soon she could reasonably do so. She had at least six husbands - one still missing. Another caught her having an affair on camera with the bar tender of his restaurant and ended up in the hospital due to all the stress. Unfortunately, he died from a tumble down the stairs soon after he returned home. He did have plans to divorce her but she hadn't moved out yet. No need to now. All of her husbands were financially well off and she was able to obtain enormous wealth one way or another. Unfortunately for her son and daughter, generosity is not one of her virtues.

Once again, Jody was starting over. He borrowed his dad's truck to find a job. He saw construction going on at the General of the Confederate Army Mansion. They were looking for a sub to do some of the work. Jody bid the job, hired a couple guys, and within three months had made $54,000. Word of his craftsmanship traveled fast and Jody was back in business.

He set up housekeeping again in a duplex down the street from his parents and then his third daughter, Mia, was born. Although he didn't trust Teri, he felt that their relationship was stronger than it had been in the past and things with her were going much better.

A phone call came from the building supplier in Texas. "Mr. Rhorer, we are looking for your Brother. He owes us over $30,000 for purchases he made for his construction company. We have your name down as a contact."

"I wish I could help you but we aren't in touch right now," Jody Responded.

"Look buddy, I don't think you know how serious this really is!" The Supplier was getting more forceful.

"I said we aren't in touch!" Jody forced back.

"If I don't get more help out of you than that, I have a baseball bat with both you and your brother's names on it." The supplier was not messing around.

"All I know is he is living in Saatchi, Texas," Jody said, now humbled. "That's all I can tell you, I promise."

Now Jody understood that if Brother and the supplier would just talk, they could put mechanics liens on the homes that they were never paid on as well as go after the contractor that hadn't paid them. He also still had the fresh wounds of his truck being taken as well as the likely chance that Brother had embezzled his unfair share of money from the company. The supplier took down the information and hung up. Jody never heard from them again.

When Brother found out that the past was on his trail. He took off from Saatchi and moved into an expensive home in Garland. Still no job but somehow managing to maintain a lifestyle status. All good things must come to an end though, and the truck he had taken from Jody was repossessed when Brother didn't make those payments either. Ultimately, Brother and his wife and new baby girl moved in with his mother-in-law. You know what they say about paybacks.

Tough Coat Plastering and Stucco was now running full force and taking many large commercial jobs and custom homes in Columbia, Lake of the Ozark's, and surrounding areas. They added tuck pointing, which is restoration of brick, and stone masonry to their service menu.

The family stayed in the duplex long enough to get their feet planted on the ground and then, again, Jody went looking for a better home and larger yard for the growing girls and company vehicles.

More business was coming in than Jody and his limited crew could handle and finding responsible, skilled workers was tough. Many of the contractors kept asking if Jody could also do their sheetrock work so demand, once again, expanded his business. Jody went outside of the area to find help. He brought up a friend, Kenny, from Texas once he had moved into a larger home in New Franklin, Missouri, that could house the family, equipment, and workers, as needed.

"Kenny," Jody promised, "If you stay with me for a year, I'll give you my dirt bike as a bonus."

Every weekend was motocross racing from then on out. Hard work, hard play, healthy babies. The perfect combination to happy times. On September 11th, 2001, Tough Coat Plastering was working full force on their largest custom home job thus far. That morning, Jody went to fill the stucco order.

"I'm here to pick up my stucco." Jody requested to the attendant.

"Don't you know what just happened?" the attendant responded. "We've just been bombed by terrorists!"

"I don't care. Just give me my stucco," answered Jody, not realizing the extent of what had taken place and fully committed to the job.

That day, as with most people in this country and many from around the world, the crew was glued to the radio as they plastered away, unsure as to what the future was going to bring.

After a long and draining day, Jody and Kenny returned home. Teri was drunk, which seemed to be her usual state as of late. She was sporting a halter top and Daisy Duke shorts and had the neighbor man in the yard with her as she attempted to do yard work. Upset by what Jody has come home to, a fight ensued between the couple.

After that incident, the fighting became more and more frequent. Jody spent many nights at his parent's home and would pick up Kenny in the morning for work. He really wanted to avoid the controversy and began ignoring the fact that Teri was drunk much of the time. It was a survival method to keep their family intact.

A good friend, Johnny, called. He was thinking about relocating from Texas to Missouri and wanted to come check things out. The plan was for him to spend a week with Jody and if he liked it and thought he could get employment, Johnny and Kenny would get a place together.

Johnny enjoyed the visit, but didn't find any work and didn't like the manual labor Jody offered him, so he returned to Texas.

Brother had now bottomed out and burned all bridges. He had pawned anything of value to get by. He was still at his wife's mother's home and heard that Kenny was up in Missouri working for Jody. Pride and conscience did not dwell in Brother at that time - he called Jody and begged for redemption.

"Hey Little Bro! I hear things are going pretty good up there for you."

"Oh, yeah?" Jody replied, still skeptical.

"I'm really missin Dad. It would be great if we could all be together again, just like the good times. Don't you think?" Brother continued.

"Uh, well…" Jody knew where this is leading.

"Bro, look, I'm sorry about what happened. It wasn't my fault. It wasn't anyone's fault but that bastard contractor. I really need a fresh start. I've got no car and no work down here. What do you think? Can you give me one more chance? You and Dad are all I got. You know my mom, she's got her own life and her own problems," Brother pleaded.

Jody conceded and he and Teri made the ten-hour drive while Jody's parent's, Naana and Paapa cared for the girls.

They met at a hotel - the typical Bates style side of the road joint with pay-by-the-hour rooms. Brother and family were thrilled to see their rescuers pull into the parking lot.

"Bro!" Brother yelled, a hand in the air.

They loaded up what possessions Brother's wife had managed to hang on to, mostly baby items.

"Glad you brought the truck, Jode, cuz there is one thing down there at the pawn shop that I can't leave town without and you will know why once we get there." Brother had one cunning surprise after another.

They got a room in Jody's name for the night before they started the long, long drive back, but Jody noticed Brother was fidgety. They headed to the pawn shop while the girls got the room situated. In the back of the shop was Brother's Yamaha YZ 250 motorbike.

"Just $600.00 will set this girl free," Exclaimed the pawn broker.

Jody gave Brother a look. Brother shrugged.

"You know I can't leave town without my bike. It's gonna be just like the good times and I promise I'll work it off, Bro."

Jody pulled out his wallet and payed with hundred-dollar bills. Scammed again. When Jody and Brother returned, there was a Mexican man waiting in the parking lot. Brother was antsier than ever.

"Jody, you go check on the girls, I got a little business here I gotta handle," Brother continued. "I'll just be a sec."

Jody went inside while Brother approached the window of a low riding car. The Mexican discretely handed him a bag - one that happened to weigh a quarter pound. Brother didn't hand the Mexican anything back. The car pulled away. Brother hopped up into the back of the truck, feeling around in the bag and pulled out a little pinch. He stuffed the bag and its contents into the air box of the Yamaha.

Brother hurried into the hotel room and made small talk for a while. Once his nerves settled, he took the pinch from his pocket and rolled a joint then lit up. He took a long drag then handed it to his wife. She followed along. They looked at Jody in a way to inquire if he was next. He batted the offer away with one hand.

"What are you doing? Is that what that was about out there in the parking lot? How'd you pay for that, Bro? I thought you were broke!" Jody was beside himself with anger.

"I thought we could use a little stress reliever," Brother responded. "Besides, Dipshit don't know I'm leaving the state - thinks I'll be bringing the money by tomorrow. Told him you were coming to town and we needed to do some celebration. See, it's all good."

"None of this is good and I'm not sittin here and takin the rap for you if the police show up." Jody left and sat in the truck.

After he cooled down and the room aired out, Jody returned to the hotel. They left early the next day. A very wise person once said, no good deeds go unpunished.

The Dos Hermanos do have one thing going for them, they can accomplish a lot of work together and they resumed the good times, as promised. Work during the week, camp trips and motocross on weekends.

A few months later, during a camping and motorcycle trip to Finger Lakes, it began to rain. Everyone crowded into Jody's tent. Teri had to go to the bathroom and chose the entrance of the tent to do so. She dropped her pants in front of the entire group and peed. Disgusted and embarrassed, Teri and Jody had words and he left for home. The next day he expected Teri to show up, but she stayed at the lakes and partied with the group. Jody had had enough once again and moved his things out of the house and into a storage shed. After the weekend ended, Brother and the clan showed up to an empty house. They found Jody at his parent's home.

"Bro, we missed ya this weekend," Brother said, trying to mend the bridge.

"Well I'm pretty much done," Jody responded.

"Ya, we saw the house," Brother continued. "Ya know me and my woman, we been talkin and I think we are gonna head on back to Texas"

"Oh yeah?" Jody replied, unimpressed.

"Yeah, I think things have settled down down there and you and Teri need your space," Brother said. "Besides, Kenny wants to go back too.

What was done was done. Jody presented Kenny with the dirt bike as he had promised for sticking by him for a year. Jody and Teri moved back into the house; this time just them and the girls. Jody was relieved to not have to start from scratch again and just wanted a normal life and stability for his daughters. Only a few days had passed before Brother called to reveal some very bad news.

"Hey Jode," brother stammered, "we got here safe and there is something I really need to tell you."

"Oh great, here it comes," Thought Jody.

But the news is not what he was expecting.

"Bro, you really shouldn't have left the way you did when we were up there camping," Brother said, pointing a finger.

"What d'ya mean? It was a lot better than fighting with Teri. I didn't wanna bring all you guys into it." Jody defended.

"Well Kenny and Teri hooked up. I though you should know because you just gave him your bike and he was your best friend and all." Brother spoke so matter-of-factly, void of any empathy for the situation he just placed his only brother in.

"Hooked up? What do you mean?" Jody was shocked and didn't want hooked up to mean what he knew hooked up meant.

"You know, they were doin it the whole weekend," Brother continued. "Anyway, if it were my woman I would want to know. That's why I told you."

What to do now. Kenny was too far away to kill. Teri was not but he knew what that would get him. Why does she keep doing this? Can't she see he's committed to having a happy family? Can't she see he loves these little girls? Can't she see how hard he works to provide a good life for them? Can't she see past herself? Of course, Teri denied everything. Jody just didn't know what to believe so he followed the path of water, the way of least resistance and gave her the benefit of the doubt.

And then she made this announcement: "I think it's time for us to start going to church."

CHAPTER 5
BEGINNINGS, ENDINGS, BEGINNINGS

Pastor Brother Haggett at the Bible Baptist Church in New Franklin, Missouri, welcomed the family with open arms and on Sundays and Wednesday nights the family showed up to worship regularly.

Jody's business was booming in spite of the World Trade Center fiasco and he was now shorthanded with the loss of Kenny and Brother. But winter brought a small reprieve from work and Jody took the family to Utah for a visit. While there, he got the girls a golden retriever puppy and named him Max - the family's first dog. They also paid Mother a visit, which for once, was uneventful. After Christmas their little family returned home.

Spring came; Jody resumed life and work and Brother and his wife paid them a visit. This time all went well. They rode dirt bikes, BBQ'ed, and talked about the good times. No fighting, no drama.

Mother began calling again. She wanted to move to Missouri and live with the family. The Utah visit opened a can of worms that Jody had worried might surface. He refused Mother's persistent requests as he knew this leopard would never change her spots.

One evening, the Pastor stopped by the house. "Good evening, Jody, Teri," Pastor began. "I wanted to stop by and let you know how much we enjoy having your family in our parish."

"It's been good for us," Jody responded. "The girls really love it."

"And what about you, Jody?" Pastor asked.

"I do too. I think it's what we needed in our lives."

"So, if you don't mind me asking," the Pastor continued, "are y'all married?"

Teri shook her head no, her eyes darting downward.

Jody was quick to respond, "No way! She cheats on me, ain't never been faithful. I'm with her for those girls."

Pastor calmly said, "I understand. But you know, the past is the past and it looks like your family has turned over a new leaf. It's something you should consider."

Jody wanted to consider it. But the scars ran deep and the cuts kept reoccurring.

Summertime didn't bring the new construction Jody expected and work dwindled. He joined the Union to try to get steady work. He worked whatever hours he could get along with any side business his company could muster up but it wasn't quite enough. Jody's dad had a brother in Oregon with an extra house. The economy was much better there so the family made plans to relocate and loaded up their belongings to start the long trip. On the way to Oregon, they stopped in Utah to visit. Great Grandma Irma was always glad to see them and was a great hostess. Jody loved to BBQ and planned a dinner for their Utah friends and family. It had been three years since Teri had heard from her father so when Father found out they were in town, he decided to show up at Great Grandma's and surprise her.

NOTE: There was a tendency for the majority of the relatives both blood and through relationships to have no accountability or remorse for any of their bad deeds. They believed that, given a little time, all would be forgotten and forgiven without restitution or acknowledgment.

Jody and Teri left for the grocery store to get dinner supplies for the party. Jody, still steaming over the stolen tools, refused to buy food for Teri's dad.

"That's water under the bridge Jody, you need to just forget about it," Teri pressed.

"That *water* cost us our family's livelihood and set us way back," Jody shot back. "He don't care what he did. He shows up like nothin happened and I'm s'posed to just smile and pay for his steak? No way!"

Jody parked his truck just in time to be punched square in the nose by Teri. He clenched the steering wheel, pressing back his urge to strike back. Nose bleeding, he went into the nearby Wendy's restaurant to clean up and cool down. When he returned to the truck, he had made up his mind not to fight about this. Teri sat there with a smug look, staring out the window.

"C'mon, let's go get the groceries and get this done." Jody said, holding a napkin up to one nostril.

They got pork steaks, one of Jody's favorite specialties, and other fixings and started back to Grandma's. Once on the road, Teri, grabbed Jody by the hair, which he still wore in long naturally curly ringlets. She kept pulling and jerking his hair and trying to grab the steering wheel, nearly causing him to wreck the truck. Jody grabbed her by the back of the head and forced her head toward the seat, accidentally banging her eye on the stick shift on the way down while looking for a safe place to pull over.

"What the HELL, Teri!" Jody yelled. "I thought we were done with this.

When the truck came to a full stop, Teri jumped out and ran down the street. She managed to get to her mother's and phone the police. When Jody got to Great Grandma's, she had already been notified of the situation. The police had been told that Jody had given Teri a black eye and they were on their way to look into domestic violence charges. Grandma had emptied most of the belongings out of the families moving trailer into the house, leaving only Jody's clothes, scaffold, and cement mixer, and taken half of the cash in Jody's bag to keep for Teri.

Jody took what he had left and headed to Oregon, alone. He made it as far Portland and dropped off a hitchhiker he had picked up going through Idaho in the downtown district - as downtown as you can get. Low on cash and the only phone available being the kind that are now extinct, the good old pay phone usually near a mini mart, Jody found a sandy place in Troutdale on the river and slept there. Luckily, three good Samaritan black women woke him the next morning and warned him about the danger he was in.

"Hey! What's your name and what are you doing sleeping out here?" The girls mused as if they had found a treasure that had washed up to shore.

Now Jody had spent plenty of nights fishing and sleeping on the side of the Missouri River or a sand barge in the middle of the Big Muddy so to him this felt like home.

"Got in late and didn't know my way around. I'm try'in to find my uncle and get a job." Explained Jody.

"Say, where's that cute accent of yours from?" The girls inquired.

"Originally I'm from Texas but I came out here from Missouri."

"Well you done came to the wrong place cute cowboy. It's a damn good thing we stumbled on you. Get up and brush yourself off. You're coming home with us. We got a phone and we can make you something to eat while you're tracking down that uncle of yours." The women taunted over their new find.

Jody stayed several days on the couch of those three motherly girls. They all had professional jobs, rented a large house together, and kept him out of sight from the neighbors. He tried and tried to contact his uncle but with no avail. Uncle Larry's phone rang and rang. With no answering machine to leave a message and no address to drive to, a discouraged Jody turned around and headed back to Salt Lake.

"Bye cowboy! Come back and see us. You always have a place to stay." The girls waved as Jody backed his truck out of their driveway.

Dino had been a friend since the sixth grade. He was the kind of guy you would want on your side. Pretty scary looking, large around with plenty of tattoos and a long goatee, but his heart was golden.

Dino let Jody move in and store his things in the back yard. It wasn't a week or so until Jody was working as a stucco and plasterer. The first thing Jody wanted to do was see his girls. Instead, he was served a protective order and, having no previous experience with protective orders, he wasn't really sure what it meant.

The girls were being hidden from Jody at a drug dealer's house named Cort. Jody had been told where they were by Vino's girlfriend. Concerned about their safety, he went straight there. He had a plan, call the cops for a wellness check on his kids and that would give him the opportunity to take them, or at least see them and make sure they were ok.

He could see Teri through the window and thought the protective order she had placed on him pertained only to her, so he waited around the corner after he called the police. But when they showed up, Jody was the one arrested. When the police inquired about the kids, Teri told them Jody had been freaking out and threatening her even though he hadn't so much as spoken to her.

He was booked into jail for violation of a protective order and domestic violence. Fortunately, he had stashed all the money he had earned since arriving to Salt Lake in a dresser at Vino's house and Vino's girlfriend brought down the $800.00 needed to bail Jody out.

From jail he went straight to a lawyer's office. He knew he was "done wrong" and was going to fight for his rights to his little girls. For the first time he realized that unless he had the law on his side, it would always work against him.

Society tends to believe a woman when she cries wolf. She can tell any story she fabricates and the man will be arrested on the spot. She can get a protective order with no proof of a real threat. She can keep her kids from their dad, take his money and destroy his property and who is going to believe the male? If a man is struck by a woman, he most likely won't call the authorities as it would appear to be a sign of weakness to be beat on by your girlfriend. Society also believes men, on a whole, can't possibly be fit to raise kids on their own nor would they have a desire to do so -especially little girls.

"I'm Jody Rhorer and I want to get custody to my three daughters, and, uh, I 'm not a rich man." Jody explained.

"What do you do for a living, young man?" Steve K inquired.

"I'm a stucco and stone mason," Jody responded.

"Well I happen to be in need of some stucco work on my house. Sounds like you need me and I need you," Steve K explained.

And the two were in business. Steve began work on getting Jody custody to his girls and Jody began work on Steve's home. That was Jody's first dealing with Steve K, who would be with him off and on for the continuation of this book.

School was starting and Teri called Jody, in violation of her own protective order. "I need money." The girls need clothes to start school," Teri demanded.

"Well I'll take them to get them some school clothes." Jody said with hope. "But I ain't just giving you the money. When can I pick 'em up?"

"How soon can you come get them?"

Jody took the girls and got them each seven new outfits, one for each day of the week. Shirts, blouses, underpants, shoes, socks - everything they needed to be ready for school. They were excited about their new clothes and being able to spend time with Daddy. He brought the girls back well within the time frame Teri had allotted to ensure there would be no problems with the police. After kissing them all goodbye, the girls proudly brought their bags into the house.
"Gimme those bags. I want to see what you got," Teri said.

"I can show you, Mom." Mo responded, suspicious that her mother might take some of her new things for herself. The younger girls had nothing to worry about as their clothes would be too small for her.

Teri snatched Mo's bags from her and then took the two younger girl's sacks as well. Teri went through all the bags with a disapproving look on her face, discarding each item onto the floor. She rummaged through the sacks for the receipts, but found none. Jody had kept them. Teri, furious, threw all the clothes out into the front yard and then called Dino's girlfriend.

"You need to tell Jody to bring them receipts over to me right now for these shitty clothes he bought the girls!"

"Hey, Jody, "Dino's girlfriend yelled, "Teri's on the phone and wants those receipts for the girl's clothes."

"Tell her to F off," Jody yelled back.

"I heard that. Let him know that if he don't get them receipts over here now I'm calling the cops and telling em that he stole all them clothes and they'll be hauling his sorry ass off to jail!" Screamed Teri. Dino's girlfriend didn't need to repeat Teri's request, Jody could hear loud and clear.

Jody sent Dino's girlfriend to deliver the receipts. When she arrived at the house where the girls were staying, they were crying at the sight of their new school outfits strewn all over the front yard. She couldn't believe what she saw. She tried consoling the girls but Teri ushered her off the property as soon as she had what she wanted. Teri carefully picked up each item of clothing, shaking them clean of any debris and placing them back in the bags. She left the girls and headed to the store with the receipts to return the clothing.

Now armed with a billfold of cash, she went to the liquor store and bought her booze of choice - beer, whiskey, and cigarettes. Working on getting herself loaded, she headed to Cort's, the drug dealer's house. Cort was leaving for a funeral so Teri asked if she could tag along. On the way back to Chesterfield, driving with no driver's license after the funeral, Teri rear-ended the car in front of her. Knowing what was in store if she was caught, she exited the car and took off running. It didn't take long for the police to apprehended her. She was booked for a hit and run, fleeing the scene of an accident, driving under the influence and driving without a driver's license. Luckily for Teri though, someone bailed her out of jail shortly after her arrest - but she wasn't going to get off that easy.

The timing was perfect. Teri's reckless behavior and neglect of the children were the ammo Jody needed to win the fight for his daughters. Steve K advised Jody that he needed to file for divorce under common law even though there had never been an actual marriage. This would ensure Jody's paternity without having to go through DNA testing. This was a great plan since the actual paternity of the girls was in doubt.

Steve's style was quick and brutal. He never wasted time or minced words. Results came quickly and he had a plan for every scenario.

Teri came into the court room dressed like a hooker. Steve eyed her and then shot a disapproving look at Jody. Jody just shrugged.

"Miss, do you have anything you would like to add?" The judge asked Teri after Steve presented Jody's case.

"Ya," Teri replied, "Ya I do."

"Then please approach the podium," the judge responded.
Teri strutted to the microphone stand, doing her best to look appealing, innocent, and vulnerable.

"I wanted to say, your honor, that Jody shouldn't have those kids cuz he's not really their father. I mean, they have different dad's than him. That's why he shouldn't have custody."

"Who has raised the girls, ma'am?" The judged asked.

"Well, he did," Teri said.

"Then he is their father," The judge stated.

Jody won everything he had been seeking. His divorce was granted with no alimony or child support going to Teri. Next, Jody wanted full custody of the girls and court approval to move them back to Missouri.

Winter was approaching and Jody knew work in Utah would be ending and wanted to get a place lined up for the girls in Missouri as well as begin a search for work, since the seasonal weather was much milder there. Jody left Steve to do the job of winning him custody and ensured him he would return when there was a court date set.

He established himself again in Missouri, got a new car, settled in with his parents and landed a large stucco job. He was already set up with the scaffold, tools, and the mixer he needed so this time he had a head start.

Jody has one younger sister, about two years younger, named Mini. Mini was talking to Brother after Jody had returned to live with his parents. Apparently, Brother had become quite the methamphetamine addict in Texas and the authorities wanted to take away his little girl so he ran. Brother took his family to Oklahoma City and was living at a campground in a tent.

He was able to get BM and the Mother-in-law to lend them enough money to get an apartment until he got a job. But Brother didn't care for Oklahoma City and wanted out of there badly.

Once again, Jody to the rescue. He drove to the city and helped Brother load everything up, including the Yamaha motorcycle. That night, the truck and all Brother's belongings were stolen. The thieves had pushed the truck around the corner and cleaned everything out once they were out of view. One thing you don't want to do is steal from a meth addict. Brother began asking around. He was given a lead about a few guys that knew something, but a confrontation with them lead nowhere.

Brother was quite sure it was an inside job. There was a girl in the apartments that he was confident knew something. He went to her door, demanding answers. It was her boyfriend, he was sure of it. She would only open the door a crack. Brother could tell she knew what had happened but instead of helping him, the tables were turned and the neighbors called the police on Brother.

When the cops arrived, Brother was really worked up and started in on the police. He began yelling and swearing. A female officer, feeling threatened, tasered him and, in the process, he grabbed her hand, breaking some of her fingers. As usual, he was the one arrested and booked into jail. It took all the money Jody had as well as what Brother's girlfriend could muster up to bail him out.

Once out of jail, Brother decided he didn't really want to leave Oklahoma City after all. Jody was frustrated that he had come all this way and now he had no money to get home. The bail bondsman warned Brother that this was his chance to leave or he may incur more charges. He just needed to make sure he showed up for court and paid his fines.

The motley crew made it as far as Sedalia, Missouri before they ran out of gas. Now stranded with no money, they hatched a plan to bum change off enough strangers at the gas station to get home. In Jody's words, "Thank God there were some helpful people."

Brother and his family moved in with Jody, Naana and Paapa and after a few days of hard labor, Jody and Brother had earned enough money to get a house and start the cycle all over again.

CHAPTER 6
WHAT COMES AROUND GOES AROUND

Jody returned to Salt Lake to face the domestic violence charge from the previous summer. All charges were dismissed at the hearing. Steve K had done his job again.

Once back in Missouri, Jody joined the Plasterers and Cement Masons Union and started work for a reputable company that he was quite happy with. The benefits were great, pay was good and he prepared his home for his girls.

Jody flew back to Utah again to a hearing to remove the protective order, at Steve's request, in preparation for the custody case. And again, his request was granted.

Teri was in attendance at the hearing and wanted to reconcile and go back to Missouri with Jody. Jody saw this as an opportunity to be with the girls while Steve worked on getting him full custody. It would also be easier to already have the girls in his home and out of Utah once the Judge, undoubtedly, granted him custody rights. He had no intention of starting up the relationship with Teri again but certainly knew an opportunity when it fell into his lap.

There was no welcoming committee waiting for Teri in Boonville. She was beyond forgiveness in the eyes of Jody's family and no one was happy to see her. Having Teri around was a small price to pay for Jody, who now was able to hold his little girls in his arms at night as he slept.

There was one person who was particularly not happy about the situation, Brother's girlfriend's best friend who had moved up to Missouri from Texas and had taken the role as roommate and now Jody's girlfriend. Imagine her surprise when Jody came home from Salt Lake with three kids and their mother in tow.

Teri wasted no time continuing her irrefutable behavior. On the second night home, she got drunk in the garage with some neighbors and decided to give them a show. Texas girl ran right into the house and tattled.

"Jody, you won't believe what Teri just did. She hocked up a big logy, spit it on the floor, then pulled down her pants and peed in front of everybody."

Jody wasn't rattled or even slightly surprised. "Yup, that's Teri for you".

The Texas girl continued to attempt to gain favor in Jody's eyes, but he knew if he was anything besides friends with her from this point forward until he gained full custody and put Teri out for good, she could mess everything up in a hurry. She took it pretty hard when Jody explained his reasoning for their now platonic relationship and she moved out with Brother's family as soon as they got their own place.

But life goes on and the bills must be paid. Everyone was working, even Teri. She got a job at a little cafe in town.

This part gets a little shady. Another friend from Texas, Matt, showed up. His mantra was to couch surf between Jody's house and Brother's place. Just a good ole' hang out kind of guy.

Brother's girlfriend went to Paapa and told him that she found out that couch-surfer, Matt, was sleeping with Teri. Mini had also confiscated some letters to Matt written by Teri as further evidence. Paapa immediately went to Jody's house to confront Matt. Matt and another guy were home drinking with Teri while Jody was at work.

"Boys, you get your things and get out of town while you can cuz I know what's going on here and Jody will know soon as well."

You don't mess with three times Mr. Corpus Christi, Texas. Matt and his buddy hightailed it out of there in a hurry. Paapa was waiting for Jody when he got home.

"Need to talk to you, son."

Paapa wanted Jody to be calm and not do anything that would jeopardize the custody case as it was so close to being done. He explained the situation to Jody between Matt and Teri and what he had done about it. Jody was disappointed but not surprised. He wanted to knock Matt senseless for doing the mother of his kids under his roof but he was long gone now. The matter at hand was what to do about Teri.

One thing that was really bothering Jody was the fact that Teri was living there with him and he was supporting the family in a traditional manner even though he had been granted a civil divorce. This could really work against him in court. He came up with a plan that he thought would fix things once and for all.

"Teri, there's drag races coming up in Cheyenne. What about us going? Just me and you?" Jody asked.

Cheyenne, Wyoming was a good day's drive round trip if you drove fast enough. The two would go together. Just them. All cozy and stuff. Yeah right!

They arrived in Cheyenne on a Saturday. Jody got a room - the cheapest he could find. He brought in Teri's bags and told her to get into the shower and get cleaned up. Jody set a $20.00 bill on the night stand next to the bed, quietly closed the door, got into his Mazda, and drove away.

Teri found a ride to Salt Lake with a guy she met at the hotel. Once she got to her mothers, she phoned Jody. "Damn you asshole I'm pressing charges for abandonment."

"Whatever," he hung up the phone. Jody didn't care. He was free. He had his girls and Teri was 1200 miles away. The family was relieved and celebrated when Jody returned. The dirty deed had been done. To be on the safe side, Jody moved the girls to Fayette, Missouri and enrolled them in a new school. He didn't want Teri to know where they lived. And now he could live happily ever after with his three little princesses. But if that happened then this book would end here and you haven't even have been introduced to Payshence yet. So, lets continue.

After about five months, Teri came to Fayette. While Jody was at work she went to the girl's new school and checked them out. She looked up Pastor Hagget and asked for the church to pay for bus tickets for her and the girls to return to Salt Lake.

When the school day was over, Brother's girlfriend went to pick up the girls only to be told that they had been checked out earlier by their mother. Jody called the police, but because the court hearing hadn't occurred yet, the police could do nothing to stop Teri from taking them away. They did tip Jody off though that Teri was at the Greyhound station but when he got there, the bus was already gone with his babies.

This time it is Paapa to the rescue. Now Jody knew that the hearing was coming up and that was what most likely prompted Teri to do what she did so he needed to keep working so he could provide for the girls once he got them - his faith in Steve K ran that deep. Maama and Paapa decided they would go to Utah to keep an eye on the girls and Paapa got himself a job there and moved.

Something that hasn't been mentioned about Jody up to this point. He is one beautiful man. He has these ice blue eyes that can melt steel and all the years of gymnastics and hard work formed a well chiseled physic that bulges through his clothing in all the right places. His jaw is square and strong and there is a little dimple in his chin. To top it off, he has the deepest voice with a Texan drawl. To state the obvious, the chicks just can't keep their hands off this man.

Knowing that it was over permanently with Teri, Jody took up with a girl named Selena from Kansas City. Since his current job was much closer to KC than it was to Fayette, he stayed at Selena's place during the week, and returned home on weekends. Brother and Jody decided it would make better sense to get a house in between KC and Fayette so he and Selena got a house together in Warrensburg.

To celebrate their new home, Jody threw a BBQ and invited some of their friends over. This would be a great place to raise the girls and he seemed to have found a great woman to do it with. The food was good, the party was on and everyone was enjoying themselves. He felt so happy and settled as he looked around for Selena. He felt the urge to kiss her and share the moment but she was nowhere to be found so he went into the house to look for her.

The bedroom door was closed but he could hear people talking. He could hear Selena laughing. Jody put his hand on the knob and slowly turned. His girlfriend was sitting on the bed with two men, smoking meth off of some tin foil. She looked up as the door opened. Jody's face must have said it all.

"What!" She said.

Jody said nothing. He closed the door and went back to the guests. His mind raced but he didn't want his friends evening ruined so he continued to play host to his guests. All those years putting up with Teri's BS had taught him something - intolerance. His life had been ruined by drugs over and over again. This is NOT what he wanted. He went about the night as if nothing happened. Said goodbye to his friends. Put his stuff in his truck and left.

Paapa had made contact with uncle Larry up in Oregon. There was a big stucco job close by that was looking for masons. Jody drove to Oregon again, this time with Uncle Larry's address.

The custody hearing always seemed to be in the not-so-distant future. Jody now had to resettle but Uncle Larry had a great little cottage with a barn and cows. Jody worked all winter until the union called him back for work in Missouri. He had learned a lot about the area and fell in love with the ocean - a love that would stay with him.

Jody sent regular payments to Steve K and kept him up to date as to what was happening in his life in hopes for good news. The girls missed their dad and he spoke to them on the phone as much as he could. Mo, was very distressed by her mom's boyfriends. She made frequent calls from inside her bedroom closet to her dad complaining about the drug use going on in the house.

Jody documented everything at the recommendation of Steve. He also discovered that Teri's only job was giving plasma and she was recently cut off from this income source when it was discovered she was infected with Hepatitis C. Another arrow Jody could give Steve to put in the courtroom quiver.

This would be the last time Jody would go to work for the union in Missouri. He stuccoed a hospital and buildings at the university. He was up 18 feet in the air on the scaffolding along with a five-gallon bucket of stucco mud when a fat guy, who had no business being up there with him, climbed aboard. The scaffolding and stucco and Jody went crumbling to the ground. The boards, fortunately, broke and fell around Jody, but the stucco bucket had perfect accuracy and hit Jody in the back. His right leg came down at an angle and struck a rock. Jody was so concerned about the job, what the bosses would say, and the partially stuccoed wall, that he fashioned a make shift scaffold, refilled the bucket and finished the job.

That night was the motocross races and he was competing. His leg was bothering him a little but he didn't pay it much attention. Instead he suited up, loaded his bike in the back of his truck, and got ready to race. He kicked butt, taking first place as he usually did; only on occasion did he take second.

BM had thrown Brother a wedding down in Texas so the girlfriend was now his wife and they had a cute little boy, honoree as hell, that loved motorcycles.

Jody went to Brother's and was jumping on the trampoline with his nephew and teaching the neighborhood kids gymnastics. He enjoyed some BBQ and his family knowing that he would soon be going to Salt Lake for what could be a bumpy ride.

The next morning, the alarm clock went off, as usual. Jody stepped out of bed and went flat to the floor. His right leg collapsed from under him. He yelled for Mini, who had been staying with him off and on since Maama and Paapa had left. Thinking it was just dislocated, he had Mini push it back into the socket and he went off to work.

In the shower after work, his leg got stuck and after some time, he was able to work it out so it would move again. A few weeks later, while watching Mini's son box the neighbor boy on the front deck, Jody tumbled off when his leg came apart again. He put it back in place and went about his business.

Two months passed and Jody left for Utah. The reunion with his parents was long coming. They had rented a large home and decided Jody would stay there when he got the girls back. He went back to work for a company that had previously employed him and while up on a scaffold, his leg came apart again. He finally realized that the problem was not fixing itself and sought the advice of a doctor. They took x-rays.

"Jody, how long has this been going on?" the Doc asked.

"Oh, about 4 1/2 months," Jody told him.

"Son, your leg isn't dislocating, it's flat broke! You're gonna need immediate surgery."

Not knowing that a metal rod and three large screws were going to put him out of commission for the next six months, Jody went through with the surgery expecting to be better than new when it was over. One good thing came with being bedridden though, he had plenty of time to think and to plan. Think and plan, plan and think.

You know how I mentioned that one part of this story got shady, this part gets down right dirty. But no one would say she didn't deserve it.

Teri was working at a bar. Jody knew she had no driver's license so he hobbled to the bus stop with his crutches, took the bus to the closest stop to her work and once she got in the car to drive home, he called the police and reported her. He did this twice and both times she was arrested. That's all it took. The police were on to her and took it from there.

Jody also recorded all conversations he had with Teri concerning the girls. He was able to repeat what the girls would tell him and get her confessions - all on audio tape. When the girls came to visit, he noted their condition. They often had bad cases of head lice and this was reported to DCFS. Also, the new boyfriend has been hitting the girls and making sexual remarks to them. Both Teri and the boyfriend had Hepatitis C. Finally, DCFS intervened. The court date was just three days away. The girls were taken to the Christmas Box house based on the living conditions of Teri's home, flea bites covered the girls, and they had severe infestation of lice. Jody visited his girls at the Christmas Box House and got all the reports from DCFS to give to Steve.

Finally! Jody got his day in court. DCFS was there to testify. Teri, of course, showed up to. She didn't give much thought to first impressions though with her mini skirt, knee high boots, and a low-cut shirt showing off all the cleavage she could muster.

"I see why you dropped that off in Wyoming." Steve K leaned over and said in Jody's ear.

"Please rise for the Honorable Judge O," The clerk announced.

All rose. It was Steve's time to shine. He presented his case and then Teri's attorney presented his case. It was not going to well for her. She knew that and pulled her wild card.

"They aren't even his kids!" Teri blurted out.

"Miss, has Mr. Rhorer provided for and supported those girls since the time they were born?" Inquired Judge O.

"Yes," Teri responded, more sober than she knew she could ever be.

"Then they are his! Full custody is granted to Mr. Rhorer." The judge let down his gavel.

AUGUST 2ND, 2005: 14 years of heartache and frustration over with the tap of a wooden gavel. You would think one would learn. You would think one would be wise. You would think one would not repeat the same mistakes. You would think.......

In November of 2005, Jody Rhorer was given full custody of his 3 daughters due to being "abused and neglected as to the mother" (Third District Juvenile Court SLC, UT). Mia turned 5 years old the next day.

Jody raised his three girls himself - always maintaining employment, getting them to school, feeding and caring for them. He loved being a devoted dad and fought for several years to get full custody so he could protect them from their mother, grandmother, and the revolving door of men coming in and out of their lives.

APIL 17TH, 2003: Kirk and Kelly are married. He is 24, she 23.

APRIL 19TH, 2005: UNIFIED POLICE DEPARTMENT, Domestic Violence call

I responded to investigate a possible domestic dispute. When I arrived, I observed Kirk J and Kelly H in the front driveway speaking. I separated the two and spoke with each of them. It was apparent that the verbal argument had occurred and that no physical contact had been initiated by either party.

Kelly H had recently moved out of the home and returned to obtain property for the couple's mutual child. During the course of that exchange emotions had risen and a fight ensued. Kelly H had initially phoned the police from her cell phone as a precaution. The parties voluntarily separated and no further action was taken.

FEBRUARY 2ND, 2006: UNIFIED POLICE DEPARTMENT, Domestic Violence call

On 2 February 06, I was dispatched on a phone detail. Kirk J called to report that his wife damaged the front door to their house. He slammed the door in his wife's face. She immediately then kicked the door, damaging it. Kirk stated that it was an easy fix and he only wanted it reported. No police action taken. No evidence processed. Case closed.

CHAPTER 7
EVERYTHING OLD IS NEW AGAIN

Everything was great. Jody was back to work, although limited in what he could do since his knee was not a hundred percent yet. Mainly he was protecting the owner's son who had been beat up by some of the co-workers.

A large job came up in Colorado Springs and the whole crew was sent there to knock the job out fast. After three days, the job was done and the crew headed home. It was on that drive back that Jody called home to check on the kids. Mini had moved to Salt Lake and was also living with the family.

"Guess who's here to see you?" Mini exclaimed.

It was Kelly - the girl from the 49th Street Galleria Jody had dated for a couple months back when he was a teenager. Mini had kept in touch with her over the years. Kelly waited there at the house until Jody arrived.

Jody and Kelly started spending a lot of time together. She was always coming over to the house. He took her motocross racing with him frequently and they became good friends but Jody was taking it slow this time.

Summer was coming and the kids were getting out of school. Jody planned a trip to Missouri and invited Kelly along. She said she had business in Utah and she needed to stay there.

Jody and the girls went anyway. While they were there, the transmission went out on the truck so Jody called Kelly and she rented a truck in Salt Lake and drove out to pick up him and the girls. He left his truck with his brother with intentions of going back out and fixing it in the future. On the ride home Jody and Kelly talked about going to Oregon and spending the summer in his uncle's cottage. They still had a platonic relationship at this point.

Once in Oregon, they spent the summer visiting the beach, playing with the girls, raising cows and growing a garden. Jody took his old job back with the union and work was good. Their relationship had developed into more than friends but Jody wasn't in love.

Kelly was looking for work too and he found it. It paid really well. She started work as a stripper. Since Jody looked at their relationship more along the lines as friends with benefits, he really didn't care at that time what she did and he became part of "the pack". Jody and lots of beautiful strippers. Since he basically missed the single teenage and young adult years, it was makeup time for him.

Kelly had a couple little boys she had left behind in Salt Lake with a man Jody presumed was their daddy. From time to time she would fly back to Salt Lake to see them. On one of these trips she got breast implants - double D's.

There were signs in hind sight that were mostly ignored or unrecognized at the time. Kelly's trips to Salt Lake became more frequent. They seemed to be centered much more on partying than on visiting her sons. The partying continued when she would return to Oregon. Jody didn't like the cycle and began to withdraw.

Maama and Paapa came to visit and they went to see the Malamoth Falls and Mount St. Helen's lava tunnels. It felt like a family and the time was greatly enjoyed. It was after this trip that Kelly and Jody had a heart to heart. She wanted to know why he had become distant.

"Look Kel, if we are going to be together, and if that's what you really want, some things will have to change."

"What kinds of things?" Kelly inquired. She seemed open and honest.

"Well first of all, you gotta quit your stripping job," Jody said. "I can't be with a woman that's always partying and working in those kinds of places. Then you need to work on getting your boys up here so you don't have to go to Salt Lake all the time."

Kelly agreed and their relationship finally bloomed and she got a new job in a hospital. Every weekend Jody took the family on trips to enjoy the beautiful countryside and ocean. It was a few months later that Kelly found out she was expecting.

Jody wasn't happy. He didn't want to have a child with her at that point. He didn't trust her and she had told him she had an IUD - and she had, for a while. But she wanted a baby with Jody and had the IUD removed without his knowledge. But the act was done, a child was coming into the world.

Another trip to Salt Lake. While Kelly was on the phone with Jody, he could hear the party going on. She was staying with her sister, who was a meth addict. The trips were getting longer too. She was bringing her little boys with her to wild parties. By this time Jody had excepted that he was going to have another child and was greatly concerned about what pregnant Kelly was doing and partaking in.

When she would return from her trips, they would mainly fight. When she was home, she was always on the phone with her drug friends back in Salt Lake. Jody knew she was doing her share of partying on these trips, what he didn't know was the drugs were hard core - methamphetamine, and her favorite, heroine.

Christmas came. The house was decorated for the girls. Kelly's pregnancy was very apparent now. She kept hounding Jody to move back to Salt Lake. Jody had a large tax return coming and gave Dino a call. Dino agreed to let the family stay at his house while they made living arrangements. Not one day after they got to Dino's, Kelly took all of the money from Jody's wallet, all his bags, and disappeared. Jody called around until one of her friends tipped him off on her whereabouts.

Kelly was staying at Lena's. Lena had three kids of her own and was what is called a "hard core" addict. Now if you are reading this book you may get a really quick education on certain elements of the druggie lifestyle. I know that in writing it, I sure did!

This part gets a little gross. Ok it's just plain disgusting and I'm not sure who would think this stuff up and actually do it, but it is apparently going on out there. Lena does what is called a Booty Bump. That is where meth is taken in through the rectum and is one of the most potent ways for an addict to get high.

Stop reading; take a break; throw up; come back; read some more.

The police recovered half of Jody's money and his bags from Kelly. Jody and the girls turned around and went back to their cottage in Oregon. He wasn't doing this again. He liked that family, farm boy lifestyle he had at his uncle's spare house. The barn, the cows, the grape orchard, and fishing the river and ocean were not worth giving up for this messed up girl.

Months passed. The winter rains were nearly daily. Conversations between Jody and Kelly were rare, but the due date was approaching. When Jody won his custody fight, he did agree upon allowing Teri to see the girls during the summer. She did have conditions she had to meet at the order of the courts. She also couldn't have any live-in boyfriends if she wanted to have the girls stay at her house. To her credit, she did as the court said. Jody didn't want to jeopardize any of his rights with the girls and made sure he had them back in Salt Lake for their visitation. He went to work there again at Western Architectural Services and rented a house in Kearns.

Mini had still been in touch with Kelly. In fact, to she still sends her son's hand me downs to Kelly's boys and keeps in touch with her. She let Kelly know that Jody was back and where he was living. Kelly showed up, uninvited, to Jody's home. She was nearly to term now and he decided to let her move in. They agreed to make a go at it again. Jody didn't want the baby growing up without it's Daddy.

A week after Kelly returned, she moved her mother in and her heroine-addict sister, Abbey. Jody put his foot down, but they wouldn't leave. He knew they had nowhere to go so he considered finding another house and seeing if the landlord would lease to Kelly's mother. Kelly and Jody ended up in a fight and Jody went to bed. A few hours later, he woke up. Everyone was gone - they went to Lena's, the Booty Bump girl.

"Where were you guys last night?" Jody asked.

"Oh, you woke up? We went over to Lena's. She was really down and needed her friends. She just had her kids taken away."

"In the middle of the night? You expect me to believe that? I ain't stupid," Jody clearly wasn't buying it. "You didn't do any partying at all? Look at your belly! You know our baby is gonna be born pretty soon. You want it all messed up?"

"All we did was smoke a little weed, Jody. I promise."

Jody knew she was lying and knew he had to get her away from her family. He arranged to have them take over the lease and he got him and Kelly a house in Salt Lake.

Brother had started up the stucco and stone business again in Missouri. He had a really big doctor's house he was working on and begged for Jody to come help. It was June. The baby's due date was at the end of July. He thought he could swing it and be back for the baby's birth. A week into July, Kelly called Jody to let him know she wanted him back there by July 16th. She said she talked to the doctor about having the baby early. Jody reassured her that he would be home by the 18th and to hang tight. The baby wasn't due until the 23rd but Jody had asked the doctor if Kelly could be induced on the 26th if the baby hadn't come naturally yet, as that was his birthday.

Kelly had scored no points with any of Jody's friends or family, besides Mini. They all recognized that she didn't deserve a man like him. That didn't keep him from trying though, for the sake of the new baby.

JULY 16, 2007 1:00 PM: Payshence Rhorer was induced at the Pioneer Valley Hospital, weighing in at 7 pounds 6 ounces. It would be days before her Daddy, who was on the birth certificate and later removed by the State of Utah, would know that she was in the world and healthy.

On the 18th of July, Jody got back to Salt Lake City, two days too late. At no time was Jody informed that Kelly was having the baby. He didn't know until arriving home to find Kelly, her mom and sister there with the infant.

"What is this? You had the baby and didn't tell me!" Jody was furious, "And what is your mom and sister doing here?"

It was clear they were not just visiting the baby. They had taken over the girl's bedrooms. Their belongings were everywhere. The two women were covered with scabby sores from shooting up and they were touching Jody's new little baby girl!

"I told you that you better be home by the the 16th," Kelly responded. "And *you* set them up to fail leaving them in that big house in Kearns. They couldn't afford that place. This is *your* fault so don't come walking in here yellin at me!"

If you don't know this already, addicts cannot be alone. There is some type of built in paranoia that sets in with drug use and they have to have a support group of drug users around them. Druggies travel in packs.

The name Jody and Kelly had decided on was Payshence Ann Rhorer prior to her birth. "You gave her the name we agreed upon, right?" Jody asked.

Kelly held her up so Jody could see her tiny blue eyes, her daddy's eyes. "Her name is T____ A__ H_____." She said.

Now Jody was livid. "You named her after a convict POS druggie who was murdered by her creep of a boyfriend? You didn't even give her my last name? Did you even put me down as the dad on the birth certificate?"

"Hey that was my sister! And yes, you are on the birth certificate."

"Well your sister didn't deserve a namesake and I will never call her that. Her name is Payshence."

Jody's friendships run deep. This man has had the same friends since 6th grade and still has them to this day. One of those friends, Riley, had just arrived at the house to see Jody, but what he found was a man that was about to lose it.

"Hey Jody, let's go about this the right way, man," Riley reasoned. "Let's get the cops over here and have them remove Kelly's mom and sister. They'll take care of it and then you can spend some time with your new daughter. I'm sure her sisters will be super excited too."

They called the police, but when they arrived, Jody was the one interrogated. "Are these women residents in this home?" The policeman asked Jody.

"No, they *are no*t residents! It's my house! I'm on the lease. I've been out of town working and they just moved in."

"So, they have their belongs here and they have been staying here," the cop responded with an answer that seemed like a question.

"Without my permission or knowledge," Jody argued.

"Regardless, this is their current home and the daughter has invited them to stay. We are going to have to ask you to leave, sir. You are clearly a threat and need to cool off. You need to find somewhere else to go for the next 12 hours. Do you understand?" The cop pointed Jody to his truck.

"Let's go, Jody. You can spend the night at my house," Riley offered.

The next day, when the cooling off period was over, Jody returned to the house. He took every light bulb out, turned the gas off at the meter and padlocked it, put a temporary shut off on the power, then went back to Riley's.
Later that night, when Kelly, her mom and Abbey got back to the house, they saw a note from the power company on the front door stating the power has been shut off. Kelly called Jody, madder than Hell.

"What did you do? How do you expect us to live and take care of your new baby with no power?"

"I am not going to pay for your mother and sister to live in *my* house that I rented to take care of *my* girls. I won't turn anything back on until *they* are gone." Jody was firm.

"Wudd are me and the baby supposed to do?" Kelly inquired.

"Riley said you and Payshence can stay here until the druggies move out. I won't have druggies around my family."

Kelly still had a step-sister to turn to. The family had full support of our governmental system. They all received welfare, food stamps, and the step-sister, got Section 8 housing. Step-sister had 3 kids with three different fathers and also was a drug addict. A perfect example of our hard-earned tax dollars at work helping the "poor have-nots." This is not a blanket statement about everyone receiving government assistance as many people legitimately need it, however, there are infinite number of people taking advantage of the system and being enabled by it as well.

"Forget you, Jody! You can kiss my ass. I'll take your baby and we'll go live with my step-sister." And they did.

Jody set up housekeeping again for his girls. Kelly had left all her things behind, but the necessities. Jody went to work, like always, and over the next several months he did what he could to see Payshence and patch things up with Kelly.

What happened next gets crazy and you may want to skip it altogether:

OCTOBER 19, 2007: It was a Saturday but Jody had to work. When he got home that afternoon, there were cops at the house. Kelly had picked up her two boys and brought them to Jody's house. She put the boys in the backyard and went to the basement where there was a window she could see and hear out of. She locked herself and the baby in a room and injected herself with a syringe. She was in a heroine stupor. She could see and hear but she couldn't move.
An older neighborhood boy in his early teens came into the yard and began playing with the boys. After he was sure no one was watching, he took the five-year-old aside and forced him to perform oral sex. Kelly could hear everything that was going on, but was so high she couldn't do anything about it.

POLICE REPORT: MOLESTATION INVESTIGATION

This is a report of sex offenses against 4, 5, 7, year old children with the suspect being 13 years old. The suspect was located and booked into DT for Sodomy upon a child and indecent exposure. Parents were notified of these events.

I was dispatched to a molest investigation...We met Kelly H at the listed address...She states that she did reside in a basement apartment with her two children, but was moving out and would be leaving the apartment.

Kelly H and Kirk J were husband and wife and are now divorced with J1 and J2 being common children.

Kim J and Kirk J are now in a relationship with Kim's son residing with them.

Kelly H was babysitting Kim's son at the time of the incident.

Kelly H states that she was moving items at her apartment and the three children were at the address.

Later in the evening, J1 stated to his dad that David made him, "suck on his weeny." J1 stated he did not want to, indicating, "No, I'm going to tell my mom." The child did state to her that David did place his penis in J1's mouth.

J2 and Kim's son both stated that David had showed him his genitals. They both stated that David had hair upon his genitals.

Kelly stated that the children explained that David had taken them to the outside of the home on the east side and met with them one at a time.

David was booked into DT for Sodomy of a child, one count and two counts of indecent exposure...David's mother...was uncooperative to the point where charges against her for interfering may be filed. She refused entry to Officers, she refused to get David when asked, and continually talked on the telephone in an effort to ignore and delay our investigation.

The police had the teenager in their custody and the boys presumed dad, Kirk, showed up at the house and began tearing into Jody.

"What the *hell* did you let happen to my kids?" Kirk accused.

"Wait a minute, I've been at work all day. I just got here. What are your kids doing at *my* house and what are *you* doing letting that drug bitch take 'em?' Jody yelled back, "This is your fault as much as anybody's. *You* put up with her shit for too long."

NOTE: It had become apparent to Jody that Kelly had a problem long before he had met her. She claimed her babysitters were shooting her up with meth starting at age 12. She had seen her mother do it so she didn't think much about it. She even suspected that the babysitter and her husband may have raped her when she was passed out on heroine. When she was 16, she won a date on a local radio station. The man was over 21, got her drunk and raped her. She told these stories like there were bragging rights attached to them. Maybe she needed excuses to fall back on for the rest of her life.

NOVEMBER 2ND, 2007:   INVESTIGATIVE REPORT

I interviewed the victim in this case at the Avenues CJC. Prior to the interview, I spoke with Kelly and Kim J.

Kelly H told me that she and her boyfriend, Kirk J, were residing at...Wright Circle with their two children, J1 and J2. Kirk has another son, TC - Kim J's son. On the date of the incident, Kim's son was over at the house visiting.

Kelly H states that they were moving out of the apartment that very day that this incident happened. The children were outside playing.

Notice the changes in Kelly's story. Notice that Kirk is now considered Kelly's boyfriend and the third boy is supposed to be - but is not - Kirk's. Notice Kelly didn't report the incident to the police for several hours - stating she was "moving things". When the truth was, she just couldn't move at all.

CONTINUED:

Kelly sates that she heard a conversation outside her bedroom window, it was J1 and David....was telling him to, "Do it now!" J1 replied, "No, I don't' want to. David said, "Don't go tell your mom, it's okay."

After being questioned by the police, the teenager was released to his parents. The cops found another child at the teenager's school that had also been molested by the same teen. Instead of cooperating with police, the family of the teenager, who had only lived in the house for 2 1/2 months, packed up and moved the boy out of state before the cops could press charges.

Jody wanted out of the neighborhood too. He found a nice house on Mockingbird Way and moved all four girls with him. Kelly was part of the package too, but spent much of her time with Lena and her drug addict sister. Jody didn't like it but he also knew he couldn't control it and saying anything only started fights.

JUNE 24TH, 2008: UNIFIED POLICE DEPARTMENT, Public Ordinance Civil Call

Dispatch initially received a call from Ms. Kim KJ who told them she was trying to move out of the residence but her boyfriend would not let her leave. While dispatch was on the line, Kirk J called stating he was the boyfriend and the reason he would not let her leave was because she was high on some drugs and he didn't feel it was safe.

I arrived at the residence and made contact with Kirk who told me Kim just left in a black ford truck. He did not know her direction of travel or anything about the truck, but she had her seven-year-old child in the vehicle. Kirk explained he has two boys of his own, ages six and seven and when he got home from work the boys were there and Kim was passed out on the bed. She had white stuff around her mouth and on her tongue and her mouth and eyes were wide open. Kirk said he was worried about her, so he woke her up and told her he didn't want her living at his house anymore. Kirk said she started packing up her stuff right away, and when she tried to leave, he hid her keys because he did not want her driving. Kirk said she had called a friend to come and pick her up. Kim tried to leave in the truck and when Kirk was on the phone with dispatch she left.

Kirk gave us a phone number for her and we were able to make contact. She agreed to meet with us at the Kearns Substation, however she never showed up. We called again and she told us she was at the McDonalds. She sounded very groggy and slurred on the phone. We went to McDonalds but we were unable to locate her. I found the truck listing, however, and requested dispatch broadcast an Attempt to Locate for the vehicle and if stopped, check the driver's welfare. Case Complete.

SEPTEMBER 8TH, 2008: UNIFIED POLICE DEPARTMENT, Domestic Violence Non-Violent call

I was dispatched to investigate a domestic in progress. Information given, open line, can hear female crying (Kim K), saying husband, Kirk J, won't leave her alone.

Upon my arrival I was met at the door by Kirk and Kim. Kim was crying and asked me if I could stay while she moved her things out of the house. She told me she had been in a verbal argument with Kirk and he told her to leave. She told me when she started to pack, he changed his mind and told her to stay and started to move her items back to the room. She said that was when she called 911.

Kirk said they had been fighting off and on for the last couple of days. He told me the relationship was coming to an end and he didn't want it to come to that. Kirk said the argument they had today was verbal only. He said he told Kim to move out because he was tired of fighting. He told me after he told her to move out, she started to pack and he realized that wasn't' what he wanted. I told both Kim and Kirk I would stay until she removed her belongings from the house. Kim was able to remove her things without further incident. Case closed.

Jody decided that if he was going to have any rights to his baby girl, he better be her legal father and began planning a wedding with Kelly, only there was just one small problem that Kelly forget to mention - she was still married to Kirk. Not only were they married but he had her two boys a majority of the time and she dropped off baby Payshence at his house too. Another rather important revelation that Kelly hadn't told Jody, only one of those boys was Kirk's, the other was some other mans who isn't getting to see him. (More information on this comes later in the story.)

"Sign the f___ing papers, Kirk," Jody overheard Kelly yelling one day.

While the couple was living in Oregon, there were many trips back and forth to Utah where Kelly claimed to be visiting her boys and family. Jody would later learn that during that time, Kelly and Kirk had filed for divorce and there were divorce proceedings happening. It is not known why it didn't come to fruition at that time.

Kelly assured Jody that Kirk would give her the divorce and wedding plans commenced. They purchased a dress, wine glasses, napkins, all the fixings for the big day. Kelly insisted they have each other's names tattooed on the insides of their wrists. So they did. There is a nice cover up tat on Jody's left inner wrist of a tribal dragon now - no one would ever suspect that engraved under that dragon is the word *Kelly*.

They put the wedding date out a ways so that there would be plenty of time to get the divorce done, but Kirk didn't make good on Kelly's promise to Jody and had no intention of giving her a divorce. Kirk was and most likely always will be obsessed with this woman. He fantasized about getting her back and knew keeping her kids and staying legally married to her would give him some control. She played along too, continuing a physical relationship with him from time to time. They were both puppets on each other's strings, he just happened to have one tied around her neck.

It would take an act of the court ordering them to get divorced for it to finally happen in 2012, and within a few months, Kelly would be married to another man - the possible father of her fifth child, also born under wedlock to Kirk.

Life resumed with some normalcy. The priorities were the kids, work, working out, church. The family attended church regularly. Jody and Kelly were baptized together and began marital counseling. It was as normal as things could get for that time. Jody was working for Big-D Construction in Park City and Kelly was working as a nursing assistant.

They had plans to meet up at Kelly's brother's after work. Jody stopped at the store and picked up flowers, cheese, drinks, and snacks. He looked forward to a relaxing evening. He called Kelly to confirm that their plans were still on. What he didn't know was that Kelly's fun had already begun. Her cousin, Cuzzy, had come to her work and begged her to go party with her, unable to resist, Kelly walked out in the middle of her shift at the nursing center to go get high with Cuzzy.

When Kelly didn't show up for dinner, Jody called around attempting to find her. Her friends knew where she was but were her accomplices. For four days there was no sign of Kelly. Jody had all the kids including baby Payshence, his older three girls, and Kelly's two boys.

On the fourth day, Kelly called Jody. "Hey, I'm at Cuzzy's. Come get me."

Jody didn't say much, just got in his truck and drove to Cuzzy's apartment. He was disgusted by what he saw when Kelly walked out. She was filthy and clearly hadn't showered or changed her clothes since she disappeared, and her arm was full of puncture marks from shooting up. He counted at least nine holes. Jody hesitated about even allowing her in his truck. Kelly was oblivious to all of it. It didn't take long for an argument about her whereabouts to break out. By the time they reached home the fight had escalated to a category five tornado.

"I can do whatever the f____ I feel! If I wanna kick it with my Cuzzy you ain't stoppin me. Just cuz we got a kid don't mean you own me."

The neighborhood was now in on the chaos and a neighbor called the cops. Jody knew he needed to leave so he grabbed the girls and left the house for a while. After they both had time to cool down, the family went back home and resumed their un-normal life. A few weeks later, Jody was riding in the car with Kelly when he saw a police car up ahead. He figured if the cops pulled them over, he most likely had a warrant for his arrest.

"Kelly, slow down a bit and stay behind that cop," Jody said.

"Why?" Kelly responded.

"Just do what I say," Jody said.

Kelly pushed harder on the gas pedal.

"What the hell? Slow down. I don't want them cops running my plates!"

Kelly went faster.

"What happens if they run your plates?"

"You know what happens. They probably arrest me for coming out to the house last week when the neighbors called them," Jody responded.

Kelly hit the gas and pulled in front of the police car. It was only a minute or two before the lights and siren flipped on. Kelly pulled over and watched, amused, while Jody was handcuffed and taken away.

For three days Jody sat in jail. Kelly ignored his calls. One of his best friends, Brad, kept a good eye on Kelly though. He spent those three days partying with her at Jody's house and spending his money.

Jody got a hold of a bail bondsman that said he would take his boat for collateral. When he got out of jail, he got his boat and brought it to the bail bondsman.

There was the issue of Brad and Kelly, but Jody was mainly concerned about paying his bills. He knew in his heart what she was and that there would be no wedding, no happily ever after. What was the point in fighting? She was never wrong, never sorry, and never wanted to change. He had mouths to feed. He sold the boat to pay off the bail bondsman and sold a motorcycle that he had been putting together to pay the rent.

The next few months flew by. Payshence had her second birthday. They threw a party and had friends over. The wedding date was still pending but there were so many setbacks. An old friend showed up out of the blue and Kelly disappeared once more on a party binge.

When she drug herself back to the house after a few days, the fighting began again. Kelly called the cops and Jody was put in jail for 30 days. According to the police, if someone called the cops during a domestic dispute, someone has to be taken away from the home and potentially arrested. *Someone* just seemed to always be Jody.

While Jody sat in jail the proposed wedding date came and went. Jody sat and thought. He wondered about his kids, the church members, what everyone was thinking about him. He was embarrassed and humiliated. Kelly didn't want to take care of Jody's girls and called up Teri to come and get them instead of his parents. Jody was furious but could do nothing. At that point he decided to make the best of a bad situation and got a job in the jail. It helped pass the time and kept his mind off what was happening at home. Thirty days in the box can feel like an eternity.

Court day came and Jody expected to be released. He was surprised to find Kelly at the hearing. For the first time he heard why he was being held, Kelly had claimed that Jody beat her up because, and this is a direct quote, "I quit sucking his dick". Now her story had changed. Kelly was begging the court to release Jody and saying nothing had happened.

"Please your honor, I really need you to let him out cuz rent is due and I need him home to pay the bills."

Not only did Jody miss the wedding date, he lost his job while in jail. The judge gave him 30 days to get a new job. He was fitted with an ankle monitor as he would not plead guilty - which he had to pay $17.00 a day for, and he also had to post bail - another call to the bail bondsman.

Home again never felt so good - for about three minutes any way. Jody looked through the window into the yard just in time to see Kelly giving money to three Hispanic men. He could only guess that it was for drugs. As he walked through the house, he could see that Kelly's mother and sister had moved in - again. He went to the master bedroom. There were men's clothes strewn around the room, but they were not his. All his clothes were gone from the closet and the dresser. The bathroom hadn't been cleaned for the month Jody was away and the sink was littered with what appeared to be pubic hair.

None of it mattered though because, somehow his baby girl was ok. He wondered what was happening to her while he was gone. Who was tanking care or her? Jody was at the bottom of the barrel. He had no money, no job, no boat, no motorcycle, and no clothes.

At least he had his truck. He went to the back yard to check on it and sort through his tools that were in his work trailer that had been hooked up to the truck. But instead, there was an empty spot where the truck and trailer had been. He called his parents.

"Mom, do you know where my truck is?" Jody asked.

"Well me and Dad wanted to talk to you about that when we saw you cuz you are gonna be really upset and Dad didn't think you should know while you were in jail."

"Know what, Mom?"

"From how I understand it, Kelly gave the truck and trailer to this illegal for drugs. We called the cops as soon as we saw it was gone and reported it stolen and let the bank know," Maama George said breathing out a huge sigh. "The cops caught the guy driven the truck and everything. He had torn out the ignition since Kelly didn't have any keys."

"They got my truck back then?" Jody said. "Where is it?"

"No, we just told the bank to take it since it was all messed up and the cops weren't gonna do nothin cuz Kelly said she gave it to the guy."

Jody dropped his head in his hands. Now what? He called the pastor that was supposed to marry them to apologize. The pastor requested they meet.

"I can't go any further than the mail box since I got this damn ankle monitor on," Jody said.

"I'll be over shortly, Jody. I really want to talk in person, but I don't want Kelly to hear what I have to say, so I'll meet you outside."

Within 10 minutes, the pastor pulled up to the front of the house. Jody extended his hand for a shake.

"Hop in my car, Jody. Are we ok talking here in front of the house?"

Jody nodded.

"Son," the pastor began, "don't feel bad about missing the wedding date. The Lord works in mysterious ways. Truth is, after what I saw going on in this house while you were penned up, I wouldn't have married the two of you anyways."

"Waddaya mean?" Jody asked.

"Well I stopped over one day to check on Kelly and the kids. I hadn't seen them at church since you got locked up. What I saw going on here was nothing like I was expecting. There were people everywhere in the house. It was apparent by the empty booze bottles what was going on. To me it looked like drugs and a non-stop party. I think Kelly even had some people living in the garage."

Jody was speechless. Minute by minute things just kept getting worse.

"The best thing you can do, son," the pastor continued, "is to get your kids and get your things and get as far away from this woman as you can."

Jody thanked the pastor for watching out for his family for him, shook his hand again, and got out of the car. It was all he could do to keep from breaking down. He walked to the garage and opened the door. As the pastor had said, it was clear people had been living in the garage. Blankets, empty beer cans and whiskey bottles, and worst of all, syringes, littered the cement floor. Jody shook his head then shook it all off. He was trapped. He didn't want to jeopardize little Payshence's safety and knew that her mother would always have rights over him based on the laws of the state of Utah. He also wanted to get his girls back from Teri as soon as possible and put his house back in order. On the bright side, Jody called Big-D and got his construction job back.

It was now Halloween. Kelly had managed to keep the drug use hidden and not disappear on any binges for several months. She was served to appear in court on the DCFS charges but Jody was not served. When she went in front of Judge V, he was upset that Jody was not there. Jody had no idea that he was expected to go as well. The judge postponed the hearing until the following day. Early the next morning, as Jody was getting ready for work, the sheriff showed up and served him a summons to appear that day.

"What's this?" he threw the papers on the bed.

Kelly barely looked at them and yelled, "I don't know!"

"You *do* know!" Jody yelled back. "What was happening around here when I was gone?"

"Apparently some fool called DSFS, didn't they!" Kelly was belligerent.

"Do you know what this means?" Jody asked. "They're gonna take our daughter."

"They ain't gonna do nothin. No bitches are takin my baby girl."

"We need to leave, Kelly. If we don't go Payshence is gonna get taken away. You really need to listen to me."

He called his boss to let him know he would be coming in late, and drove Kelly to the court house. At the hearing, the judge ordered DCFS to present their case.

OCTOBER 27TH, 2008: SLC 3rd District Court, Judge V Presiding

STATE OF UTAH in the Interest of J1, J2 and PR
Petitioner, State of Utah, Division of Child and Family Services, by and through counsel, hereby alleges that the above-named children are within the age of juvenile court jurisdiction...This petition is based upon the following allegations:

1. *J1 is a 7-year-old male child...J2 is a six your old male child...PR is a one-year-old child.*
2. *Kelly H...is the mother of the above-named children.*
3. *Kirk J...is the father of J1 and J2.*
4. *Jody Rhorer....is the purported father of PR...Legal paternity of the child has not been established.*
5. *There is prior DCFS history involving this family. In October, 2005, DCFS supported a finding of domestic violence related child abuse of J1 and J2 against the father, Kirk J. In November 2007, DCFS supported a finding of sexual abuse of J1 and lewdness involving J2 as the victim of a 13-year-old out-of-home perpetrator. **There are numerous investigations that have resulted in unsupported findings involving this family.***
6. *The mother has a history of being involved in relationships where domestic violence occurs. On July 21, 2008, the mother and Jody were involved in a domestic dispute after the mother refused to perform oral sex on Jody. When police arrived at the home, the mother was observed to be crying hysterically in the driveway. Police heard the mother speaking on her cell phone with an unknown individual. She stated, "I wouldn't suck his dick so he grabbed me by the hair and threw me on the ground. He choked me, hit me in the face, he pulled me around.*

This is one of Kelly's favorite stories to tell. She loves to spurt it out in court, one would guess, for reactionary purposes. Let's revisit that day. Jody and Kelly were in the bedroom and having an intimate moment Kelly had initiated, when her cell phone rang. The voice on the other end was a male asking if "his girl" wanted to go get high with him. Instead of hanging up, Kelly continued the conversation until Jody grabbed the phone away from her and threw it. At that point, Kelly went crazy on Jody and they did have a brawl resulting in the police arriving at the request of a neighbor.
CONTINUED
The mother then became uncooperative with police and told them to leave. Later, the mother reported to police that Jody repeatedly hit her in the face with an open hand and then bit her right pinky finger then tried to strangle her. Police observed scratches to the mother's neck, cuts to her lip and left cheek, and a cut on her pinky finger....

Upon reviewing dozens of pages of court documents, there appeared to be common themes that reoccurred. One was that Kelly didn't like to cooperate with police right after an incident and only after hours or days would she call to make a report. The reason for this? She was under the influence and impaired by meth or other drugs.

CONTINUED

7. The mother has been very uncooperative with DCFS. The caseworker has made at least five unannounced home visits, but the mother does not answer the door. The caseworker has called the mother and left business cards on the mother's front door, asking the mother to contact DCFS, but the mother has not availed herself to the caseworker.

8. The mother has previous convictions for illegal possession/use of a controlled substance and theft. The mother currently has two warrants for her arrest for driving infractions.

9. Kirk has prior convictions for 5 counts of illegal possession of a controlled substance, 2 counts possession with intent to distribute a controlled substance, possession of drug paraphernalia, providing false information to law enforcement, carrying a concealed dangerous weapon and driving under the influence with personal injury....

10. Jody Rhorer has prior convictions for simple assault, violation of a protective order, and domestic fighting...

11. The children are not enrolled in nor are they eligible for enrollment in any Native American Tribe.

12. It is in the best interest of the children that DCFS be awarded protective supervision over the children.

Based on the above allegations, the State of Utah, Division of Child and Family Services, respectfully move the Court to find that:

1. The above-named children are abused, neglected and/or dependent children pursuant to U.C.A 78A6-105(2008).

2. The above-named children are within the jurisdiction of the Juvenile Court

Based on the above findings, the State of Utah, Division of Child and Family Services, respectfully moves the Court to:

1. DCFS is awarded Protective Supervision over the family.

2. Appoint a Guardian ad Litem to represent the best interests of the children.

3. Substantiate the supported findings of the Division of Child and Family Services,

4. Set this matter for an expedited hearing...and to address the immediate protection of the children.

5. Make whatever other orders are in the children's best interest.

Jody's court date came. Kelly, her mother and sister had been tormenting Jody since he had gotten home. Prior to Jody's court appearance, Kelly scratched Jody's face so badly that there were fresh scabs and red claw marks running down the side of his head.

"All rise for the Honorable Judge S," the court bailiff stated.

Jody stood, representing himself; the fresh wounds on his cheek visible to the judge.

"So, young man, you can't get out of jail for a few weeks without more trouble?" the judge asked, referring to his facial wounds.

"Look Judge, no police got called since I got out. I didn't cause no trouble. I just need this damn ankle monitor off my leg so I can get on with my life," Jody explained. "If you look at the court record, you'll see that Kelly made all that up and even said so in court. She also told my PO that she made that all up just to get me in trouble. I spent a month in jail for basically nothing. The drug charges and the DCFS investigation all happened when I was locked up."

The judge laughed with some amusement and granted Jody's request.

Jody had a plan to take all the girls to Missouri, like the pastor had told him to do. But now Jody worried about leaving the state with the DCFS summons looming overhead. Rent was due again and Jody was not going to pay another month for Kelly's mother and sister. Looking back, Jody has always regretted not taking Payshence out of the state at that moment in time. Had he done so, the entire course of this story would have changed. But fear of what the government might do prevented him from following his heart.

Jody asked Teri if he could come and stay with her until the DCFS investigation was over. Teri agreed, since she already had the other girls with her. Jody took Payshence and left Kelly and her family behind.

It didn't take long for Kelly to be evicted from the house and come begging for Jody and Terri to take her in. To his surprise, Teri said she could stay with them. Teri had been taking care of Payshence when Jody was at work., but Kelly brought with her drama and drugs. She hooked up with Cuzzy again for another party binge and disappeared.

As usual, Jody went out to find her, only this time, Kirk and his current girlfriend, Kim, were also part of the search as they had Kelly's two older boys. No one had success, but after a few days, she showed up at the house like road kill that wasn't quite dead yet.

As the zombie-like figure stumbled sideways down the street toward the house, the whole family looking on from the front yard, Teri exclaimed, "This is it, Jody. She needs to go." Interesting how the shoe looks different being worn on someone else's foot.

Jody knew Teri was right though, and that the situation was not going to work much longer, but he also didn't want to rent another place as he planned to leave the state with all the kids once he straightened things out with DCFS. The logical solution was to get temporary housing, so he bought a fifth wheel trailer and moved his girls and the "druggy," as he referred to her, to the KOA Campground.

NOVEMBER 4TH, 2008: 3RD DISTRICT COURT, Motion for Appointment of Counsel

Kelly submitted to the court a Motion for Appointment of Counsel. She stated that she was currently "separated" and was "financially responsible for the care of __1__ child. She stated that her "monthly income of all members of *her* household was $800 to $1100. Most of the form was left blank.

NOVEMBER 7TH, 2008: ORDER OF APPOINTMENT OF CONFLICT COUNSEL

*The Court having determined that conflict counsel is necessary in this matter… is hereby ordered that Attorney JN be appointed in this matter to represent the **father**, **Jody Rhorer***

CHILD WELFARE PRETRIAL HEARING
The matter comes before the Court for a Child Welfare Pretrial Hearing.
Ms. L (appointed counsel for Kelly H) was excused with the mother to speak about the allegations in the petition.
The Court tried to locate conflict counsel for the father (Kirk) but was unsuccessful.
Ms. Nickel advised the court that service was not made to the father, Jody Rhorer.
The court inquired where the children were currently living.
Ms. Nickel advised the Court that Payshence is in Kelly H's custody and J1 and J2 are in Kirk J's custody.
Ms. L advised the Court that the mother is in dispute with the petition but would stipulate to post services and would submit to a UA test if ordered by the Court today.
Kirk expressed concern of why the children were not removed and gave basis. Kirk furthermore requested that the child, PR, be removed at this time due to the mother not providing the child to the Division of Child and Family Services and further expressed that the mother is not taking court involvement seriously and there is belief that the child…is in substantial danger and removal would be warranted.
Ms. L expressed that the mother is willing to participate with DCFS and addressed that there is nothing to warrant the removal of the child.
Ms. Nickel advised the Court that there is an active warrant for the mother and there are allegations that the mother is currently living with the father, Jody.
The paternal grandmother addressed the Court that she would be willing to take the child.
Mr. J, Guardian ad litem, had no objections to placing the child with the paternal grandmother.
The mother, Kelly H, is taken into custody due to an active warrant for failure to appear before another Judge.
ORDERS: *The protective custody of PR is placed with DCFS. The removal of said child from the home and placement of the child in the custody of an agency or individual other than his or her parents was in the best interest of the child. The parents are ordered to contact ORS to determine a support amount for the child. Kirk J is ordered to submit a random UA test. Kelly H is to have supervised visitation.*

NOVEMBER 7, 2008: SHELTER HEARING

This matter comes before the court for a shelter hearing. The court finds that appropriate notice was given to the father and/or mother in regard to this shelter hearing, and that all preliminary requirements have been met.

Ms. Nickel, Attorney for the State of Utah proffered testimony in regard to placing said children in shelter. Attorney Connie indicated that she would like more time for discovery. Further, Kirk J will cooperate however necessary.

(Remember this name. November of 2008 is when Attorney Connie was assigned as free legal counsel to Kirk and would continue at his beck and call to administer free legal services for the next 10 years.)

Mr. J, GAL, agreed with the continued removal of the children. Further, Mr. J indicated that he believes the grandmother is an appropriate placement. Ms. K, appointed attorney for Kelly, indicated that the mother does not stipulate to the removal and will drug test. Further, Mr. Rhorer lives with her. The father, Mr. Rhorer, was served a copy of the petition in open court. Mr. Rhorer stated that he would vacate the mother's residence if that is what the court ordered.

FINDINGS: Whereas, a verified petition has been filed in the above-entitled Court in the interest of the above-named children alleging facts or circumstances of neglect, abuse, or dependency that bring said children within the jurisdiction of the Juvenile Court, and based on information presented at the shelter hearing and available to the Court it appears that:

Continuation in the home would be contrary to the welfare of the children and removal is in their best interest; Removal was reasonable in that there is a substantial danger to the physical health or safety of the children and that the children cannot be protected without removal from the custody of the parents and that an emergency existed justifying the removal. It is in the best interest of the child to be placed in the temporary care and custody of DCFS pending further hearing on the matter.

ORDERS: PR is to remain in the protective custody of DCFS with authorization for placement with the Grandmother, Georgia Rhorer.

J1 and J2 are to remain in the custody and guardianship of Kirk J. Sibling visitation is authorized through DCFS.

DCFS may consider returning custody to the mother if the father moves out of her residence and there is verification to that effect. The Guardian ad Litem is to be notified.

Mr. Rhorer is to have no contact with the mother, directly or indirectly.

Restraining orders were put in place against Kelly and Jody and they were ordered not to have any contact with each other. Payshence was ordered to be taken away and put in the Christmas Box House. What had happened while Jody was in jail? He still didn't know and wasn't privy to the DCFS report. The judge gave Jody 3 hours to get his things packed and ruled that Kelly could continue to reside in Jody's fifth wheel at the North Temple KOA.

About the time that Jody and Kelly arrived back at the KOA, Kelly's mom showed up with Payshence. Jody began packing up his things and the girl's belongings. He wasn't sure what was going to happen with Payshence. He was getting her clothes and toys together when there was a loud knock on the door. Jody opened the trailer door to find two police officers in bullet proof vests and body armor.

"We have orders to remove Payshence Rhorer from this home," barked one of the officers.

They eyed Jody suspiciously; waiting for him to make a move so they could use blunt force against him. Jody clutched his precious little girl, tears welling in his eyes; fear welling in Payshence's. One officer reached out and carelessly plucked her out of Jody's grip. Jody handed the other one her bag. He felt so angry and helpless at the same time. He wanted to fight to the death for his little girl - but he knew he would come out on the losing end of that battle. He could do nothing but hold back the tears and tell his baby girl that everything would be okay and he would come and get her soon.

Jody left his trailer and Kelly behind at the KOA and he and the older three girls moved in with his parents. There was a placement hearing shortly after Payshence had been taken.

NOVEMBER 12, 2008: SHELTER ORDER

State of Utah, in the interest of: J1, J2, PR

The above matter came before the court for a Shelter Hearing on the 7th of November. The following persons were present: Ms. Nickel, Assistant Attorney General; Mr. J, Guardian ad Litem; Ms. L, attorney for mother, Kelly H; Connie, counsel for the father, Kirk J; Jody Rhorer, father of PR; Kirk J, father of J1 and J2; and grandmother. Notice was served on the mother and Mr. Kirk J.

A Verified Petition, dated November 6, 2008, was filed. Counsel was appointed to represent the mother. Conflict counsel was appointed to represent Mr. Kirk J. Mr. JN was appointed to represent Jody Rhorer.

PR had been placed in protective custody by the court. The parties stipulated to the reasonableness of the removal. The parties discussed the need to continued removal. The State argued that in spite of the history of domestic violence, the mother has chosen to be with Mr. Rhorer, resulting in the need for continued removal. The Guardian ad Litem supported continued removal of PR and requested she be placed in the temporary custody and guardianship of DCFS. Ms. L - Kelly's attorney, opposed continued removal and indicated her client would cooperate with the Division of Child and Family Services. She disputed the factual allegations. Mr. Rhorer indicated he would move out of the house.

FINDINGS:

1. The jurisdictional requirements have been met.

2. In accordance with Utah Code, a preponderance of the evidence shows that one of the following circumstances exists:

A. There is a substantial danger to the physical health or safety of the child, and the child cannot be protected without removal from the custody of the parents.

B. The child is suffering emotional damage, as a result of a parent engaging in or threatening the children with unreasonable conduct, and there are no reasonable means to protect the child's mental health without a removal from custody.

C. The child or another child in the same household has been physically or sexually abused, or is at substantial risk of being physically or sexually abused by a parent or a person known to the parent.

D. The parent(s) is/are unwilling to have physical custody of the child.

E. The children is/are in immediate need of urgent medical care.

F. The parent's actions, omissions, or habitual action create an environment that poses a threat to the children's health or safety.

G. The parent's action in leaving a child unattended would reasonably pose a threat to the children's health or safety.

H. The child or another minor in the same household has/have been neglected.

3. Continuation in the home would be contrary to the welfare of the child, PR, and removal is in her best interest. The lack of preventive efforts was reasonable because one of the following emergency situations/aggravated circumstances occurred:

a. Any of the grounds for removal or circumstances listed under 78-3a-301, or 78-3a306(9) or (12).

The truth is, the court had no reason to take Payshence away from Jody. She was not neglected by him, left alone, denied love, attention or affection. Her safety was not in jeopardy. Kelly had a drug problem. The two argued about it to the point of fighting. Kelly made up stories about Jody to get the attention off of herself and her problem. Neighbors complained about the partying going on at the residence when Jody was out of town working on a job and while locked up for Kelly's false allegations. If there was truly a problem in the home, why weren't Jody's other children taken out of the house? Why was only the baby removed? The court stated that Kirk had child abuse charges, but the two older boys were both released to his custody.

CONTINUED:

4. There is not a natural parent available, with whom the child, PR, was not residing in the time the events or condition that brought her within the court's jurisdiction occurred, and who desires custody of the child.

5. The Division of Child and Family Services is to conduct an investigation regarding the safety and appropriateness of placement with a relative who requests placement. DCFS shall report it's findings to the Court. Pending such report, the child shall remain in the custody of the agency.

At no time is the reason revealed as to why Payshence was removed. Instead, only lists of code are given with scenarios - none of which matched the truth. The truth was, while Jody was gone, DCFS showed up at the house and Kelly refused to come to the door, instead, yelling out the window and provoking the case worker. She was entertaining two recently released prison inmates and her cousin, Cuzzy, and they were all having a drug fest. Later, Jody would find photos Kelly had taken of the four of them in his bedroom.

CONTINUED:
It is hereby ordered, adjudged, and decreed:
1. The initial removal of the child, PR, was necessary pursuant to the specific findings herein included.
2. It is in the best interest of the child to be placed in the temporary legal custody and guardianship of the grandmother, for continued care and placement pending the adjudication hearing. Temporary Custody and guardianship of the boys continues with their father, Kirk J.

Once again, there were no specific findings ever mentioned. Payshence was recommended to be placed with Kirk's lesbian mother and her live -n partner - neither of whom were related to her. However, Kirk's mother told Jody she didn't want to be a part of this and Jody's mother had spent so much time with Payshence and had a safe home to take care of her in. It was at the request of Kelly that Payshence go to Kirk's mother. Her motive being that if Jody and his family had her, she would lose control and Payshence could be kept from her because of her drug habits. She always knew that if Payshence was at Kirk's or his relatives, she could take her as she pleased.
Secondly, Kirk's issues are being brought into a case that has a direct effect on Jody and Payshence. Shouldn't Kirk's issues with the two older boys have been a completely separate hearing?

CONTINUED:
3. The parents are ordered to contact the Office of Recovery Services (ORS) to determine a support amount for said children for the period that the custody of the said children is given to an agency or individual other than his or her parents...
4. The parents shall cooperate with DCFS within five working days, to provide information regarding relatives who may be able and willing to care for the children.
5. DCFS shall provide protective supervision services over the children.
6. The parents, Kelly H and Jody Rhorer, may have supervised visits with the children, supervised by DCFS or the grandmother. However, all visits shall be coordinated through DCFS.
7. DCFS has the authority, if in their discretion, and with the approval of the GAL, to return the child to the mother, after Mr. Rhorer has moved out and they feel it is safe for the child.
8. The siblings may have visits supervised by DCFS.
9. There shall be no contact of any sort between Kelly H and Jody Rhorer.
10. This matter is set for pre-trial on November 20th, 2008.

Another point that is hard to comprehend - How does the government tell two people with a child together and in a relationship that they are not allowed to speak to each other, see each other, or have any type of contact whatsoever? Who is the government to say whom we can or cannot associate or carry on a relationship with?

NOVEMBER 20TH, 2008: STATE OF UTAH IN THE INTEREST OF PR, J1, AND J2; MINUTES, FINDINGS, AND ORDER

Before Judge V these cases came before the Court for a hearing on the following: **CHILD WELFARE PROCEEDING** *- Pretrial*
MINUTES: *Present Ms. Nickel, Assistant Attorney General; Connie, Attorney for Kirk J; Mr. J, GAL Attorney; Georgia Rhorer, Grandmother; Kelly H's mother; Mr. JN, Attorney for Jody Rhorer; Attorney for Kelly H; Ms. I and Ms. S, Division of Child and Family Services;*
Regarding PR: The matter comes before the Court for a Child Welfare Pretrial hearing.
Mr. Rhorer's attorney requested that appointed counsel be vacated as the father is not proven the legal father. Mr. JN further advised the Court that the mother has advised counsel that the father has moved out of state.
Kirk J advised the Court that the father has quit his job and allegedly moved out of town.

(Why was Jody's attorney taking advise from Kirk? Why didn't he consult with Jody?)

The Court advised counsel that the Court is inclined to issue a bench warrant with bail set at $20,010 for the father, Jody Rhorer. Mr. JN rescinds the withdraw of counsel request. The Court authorizes Mr. JN to withdraw as counsel. Mr. JN is excused.

Ms. Nickel amended the petition on the record.

Regarding J1 and J2: Kirk J was informed on the right to trial and the right to present evidence. Connie entered admissions to paragraphs 1, 2, 3, 9, 11, 12 and 13 on behalf of her client. The GAL requested Kirk J be granted permanent custody of J1 and J2 and that the Court terminate jurisdiction. Kirk J and Connie are excused.

Kelly H was informed of the right to trial and the right to present evidence and her attorney entered admissions to paragraphs 1 through 8, 11, 12 and 13 and entered a 34e response to paragraph 9 on behalf of her client. Ms. Nickel requested that Payshence Rhorer be returned to the mother with PSS services. A Court report was submitted by DCFS. The GAL advised the Court that the grandmother, Georgia Rhorer, was voluntarily submitting to a urine analysis test and will continue to UA and will further submit.

FINDINGS:

Regarding J1 and J2: In regard to the father Kirk J - based on the clear and convincing evidence presented, the Court finds the petition to be true. The above children are dependent and neglected and come within the provisions of the Juvenile Court Act.

The Court concludes that J1, J2, and PR are neglected by mother, Kelly H. The Court finds that reunification services are appropriated for the children and the mother.

ORDERS:

J1 and J2 are placed in the permanent custody of the father, Kirk J - Court jurisdiction is terminated.

Regarding PR: The paternal grandmother, Georgia Rhorer, is to provide daycare. A bench warrant for Jody Rhorer is issued. There is to be no visitation with Jody and the child until Jody appears in court. A service plan is to be completed and implemented by DCFS and is to address psychological and domestic violence component. PR is released from the custody of DCFS and DCFS is to provide Protective Supervision services and will make reasonable efforts to provide services to the children and the mother for the purpose of reunification of the family. A review hearing (mother) is set for 02-12-2009.

What about the dad, Jody? Isn't he part of the "family?"

NOVEMBER 24TH, 2008: NOTICE OF WITHDRAWAL OF COUNSEL

Mr. JN, Attorney at Law, hereby withdraws as counsel for Jody Rhorer in the above-entitled matter.

JN was the *court appointed* attorney for Jody. He withdrew 2 days prior to the next court hearing. He did not discuss it with Jody or give a reason. Jody needed him to be in court to represent him as he had gone back to Missouri to work to help Brother with a job. George planned on attending to fill Jody in on the details. His attorney should have been able to represent him in his absence but was told to withdraw from the case and, instead, the judge issued a warrant for Jody's arrest.

DECEMBER 5TH, 2008: ADJUDICATION ORDER

STATE OF UTAH, *in the interest of J1, J2, and PR*

The above-entitled matter came before the court in an Adjudication Hearing on the 20th day of November, 2008. Mr. JN moved to withdraw due to paternity not yet being established for Mr. Rhorer. There was no objection. That motion was granted. The State moved to dismiss Mr. Rhorer in that he has not established paternity for PR. There was no objection. Kirk J indicated the Mr. Rhorer had quit his job and moved out of state.

The father, Kirk J, and the mother, Kelly H, were asked if they were under influence of any drugs or alcohol. Both denied being under the influence of drugs or alcohol. They were advised of their rights to trial, to have the State prove the petition by clear and convincing evidence, to call witnesses, to cross-examine witnesses and to appeal the finding of the court. They voluntarily waived those rights, expressed satisfaction with their attorneys and admitted the allegations in the petition. Except Kelly for those allegations contained in paragraph 9, which she neither admitted nor denied pursuant to Rule 34(e) of the Utah Rules of Juvenile Procedure.

The Guardian Ad Litem requested that permanent custody and guardianship of the boys be awarded to Kirk J and that jurisdiction be terminated as to those two children. The mother stipulated to permanent custody and guardianship of the boys being awarded to Kirk J. Kelly's attorney requested a return of custody and guardianship of PR to her client, with Protective Supervision Services in place.

FINDINGS OF FACT

1. J1 is a seven-year-old male child, J2 is a six-year-old male child. PR is a one-year-old female child...

2. Kelly H is the mother of the above-named children....

3. Kirk J is the father of J1 and J2.

4. Legal paternity of PR has not been established.

5. In November 2007, DCFS supported a finding of sexual abuse of J1 and lewdness involving J2 as the victim against a 13-year-old out-of-home perpetrator.

6. The mother has a history of being involved in relationships where domestic violence occurs.

8. The mother has a history of drug abuse and the mother has admitted to DCFS that she has a history of drug use. The children have been exposed to the mother's illegal drug use and the mother has parties involving drug use in her home.

9. The caseworker has made at least five unannounced home visits in August 2008. The mother did not answer the door. The mother moved out of the residence and did not return the calls to the Division. There is concern that the mother is abusing methamphetamine.

10. The mother has previous convictions in 2001 of illegal possession/use of a controlled substance and theft. The mother currently has two warrants for her arrest.

11. Kirk J has prior convictions for illegal possession/use of a controlled substance X5, possession with intent to distribute a controlled substance X2, possession of drug paraphernalia, providing false information to law enforcement, carrying a concealed dangerous weapon, and driving under the influence with personal injury.

13. It is in the best interest of the children that DCFS be awarded custody and guardianship of the children for out-of-home care and placement.

15. It is in the best interest of J1 and J2 to place them in the permanent custody and guardianship of the father, Kirk J.

CONCLUSIONS OF LAW

1. J1 AND J2 are dependent children in that they are minors who are homeless or without proper care through no fault of their father.

2. The above-named children are neglected children in that they lack prior parental care by reason of the fault or habits of the mother.

ORDER

1. Custody and guardianship of the child, PR, are returned to her mother, Kelly H.

2. Permanent custody and guardianship of J1 and J2 are awarded to Mr. Kirk J.

3. The petition making allegations against Mr. Rhorer is amended to dismiss all references or allegations to Mr. Rhorer, in that he has not established paternity.

4. A warrant for Mr. Rhorer shall issue in the amount of $20,101, for his failure to appear.

5. The mother shall submit to a drug screen. It shall be a hair test. If it is negative, then DCFS has the discretion to limit further requests for drug screens.

6. DCFS shall provide Protective Supervision Services over PR.

7. Jody Rhorer may not have any visits with PR until he establishes paternity and enters an appearance in this case.

8. The mother of Jody Rhorer may have visits with PR. Visits are not mandatory and are not specifically ordered. There is no prohibition of her having visits.

9. The siblings may have visits supervised by DCFS.

10 There shall be no contact of any sort between Ms. Kelly H and Jody Rhorer.

11. The Division of Child and Family Services involvement with J1 and J2 is terminated.

12. Court jurisdiction over J1 and J2 is terminated.

13. *The appointment of the Guardian Ad Litem for J1 and J2 is vacated.*
14. *This matter is set for review on February 12, 2009.*

     Jody had already applied for full custody and his court appointed attorney had filed the necessary documentation. By this time, he realized he needed official court orders and since he had already been through this with his older daughters, he knew how it had to be done. But what didn't make sense is why the court would allow Payshence to see her sisters and grandmother, but not her daddy - who had done nothing but love for her.

     Another court hearing was held in West Jordan with Judge K. This was a completely different Judge and different court house. Kelly was a no-show and the judge awarded full custody of Payshence to Jody. The family went home and celebrated. Life could resume now. Life could move forward. The past was behind them...for about seven months.

2009

When Judge V became aware of the custody appointment, he ordered a hearing in his court. Jody, wondering what any of this was about, appeared with his court appointed attorney. Apparently, Judge V had instructed JN to reverse the custody appointment in Judge K's court room without Jody's knowledge. During the hearing with V, there was dialog exchanged between V and JN. Jody could not follow any of what was said as it was legal ease. He left thinking everything was fine. By this time Jody had already moved in with his parents. He was so fed up with the lies and games.

A few days later, Jody was served another summons to appear before Judge V. He and his attorney appeared, once again. Jody was surprised and suspicious to see Kelly and Kirk at the hearing. The attorneys met together prior to all parties entering the court room.

"Jody Rhorer, please stand up." Judge V ordered. Jody stood.

"Mr. JN, did you do as I instructed you to do?" V asked.

"Yes, your honor, I did."

V turned toward Jody and grinned. "Mr. Rhorer, you have no further rights to the child, Payshence Rhorer. You are now ordered to leave the court room or you will be arrested."

Jody turned towards the attorney that had betrayed him, shrugged his shoulders and gestured with his hands outstretched. JN just looked away.

"Did you hear my orders Mr. Rhorer?" the judge repeated.

Jody turned and walked out. It was like being hit by a fast-moving train. He was completely derailed. How could he go from being so elated with entire protective control over his daughter to having no paternal rights and not even be recognized by the courts as any relation to his child in such a short period of time? Seven months of bliss with his little Angel and now devastation.

Another hearing was held in V's courtroom shortly thereafter involving Jody's parents. The judge ordered that they have no rights to their granddaughter. Judge V single handedly removed all relatives from Payshence Rhorer's life on her father's side of the family.

Jody was emotionally distraught and physically exhausted. DCFS wanted to meet with both Jody and Kelly. Jody contacted Kelly to find out what had happened in court and what she thought DCFS would want to meet about. He then found out that Kelly had been appointed rights to Payshence by Judge V after his custody had been removed.

Kelly wanted to talk to Jody in person and wanted that talk to take place at a dance club called Habits. Before going to the club, she dropped Payshence off at Jody's parent's house. But when Jody arrived, he soon found out it was all a set up. There was not a discussion of DCFS or any details about the hearing or why Jody's custody was taken away. Instead, she acted strange and something seemed shady. Kelly said she was going to report Jody for violation of the restraining order for being in the club at the same time she was. Flashbacks of Teri and her restraining order ploys flew through Jody's mind. He panicked, thinking he would be arrested and thrown back into jail, so he called his best friend, Shawn, to pick him up. With Shawn's help, he got a hotel and a bus ticket to Florida for the next morning. He would go to his grandma's until things cooled off.

In the meantime, Kelly went to Jody's parent's home to retrieve Payshence. She was very intoxicated and shouldn't have been driving at all let alone picking up her baby daughter.

"Why don't you go home and come get Payshence in the morning, Kelly," George asked. "You shouldn't be driving like this with the baby."

"I'm not drunk. Give me my kid or I'm calling the cops," Kelly insisted.

Paapa stepped in, "C'mon now, she's sleeping and you need to sleep this off too. So, come back in the morning."

That is when Kelly freaked. "You're kidnapping my kid! Give me my kid! You kidnappers!"

Paapa called the cops while George tried to calm Kelly down. When the police arrived, they questioned Kelly then ordered Jody's dad and mom to hand Payshence over to her.

"Are you drunk ma'am?" the officer asked.

"I was at a club but I'm fine."

"Well you need to take your child straight home," the officer said.

"I want you men of the law to understand that if anything happens to our granddaughter because you are handing her over to a drunk, I will hold you legally responsible," Paapa insisted.

The officers looked more carefully at Kelly and questioned her again.

"Are you sure you're fit to drive?"

"I told you I'm fine!" Kelly slurred.

"Well for precautionary measures, I think it is best for you and your daughter to take a cab home and come back to get your car tomorrow."

The officer called for a cab and tipsy Kelly rode away with little Payshence in the back seat of the taxi.

The next morning Riley drove Jody to the bus terminal in Grand Junction, Colorado. Two days later, still on the Greyhound crossing the middle of Missouri, Kelly called.

"Where the hell are you?"

"None of your business. Don't call me no more." Jody said.

"Well I never called your parole officer, asshole. You should be grateful. I coulda got you in hella trouble but I didn't," Kelly quipped. Jody hung up on her, not believing a word she said.

A few minutes later, George called. "Jody, come back home, they ain't after you."

"You sure, mom?"

"Yeah. Everything's ok. Get off in St. Louis, I already got you a plane ticket home."

"Well shit! This stuff is gettin old," Jody said with some relief.

"For me and Paapa too," George agreed.

Monday night Jody arrived at the Salt Lake City airport and who is there to pick him up? You guessed it! He didn't know what to do or think. Instead of taking him to his parents, she took him to the fifth wheel trailer at the KOA. Jody didn't want to be there and was suspicious that she was setting him up again, but the next morning, she took him to Riley's to pick up his car. Jody left for work - fortunate not to lose his job again.

That evening he meet with his probation officer and Kelly showed up to that as well. He asked the PO to see if the restraining order to keep him and Kelly from communicating was still in effect. The PO said he could not see anything pending.

The second week back, DCFS began contacting Jody. Then came word that it had been reported that Jody had violated the restraining ordered. Again, he got screwed and would take no chances that he might end up jailed again. It was Kelly that showed up at the airport and then again at the PO meeting. Had his PO turned him in after telling him he didn't think the order was in effect any longer or was this Kelly's master plan all along? Jody wasn't taking any chances. The older girls were with their mother until Jody could get everything figured out. That night he loaded up his SUV and headed to Florida.

CHAPTER 8
FISHING LIFE AWAY

Two and a half days later, Jody arrived at Grandma Arlene's trailer park in Palmetto, Florida. Grandma Arlene was always happy to see Jody as he was her favorite. He explained to his grandparents what was happening back in Utah and they did their best to comfort him. He went to visit his cousins, did some fishing, and tried to put everything behind him.

Not too long after he arrived, George called to tell Jody that Kelly was looking for him and that he needed to call her.

"My mom said you were looking for me," Jody said to Kelly.

"Yeah! You didn't show to the DCFS hearing, fool! Where the hell are you?"

"I'm in Florida."

"You are not in Florida," Kelly responded.

"Really? Look at the area code, Bitch!" and Jody hung up.

For the rest of the winter Jody worked odd jobs and fished on the ocean. His parents kept him abreast of what was going on in Utah. He talked to the older girls regularly on the phone and reassured them he would return in the spring. He used this badly needed break to get his strength back and come up with a plan to reunite his family. He worked out regularly and started to feel like himself again.

As soon as it got warm enough for work to resume, Jody headed back to Missouri. He got employment doing stucco for Dickerson Plastering and worked weekends as a bar tender. Kelly heard that Jody had moved and was doing well. She called and wanted to reconcile, apologizing for everything and said she had changed and wanted to bring Payshence to Missouri so they could be a family. She also offered to bring Mona out with her.

"Honestly babe, things are gonna be so different now. I miss you. I miss us. Don't you wanna see your baby girl? She's growing like a little weed, you know," Kelly chided.

"I don't trust you."

"You should. I'm clean now…promise," Kelly went on, "I'll bring Mo out with me. I'm sure you're missin the girls."

"I dunno," Jody said.

"It will be just like it was in Oregon, only we'll have Payshence too. Please Jody."

Jody finally broke. "This is the last time. I'm only doing this for Payshence."

He agreed to take her back again and she set up housekeeping in a little home Jody had rented. But meanwhile, back in Utah, Kelly's absence had been noticed by DCFS.

FEBRUARY 12, 2009: CHILD WELFARE PROCEEDING

The Court addressed preliminary matters. Reports and recommendations are submitted to the Court. The Court is informed that the mother left the state with the child.

The Court indicated the mother is testing positive for drugs, and has been non-compliant, therefore, issued an adult bench warrant and pick up order.

ORDERS
A warrant is issued for Kelly H. The bail amount is $20,101.00
A shelter warrant is issued for PR.
The Court retains the right to impose further disposition.
All previous orders of the Court consistent with this order are hereby continued.
PR is continued in the custody of DCFS.

FEBRUARY 12, 2009: WARRANT TO TAKE CHILD INTO PROTECTIVE CUSTODY

ORDER OF CUSTODY TO ANY PEACE OFFICER AND THE PERSON IN CHARGE OF SHELTER HOME:

Whereas, a verified petition has been filed in this Court in the interest of the above-named child alleging facts or circumstances of abuse, neglect, or dependency that bring the child within the jurisdiction of the Juvenile Court, and based on information available to the Court, it appears that:

Continuation of the child in the home would be contradictory to her welfare and removal is in the best interest and/or, due to an emergency situation, which amounts to aggravated circumstances, the lack of preventative efforts was reasonable, and there is an eminent risk of harm to the child.

You are therefore commanded to execute this WARRANT and take PR, a 1year old, female child, into protective custody from the address listed above or any other place where you may find her and place said child at the CHRISTMAS BOX HOUSE SHELTER.

State of Utah and the person receiving said child, are ordered to receive said child into your custody and to keep safely said child until further order of this Court or until otherwise legally discharged.

CHAPTER 9
REUNITING DOESN'T FEEL SO GOOD

FEBRUARY 25TH, 2009: MOTION FOR ORDER TO SHOW CAUSE FOR CONTEMPT OF COURT

Petitioner, State of Utah, Division of Child and Family Services, by and through its counsel, Ms. Nickel, Assistant Attorney General, hereby moves this court to issue an order to show cause if any she has, why Kelly H, should not be held in contempt of this court.

This motion is based on the following and the accompanying affidavit of Ms. I of DCFS.

1. Kelly H has violated the orders of the Court including the following:

a. Allowed PR to have visits with the purported father Jody Rhorer prior to establishing paternity. b. Kelly has had contact with Jody Rhorer.

***THEREFORE,** the State prays the court issue an order directing Kelly H to appear before the court to give cause why she should not be held in contempt of court for violating the Court's order.*

AFFIDAVIT OF MS. I

I, Ms. I, being duly sworn, depose and state:

1. I am a caseworker for DCFS and am assigned to the above case.

2. This affidavit is in support of a Motion for an Order to Show Cause for Kelly H failing to comply with court orders.

3. On February 19, 2009, I spoke to Kelly H. She informed me she and PR were in Missouri with Jody Rhorer. This is a violation of the Court's order there would be no visits until paternity was established. Kelly was to have no contact with Jody.

4. Kelly told me that she left the state impulsively because she wanted to be with her family, meaning PR and Jody.

5. She claimed that she and Jody were not fighting or using drugs.

A few weeks after Kelly and Payshence arrived, Jody got a phone call while he was at work from a hysterical Kelly. A DCFS worker flew into St. Louis, took a taxi cab to Pilot Grove, came to the house, and took Payshence from the house. As they spoke, his baby girl was on her way to the airport to be flown back to Utah with a complete stranger claiming to be a government employee.

Duped again, Jody was ready to go ballistic. Kelly's motive was not to be a happy family, the truth was, Kelly was on the run for failing a drug test and Payshence was supposed to be taken from her. Once she got to Missouri, she filed for financial assistance and food stamps from the state and the welfare office in Missouri contacted the welfare office in Utah, where she was also getting government assistance, and reported her whereabouts.

Jody went home - without knowledge of the things mentioned above. Kelly ensured him that she was going to go back to Utah to get Payshence and then return with her so they could resume their family life. She just needed some work done on her car first. On Saturday, Jody got the car ready for the road trip.

Mona wanted to spend the night at her friend's house in Prairie Home. It was about a 45-minute round trip. Jody told Kelly he would be back in about an hour and left. When Jody returned home, Kelly's car was not in the driveway. When he entered the house, he noticed his flat screen television was missing and looked around to see what else was gone. Kelly had taken the kids new X Box 360, all the games, and anything else of value she could use or sell.

Jody called the police and made a report. There was an APB put out and Kelly was apprehended in Park City, Utah a day later. She was arrested for a third-degree felony and booked into jail until Missouri State Police extradited her. Kelly's drug dealer friend, Henry, put up her bail and she flew back to Utah.

MARCH 2ND, 2009: TRANSPORTATION ORDER

It is hereby ordered that an officer from the Salt Lake County Sheriff's Department transport Kelly H, from the Summit County Jail to the Salt Lake County Adult Detention Center, to the Third District Juvenile Court for a hearing to be held on March 12, 2009.

SHELTER HEARING

Present: Judge McC; Brent N, GAL; Georgia and Terry Rhorer, Grandparents; Mr. F, Attorney for The Division; Ms. I with DCFS

Mr. F addressed issues regarding paternity.

The court noted that paternity has not been established and addressed visitation issues.

Mr. F noted that Georgia and Terry Rhorer are going to be out of state for a short time.

Ms. Rhorer requested the Court to allow her to take the child with them to Florida on vacation. The Court indicated that Judge V would have to approve the vacation. The Court instructed Mr. and Mrs. Rhorer to contact the caseworker upon returning from vacation.

The child is to be placed with Mr. and Mrs. Rhorer with the specific approval of Judge V and the GAL. A Pretrial Hearing for the mother is set.

MARCH 12, 2009: STATE OF UTAH, in the interest of Kelly H and PR

Present: Judge H; Brent N, GAL; Ms. Nickel Attorney for The State; Ms. L, Attorney for The Mother

Ms. Nickel addressed the Court regarding the notice of this hearing not being served and the mother being incarcerated at that time. Ms. Nickel moved to the Court to reset the matter and gave basis.

GAL Brent N addressed the Court regarding the release of the mother. Brent N further addressed the record reflecting that the mother is not present at this time.

Ms. Nickel advised the Court of the information that was received and moved the Court to amend the record due to that current information. Ms. Nickel further advised the Court that the mother is apparently in the Summit County Jail at this time waiting to be extradited to another state.

ORDERS

The court retains the right to impose further disposition. All previous orders of the Court consistent with this order are hereby continued. In regards to Kelly, a Contempt hearing is set.

MARCH 16TH 2009: TRANSPORTATION HEARING

It is hereby ordered that a person from the Salt Lake County Sheriff's Office transport Kelly H from the Summit County Jail to the 3rd District Juvenile Court for a hearing to be held on March 19, 2009 before Judge V.

MARCH 23RD, 2009: ORDER

The above-entitled matter came before the court for a Review Hearing and a Pre-trial on the State's motion for Order to Show Cause on the 19th day of March, 2009 with Honorable Judge V presiding.

The mother was asked if she was under the influence of any drugs or alcohol. She denied being under the influence of drugs or alcohol. She was advised of her rights to a trial, to have the State prove the allegations by a preponderance of evidence, to call witnesses, to cross-examine witnesses and to appeal the finding of the court. She voluntarily waived those rights, expressed satisfaction with her attorney and admitted the allegations in the Order to Show Cause.

The court received two letters from Kelly H.

The Guardian ad Litem moved to terminated reunification services based upon mother's incarceration and extradition proceedings to Missouri. He also requested that the court update the shelter findings since the prior shelter hearing was done with a reservation of rights. The mother stipulated to the shelter findings being entered.

FINDINGS OF FACT

1. Kelly H knew of the court order that there were to be no visits between PR and Jody Rhorer until paternity was established and that Kelly was to have no contact with Jody Rhorer

2. *Kelly had the ability to comply with the order of the court and chose not to comply.*

3. *Kelly had contact with Jody Rhorer and allowed PR to have contact with Jody Rhorer.*

4. *Kelly H is in contempt of this court's order.*

5. *There is substantial danger to the physical health and safety of the child, and the child cannot be protected without removal from the custody of the mother.*

6. *Reasonable efforts were made by DCFS /other agency to prevent placement outside of the home including Protective Supervision Services to the mother.*

7. *It is in the best interest of the child to be placed in the temporary legal custody of DCFS for continued care and placement.*

ORDER

1. *Custody and guardianship of the child, PR, are placed with DCFS.*

2. *The mother is sentenced to 30 days in jail for her contempt. She is to be given credit for time served.*

3. *Reunification services to the mother are terminated.*

4. *The mother is ordered to contact the Office of Recovery Services to determine an amount for child support.*

5. *This matter is set for a review/pre-trial on April 21st, 2009.*

The Christmas Box House held Payshence until a foster family picked her up and for the next nine months she was in foster care. Kelly had a list of requirements she was expected to fulfill to get her back and she now had a fourth child, BS, who would also find himself following in the same fate as Payshence.

George and Terry's plan to become foster parents was not accepted by the court for placement of Payshence. Instead, the foster care agency tried to place other children in their home when they clearly expressed their only intention was to take their granddaughter.

MARCH 25TH, 2009: VERIFIED PETITION FOR TERMINATION OF PARENTAL RIGHTS

The Division of Child and Family Services by and through its undersigned counsel, Ms. Nickel, Assistant Attorney General, hereby petitions the court to terminate parental rights of Kelly H. This petition is based upon the following allegations:

1. *This Court has jurisdiction and child is a resident of Salt Lake County, Utah.*

2. *PR is an infant female.*

3. *The mother of the child, Kelly H, is currently incarcerated in the Summit County jail.*

4. *Legal paternity of the child has not been established.*

5. *On November 7, 2009, a shelter hearing was held. The Court ordered PR into the temporary custody and guardianship of her grandmother, Georgia Rhorer. The Court also granted custody of the mother's other two children, J1 and J2, to their father, Kirk J.*

6. *On November 20, 2008, an adjudication hearing was held wherein the Court made the following finding of fact:*

   a. *On July 21, 2008, the mother and Jody Rhorer were involved in a domestic dispute after the mother refused to perform oral sex on Jody. All three of the children were present at the time of the incident.*

   b. *On October 8, 2008, the mother reported to DCFS that Jody has been physically and mentally abusive towards her throughout her entire relationship with him.*

   c. *The mother has admitted to DCFS that she has a history of drug use. The children have been exposed to the mother's illegal drug use and the mother has parties involving drug use in her home.*

7. *At the adjudication hearing the Court found PR to be neglected and returned custody of PR to the mother. The Court also ordered that there was to be no visits between PR and Jody Rhorer until paternity was established and that there was to be no contact between the mother and Jody Rhorer.*

8. *On or about February 12, 2009, the mother, instead of appearing at the review hearing, traveled to Missouri with PR to be with Jody Rhorer. The Court issued a shelter warrant to take the child into protective custody.*

9. *On February 19, 2009, the caseworker spoke to the mother and confirmed that she and PR were in Missouri with Jody Rhorer.*

10. *On or about February 29, 2009, with the assistance of Children's Services in Missouri, Ms. I from DCFS traveled to Missouri to pick up the child.*

11. *A shelter hearing held in front of Judge McC. PR was put in custody of the Division.*

12. *On March 19, 2009, at a pretrial hearing, the Court found the mother to be in contempt of court in that she had contact with Jody Rhorer and allowed PR to have contact also. The mother was sentence to thirty days in jail. Reunification services were terminated.*

13. *The mother has convictions for possession - 1999 and theft - 2000. On March 16, 2009, the mother signed a Consent and Waiver of Extradition related to a warrant out of Boonville, Missouri for larceny. She will be extradited and face felony charges in Missouri.*

14. ***It is in the best interest of the child to be adopted by her foster parent or other appropriate individual where she is loved, properly cared for, and protected from neglect and abuse.***

WHEREFORE, Petitioner respectfully prays the Court find the following:

1. *That pursuant to Utah Code PR has been neglected by Kelly H thereby justifying termination of her parental rights.*

2. *That pursuant to Utah Code Kelly H is a unfit or incompetent parent, thereby justifying termination of her parental rights.*

3. *That pursuant to Utah Code PR is being cared for in an out-of-home placement under the supervision of the Division of Child and Family Services. The agency was willing to provide appropriate services to Kelly H but she has willfully refused, or has been unable and there is a substantial likelihood that she will not be capable of exercising proper and effective parental care in the near future, thereby justifying termination of her parental rights.*

4. *That pursuant to Utah Code, Kelly H has failed to make a parental adjustment, thereby justifying termination of her parental rights.*

5. *That is is in the best interests of PR to be adopted by her foster parents or other appropriate individuals where she is loved, property cared for, protected from neglect and abuse.*

6. *That it is proposed that an order by entered permanently terminating the parental rights of Kelly H with regard to PR.*

The State of Utah intentionally kept Payshence away from her real family. The State had no consideration for Jody at all, even to the point of suggesting his daughter be adopted out to strangers. She had a family, three sisters, grandparents, cousins, and a daddy who loved her. Who was the government to tear a little girl away from the biological people she belonged with?

Put yourself in those shoes for just a moment. Which child of yours would you hand over because the government said so? The Court was aware there was a father. The father was not questioned regarding the allegations Kelly made about him. He was found guilty and sentenced by the Courts, by DCFS, by the State, all because Kelly said so. Kelly's rights were proposed to be terminated and Kelly's lies could also cause Jody to lose his. Not his three other children, but just this one. If he was such a threat, why was the State not concerned over safety of his other girls?

In hindsight, Jody would admit that it would have been better for Payshence to have been adopted by a loving family at that time, then to be subject to the hell that would become her life.

MARCH 31ST, 2009: ENTRY OF APPEARANCE OF COUNSEL

Mr. Ward, attorney at law, does hereby enter his appearance of counsel for Georgia Rhorer in the above matter. The interest of Georgia Rhorer is that she is the paternal grandmother to the above-named minor child and seeks to establish legal rights as the child's grand-parent including, but not limited to the right to seek and be appointed as the child's legal custodian and guardian.

When the court date arrived in Missouri, Jody and Mona went together expecting to get justice and their belongings back. Kelly and Henry were there with a hired attorney. The lawyer made the argument that since Kelly lived with Jody, the property in the house belonged to her as much as it did to him. The judge went along with that argument and Kelly got to keep all of Jody's property and the case was dismissed. Still today, the stolen children in Kirk's house get to play with the stolen games, on the stolen X-Box, on a stolen flat screen television.

APRIL 2, 2009: TRANSPORTATION ORDER

It is hereby ordered that an officer from the Salt Lake County Sheriff's Department transport Kelly H from the Summit County Jail to the Matheson Courthouse for a hearing before Honorable Judge V.

Several stamps appeared on this order which stated "NOT IN CUSTODY." Apparently, the Court hadn't verified that Kelly was still in jail when they sent the Order as she had beat the charge and was released.

APRIL 13TH, 2009: UNIFIED POLICE DEPARTMENT, Domestic Criminal call

I contacted the Victim, Kim K, by telephone at her request. She told me that she was just assaulted by her ex-boyfriend, Kirk J, who she used to live with. Kim said she was hit 3 or 4 times and then dragged by her hair. Kim said that she was finally able to get away from him and drive away.

I asked Kim if she had any injuries and she said yes. I requested that she come to the Kearns Precinct so I can have the injuries photographed and she can fill out a witness statement. Kim asked if the precinct was the one on 5400. I told her yes and she said that she would be there shortly.

I waited until around 1700 hours and had not heard or seen Kim so I decided to call her back on the phone number in the detail. After several rings I got a voice messaging system. I explained to Kim who I was and that I was wondering why she did not come to the Kearns Precinct. I left the number to my voicemail pager system so she could call me back.

I made contact with Kearns Deputies working that night and explained to them if Kim shows up to have her fill out a witness statement and have ID photograph any injuries.

I talked to the Kearns Deputies the next day and they said that she never showed up. I also check my messages on my voicemail pager system and did not have a message from Kim. Case closed. Unable to contact the victim.

APRIL 29, 2009: CHILD WELFARE PROCEEDING; TERMINATION OF PARENTAL RIGHTS

The Court clarified what type of permanency hearing is being held.

Ms. L, Kelly's Court appointed attorney, moved the Court to reinstate reunification services for the mother and gave basis.

The Court addressed matters regarding open charges in Missouri.

Mrs. N, Attorney for the State of Utah, addressed the Court regarding the behavior of the mother and submits to the motion. Brent N, GAL, objected to the motion and gave basis.

The Court addressed matters regarding employment of Kelly H and income. The Court denied the motion. Kelly's attorney addressed the Court with matters regarding visitation.

Mr. Ward, Georgia's attorney, addressed the Court regarding DNA testing for the father.

The Court addressed and accepted comments from all parties present.

ORDERS

PR is continued in the custody of the Division of Child and Family Services.

PR shall have no contract with Jody Rhorer.

Kelly may have supervised visits if her drug tests from DCFS come back clean.

Jody Rhorer and Georgia Rhorer have no legal standing until a DNA test has been done.

Kelly H is to get a job, and have stable living arrangements.

The Court retains the right to impose further disposition.

All previous orders of the Court consistent with this order are hereby continued.

When spring came, Jody and Mo returned to Utah and Jody planned to begin work on the Core Project in Provo - a highway renovation that would take four years to complete. But first things first - he needed to clear his name which meant turning himself in to the authorities for the bench warrant, which resulted in his arrest and booking into jail. His court appointed attorney was Ms. Hardling. He also had clarity, finally, on what he needed to do to be recognized as Payshence's father, since being on the birth certificate was not enough.

JUNE 8TH, 2009: REQUEST FOR PRODUCTION OF DOCUMENTS, WITNESSES, EXHIBIT LISTS

Comes now the Respondent, Jody Rhorer, by and through counsel, Ms. Hardling, and hereby submits the following Request for Production of Documents to the Attorney General and the Utah Division of Child and Family Services and the Guardian ad Litem's office.

REQUEST FOR PRODUCTION OF DOCUMENTS

Pursuant to the Utah Rule of Civil Procedure, 34, Respondent hereby submits to the following Request for Production of Documents upon the Utah Division of Family Services. In answering this Request, the law requires that the answering party utilize all information that is available to the answering party, including information in the possession of the answering party, it's agents or attorneys, as well as any information over which they exercise control.

Note also that this Request is deemed continuous and shall request supplemental answers pursuant to Rule 26 of the Utah Rules of Civil Procedure. In the event that further responsive documents come into the possession, custody or control of an answering party after this Request has been answered, the answering party is required to supplement its response within a reasonable period of time after receiving such documents.

Respondent hereby requests the following documents from the answering parties: above-named child conceding the allegations of the Verified Petition or any other substantive pleading filed in this matter.

1. Any documents that summarize, record or reference statements made by the above-named child concerning the allegations of the Verified Petition or any other substantive pleading filed in this matter.

2. Any documents that summarize, record or reference statements made by Respondents concerning the allegations of the Verified Petition or any other substantive pleading filed in this matter.

3. Any documents that summarize, record or reference any information you relied upon in formulating the allegations of the Verified Petition or any other substantive pleading filed in this matter.

4. Any documents that summarize, record or reference any information upon which you plan to rely to establish the truth of the allegations of the Verified Petition or any other substantive pleading filed in this matter.

5. Any documents that summarize, record or reference any information that does not support the allegations of the Verified Petition or any other substantive pleading filed in this matter, including any and all information that tends to refute the truth of the allegations of the Verified Petition or pleading.

6. Any CPS or DFS activity logs, transportation logs, referral forms, risk assessment forms, or other documents pertaining to this matter.

7. Any medical of psychological evaluations pertaining to this matter.

8. Any police reports pertaining to the matter.

9. Any documents derived from any foster parent, shelter parent, or kinship placement pertaining to this matter.

10. Any other letters, reports or summaries, generated from any source, pertaining to this matter.

11. Any photographs that summarize, record, or reference any information that does or does not support the allegations of the Verified Petition or any other substantive pleading filed in this matter.

REQUEST FOR WITNESS AND EXHIBIT LISTS

The Respondent, by and through counsel, Ms. Hardling, hereby requests the State of Utah and the Guardian ad Litem's Office provide a list of the individuals who they intend to call as witnesses to testify at the trial in the above-entitled matter, and a brief summary as to what each individual will testify, and a list of all Exhibits planned to be produced.

Finally, an attorney that took her job seriously and demanded proof of the bogus allegations. Every attorney has their own style of pleadings and presentation. Some are straight and to the point. Some ramble and repeat. Some speak in clear and precise language for most to comprehend; while others use hard to decipher legal jargon. Some seek truth and some aim to deceive. All of these will show up within the pages of this book.

JUNE 22ND, 2009: THIRD DISTRICT JUVENILE COURT FOR SALT LAKE COUNTY, Transportation Order

It is hereby ordered that an officer from the Salt Lake County Sheriff's department transport Jody Rhorer, Inmate #165790, the father of the above-named child from the Salt Lake County Adult Detention Center, to the Third District Juvenile Court.

But the hearing scheduled for June 23rd was put off until July and then put off again until August. All the while, Jody waited in jail for unexplained reasons. Ms. Hardling, with all her demands and gusto, never got an opportunity to present her findings from the lists, reports, experts, photographs, witnesses, etc., because she was removed from the case and apathetic attorney JN was reassigned. Had Hardling been able to move forward, would a different outcome have taken place? Would this book have even been written? One small action that may have changed the entire course of lives. A zealous attorney gave Jody hope. JN's style was far less exuberant. He was not interested in lists, witnesses, reports, or proof in general and had left Jody hanging in the past.

JULY 19TH, 2009: NOTICE OF APPEARANCE OF COUNSEL

Mr. JN, Attorney at Law, hereby appears as counsel for Jody Rhorer in the above-entitled matter.

AUGUST 5TH,2009: MOTION FOR PATERNITY

Petitioner, Jody Rhorer, by and through counsel and pursuant to Section 78B0-15, Utah Parentage Act, Utah Code Annotated, and other pertinent statutes, hereby petitions for relief against the Respondent, Kelly H, alleging as follows:
1. Petitioner is a resident of Salt Lake County, State of Utah.
2. The natural mother of the minor child is Kelly H.
3. The parties are not and have never been married to each other.
4. The parties engaged in sexual intercourse in the State of Utah and the minor child was born in the State of Utah, and therefore, the State of Utah should have exclusive jurisdiction in this matter.
PATERNITY
5. Petitioner is and should be declared and adjudged the father of the minor child, PR. **The birth certificate should be changed to list Petitioner as the natural father.**
CUSTODY AND PARENT-TIME
6. Petitioner is a fit and proper person to be awarded the sole physical and legal custody of the minor child.
WHEREFORE, Petitioner prays for judgement against Respondent as set forth in the Petition and for such other and further relief as the Court deems just.

But the truth is, Jody and Kelly didn't consummate their relationship in Utah. It was not until the move to Oregon that the two became a real couple and that is when Payshence was conceived. Could this have been a game changer had JN gotten it right? With the filing of the Motion of Paternity by Jody, came the effort by Kelly's attorney to get *her* back in the parenting game as well.

AUGUST 25TH, 2009: MOTION TO REINSTATE REUNIFICATION SERVICES

COMES NOW, Respondent, Kelly H, by and through counsel, and hereby moves this Court for an Order directing the DCFS to reinstate reunification services to the natural mother.
FACTS
1. At the pretrial on November 20, 2008, the parties reached a resolution. This matter came before the court on a Protective Supervision Services petition, "PSS." The court found that the children were neglected relative to the mother and DCFS was ordered to prepare and submit a service plan for Kelly H. The natural father of the two oldest children was awarded permanent custody and guardianship. The younger child, PR, was returned to the custody of the mother and PSS services ordered.
2. A hearing was held on February 12, 2009. There was issued a warrant for the mother's arrest and an Order to pick up the minor child from Missouri.
3. On February 24, 2009, the Assistant Attorney General filed a Motion for Order to Show Cause against Kelly H, alleging that she was out of compliance with the court's orders.

4. On March 19, 2009, the State's Motion for Order to Show cause came before this Court for a hearing. The Court found Kelly H in contempt of court and sentenced to jail time in the Summit County jail. At this hearing, the Court denied a request for reunification services and set the matter for a Permanency Hearing on April 21, 2009.

5. On March 26, 2009, the Assistant Attorney General filed a Verified Petition for Termination of Parental Rights.

6. At the April 21, 2009, hearing the Court again denied a request for reunification serves and set the matter for trial on the State's Verified Petition for Termination of Parental Rights.

7. Kelly H has been enrolled in the Women's Program at Catholic Community Services since June 8, 2009, and is participating in four different therapy sessions per week.

8. Kelly H's counselor at Catholic Community Services reports that "Kelly is an active participant in the treatment groups." The issues of domestic violence and substance abuse are addressed in therapy.

9. Kelly has been keeping in regular contact with DCFS caseworkers.

10. Kelly is employed as a Certified Nursing Assistant with Quality Staffing Services.

11. Kelly completed the Love and Logic parenting class on June 24, 2009.

12. Kelly has stable housing.

13. Kelly's criminal matter in Missouri was dismissed without prejudice.

14. Kelly has been consistently exhibiting substantial progress in her therapy and is complying with the service plan and court orders.

ARGUMENT

According to Utah Code Annotated Section 78A-6-312(4)(b), the court is determining if reunification services are appropriate and shall also consider whether the parent has expressed an interest in reunification with the child. In this case, Kelly H was initially offered reunification services prior to her failure to previously comply with court order. Based upon her failure to comply, the court determined that she should not be offered reunification services. Kelly H has, however, sought out and participated in the services on her own. She has made remarkable strides to better her life and to meet the needs of her child, PR. She is participating in four different therapy sessions a week, substance abuse treatment, parenting classes, domestic violence counseling, she is employed, she has stable housing, her criminal matter in Missouri is resolved, and she is actively striving to better the situation for her child. Throughout these proceedings, Kelly has always demonstrated her concern for the well-being of her child. The work, time and effort Respondent has put into services to reunify her with her child shows her determination and intense desire in reunification with the child. Furthermore, the Assistant Attorney General and the GAL have no objection to this Court entering an order directing DCFS to provide reunification serves to the natural mother, Kelly H.

WHEREFORE, Respondent respectfully requests that this Court enter an Order directing DCFS to offer reunification services to the natural mother.

EXHIBIT 1 - Letter from Catholic Community Services, July 21, 2009, RE: Kelly H

To Whom it May Concern,

Kelly H was enrolled in the Women's Program at Catholic Community Services on June 8, 2009. She attended one process group, one individual therapy session and one case management session per week. In addition, she is requested to attend one self-help group per week. Kelly has had no absences to group and individual sessions to date. Kelly is drug tested at this facility on a random basis twice per week. All urinalysis tests are negative for all drugs tested.

Kelly is an active participant in the treatment groups. She appears to be open to feedback and has demonstrated the ability to relate personal experiences to other clients. She has attended group, individual, and case management sessions with no absences. In individual sessions, she is engaged and open to input. We are addressing the instances of domestic violence in her past and uses of substances. It is my feeling that Kelly is currently stable and making progress on both these issues.

Clinical Psychology Intern

EXHIBIT 2 dated August 13, 2009, contained a statement from Quality Staffing Services that Kelly had been employed as a Certified Nursing Assistant since September 28, 2009. However, it was not signed by the person that supposedly wrote it.

EXHIBIT 3 - Certificate of Completion for the *"Love and Logic Parenting Class"* dated June 24, 2009.

EXHIBIT 4 dated August 14, 2009, showed that Kelly had made application for an apartment at Sunset Vista and had been approved.

EXHIBIT 5 - the Missouri State Public Defendant letter dated July 2, 2009:

Dear Ms. Kelly H,

Please find enclosed an Authenticated copy of the dismissal of your case which you should share with your child custody attorney. The Prosecutor dismissed the case without prejudice which means he can refile the charge at any time during the next 3 years. I am also retiring to you those documents (receipts, fax documents, bond and hospital papers) you gave me along with the lien for Public Defender services. You can make payments on the lien via the enclosed envelopes, just make sure you include your case number on all money orders.
        District Defender

AUGUST 25TH, 2009: ORDER

Based on motion by Respondent and for good cause shown. IT IS HEREBY ORDERED that DCFS shall provide reunification services to the mother, Kelly H, effective immediately.   Signed by Judge V
AUGUST 27TH, 2009: CHILD WELFARE PROCEEDING

Ms. L, Kelly's attorney, addressed the Court regarding the progress made by the mother and the charges in Missouri being dismissed.
The Court addressed the involvement of Georgia Rhorer with the child.
Ms. Nickel, Attorney for the State of Utah, addressed the court regarding a motion filed for paternity by Jody Rhorer.
The Court addresses reinstating reunification. All partied addressed visitation matters.
Brent N, GAL, addressed the mother complying with the service plan.
Ms. Nickel moved the Court to have unsupervised visitation for the mother. There were no objections. The Court denied the motion.
The Court addressed and accepted comments from all parties present.

ORDERS:
PR is continued in the custody of DCFS.
The Motion to Reinstate Reunification Services filed on August 25, 2009, is granted.
Kelly H is restricted from having contact with Georgia Rhorer. Failure to comply with this matter may result in either party being found in contempt.
The Court hereby orders Georgia Rhorer, paternal grandmother, not to attend team meetings which Kelly H is currently attending.
The Court hereby orders DCFS to perform drug testing on Kelly H.

Aren't' second chances wonderful? Not even two months out of jail and Kelly was back in the mommy saddle. You must give her credit for putting forth the effort and the State of Utah for allowing it. The question remained, could she keep it up long enough to be the mother her children deserved? But why would the State ban her from George who was clearly trying to help her comply by offering her support?
    To add to the chaos, Kelly had been with a man named Brock that was Jody's friend's younger brother. Brock was named as fourth child, BS's father and had paid child support and claimed BS as his son, only to find out after DNA testing that the real biological father was Kirk's best friend.

OCTOBER 27TH, 2009: PERMANENCY ORDER, Judge V presiding

The above-entitled matter came before the court for a Review Hearing and a Permanency Hearing on the 29th day of October, 2009, with the Honorable Judge V presiding. The following persons were present: Ms. Nickel, Assistant Attorney General; Mr. Brent N, GAL; Ms. L, attorney for the mother; Kelly H, mother; and Ms. I, of DCFS.

FINDINGS OF FACT
1. The services offered to the mother in the service plan constituted reasonable efforts on the part of DCFS to reunify the mother with her child.

2. The duties and responsibilities of the mother under the service plan are clearly set forth in that document and have been communicated to the mother on the record in these proceedings.

3. The permanency goal for the child has been to return home.

4. DCFS has made reasonable efforts to finalize the permanency plan or goal for the child.

5. The mother has made substantial efforts to comply with the service plan.

6. There is a substantial likelihood that the child could go home in the next 90 days.

7. It is in the best interest of the child to continue reunification services.

ORDER

1. Custody and guardianship of the child, PR, are continued with DCFS.

2. Reunification services to the mother are continued.

3. A trial home placement for the child with the mother is authorized.

4. This matter is set for review/pre-trial on December 17, 2009.

DECEMBER 17TH, 2009: TERMINATION OF PARENTAL RIGHTS - REVIEW

Present were the GAL, Attorney General, Jody, Kelly, Kirk, Kelly's Attorney, an Aunt, Payshence's Foster Family, DCFS Representative

Reports and recommendations are submitted to the Court by DCFS. The District Attorney advised the Court to continue monitoring and provided basis for the recommendation. The GAL concurred with the recommendations of the Court and commended the family for the support of the process. The Court admonished Kelly H for her continued behavior and decisions.

ORDERS

PR is continued in the custody of DCFS.

All previous orders for the Court consistent with this order are hereby continued.

2010
CHAPTER 10
THE ENDING IS THE BEGINNING

JANUARY 15TH, 2010: DECREE OF PARENTAGE, Judge K presiding

The above-entitled matter comes before the Honorable Judge K in the above-entitled Court, neither party appearing in front of Judge K, but Respondent having been duly served with a Summons and Petition for Decree of Parentage, and having failed to answer or otherwise plead to said Petition within the period of time permitted therefore by law, and the clerk of the court having heretofore entered the default of said Respondent, and good cause appearing therefore.

IT IS HEREBY ORDERED, ADJUDGED AND DECREED:

1. Petitioner is a resident of Salt Lake County, State of Utah.

2. Respondent is the natural mother of the minor child.

3. The parties are not and have never been married to each other.

4. The parties engaged in sexual intercourse in the State of Utah and the minor child was born in the State of Utah, and therefore, the State of Utah shall have exclusive jurisdiction in this matter.

PATERNITY

5. Petitioner is and shall be declared and adjudged the father of the minor child, Payshence Rhorer. **The birth certificate shall be changed to list Petitioner as the natural father.**

CUSTODY AND PARENT-TIME

6. There is currently pending in the Third District Juvenile Court in Salt Lake County an action that granted the State of Utah DCFS custody of the minor child.

TAX EXEMPTION

7. Petitioner shall be allowed to claim as a dependent for income tax purposes.

FEBRUARY 5, 2010: NOTICE OF FILING DECREE OF PARENTAGE

PLEASE TAKE NOTICE that the attached Decree of Parentage has been entered in the Third Judicial District Court, wherein Jody Rhorer was determined and adjudged to be the biological father of Payshence Rhorer, the minor child herein. (Although the Decree of Parentage was filed at that time, the court could never locate it for future proceedings.)

Jody had established that he was legally Payshence's Daddy! Now just the issue of DCFS having custody. Soon he should have his darling baby girl back in his arms. Soon his girls would have their little sister back. Then he could move on with his life and put his focus on taking care of his family - maybe someday find a good woman to help him raise them. No more attorneys, or judges, or court, or missing work.

FEBRUARY 16TH, 2010: PERMANENCY ORDER, Judge V presiding

The above-entitled matter came before the court for a Review Hearing and a Permanency Hearing with the Honorable Judge V, presiding. The Court received a court report and a Decree of Parentage for Jody Rhorer. The Assistant Attorney General informed the court that Kirk J and Kelly H are still married. The Petition filed by Mr. Rhorer in District Court to establish paternity didn't provide any notice to Kirk J. The Assistant Attorney General requested counsel be appointed for Kirk J.

FINDINGS OF FACT

1. The permanency goal for the child has been return home.
2. DCFS has made reasonable efforts to finalize the permanency plan or goal for the child.

ORDER

1. Custody and guardianship of the child, PR, are returned to the mother, Kelly H.
2. DCFS shall provide protective supervision services over the child.
3. Conflict Counsel, Connie is appointed to represent Kirk J.
4. This matter is set for a review hearing on April 15, 2010.
5. This matter is set for hearing on the issues of paternity between Mr. Rhorer and Kirk J on April 27, 2010.

The Assistant Attorney General advised the Court of paternity matters pertaining to the child. The Court addressed matters pertaining to the pending paternity issues and divorce matters. The Court addressed and accepted comments from all parties present. DCFS has made a reasonable effort to finalize the permanency goal or plan for the child. The permanency goal is reunification with a concurrent goal of guardianship with a relative. The Court finds that reunification services are appropriate for the child and family.

PR is released from the custody of DCFS. Custody of PR is placed with Kelly H. The protective supervision of PR is placed with DCFS and they will make reasonable efforts to provide services to the child and parent(s) for the purpose of reunification of the family. Connie is appointed as conflict counsel to represent Kirk J.

April 17th, 2010, ORS filed a child support claim to cover the period that the state had taken Payshence from Jody and held her in their custody at the Christmas Box House and in foster care. ORS began garnishment of $245.00 per month from Jody's paycheck. As soon as Jody was able to file as her biological father, the State, through the Assistant Attorney General, assigned a court appointed attorney for Kirk J. Just as the Court told him to do, Jody established paternity. Then the Court went straight into action to take that away from him. Although Jody currently had been given his rights as Payshence's father, he still had the custody issue to deal with.

Jody hadn't had contact with Kelly for some time when, out of the blue, she called George.

"George, it's Kelly! I know it's your birthday so why don't you come out to the Westerner with me and celebrate."

"Well how ya been?" George inquired. "We do need to do some catchin up!"

George agreed to meet at the country western bar so she could find out what was going on with Payshence and, hopefully, open the door again for Jody to see his daughter.

APRIL 20TH. 2010:   MOTION FOR PARENT TIME

Jody Rhorer, natural father of PR, by and through counsel, JN, hereby requests that the court grant him parent-time with the minor child.

This Court had previously issued a No-Contact Order between Jody Rhorer and the minor child because Jody had not established paternity of the minor child. However, on or about January 25, 2010, a Decree of Parentage was entered declaring Jody Rhorer as natural father of minor child. Therefore, Jody Rhorer comes before the court to request that court initiate parent-time for him with the minor child.

APRIL 27TH, 2010:   CHILD WELFARE PROCEEDING - Review (Father)

This matter comes before the Court for a CW Review hearing. The Court addressed preliminary matters and informed all parties as to father's Motion for Parentage. An oral report, status of the proceeding, and recommendation was given to the Court by the GAL. The Court accepted and reviewed the submitted report. The Court informed all counsel to discuss paternity and parentage prior to the next hearing.

ORDERS

PR is continued in the protective supervision of DCFS. The Court hereby continues the no contact order between Jody Rhorer, father and Kelly H, mother. All previous orders of the Court consistent with this order are hereby continued.

MAY 20TH, 2010: CHILD WELFARE PROCEEDING - Review (Mother/Father)

The Court and JN addressed matters pertaining to the legal father and matters in District Court. Kelly H's attorney addressed the Court regarding notice of hearings as to the mother. The Court addressed all parties regarding the No Contact Order between the mother and father. All parties discussed the present proceedings and orders pertaining to the District and Juvenile Court. The Assistant Attorney General addressed the Court regarding the involvement of DCFS in the case. The Court acknowledged the presence of the GAL and informed him of the present proceedings. The GAL and JN discussed the paternity matter with the Court. PR is continued in the custody of Kelly H. PR is released from protective supervision with DCFS.

The Court hereby continues the no contact order between Jody Rhorer, father, and the mother, Kelly H. PR is continued under the Courts jurisdiction for further review in Sixty days.

JUNE 16TH, 2010: STATE OF UTAH, ORS; ORDER: Paternity and Child Support

Based upon consideration of the alleged facts in the Notice of Agency Action, and Jody Allen Rhorer, having provided information through participation in an adjudicative proceeding:

Genetic testing having been conducted having been found to be the biological father of PR based upon a paternity index of at least 100, It is ordered:

That Jody Allen Rhorer is the father of the following child born to Kelly H: **Payshence Rhorer.**

JULY 8TH, 2010: MOTION TO SET ASIDE DECREE OF PARENTAGE & DISMISS ACTION

The parties to this action, Petitioner, Jody Rhorer, by and through counsel, and Respondent, Kelly H, by and through counsel, hereby stipulate that the Decree of Parentage entered on or about January 25th, 2010, shall be set aside. The parties further agree that this action shall be dismissed.

*Grounds for the Motion are at that the time that Petitioner filed his Petition for Paternity, Respondent was still married and therefore, a **legal father** existed who was not made a part of the previous action. Accordingly, the order should be set aside and the case dismissed.*

JULY 20TH, 2010: CHILD WELFARE HEARING - REVIEW

JN addressed the Court regarding the proceeding at present. The GAL addressed the Court regarding custody and paternity matters and gave a verbal report and recommendations. JN addressed the possible stipulation between all parties. Kelly's attorney informed the Court of the position of the mother regarding the case.

ORDERS

PR is continued in the custody of Kelly H. All previous orders of the Court consistent with this order are hereby continued. Court jurisdiction is terminated.

JULY 21TH, 2010: ORDER SETTING ASIDE DECREE OF PARENTAGE AND DISMISSING ACTION, Submitted by Attorney JN

Pursuant to the joint Motion, and good cause appearing therefore, **IT IS HEREBY ORDERED, ADJUDGED AND DECREED** *That the Decree of Parentage is set aside and this case dismissed, without prejudice.*

Filed by Jody's own attorney! As Jody recalled it, when he entered the Court, Judge V called JN up to the bench and muttered some information to which JN agreed. When Jody's Motion was dismissed and his rights removed, he was dumbfounded. His attorney offered no explanation as Jody stood there with his hands out at his side shrugging his shoulders.

But still ensued the State's attempt to collect support for the period of time that Payshence was in their custody. June 16, 2010, ORS had submitted a request to collect support from both Jody and Kelly, but on August 12th, that Order was rescinded because *"Evidence indicates that there is good cause to set aside the Order listed above for the reason that Prior to establishment of the Administrative Order there was pending paternity action pursuant to ORS policy."* Referring to the fact that the state recognized Jody as the father, and then, by the hand of his own attorney, took that away from him.

Laboratory Corporation of America
P.O. Box 2230 Burlington, NC 27216 Telephone: (336) 584-5171   Relationship Report

Account Information
Acct #:   43706255
ORS/CSE TEAM 29
Acct Ref 1: C000965874
Acct Ref 2:
Acct Ref 3:
SALT LAKE CITY, UT 84145

LabCorp Case #   C0L-015000

Relationship	Party		Race	Date(s) Drawn
		04C-3403-0	Caucasian	04/08/2010
		04C-3404-0		04/08/2010
Alleged Father	RHORER, JODY A	03G-3141-0	Caucasian	03/11/2010

DNA Analysis

D3S1358	D7S820	vWA	FGA	D8S1179	D21S11	D18S51	D5S818	D13S317	D16S539
14, 17	10, 12	17, 19	18, 20	12, 14	29, 31	12, 18	11, 12	8, 9	11, 13
17	10, 12	17, 18	18, 23	12	31, 32.2	14, 18	11, 13	8, 11	9, 11
15, 17	10, 13	17, 18	23	12, 15	31.2, 32.2	14, 17	9, 13	11, 12	9, 13
2.54	1.21	2.43	7.11	3.52	5.80	2.96	9.11	1.65	4.13

DNA Analysis

TH	TPOX	CSF1PO
8, 9.3	8, 12	10
6, 8	8, 13	10
6, 9.3	8	10, 13
2.31	1.75	1.91

Conclusion:

Combined Paternity Index: 513,412 to 1   Probability of Paternity: 99.99% (Prior Probability = 0.5)

The alleged father, JODY A. RHORER, cannot be excluded as the biological father of the child, TRACY   since they share genetic markers. Using the above systems, the probability of paternity is 99.99%, as compared to an untested, unrelated man of the Caucasian population.

I, the undersigned Director, upon being duly sworn on oath, do depose and state that I read the foregoing report on the analysis of specimens from the above named individuals, signed by myself, and under penalties for perjury it is my belief that the facts and results therein are true and correct.

_____
Gary M. Stuhlmiller, Ph.D., Director

State of North Carolina
County of Alamance

I,   Richard R. Long   , certify that Gary M Stuhlmiller, Ph.D. personally came before me this day and acknowledged that he (or she) is an employee of Laboratory Corporation of America Holdings, a corporation, and that as an employee being authorized to do so, executed the foregoing on behalf of the corporation.

Subscribed and sworn to [or affirmed] before me this _____ APR 1 9 2010 _____ at Burlington, NC.

_____
Notary Public

RICHARD R. LONG
Notary Public, North Carolina
Alamance County
My Commission Expires
February 23, 2015

Laboratory Corporation of America is accredited by the AABB.

2011

JUNE 7TH, 2011: COMPLAINT FOR SUPPORT

STATE OF UTAH, Office of Recovery Services ex rel. Kelly H v. Kirk J, **WHEREFORE**, the Office requests:

1. *Ordering that the parent(s) without physical custody shall pay the amount of support set forth in the paragraph. Beginning December 1, 2009, the alleged father's base support obligation is a least $315.00 per month and the mother's base child support obligation is at least $117.00 per month. The support obligations continue through the end of the month the child becomes 18 years of age, or through the end of the month of the child's normal and expected date of graduation from high school, whichever occurs later. When physical custody changes, the parent without physical custody shall pay as required above without the need to modify this order. This automatic change does not apply to situations involving joint or split custody or periods of court-ordered parent-time.*

<u>*2. Alternatively, if genetic testing determines that the alleged father is the actual biological father, an order should be entered finding the alleged father is not the child's father.*</u>

3. *Ordering immediate and automatic income withholding for the payment of child support.*

4. *Ordering that all child support payments shall be made to the ORS unless the Office gives notice that payments should be sent elsewhere.*

5. *Ordering that if insurance for medical and dental expenses is available the parent(s) shall be responsible for maintaining insurance for the dependent child.*

6. *Ordering that if child is covered by health, hospital or dental insurance plans insurance of the father shall be primary coverage. If a parent remarries and his or her child is not covered insurance plan of the step-parent shall be treated as if it is the plan of the remarried parent and shall retain the same designation as the primary or secondary plan of the dependent child.*

7. *Ordering that both parents provide cash medical support by equally sharing all reasonable expenses.*

8. *Ordering that both parents share equally out-of-pocket costs.*

9. *Ordering that written verification of insurance be provided to the Office.*

10. *Ordering that unless and until verification is provided to the Office, no credit will be given to the Office.*

11. *If child care costs are incurred, the father and mother share equally all reasonable work-related child care costs.*

12. *Ordering that interest shall accrue on judgments at the lawful rate.*

13. *Ordering the father and mother to notify the Office of any change in residence, employment, income and custody.*

14. *Reserving issues regarding reimbursement of support, custody, parent-time, tax exemption and any other issues related to the rights of the parents for separate determination upon application to the Court by either parent.*

Well this was not what Kirk was bargaining for. If his pocket book was going to be involved, he wanted no part of Kelly's plan to keep Payshence from Jody. Kirk petitioned the court with a hand-written note dated July 11th, 2011. The following is in accordance to his own writing and includes all grammar and punctuation:

"To whom it may concern,
I am writing this complaint to the summons. For Civil No. 114, between ORS & Kelly H vs Kirk J. I Disagree with the information and this is my 2nd Response to this matter 1st I filed at West Jordan Ut. Court.
Kirk J"

Kirk was adamant that he not be made to pay for Payshence's care so the State ordered Kirk to take a DNA test, although Jody had already taken the test that proved *he* was the father.

SEPTEMBER 12, 2011: ORDER FOR GENETIC TESTING

This matter came before the Court on August 22, 2011 for rehearing on the Office of Recovery Service's Motion for Genetic Testing, District Court Commissioner presiding. The ORS was represented by Assistant Attorney General Hunt. Kelly H "mother" was not present nor represented by counsel. Kirk J "alleged father" was present pro se'.

Based on a stipulation of the parties present and the Court being advised, therefore:

IT IS ORDERED:

1. Kirk J, Kelly H, and PR shall submit to genetic testing to be scheduled by the Office.

2. Lab Corp is appointed to conduct the testing.

3. The issue of reimbursement of cost is reserved.

Five months later, and five months in a little child's life is a very long time, ORS returned to court with their findings....

2012

FEBRUARY 9, 2012: ORDER OF DISMISSAL

This matter came before the Court on January 23, 2012 for hearing on the Office of Recovery Service's Motion to Exclude Respondent from Paternity. The ORS was represented by Assistant Attorney General Hunt. Kelly H "mother" was not present nor represented by counsel. Kirk J "alleged father" was not present nor represented by counsel.

Based on the party's failure to appear and subsequent default and the Court being advised,

IT IS ORDERED that the Respondent Kirk J is not the father of the minor child PR and that the Office's Complaint for Support is dismissed.

Herein lies and new problem. The State wants money. They want the daddy to pay them back for taking his baby away from him, ordering no-contact, ignoring the fact that the DNA test shows who the daddy is, and then assigning her the "alleged father" that they want her to have, per the UUPA. The "alleged" - who's piece of paper that united him with Kelly in marriage was not nullified properly - and therefore little Payshence should be assigned to this felon, and not just her, but 3 of her half-brothers as well. So, the State wanted money from Jody, but wouldn't sanctify the fact that he is the father and allow him legal visitation or custody rights, therefore, they had to rescind their collection attempt and move it over to Kirk, who was having no part of that and didn't even show up in court to try to fight for his right to be the "alleged father".

Money, money, money, money. If they can't get it from Jody or Kirk, maybe they can get it from Payshence's newest brother, BS's, alleged father? While all this was going on with Payshence, this new baby boy was also affected by similar events. I'm not sure how much money his daddy could make in jail, but the State was going to give it a shot anyway.

By now, the state had placed BS into Kirk's possession as well. It was all good with Kelly, as long as she could see the kids when she wanted, but she just couldn't give up her partying lifestyle and her job as a stripper didn't allow her to have four kids in need on a regular basis. She never did give up an interest to be called their mother, but just couldn't stay out of trouble long enough to get them back….

FEBRUARY 9TH, 2012: VERIFIED PETITION FOR PROTECTIVE SUPERVISION

STATE OF UTAH, in the interest of PR and BS

Petitioner, State of Utah, Division of Child and Family Services, by and through its counsel, Assistant Attorney General, hereby alleges that the above-named children are within the age of juvenile court jurisdiction and that the above-named children are within the provisions of Utah code. This Petition is based upon the following allegations:

1. PR is a four-year-old female child. BS is a one year old-male child.

2. Kelly H is mother of the children.

3. Kirk J is the father of PR.

4. Brock S is the father of BS. He is currently incarcerated at the Salt Lake County Jail.

5. PR was removed from the custody and guardianship of her mother in 2008 due to domestic violence and drug use by her mother.

6. On November 8, 2008, Judge V adjudicated PR as a neglected child as to her mother.

7. The Division provided reunification services to the mother. Judge V restored custody and guardianship of PR to her mother, and on May 20, 2010, court jurisdiction was terminated.

8. Since the mother's case closed in 2010, law enforcement has responded to at least seven calls regarding domestic violence between the mother and Brock S.

9. On October 29, 2011, the mother and Brock S were punching each other and swerving across all lanes of traffic in a car on the freeway. PR and BS were in the car. The mother has pending charges for domestic violence in the presence of a child as a result of the incident. Brock S pled guilty for violation of a protective order and is scheduled to be sentenced on February 21, 2012.

10. *The mother obtained a protective order against Brock S; however, Brock S has been found to be in violation of the protective order on at least two occasions. Brock S is currently incarcerated due to a violation of the protective order against the mother as well as other charges.*

11. *In January, 2012, DCFS began investigating allegation of domestic violence, related child abuse, and child endangerment by the mother.*

12. *The mother is currently living with her stepmother and stepmother's son, **who is a convicted sex offender.***

13. *Kelly H has a criminal history with convictions of Illegal Possession/Use of Controlled Substance in 1999; Theft in 2000; Driving under the influence of Alcohol in 2009.*

14. *Kirk J has a criminal history with convictions for Carrying concealed Dangerous Weapons and Illegal Possession/Use of Controlled Substance in 1997; Intent to Distribute Controlled Substance in 1998; Illegal Possession/Use of Controlled Substance, a Third-Degree Felony, in 1999; Illegal Possession/Use of Controlled Substance, a Third-Degree Felony, in 2000 and Driving under the Influence with Personal Injury in 2009.*

15. *Brock S has a criminal history with convictions for Simple Assault in 2005; Criminal Mischief in 2006; Unlawful Detention in 2007; Fighting and Criminal Mischief in 2007, Simple Assault in 2009; Impaired Driving in 2011; Criminal Mischief in 2011 and Violation of Protective Order in 2011.*

Based on the above allegations, the State of Utah, DCFS moves the Court to find that:

1. *The children are abused and/or neglected...*

2. *The children are within the jurisdiction of the Juvenile Court.*

***WHEREFORE**, based on the findings, the State of Utah, DCFS, moves the Court to:*

1. *Order Protective Supervision Services or other appropriate services over the children.*

2. *Appoint a GAL to represent the children.*

3. *Make whatever other orders are in the children's best interest, including removing the children from the home if their health and safety continue to be at risk.*

4. *Substantiate the supported findings of DCFS.*

FEBRUARY 10, 2012: TRANSPORT ORDER; STATE OF UTAH

It is hereby ordered that the Salt Lake County Sheriff transport, BROCK S, father of the above-named child, from the Salt Lake County Adult Detention Center to the Third District Juvenile Court for a hearing to be held on February 14, 2012, before Judge V.

FEBRUARY 10, 2012: SUMMONS AND NOTICE

STATE OF UTAH TO: Kirk J

PLEASE TAKE NOTICE *that the State of Utah, DCFS has filed a copy of the attached Verified Petition with regards to the above child, PR.*

Also take notice that the following pre-trial hearing will be held February 14, to consider whether the allegations contained in the State's Verified Petition with regard to the above-named child are true, and whether protective supervision services over the above-named child should be granted to the State of Utah, Division of Child and Family Services.

You are hereby summoned and required to appear in person at the place, date and time specified, and to answer the petition in open court pursuant to Rule 34, Utah Rules of Juvenile Procedure or by written answer filed with the Court and provided to all parties within 10 days after the pre-trial hearing or 30 days after service of the petition, whichever comes first.

You are entitled to have an attorney present at this hearing. If you cannot afford an attorney, you should complete the application for appointment of an attorney available at the Juvenile Court at the above address, and if you qualify, an attorney will be appointed to you. The Court will also appoint a Guardian ad Litem to represent the child.

Furthermore, you are hereby notified that the parent or legal guardian is liable for the cost of support of the child in the protective custody, temporary custody, and custody of the division, and for legal counsel appointed for the parent or guardian.

Valentine Day was very busy in Juvenile Court in 2012. A new GAL was appointed to Payshence and BS. Kirk applied for another court appointed attorney and one was also assigned to Kelly and BS's alleged father and a warrant was issued.

FEBRUARY 14TH, 2012: WARRANT TO TAKE CHILD INTO PROTECTIVE CUSTODY. **STATE OF UTAH**, in the interest of PR and BS

ORDER OF CUSTODY TO ANY PEACE OFFICER AND THE PERSON IN CHARGE OF SHELTER HOME:

Whereas, a verified petition has been filed in this Court in the interest of the above-named children alleging facts or circumstances of abuse, neglect, or dependency that bring the children within the jurisdiction of the Juvenile Court it appears that:

Continuation of the children in the home would be contrary to their welfare and removal is in their best interest and/or, due to an emergency situation, which amounts to aggravated circumstances, the lack of preventative efforts was reasonable, and there is an eminent risk of harm to the child. You are therefore commanded to execute this Warrant and take PR and BS, a 4-year old female and a 1-year-old male child, into protective custody and place at the   CHRISTMAS BOX HOUSE SHELTER

State of Utah and the person receiving said children, are ordered to receive said child into your custody and keep safely until further order of this Court or until discharged.

FEBRUARY 16, 2012: SHELTER HEARING

Removal was reasonable in that there is a substantial danger to the physical health or safety of the children and that the children cannot be protected without removal from the custody of the parents and that an emergency existed justifying the removal.

Continuation in the home would be contrary to the welfare of the children and removal is in their best interest; due to the substantial danger which exists, the lack of preventative efforts is reasonable.

It is in the best interest of the children to be placed in the temporary care and custody of DCFS pending further hearing on the matter.

ORDERS:

PR, BS are placed in the interim custody of DCFS. The removal of said children from the home and placement of the children in the custody of an agency or individual other than his or her parents was in the best interest of the children. The parents are ordered to contact the Office of Recovery Services to determine a support amount for the children.

The Court orders supervised visitation for the parents. The parents are to have separate visitations with the children. The Court orders the mother to submit to random UA's. The Court orders a hair follicle test on the mother.

All previous orders of the Court consistent with this order are hereby continued.

FEBRUARY 21ST, 2012: SHELTER HEARING, Judge V presiding

The above-entitled matter came before the court for a Shelter Hearing on the 16th day of February, 2012. Judge V presiding. The Children were removed by warrant issued by this court after a hearing on the State's protective supervision services Petition pretrial on February 14, 2012. The parties acknowledged the reasonableness of the removal and argued the need for continued removal.

The GAL expressed concern over who was watching the children, specifically that a registered sex offender was babysitting the children. The GAL discussed Kirk J and the fact that he is married to Kelly H, but is not the biological father of either child. He is living with Jill C and has a child with her, but she is still married to someone else. He discussed the grades and school attendance of the children living in the home of Kirk J. Kirk's attorney commented on the home study for Kirk J that was very favorable. Kelly's attorney indicated that his client had housing with a lease but she is living at the grandmother's home. She has employment through a temporary staffing agency and works from 8-30 hours per week.

FINDINGS

1. The jurisdiction requirements have been met.

2. In accordance with Utah Code a preponderance of the evidence shows that there is a substantial danger in the physical health or safety of the children, and the children cannot be protected without removal from the custody of the parents.

3. Continuation in the home would be contrary to the welfare of the children and removal is in their best interest. The lack of preventive efforts was reasonable.

*4. **There is not a natural parent available, with whom the children were/was not residing at the time the events or conditions that brought them within the court's jurisdiction occurred, and who desires custody of the children.***

*5. **DCFS is to conduct an investigation regarding the safety and appropriateness of placement with a relative who requests placement. DCFS shall report its findings to the Court. Pending such report, the children shall remain in the custody of the agency.***

ORDER

1. The initial removal of the children was necessary pursuant to the specific finding herein included.

2. It is in the best interest of the children to be placed in the temporary legal custody and guardianship of DCFS for continued case and placement pending the adjudication hearing.

3. The parents are ordered to contact the ORS to determine support amount for said children.

*4. **The parents shall cooperate with DCFS within five working days, to provide information regarding relatives who may be able and willing to care for the children**.*

5. The mother shall submit to drug screens as requested by DCFS.

6. The parents may have supervised visits with the children, supervised by DCFS.

Payshence and BS were taken to the Christmas Box house. Jody was not notified. Although the State knew Jody was trying to get his daughter and had a safe and loving environment to take care of her, he was, once again, left out of the picture, and little Payshence was, once again, carted off to strangers. Jody and his family spent regular time with Payshence but were never informed when there were issues, as Kelly did all she could to keep the truth from them.

FEBRUARY 28, 2012: PROCEEDINGS TRANSCRIPT

THE COURT: *All right. This matter is in the interest of the children, PR and BS. Mr. Brent N, GAL is here representing the children. Ms. Nickel is the attorney general. Ms. D is here from DCFS, and Ms. I is also here from DCFS. Mom is here ...(Interruption.)*

THE COURT: *The mom is here with Mr. H. And Kirk J, the father of PR is present with Ms. Muir (his court appointed attorney). Petition was filed February 10th. We've had two hearings since that filing. I believe two. Maybe not since, but we've had two hearings. Today is the time and date set for pretrial. Has the petition been resolved?*

MR. H, Kelly's attorney: *We're close, your Honor, but no. And I just want the record to reflect this is our first pretrial hearing. The last two hearings were - - one was a shelter; one was a warrant hearing. So, I can file an answer. There's one line that we're in disagreement about that we are trying to resolve, but there will be enough for jurisdiction, just from what my client has told me, so that's not going to be an issue. It's an issue of how culpable.*

In the meantime, my client - - I just wanted to let the Court know that she has contracted with FACT, the Family Abuse Center for Treatment. Ms. Taylor who I've worked with in the past, is her domestic violence therapist, and I have some confirmation that she's begun that process, domestic violence therapy. I can provide that to counsel, if necessary.

THE COURT: *Well, it looks like we need to set it for adjudication for April 16th, 2012. Let's give them an adjudication date. I did receive a letter from your client, Ms. Muir. I didn't read it. I don't want him writing to me, so I'll give it to the lawyer for - - to decide what they want to do with it, but - -*

MS. MUIR: *I do have a copy of it, your Honor. It looks like, from looking at the file, Ms. Connie represented Kirk J before, and I don't know why the case didn't go back to her to represent - - this case has a lot of history, and she knows more about it than I do. I think all parties are fighting about - -*

THE COURT: *Isn't that determined by the - - Locket & Associates?*

MS. MUIR: *No, your honor, it's based on a - -*

BRENT N: *A rotation.*

MS. MUIR: *- - a rotation. And Ms. Connie would have been next in line. I'm not sure about (inaudible) it came during shelter, and so perhaps it was just a real easy time (inaudible).*

THE COURT: *I don't know. Okay. Well, that's fine. I'll go ahead and appoint Ms. Co, but - -*

MS. MUIR: *And I'll make sure she gets the file.*

THE COURT: *Yeah. I'm not going to read his (Kirk's) letter, regardless of what the lawyers want today. No offense to the lawyers, but I think Ms. Connie should be the first one to look at it to see if it's appropriate or not, since she's going to be representing him. So, we need to set the adjudication by April 16h. Mr. Michael, what do you got, sir?*

MR. MICHAEL: *April 12th at 10:00.*

THE COURT: *April 12th. All right. Thank you. Yes?*

UNIDENTIFIED SPEAKER: *Your Honor, we've got the children in the Christmas Box House.*

THE COURT: *Uh-huh.*

UNIDENTIFIED SPEAKER: *And we have an obligation to try and place with the non-offending parent unless it's clearly unsafe.*

THE COURT: *Uh-huh.*

UNIDENTIFIED SPEAKER: *And it's still our recommendation that the children be placed with the father during this time.*

THE COURT: *Father of the one?*

UNIDENTIFIED SPEAKER: *Kirk J.*

THE COURT: *He's the father of just one, correct?*

UNIDENTIFIED SPEAKER: *Well, he's the legal father - - of both - - of PR and BS, so - - and our investigation doesn't show that it's clearly unsafe. I know we visited last time, but I just - -*

THE COURT: *<u>I know, and, you know, I hate to go back and dig out all the reasons I didn't do it before, so - - you know, I'm not sure that - - you know, every time this is raised, do I have to go back and say, "All right. This is why I'm not doing it"? I can't' remember. You know, I've had 50 hearings since then, so - -</u>*

UNIDENTIFIED SPEAKER: *I think it was the issue of the domestic viol*ence issue in his home - -

THE COURT: *In his home?*

UNIDENTIFIED SPEAKER: *- by his significant other against his father.*

THE COURT: *<u>Well, I don't' remember. I'm just - - you know - -</u>*

UNIDENTIFIED SPEAKER: *Any way, I'm just raising it.*

THE COURT: <u>*I'm not inclined to keep revisiting that issue. I mean, I've already made a decision that the*</u> <u>*children don't go with him, so every time you raise it - - I'm just trying to figure out, "Okay. Why are we doing this*</u> <u>*again when I've already made my decision?"*</u> *Somebody. Go ahead, Mr. N.*

BRENT N: *And, Judge, I - - I concur, and I think that what needs to happen, because I've been trying to pull together information, and the only way I would slightly amend or ask the Court to amend what the Court indicated is at* *some point I would like the Court to reconsider the issue.*

THE COURT: *Uh-huh.*

BRENT N: *But I think it is appropriate that when that request is being made, that the documentation be made to indicate what those concerns were in the first place and why they've been resolved. One of those issues, for example, did deal with a domestic violence situation, and there was a letter that was provided to me just today indicating that a completion, but I'm not yet ready with a motion in order to do that. But just in response to the Court's questions, there may come a time when I do come before the Court, either joining or by my own motion, making that request, but, you know, in those child welfare proceedings it sometimes is appropriate for the Court to reconsider, even though issues have been identified when they're resolved.*

THE COURT: *Yeah. Well, I - - I certainly don't dispute that at all. I'm looking at my notes, and specifically I do have "Kirk J, underlying domestic violence incident in the home. Removed from the mother two times previously because of domestic violence relationships and problems. And I don't recall for sure, but it seemed to me by taking children out of one domestic violence environment and placing in another domestic violence environment - it doesn't make sense to me to do that, so - - I just had my notes. I don't have the last order that was submitted by DCF - - or by the AG's office.*
Do you have something there? You know, I just think that what we did is - - we were real concerned about the mother's seven referrals to DCFS for domestic violence, as well as the encounter that she had in an automobile where the children were present and other domestic violence in a dangerous situation, **and then the alternative was to place the children with the father, Kirk J, who was also involved in some kind of domestic violence incident most recently, so that's my recollection.**

UNIDENTIFIED SPEAKER: *Your Honor, actually (inaudible) other (inaudible) domestic violence issues.*

THE COURT: *Is she here? (Referring to Kelly)*

UNIDENTIFIED SPEAKER*: She is here, and she did bring a letter today (inaudible) that she had completed her domestic violence course. I think that's one of the things the Division wanted to know and one of the reasons they were (inaudible).*

THE COURT: *Didn't we have another sister here at the last hearing who the bailiff almost had to take into custody because of her mouthing off? Was it one of these ladies here?*

BRENT N: *It isn't anyone who is here, Judge.*

THE COURT: *So, what are the facts? I mean, this tells me the issues they dealt with, but I don't know what the facts are. What was the incident? What do the police reports say? What was the involvement with Kirk J? What was DCFS's involvement? How many times have the cops been over there? This tells me she went in and completed an eight-lesson parenting cycle educational program. Okay. Intensive treatment, you know, issues that play - - past behaviors that place her at risk for violence, progress towards treatment goals, thinking errors, stress management, listening skills., cog - - I don't - - this doesn't - - this tells me you went to treatment, but I still don't know what this was all about.*

UNIDENTIFIED SPEAKER: *Your Honor, my understanding from reading the police report is that there was an incident where she (Jill C) had called the police because she got in a fight with her - - with Mr. Kirk J's father.*

THE COURT: *Uh-huh. In the home?*

UNIDENTIFIED SPEAKER: *In the home, and had hit him both with a coffee pot and a picture on the wall. It was - - whether it was after the birth of the child and due to postpartum depression or some hormonal imbalance, I don't know, but she had also called the police to tell them what she had done, and then obtained treatment, I think, for that.*

THE COURT: *So, was she arrested?*

BRENT N: *I think she was cited.*

UNIDENTIFIED SPEAKER: *She was cited, uh-huh.*

BRENT N: *I can't' remember if she went to jail.*

UNIDENTIFIED SPEAKER: *I don't know.*

THE COURT: *Has anybody called the victim of that domestic violence, the father, and talked to him about the incident. Because they can tell us whatever they want. I - - you know, I just - - I need both sides of the story here.*

UNIDENTIFIED SPEAKER: *Well, Judge, I was the investigator in that case, and I was able to speak with Dan.*

UNIDENTIFIED SPEAKER: *He was living there at the times, yes?*

THE COURT: *Okay. And so, she did this to him?*

UNIDENTIFIED SPEAKER: *She broke the coffee cup - -*

THE COURT: *How old is he?*

UNIDENTIFIED SPEAKER: *I want to say he's in his 70's.*

THE COURT: *Where were the kids when this was going on?*

UNIDENTIFIED SPEAKER: *In the home. They saw it.*

THE COURT: *Where was Mr. J at the time?*

UNIDENTIFIED SPEAKER: *In the kitchen.*

THE COURT: *And what was his involvement?*

UNIDENTIFIED SPEAKER: *Not this Mr. J (Referring to Kirk). I'm sorry, Dan J.*

THE COURT: *The grandpa.*

UNIDENTIFIED SPEAKER: *Grandpa was in the kitchen.*

THE COURT: *But Kirk J wasn't present?*

UNIDENTIFIED SPEAKER: *I believe he was at work.*

THE COURT: *Okay. And?*

UNIDENTIFIED SPEAKER: *And I spoke to the victim, he said that he's had some problems with the mother. His opinion was there was a substance abuse problem with pills and alcohol.*

THE COURT: *Uh-huh.*

UNIDENTIFIED SPEAKER: *And he said that she was unpredictable. They - - they - - I got the feeling they sort of butted heads, personality-wise.*

THE COURT: *Uh-huh.*

UNIDENTIFIED SPEAKER: *But that was his home and he had lived there for quite some-odd time and was - - was a huge help taking care of the children, provided child care, because he was HIV positive and not working.*

THE COURT: *What was he HIV positive from? From drug use himself?*

UNIDENTIFIED SPEAKER: *I don't believe so.*

THE COURT: *Because of sexual relationships?*

UNIDENTIFIED SPEAKER: *I believe so.*

UNIDENTIFIED SPEAKER: *Yes.*

THE COURT: *So, he is a registered sex offender as well?*

UNIDENTIFIED SPEAKER: *No. No, Judge.*

THE COURT: *Does he live there?*

UNIDENTIFIED SPEAKER: *I think he is just - - leads a homosexual lifestyle, and I think that's how he contracted - -*

THE COURT: *Does he live there?*

UNIDENTIFIED SPEAKER: *Not any more. They've asked him to leave.*

THE COURT: *Well, you see, all that stuff, it just kind of stirs the pot a little bit, doesn't it? Allegations of drug use, allegations of erratic behavior, allegations of whatever is going on in that home.*

UNIDENTIFIED SPEAKER: *I believe - - I believe Jill was taking some medication for some mental health problems that she feels - -*

THE COURT: *What kind of mental health problems?*

UNIDENTIFIED SPEAKER: *Depression (inaudible).*

JILL: *They put me on (inaudible) OB put me on Wellbutrin for my postpartum depression, I experienced, and I'd been on it for a week and a half and had a lot of anger, so I went right back -*

THE COURT: *Anger at what?*

JILL: *What was that?*

THE COURT: *Anger at what?*

JILL: *Everything. I - - except for my kids. I just - - everything set me off.*

THE COURT: *When did this happen?*

JILL: *This happened last April. The beginning of last April.*

THE COURT: *Go ahead, Ms. Dalton. Thank you.*

MS. DALTON: *Well, we did open the PSC case, voluntary caseworker, and I believe that Ms. Rapp was the caseworker on that, and she - - she thought there was some progress being made, and because the victim was no longer in the home - - he had been relocated somewhere else - - that it was safe to close the case, because there had been no more instances. The other thing that I do know is that we requited for her to complete a substance abuse program, and I believe **she said that those classes were too expensive. She did drop out of them, and at this point she would have to start all over again with a new - - for her to get any kind of letter of completion for that.***

THE COURT: *Okay. Thank you. Well, that's more information than I had ten minutes ago. Anything else? Anybody also? No? **What's the prognosis for placing these children in a home besides the homes that's been requested?***

UNIDENTIFIED SPEAKER: *I'm in the process of placing the kids. They did have an overnight visit over the weekend that went well with the family. Payshence was sick yesterday, so we didn't proceed with anything additionally yesterday just because of how - - her not feeling well, so today the kids have visits with their parents, and then we'll go from there. So, they will likely be placed before the end of the week.*

THE COURT: *They'll be together?*

UNIDENTIFIED SPEAKER: *Yes.*

THE COURT: *And how are they doing?*

UNIDENTIFIED SPEAKER: *They're doing well. Payshence misses her mom a lot. It's really difficult for her in the late afternoons and evenings. She has a hard time going to sleep. BS is doing really well. His - - he had a pretty bad rash on his scalp and on his body and (inaudible).*

THE COURT: *A what? A rash?*

UNIDENTIFIED SPEAKER: *A rash.*

THE COURT: *Did he have that when he was picked up?*

UNIDENTIFIED SPEAKER: *He had it when he came to the Christmas Box House, yeah.*

THE COURT: *And what was that attributed to, that rash? Do you know?*

UNIDENTIFIED SPEAKER: *It was - - I think he had a fungal rash on his scalp, and then we've had a conflicting diagnosis of the rash on his body. One doctor said that it was scabies. Another doctor said that they didn't think it was scabies, and they're using a topical ointment to - - that's helping clear it, and I believe that he was supped to be on antibiotics for a period of time.*

THE COURT: *Uh-huh. He was supposed to be prior to us intervening or -*

UNIDENTIFIED SPEAKER: *It's my understanding that he already was receiving treatment for whatever the rash was when he came to the Christmas Box House, because he came with medication.*

BRENT N: *That was the report that the Christmas Box House gave me.*

UNIDENTIFIED SPEAKER: *Right. He did have some medications, and the Christmas Box House - - I - - if you remember, Judge, I had to pick those kids up - - drop them off, and come back. When I went back to check them in, they said that they had spoken to the doctor who had prescribed the medication, and they described what he looked like. The doctor said her instructions were, if it looked worse or got worse, for him to come back in, and that's - - and so I had to take him to Primary Children's that night, and indeed it was worse than what the prescribing doctor had seen. They diagnosed impetigo and the fungal infection.*

THE COURT: *So, they had a different diagnosis?*

UNIDENTIFIED SPEAKER: *Right. Payshence has been diagnosed with a fungal infection. A vaginal fungal infection.*

THE COURT: *A vaginal what?*

UNIDENTIFIED SPEAKER: *Fungal yeast infection.*

THE COURT: *The - - the - - PR?*

UNIDENTIFIED SPEAKER: *Right.*

THE COURT: *And is this a recent diagnosis?*

UNIDENTIFIED SPEAKER: *Since she's been in the Christmas Box House. So it may be that there is a fungus in the home of that - - something is causing these kids to get this fungus.*

THE COURT: *Well, the mother was allowing a registered sex offender to watch PH, so have we done any further investigation on that case like talking to PR about, you know - -*

UNIDENTIFIED SPEAKER: *Judge, we couldn't get a detective during the time period that you requested, but we did have a DCFS - - a CPS worker who has worked in sex abuse speak to PR. The problem is, she - - is her age. She's very hard to interview. The only thing that came up that was questionable was a peeking game that she talked about that she couldn't describe. She just said she doesn't like it. It scares her.*

THE COURT*: Uh-huh.*

UNIDENTIFIED SPEAKER: *But she couldn't tell us how the game was played, and another problem was she didn't have any names for her private parts. We usually ask them where the bathing suit covers, and she would say "my back" or "my arm" and so, without having any labels to refer to, it is not the Division's policy to start giving names to places for children.*

THE COURT: *Yeah. I - - and I appreciate that sensitivity. The peeking game, was she saying she was playing this game with her caretaker?*

UNIDENTIFIED SPEAKER: *She said it was - - it was played with somebody named - - I believe it was Anthony and Mike.*

THE COURT: *Uh-huh. Who is Anthony?*

UNIDENTIFIED SPEAKER: *She couldn't say.*

In the background on the tape a woman began to cry.

THE COURT: *Who is Anthony? Ma'am, why are you crying? Who is Anthony? Ma'am, I'm talking to you. Stand up, ma'am. Who is Anthony?*

UNIDENTIFIED SPEAKER: *He was a friend of the sex offender's?*

THE COURT: *Okay. And who is Michael?*

CRYING WOMAN: *I don't know who Michael is.*

THE COURT: *And why are you upset?*

CRYING WOMAN: *Because she used to call him her "boyfriend".*
THE COURT: *She used to call who "boyfriend"? Anthony?*

CRYING WOMAN: *Yeah.*

THE COURT: *So, the five-year-old was calling Anthony "boyfriend" - Okay. These - - these hearings are sometimes very disturbing, and you have a right to your feelings, but unless we get all this information out, we're not able to help children and families, okay? This isn't a criminal court. This is trying to figure out, you know, who surrounds the child, who is responsible, who is not responsible, what are the issues, how do we protect kids. Okay?*

UNIDENTIFIED SPEAKER: *Would it be appropriate for her to be in some intensive trauma treatment with a professional who deals in this before we get more information, given her young age and her verbal skills?*

THE COURT: *Yeah. She's five. Well, okay.*

BRENT N: *Four.*

THE COURT: *Four? Only four? Jeez. Well, let's go ahead and pursue that, okay? And not to put anything in the child's head, but just give her an opportunity to talk. I'm going to go ahead and deny the request to place the child with Kirk J at this time, the children. And I just have concerns about that home environment, and maybe it was just a one-time incident, but there seems like there's been a lot of other issues that have been at least flushed out, not necessarily proven, but it just seemed to me that what we really need to do with these children is place them in a home environment that we know is safe and stable in terms of some of the other issues that's been raised today with respect to not only the mom's care for the children or lack thereof, and also Kirk J's (inaudible), so **I'm not going to pull kids out of a domestic violence situation and place them in another one with - - maybe not currently, but where there's a history of that. I'm not going to do that.** The number one thing in this case is to try to get these kids some help, and believe it or not, once mom is adjudicated on this petition, then we look at reunification. What does she need at this particular point? And, of course, I'm not saying I'm going to order reunification services, because there's a bunch of stuff that's not going to go away in terms of history, but that's what we're trying to do here. Now, how old is BS? He's just a baby, right? He's - -*

BRENT N: *Yeah, BS is one.*

THE COURT: *Only one. All right. Well, you have the date, and I'll see you then.*

BRENT N: *Judge, I assume if we do get a resolution, we could file a motion.*

THE COURT: *Oh, yeah. I'll see you even sooner than that if you resolve it. I mean, I said April just because the time frame - - if you need me to see her next week or two, I'll do it.*

UNIDENTIFIED SPEAKER: *Judge, I'm going to speak to my client on this one. I'm scheduled - - I'm still reporting on the Lopez case, but my client hasn't appeared at the last two or three hearings, so if she's not here today, I'm going to keep trying to reach her.*

THE COURT: *This letter, should I hang on to it Ms. Muir?*

MS. MUIR: *Yes, your honor, if you would. I think it's (inaudible). I'll make sure Ms. Connie has a copy of it.*

THE COURT: *Where did Mom go?*

UNIDENTIFIED SPEAKER: *Well, she's still here. Let's ask.*

End of transcript.

The entire hearing was summed up below in one short paragraph. So much goes on in a court room and very little makes it in to the summary.

FEBRUARY 28TH, 2012: CHILD WELFARE PROCEEDING, Judge V presiding

This matter came before the Court for a pretrial. The Court addressed preliminary matters. Kirk J's attorney moved the Court to re-appoint Ms. Connie to represent the father in this matter. There were no objections. The Court granted the motion.
PR and BS are continued in the temporary custody of DCFS. The Court hereby re-appoints Connie to represent the father in the case.

FEBRUARY 29TH, 2012: MOTION TO WITHDRAW AND ORDER

*Comes now, Ms. Muir, appointed counsel for the respondent, Kirk J, and hereby moves the court for an order vacating her appointment and allowing her to withdraw in this matter. **The Court appointed Connie to be Kirk J's attorney, as she had represented him in the past.** Thus, Counsel asks the Court for an order vacating her appointment and allowing her to withdraw in this matter.*

MARCH 6TH, 2012: CHILD WELFARE PROCEEDING

This matter came before the Court for a Continued Pretrial and an Amended Verified Petition is submitted to the court. Upon motion of counsel, the petition was amended by interlineation. The parties are informed of the right to trial and the right to present evidence. The allegations in the petition are admitted by Kelly H, mother.
ORDERS
PR and BS are continued in the interim custody of DCFS. The Court retains the right to impose further disposition.

MARCH 7TH, 2012: ADJUDICATION ORDER

The above-entitled matter came before the court for a Pre-trial Hearing on the mother the 6th day of March, 2012, with the Honorable Judge V presiding.
CONCLUSIONS OF LAW
1. The above-named children are neglected children within the meaning of Utah Code...in that they lack proper parental care by reason of the fault and habits of the mother.
From the foregoing Findings of Fact and Conclusions of Law, the court enters its order.
ORDER
1. The children shall continue in the custody and guardianship of the Division.
2. The parents may have supervised visits with the children, supervised by DCFS.
3. The mother shall submit to drug screens, including hair tests, as requested by DCFS.
4. This matter is set for Pretrial on the father and a dispositional hearing on the mother.

APRIL 12, 2012: DISPOSITION HEARING

The Father, Kirk J, was asked if he was under the influence of any drugs or alcohol. He denied being under the influence of drugs or alcohol. He was advised of his rights to a trial, to have the State prove the petition by clear and convincing evidence, to call witnesses, to cross-examine witnesses and to appeal the finding in court. He voluntarily waived those rights, expressed satisfaction with his attorney and admitted the allegations in the petition.

The parties submitted the matter for the court to enter its Conclusions of Law. The court received a child and family plan, a domestic violence assessment on the mother, 2 letters from...Family Abuse Center for Treatment, prescriptions, and an assessment on PR.

The Assistant Attorney General requested that the child and family plan be amended to include the requirements that the mother have legal employment, **that the parents be required to divorce each other and that the mother obtain drug treatment**. _The AAG also suggested that Jill C, paramour of Kirk J, divorce her husband, and notified the court that Kelly H was again pregnant and the biological father is **not** Kirk J._

Kelly's attorney noted that the letter from the therapist for the mom recommended reunification services for the mother and children, when she had never even seen the children and that the mother provided a clean hair test the day prior to providing a positive drug screen.

The parties discussed visitation for the father Kirk J, and the need to look to placing the children with him, sooner rather than later.

FINDINGS

1. PR is a four-year-old female child. BS is a one-year-old male child.
2. Kelly H is mother of the children,
3. Kirk J is the father of PR. He is the legal father of BS.
4. Kirk J has an extensive criminal history.
5. The children are not members of any Native American Tribe.
6. The petition, as amended, is true as to Kirk J.
7. The services offered to the parents in the child and family plan constitute reasonable efforts on the part of the Division to reunify the parents with their children.
8. The duties and responsibilities of the parents under the child and family plan are clearly set forth in the document and have been communicated to the parents on the record in the proceeding. The amendments to the plan that the mother obtain drug treatment, a divorce and legal employment and **Kirk J obtain a divorce from Kelly H** were also communicated to the parents on the record in these proceedings.
9. The permanency goal for the children is return home.

CONCLUSIONS OF LAW

1. The above-named children are dependent children in that they lack proper care through no fault of the father.

ORDER

1. The children shall continue in the custody and guardianship of DCFS.
2. **The father, Kirk J, may have extended visits with the children, but the visits shall be set up and structured with written rules that include no alcohol or domestic violence in the home.**
3. Prior consistent orders shall continue.
4. The child and family plan is amended to include requirements that the mother obtain drug treatment, the parents obtain a divorce from each other and legal employment for the mother. Reunification services are ordered for Kirk J and Kelly H.
5. The mother shall obtain pre-natal care.
6. The DCFS shall sort out the mother's residence, facts surrounding the multiple residences and how she pays for them.
7. There shall be no people with criminal convictions in the father's home when the children are present.

MAY 22ND, 2012: CHILD WELFARE PROCEEDING

The Court reviewed the submitted reports. The Attorney for DCFS informed the Court that the Division is recommending a trial home placement of the children with Kirk J and gave basis. The GAL concurred with and supported the recommendation. Kelly's attorney spoke on her behalf and further moved the Court to expand her visitation and gave details.

ORDERS

PR, BS, are continued in the custody of the DCFS.
The Court authorizes a trial home placement for BS and PR with Kirk J.
The Court hereby orders that visits between Kelly H must be clean and sober.
That reunification services continue to be provided.

JULY 31ST, 2012: CHILD WELFARE PROCEEDING, Custody given to Kirk J

The Court addressed all preliminary matters. Reports and recommendations are submitted to the Court by DCFS. All parties discussed the letter regarding the mother's therapeutic progress. The Court addresses and accepts comments from all parties present.

ORDERS
Permanent Custody and Guardianship of PR and BS are placed with Kirk J.
Visits between Kelly H, BS, and PR will be determined by Kirk J.
PR and BS are released from the custody of the DCFS.

From this point forward, nothing would be the same for little Payshence. Her family, as she knew it, would unravel and dwindle away under the control of Kirk and his current live-ins. She would be a tool and a pawn to get what he wanted from Kelly who would be able to see her children sparsely, and only if she provided "favors." Jody would be completely cut off from his little darling with every effort made to erase his existence from her memory.

CHAPTER 11
A NEW MRS. RHORER

SEPTEMBER 21, 2012: Enter Me. The biographer, narrator of this book and now the wife of Jody Rhorer.

We met the new traditional way - Match.com. Our first date was about a week from the time we made our first connection on Match. I always believed in love at first sight and I had held out hope for a soul mate. I studied the happiest couples I knew as I had a miserable 24-year marriage and I was determined to get it right, or be alone. At least alone, a person is not subject to the cruelties of the very human being that vowed to adore and protect them.

I must admit that I was so taken aback by Jody when he stepped out of the car to pick me up for dinner, that my initial reaction was that this man couldn't possibly be looking for a serious relationship. His appearance and charisma, the way he smelled, down to his square-toed cowboy boots caught me completely off guard. I didn't want to confuse lust with love and decided at that moment that there would not be a follow up date as a man this fine must have so many options he wouldn't possibly settle for just one - especially one 12 years older. I, being a well-known and respected business woman in my community, could not show up in public with a "cowboy toy" on my arm and be taken seriously. I would be polite, enjoy the dinner, say thank you and goodbye.

Three hours later, he held my heart in his hands. Never had I met someone so sincere, open, ready to love and be loved. Jody told me his story, from the beginning up to that moment. He told me about the three woman who had impacted his life; about his three oldest girls and his little five your old daughter, Payshence, who he was still seeing regularly but planned on starting yet another legal fight to gain custody. He explained how he had been told several times by attorneys that he had no possible chance at getting her unless Kelly and Kirk either divorced or were incarcerated due to the Utah Parentage Act.

The restaurant was shutting down so our date came to a close, but not before Jody informed me of the things in his past - he wanted to be one hundred percent transparent and honest. I learned a valuable lesson that night - a girl who had never been in trouble for anything; a Mormon mother of 4 sons that weren't even allowed to say "shut up". I learned there are two sides to every pancake.

Just because someone is arrested and a mug shot is produced, doesn't make that person bad, guilty, evil, or a number of other adjectives I had given those people up to that moment. No, it's often just a procedure without merit, proof, fairness. A fleeting moment where judgement is made, often incorrectly and without consideration and accountability. But the trail left behind is one that never fades and follows the accused around like a looming shadow that always requires justification and explanation. Once all details have been revealed, often one finds that a law is ludicrous or that gray areas open the way for incarceration without guilt and even a chance to prove otherwise.

But this is not a story about my love affair with Jody; it's about his battle to get his little girl back. I felt a need to go into great detail about his life with his other 3 daughters; about how a life partner can make or break you; about time and circumstances and how, try as you might, things can happen that are just out of your control - things that do unrepairable hurt to a person, both child and adult alike.

Four days after we met, Jody asked me if I would be "exclusive" with him. Of course I said yes! He had asked on the phone and called me back 3 more times to make sure I meant it.

"Do you know what exclusive means?" He asked.

Silly question. I wear your sweater - the one with letterman patch. I wear your ring around my neck, like Elvis said.

"Yes, I know what it means," I answered.

"What does it mean?" Jody responded. He just needed to hear me say it, I supposed.

"It means we only see each other," I said.

"That we don't date anyone else," he added.

"Right."

"So, are you sure?" he asked again.

"I'm sure!" I insisted. And I was. And we basically have never been apart since. That's how true love works - it is easy, it is effortless.

Many times I have wondered how this man could be so open and trusting as opposed to bitter and jaded. Especially after he told me about his last wife, Krista. Jody had been working in Salt Lake when he met Krista. He thought she was a good church-going girl. She had a daughter Mia's age and also a son. She was cute and sweet and fun. They had only dated a few months when time came to return to Missouri to work, as he was accustomed to doing when the cold came. There were two reasons for his annual southern migration; he usually was laid off because construction was seasonal, and, he hated the winter weather in Utah.

When he said he was leaving, Krista wanted to go too, only she thought it would be best if they were married as it would look better for the custody purposes of her kids as she would be taking them out of state and their father's may object to that if she were just following a boyfriend. They quickly pulled together a celebration and were married in the city park. Jody was happy. He wanted to be settled. He wanted a good mom for his girls.

Once in Missouri, Jody rented a house for the family and went to work. It wasn't long until Krista got a job as well and for the first several months, things seemed okay. Krista didn't get along with George and Jody's girls were not particularly fond of her and also fought with her kids, but this isn't too out of the ordinary for a blended family early on when everyone is still getting to know each other. However, some red flags began to pop up. Krista never had any money left from her paycheck and wanted to quit her manufacturing job and get a job in a bar - which Jody was completely against. She also was spending a lot of time with Brother and his wife. Krista's behavior was becoming more erratic and there was some strain in the relationship but Jody was committed to making this work.

The union call came early that year and Jody had to fly back to Utah to start work again. The plan was for him to come back in a few weeks when he had a three-day weekend, pack up the family and their belongings, and all make the 22 hour drive to Utah together.

"I want to come back now, Jody," Krista demanded. "I want to see my boy so I'm gonna pack the trailer myself."

"Krista, you need to listen to me. That's too long of a trip for you to drive with the girls by yourself. It ain't that easy pullin a full trailer in that big-ass truck. You can wait a few weeks. You'll be fine."

"You don't understand. I can't be here with your family and not have you here. Your mom doesn't like me," Krista argued.

"Of course she does," Jody continued. "Now put a smile on your face and be my tough girl."

What Jody didn't read into his conversation with Krista was that she had excessive anxiety due to a recent methamphetamine habit she picked up a couple months after they had moved to Missouri. She quickly disregarded her conversation with her husband and loaded up the large utility trailer with their belongs. This would include their furniture, a new bedroom set, large screen television, all Jody's personal items, including clothing, important documents, tax documents, tools, fishing gear pretty much everything Jody and his girls owned with the exception of the clothes he brought for work.

Fortunately, only Tina and her turtle and Krista's daughter were passengers in the truck as they headed out on their journey to Utah that day. The other girls would come out with Jody's parents later. But the trio did not get far. About 15 miles out of Boonville, Krista lost control of the truck, the trailer fishtailing wildly. She tried to straighten out but miscalculated and the truck and trailer flipped, flinging all the Rhorer belonging across the highway and into the trees and surrounding brush.

Krista checked the girls. Everyone was okay but she knew she needed to get away from the accident before the police showed up. She was under the influence of narcotics and driving on a suspended license. Tina's main concern was recovering her turtle. Krista's main concern was disappearing.

Jody would never see Krista again. She took her daughter and fled back to Utah, leaving Tina behind. Jody's truck and trailer and all his belongings were a complete loss. Insurance didn't cover anything since Krista's license had been suspended. Once again, Jody found himself heartbroken, and starting over again. Three months later he met me.

CHAPTER 12
OPERATION TAKING BACK PAYSHENCE

A couple weeks after we began our love affair, Jody and I were at my youngest son's high school football game. We were sitting in the bleachers watching him play. The crowd was cheering loudly when his phone rang. It was Payshence. She was now five years old.

"Hi honey, I miss you," Jody said.

"When do I get to see you, Daddy?" Payshence asked.

"I just need to talk to your mom about that, but it will be soon. How do you like school? Are you wearing the new clothes I got you?"

"I like it. My teacher is nice. I just want to see you and my sisters," Payshence pleaded.

"Ya, we are gonna do that soon. I'm just waiting for your mom to tell me when and I'll be there. I want to see if I can take you with me to meet my new friend too," Jody said. "I sure love you."

The noise of the crowd made it hard to continue the conversation, but had he known that would be one of the last conversations he had with his little girl, he never would have hung up the phone.

The next several months were a cat and mouse game. Kelly would promise Jody he could see Payshence, they would set up a meeting place, and then she would either not show, or not answer his texts or calls the day of their appointment. What we didn't know and what she didn't tell us was that Kirk had been given complete control over Payshence and her other children and that only through Kirk's permission, could she take Payshence to see Jody - and he wasn't cooperating.

Jody and Payshence had a special ritual they did whenever they were saying their goodbyes. This is something that Payshence came up with. She would put her thumb and pointer finger together tightly and say, "I love you this much! Nothing can come between us." That was their special saying. The day Jody had taken her to get her school clothes would be the last time Payshence would be able to tell him this. Kelly came to Jody's house to pick her up.

"Mommy, look at what daddy got me!" Payshence held up her bags of new school clothes.

"Nice baby," Kelly said, "We gotta go though."

Payshence held up her thumb and finger, "I love you this much Daddy. Nothing can come between us."

Kelly shot a look of disdain at Jody. Her biggest fear was for Payshence to be in Jody's custody. She knew if it were up to him, she wouldn't see her daughter unless she was clean and history showed that she couldn't stay clean for long.

Kelly brought Payshence to Kirk's and dropped her off. Jody wasn't aware of the new arrangement that the court had implemented. Kelly certainly didn't want him to know that she had lost custody and visitation was to be supervised (which neither she or Kirk adhered to). It would be some time before he figured out what was going on.

"Mom, why do I have to stay here?" Payshence cried as Kelly tried to peel her from her leg.

"It's just for now until I can get some things worked out," Kelly told her.

In her mind I'm sure she was convinced things would change and the state would give her custody back. She now had a fifth child as well - another boy - she was at risk of losing to Kirk.

Payshence began to cry, "I don't wanna stay here!"

At this point Kirk had come outside. He grabbed Payshence by the arm.

"C'mon," He demanded.

Payshence jerked away. " My daddy is gonna stab you in the neck!" she yelled.

"What?" Kirk said, "That ain't gonna happen cuz you ain't gonna see your daddy no more."

He picked Payshence up and took her in the house. This incident would come up again and again. It would be twisted around to look like a threat that was repeated from Jody. This was not the case. Jody didn't even know Kirk had custody but he did start to suspect something after so many put offs from Kelly.

The holidays were coming and the girls were still able to see Payshence regularly. However, there were rules. They could never talk about their dad; they could not tell their dad that they were told not to speak of him. If Payshence brought him up, they had to brush it off or change the subject.

Tina had formed a strong bond with Kelly and was able to see Payshence more than the other girls. Kelly would pick her up, usually without Jody knowing as he didn't approve of their continued relationship. During one of these incidents, Tina had asked to see Payshence. Kelly took her to Kirk's house and all Kelly's and Jill's kids were there. Shortly after they arrived, Kelly, Kirk, and Jill got in the car and left, not mentioning a thing to Tina. She was left there for the next six hours watching the kids while the adults went out to party. After that, Tina was much more wary about going with Kelly.

Mona also paid a visit to Kirk's house at Christmas to see Payshence. By this time, the girls began reporting what they were seeing and what they had been told about not discussing Jody. It was clear that there was a conspiracy to get Payshence to forget about her dad.

OCTOBER 2ND, 2012: VERIFIED PARENTAGE PETITION, Kelly H vs. Shane S

Kelly had one last child - a son - for a total of five. The father appeared to have had a tough life and showed signs of gang affiliation, including many tattoos visible on his arms and neck. He walked with assistance of a cane - I was told because of a gun-shot wound. He appeared to support Kelly's stripper lifestyle, accompanying her out of state to the Sturges motorcycle festival and posting a picture of his grinning naked body covered in small bills lying on a bed on Facebook.

However, he did appear to be a concerned father that wanted very much to love and raise his son. At first, the boy was also being left at Kirk's house and when Shane and Kelly were on the outs, it seemed Kelly was going to invoke the Utah Uniform Parentage Act for this child too. Shane knew what had taken place with Kelly's last two kids as he had attended several of the court hearings - so he was ahead of the game. His roots were from Mexico and he was planning to take the baby away if he wasn't given proper legal parentage. His plan worked and his rights to his son were secure.

OCTOBER 14TH, 2012: UNIFIED POLICE DEPARTMENT, Disorderly Conduct

The complainant said that there was a domestic across the street from his residence. Officer W.W. and I arrived and made contact with Jill C in the garage. Jill said that she had a large verbal argument with her best friend in the front yard and then her friend left. I asked Jill who else was at the residence and she said her husband was also there. I asked her to have him come out so I could make sure there had not been a domestic. Jill's husband, Kirk J, came into the garage. Kirk was intoxicated and belligerent. In spite of this it did not appear that there had been a domestic between Jill and Kirk and they confirmed that the argument had been between Jill and her friend that was now gone. Case Closed.

OCTOBER 25TH, 2012: UNIFIED POLICE DEPARTMENT, Burglary, No Forced Entry call

While on patrol I was dispatched to a custody dispute. According to the detail, the complainant stated there was a woman on the porch arguing over the custodial rights of kids. Upon my arrival I saw a red passenger car leave the scene before I could make contact. I later learned the suspect, Kelly H, was in this car.

I spoke with Kirk J, who is the ex-husband to Kelly H, and his new wife, Jill C. Jill told me while they were sitting in their home tonight, Kelly walked in, unannounced and uninvited and stormed through the residence. Jill was downstairs in the bathroom when suddenly the door flew open and there stood Kelly. She was yelling she wanted the kids and had one of the little kids in her arms. Kirk was able to get the child away from her and got her to go upstairs and out of the home. The neighbor called the police as this was happening.

Jill stated Kelly left without taking any of the kids. Kirk explained to me there has been guidelines and rules set up if Kelly wants to see the kids. She has not been following these rules, so Kirk is refusing to let the children see their mother. Kirk stated Judge V removed Kelly's paternal rights and has told him to make sure she follows the rules in order to get visitation.

I asked Jill and Kirk what they would like done tonight and I explained to them since Kelly entered the home unlawfully, I could file charges on her for burglary. Kirk did not want to press the issue, but Jill stated something needed to be done. I explained I could hold off on charges, but if something like this happens again, I could file down the road. Both liked this idea, so I provided them with a case number for reference.

Certainly, in Kirk's mind he could defy the Court's order of no alcohol or domestic violence but he was quick to turn Kelly in when she showed up to see her children. Something else that was going on at this time was the court-ordered divorce of Kelly and Kirk. A long time coming.

<u>NOVEMBER 21ST, 2012:</u> VERIFIED PETITION

Petitioner complains and alleges as follows: During the course of the marriage the parties have experienced difficulties that cannot be reconciled that have prevented the parties from pursuing a viable marriage relationship. The parties did not acquire any real property during the marriage. Neither party should be awarded alimony from the other. There has/have been 4 children born or adopted of this marriage. Utah has jurisdiction over the custody and parent-time issues in this case. The statute for jurisdiction in Utah is: The Uniform Child Custody Jurisdiction and Enforcement Act. PR began living with Kirk J 05/31/2012.

Pursuant to Rule 100 of the Utah Rules of Civil Procedure, The Uniform Child Custody Jurisdiction and Enforcement Act and The Uniform Interstate Family Support Act. The Petitioner, Kelly H, states upon information and belief, that:

a. The Petitioner has not been a party or witness to, or participated in any other litigation concerning the custody, child support or parent-time of the parties' minor children nor does the Petitioner have information about any custody, child support or parent-time proceeding concerning the minor children in this State or any other state or country.

b. There are no criminal or delinquency cases in any court in this State or any other state or country in which a party's child is a defendant or respondent.

c. There are no protective order cases in any court in this State or any other state or country involving a party regardless whether a child of the party is involved.

d. There are no protective order cases in any court in the State or any other state or country involving the parties children.

e. There are no cases involving the parties' children filed or pending in any Juvenile Court in this State or any other state or country.

f. The Petitioner does <u>not</u> know of any person, not a party to these proceedings who has physical custody of the parties minor children and who claims to have custody, child support, or parent-time or visitation rights with respect to the children.

The following provision shall be part of the parties parenting plan:

"three of my children are not biologically his one being my two-year-old he had had custody for about 3 months of them because of the situation I was in I would like to have my baby at least half of the time. (Manually written by Kelly in the court document.)

The Petitioner is not employed and currently receives no countable income from any source. The Petitioner receives $700 per month non-countable public benefits. The sole custody worksheet was used in calculating the child support in this matter. Petitioner's base child support amount is $30.00 per month.

WHEREFORE, _Kelly H prays that a divorce be granted pursuant to the terms set forth in the Petition._

On the same day, Kelly and her boyfriend, Shane, showed up at Kirk's house resulting in a call to the police. On November 23rd, 2012, Kirk filed for a protective order against Kelly. Jill and eight children were listed as protected from Kelly. Since this incident occurred on the same day as the Divorce Petition was filled out, it leaves one to wonder if the papers being flung in Jill's face were those same papers.

The following is from the protective order:

"Has the Respondent (Kelly) used weapons or been violent in the past?
{X} Yes
If yes, describe here:
She walks into house uninvited knowing she is not supposed to be there verbally assaults visitors in my house takes hold of kids won't let them go. came to house throwing papers in girlfriends face, has had many domestic violence she is very unpredictable don't know what she will do next. have had to call the cops three in two weeks. lots of phone harassment.:
Describe the abuse or domestic violence:
she opened the door and threw paper work in calling my girlfriend horrible names. she grabbed J1 would not let him go while he was asking her please to stop.

Kelly had contacted Jody to get his support. Suddenly Kirk was calling the shots and not conforming with her wishes when she wanted to come and go with the kids. Jody calmly listened to her frustrated pleas and saw a small crack of light. His plan was to carefully and calculatively make sure that crack didn't close up. He agreed to go to court and testify in her behalf at the divorce hearing, but he also had plans of his own. Over and over Jody's attorneys told him he didn't stand a chance of getting custody of Payshence unless Kirk and Kelly were either divorced or incarcerated. Since the former seemed most likely in the short term, now was time to act and certainly having Kelly on his side for once could make a huge difference.

NOVEMBER 28TH, 2012: UNIFIED POLICE DEPARTMENT, Public Ordinance Civil Case call

The complainant, Jill C, said she had questions about Protective Orders. She requested phone contact and I made contact by phone. Jill said she lived with her boyfriend, Kirk J. She said they have been having problems with Kirk's ex-wife, Kelly H. Jill said Kirk was given custody of his and Kelly's child, plus Kelly's other three children. She said Kelly is using drugs and this was the reason custody was given to Kirk and it is up to Kirk to decide if Kelly can have visitation. She said a couple weeks ago, Kelly picked up her daughter from school without permission from Kirk and she did return her daughter but caused a scene at their house. She said since then Kirk has not allowed Kelly to see any of the children. Jill said Kelly keeps calling and harassing them about seeing the children.
Jill said they did get a protective order against Kelly. She asked if the protective order had been served. I checked for a protective order and found there was one but it had not showed as served. I provided Jill with this information. She asked how they could get it served and I advised if she knew where Kelly was at, she could have whatever jurisdiction she was in serve the protective order. Jill said she didn't know she could do this and she was going to make some calls to find Kelly's location and have the protective order served. This case is cleared as a civil problem.

DECEMBER 1ST, 2012: ANSWER TO PETITION

Respondent, Kirk J, states the following:

 The correct marriage date is April 17, 2003.I have had full custody of J1 and J2 (the two older boys) since November 2008. Permanent custody and guardianship of PR and BS was awarded to me by Judge V in Third District Juvenile Court on July 31, 2012.

 As stated in the Juvenile Court Order, all visitation will be determined by me. Also, there is a protective order in place barring the Petitioner from having any contact with the children at this time.

 My gross monthly income currently is $3,500 per month. Petitioner has stated to me that her income, paid "under the table" is approximately $2,500 per month. As far as public assistance received by Petitioner, that assistance was for children that were not my legal financial responsibility at the time.

 REQUEST

 I request the court grant the divorce. I request that the Court leave the custody matter within the Juvenile Court. I request child support for the four children in my custody in the amount of $692.00 per month.

 To my knowledge, the older two boys have not been genetically tested as to paternity. They were born 14 months apart in 2001 and 2002 and it wasn't until 2003 that Kelly and Kirk were married.

 Throughout the future court proceedings, many stories are told. One story repeated over and over was that Kirk had raised Payshence since she was a baby and that he had also raised Kelly's older children as well, claiming that he was the father. Kirk's response to the Divorce Petition sets the record straight by his very own hand.

DECEMBER 20TH, 2012: HEARING ON REQUEST FOR CUSTODY OR PARENT TIME - Kelly H vs. Kirk J, Commission Bloom Presiding

 Hearing is held on Ms. Kelly H's request for custody, or at least parent-time with the children. The Court finds there are two Juvenile Court orders regarding these children, granting permanent custody of the children to Kirk J. This Court will contact Judge V regarding these orders, and obtain certified copies for the District Court file.

 *The Commissioner, after hearing argument, **RECOMMENDS**:*

 1. The Court finds the Petitioner has not met her burden to prove immediate and irreparable harm if the final juvenile court orders are not amended regarding custody and parent time. The Petitioner's motion is NOT granted with regard to change of custody.

 2. The Respondent shall cooperate with the Petitioner to allow parent-time as the parties agree.

 3. The Petitioner shall provide any documentation to the court regarding what was required of her by the Juvenile Court, and proof of her full compliance.

 4. The parties may request a further hearing if needed, or move this case to trial.

 Kirk J is directed to prepare the order. After the hearing, the Court will obtain certified copies of the juvenile court orders, which shall be scanned and docketed into this case.

Hearing transcript:

THE COURT: *Matter No. 4 is Kelly H vs. Kirk J*

KELLY: *Present.*

THE COURT: *Are you representing yourself today?*

KELLY: *Yes, ma'am.*

THE COURT: *And your name?*

KIRK J: *I'm very deaf.*

THE COURT: *Okay. Are you representing yourself, sir?*

KIRK J: *I can't hear you.*

THE COURT: *Are you representing yourself today?*

KIRK J: *Yes.*

THE COURT: *You don't have an attorney representing you; is that correct?*

KIRK J: *I don't.*

THE COURT: *Okay. And what is the status of this matter?*

KELLY H: *We're not agreeing on anything.*

THE COURT: *Okay. One thing I do need to address, Ms. H, it is your request with regard to custody, parent-time, et cetera. I have reviewed the protective order minutes from a hearing that was held December 11th, 2012. The commissioner in that case found that there is a juvenile court case pending. Is that correct?*

KELLY H: *Uh-huh. It's been - it's final. It's been done since like July, I think.*

THE COURT: *Okay. And sir, did you know of any juvenile court case that may be pending?*

KIRK J: *What's that?*

THE COURT: *Do you know of any juvenile court case that is currently pending?*

KIRK J: *I think there is one. I'm not sure if it is pending or not.*

THE COURT: *Okay. As of December 11th, 2012, Commissioner Sagers found that there is a custody action pending in Third District Juvenile Court.*

KELLY H: *It was final in July.*

KIRK J: *It's, it's actually I think a closed case, because he had made - I've got orders right here where - from him, Judge V - - on these if you want to look at them.*

THE COURT: *And is that a final order where he terminated jurisdiction?*

KELLY H: *Yes.*

KIRK J: *Yeah, that's what these are.*

THE COURT: *Okay. It appears from this minute entry that Kirk J, you were awarded permanent custody of BS and PR is that correct?*

KIRK J: *And J1 and J2.*

THE COURT: *Okay. It does not state that.*

KIRK J: *It's, it's in one of those that I just gave to you.*

THE COURT: *This one is from 2008.*

KIRK J: *Right. That was the first case. And then the next one is for the last case.*

THE COURT: *We've been going to court for almost four years over this - these cases. (Pause) Okay. I have reviewed these. So, you don't have any agreements, so Mr. J, go ahead and have - well. I'm going to actually have you stand right there so you can hear. Ms. H, you can go ahead and make your argument regarding what you're requesting today. And make sure you speak loudly so he can hear. And Mr. J, I will ask you, do you have others here with you today?*

KIRK J: *Yeah.*

THE COURT: *I'm wondering if one of them can be next to you and make sure that they speak to you what is said so that you can hear. Would you like that, sir? Would that assist you? You go ahead and have a seat at the table. And I'll allow this young lady - to sit next to you to state to you what is stated if you cannot hear.*

KIRK J: *What's that?*

THE COURT: *Why don't you go ahead and state to him what I just stated, ma'am.*

SPEAKER UNKNOWN: *She wants me to tell you what she's saying.*

KIRK J: *Okay. Thank you.*

THE COURT: *Okay. Go ahead, ma'am.*

KELLY H: *For the temporary orders I put in there that, um. Well, mostly I want parent-time. He's not letting me see my kids. **They're not even his kids, but because we're legally married, he stepped in.** I was having domestic violence problems with my ex-boyfriend, so the State got involved. And instead of them being in foster care they went and stayed with him. And so, the judge - and I'm having the case pulled from Judge V because I don't believe what he did was right. Like one court date he said one thing, then he'd go back to something else and he'd do something else. And DCFS, they're - what the main thing was to have my kids back with me. It's not right.*

THE COURT: *Okay. Have you filed any petition other than this petition for custody of the kids?*

KELLY H: *Not yet, no. Uh-huh.*

THE COURT: *But this petition for divorce is pending, and you're asking for custody.*

KELLY H: *Yes. Custody of my two -*

THE COURT: *- of -*

KELLY H: *Well, I put on there BS -*

THE COURT: *You said one.*

KELLY H*: *- but I want to change that to Payshence also. **He's had Payshence for five months only**. And he's in contempt of the order right now anyways. My daughter is not being treated like she's supposed to be. My two-year-old little boy stayed with me up until October. And that's contempt that he wasn't supposed to. He got mad at me in October and stopped letting me see my kids. In the last two months I've seen them one time. He went to the school and took me off their things so that I can't go there and go have lunch with them or whatever. They're telling everybody there's a protective order, which there isn't. And like I said, he's only had my two-year-old for two months. He won't let me talk to him. He's not letting me see him. **And they're my kids, they're not his**.*

THE COURT: *Okay. Ma'am, why don't you list all of the children that are in question. I have two orders here. One order includes J1 and J2. The other is BS and PR.*

KELLY H: *Okay. J2 is not his child either, but we were mar - we - they've been - he's had them for seven years. J1 and J2, when I went to court my little girl's dad, same thing, he was abusive in the relationship. And I stayed with him, so the State got involved. And at that time in there, there was no reason - we didn't fight for custody. We were good friends for a long time, and I didn't think that I had to. I didn't think that this would go on. So, I didn't argue or try to fight for custody for my two older boys and that's why they just gave him the custody of J1 and J2.*

THE COURT: *Okay. Let's get back to which children are at issue here. Because there are - four here, and you mentioned a fifth.*

KELLY H: *I want visitation with my two older boys. Payshence and BS I want custody back of. To do whatever it takes or whatever I have to do to raise my children and be a mother to my kids.*

THE COURT: *I have - BS and is PR? I wanted to make sure we were talking about the same children. But we currently have orders from the juvenile court awarding permanent custody to Mr. J, correct?*

KELLY H: *Uh-huh. What I need to know is I want to do whatever I need to do, file what I need to do to get custody of my two children back. Payshence and BS.*

THE COURT: *Okay. All right. Anything else, ma'am?*

KELLY H: *Yeah. Um. I went - I filed for divorce. Two days later he tried to go get a protective order. I think he has a huge, like, control issue. He tried - called the cops. Making up lies - tried to get a protective order. Which was denied, because obviously he was just doing whatever. Yeah. I went to the house. Walked in. Tried to see my kids. He called me up. "Do you want to hear my demands?" And I said, "I'm not - you're not demanding me to do anything." He was drunk and hung up on me. I went over to his house, and walked in, and tried to see my kids. And I have the right to be with my kids.*

THE COURT: *Okay. And these orders do not grant you any -*

KELLY H: *No.*

THE COURT: *- parent-time.*

KELLY H: *Well, and the thing is, is he left it up to him. And I was okay with that, because we were friends at the time. And I didn't think he would ever try to use my kids as a tool, and hurt my kids and not let me see my kids. For him to just say that he can decide parent-time, that's not right either.*

THE COURT: *Well, this order....it does say that. It says visits between Kelly H and BS, and PR., will be determined -*

KELLY H.: *By Kirk.*

THE COURT: *By Kirk J.*

KELLY H: *Yeah. I know that - what it says.*

THE COURT: *That's what the order says.*

KELLY H: *Yes.*

THE COURT: *So, he's following the order and doing that, apparently.*

KELLY H: *He wasn't following the order, though, because BS stayed with me the whole time. He - - the judge told him he couldn't live with me at that time, do you know what I mean? But I've done my domestic violence classes. I've done everything I'm supposed to do. My, my parenting classes. And I just want custody of my kids back.*

THE COURT: *Okay. Anything else?*

KELLY H: *No. That's it.*

THE COURT: *Thank you. Mr. J, your response?*

KIRK J: *Um. Well, I'm not - - I'm - - the whole time I have not wanted to take the kids from her. We've been going through courts with Kelly back since 2008. You can see that. I mean, it's repeated times over and over. I've been to every court case, every hearing. Most, most all the time sitting right next to her. We've - - I've been to DCFS places to see PR and BS over and over. Been to the Christmas Box House. We've been, um. I mean, and that's not the first time to the DCFS place where they've been taken away. The judge ordered the two older boys, because I've had them since they were born. I mean, with me.* **We, we got married in 2003, and she left in 2003.**

I mean, we, we haven't even been together since then. I've had those babies ever since they were born (**This is in direct conflict with his written testimony in the Divorce Petition where he states that the boys started living with him in 2008**). *He ordered that, that first order for permanent custody probably because of that. With PR, I've had her pretty much since she's been born, off and on. Except for most of the time when she's been taken away from Kelly it's been pretty much there.* (**Also in conflict with what he and Kelly wrote on the divorce decree stating July of 2012 when the court ordered her into his custody.**)

The, the biological father, I - we, we've been to court with Judge V to, to do the legal father rights, and he ended up ruling me as legal dad. The next case that she ended up having PR and BS taken away, he - - at the end of the case we, we, we went through for about four months, and he ended up just giving me permanent custody. With orders that if she is - - if she does drugs, or if she has any violence, or - I'm not to let her see them. And all I am doing is following the Judge's orders.

I mean, I watched her drop her baby and, and go after PR looking like she wanted to attack her. But she dropped the baby in the car seat. She ended up going out and doing drugs, and then - - and she had BS. at the time. And I - - Jill had to leave work just to pick him up where she was hitting, hitting Shane, the baby's dad, in the house. The cops ended up getting called and she ended up getting removed from the house. So, we just - - we ended up not letting her see the kids. And it's, it's been lots of harassment since then. You know, coming to the school, the house. I mean, we've had to call the cops, of course, over every time. And DCFS told me that's exactly what I should be doing, so. The only thing I'm doing is what Judge V has said in the court. I mean, and DCFS has told me to do.

THE COURT: *Okay. Thank you, sir. What do you believe should happen regarding parent-time between Ms. H and the children?*

KIRK J: *Well, I think that she should finish all the classes that Judge V has ordered, because after the case that, uh, he told me - - or he told her he'd have another review later on down the road. She said she didn't want to finish none of the classes. She's not going to go back to that court...*

KELLY H: *Your Honor, he - -*

KIRK J: *...From that point on.*

THE COURT: *And I'll turn to you in a moment, ma'am. Anything further?*

KIRK J: *It was the drug classes and stuff like that, yeah.*

THE COURT: *Okay. Anything else you'd like to say, sir?*

SPEAKER UNKNOWN: *No. Anything else?*

THE COURT: *Okay. Thank you. Final argument, ma'am?*

KELLY H: *He's so full of crap. I've done everything I was supposed to do. There's final things that I finished my stuff in V's court. I wasn't required to do drug classes because I haven't been doing drugs. That was four years ago. And yes, they called the cops because I would go to the schools and see my kids because he's not letting me see my kids. They're my kids. I need to know what I need to do to get my babies back. **They shouldn't be with an adoptive family** when I want to be a mother to my kids.*

And I realize that Judge V ordered him to say what - - when I can visit. But then you get mad at each other, and then he uses my kids as a tool. And it's not fair to my kids. Brainwashing them. My son told me, "My dad tells me things and wants me mad at you so that I'm on his side." He's just doing things that he shouldn't be doing. And my kids are caught in the middle of it, and they're the ones being hurt.

THE COURT: *I am prepared to make my recommendations. Ms. Kelly H had requested that on a temporary basis she be awarded custody of one of the parties' children - - one of the children in question. And that - - or that she at least be allowed parent time-with the children. Mr. Kirk J has provided two orders to the Court. One is an order entered by Judge V on November 20th, 2008. That order was with regard to three of the children. PR, J1, and J2. This 2008 order indicates that Kirk J should be awarded permanent custody of J1., J2, and the Court terminated jurisdiction with regard to these two. In this order PR was awarded to Kelly H.*

The second order from the juvenile court was entered July 31st, 2012. This order is with regard to BS and PR. This order does indicate that permanent custody and guardianship of PR and BS is placed with Kirk J. Visits between Kelly H and these two children is to be determined by Kirk J. The orders indicate that Kelly H has found to have neglected the children. And so custody was awarded to Kirk J with him having full discretion regarding parent time.

Kelly H is now requesting that she be awarded custody of two of the children, or that at least she has parent-time. Kirk J has objected to that. I do need to address some procedural issues. We do have permanent orders with regard to all of these children. The statutes request that once a permanent order has been entered that is must be filed in the district court case, and the Court can proceed accordingly. These two have now been provided to the Court. They are not certified copies, so I will contract Judge V's clerk to determine if indeed these are actual representations of the court orders. If they are, I will file those certified copies that I'm able to obtain with this court.

Now that this Court has determined that there are permanent orders regarding custody and parent-time, we have a certain standard I must follow in determining whether that should be changed. Rule 106 of the Utah Rules of Civil Procedure states: "If a party is seeking modification of a final order, they must file a petition to modify." In this case, those orders had not been included in the district court's orders, so I do not believe a petition to modify is necessary, possibly. The main concern I have, however, is Rule 106 states that if there is a final order entered, that final order shall remain in effect until the parties go to trial. Certain exceptions are included in the rule, including if a party shows that immediate and irreparable harm will occur if the order isn't changed. In this case we have final orders of the juvenile court indicating Kelly H has been found to have neglected these children. Her sole request is that she be allowed parent time-because it's not right for the children to not see their mother.

She also asserts that Kirk J had been inappropriate in his decisions regarding parent-time. She also asserts that she has complied with all of the requirements the juvenile court has placed upon her. In these orders I see no requirements the juvenile court has placed on Kelly H to change the parent-time. However, in one of the orders it does state that the court retains the right to impose further disposition. That was retained with regard to one of the children in the 2008 order. However, the 2012 order awarded permanent custody of the other two children to Kirk J. I am finding that Kelly H has not shown immediate and irreparable harm to the child or children if Kirk J is not given the discretion to determine how parent-time shall go. This is on a temporary basis. What I recommend is that Kirk J continue to work with Kelly H to allow parent-time, pursuant to these orders.

I would like to see from Kelly H any documentation showing what the juvenile court required her to do, so that I can make a determination as to whether there should be any changes in custody and parent-time on a temporary basis. Or the parties simply can take this to trial to show if these orders from juvenile court should be changed or amended. The recommendations of the Court are that the orders from juvenile court will be implemented into this case. That Kirk J will work with Kelly H to award parent-time to her as the parties agree. So those are the recommendations of the Court. I do need one of you to prepare the order. I would typically ask Kirk J to do so: however, I don't know if he heard me very well.

SPEAKER UNKNOWN: *Yeah. I lost track. Prepare the order to go into trial, right?*

THE COURT: *From my recommendations today, what temporarily will happen as this divorce case is litigated and prepared for trial. There needs to be a temporary order prepared reflecting what I've just recommended.*

KIRK J: *What was recommended?*

THE COURT: *I am going to ask Kirk J to do so. My clerk will have the minute entry completed by the end of the day. That may assist you in understanding the terms.*

SPEAKER UNKNOWN: *Okay.*

THE COURT: *There's also an ability to retain a recording of what was said - - everything that we do in here is recorded. You can get a copy of the recommendation portion of this hearing and review that to prepare the order if you choose to do that. The minute entry may be sufficient to have all of the details of that. And we're just before Christmas, so I strongly support the parities in talking to determine what parent-time Kelly may have during the holidays. If you want to talk and see if you can reach an agreement as to what time Kelly H should have with the children over the holidays, you may do so.*
If you reach an agreement on that you can put it on the record today and that will become the order of the Court. If you want to take some time to do that right now, you may, but my recommendations regarding the motion are complete.

SPEAKER UNKNOWN: *Your Honor, there's a restraining order. So how would they work around that?*

THE COURT: *Is there a protective order?*

KELLY H: *No, there's not. It was denied. There's no restraining order. There's no protective order.*

SPEAKER UNKNOWN: *Oh.*

THE COURT: *I have reviewed the minutes from the protective order hearing from December 11, 2012, showing that the protective order was dismissed.*

THE COURT: *If there's no other order except for this case, you two can communicate without any violation of the protective order. Okay?*

KELLY H: *Oh, yeah. Ma'am, I have one more question.*

THE COURT: *Okay. Go ahead and stand, ma'am.*

KELLY H: *We're supposed to, um. He was supposed to go in and sign off on the birth certificate of this baby.* ***And so he don't try to come in and steal this baby can you order him to go in?*** *All three of us have to go and sign a piece of paper to take him off the birth certificate so my baby -*

THE COURT: *Which?*

KELLY H: *I have an almost four-month-old baby. His father is here. He's supposed to go in and sign off of it.*

THE COURT: *And that issue wasn't before me.*

KELLY H: *Because it wasn't in there, so.*

THE COURT: *Yeah. It's not before me, so I cannot compel that. If the two of you agree to that, you most certainly may proceed. But if it's not in the motion I can't address it unless there's an agreement to do so.*

KELLY H: *Okay. And then can we instead of, um. If I get my stuff showing that I've done my parenting class and stuff like that - do I bring it to the Court and try to get - to show it to you? Or how do I make things more permanent and to where it's not in his choice? Because if it's up to him, he gets mad at me, and I don't see my kids.*

THE COURT: *You have to prove to the Court that it's in the best interest of the children to make it so you have more rights with regard to seeing them. Either on a temporary basis or permanently. I will tell you, ma'am, the juvenile court found on two occasions that you neglected the children.*

KELLY H: *Because I was in an abusive relationship. I understand that.*

THE COURT: *You're going to need to show to either myself or the judge that the children are not at risk in your care. That will be your burden to prove.*

KELLY H: *When I have those how do I get another court date?*
THE COURT: *Simply completing certain classes may not be enough to show the Court.*

KELLY H: *I know that. I realize, yeah.*

THE COURT: *Okay, but I'm going to ask that you speak to an attorney or other legal advisor to assist you in knowing what to do. I can't give you legal advice with regard to how to do that. I'm ethically precluded. But downstairs there is a clinic. If you want to go down there today and talk to them, they may be able to assist you in what you need to do.*

KELLY H: *Okay, one more question. If we don't agree on what he thinks that I should have parent-time, what do I do then? Just file another -*

THE COURT: *Seek to change this order. The order gives him that right, ma'am. And it's a final permanent order.*

KELLY H: *So get the tapes from Judge V's thing, seek to change that?*

THE COURT: *You'll need to file a motion, or go to trial to prove to the Court that this order should change. But as of this point, I am not showing that you met the standard of showing immediate and irreparable harm if it is not changed, so he continues to have that right. Okay? Thank you all.*

On **December 26th, 2012** Kelly filed a Petition to Modify Child Custody, Parent-Time:

*"I filed for divorce since he won't let me see or talk to my kids. He has only had Payshence for 5 months and BS for 2 1/2 months. He is a raging alcoholic. My babies need me and I need them. Kirk J is in contempt. He decides based upon his own happiness not the children's. I want a divorce. We no longer talk and **he's using my babies as a tool and putting things in their little heads**. It's not right. "*

DECEMBER 26TH, 2012: FACEBOOK POSTS by Kelly H in response to a photo she posted with her five children

S.T.: hey this is the way u need to be forever get it together girl i love u dearly and only want u to be happy ur kids r awesome i realy do want u to be happy
KELLY H: It's Kirk he's bein a bitch keeping them from me if any time in my life I maybe shldnt have had my kids it wldnt b now fuk him it's only temporary that he has any say. Hope ur doin well
S.T.: like i said girl i love u and i think of u like my family i hear and see both sides just keep doing what u need to do and thats all u r responsable for ur kids love both of u guys time will bring things out to be the way they r supposed to ur baby is so cute and ur daughter i hang out with on thanksgiving and she is to cute i can tell she is urs for sure

KELLY H: Yea u hear them punk ass bitches tlk shit let em know dnt be pussy's come run their mouth to me they dnt know what the fuk is goin on except what Kirk lame worthless bitch made ass says N thanks yea my bby is beautiful hrs the most wndrfl thing ever One day he gonna b sorry it ain't over I'm not gonna give jst fight harder n one day the kids are gonna hate him no doubt in my mind n I'm koo with that cause he deserve to b hated. Sorry lame excuse for a daddy waste of space pathetic reality

A.B.: You tell him nobody should keep the kids away from there mom.

KELLY H: Yea he is a piece of shit n his nasty fat lame fake bitch Jill is only making him be worse but it's ok karma a bitch in the end the right judge will see through his bullshit n know what's right n change this shit

2013

JANUARY 7TH, 2013: UNITED POLICE DEPARTMENT, Domestic Criminal call

I was dispatched on a domestic violence detail, arrived at the listed address and was met in the front yard by Kirk J and Jill C. Jill had called police to report Kirk's ex-wife, Kelly H, had come to the home and thrown a plastic yard decoration candy cane through the front window. According to Kirk, Kelly had come to the residence to take their children from the home. Custody of the children is fully Kirk's. Kirk said when Kelly knocked on the front door their small son answered the door and let Kelly partially inside. At this point Kelly said he went to the front door and took the boy away from her, told her to leave and closed the door. Kirk said he had to push the door closed because Kelly was trying to stay inside the residence.

Once the door was closed the young boy sat down on the couch in the front room with his back to the front window. Kirk said he could hear Kelly screaming outside and he was trying to calm down the children when he saw Kelly throw the yard decoration at the window, which broke through the window and struck the boy in the head as he was sitting on the couch. He had no injury, but did have a small red mark on the back of his head. This was photographed by ID. Kirk said Kelly then ran to her car and drove off.

While I was interviewing Kirk and his family Kelly showed up at the Kearns Substation to report she had been strangled by Kirk when he took her son away from her. I had ID photograph the scene and the boy's head. I also had both Kirk and Jill fill out witness statements. I went to the Kearns Substation and met with Kelly who was there with her boyfriend. ID photographed some red marks on Kelly's neck and shoulders. Kelly also had a small scratch on her right forearm which she believed came from hitting the brick exterior of the home when she was pushed out.

I asked Kelly how she was strangled during the incident. She explained when her son answered the door, he ran up to her and she picked him up. Kirk then came up to her and wanted her to release the child. She refused to do so and Kirk then wrapped one arm around her neck and head while the other arm took hold of her son. Kelly said he then pulled them apart. She said she was inside the front door of the residence when this occurred. Kelly's boyfriend said he saw the whole thing happen while sitting in their car in the driveway.

Kelly said once Kirk had her son in his arms she was pushed outside and then the door shut. She was so angry she grabbed a large plastic candy cane, and threw it through the front window. When she saw that the window had shattered, she left the residence.

Kirk and Kelly have a history of domestic violence and are currently disputing custody of their children. I explained to both Kelly and Kirk this incident would require follow up investigation and detectives would be in contact with them. I told Kelly at this time I feel it was necessary to file Domestic Violence-Criminal Mischief charges with the District Attorney for her part in this incident. I explained that once the door was shut, she should have left and called the police rather than add to the incident by destroying property. She understood and I also explained the allegations of assault on her by Kirk would need further investigation before charges could be filed. She understood and was given a domestic violence pamphlet and resources for a victim's advocate. I also explained if she had any further pain, she should seek medical help.

I received a call from DCFS about this incident. Jill C had called to report child abuse on the boy due to the item coming through the window and hitting him. I explained ID had taken photographs of the mark and gave the case number. I will be filing charges on Kelly for the DV-Criminal Mischief. I was not able to determine at this time if charges need to be filed against Kirk for his involvement. Sent to the Special Victims Unit for follow up.

JANUARY 13TH, 2013: HEARING, Divorce proceeding - Kirk and Kelly, Commissioner Bloom presiding

A Juvenile Court judge has awarded custody of the parties two children to the Respondent, Kirk J. Further, the Respondent is awarded custody of the Petitioner's two children (not Respondent's) in another Juvenile Court Order. Parent-time is awarded as Kirk J deems appropriate. The Court has no information as to whether Kelly H has fulfilled the Juvenile Court's requirements for her.

The Commissioner **RECOMMENDS**:

1. Whether the Petitioner's children will be returned to her is a decision for the Juvenile Court Judge. The Petitioner is referred to that court regarding those two children.

2. *Regarding the children of the parties in this action, this Court will confer with Judge V of the Juvenile Court pursuant to Rule 100.*

3. *After conferring with Judge V, this Court will prepare a minute entry, which will be mailed to the parties.*

4. *All exchanges of the children for parent-time will be through a third party, and NOT at the residence of the Respondent.*

5. *If the Petitioner has not served the Respondent with her petition to modify, she shall do so.*

Jody attended the hearing with Kelly. Commissioner Bloom presided. Kelly asked for time with her kids and pointed out that Jody was the father of Payshence. Bloom ruled that Kelly had not completed the paperwork and requirements that the court had ordered her to. She also said that Juvenile Court still presided and so there was nothing she could do regarding custody or parent-time. All in all, it was a fairly unproductive hearing, as many are.

FEBRUARY 7TH, 2013: HEARING RECOMMENDATIONS - Kelly H vs. Kirk J, Commissioner Bloom presiding

This matter came before this Court on Kelly H's Motion to Amend Temporary Orders at a hearing on January 31st, 2013, in the parties action for divorce. Kelly H was present representing herself. Respondent, Kirk J, was also present, representing himself.

At a hearing on December 20, 2012, the Court determined that there are two juvenile court cases involving the children of the parities. In both cases, Kirk J was awarded custody of the children. Parent-time of the children was to be by agreement.

Kelly H initially requested that this Court award her temporary custody of her two children, who are not the biological children of Kirk J, and at least parent-time with the children of both parties. The Court found that final orders had been entered in juvenile court regarding all of the children and that Kelly H had failed to prove that immediate and irreparable harm would occur to the children if the final orders were not modified. Wherefore, pursuant to Rule 106 of the Utah Rules of Civil Procedure, the Court recommended that parent-time be consistent with the final orders entered in juvenile court.

Kelly H has filed a second motion to amend the final orders of the juvenile court in the present case, which motion was heard on January 31, 2013. She asserts she has done all that is necessary to allow her to have custody of the two children that are her biological children and not the biological children of Kirk J and at least standard parent-time of the children she and Kirk J share. Kirk J opposed this motion.

This commissioner recommended that a Rule 100 conference occur between her and Judge V to discuss the cases before the court. Judge V and the Commissioner discussed the cases before the Court. Based on their discussion, both courts agreed that there is a significant amount of information in the juvenile court files to which the district court does not have access, and that the district court has little information about the parties and the children, which would limit the district court in determining whether a modification of the juvenile court orders would be appropriate.

Wherefore, both courts agreed that the issues regarding the children should be considered by the juvenile court. This commissioner hereby refers the child-related issues in the divorce petition, including Kelly H's petition to modify the juvenile court orders, to the juvenile court. All other issues in this divorce case shall be litigated in district court.

FEBRUARY 7, 2013: ORDER APPOINTING GUARDIAN AD LITEM - BS, J1, J2, Payshence

Upon review of the petition filed concerning the above-entitled children, the Court hereby determines that it is in the best interest of the children that a Guardian ad Litem attorney be appointed to represent the best interest of the minor children named above until final disposition of the case or until dismissed by the Court.

FEBRUARY 7, 2013: LETTER to The Court from Kirk J

The following letter was sent to the court with Kirk's name on it, but not written in his handwriting. The penmanship was very neat and precise, with proper spelling and punctuation, contrary to other papers penned by Kirk:

Your Honor,

I am writing you this letter in hopes of a review on the Kelly H case. I think that it is very important that you hear what has been going on mostly because you have had lots of cases with her for the last 4 years. I thought for sure that the last order you gave her would be the end to this nightmare we are going through.

Right after she had her baby she went out and got high. She was doing so while I thought that she was over all that. Anyway, her boyfriend called me while I was at work letting me know about all this, and that he had BS. My girlfriend had to immediately leave work to go get him. Kelly ended up getting there first. When my girlfriend got there there was screaming and yelling. The cops were called. BS was given to my girlfriend and Kelly was removed from the house. After all of that I limited her visits. That made her very mad. We have had to call the cops many times. She has gotten out of control. She has been to my house many times screaming and yelling mostly in front of at least one of the eight children we have here. She has been very harassing. I have called DCFS and got a protective order. It was very hard to get the protective order, but now we have one.

I took what you told me in court very serious. I promised Payshence she will never live in another foster home again. I intend to keep that promise to her.

Kelly has gone as far as throwing a really heavy Christmas decoration through my front window hitting the ten year old in the back of the head, shattering glass over 3 of the babies. Then she told the police that I choked her. <u>Charges</u> have been filed against her for this. She has taken her protective order off of Jody so that they could try to change the custody order. I have been told I need an attorney. But you honor I am raising eight children it is very hard for me to come up with a retainer. My girlfriend and I have been doing this with no help from any of the other parents. I am hoping that this matter can be settled with a review in your court.

Thank you,
Kirk J

FEBRUARY 21ST, 2013: DISTRICT COURT TRANSFER - Judge V

*The matter came before the court for a pretrial. **The court noted the absence of the petitioner**, Kelly H. The Court addressed and accepted comments from all parties present. The Court finds that allegations 2, 3, 8 (for all four children) should be dismissed.*

All the fuss Kelly made to the Court and she didn't even show up for the hearing. For Jody, the time to act had finally come. With the divorce pending there was a chance to open up the parentage and custody action. After Jody went to court with Kelly, we hired David B, an attorney in Salt Lake who came highly recommended from a friend.

MARCH 8TH, 2013: NOTICE OF COUNSEL - Attorney David B, Judge V presiding

David B, hereby enters his Notice of Appearance of Counsel for Jody Rhorer, the biological father of Payshence Rhorer, the minor child in this action.

MARCH 8TH, 2013: LETTER to The Court from Kelly H

Your honorable Judge, please take a minute to read my letter, hear my concerns and requests. I very much so are asking and praying that another judge can and will hear my case with regards to custody and parent time with my children. Your honor first of all, yes I do have a long history with the juvenile courts and Judge V over the last four years. The first was Feb. 2009 which involved my 19 month old daughter Payshence. The DCFS case, because I was involved in an abusive relationship. Then again Feb. 2012 and yes again because I choose to be in violent relationships. This time six months later then the last incident. DCFS involved and again removed my babies. Judge V ended up giving my husband **Not** the biological father custody of the babies and also left parent time up to him. Since then we have become unreasonable with each other and no longer have an understanding friendship and he has chose to use his power with the kids to hurt me and won't or hasn't since October 2012 let me see, visit with them, also had stopped all means of communication, school, phones, Facebook, etc. I 100% accept and know my fault in staying involved in abusive relationships.

Its a brutal cycle to become strong enough to get out of and away from the abuse, but after four long years I did. Judge, Its been 17-18 months that I've not been involved with that life style. I've done and completed parenting classes, group DV treatment, anger management and also individual treatment. I've made some life changes and are aware of the choices not to make and know the signs of abusive men. Judge V has been the judge and I feel strongly that he doesn't like me, has judged and labeled me in a category that to him are scum of the earth. I don't' know how aware or how much he remembers of me, my cousin and some of his children years ago partying together. I believe some and that he's let that influence his decisions. He's labeled me and won't reconsider his opinions. Almost every court hearing Judge V has talked bad to me and about me to others in the courtroom. Protective Order hearing he said "if he had jurisdiction and it were up to him he'd protect my baby from me, like he has three of my other kids." There are two. He said "I'm sure she's the most difficult person you've ever had to deal with" meaning me to courtroom members. Even after his ruling continued to talk down about me to my babies father and grandfather. He said "Que lastaema" in Spanish meaning how sad, to them as they were leaving, saying how sad he didn't have the choice to take my baby away from me. The judge on Feb. 21 told my husband "no matter what I do he is not gonna let it leave his courtroom - no matter how many appeals I do it will always go back in front of him." Your honor to me, this is very threatening. Judge please consider all I have said and allow me and my children, whom I love so very much and miss more then words could say, a chance to be heard by another judge. Please allow me to be given the chance to be the mother I can be and want to be as well as, the mother my babies need and miss. My parental rights were never, have never been taken away, but still are being denied parent time and hopefully custody back of my two beautiful babies. Thank you Judge for taking time to read.

Sincerely,
Kelly H

I have never been an addict. I don't know what it is like to have a substance control you to the point that you abandon and betray the most precious things life has offered up - your very children. All the words, begging and pleading, couldn't put Kelly's kids back in her life again - only Kirk had that power. And it was all about that power that drove a man in his mid 30's to want to possess the children of other men. It was not about love, not about wanting the very best for these fragile and confused kids. It was 100% about control over Kelly. I suppose in a way, at this point in time, Kelly was fighting a similar fight to Jody's - only she had created the situation.

Just a couple months after the divorce was finalized, Kelly married Shane S, crippled by his lifestyle in gangs and reduced to walking with a cane, tattoos up his neck and face and a body shriveled by abuse; a braid of hair hanging from the back of his neck like a rat's tail. If I sound harsh, if I sound judgmental, it is only because I want you, the reader, to have a clear vision of what we were dealing with. This would be the newest "daddy" in Payshence's life.

MARCH 8TH, 2013: KELLY H vs. SHANE S - VERIFIED PARENTAGE PETITION Filed - Commissioner Kase assigned

The parent/child relationship of DS (Kelly's fifth child) is as follows:
a. Shane S is the biological and legal father of DS.

MARCH 18TH, 2013: UNITED POLICE DEPARTMENT, Violation of Protective Order call

The complainant said there was a female at the elementary school trying to pick up a child. There is a court order in place that says she is not to have contact with the child. Upon arrival, I was approached by a female, who identified herself as Kelly H. She said she is the one the school was calling about and was married to Kirk J. Kelly said they have children together but they are no longer together. Kelly said Kirk was given custody of the children. She said he has a protective order against her and they already had their hearing. She said the judge took the children off the protective order. Kelly said she came to the school to see her 6-year-old daughter. She said she just wanted to give Payshence a hug and a kiss. Kelly said the judge did not say she couldn't go to the school. She said when she got there, she was yelled at by the staff that she wasn't supposed to be there. Kelly said she knows Kirk has lied to the school about her.

I went inside the school and made contact with the daughter's kindergarten teacher and Jill C, Kirk's current girlfriend. The teacher said she was walking her students back inside the school when Kelly walked around behind her and grabbed Payshence from behind. She said Kelly carried Payshence to her car and put her inside and Payshence was crying and was very upset. She said she walked to Kelly's car and told Payshence to get out of the car. The teacher said she had been told about the protective order prior to this incident. She said Kelly told her "I am taking my child." The teacher told Kelly she wasn't taking Payshence anywhere and Kelly finally did let her out of the car. Kelly was using foul and vulgar language in front of the children.

Jill said the school contacted her about what was going on. She said she came to the school right away and showed me a copy of the protective order. It listed Payshence as a party and listed the elementary school as a place Kelly is not allowed to go. I checked the protective order on the statewide system and found there was a valid protective order. Jill said Kelly has violated the order several times since it was served on her. She said last night the police were contacted because she had violated the protective order using FaceBook. Jill said Kirk is out of town right now working at a job site. She said she believes Kelly found out he was out of town and this is why she is at the school.

I took Kelly into custody without incident. I checked the cuffs for proper fit and double locked the cuffs. She was transported to the Salt Lake Jail where she was booked in on the charge of Violation of a Protective Order. This case is cleared with an arrest.

It's ironic that Jody can be jailed for accepting a phone call from Teri when she had put a protective order against him, but Kelly can violate hers time and time again and also have domestic violence charges and still not get jail time! Of course, she did lose custody of all her children - which is a far bigger punishment than being locked up.

APRIL 3RD, 2013: UNIFIED POLICE DEPARTMENT, Keep the Peace call

On 4/3/13 at 1716 hours, I was dispatched on a Keep the Peace call. Kelly H wanted to pick up two of her kids from her estranged husband, Kirk J. Both parties have protective orders against each other and both children appear to be protected from both parties. The children were left in the care of Jill C, who is Kirk's girlfriend. Kirk was out of town. Kelly was advised to contact the court to fix the problem with the orders. Case closed.

APRIL 10TH, 2013: NOTICE OF HEARING - PR and BS, Judge V presiding

Notice is hereby given that a Pre-Trial regarding the Petition to Modify Parent-Time filed March 27, 2013, by the natural mother, Kelly H, in the interest of said children, is scheduled on May 21, 2013 before Judge V.

MAY 10TH, 2013: MOTION TO INTERVENE - Divorce Proceeding: Kirk and Kelly, Jody Rhorer Intervener -Commissioner Bloom presiding

Jody Rhorer, by and through his counsel of record, David B, and pursuant to Rule 24 of the Utah Rules of Civil Procedure, hereby moves this Court to intervene in the above-entitled matter. The purpose for the intervention is that Jody Rhorer is the biological father of Payshence Rhorer, a minor child.

The Intervenor is aware of a Juvenile Court proceeding concerning his status as a parent of PR, however the Intervenor is not aware that there is a final order or that he was actually served with appropriate service of process to deprive him of any parental rights of PR.

MAY 31ST, 2013: FACEBOOK POST by Kelly H

"So I'm just sitting n I'm so pissed or am I hurt my kids have been takin away n kept from me for goin on 8 mths n for what accusations n excuses N you try to justify it get real I dnt think they realize wht they have done they have takin away so much from not only me but my kids I didn't get to take my bby grl to school be there for a kindergarten graduation missed out on the 2-3 yrs w my bby boy my boys b days x mas many other holidays so so much more none of them know there 8 mth old bby brother what a shame N now after all this time now u wanna send pictures n tlk about ur feelings excuse my language but fuck off All I know is its in gods hands n I have court in 11 days. To my babies I love u guys more then u will ever know"

JUNE 3RD, 2013: MOTION TO BIFURCATE Divorce proceeding: Kirk and Kelly, Commissioner Bloom presiding

Hearing is held on the Petitioner's motion to bifurcate. The Respondent Kirk J, indicates he agrees with the Petitioner's request to bifurcate. The parties had not yet attended the divorce education orientation courses, but indicate they plan to do so soon.

*The Commissioner **RECOMMENDS**:*

1. The parties shall attend the divorce education/orientation courses.

2. The motion to bifurcate is GRANTED.

The Petitioner, Kelly H, is directed to prepare the order, including Findings, Decree, Affidavit of Jurisdiction, and roof of divorce education for both parties.

JUNE 11TH, 2013: ORDER ON PRE-TRIAL HEARING in the interest of Payshence Rhorer and BS - Judge V presiding

***THIS MATTER** came before the Court for pre-trial hearing on Ms. Kelly H's Motion on the 11th day of June, 2013. Ms. H appeared personally. The father, Kirk J, appeared personally, and by and through counsel, Connie, the minors appeared by and through their Guardian ad Litem, Mr. Newt.*

The Court heard comments from the Guardian regarding the conclusion of his investigation, and argument from all parties regarding whether to set the Motion for evidentiary hearing, or whether to adopt the recommendation of the Guardian ad Litem for visitation of Kelly H by a professional visitation supervisory service established such as Willwin or Renaissance, Kelly H having expressed her concern that she cannot afford professional visitation supervision fees, and the Court having heard and considered comments of all present that visitation between Kelly H and the minors would be ideal if it could be made safe.

***IT IS HEREBY ORDERED** that the visitation order in this matter SHALL be and the same hereby is modified to allow visitation for Kelly H is to pay any fee for the intake appointment or evaluation at the supervision agency. Thereafter, Kirk J is to share the cost of weekly supervision fees, up to $25.00 per week.*

Kelly H shall cause the supervisory agency to prepare a report of her interactions with the children for submission to and consideration by the Court for the next hearing.
    ORDERS:
    Motion and Affidavit to Waive Fee filed on March 27, 2013 is granted.
    Motion to change Custody Order filed on March 8, 2013 is denied.
    The Court orders professional visitation. Further Kelly H is to pay any fee for the intake appointment, or evaluation.
    Kirk J is to share the cost of weekly supervision fees, up to $25.00 per week.
    All previous orders of the Court consistent with this order are hereby continued.

    JUNE 24TH, 2013: ORDER FOR INTERVENTION - Kelly H vs. Kirk J, State of Utah, Office of Recovery Services, Intervenor

    The State of Utah Office of Recovery Services Motion for Intervention having come before the Court, and the Court having considered the same:
    IT IS ORDERED *that the Office is joined as an Intervenor and is permitted to file a pleading or take another appropriate action.*

    JUNE 24TH, 2013: ORDER ON PRE-TRIAL HEARING - Attorney Connie, Judge V presiding

    THIS MATTER *came before the Court for pretrial hearing on Kelly H's Motion on the 11th day of June, 2013. Kelly H appeared personally. The father, Kirk J, appeared personally, and by and through counsel, Connie, the minors appeared by and through their Guardian ad Litem, Brent N.*
    The Court heard comments from the Guardian regarding the conclusion of his investigation and argument from all parties regarding whether to set the Motion for Evidentiary Hearing or whether to adopt the recommendation of the Guardian ad Litem for visitation for Kelly H by a professional supervisory service establishment, Kelly H having expressed her concern that she cannot afford professional visitation supervision fees, and the Court having heard and considered comments of all present that visitation between Kelly H and the minors would be ideal if it could be made safe;
    IT IS HEREBY ORDERED *that the visitation order in this matter* **SHALL** *be and the same hereby is modified to allow* **visitation for Kelly H if it is supervised by a licensed professional visitation supervisory business***. Kelly H is to pay any fee for the intake appointment or evaluation at the supervision agency. Thereafter, Kirk J is to share the cost of weekly supervision fees, up to $25.00 per week. Kelly H shall cause the supervisory agency to prepare a report of her interactions with the children for submission to and consideration by the Court for the next hearing.*

    This is all it took for Kirk to stop restricting the children from Kelly - an order demanding he pay one half of the cost for supervised visitation. The only thing missing from the Order was someone to enforce it and ensure that it would happen the way it was specified - but it never did. Kirk would continue to allow Kelly to take Payshence and her other children at will provided she was in his good graces.

    We met David B at the courthouse. This was my first hearing and I had high expectations. I am not sure about what, but for some reason I always held out hope that the judge would see what a gross injustice was being done to Payshence and immediately order her removed from captivity and placed back in the right place. But Payshence wasn't really the issue at hand to the court - it was always about the proper paperwork, jurisdiction, rules, procedures, technicalities - but *not* the baby girl.

    JUNE 25TH, 2013: MOTION TO INTERVENE - Submitted by Attorney David B, Commissioner Bloom presiding

    Intervenor, Jody Rhorer, by and through his counsel of record, David B, appeared before the Court on his motion to Intervene on June 2nd, 2013. Respondent, Kirk J, appeared Pro Se. Petitioner, Kelly H did not appear. Mr. Hunt appeared on behalf of the State. There have been no objections filed to the motion to intervene for Jody Rhorer.

    ORDERED *that Jody Rhorer's Motion to Intervene regarding custody and related matters of the minor child is hereby granted.*

We were only with David B for 8 months. Much of the time he was on vacation and things were not progressing. Also, we were quoted $250 then charged $300 an hour instead. On April 16th, we were charge $300 for sitting in his office for forty minutes while he explained what he had spent the $1000 retainer on and the first 10 minutes he spent on the phone with someone else. Ultimately, we ended up letting him go due to little action on his part. To his credit, he did know what he was doing when he filed the Motion to Intervene that got Jody's foot in the door to begin the long journey to take back Payshence and several attorneys told us that had he not done that, we wouldn't have had an in at all. Thank you, David.

JUNE 29TH, 2013: UNIFIED POLICE DEPARTMENT, Simple Assault call

    On June 29, 2013, at approximately 1600 while patrolling Kearns Township I was dispatched on a domestic dispute. The complainant, Jill C, said her live-in-boyfriend, Kirk J, grabbed her shirt and ripped it. Jill C advised Kirk J was still on scene.

    Upon arrival Jill C was standing in the driveway, her shirt was ripped down the right side. She was crying and claimed she came over to feed her dog. Jill C and Kirk J's relationship is in turmoil and they have been separated for two weeks. They have a child together and have lived together for four and a half years.

    When Jill C came into the residence she saw another female inside with Kirk J. She began yelling at him because she thought he may be cheating on her. Jill said Kirk J had been drinking and didn't want him to drive his truck while intoxicated. Kirk's vehicle was parked impartially in the road with the hazard lights on. Jill claimed she was taking the keys to move the vehicle, and not allow Kirk J to drive it to pick up their child today.

    Kirk said Jill C took his keys so he closed the front door when she tried to leave. Jill opened the door to go outside. Kirk J grabbed Jill C's shirt and pulled her back inside the house. The shirt ripped. Jill got away from Kirk, went outside, and got into her vehicle. Kirk opened the hood of her vehicle and started unplugging wires while yelling to give him back his car keys. Jill C informed Kirk J she dropped the keys on the porch. Kirk J put the wires back in place so the vehicle could run, retrieved his keys, and went back inside. Jill then called police.

    Kirk J saw I was on scene and exited the house to speak with me. He was very angry and had a very hard time listening to my repeated instructions to sit down on the porch until I was finished speaking with Jill C. He eventually complied. I spoke with Kirk J and could smell the distinct odor of alcohol emitting from his breath.

    Kirk J claimed Jill C came over today and saw his female friend on scene. Jill C got very upset and tried to leave the house with his car keys so he closed the door to take his keys back. Jill opened the door and walked out on the porch. Kirk admitted he grabbed Jill's shirt, but he only did this so he could get his car keys back and claimed he did't mean to rip the shirt. He saw Jill get into the vehicle, and he claimed he wanted to stop her and get his keys back. He admitted he opened the hood of Jill's vehicle and started unplugging wires. She informed him his keys were on the porch so he put the wires back where they go, retrieved his keys, and went back inside.

    I had a forensic technician respond to take photographs of Jill C and her torn shirt. She got a new shirt and left the scene to stay at a friend's house for the day. I issued Kirk J a citation for: Assault [Domestic Violence]. I instructed both Kirk J and Jill C not speak with each other for the remainder of the day. Case Closed/Citation Issued.

CHAPTER 13
AN ENDLESS JOURNEY

When Jody was a child, his parents took him to visit some relatives in Oregon. It was on that trip that he first set eyes on the breathtaking landscape of Cannon Beach. From the lookout above Haystack Rock he promised himself that this would be the place he would someday marry the love of his life.

Twenty-eight years later, on another trip to the Oregon coast, Jody took me to the same place he had made that vow to himself and knelt down on a knee and asked me to be his wife.

"This is the place I have wanted to bring the woman of my dreams since my parents brought me here when I was 8," Jody explained.

"You didn't want to marry Kelly here? You were living so close by. And Krista? Why didn't you bring her here?" I asked.

"Because until now, no one has been worthy of this place until you."

Yes, Jody promised me poetry and he delivered.

It was on this trip that we made the decision to let David B go and hire Steven K. Steven had done an exceptional job getting Jody's other daughters but we didn't call him initially because he had moved to St. George and we were concerned with the proximity.

"Hi Steve, this is Jody Rhorer's fiancé and we need some help." I briefly explained the situation with Payshence as Jody drove down the scenic coastal highway.

Steven K was a no nonsense, bottom line, straight shooter.

"I can look up what I need on the court website. How soon can you get me a $2,500 check? I'll review your case and send you over your options. You choose the one you want to go with and I'll get it filed," Steve instructed without even taking a breath. "I do have this thing I am dealing with and I'm not sure how it's all going to end up, but for now, I'll take your case."

The "thing" Steve was referring to was a potential dis-barring for involvement with a teenager. From what we were told, she was not honest about her age and he was set up. But knowing his great skills as an attorney, and not knowing the details of his situation, we moved forward.

CORRESPONDENCE from Steven K:

Below is an email I sent to Judge V's Clerk today. I have also attached the documents I submitted today. Thank you, Steven K

STATE OF UTAH, in the interest of
Payshence R and BS

I am the attorney for Jody Rhorer in the above-entitled matter. I have enclosed a copy of my Appearance of Counsel.

AUGUST 2ND, 2013: APPEARANCE OF COUNSEL, Attorney Steven K

COMES NOW, Steven K, and hereby makes and enters his appearance of counsel on behalf of Jody Rhorer in the above-named matter.

AUGUST 27TH, 2013: REPORT ON REVIEW OF JUVENILE COURT FILE - from Steven K

Dear Jody,
I had a chance to go through the 333 pages of the Juvenile Court file. The Juvenile Court charged me $83.25 for the file. Enclosed please find a statement for services rendered reflective of the $2,500 you paid me.
As you may recall, in October 2008, a petition was filed regarding your child and Kelly H's children. There were allegations that you committed domestic violence. After the petition was adjudicated in court (admitted by Kelly), you were basically taken out of the paperwork. You were initially described as the father of the child. The petition indicated that you had not established your paternity.
There was a pre-trial on November 6, 2008, and a shelter hearing on the same day. You appeared at the shelter hearing and you were served in open court. You were ordered no contact with Kelly H. The file also contains a return of service indicating that you were served at the KOA campground on North Temple on the same day as court.
JN was appointed as your representation and then withdrew because you had not established paternity, leaving you hanging.
At the hearing on November 7, 2008, you were awarded supervised visitation through DCFS. On November 20, 2008, there was a hearing which you did not attend and JN withdrew as your lawyer.
Apparently, you did not appear at a subsequent hearing because you reportedly moved to Missouri. A warrant was issued for your arrest for failure to appear. Your child was returned to Kelly and the older children were returned to Kirk J. In February, 2009, apparently Kelly relocated to Missouri and was living with you. DCFS found out and a new petition was filed, as a result, the children were once again removed. Then a petition to terminate parental rights was filed against Kelly but not you because you had not established paternity and were not the "father."
Clark W then got involved in the case representing your mother at a hearing on March 19, 2009, as a result of the fact that you did not establish paternity. The Court appointed a lawyer for you, S Hardling, and apparently you were arrested and brought in to Court. Kelly had cleaned up her past including the criminal case in Missouri. Even though the State filed a petition to terminate her parental rights and ultimately Payshence was given back to her. In August, 2009 on your behalf, JN filed a Petition for Decree of Parentage. The Decree was signed giving you paternity in January, 2010. That July, JN and Kelly's lawyer agreed to vacate the order for some unknown reason. The Court dismissed the petition against Kelly.
The Decree may have been set aside because Kirk was not given notice.   Under common law, a child born during a marriage, even if it was born the day after the husband and wife were married, is presumed to be a child of the marriage. We will proceed with a new Complaint to establish your parentage unless Kelly will sign a Voluntary Declaration of Paternity form. You told me Wednesday that you had requested the form and you would try to get Kelly to sign it. We can file a separate action or we can file it within the confines of Kirk and Kelly's divorce case that Dave B intervened in. I have prepared a petition for both cases.
In May, 2010, Judge V gave custody of Payshence back to Kelly and on May 20, 2010, the Court terminated jurisdiction. In February, 2012, Kelly made some bad decisions regarding her paramour, Brock S, and the children were picked up again and placed in the Christmas Box House. Thereafter they were all three returned to Kirk at a shelter hearing in February, 2012.
Based on the divorce filing between Kirk and Kelly, there was a conference between Judge V and Commissioner Bloom (the assigned Commissioner in the divorce case) and it was decided that the custody question between Kirk and Kelly would be decided by V. The last thing in the Judge V file shows that the District Court cases were transferred to him but then they may have been dismissed after he denied Kelly's request for custody.

I recommend that you get Kelly's signature on a Voluntary Declaration of Paternity. You tell me that you talked to Kelly and she is a stripper in North Dakota and as long as you are fighting Kirk for Payshence, she will be on your side. Take a look at the paperwork that is enclosed and we will talk after you read it.

Thank you,
Steven K

SEPTEMBER 27TH, 2013: BIFURCATED DECREE OF DIVORCE, Kirk and Kelly, Signed by Judge Stanley

This matter came for hearing on the Petitioner's Motion to Bifurcate the Divorce held on June 3, 2013, before Commissioner Bloom. The Petitioner was present and represented herself. The Respondent was present and represented himself.

The Court, having heard from the parties, having accepted the Respondent's indication that he agrees with the Petitioner's request to bifurcate the divorce, and having reviewed the court docket file in this matter.

ORDERS:
The Petitioner's Motion to Bifurcate is granted.
The Petitioner and Respondent shall attend the divorce education/orientation courses.
All issues including those related to the parties children are reserved.
All other issues not specifically addressed herein are reserved for trial.

OCTOBER 1ST, 2013: EMAIL from Steven K

Jody: ORS will be contacting you. They have the results of the paternity test however, they will not release them to me. They will only release them to you. Once you received them please email a copy to me. Steven

OCTOBER 2ND, 2013: UNITED POLICE DEPARTMENT, Public Peace, Ungovernable call

At about 2018 hours on Wednesday night I responded to a call at the request of Ms. Jill C, the complainant. It was regarding her teenage son and daughter being ungovernable.

Dispatch informed me that they received a call from the boy and girl who were currently waiting for an officer at the Kearns Olympic park. Upon my arrival at the playground, I spoke with the children. Both parties involved told me that they ran away from home because their parents were physically being mean to them.

I spoke with Jill C by telephone. She informed me that her son was verbally abusive toward her so she slapped her son in the mouth then he and his sister took off running away from the house. Jill C requested I transport them back home. I shuttled both juveniles back home. Upon my arrival at the residence, both of the juveniles informed me that they have suicidal thoughts because they can't stand living at the house with their parents.

I requested Unified Fire Authority out at the scene to further medically check them out. Both juveniles were in fair condition and transported by UFA to Pioneer Valley Hospital.

Case closed.

Surely if the children in the home were suicidal, DCFS should have been brought in but instead, they were returned home and the case was closed.

OCTOBER 7, 2013: REQUEST CUSTODY CHANGE - Payshence, BS, Judge V

This matter came before the Court for a review. The Court addressed preliminary matters. All parties addressed the Court in regards to modifying the Court's order of visitation. The Court addressed and accepted comments from all parties present.

ORDERS:

The Court orders that visitation is to remain the same, as previously ordered.

The Court authorizes Ms. Kelly H and Mr. Kirk J to submit a motion for third party visits. All previous orders of the Court consistent with this order are hereby continued.

OCTOBER 10TH, 2013: Letter to Governor Herbert and Congressman Rob Bishop:

It is in desperation that I write this letter. My name is Jody Rhorer. I am the father of a beautiful 6-year-old little girl named Payshence. For the first 3 years of my daughter's life I got the privilege of raising her, but all that changed one day when I came home and her mother, once again, was passed out from injecting meth. There were 9 fresh needle marks in her arm. My daughter and her half-brothers were left unattended while their mother slept in the bedroom.

Looking back now, I should have called the police but instead I reacted and, wanting to remove her from their presence, I picked her up and tossed her out the front door. In turn, she called the police. I was arrested and served 6 months in jail for domestic violence - she, on the other hand, received no punishment.

During that time Payshence's mother requested paternal rights be removed from me and allotted the estranged husband who (allegedly) fathered only one of her 5 children but has custody of 4 of them, instead of their biological fathers. Utah has a law that still exists referred to as a "Bastard Law" from the 1800's that gives the legal husband rights to a wife's child even if he is not the biological father. For the past 3 years I have been fighting to get my daughter back. I was awarded my right to custody, just to have it taken away by Judge V based upon this outdated law and as revenge from her mother.

Kirk J has a long criminal record for drugs, weapons, and violence and uses the children for financial means. Payshence has been in and out of foster care and the Christmas Box House whenever Kirk's residence is found unfit for children for a multitude of reasons but then returned to him again. The mother has lost all custodial rights to her children. In essence, you have 3 kids being held hostage for money for financial assistance from the State by a felon that is not even related to them.

I am a hard-working father with a stable union job. I do not do drugs. I live in a clean and safe home in Eden, Utah with my fiancé who is the broker of her own real estate company and who I am marrying in June. This year alone, I have already spent $5,000 on attorneys and NOTHING has transpired. I'm sure you have a little grandchild that you love very much. What measures would you take to get that child back if she were taken from you? What if you knew where she was, and the circumstances that she was living under and you were not allowed to see her - you couldn't talk to her on her birthday, tuck her in at night, see her off on her first day of school?

The State of Utah has done a huge injustice to fathers who aren't able to see their own biological children, let alone raise them. I have taken 2 DNA tests that and they show that I am 99.99% Payshence's father as well as being on her birth certificate. I am pleading that you will bring these kids to their rightful families. Kirk J is not fit to be a parent to these children and their future is doomed if they are left there.

My worst fear is what my daughter is thinking every day about her Dad - that he doesn't care and that he has forgotten her. Please grant me the right to have my little girl back. To go another Christmas without her is more than I can take. I thank you for the time you have spent reading my letter. I know you have many important things to do - I just pray that you are able to take action soon.

Kind regards,

Jody Rhorer

The only response we received from either party was a generic reply stating they do not handle "these kind of complaints". Our elected government officials make the laws and yet when there are flaws and negative consequences of government-imposed regulation, they claim to have no power. I think they just have no empathy. Certainly, if one of their own was affected by the Utah Uniform Parentage Act, they would waste no time in correcting this erroneous rule.

Coincidentally, shortly after this letter was sent out, we received a phone call from Steve K. "Jody, great news. I can't believe it! Judge V just retired! It's just out of the blue - there was not even a hint this was going to happen."

"Does that mean we don't have to be heard in the juvenile court?" Jody asked.

"That's right. We will be pursuing our case in district court."

OCTOBER 15TH, 2013: EMAILS from Steven K to custody evaluator and to Jody:

Subject: My Client, Jody Rhorer
I am filing a Motion for Custody Evaluation and would appreciate if you would provide me with the following information:
1. Approximately when you could commence a new evaluation;
2. Retainer required and hourly amount:
3. Approximately how long it will take to complete the evaluation.
Thank you,
Steven K

RESPONSE:

October 21st, 2013

Hello, I am sorry that I have not replied before this. I cannot start a new case until the first of December. My retainer is $3000.00 and I bill at $160.00 per hour. This fee will change beginning in January to $170.00 an hour. Thank you. Hope you are hanging in there. Heather W, PhD.

November 15th, 2013

Jody: I have made the revisions - motions attached. Let me know what you want to do. Have you spoken to Steve O about a custody evaluation? If not, then we should go with Dr. Heather W or Anna T. I have exhausted the $2,500 you paid me but I can have an associate attend the hearing for under $500.00. Steven K
November 21st, 2013

Jody: I have attached the revised Affidavit. Please review it and fill in the blanks and get back to me. Once I have all the information in the Affidavit and it has been signed and notarized by you and the documents are filed you can contact my associate, Nancy S or her secretary, Deanne, regarding representing you at the hearing. Steven K

NOVEMBER 21ST, 2013: AFFIDAVIT OF JODY RHORER

COMES NOW, Jody Rhorer, and being first duly sworn upon his oath, reposes and states as follow:
1. I am Jody Rhorer, the Intervenor.
2. I am the biological father of the minor child and awarding custody to me is in her best interest.
3. My daughter lived with me and her mother and her three half-sisters from the time she was born until she was approximately 3 years old. Because the Petitioner was using drugs the Petitioner and I separated. Unbeknownst to me, Petitioner was being investigated by DCFS for neglect and ultimately our daughter was placed into foster care. I was ordered to stay away from the Petitioner by Judge V.
On or about February, 2011, the Court awarded custody of our daughter to the Respondent, Kirk J, who has a significant criminal history. Petitioner and Respondent were legally married at the time. At that time, I hired an attorney and filed a paternity case seeking to have my custody rights restored. I was advised that it was because the Petitioner and Respondent were still legally married and there was a "presumption" that the child was Kirk's.
On or about June, 2011, Petitioner and I resumed our relationship and had our daughter with us again as judge V awarded custody to Kelly. Kelly started having difficulties in her life again and we discontinued our relationship. DCFS became involved and, once again, custody of our daughter was awarded to Kirk J.
At that time, I contacted my attorney again to attempt to get custody of my daughter and was told that until the Petitioner and Respondent were legally divorced there was nothing I could do.

During the entire time our daughter's half-siblings, ages 13, 16, and 18 continued to see her and I was able to visit her during times when Respondent allowed Petitioner to take our daughter for days at a time. I spent time with my daughter. I bought her clothes to start kindergarten and toys for her birthday and Christmas.

I was restricted from regular visitation by the Respondent and was only able to see my daughter when the Petitioner had her.

I continued to have contact with my daughter through her half-siblings and the Petitioner recently re-married. Kelly has again lost the right to see our daughter and Kirk has never cooperated with me being involved in my daughter's life.

My daughter and I talked on the telephone approximately one month ago, which was the last time I was able to have contact with her.

4. My daughter knows that I am her father and I am ready, willing and able to provide the support, education and emotional needs of my child.

5. If the Court deems it necessary to obtain a custody evaluation or appoint a Guardian ad Litem, I should have interim parent-time not less than standard.

6. I realize that I have not had court ordered parent-time for several years but the child has lived me for the majority of her life and I believe that a custody evaluation should not be necessary.

DECEMBER 9TH, 2013:   FILED: Motion to Establish Jody Rhorer as Father; Motion for Determination of Parentage; Motion for Custody and in the Alternative Parent-Time; Affidavit/Declaration of Jody Rhorer filed by Steven K, Commissioner Bloom Presiding

COMES NOW, *Intervenor, Jody Rhorer, by and through his attorney, Steven K, and requests that this Court enter an order establishing Jody Rhorer as the natural and biological father of PR.*

This Motion is based upon the fact that in April, 2010, Kelly H, Payshence Rhorer and Jody Rhorer submitted to genetic testing with LabCorp. As a result of the genetic testing, Jody Rhorer could not be excluded as the biological father of the child, and the probability of paternity is 99.99%.

The minor child currently is in the custody of Respondent pursuant to order of the Third District Juvenile Court.

As a result of the motion for custody filed by Kelly H in this case, the matter was remitted back to the Third District Juvenile Court following a Rule 100 telephone conference between the Honorable Judge V and Bloom. Recently, it was announced that the Honorable Judge V was in retirement effective November 1, 2013. Based upon Judge V's history with the minor child in this case and all of the parties, it was determined that the juvenile court would be the appropriate forum for custody determination in this case. However, with the impending retirement of Judge V, those considerations no longer are appropriate.

The process of reassigning or appointing a new Judge will result in none of the benefits having Judge V hear the matter due to his experience with the parties and the child. Additionally, this Court is the appropriate forum for the determination of custody between Kelly H and Jody Rhorer. Kirk J is not the biological father and pursuant to the Utah Supreme Court case of Hutchison v. Hutchison, *Jody Rhorer has a parental presumption of custody.*

Based on information and belief, Judge V denied Kelly H's motion for custody made adverse to the Respondent. For all of the foregoing reasons the Court should enter an order judicially declaring that Jody Rhorer is the natural father of the minor child, awarding him custody and in the alternative order a custody evaluation (if necessary).

COMES NOW, *the Intervenor, Jody Rhorer, by and through his attorney, Steven K., and hereby moves this Court for an order determining parentage of the minor child, PR.*

This Motion is based upon the fact that genetic testing performed by LabCorp has determined that the Intervenor is 99.99% probably the father of the minor Child and therefore, the Court should, as a matter of law, enter an order in favor of the Intervenor and grant his motion, judicially declaring and establishing parentage in favor of the Intervenor regarding the minor child, PR. A copy of the genetic testing results and affidavit are attached hereto and incorporated herein by reference.

COMES NOW, *Jody Rhorer, by and through his attorney, Steven K, and hereby moves this Court for entry of an award of custody or in the alternative a custody evaluation and for interim statutory parent-time during the pendency of the evaluation if the Court finds an evaluation is necessary.*

The Motion is based upon the fact that currently the Respondent has physical custody of the minor child PR, pursuant to orders of the Third District Juvenile Court. The Petitioner's motion for custody was denied by the Juvenile Court after this matter was remitted back to Juvenile Court to determine custody between Petitioner and Respondent. Intervenor, however, has not motioned the Court of custody and based on the impending retirement on November 1, 2013, of the Honorable Judge V, it is no longer appropriate for the Juvenile Court to exercise jurisdiction in this matter. The Juvenile Court has made no finding as to Intervenor, Jody Rhorer, except to find him in contempt for failing to appear at a court hearing.

Pursuant to the Utah Supreme Court case of _Hutchinson c. Hutchinson,_ 649 P. 2d 38 (Utah 1982), there is a parental presumption of a natural parent regarding custody of minor children. The Intervenor never agreed to an order of custody in factor of Respondent and his rights as to being the custodial parent against the other natural parent, Kelly H, has never been determined. Based on the fact that the child is currently in the custody of a non-parent, and by virtue of the fact that Petition's motion for custody filed in this Court was denied by the Honorable V, any custody determination must be between the Respondent and the Intervenor. Because of the parental presumption, Intervenor, Jody Rhorer, should be awarded custody and interim parent-time not less than as described in 30-3-35.

Alternatively, based upon the foregoing, the Court should order a custody evaluation (if necessary) and submits that Dr. Heather W and Dr. Anna T are fit and proper persons to submit as custody evaluators.

CHAPTER 14
THE CIRCUS COURT

DECEMBER 19TH, 2013: APPEARANCE OF CO-COUNSEL, filed by Nancy S, Commissioner Bloom presiding

Nancy S hereby enters her appearance as co-counsel for Intervenor, Jody Rhorer, in the above-entitled matter.

2014
NANCY S

JANUARY 2ND, 2014: SUPPLEMENTAL AFFIDAVIT OF JODY RHORER IN SUPPORT OF MOTIONS, filed by Steven K, Commissioner Bloom presiding

Jody Rhorer, being first duly sworn, and upon his oath swears and states as follows:
1. I am the intervenor in the above matter.
2. I am the biological father of the minor child, PR, my name was placed on the birth certificate of the minor child as her father immediately after she was born. I have since taken a DNA test that proves I am her biological father.
3. At the time PR was conceived and born I did not know that the petitioner was married. The petitioner and I had moved together to Portland, Oregon and we were residing together when the minor child was conceived and were residing together in Salt Lake City when the minor child was born. Approximately 18 months after the birth of our daughter the petitioner and I were planning to marry and I overheard the petitioner speaking to the respondent by phone about getting a divorce. I then learned that the petitioner was married.
4. For the first three years of the minor child's life the minor child lived with me in my household, and then again in 2011.
5. From the time the minor child was born in 2007 to 2011 the respondent was not in the child's life. Kirk J was awarded custody of the minor child in 2012 pursuant to order of the Juvenile Court. I tried to intervene in the Juvenile Court matter in order to have custody of my daughter, but I was not allowed to intervene at that time.
6. The minor child was placed in foster care, but thereafter in August, 2012, the respondent was granted custody of the minor child. Since August, 2012, the respondent has not allowed me to visit with the minor child.
7. Awarding custody of the minor child to me is in her best interest for reasons including, but not limited to, the following.
8. The minor child resided with me since birth to 2009 and then again in 2011 during which time the petitioner and I resumed a relationship. During 2010 the petitioner would bring the minor child to my mother's house and I would spend time with my daughter.
9. It is undisputed that I am the biological father of the minor child.
10. The minor child has always called me "Daddy" or "Dad" and still refers to me as "Dad." She knows that I am her father.

11. The minor child and I have developed a deep and loving relationship as father and daughter. During the time we lived together we did many things together, like playing ball, going to the park and having family outings, either alone or with my other three daughters and family members. The minor child knows my other three daughters as her sisters. Attached as Exhibit 1 are photographs of the minor child with me and other family members.

12. *After custody of the minor child was awarded to the respondent, I have kept in contact with her as much as I have been allowed. The last time I talked to my daughter was in approximately October 2012, when I spoke with her on the phone and told her that the petitioner was going to let her visit with me the next day. The following day the petitioner never called me back and never followed through with our plans to allow my daughter and I to spend time together.*

13. *Thereafter, neither the petitioner nor the respondent will allow me to speak with the minor child or to visit with her. Nevertheless, I have sent her cards and letters. Her sisters, who reside with me, also send her cards and letters. We try to always let her know that we love her and want to be with her.*

14. *I would be cooperative in allowing the petitioner and respondent to have any visitation time the court awards to them, allowing the minor child to feel loved and wanted by everyone in her life.*

15. *I am engaged to be married to Deone Smith in June 2014; Deone is a loving mother to her own children and to my three daughters of whom I have full legal custody and who live with me, to wit: MR age 19 years; TR, age 16 years, and MR, age 14 years.*

16. *I live with my daughters in a home in Eden, Utah, where we have a bedroom for the minor child. We also have toys and clothes for her. Attached is a photograph of the home and the bedroom from my daughter. Her sister's bedroom is across the hall.*

17. *I have visited Valley Elementary School in Eden where the minor child would attend school in anticipation of her living with me and to arrange for her education.*

18. *I am a fit and loving father and I have never had a complaint against me to DCFS.*

19. *It is my understanding and belief that both the petitioner and respondent have had DCFS complaints against them.*

20. *Both the petitioner and respondent have histories of criminal activity. It is my understanding that the respondent has served time in prison and has had recent DUI charges. I have no criminal history other than in 2010 I was accused of domestic violence against petitioner when I forced the petitioner to leave our home because she was under the influence of drugs and I found drugs in the petitioner's clothes and in the laundry.*

21. *The minor child currently resides with the respondent in a home with two adults and at least one or two boys who are both older that she is. I was given this information by my other daughters, the minor child's sisters, when they were allowed to visit the minor child in the respondent's home.*

22. *I am a fit and proper person to have permanent custody of the minor child; in the alternative, I should be awarded temporary custody pending a final declaration by the court, or in the alternative I should be awarded parent-time visitation with the minor child pending a final declaration of the court.*

23. *The minor child has known me and my daughters as her family and it would be in her best interest to be reunited with me and her other family members.*

We met Nancy S for the first time at the court house. She was a pleasant looking large lady in her late 50's with black hair and red lipstick and wearing a suit with a skirt. The hearing was only a matter of minutes but what happened there would change the outcome of what could have been a short and successful custody change.

In the hallway before we entered the courtroom, Kirk saw an old familiar face, that of Connie, his court appointed free attorney from the juvenile court.

"Hi, Kirk. What do you have going on here?" Connie inquired with a Holly Hunter sounding drawl.

"Uh, I'm not really sure. Somethin 'bout custody of Kelly's little girl."

"Well I've got a few free minutes if you want me to sit in on the hearing with you."

"Ya, that would be great - but I don't have any money to pay you," Kirk replied.

"Don't worry about that right now, I'm sure it won't take long."

In the courtroom Connie quickly skimmed over the matter at hand and then gave her verbal notice of appearance to the judge stating that she was stepping in as Kirk J's attorney. I watched the whole thing unfold, baffled that Kirk could be unrepresented one minute and literally have someone step in and take over without any pre-notice whatsoever while we had been preparing for this for months. Had Connie not been at that exact place at that precise moment; had Nancy gone straight to the juvenile court to release our case first, I am sure I would not be writing this book today as the court system is so complex that surely an uneducated person such as Kirk would have been at a loss had he tried to maneuver through it on his own.

Had Connie not stepped in and taken a personal interest in this case and worked entirely pro bono for the next seven years and counting, he surely would have given up long ago. Had he been forced to contribute one dime of his money towards the cause of keeping custody of Payshence, he certainly would have bowed out. Remember, this is the man that took a DNA test to prove he *wasn't* Payshence's father so he wouldn't have to pay ORS back for the foster care expenses.

JANUARY 16TH, 2014: HEARING - Attorney Nancy S, Commissioner Bloom presiding

The following facts are stated:
1. The Intervenor, Jody Rhorer, is the biological father of one of the children of the Petitioner, Kelly H.
2. The Juvenile Court has jurisdiction over that child, their jurisdiction has not been terminated.
3. The Respondent, Kirk J, has been awarded custody of the subject child by the Juvenile Court.
4. The Court has no jurisdiction over the child until Juvenile Court jurisdiction is terminated.
*The Commissioner, after hearing argument, **RECOMMENDS:***
*1. This Court can look at the best interest of the child ONLY after jurisdiction has been terminated by Juvenile Court. The Court will NOT proceed until that time. The motion is **RESERVED** pending Juvenile Court termination.*
2. Mr. Rhorer may go to the Juvenile Court to seek relief.
3. If the Juvenile Court relinquishes jurisdiction, the Court should be notified so the URCP Rule 100 conference can be held with the Juvenile Court Judge.

Strike one against Nancy. What a waste of time and money. My expectations were so great I had purchased clothes for Payshence - jammies, pants and shirts for school and a purple velvet jogging suit. All I could do was shake my head that this new attorney we had inherited didn't do her homework and see that we had to have a release from juvenile court in order to proceed in district court. A seasoned attorney certainly should know that.

JANUARY 20TH, 2014: WITHDRAWAL OF COUNSEL, filed by Steven K

COMES NOW, *Steven K, and hereby withdraws as counsel for Jody Rhorer, in the above-named matter.*

Unfortunately for us, Steven's license was suspended and he was no longer able to represent us. We were now with Nancy - we thought because she was an outstanding and astute attorney with extensive knowledge of family law. But we would later learn that the reason Steven asked her to sit in for us was because Deanne, his former legal secretary, had gone to work for Nancy when he had moved out of the area. Steven merely wanted Nancy to sit in for him at the hearing as a matter of convenience. She was, in fact, not a family law attorney at all but a lawyer that dealt with insurance agency claims.

JANUARY 28TH 2014: MOTION REQUESTING ORDER TERMINATING JURISDICTION - STATE OF UTAH, in the interest of Payshence Rhorer - Attorney Nancy S

Jody Rhorer, by and through his attorney, Nancy S, requests that this Court enter an order terminating jurisdiction in the above-entitled matter. The Motion is based upon the fact that all matters have been resolved and there are no matters pending before this Court and pursuant to the Minutes and Order of the Court regarding the review hearing on September 10, 2013, no future hearings are set, withdrawal has been filed in this matter.

In addition, there is currently a case pending in the Third District Court, Salt Lake County, wherein the Honorable Judge Stanley granted Jody Rhorer's request for intervention. Jody Rhorer is the biological father of the above-named minor child. A copy of the genetic test results is attached hereto and incorporated herein by reference.

JANUARY 28TH, 2014: ORDER-RECOMMENDATION, Commissioner Bloom

Intervenor's Motion to Establish Jody Rhorer as the Natural and Biological Father of PR, Motion for Determination of Parentage, and Motion for Custody and in the Alternative for Custody Evaluation and Motion of Interim Parent-Time having come on for hearing before Commissioner Bloom, on the 16th day of January, 2014, the Petitioner and Respondent having appeared pro se, the Intervenor was present and represented by counsel, Nancy S and Mr. Hunt for ORS appeared on behalf of the State of Utah, the Court having read and reviewed the file, and having heard argument of the parties.

NOW, THEREFORE, IT IS HEREBY ORDERED as follows:

1. Intervenor's Motions are hereby reserved pending termination of jurisdiction by the Juvenile Court regarding the minor child PR. This Court will not proceed until the Juvenile Court has terminated its jurisdiction.

2. Intervenor may seek relief in the Juvenile Court as to establishing paternity and custody or he may request that the Juvenile Court terminate jurisdiction.

3. If the Juvenile Court terminates its jurisdiction, Intervenor shall notify this Court so that a URCP Rule 100 conference can be held with the Juvenile Court Judge.

4. If the Juvenile Court enters an order terminating its jurisdiction, Intervenor shall provide a copy of said order to this Court.

JANUARY 28TH, 2014: ORDER TERMINATING JURISDICTION, Juvenile Court, filed by Nancy S

Based upon Jody Rhorer's Motion Requesting Order Terminating Jurisdiction, and good cause appearing therefore; **IT IS HEREBY ORDERED** this Court's jurisdiction of the minor child, Payshence Rhorer, is terminated.

MARCH 14TH, 2014: ENTRY OF COUNSEL Connie C, Opposition to Establish Paternity

Comes now, Connie C, Attorney at Law, and on behalf of the Respondent, Kirk J, filed the foregoing Entry of Appearance.

MARCH 18TH, 2014: AFFIDAVIT OF KIRK J, fabricated by Connie, Commissioner Bloom presiding

STATE OF UTAH
COUNTY OF SALT LAKE

I, Kirk J, being first duly sworn, depose and say:

1. I am over 18 years of age and a resident of the State of Utah and all statements made in the affidavit are based on my personal knowledge or belief.

2. I married Kelly H in April of 2007. **(The factual date was 2003.)**

3. Among the children born during that marriage was my daughter, PR, who was born July 2007.

4. I have raised PR as my child, she calls me "Daddy."

5. She views the other children born of my marriage to Kelly H as her siblings.

6. I was not aware that PR might not be mine until during a Juvenile Court hearing and test result ordered indicated Jody Rhorer was PR's biological father. **(This is a bold-faced lie!)**

7. *Mr. Rhorer is a person who had a relationship with my former wife, Kelly H, while she was married to me.*

8. *That PR is the biological child of Jody Rhorer is immaterial to me in that I have always embraced her as my own daughter, and I always will.*

9. *As part of that attachment and relationship, I have financially provided for PR whether she was living with me or Kelly H, and irrespective of whether Kelly and Mr. Rhorer or any other man was living with her.*

10. *This support included money, clothes, presents for birthdays and Christmas, essentially, anything that was needed. (Because we were only recently divorced, there was no Court Order about support).* **(LIES!)**

11. *Physical custody of PR was placed with me in May, 2012, as part of the Juvenile case, and I was given Permanent Custody and Guardianship in July, 2012.*

12. *PR knows Jody Rhorer's name, and that is about it, and because I was very involved with raising her with Kelly H despite the fact we did not live together, I do not believe he lived with Kelly and PR for her first three years of life, as he has attests in his affidavit.*

13. *PR and I are very close; she trusts me, comes to me with problems or bad dreams.*

14. *PR has a close bonded relationship with my extended family, many of whom do not know she is not biologically my daughter.* **(Another lie.)**

15. *Other of my children with Kelly H who are also not biologically mine do not know it either, and all are treated exactly the same, as my children, and all recognize each other as my children, and as a family.*

16. *If in fact Mr. Rhorer knew he was PR's father when she was a baby, he did nothing at all to act as a father, such as to make some legal effort to establish paternity.* **(LIE.)**

17. *Instead he seemed content enough with the situation that I raised her as my own and provided the things she needed.*

18. *It was only after it appeared Kelly's relationship would be disrupted with the children that he took any efforts.*

19. *PR is safe, protected, assimilated, and loved in my home with her siblings, and contact with Mr. Rhorer would be confusing, hurtful, and disruptive to her.*

20. *The many ups and downs and parenting deficits on the part of PR which caused repeated DCFS intervention and placement of PR in a foster home have already disrupted her young life, and she has done well in my home and in my care since May, 2012, and the status quo should not be disrupted in her best interest. Further, your affiant sayeth naught.*

I suppose I don't need to point out that nearly all of this sworn affidavit was concocted. Little did I know our entire case would be littered with this type of off-the-cuff presentation by Connie. What in the world would a 34-year-old man want custody of other men's children for? What reason would he have to keep them from their REAL families?

It was not out of love as this is clearly not a loving person. A loving person would want what is best for a child; would want the child to be happy and secure. This is a drunk with a history of violence and illegal activities and strip clubs and abuse.

I wondered as I read the carefully crafted wording of the attorney if Kirk even participated at all in formulating the affidavit. Most of the words chosen he most likely didn't even know the meaning of and every detail, down to the wedding date, was incorrect. What was Connie's motive? Why would she blatantly lie? How could she feel good about keeping this little girl away from her family? Why was she doing this all for free?

We attempted to get a copy of Payshence's birth certificate. We first tried ordering it from the county website. Then we ordered it from a private company on the internet that charged us $90.00. After several weeks, we received this note:

"Thank you for using our website to order a birth certificate. However, our records show that there is a pending order from the Office of Recovery Services on the record you are requesting. Your credit card has been refunded any amount you were charged."

We then went to the Office of Vital Statistics in Salt Lake and attempted to get a copy of the certificate in person. The office staff was helpful but also cautious. We were told we couldn't get a copy and that Jody's name had been removed as father.

MARCH 21ST, 2014: OPPOSITION TO JODY RHORER'S MOTIONS TO ESTABLISH HIM AS "NATURAL AND BIOLOGICAL" FATHER OF PR AND FOR DETERMINATION OF PARENTAGE, Submitted by Connie C, Commissioner Bloom residing

Comes now, Connie C, Attorney at Law, and on behalf of the Respondent, Kirk J, files the foregoing Opposition to Jody Rhorer's Motion to Establish himself as "natural and biological" father of PR.

FACTS

(I) Respondent, Kirk J, was legally married to the mother of PR at the time of the child's conception and birth.

Mr. Rhorer's request that he be established as "natural and biological" father of the child would have no legal effect whatsoever as the **legal** paternity is the touchstone which confers rights and responsibilities which this Court can recognize.

Mr. Rhorer's pleadings cite either case law or statutes which would apply only to legal parents. He demands rights which might be conferred upon legal parents, such as right to visitation, custody, or a right to request modification of Orders related to the same. Mr. Rhorer declares this Court should recognize his paternity "by operation of law," due to a DNA test which shows he is biologically the father of PR. Biological paternity does not confer legal parental rights, particularly where there is a legal presumption of paternity to another.

In addition to the plain language of the Uniform Parentage Act, a recent Court of Appeals case makes clear a person in the position of Mr. Rhorer has no standing to contest paternity. Mr. Rhorer had an affair with Kelly H while she was married. Kirk J, as husband of Kelly H, acted as father of the child, even at times when Kelly's parenting skills were found deficient by the Juvenile Court. It is Kirk J who has had custody of PR, and to allow a challenge by Mr. Rhorer in this forum, simply because Kelly H has finally gotten around to divorcing Kirk J (after having what she asserts are three of four children born of the marriage with other men) would be nothing more that "disruptive and unnecessary."

A review of the Utah Uniform Parentage Act leads to the conclusion that Mr. Rhorer is a legal stranger to the minor, PR. "A man is presumed to be the father of a child if he and the mother of the child are married to each other and the child is born during the marriage." Kelly H and Kirk J were married in April, 2002 **(Wrong again, it was 2003)**, and were married during the conception and birth of PR.

A presumption of paternity thus established may only be disputed pursuant to 78B-15-607, U.C.A., 2008, 78B-15-204(2), U.C.A., 2008. Paternity of a child conceived or born during a marriage "may be raised **by the presumed father or the mother** at any time prior to filing an action for divorce or in the pleadings at the time of the divorce of the parent."

Therefore, by its plain terms, the Paternity Act does not provide standing to an "a man who alleges himself to be, or is alleged to be, the genetic father or a possible genetic father of a child but whose paternity has not been determined," to attempt to rebut a presumption which arises based on marriage.

Clearly, Kirk J does not wish to rebut the marital presumption of paternity of PR in him. He has had custody of her and raised her as his own child. It is equally clear that the only other person with standing to attempt to rebut paternity, the mother, Kelly H, has failed to do so "prior to filing an action for divorce or in the pleadings at the time of the divorce of the parent."

Though Mr. Rhorer claims that the minor lived with him "and her mother and her three half-sisters from the time she was born until she was approximately 3 years old," Kelly H, the mother, and person with standing to challenge the marital presumption of paternity, attested that the child lived with her. She has failed to even identify Mr. Rhorer as PR's biological father, let alone plead, and assert that she could prove by a preponderance of the evidence "that it would be in the best interest of the child to disestablish the parent-child relationship." As such, Kelly H has failed "prior to filing an action for divorce or in the pleadings at the time of the divorce of the parent, to seek to rebut the legal presumption of paternity in Kirk J.

WHEREFORE, because only Kelly H and Kirk J had standing to raise the issue of paternity of PR before the divorce, and because neither party with standing has, Mr. Rhorer's Motions regarding paternity must be dismissed. Further, because as a legal stranger to PR, Mr. Rhorer is not entitled to visitation, custody, or an Order Appointing a Custody Evaluator, his Motions with regard to the same must be dismissed as well.

But in actuality, Kelly not only listed Jody on Payshence's birth certificate, she also brought it up in her divorce paperwork. So, technically, she did address paternity in the divorce proceeding.

MARCH 21ST, 2014: MOTION TO DISREGARD DNA TEST; AFFIDAVIT/DECLARATION OF KIRK J; MOTION TO RECONSIDER ORDER GRANTING INTERVENTION OF JODY RHORER, submitted by Connie C, Commissioner Bloom residing

Comes now, Connie C, Attorney at Law, and on behalf of the Respondent, Kirk J, files the foregoing Motion to Reconsider the Order Granting the Motion filed by Jody Rhorer to Intervene,

FACTS

(1) Respondent, Kirk J, was legally married to the mother of PR, at the time of the child's conception and birth.

(2) Neither the mother of PR, nor Kirk J, to whom she was married during the conception and birth of PR filed any pleadings prior to, or contemporaneous with the divorce filings to attempt to rebut the "marital presumption" of legal paternity which arose in Kirk J by virtue of his marriage to the child's mother at the time of the child's birth.

(3) This matter is a divorce action between Kelly H and Kirk J, in which neither of them has filed any pleadings regarding paternity of PR, despite the fact that Kelly H's pleadings have suggested that PR is not biologically Kirk J's.

(4) Mr. Rhorer moved to intervene such to attempt to establish Paternity of PR to ask for Custody, and/or a Custody evaluation and visitation.

(5) Kirk J was unrepresented at the time of the hearing on the Motion for Intervention, and did not object to the Court's Order allowing Mr. Rhorer to intervene.

(6) Kelly H did not appear at that hearing.

(7) The divorce has been granted to Kelly and Kirk.

DISCUSSION

By virtue of his lack of standing regarding Paternity, he also lacks standing regarding any rights which inure to parentage, such as a right to Petition for Custody, modification of custody order and/or visitation.

Because Kirk J is the presumed father by virtue of marriage, and Mr. Rhorer has no standing to contest paternity, he is an improper party to this proceeding.

The Court should disregard any DNA/Paternity Test Results. "In a proceeding to adjudicate the parentage of a child having a presumed father the tribunal may disregard genetic test results that exclude the presumed or declarant father if the tribunal determines that the conduct of the other or the presumed or declarant father estops that party from denying parentage and it would be inequitable to disrupt the father-child relationship between the child and the presumed declarant father." 78B-15-608(1), U.C.A., 2008.

To the contrary, in considering whether it should disregard a genetic test the Court shall consider the best interest of the child, including the following factors:

(a) the length of time between the proceeding to adjudicate parentage and the time that the presumed or declarant father was placed on notice that he might not be the genetic father;

(b) the length of time during which the presumed or declarant father has assumed the role of father of the child;

(c) the facts surrounding the presumed or declarant father's discovery of his possible non-paternity;

(d) the nature of the relationship between the child and the presumed or declarant father;

(e) the age of the child;

(f) the harm that may result to the child if presumed or declared paternity is successfully disestablished;

(g) the nature of the relationship between the child and any alleged father;

(h) the extent to which the passage of time reduces the chances of establishing the paternity of another man and a child-support obligation in favor to the child; and

(i) other factors that may affect the equities arising from the disruption of the father-child relationship between the child and the presumed or declarant father or the chance of other harm to the child.

As attested in Kirk J's attached affidavit, he is the presumed father of PR by virtue of the marriage to the child's mother at the time of the child's conception and birth. Kirk J was unsure as to whether he was the child's father, but treated her as if she was his child, including identifying himself to her as father, and assimilating her into his family, including identification of her as siblings to the other children of the marriage. Even during times that the child's mother and Kirk J were not together, he "split time" as the parents shared time with the children of the marriage, including PR.

Kirk J developed a father/daughter bond with PR which is enjoyed by both. PR resorts to Kirk J in times of trouble and need, and looks to him for protection, security, and comfort. Kirk J has provided for PR financially, including the necessities of everyday life, as well as gifts on gift giving occasions.

Kirk J learned that he was not biological father of PR as part of a Juvenile Court matter in which the Juvenile Judge ordered paternity testing of alleged father, Jody Rhorer, in 2010. Though biological paternity in Mr. Rhorer may be a scientific fact, Kirk J's acceptance of his legal responsibilities to PR, a child born of his marriage, and his enduring and unwavering emotional commitment to PR is not bound by mere biology. His acceptance of her as a daughter extends to her siblings, as well as Kirk J's extended family, grandparents, aunts, uncles, cousins, many whom do not know PR is not Kirk J's biological child.

In fact, Kirk J has had sole physical custody of PR for nearly two years. As such, PR is settled and secure in her life as daughter of Kirk. PR is now almost 7 and continuity and stability are key for a healthy life including secure emotional bonding.

Alleged father, Jody Rhorer, asserts through an affidavit filed in this case that he co-habited with the child's mother, Kelly H and PR until the child was three years of age. By virtue of Kirk J's constant interaction with the child, he can attest that Mr. Rhorer did not live with Kelly H that long. Further, during this time, Kirk J had regular visitation, including overnight and extended visitation, sometimes for protracted periods of time.

Mr. Rhorer asserts he had been residing with Kelly H and PR, and at times he asserts he knew he was PR's biological father (whereas Kirk J did not know at the time) Kelly H did absolutely nothing in furtherance of disestablishing Kirk J's presumption of paternity. Though Mr. Rhorer later was forced to appear before the Juvenile Court, he did nothing in an attempt to establish paternity before the Division of Child and Family Services intervened with the family. During the time he asserts that he was in a relationship and a "couple" with Kelly H, he did nothing to move toward establishing paternity in himself, and disestablishing it in Kirk J, content enough to allow Kirk J to serve as father in all emotional and financial ways. Mr. Rhorer has failed to demonstrate that the Court's recognition of the DNA test would serve the child's best interest. Disregarding the DNA test is the only way the Court can ensure the continuity and stability of PR's home life and emotional relationships.

__WHEREFORE__, Kirk J prays the Court reconsider its Order allowing the Intervention of Mr. Rhorer, that the Court issue its Order denying the Motion to Intervene, and for such other and further relief as the Court deems appropriate in the premises. Kirk J prays that the Court disregard the DNA test submitted by Jody Rhorer, and that the Court adjudicate Kirk J as legal father of PR.

MARCH 25TH, 2014: MOTION TO STRIKE RESPONDENT'S MOTION TO DISREGARD DNA PATERNITY TEST SUBMITTED BY INTERVENOR; MOTION TO STRIKE RESPONDENT'S MOTION TO RECONSIDER ORDER GRANTING INTERVENTION OF JODY RHORER; MOTION TO STRIKE RESPONDENT'S OPPOSITION AND AFFIDAVIT IN RESPONSE TO INTERVENOR'S MOTIONS, submitted by Nancy S, Commissioner Bloom presiding

Jody Rhorer, by and through counsel, Nancy S, hereby moves the court for an order striking the Respondent's Motion to Disregard DNA Paternity Test Submitted by Intervenor Jody Rhorer. Intervenor's motion to establish paternity was evidenced by a DNA Paternity Test results attached to his motion. This motion to strike is based on Rule 101 of the Utah Rule of Civil Procedure which states that a responding party to a motion shall file and serve the moving party with a response and attachments at least 5 business days before the hearing. The hearing on Jody Rhorer's motions is scheduled for Wednesday, March 26, 2014 at 9:00 a.m. Respondent e-filed his Motion to Disregard the DNA Paternity Test on the afternoon of Friday, March 21, 2014, only two business days before the hearing, although counsel for Respondent entered her appearance in this matter on March 14, 2014. This untimely filing does not allow the intervenor the request time to reply.

Subparagraph (f) imposes sanctions for failure to timely file including continuing the hearing, rejecting the papers and imposing costs and attorney's fees caused by the failure and the continuance and impose other sanctions as appropriate. The Respondent's failure to file documents timely has caused an undue burden on the Intervenor and his attorney and any delay in adjudicating the matters before the court by continuing the hearing will further cause distress and burden the Intervenor, causing him additional attorney fees. Intervenor requests the court to strike the Respondent's Motion to Disregard DNA Paternity Test Submitted by Intervenor Jody Rhorer and award the Intervenor attorney fees and other sanctions as the court deems appropriate.

Jody Rhorer filed a motion to intervene in the divorce action between Petitioner and Respondent in order to establish paternity of minor child, PR. A hearing was held before Judge Stanley on June 25, 2013, in which the Respondent was present as well as Jody Rhorer and his attorney. The Petitioner, Kelly H, is not a party to this Motion to Reconsider; nonetheless, Kelly H was given notice of the motion to intervene and had an opportunity to attend and be heard. Kirk J did not object to the intervention. ORS did not object. The court ruled that Jody Rhorer had standing to intervene and an order granting Jody Rhorer's motion to intervene was entered on July 1, 2013. The Respondent's Motion to Reconsider is not well taken, such a motion is not provided for in the Utah Rules of Civil Procedure. The Respondent's Motion to Reconsider is merely an end run to avoid time constraints of Rule 60(b) URPC.

Respondent failed to file a motion to set aside the order as provide by Rule 60(b) within three months after the order was entered. Respondent had ample time to timely file a motion to set aside the order, but failed to do so; further, the Respondent had been a party to Juvenile Court proceedings in which he was represented by his current counsel in this case and had the opportunity to consult with counsel and hire the assistance of counsel to bring a timely motion as provided by the Utah Rules of Civil Procedure. Since both the Juvenile Court case and this case in which the intervention was granted were proceeding concurrently, it is likely that Respondent would have consulted with his current counsel regarding Jody Rhorer's Motion to Intervene.

The Respondent's failure to timely comply with the procedure set forth above precludes any attempt now to set aside the court's order. Neither the Petitioner nor Respondent objected to Jody Rhorer's intervention and thus agreed to his intervention. The court's order granting Mr. Rhorer's right to intervene is a final determination of his right to assert his parentage of the minor child. **Without his intervention he will be forever barred from bringing an action to assert his right.**

The order entered by Judge Stanley was based on facts that remain the same today. There is no new evidence that would change or alter the court's order. Respondent has not presented to the court any exemption that would permit a reconsideration of the final order granting Jody Rhorer's motion to intervene.

For the reasons set forth above the Respondent's motion to reconsider should be stricken. Intervenor requests an award of attorney's fees of the cost of opposing this motion. Jody Rhorer hereby moves the Court for an order striking the Respondent's Opposition to Jody Rhorer's Motions to Establish him as Natural and Biological Father of PR and for Determination of Parentage, fees caused by the failure and by the continuance and impose other sanctions as appropriate. Intervenor requests the court to strike the Respondent's Opposition and Affidavit and award the Intervenor attorney fees and other sanctions as the court deems appropriate.

MARCH 26TH, 2014: ORDER OF MOTIONS HEARING AND GRANTING CONTINUANCE; compiled by Connie C, Commissioner Bloom presiding

THIS MATTER came before the Court on March 26th, 2014, for the hearing on Motions filed by Intervenor Jody Rhorer, that he be declared the natural and biological father, for custody and/or a parenting evaluation, and for an order of parent time; Kirk J appeared personally and by and through his Counsel, Connie. Kelly H appeared personally. Mr. Rhorer appeared personally, and by and through his counsel Nancy S.

Nancy S argued that Kirk J's responses to her Motions are untimely based on the filing date of the Motions, and that the responses should be stricken. Further, she argued that Kirk J's motion to disregard the DNA testing and motion to reconsider the Order allowing Intervention by Mr. Rhorer are untimely since they were filed three business days before the hearing.

Connie conceded that because the Intervention occurred months ago, and Kirk J recently retained her as counsel, the responses and motions are untimely, and that a continuance would be the appropriate remedy should Mr. Rhorer's counsel wish for more time. Connie further argued that the court may not grant the remedies (declaration of paternity/custody/custody evaluation) Mr. Rhorer prays for in his motions in light of the fact that they fail to address both provisions of the Uniform Parentage Act which apply, and a recent Court of Appeals case which is binding of the Court as to whether the Juvenile Court issued an adjudication related to paternity or other relevant matters.

Kelly H addressed the Court to the effect that she believes that it would be in the best interest for the minor, PR, to remain in the custody of Kirk J and that visitation or contact with Mr. Rhorer would not be in the minor's best interest because the minor knows Mr. Rhorer's name, but does not know him, Mr. Rhorer has untreated issues related to domestic violence which would impair his ability to have safe interactions with PR, and that the last time she permitted Mr. Rhorer to have contact with PR he told her he was going to "stab Kirk J in the neck" or words to this effect.

Nancy S indicated she wished to have more time to address the issues presented to the Court, and as such the Court granted a continuance of this matter. The Court further indicated that it desired involvement of the GAL involved in the Juvenile case, Brent N (or someone in his office with knowledge of the case), and would like him to appear at the next hearing. The Court indicated it would like a review of the Juvenile file conducted, and relevant Orders lodged with the District Court.

***IT IS THEREFORE ORDERED** that continuance of the pending motions shall be **GRANTED**. The matter shall be heard the 29th day of April, 2014, and Connie shall notify the GAL of that hearing, and that Court requests that he appear.*

***IT IS FURTHER ORDERED** that Connie C investigate the Juvenile Court file and provide any Orders to the Parties and the Court.*

MARCH 26TH, 2014: HEARING ORDER - Commissioner Bloom, Petitioner Kelly H, Respondent Kirk J, Intervenor Jody Rhorer

Hearing is held on the Intervenor's motion to be established as the father of the child, and that he be given custody or a custody evaluation be performed, with interim parent-time. Other motions filed were not timely of today's hearing.

*The Commissioner, after hearing argument, **RECOMMENDS** that:*

*1. The hearing be **CONTINUED**. Counsel and the parties agree to 4/29/14.*

2. Brent N (GAL on the Juvenile Court case) or a GAL that would have the information be present to provide the court information on the Juvenile Court case. Attorney Connie to notify the GAL office.

3. Counsel are directed to determine if there are any orders addressing this issue.

Between April 10, 2014, and May 12, 2014, Nancy filed over 700 pages with the court including: Demand for Discovery to ORS, Intervenors Memorandum of Opposition; Jody Rhorer's Reply Memorandum and Exhibits; Affidavit/Memorandum of Jody Rhorer; Notice of Lodging (Kirk J's criminal history); Notice of Lodging (Kelly H's criminal history); Notice of Lodging (Jill C's criminal history); Notice of Lodging (Jill's Husband's criminal history); Notice of Lodging (Kirk's father's criminal history); Lodging of CD of Juvenile hearing; Lodging of Juvenile Court records parts one and two; Proposed Order; Motion/Stipulation to Continue; Affidavit/Declaration of Mona Rhorer, and many more.

APRIL 14TH, 2014: NOTICE OF LODGING

Intervenor, Jody Rhorer, by and through his attorney, Nancy S, hereby lodges the following documents with the Court:

1. Order for Genetic Testing (filed September 12, 2011).

2. Order of Dismissal (filed February 9, 2012) declaring that Kirk J is not the father of PR, born in July 2007. Based on the parties' failure to appear and subsequent default and the Court being advised, now therefore,

***IT IS ORDERED** that the Respondent, Kirk J, is not the father of the minor child PR and that the Office's complaint for Support is dismissed.*

A man portraying himself to be wise who will make his appearance later on in this book said "If you get in a shitting contest with an asshole, you are bound to lose." So, to that end I ask you, what happens when two assholes get in a shitting contest? It becomes a shit show. For the record, I'm not much of a potty mouth but I don't think it could be said any better.

Connie rebutted Nancy's lodgings by filing back copious amounts of her own rhetoric. Much of her voluminous motions were packed with her own fabrications and inaccuracies. She would pose "facts" without proof and with no case reference or date references, or any sort of backing whatsoever for that matter and no case law to prove it up.

APRIL 21ST, 2014: NOTICE OF LODGING OF JUVENILE COURT DOCUMENTS.   Connie submitted 24 pages of Juvenile Hearing documents from 2008 to 2012 - the same documents included previously showing the hearings where Kelly was being investigated.

With every Motion, Lodging, Memorandum, etc., that Connie would file, Nancy would react with a repetitious rebuttal. Certainly, that seemed like the reasonable thing to do, and, at the time, we agreed that something had to be done - even if it did cost us tremendously. What I now know is this, unless there is a hearing scheduled to address the Motion, Lodging, Memorandum., etc., they are practically meaningless and if attorneys really think a judge or commissioner is going to read the dozens upon dozens of rambling pages submitted to the court queue they certainly should know better.

APRIL 22, 2014: INTERVENOR'S MEMORANDUM OPPOSING MOTION TO DISREGARD DNA TEST, submitted by Nancy S, Commissioner Bloom presiding

Jody Rhorer, by and through his counsel, Nancy S, hereby submits this Memorandum in Opposition to Motion to Disregard DNA Paternity Test Submitted by Intervenor Jody Rhorer.
FACTS
1. Jody Rhorer is the biological father of PR, the minor child born July, 2007.
2. Jody Rhorer and Kelly H were cohabiting in Oregon during the time of PR's conception. Kirk J resided in Utah at the time of PR's conception.
3. Jody Rhorer and Kelly H were living together in Salt Lake City at the time of PR's birth, and they continued to live together with PR after the child's birth. Mr. Rhorer and PR have established a close and loving bond as shown in Jody Rhorer's Affidavit previously filed with the court.
4. Neither Kelly H nor Kirk J told Jody Rhorer that they were married, and at all times relevant Jody Rhorer believed that Kelly H was not married.
5. During the 2008 Juvenile Court proceedings neither Kirk J nor Kelly H informed the court that Kirk J was the presumed father of PR and never told the court that they were married. The Court was informed of their marriage by the attorney for the State of Utah after Mr. Rhorer established paternity of PR.
6. The Juvenile Court records show that Mr. Rhorer was told by Judge V to establish paternity of PR and was ordered to submit to DNA genetic testing. Mr. Rhorer could not afford to hire counsel for that purpose until late 2009. On January 15, 2010, an Order was entered in the Third District Court declaring Mr. Rhorer the father of PR.

7. Mr. Rhorer submitted to DNA genetic testing in an Office of Recovery Services proceeding and was declared to be the father of PR by Order dated June 16, 2010. The Order stated that Kelly H provided information through participation in that proceeding.
8. Kirk J voluntarily participated in a judicial proceeding in the Third District Court and stipulated to DNA genetic testing and as a result was declared not to be the father of PR. Both Kirk J and Kelly H were given notice and opportunity to object to the final Order, but neither objected. This Order is res judicata that Kirk J is not the legal father of PR.
9. Both Kirk J and Kelly H have raised the issue of PR's paternity on many occasions, including the following:
a. Verified Divorce Petition by Kelly H wherein she states that three of her four children are not the biological children of Kirk J, one of them being the two-year-old child PR.
b. Verified Divorce Petition, paragraph 9.1c in which Kelly H references PR and lists Kirk's relationship to PR as "other."
c. Answer to divorce petition filed by Kirk J does not deny the allegations contained in paragraph 9.4h and 9.1c and therefore admitted the same.
d. Answer to divorce petition, paragraph 7 in reference to paragraph 12 of the Verified Divorce Petition, Kirk J stated public assistance provided to Kelly H was for children who were not his legal financial responsibility at the time.
e. In Juvenile Court proceedings, at the initial hearing on November 6, 2008, both Kelly H and Kirk J were present and agreed that Jody Rhorer was the father of PR. This was prior to filing the action for divorce.
f. Kirk J voluntarily submitted to DNA paternity testing with ORS which showed he was not the biological father of PR. Third District Court. Orders dated September 12, 2011 and February 12, 2012. This was prior to filing the action for divorce.

g. *Kelly H provided information to ORS and voluntarily participated in an ORS proceeding with Jody Rhorer at which time Mr. Rhorer submitted DNA testing and ORS determined that Mr. Rhorer was the biological father of PR. Order dated June 16, 2010. This was prior to filing the action for divorce.*

h. *Neither Kirk J nor Kelly H objected to Jody Rhorer's motion to intervene in the divorce proceedings knowing that the reason for his intervention was to determine parentage of PR.*

ARGUMENT

U.C.A. 78B-15-608, **the statute governing whether to disregard genetic test results, states that the conduct of the parties may be looked at to determine whether to accept the DNA genetic testing.**

Jody Rhorer and Kelly H began their relationship in 2005. Kirk J and Kelly H failed to inform Mr. Rhorer that they were married. During Jody Rhorer's and Kelly H's relationship PR was conceived and born. Mr. Rhorer has stated that he signed a Voluntary Declaration of Paternity and upon knowledge and belief, his name was placed on PR's original birth certificate. Jody Rhorer, in reliance on Kelly H's and Kirk J's conduct, believed that he had established paternity by signing a Voluntary Declaration of Paternity.

Kirk J and Kelly H failed to inform the Juvenile Court that they were married and Kirk J was the presumed father of PR. Their conduct constitutes fraud and fraudulent misrepresentation, as well as perjury upon the court.

Given the conduct of the parties since PR's birth and the conduct of Kirk J in disestablishing paternity, and the conduct of Mr. Rhorer in establishing paternity pursuant to ORS Order, Kirk J and Kelly H should be estopped from denying Mr. Rhorer an opportunity to establish parentage in this matter by DNA genetic testing. Kirk has voluntarily used genetic testing to disestablish paternity, and Jody Rhorer and Kelly H have previously agreed to establish Jody Rhorer's paternity using genetic testing in other court proceedings.

During the 2008 Juvenile Court proceeding Kirk J did not acknowledge his presumption of paternity for 2 1/2 years after PR's birth, and only acknowledged the presumption after Jody Rhorer filed for paternity in August 2009, and after Ms. Nickels, the attorney for the State of Utah, informed the Juvenile Court at a hearing in August 2009, that the parties were married. During that time PR was never in Kirk J's household and Kirk J did not hold out PR as his child.

Kirk J attended hearings in the Juvenile Court proceedings and held out two other children, including one whom they acknowledge as having a father other than Kirk J, as his own children; however, he never held out PR as his own child. Kirk J in his Answer to the Verified Divorce Petition states that PR began living with him on July 31, 2012, at which time the Juvenile Court awarded him custody and guardianship of PR. Furthermore, Kirk J has not accepted his legal responsibility for PR as evidence by his voluntary participation to disestablish himself as the biological father of PR

Conversely, Mr. Rhorer has always held himself out to be the father of PR. He has established a close and loving relationship with PR. Mr. Rhorer's other children have established a close and loving bond with PR. Jody Rhorer and Kelly H lived together with PR from PR's birth in July 2007, until 2010, and thereafter Jody Rhorer had extensive visitation with PR. Jody Rhorer's mother and other family members have established close loving relationships with PR. These relationships with PR are evidenced in the photographs attached to Mr. Rhorer's previous affidavit and his averments therein. Jody Rhorer continued to have visitation with PR until approximately April, 2013, when Jody Rhorer assisted Kelly H in a hearing before the court and Kirk J thereafter refused visitation.

PR has known Jody Rhorer as her father for all her life. Kirk J was given custody and guardianship of PR in 2012 in a Juvenile Court action only because Mr. Rhorer could not establish his paternity because of the marital status of Kirk J and Kelly H. Once a divorce action was initiated, Mr. Rhorer intervened, with the parties' permission, in order to establish paternity.

Mr. Rhorer's establishment of PR's paternity in this divorce proceeding will not disrupt the child's life; in fact, her life was disrupted in 2012 when Kirk J was given custody and guardianship of PR and thereafter in 2013 when Kirk J refused to allow PR to visit with her natural and biological father, Jody Rhorer. Kirk J has acknowledged that he has been involved with PR's life only in the past 1 1/2 years. PR knows Mr. Rhorer as her father. No harm will result to PR if Jody Rhorer establishes paternity in these divorce proceedings; to the contrary, allowing Mr. Rhorer to establish paternity would serve to re-enforce the father-daughter relationship PR has known since her birth.

WHEREFORE, *Jody Rhorer prays that the court deny Kirk J's Motion to Disregard the DNA Paternity Test Submitted by Jody Rhorer, and further that the Court acknowledge that Kirk J has disestablished paternity of PR pursuant to the Court Order in Case No. 114903342, that Jody Rhorer's establishment of paternity in Case No. C000965874 is res judicata, or in the alternative, to allow Jody Rhorer to establish paternity of PR in this matter.*

APRIL 23RD, 2014: JODY RHORER'S REPLY MEMORANDUM TO OPPOSITION TO HIS MOTIONS TO ESTABLISH HIM AS NATURAL AND BIOLOGICAL FATHER OF PAYSHENCE RHORER AND DETERMINATION OF PARENTAGE, submitted by Nancy S

Jody Rhorer, by and through counsel Nancy S, hereby submits his Reply Memorandum to Kirk J's Opposition to Mr. Rhorer's motion to establish himself as the natural and biological father of PR and for determination of parentage. Additional facts have become known since Mr. Rhorer's initial Petition was filed.

ADDITIONAL FACTS

1. On February 9, 2012, Kirk J was adjudicated not to be the father of PR born July, 2007, in judicial proceedings in the Third District Court wherein Kirk J and Kelly H raised the issue in PR's paternity. Kirk J voluntarily participated in and stipulated to DNA genetic testing to excluded himself as the father of PR. This adjudication was prior to filing the action of divorce. Copies of the relevant Orders are attached as Exhibit 1.

2. On June 16, 2010, Jody Rhorer was adjudicated the father of PR in an Office of Recovery Services proceeding wherein Kelly H raised the issue of PR's paternity and participated in the adjudicative proceeding. This action was prior to filing the action for divorce. A copy of the Order is attached as Exhibit 2.

3. Both Kirk J and Kelly H have raised the issue of PR's paternity in the divorce action.

a. Verified Divorce Petition filed by Kelly H, paragraph 9.4h wherein she stated that three of her four children are not the biological children of Kirk J, one of them being the two-year-old child PR and paragraph 9.1c in which Kelly H lists Kirk J's relationship to PR as "other."

b. Kirk J in his Answer to the Verified Divorce Petition does not deny the allegations contained in the paragraphs 9.4j and 9.1c and therefore admitted the same.

c. Kirk J's Answer to the Verified Divorce Petition, paragraph 7 in reference to paragraph 12 of the Verified Divorce Petition, Kirk J stated public assistance provided to Kelly H was for children who were not his legal financial responsibility.

d. Neither Kirk J nor Kelly H objected to Jody Rhorer's motion to intervene in the divorce proceedings knowing that the reason of his intervention was to determine parentage of PR.

4. Jody Rhorer and Kelly H began their relationship in 2005. Kirk J and Kelly H failed to inform Mr. Rhorer that they were married. During Jody Rhorer's and Kelly H's relationship PR was conceived and born. Mr. Rhorer has stated that he signed a Voluntary Declaration of Paternity and upon knowledge and belief, his name was placed on PR's original birth certificate. Jody Rhorer, in reliance on Kelly H's and Kirk J's conduct, believed that he had established paternity by signing a Voluntary Declaration of Paternity.

5. At the Juvenile Court on November 6, 2008, Kirk J and Kelly H were present. Jody Rhorer was not present as he had not been served with the Petition. Jody Rhorer was identified as the father of PR. Neither Kirk J nor Kelly H told the court they were married, nor did they tell the court that Kirk J was the presumed father of PR. Two other children, one of whom Kelly H acknowledged was not fathered by Kirk J, were placed with Kirk J; PR was placed with her paternal grandmother, Georgia Rhorer. A woman who identified herself as Kim J told the court that she was "stepmother" to the two other children.

6. The Juvenile Court records show that Mr. Rhorer was told by Judge V to establish paternity of PR and was ordered to submit to DNA genetic testing. Mr. Rhorer could not afford to hire counsel for the purpose until late 2009. On February 15, 2010, an Order was entered in the Third District Court declaring Mr. Rhorer the father of PR. This Decree of Parentage has been lodged with this Court.

7. On February 16, 2010, the Juvenile Court was informed that Kirk J and Kelly H were married. This information was given to the court by Ms. Nickels, the attorney for the State of Utah, after Mr. Rhorer had established paternity in Third District Court on February 15, 2010. The Permanency Order has been lodged with this Court.

8. Jody Rhorer and Kelly H were living together in a relationship as a couple and were cohabiting in Oregon during the time of PR's conception and continued to live together as a couple in Salt Lake City after PR's birth. Kirk J resided in Utah at the time of PR's conception.

ARGUMENT
Kirk J has disestablished paternity of PR and therefore there is not presumption to rebut

U.C.A. 78B-15-6-07(1) states,

Paternity of a child conceived or born during a marriage with a presumed father as described in Subsection 78B-15-204(1) may be raised by the presumed father or the mother at any time prior to filing an action for divorce or in the pleading at the time of the divorce of the parents.

Section (4) states: There is no presumption if the presumed father was properly served and there has been a final adjudication of the issue. Pursuant to an ORS action initiated by Kelly H, Kirk J raised the issue of paternity of PR and voluntarily submitted to DNA genetic testing to disestablish paternity. He was properly served with notice and an opportunity to object to the findings. He did not object and a final adjudication of the issue was entered before the divorce proceedings were filed. Kelly H was given notice and never objected to the order. Kirk J was successful in disputing his presumption of paternity. Kirk J is no longer the presumed father. Jody Rhorer is entitled to establish paternity of PR.

Kirk J could have acknowledged his paternity of PR and avoided the genetic testing to exclude himself as her father; however, he stipulated to undergo a genetic DNA test to exclude himself as her father, and was successful in his efforts. Kirk J has disestablished paternity of PR. The best interest of the child, as well as public policy, requires that Jody Rhorer be allowed to establish paternity.

On November 21, 2012, Kelly H filed for divorce from Kirk J and a bifurcated divorce was granted on September 27, 2013. They allowed Jody Rhorer to Intervene for the express purpose of establishing paternity. The legislative intent to limit standing to the presumed father and mother was to prevent the marriage from being attacked by an outsider and to preserve an intact marriage. Kirk J and Kelly H did not have an intact marriage.

The parties have agreed to allow Jody Rhorer to establish parentage

Kirk J and Kelly H agreed that Jody Rhorer could establish his paternity of PR. They did not object to his motion to intervene.

In *R.P. v. K.S.W. and D.R.W.*, the Utah Court of Appeals states:
that under this construction of Section 607, the presumed father or the
mother can, as a practical matter, determine whether to allow an alleged
father to be adjudicated as the child's parent and to have a role in the child's life.
Kirk J and Kelly H waived their challenge to Mr. Rhorer's intervention to
establish parentage of PR and are estopped from challenging the intervention at this time.

The State is unconstitutional as applied to Jody Rhorer

The action of Kirk J and Kelly H, for all intents and purposes, were those of persons who were not married to each other. The facts in the recent case of *R.P. v. K.S.W. and D.R.W.* are different for the facts in this case. In the case at hand, Mr. Rhorer and Kelly H did not have an affair; rather, they were in an established, committed relationship. At the time PR was conceived and born they had been living together for two years. Kirk J had been living with another woman who had taken his last name, Kim J, during that period of time. As evidenced by the Disposition Order dated April 27, 2012, lodged with this court, Jill C appeared in the 2012 Juvenile Court hearings and identified herself as Kirk's girlfriend. They stated to the court that they have a child together.

Kirk J and Kelly H were married on paper only. Kelly H has filed for many protective orders against men with whom she has resided during her marriage to Kirk J and she has filed paternity lawsuits against the men who fathered her children while she was legally married to Kirk J. For instance, the father of a child born to Kelly H, BS, is referred to as the child of Brock S; however, after Kelly H filed a paternity lawsuit against Brock S the ORS became involved and based on DNA testing it was determined that another man is the biological father of the child, BS. Xchange documents evidencing the criminal and protective order histories of the parties are being lodged with this Court.

The legislature did not contemplate the nature of the relationship between Kirk J and Kelly H when it enacted the Utah Uniform Parentage Act and 798B-15-607 with its limitations to the presumptive father and mother. The Utah Court of Appeals decision in *R.P. v. K.S.W. and D.R.W.*, 2014 UT App. 38 did not address whether the UUPA applies to the type of relationship that exists between Kirk J and Kelly H where there was not an intact marriage to preserve, nor when the presumed father was not continuously in the child's life. The decision does not address the facts in the case at hand when the presumed father and mother have deliberately withheld their marital status from the biological father and the Courts.

The limitations on standing in Section 607 of the UUPA are unconstitutional as applied to Jody Rhorer and others similarly situated. In the recent case *R.P. v. K.S.W. and D.R.W.*, 2014 UT App. 38, the biological father did not have an established relationship with the child. In this case, Jody Rhorer and PR have had a relationship since she was born. He was allowed and encouraged by Kelly H and Kirk J to establish a loving relationship with PR and in fact, he and PR have a close and loving bond.

The purpose for limiting standing to the presumed father and mother is to keep a marriage intact and to prevent a disruption to the child. If PR's life was disrupted it was when she was given to Kirk J in 2012 and when Kirk J refused to allow continued visitation with Jody Rhorer in 2013. The Juvenile Court records reflect that PR had difficulty transitioning to Kirk's home. Also, the records reflect that she had difficulty in the afternoons and evening and that she had difficulty sleeping. The recording to the February 28, 2012, Juvenile Court hearing in which this is addressed is being lodged with this Court.

The Utah Uniform Parentage Act and Section 607 are unconstitutional as it deprives Jody Rhorer of his due process under the law. When Jody Rhorer established paternity in January, 2010, he still believed that Kelly H was not married. Kirk and Kelly then came forward about their marital status and claimed that Kirk J was the presumptive father. The statute is unconstitutional as it applies to the type of marital arrangement between Kirk J and Kelly H. By her own admission, four of her five children born inside the marriage were fathered by men other than Kirk J.

Kelly H and Jody Rhorer began their relationship in 2005, at which time Kelly had given birth to one child who was fathered by a man other than Kirk J; Kelly H did not adopt Kirk J's surname name as her own, she has not listed Kirk J's address as her own and she has had many relationships and multiple children fathered by other men. The public policy noted by the legislature in limiting challenges to paternity to the presumed father and mother is not applicable in the present case. To allow Kirk J to invoke the "presumptive father" status in this case is to fly in the face of the legislative intent to keep marriages "intact." This was never an intact marriage.

The statute is unconstitutional in that it deprives an unmarried biological father from establishing paternity when he had been the child's only father for the first several years of the child's life and when the child did not have a relationship with the presumed father, and when the parties to a marriage failed to disclose the existence of a presumed father. The statute violates Jody Rhorer's substantive and procedural due process rights. The statute is unconstitutional as applied to Jody Rhorer inasmuch as both Kirk and Kelly have acquiesced to his establishing his paternity of PR.

It is in the best interest of the child for Jody Rhorer to have custody of PR

The following sets forth reasons why it is in the best interest of PR that custody be awarded to Jody Rhorer:

1. Jody Rhorer and his family members have had a close and loving relationship with PR since she was born.
2. Jody Rhorer has created a safe and stable environment for PR.
3. On June 11, 2013, the Juvenile Court order that visitation with PR and Kelly H be supervised by a licensed professional visitation supervisory business; however, the parties have failed to file this order with this Court in these proceedings and upon information and belief they have violated the order. A copy of the Order on Pretrial Hearing is attached. On September 10, 2013, the Juvenile Court ordered that the visitation remain the same. The minute entry is attached.
4. On April 12, 2012, the Juvenile Court ordered that Kirk J is not to have persons with criminal convictions, alcohol or domestic violence in the home, but upon information and belief he has violated that provision. The minute entry is attached hereto.
5. There has been domestic violence in Kirk J's home with Kelly H.
6. Kirk J and Kelly H have lifestyles and family members and associates who are potentially dangerous to PR:
a. RB, Kelly's stepbrother, was convicted of forcible sodomy and is a registered sex offender. Kelly H has lived with him and allowed him to babysit PR. Kirk J has allowed the children to interact with him.
b. DJ, Kirk's father, was charged with Obscene Acts, Public Intoxication, Forgery and Drug Possession. He has lived with Kirk J and has been allowed to babysit the children, including PR;
c. Jill C's husband, KC, was convicted of Attempted Unlawful Sex Activity with a Minor in 1996. He has also had charges of domestic violence, assault, and Protective Orders.
7. Kirk J and Jill C have had drinking and substance abuse allegations against them and have been charged with crimes involving drugs and alcohol and violent behavior.
8. On February 28, 2012, the Juvenile Court heard testimony of a DCFS investigation which showed that PR had a vaginal fungal infection. This recording is being lodged with the Court.
9. At the Juvenile Court hearing on February 28, 2012, a DCFS worker who interviewed PR stated that PR told her she had played a "peeking game" with persons named "Anthony" and "Michael." The worker stated that when questioned further PR said that she didn't want to talk about it, that is was scary to her. "Anthony" was identified as a friend of the sex offender who had baby sat the child. The worker told the court that PR referred to "Anthony" as her "boyfriend." The safety and wellbeing of PR is at issue and Jody Rhorer is able to provide a safe and stable home for his daughter.

WHEREFORE, Jody Rhorer prays the Court to enter an order that Kirk J has disestablished paternity of PR, that Jody Rhorer is the father of PR and award him custody.

APRIL 24TH, 2014: AFFIDAVIT OF JODY RHORER, filed by Nancy S, Commissioner Bloom residing

Comes now Jody Rhorer and swears and states as follows:

1. It is my belief that after PR was born, I signed a Voluntary Declaration of Paternity and that my name was placed on my daughter's birth certificate.

2. I was told by Judge V in the Juvenile Court to establish paternity of PR.

3. I wasn't able to afford to hire an attorney to establish paternity until 2009.

4. When I filed the paternity action in Third District Court, I believed that Kelly H was not married. The Decree of Paternity was signed on January 15, 2010.

5. In February 2010, I learned that Kelly H was married to Kirk J.

6. I was told by Judge V in Juvenile Court to dismiss the Decree of Paternity because Kelly H and Kirk J were married, so my attorney dismissed the decree.

7. In 2010 I went to the Office of Recovery Services and I took a genetic DNA test to prove that I was the biological father of PR. The results proved that I am the biological father of PR.

8. I consulted attorney JN over the course of 2011 asking if I could file to establish paternity and he told me that I would have to wait until Kelly H and Kirk J filed for divorce.

9. As soon as I learned of their divorce, I hired an attorney and filed a Motion to Intervene in order to establish my paternity of PR.

Signed Jody Rhorer

APRIL 24TH, 2014: NUMEROUS COURT LODGINGS

Jody's attorney, Nancy S, proceeded to lodge volumes of criminal records of Kirk J, Kirk's father, who had lived with him, Kirk's current live-in girlfriend, Jill C, Jill's husband whom she no longer lived with, and Kelly H's criminal records as well - totaling about 527 pages.

APRIL 25TH, 2014: EMAILS Between Connie C and Nancy S

From: Connie
To: Nancy
I noticed you lodged a CD of the juvenile Court hearing, and of course, I got the notice of lodging by email, but you can't send a CD by email. Have you mailed me a copy of the CD? If so, when was it mailed? You have filed so much stuff within days of the hearing, I fear I am not going to have time to address it, and much of it is beyond the time I have to respond.

From: Nancy
To: Connie
Hi Connie,
The CD has been mailed to you in time for the hearing. You should get it today. I believe the only things filed yesterday were copies of the court docket summary attached and Jody's affidavit, but nothing you need response to. These were filed because they were referenced in the memos previously filed. I hope that answers your concerns.
Thanks,
Nancy S

From: Connie
To: Nancy
As part of your "reply" (and only yesterday) you have lodged a constitutional challenge of the Statute. I do not find that a proper reply. That is an independent motion, and as with your other late filings which are not merely responsive to my pleadings, I have a right to reply. I would suggest you stipulate to a month continuance of the hearing and you draft a proposed motion and order.

If I must waste time with a "hurry up" response to the fillings you have produced (and I think all within five business days of the hearing) and I have to attend the hearing Tuesday to mention how hundreds of pages of exhibits AND new arguments including a constitutional challenge were served on me two business days before the hearing, I'll ask you pay my fees and I never do that. However, I feel it is entirely warranted if time is wasted because of the timing of these submissions. I have no problem with your wanting to raise the issues with the Court, but I have no intention of allowing a situation where my client's interests are sacrificed by the timing of the filing.

It is simply outlandish to expect to file your responses (with such volume) and new motions so close to the hearing date. Please advise regarding your position on this matter. It is appropriate we resolve the issue of the continuance immediately.

In response to your email, while I appreciate the additional information that the CD was mailed yesterday, it certainly does not "address my concerns" about the timing. The rules require filings be made timely before hearings, and it's not appropriate to expect me to deal with the volume of new materials you've summated in two business days before the hearing. (If the CD does in fact arrive today, it will be one business day for purposes of the CD). This is simply not reasonable. Please let me know your thoughts. Connie

From: Nancy
To: Connie
Hi Connie, Certainly, I will agree to a continuance. It is my policy to always agree to an extension of time when I'm asked for it. We should contact the court by way of conference call and set up a new date for a hearing. If you will prepare a stipulated motion for continuance, I will sign it. Thanks, Nancy S

From: Connie
To: Nancy
It dawned on me I should consult Mr. Hunt and Kelly H. I have not heard from Kelly H, but please find the attached Motion and proposed Order. Connie

From: Nancy
To: Connie
Hi Connie, The motion states that my pleadings were filed two business days before the hearing: however, they were filed April 22 and April 23. Will you please note that my pleadings were filed 4 and 5 days before the court hearing rather than two days? We can stipulate that we need more time for preparation. After that change is made you can affix my signature electronically for filing. Thanks, Nancy

From: Connie
To: Nancy
I'll modify it, but will just note it's not stipulated, ask for a continuance or in the alternative to strike all your pleadings and I'll ask for fees. The docket history is quite clear as to when these items were filed. None of it is timely, and I have attempted to avoid wasting the Court's time and be fair, but I cannot justify wasting more of my client's time. Connie

From: Nancy
To: Connie
Connie,
I have already agreed to stipulate to a continuance. I just ask that the motion state what dates my pleadings were filed. If you don't want to do that, the court can note the dates in the docket. There is enough contention between our clients, you and I should be working together amicably in this matter. - Nancy

From: Connie
To: Nancy

I agree. However, I asked you to file the order because your late filing is the cause AND because the last order I drafted, you found fault with. You told me to do it. I did it. I put in exactly that the rationale contained in my prior email, and again, you picked the order apart. I have wasted 45 minutes to an hour going back and forth with you, and then having to re-check the incorrect information you wrote me about the filing dates of your pleadings. These are my client's resources being wasted, and I cannot justify wasting his time. Connie

From: Nancy
To: Connie
Connie, I am sorry you feel that I have picked apart anything you drafted. I have a great deal of respect for you, your work and your fine reputation. Perhaps we should try to communicate better. Our goal is to have the hearing continued so that you can file responses. Let's do that. Thanks, Nancy

From: Connie
To: Nancy
The question is are you okay with the stipulation the way I phrased it previously, or would you rather I file the one I drafted after you refused to agree to the terms contained in it. As I said, I cannot justify expending any more time on something which should be simple and not controversial. Be advised that I have reached Kelly H, and she has stipulated, so if you agree to the prior form, it will be modified to the extent of including that she had been reached and she stipulates.

APRIL 26TH, 2014
From: Nancy
To: Connie
Hi Connie, I hope you're Saturday is going well. I had meetings out of the office yesterday afternoon and received your green filing notice today. I'll let the court know Monday that I don't object to the continuance. Nancy

Clearly Nancy was intimidated by Connie. I was astonished and disappointed when I found these emails in our records some months later. I recall getting a phone call from Nancy stating that our court date had been postponed for a month but she did not tell us the reason was because she cowered down to Connie, letting her walk all over her and completely forgetting that she owed us her representation and loyalty. Connie repeatedly referred to the resources and time wasted of her client, Kirk J, and threatened to ask the court for attorney fees, and yet she was not charging anything for her services. In the end, it was yet another month lost and Connie had a month to prepare for the hearing. A savvy and committed attorney would have held her ground and used the five-day filing as a strategy against the other agent - the same way Connie had used it against us.

APRIL 28TH, 2014: MOTION/STIPULATION TO CONTINUE HEARING AND REQUEST FOR CONFERENCE CALL, filed by Nancy S

PLEASE TAKE NOTICE *that the hearing previously scheduled for April 29, 2014, is continued to May 28, 2014, before Commissioner Bloom.*
Jody Rhorer, by and through counsel, Nancy S, moves the Court for an order continuing the hearing set for April 29, 2014. Nancy S, counsel for Jody Rhorer, stipulated to continue the hearing as evidenced by copies of email communication between herself and Connie, counsel for Kirk J, which are attached hereto but request the Court note the date of the filing of responses to Kirk J's motions as being four and five days to the hearing scheduled for April 29, 2014. Copies of court dockets were lodged with the Court thereafter.

Connie C, counsel for Kirk J, raised the issues presented in the case of R.P. v. K.S.W and D.R.W. which had not been decided at the time of Jody Rhorer's petition. Counsel for Jody Rhorer, in his response, addressed the issues in R.P. v. K.S.W. and D.R.W. Further, additional information vital to the matters of adjudication of parentage came to the attention of Jody Rhorer's counsel but could not be confirmed until April 22, 2014, when counsel spoke with Mr. Hunt, attorney for the State of Utah, Office of Recovery Services.

A continuance of the hearing is proper to allow Kirk J, by and through counsel, Connie, to respond to the new information and allegations presented in Jody Rhorer's response.

Nancy S, counsel for Jody Rhorer, requests a conference call to set a date for the hearing.

And so, Nancy filed the petition, just as Connie told her to. And of course, Jody was billed for it.

MAY 6TH, 2014: NOTICE OF LODGING, filed by Nancy S

Intervenor, Jody Rhorer, by and through his attorney, Nancy S, hereby lodges the following documents with the Court:

1. Deposition of Kirk J on December 15, 2011, 3rd District Court:

EXAMINATION
Q. How long have you lived at your current address?
A. Probably six years.
Q. Were you living at the address at the time of the accident?
A. Yes. It might have been like seven years.
Q. Tell me a little about your education. Did you graduate from high school?
A. Yeah.
Q. Where did you go?
A. Which time?
Q. Where did you graduate from?
A. I graduated from the prison.
Q. Okay. When did - - did you get a GED then?
A. I've got a GED and my diploma.
Q. And did you get that through - - you got that through the prison system?
A. Yeah.
Q. What years did you serve in prison?
A. It was the end of '99 through to 2001.
Q. Okay. And what were you in prison for?
A. Drugs.
Q. Possession?
A. Possession and intent. There were a few charges.
Q. Let's talk a little bit about - - have you been charged with any felonies?
A. Yes, seven.
Q. Seven felonies? Oaky. Let's go through those. What - -
A. I couldn't tell you exactly, but they all have to do with drugs, though.
Q. Okay.
A. They're mostly all possessions.
Q. How many did you serve time for in the prison system?
A. All of them.
Q. You went to prison for all of them?
A. All at one time.
Q. Okay. Are you married?
A. Yeah. Well, I'm legally separated.
Q. Who is your wife at this time?

A. Well, she's not really - - I haven't gotten a complete divorce with my wife, and I was separated with her at the time, if that's what you mean.

Q. What's her name?

A. Kelly H.

Q. When did you get married to her?

A. It was April 17, 2003, I think. It was 2002, it's 2003.

Q. When did you get legally separated from her?

A. Let's see, that would be - - I think it was 2004 or 2005.

Q. And there's been no divorce proceedings or anything like that?

A. We got a bunch of paperwork and I got - - I'm guessing what is was, was the legal separation paper.

Q. Okay. You don't know if - - could it have been a divorce?

A. No, it wasn't a complete divorce.

Q. That's fine. Do you have any children?

A. Two. I have three, two with her.

Q. So, you have two with her? What are ages?

A. Nine, ten, and a two-year-old.

Q. And you have a two-year-old? Who is the two-year-old's mother?

A. Jill C. She's current. I have six kids at home.

Q. Oh, okay. So, you live with Jill right now?

A. Yes.

Q. Okay. How long have you lived with her?

A. Three years.

Q. Do you recall what the date of the accident was that we're here talking about?

A. It was June or July - - June 31st, I think. Or June - - 2006.

Q. Okay. At that time, you lived at the same address that you do now, correct?

A. Yeah.

Q. Who were you living with at the time?

A. My brother was living there. I think Kim. Yeah, Kim, my girlfriend was living with me.

Q. Okay. Let's get into the facts of this - - Have you even seen the police report in this matter?

A. I guess against me, yeah. That would have been when I went to court.

Q. Okay. And that was for your DUI?

A. Right.

Q. Now, tell me what you were doing in the two hours prior to this accident?

A. Sitting at the bar.

Q. The bar? What bar?

A. It was a mix between Dream On and The Three Alarm.

Q. The Three Alarm?

A. Uh-huh.

Q. How long had you been at either of these establishments total?

A. It was a mix, but I couldn't tell you that. I don't' know.

Q. Would it have been more than six hours?

A. No.

Q. More than two hours?

A. Maybe more than two hours. That's not a for sure thing.

Q. So maybe between two, two to three hours, that would be a safe - -

A. Yeah.

Q. Can you give me an idea of how much alcohol you had consumed?

A. No.

Q. When you typically go out to a bar, do you have a drink of choice?

A. A couple. I like Long Islands and I like beer.

Q. On that night do you recall whether you were drinking Long Islands or beer?

A. I don't recall exactly. I'm thinking I had a Long Island and a few beers.

Q. Okay - - did you start at one bar and then move to the other?

A. We went back and forth because the one is a strip club and then the other one is a pool hall.

Q. Okay. So, you were drinking at both establishments that night?

A. Well, I had to have been at The Three Alarm to drink a Long Island, and then been at the other one because they don't sell both.

Q. So, tell me what happened after you left these establishments.

A. Well I was heading through the light and the lady to the side of me, hit the brakes...and got knocked into me...when CJ came driving up. I'm guessing that this is what he wanted to do, come in front of me like this.

Q. So, tell me what happened after your car impacted her.

A. I left the car, well, the bag burst open, and I let the car - the car died, and I let it glide because it - I just put it in neutral and let it glide off to the side of the road. I really don't know what went on between those two cars after that, because I got out and ran.

Q. Okay, tell me why you ran.

A. I wasn't thinking straight. I don't know. I really couldn't tell you. I ran to the next street then got arrested.

Q. Were you cited for a DUI?

A. Yes.

Q. What did you plead?

A. Guilty.

Q. Since this accident have you had any other DUI's?

A. Yes. One. 2008.

Q. Okay. Tell me the circumstances of that DUI.

A. I was very drunk and driving. That one, I have no freaking clue about that night. I was toast.

Q. How often...in 2006...would you frequent bars?

A. Probably once a week.

Q. Were The Three Alarm and Dream On kind of your places of choice or...

A. There are a few of them. Million Dollar, Southern Exposure, T.J.'s, that's pretty much it.

Q. Besides going to bars, did you drink at your house as well?

A. Sometimes. Probably about the same nights that I go out.

Q. So maybe once a week?

A. Yeah. A couple.

Q. Now at the time of the accident did you ever tell anybody that you weren't the one that was actually driving?

A. No. Well...I might have told the cops that that night.

Q. Tell me what your injuries were.

A. I was burned on my hand - - or my arm from the air bag.

Q. Have you been involved in any other motor vehicle accidents where you were at fault?

A. Yeah. I think it was 2002, I had one.

Q. I don't think I have anything further.

If Kirk J was in prison in from 1999 through 2001 and J1 was born in 2001, how could he possibly be his biological child?

MAY 8TH, 2014: AFFIDAVIT OF MONA RHORER, Loded by Nancy S, Commissioner Bloom presiding

Mona Rhorer, being fully sworn, and upon her oath swears and states as follows:

1. *I am Jody Rhorer's daughter and I am 19 years old.*
2. *I have known my sister Payshence all her life.*
3. *Kirk J and Kelly H have allowed me and my sisters to visit her and I have been at Kirk J's house and with Kelly H when they have had Payshence.*
4. *The last time I saw my sister was last Christmas 2013, at Kirk's house. I was also at Payshence's birthday party in July 2013, at Kirk's house and I've been at Kirk's house at other times for birthdays for the other kids. My sisters, Tina and Mia were with me. We took presents from us and from my Dad, Jody Rhorer, and gave them to Payshence. Every time I've seen her, she's asked me, "Where's Daddy?" I tell her that Daddy loves her. Last Christmas Payshence said to me, "I want to talk to Daddy." I asked Kelly if it was ok to call my Dad and let Payshence talk to him and she said it was ok, so I called and she talked to my Dad for a long time. We didn't want Kirk J to know about it because Kirk had said that he didn't want Payshence to talk to my Dad.*
5. *Whenever I've seen Payshence she wants to talk about our Dad, Jody Rhorer. She asks to see pictures of him and I show her pictures I have of our Dad on my cell phone. She always wants to talk to my Dad. She always asked about Dad and I tell her about him. I know she would recognize our Dad if she saw him now.*
6. *When I have been to Kirk J's house it was cluttered and dirty. I have seen food was all over the table and the kitchen floor, and it looked like no one had picked up after the children.*
7. *The household is chaotic. I've seen the children run around without any supervision by an adult and the children are dirty and ignored and the adults let the children cry.*
8. *I believe there are only four bedrooms in Kirk's house. One of them is a toy room. I'm not sure where my sister sleeps.*
9. *The last time I saw my sister was last Christmas 2013, at Kirk J's house. Kelly got into a screaming argument with one of the neighbors at the house and she was yelling and screaming obscenities in front of the children, including Payshence. I heard Kelly threaten the neighbor that, "You're going to get what's coming to you." The neighbor left the house.*
10. *I have seen and heard Kelly and Kirk arguing in front of the children.*
11. *I was at a birthday party for Payshence at Kirk J's house last year in July, 2013, in their backyard. There were about 15 adults and a lot of children. I saw Kirk J and Jill C, his girlfriend, drinking beer. There were alcohol bottles in the kitchen. There were lots of other people drinking in front of the kids and were always a lot of pregnant women at his house.*
12. *I know who RB (the convicted sex offender) is because I've seen him with Kelly many times in the past. He was at my sister's birthday party at Kirk J's house. I also saw RB at Kirk's house at a barbecue for BS's (Payshence's younger half- brother) birthday and a party the year before where there were a lot of children, including my sister. There was a lot of drinking at those parties. My sister and other children were at those parties.*
13. *I have seen Kelly's sister with Kelly many times and I know she has a criminal history and has been involved in using drugs. She was at my sister's birthday party. I have also seen many photos of her sister's daughter and Payshence together on Kelly's Facebook page.*
  Signed by Mona Rhorer

Out of the blue, without our consent, and for reasons unknown and without merit, our own attorney filed Jody's criminal history. It had not been ordered by the court or even requested by anyone to our knowledge.

MAY 12TH, 2014: NOTICE OF LODGING, filed by Nancy S, Commissioner Bloom presiding

Intervenor, Jody Rhorer, by and through his attorney, Nancy S, hereby lodges the following documents with the Court:

1. *Court dockets from Xchange regarding Jody Rhorer.*
*Intervenor lodges these documents **in the interest of Justice**. Since Intervenor previously lodged the Petitioner, Respondent and other's Xchange dockets, Intervenor believes it is fair and appropriate to lodge his as well.*

Had we been aware of this motion at the time it was filed, we would have fired Nancy on the spot. For a week she had sent Jody to five counties gathering every police report in his existence all the way back to a fix-it ticket when he was 16 for a broken car taillight.

We weren't sure what the purpose of this was but certainly Jody wouldn't have taken so much time from work to gather documents that his own attorney planned to turn over to the court all in the name of being "fair and appropriate!" When was Connie ever fair and appropriate?

The reason Nancy gave us for needing the records was to "be prepared" in the event Connie brought them up. We were not privy to this filing until I found it among the records I recovered from her office months after we terminated her (spoiler alert!). All the attorneys we hired were given specific instructions to copy us on all filings. I often had an underlying feeling that Nancy doubted Jody and was secretly searching for something - the same way she was searching for a motive behind Kirk's possession of other men's children. She had developed an entire conspiracy theory and now seemed to be looking at Jody and I as well.

MAY 14TH, 2014: MOTION FOR APPOINTMENT OF GUARDIAN AD LITEM, filed by Nancy S, Commissioner Bloom presiding

Intervenor, Jody Rhorer, by and through counsel, Nancy S, hereby moves the court to appoint a private Guardian ad Litem for the minor child PR inasmuch as issues of child custody and parent-time visitation are in dispute in this matter. Further, the Juvenile Court has terminated jurisdiction, and therefore it is in the best interest of the child to be represented by a Guardian ad Litem in this matter. The Intervenor moves for an order that the private Guardian ad Litem be appointed by the Office of GAL and that the court assess the fees and costs against the parties in a proportion the court determines to be just, and designate the payment to the GAL in accordance with the provisions of U.C.A. 78A-2-228.

MAY 21ST, 2014: INTERVENOR'S FIRST SET OF REQUESTS FOR ADMISSIONS TO RESPONDENT KIRK J, filed by Nancy S, Commissioner Bloom presiding

Pursuant to Rule 36 of the Utah Rules of Civil Procedure, Intervenor submits the following Request for Admissions to Respondent, Kirk J. Responses must be served upon the undersigned counsel for the Intervenor within 30 days after service of these requests. PLEASE TAKE NOTICE THAT ALL THE MATTERS IN THESE REQUESTS SHALL BE DEEMED ADMITTED PURSUANT TO RULE 36 OF THE UTAH RULES OF CIVIL PROCEDURE UNLESS A RESPONSE IS SUBMITTED WITHIN 30 DAYS AFTER SERVICE OF THIS REQUEST.

REQUEST NO. 1: *Admit that on October 2, 2013, the Unified Police Department was dispatched to your residence.*

REQUEST NO. 2: *Admit that Unified Police Department investigated an incident that occurred at your home on October 2, 2013.*

REQUEST NO. 3: *Admit that the incident on October 2, 2013, involved alleged domestic violence.*

REQUEST NO. 4: *Admit that the incident on October 2, 2013, involved yourself, Jill C, and her minor children.*

REQUEST NO. 5: *Admit that the minor children alleged that on October 2, 2013, you physically grabbed the male, age 16, by the neck and pinned him against the wall and started to strangle him and further, that you then pushed him into the garage.*

REQUEST NO. 6: *Admit that on the date of this incident, October 2, 2013, you had been drinking alcohol.*

REQUEST NO. 7: *Admit that on October 2, 2013, you witnessed Jill C slap the minor male across the face.*

REQUEST NO. 8: *Admit that after the alleged incident on October 2, 2013, Jill C's two minor children ran away from home.*

REQUEST NO. 9: *Admit that the two children called the police to report the incident.*

REQUEST NO. 10: *Admit that during the investigation of the incident on October 2, 2013, both of the minor children informed the police that they had suicidal thoughts because they couldn't stand living at the house with you and their mother.*

REQUEST NO. 11: *Admit that on October 2, 2013, the minor children were transported to Pioneer Valley Hospital as a result of their statements of suicidal thoughts.*

REQUEST NO. 12: *Admit that during the investigation of the incident on October 2, 2013, the minor male child stated he did not want to live in the house with you and his mother because of the fighting and drinking in the home.*

REQUEST NO. 13: *Admit that on July 31, 2012, the minor child Payshence Rhorer, was placed in your custody and guardianship in a Juvenile Court action.*

REQUEST NO. 14: *Admit that on April 12, 2012, the Juvenile Court ordered that any extended visits between yourself and Payshence was conditioned upon there being no drinking of alcohol in your home.*

REQUEST NO. 15: *Admit that on April 12, 2012, the Juvenile Court ordered that any extended visits between yourself and Payshence was conditioned upon there being no domestic violence in your home.*

REQUEST NO. 17: *Admit that on June 11, 2013, the Juvenile Court ordered that the Petitioner, Kelly H, could have visits with PR but only if visitation was supervised by a licensed professional visitation supervisory business.*

REQUEST NO. 18: *Admit that the Juvenile Court order referenced in the next preceding Request has not been changed and remains in full force and effect.*

REQUEST NO. 19: *Admit that you have allowed Kelly H, to have visitation with PR without supervision by a licensed professional visitation supervisory business.*

REQUEST NO. 20: *Admit that since PR was placed in your custody and guardianship on July 2012, you have not provided counseling for PR.*

REQUEST NO. 21: *Admit that on June 29, 2013, Unified Police Department was dispatched to your residence.*

REQUEST NO. 22: *Admit that on June 29, 2013, Unified Police Department investigated an alleged domestic violence assault involving yourself and Jill C.*

REQUEST NO. 23: *Admit that on June 29, 2013, you had been drinking alcohol.*

REQUEST NO. 24: *Admit that on June 29, 2013, you were issued a citation for "Assault, Domestic Violence."*

REQUEST NO. 25: *Admit that on January 6, 2013, UPD was dispatched to your residence.*

REQUEST NO. 26: *Admit that on January 6, 2013, UPD investigated a report of Domestic Violence at your residence.*

REQUEST NO. 27: *Admit that on January 6, 2013, the Petitioner, Kelly H and Shane S were at your residence.*

REQUEST NO. 28: *Admit that on January 6, 2013, domestic violence took place at your residence which was witnessed by PR and the other minor children in your household.*

REQUEST NO. 29: *Admit that as a result of the incident of, you requested a protective order against Kelly H.*

REQUEST NO. 30: *Admit that convicted child molester, RB, has been at your home.*

REQUEST NO. 31: *Admit that your father (convicted sex offender), has been the caretaker of PR.*

REQUEST NO. 32: *Admit that Jill C's husband, a convicted sex offender, has been to your home.*

MAY 21ST, 2014: KIRK J'S RESPONSE TO INTERVENORS MOTION REGARDING CONSTITUTIONALITY OF STATUTE, filed by Connie C, Commissioner Bloom presiding

Comes now, Connie C, on behalf of Kirk J, and files the foregoing Response to the Motion of Intervenor Jody Rhorer's Motion Regarding the Constitutionality as applied to him.

Mr. Rhorer's Constitutional argument is stated thusly, "[t]he Utah Uniform Parentage Act and Section 607 are unconstitutional as it deprives Jody Rhorer of his due process under the law." The Memorandum also asserts that the statute violates Mr. Rhorer's "substantive and procedural" due process rights. However, no analysis of which the procedural or substantive rights is offered.

Mr. Rhorer's argument seems to center on his assertion that he did not know Kelly H was married to Kirk J when he impregnated her. He also seems to suggest that the Utah Legislature intended, and the Courts had suggested that "degrees of marriage" are to be treated differently in Utah, with disparate protections granted to collateral attacks to paternity of issue of the marriage based on whether the union is cohesive and obviously intact or whether the spouses are separated and/or ignoring their wedding vows related to sexual fidelity. While the concept advanced by Mr. Rhorer is an interesting one, neither his procedural or substantive due process claims are sufficiently supported such that this Court could entertain them.

Mr. Rhorer has offered no support to be found in the statutes to suggest that the Legislature intended men knowingly sleeping with a married woman to be treated differently than men sleeping with a married woman through inadvertence, simple ignorance, or even trickery or deceit on the part of the adulteress. To the contrary, in that the Uniform Parentage Act provides standing to contest parentage only to the married woman and the married man (even when it comes to divorce proceedings). In doing so, the Legislature clearly signaled that the family unit, the familial relations between legal father, mother, and children would be paramount. The 'biological father' procreating with a married woman is relegated to a position where his 'rights' if any, are subservient to the parties of the marriage.

Accordingly, the statutory scheme as a whole suggests it is the legal marital relationship, and specifically, the cohesiveness and continued affiliation of the issues of the marriage which is to be ensured. Likewise, while the Legislature no doubt could have included a provision granting standing to challenge paternity to a man who could demonstrate he was unaware that the woman he impregnated was married to someone else, it did not include such a provision.

The statutes as a whole support the proposition that the Legislature intended that unmarried persons having sex are to be treated harshly. For example, the Utah State Code still criminalizes 'fornication.' 'Any unmarried person who shall voluntarily engage in sexual intercourse with another is guilty of fornication. Adultery, a married person having sex with someone other than his or her spouse, is also criminalized.' Both of the above-referenced provisions are found under the subtitle 'offense against the family.' The Legislature viewed the described conduit (which both Mr. Rhorer and Kelly H engaged in in this case, which ultimately produced PR during Kelly H's marriage to Kirk J as an affront to the family, not conduct which should be protected in any way, shape, or form.

Accordingly, even looking at the broader context of statutes including the criminal code, it is apparent that the Legislature intended to communicate the community's disdain and disagreement with sex between unmarried people, and support of the legal marriage, and the legal relationships that are born of legal marriages.

Because Mr. Rhorer's position related to constitutionality of the paternity statutes as applied to him have not been adequately supported and because review of the paternity statutes and criminal code regarding unmarried sex and sex outside marriage argue that the Legislature intended no protections, Mr. Rhorer's constitutional argument cannot be maintained.

MAY 21ST, 2014:   MOTION TO STRIKE LODGED DOCUMENTS, filed by Connie C, Commissioner Bloom residing

Comes now, Connie C, on behalf of Kirk J, and pursuant to Rule 10(h) of the Utah Rules of Civil Procedure, files the foregoing Motion to Strike the following enumerated documents lodged by the Intervenor, Jody Rhorer. Grounds and reasons are stated below:
(1) Notice of Lodging: Kelly H, Volumes I, II, III, filed April 24th, 2014
(2) Notice of Lodging: Kirk J, Volume I, filed April 24th, 201
(3) Notice of Lodging: Jill's husband, KC, filed April 24th, 2014
(4) Notice of Lodging: Jill C, Volumes I, and II, filed April 24th, 2014
(5) Notice of Lodging: Kirk's dad, DJ, filed April 24th, 2014
(6) Notice of Lodging: Juvenile Court CD, filed April 24th, 2014
(7) Notice of Lodging: Kirk J's Deposition, filed May 6th, 2014
(8) Affidavit of Mona Rhorer, filed May 8th, 2014
(8) Notice of Lodging: Jody Rhorer, filed May 12th, 2014

DISCUSSION

The court may strike and disregard all or any part of a pleading or other paper that contains redundant, immaterial, impertinent or scandalous matter. The last Order in this matter incites that the Court invited an investigation of the juvenile court file regarding PR, and ordered that, 'any relevant orders be lodged with the court.'

None of the above-referenced materials lodged by Mr. Rhorer, as listed above are orders, as called for in the Court's prior Order regarding what was to be lodged with the Court to assist it in deciding the issues pending. Items 1 through 5 and 8 are docket histories [not Orders] regarding Kirk J, Kelly H, Mr. Rhorer, and three other persons. The deposition, number seven is unrelated and seemingly immaterial. Item number eight is testimonial, and even if the Court found the content relevant to any issues in this case, it is not associated with any motion, and should not be considered by the Court unless entered by sworn testimony, with Kirk J having the opportunity to cross-examine.

None of the materials provided are relevant or helpful to the Court in determining the legal paternity issue which is before the Court. Kirk J conjectures that the voluminous materials have been offered to obfuscate the primary legal issue the court must make, i.e., whether Mr. Rhorer has standing in this matter, and more specifically, legal paternity of PR. Alternatively, it appears that Mr. Rhorer has presumed through 'lodging' materials that should only be considered as part of a contested trial (should the court even determine that one should be held). Mr. Rhorer may not advance to a fact-finding phase without establishing that he even has standing. Further, he may not side step the Rules of Evidence by simply submitting documents to the Court for consideration.

Whether the submitted materials would pass muster of the Rules of Evidence must be left for another day. Mr. Rhorer may not obtain preemptive consideration of these matters without establishing that he is even eligible to contest legal paternity in this matter. Nor should the court permit Mr. Rhorer's 'bootstrapping' any argument regarding legal paternity by inundating the Court with irrelevant materials designed to 'smear' and denigrate the character and reputation of others.

CONCLUSION

Because Mr. Rhorer has not demonstrated that he has standing to contest legal paternity in this matter, the Court's consideration of any matters that could only go to a custody determination is premature and inappropriate. Accordingly, Mr. Jacobsen prays the Court strike the above-enumerated Lodged materials.

MAY 21ST, 2014:   KIRK J'S REPLY TO INTERVENOR JODY RHORER'S REPLY IN OPPOSITION REGARDING PATERNITY DETERMINATION, filed by Connie C, Commissioner Bloom presiding

Comes now, Connie C, Attorney at Law, files the foregoing Reply to Jody Rhorer's Reply to Kirk J's Opposition to Mr. Rhorer's Motions to Establish him as 'biological father."

FACTS

(1) Kirk J did nothing to institute a 'disestablishment of paternity' case as alleged in Mr. Rhorer's pleadings. Rather, the Office of Recovery Services filed a matter related to PR, in which Mr. Jacobsen filed an answer indicating he 'disagreed with everything' in the pleading. Kirk J's reply, filed contemporaneous herewith, and incorporated in this pleading by reference.

(2) Kirk J never agreed or acquiesced in any attempts by Jody Rhorer to attempt to establish his paternity of PR.

(3) Mr. Rhorer has failed to provide any evidence of a Voluntary Declaration of Paternity regarding PR, Kirk J, as presumed legal father of PR, by virtue of his marriage to Kelly H would have to have signed same to make the same legally effective, and Kirk J did not sign such a document, nor would he have agreed to sign such document.

(4) ORS maintained separate actions and obtained DNA testing on both Jody Rhorer and Kirk J in separate actions, and never inquired of Kirk J whether he intended to stand on his legal presumption of paternity of PR arising from his marriage to Kelly H.

(5) Despite Jody Rhorer's protestations that he has 'established paternity' of PR and despite ORS's activities related to him, he has paid no child support in the years Kirk J has had permanent custody and guardianship of PR.

DISCUSSION

Mr. Rhorer's claim that Kirk J sought to disestablish paternity of PR through an ORS action cannot be supported. Rather, ORS started the proceeding on behalf of the State and in the name of Kelly H. ORS requested the DNA test without any explanation as to what it would seek to do with the results. ORS (through a different attorney) also conducted another case regarding Mr. Rhorer regarding PR without noticing Kirk J. Therefore, full determination of the issues, including Kirk J's reliance on his martial presumption of paternity was never had in any ORS proceeding. ORS is not entitled to simply disregard a martial presumption of paternity irrespective of DNA testing results.

The Juvenile Court, knowing of Mr. Rhorer's biological paternity nonetheless issued an adjudication Order which establishes Kirk J as legal father of PR. That Order of a court of competent jurisdiction in this State is entitled to full faith and credit. Mr. Rhorer has demonstrated that time and again, he has attempted to 'establish paternity' in an attempt to thwart Kirk J's marital presumption of paternity by failing to notify Kirk J of his paternity action and by his own admission attempting an unlawful voluntary relinquishment through the Office of Vital Statistics. His styling of Kirk J's initial lack of objection to Mr. Rhorer's intervention in the divorce as an acquiescence to his attempts to establish paternity, when the same has been adjudicated by the Juvenile Court is more of the same.

CONCLUSION

Mr. Rhorer's assertions as to what he knew when about Kelly H's marriage, his protestations that PR knows him as father, et cetera and so on have no legal effect. Nor does the fact that he happens to be the biological father of PR. Kirk J had a legal presumption of paternity by virtue of his marriage to Kelly H during the time of the child's conception and birth. Judge V, the only tribunal who had all individuals to this contest before it, Kelly H, Mr. Rhorer, and Kirk J, and having been made aware of Mr. Rhorer's biological parentage of PR and Kirk J's marital presumption of parentage of PR issued an adjudication order establishing Kirk J as father of PR. This Court is not at liberty to ignore that Order of Parentage for any reason.

Further, the Uniform Parentage Act is clear that this Court may undertake decision regarding parentage if and when husband or wife call into issues parentage. Mr. Rhorer's argument that because it has been merely mentioned in pleadings that Kirk J is not biological is insufficient as a matter of law to bring parentage into question such that Mr. Rhorer may attempt to establish paternity. Kelly H has indicated at hearing she has no desire to open the issue to Mr. Rhorer.

WHEREFORE, Kirk J prays the Court deny all Mr. Rhorer's Motions and rescind the Order allowing Mr. Rhorer to intervene.

EXHIBIT 1
KIRK J'S ANSWER TO ORS AND KELLY H VS. KIRK J

"7-11-11
To whom it may concern,
    I am writing this complaint to the summons. For Civil Case with Judge Quin, between ORS & Kelly H vs. Kirk J. I disagree with the information and this is my 2nd response to this matter. 1st I filed at West Jordan UT court. Kirk J"

MAY 21ST, 2014: KIRK J'S RESPONSE TO INTERVENORS MOTION TO APPOINT GUARDIAN AD LITEM, filed by Connie, Commissioner Bloom presiding

Comes now, Connie, Attorney at Law, and files the foregoing Response to Jody Rhorer's Motion to Appoint a GAL in this matter. Initially, Kirk J avers that Mr. Rhorer has no standing to move for appointment of GAL in Kirk J and Kelly H's divorce action. Moreover, the statute that allows for Appointment of a Guardian ad Litem provides that the District Court may make such an appointment if abuse or neglect has been formally alleged, and that the alleged abuse has been reported to child protective services (along with other requirements).

No neglect or abuse has been alleged in this case. Rather, Mr. Rhorer wishes to have the GAL participate in his fourth attempt at avoiding Kirk J's legal parentage of the minor child PR.

CONCLUSION
Because that statute does not allow for appointment of a Guardian ad Litem regarding an issue to settle paternity, the Court must deny the Motion.

MAY 22ND, 2014: INTERVENOR'S RESPONSE TO MOTION TO STRIKE LODGED DOCUMENTS, filed by Nancy S, Commissioner Bloom presiding

Intervenor hereby objects to the Respondent's Motion to Strike Lodged Documents for the following reasons:
1. The deposition of Kirk J taken under oath on December 15, 2011, will show by his admissions that he and Petitioner did not live together after their marriage ceremony, that he cohabited with and had children by more than one woman after his marriage ceremony with Petitioner, and that Kirk J did not consider the minor child, PR, as his own child and that PR did not reside with him in his household. The date of the deposition is relevant in that PR did not reside with him in his household. The date of the deposition is relevant in that the statements made by Kirk J were made three months after he stipulated to submit to DNA testing to disprove his paternity of PR and goes to his intent to disprove paternity and his belief that he had, in fact, disestablished paternity.

2. The court dockets and Affidavit of Mona Rhorer will assist the Court in determining the best interest of the child in the matters of custody and visitation, and the dockets show evidence of the parties' criminal histories and patterns of behavior, as well as histories and behaviors of family members and others in their households.

3. The information in the documents are evidence that the relationship between Petitioner and Respondent is contrary to a marriage relationship and as such, is not a marriage contemplated as protected by the Utah Parentage Act.

     WHEREFORE, Intervenor prays that the Court denies the Respondent's Motion to Strike Lodged Documents and for further relief as the Court deems just and proper.

     MAY 27TH, 2014: MOTION FOR ORDER FOR DCFS INVESTIGATION, filed by Nancy S, Commissioner Bloom presiding

     Jody Rhorer, by and through counsel Nancy S, hereby moves the court pursuant to U.C.A. 30-3-5.2 for an Order that the State of Utah, Division of Child and Family Services investigate allegations of child abuse of the minor children of the parties, including PR, and alleges that an investigation will aid the court in determining the best interest of the children, including PR. Since July 2012, the minor child has lived in the home of Kirk J.
     1. The attached 14 police reports show the numerous complaints of domestic violence at Kirk J's home, the violent acts of Kelly H, Kirk J, and Jill C in front of the children; the danger to the older children in the home causing them to report 'suicidal thoughts' because they can't stand living in Kirk J's home due to his habitual intoxication, the physical altercations between the parties involving the minor children, including PR, or witnessed by the minor children, the loud and disturbing arguments between and among the parties that were reported by neighbors, the violent destruction of property in front of the children, and physical injury to the children caused by the parties' violence.
     The reports of domestic violence at this address and involving the parties go back to 2005. The reports in 2008 and 2009 involve Kirk J's former live-in girlfriend, Kim, and show that Kirk has been habitually physically abusive. The police reports show a continuing pattern of behavior and abuse perpetrated by Kirk J, Kelly H, and Jill C. This abuse has either been witnessed by or has involved the children, including PR.
     2. The court dockets previously lodged with the court evidence that as recently as February 2014, Kirk J was charged with crimes involving alcohol. The police reports, Facebook photos, and the Affidavit of Mona Rhorer evidence that Kirk J has alcohol at his home, in direct violation of the Juvenile Court's order at the time he was awarded custody and guardianship of PR.
     3. The CD of the Juvenile Court proceedings lodged with the Court in which Judge V was told that a doctor diagnosed the minor child, PR, with a vaginal fungal infection and that PR said she was forced to play a 'peeking game' that she didn't want to talk about and that scared her, and further, that the game was played by men named "Anthony" and "Mike" who were identified as friends of RB, Kelly H's stepbrother who is a convicted sex offender, and whom Kelly H allowed to babysit PR. When Kirk was awarded custody and guardianship of PR one of the conditions was that he provide counseling for PR; however, he has failed to do so according to Kelly H's statements made to this court in a hearing on December 20, 2012. Kirk J has not provided any proof that he has complied with the court order.
     4. Kirk J's award of custody and guardianship of PR was conditioned upon Kelly H having visitation with PR only in a professional supervised visitation facility. Facebook pages show that Kirk J allows Kelly H to have unsupervised visits in violation of the court's order.
     5. Kirk J's award of custody and guardianship of PR was conditioned upon his not having in his home people who endangered PR. The police reports, as well as the Affidavit of Mona Rhorer, show that Kirk J has violated the court's order.
     6. Kirk J, Kelly H, and Jill C have associated with known sex offenders and individuals who have been charged and convicted of sex crimes, and they have allowed these individuals to be in contact with the minor children, including PR. Kirk J has allowed his father to babysit the children as evidenced in the Juvenile Court proceedings; RB has been seen at Kirk J's home in the presence of the minor children, including PR, on several occasions by Mona Rhorer; Jill C's current husband also has access to the minor children.
     7. The older minor children in Kirk J's home are allowed to have access to RB as 'friends' on Facebook.
     8. Kelly H's Facebook postings show that the children are exposed to alcohol. Particularly, the photo of a child drinking from a beer bottle with Kelly's caption, "Wish he had a cold one." PR's photo was included on the post as being with Kelly H at the same time.
     9. Jill C's Facebook page shows she is aligned with 'Mothers for Marijuana International.'
     Witnesses have given information regarding their observation and involvement at the home regarding Kirk J and Kelly H to support the motion; however, these witnesses have stated that they are afraid to testify in court or for their identities to become known because they are afraid of retaliation by Kirk J and/or Shane S, Kelly H's current husband.
     WHEREFORE, Jody Rhorer moves the court for an order for a DCFS investigation, or in the alternative for an evidentiary hearing so that evidence may be submitted and testimony may be heard by the court in ordering a DCFS investigation.

Many police reports were submitted as attachments to this Motion containing domestic violence and intoxication of Kirk, Jill, and Kelly. The extra month allotted to Connie by Nancy resulted in nothing more than motions to strike all of our court submissions.

MAY 28TH, 2014 - Court was held today. We were in session for nearly 2 hours. The judge needed time to review the documents issued to the court before she rendered her decision. We are impatiently waiting.

MAY 30TH, 2014 - Jody got a call today from Tina. Payshence had Kelly's phone and found her number. She wanted to know where her Daddy was. Tina said that he wasn't there with her but maybe Payshence could call him on his phone. Tina called and told Jody then called Kelly back to see if Payshence could call him. Kelly was not aware that Payshence had used her phone to try to find her Daddy and would not let her speak to him. Jody nearly cried with sadness and happiness at the same time knowing his little darling was looking for him.

JUNE 2ND, 2014: AFFIDAVIT OF WENDY C, filed by Nancy S, Commissioner Bloom presiding

Intervenor, Jody Rhorer, by and through his attorney, requests that this Court accept the Intervenor's submission of the Affidavit of Wendy C and the birth certificate of PR, the minor child, which are attached hereto. Commissioner Bloom asked counsel for this information at the hearing on May 28, 2014, however, counsel did not receive this information until today, June 2, 2014, although counsel had requested the information prior to the hearing. This documentation will show that Kirk J's name was never listed on PR's birth certificate as her father, and further that Jody Rhorer's name was on the birth certificate.

Wendy C, being first duly sworn upon her oath, hereby deposes and states as follows:

1. I am the Certification Unit Supervisor at the Office of Vital Records and Statistics.

2. I have reviewed our records regarding the birth certificate of Payshence Rhorer, Place of Birth: West Valley City, Salt Lake County, Utah.

3. Jody Rhorer was added by an ORS Administrative Order as the birth father on the birth certificate for the above-mentioned child on July 28, 2010.

4. Mr. Rhorer was later removed from the birth certificate pursuant to Judicial Court Order in the Third District Court on March 5, 2012.

5. Mr. Rhorer is the only father that has ever been on the above-referenced birth certificate.

6. There have been no other changes to this record.

Based upon Intervenor's Motion to Submit Affidavit of Wendy C and Birth Certificate of PR, the Minor Child, there having been no objections filed thereto, and good cause appearing therefore,

IT IS HEREBY ORDERED *as follows:*

1. The Affidavit of Wendy C, which was filed with the Court on June 2, 2014, as an attachment to Intervenor's Motion, is admitted into evidence.

2. The birth certificate of PR, the minor child, which was filed with this Court on June 2, 2014, as an attachment to Intervenor's Motion, is admitted into evidence.

JUNE 17TH, 2014: REQUEST TO SUBMIT, filed by Nancy S, Commissioner Bloom presiding

The following motions are now at issue and ready for decision of the Court. The documents indicated have been filed with the Court.

1. (a) Type of Motion: Motion to Amend Order; Motion to Submit Affidavit of Wendy C and Birth Certificate of PR, the Minor Child; Motion for Order for DCFS Investigation

(b) Date filed: May 27, 2014; June 2, 2014

(c) Party filing motion: Intervenor, Jody Rhorer

JUNE 17TH, 2014: ORDER REQUIRING DCFS INVESTIGATION, filed by Nancy S, Commissioner Bloom presiding

Based upon Intervenor's Motion for Order for DCFS Investigation, there having been no objections filed thereto, and good cause appearing, therefore:
IT IS HEREBY ORDERED *as follow:*
1. The State of Utah, Division of Child and Family Services shall conduct an investigation into the allegations contained in Intervenor's Motion and the police reports attached thereto.
2. The State of Utah, Division of Child and Family Services shall investigate any other information relevant to the welfare and best interest of the minor children in this matter.

JUNE 18TH, 2014: RESPONSE TO NOTICE TO SUBMIT MOTION FOR ORDER FOR DCFS INVESTIGATION, filed by Connie C, Commissioner Bloom presiding

Comes now, Connie, Attorney at Law, and on behalf of Kirk J, files the foregoing response to Intervenor Jody Rhorer's Notice to Submit his Motion for Order for DCFS Investigation.
Intervenor Jody Rhorer has failed to notice counsel for DCFS, the Utah Attorney General's Office. Noticing to Submit the Motion without necessary service, notice, and opportunity to be heard is improper. Without proper service, the Division of Child and Family Services is not a party, this Court may not make Orders against them.

JUNE 21ST, 2014: JOURNAL ENTRY

Today we were married on the null overlooking the ocean at Cannon Beach, Oregon. What a nearly perfect day. No clouds or wind. Just blue skies, family and friends. The pink dress with ribbon roses I bought for Payshence went unworn. The pink rose barrettes I made to hold back her long wavy hair wait for her in her closet. I mailed her a wedding invitation and Jody asked Kelly if she could come to the wedding. Kelly said she didn't care but it was up to Kirk. He said he wouldn't allow it, of course. That didn't stop Jody from continuing to hope. He was ready to take the first flight back to Salt Lake City to pick her up and bring her to Oregon - if only the call would come…and he didn't stop asking right up to the day before the wedding. We still did not know that Kirk had guardianship over Payshence and that Kelly had lost her custodial rights. Kelly continued to play along like she had some say in Payshence's life.

JUNE 25TH, 2014: DISCOVERY ISSUES, filed by Connie C, Commissioner Bloom presiding

Comes now, Connie C, Attorney at Law, and on behalf of Kirk J, files the foregoing Statement of Discovery Issues pursuant to Utah Code of Judicial Administration 4-502(2).
Intervenor Jody Rhorer causes to be served Requests for Admissions on Counsel for Kirk J. The Requests for Admission came on the eve of the hearing before the Commissioner. The Commissioner took the issue of paternity under advisement and a ruling is still pending.
The Requests for Admissions cite the Request for Admission Rule, and then violate it by containing over three times the number of items allowed for by that rule. The Requests also contain matters about other people, designed only to attempt to smear the reputations or character of associates or relatives of Kirk J. These tactics on the part of Mr. Rhorer have been constant through this case, with over six hundred pages of documents attempted to be lodged (which was stricken by Order of the Commissioner) which similarly sought to attack the character of the parties, and Kirk and his family members. After hearing at which the Commissioner Ordered such attempts to "lodge" such materials, Mr. Rhorer swiftly attempted to "lodge" more materials. After service of the Request for Admission, Kirk J filed an objection.
The parties have conferred toward resolving the discovery issues, but no resolution has been reached. Wherefore, as a predicate to filing a Motion for Protective Order, Kirk J files the foregoing Statement of Discovery Issues.

JUNE 30TH, 2014: OPPOSITION TO DISCOVERY ISSUES, filed by Nancy S, Commissioner Bloom

Intervenor Jody Rhorer, by and through counsel Nancy S, hereby submits this Statement of Opposition to Discovery Issues pursuant to Rule 4-502 of the Utah Judicial Administration.

STATEMENT OF FACTS

1. On or about May 21, 2014, Intervenor received police reports from Unified Police Department pursuit to GRAMA request. Intervenor received nine (9) police reports in which the police were called to the respondent's home since the minor child, PR, was place in custody of respondent.

The police reports showed investigation and subsequent charges of domestic violence and domestic violence in the present of children, as well as children being victims of domestic violence. The police reports indicate that on at least one occasion two minor children in the respondent's household called the police after the children ran away from home, and then told the police about physical abuse in their home. The police report of October 3, 2012, states that "both of the juveniles informed me [investigating officer] that they've suicidal thoughts because they can't stand living at the house with their parents." The minor children were transported to Pioneer Valley Hospital. The various police reports named Kirk J, Kelly H, Jill C and Shane S as adults involved in the police investigation. The police reports are attached as exhibits to Intervenor's Motion for DCFS Investigation.

2. On May 21, 2014, Intervenor submitted Requests for Admissions to the respondent based on the police reports.

3. On May 21, 2014, respondent filed an Objection to the Request for Admissions; however, the Objection did not address each Request individually. The respondent's Objection was that Mr. Rhorer does not have legal standing to proceed with discovery, the Requests have nothing to do with the issues before the court, and that the Requests exceed the limit pursuant to Rule 26(C5) of the Rules of Civil Procedure.

4. On June 12, 2014, Intervenor sent to respondent an email stating the following:

'Hi Connie,

Your answers to our request for admissions are due on June 21, 2014. I acknowledge receipt of your Objection stating that only 10 requests are allowed and that you do not recognize Jody Rhorer as having standing in these proceedings. However, Judge Stanley has granted Mr. Rhorer standing to proceed as an Intervenor and therefore I would appreciate receiving from you the answers to the first 10 requested. Further, will you stipulate to the additional discovery request pursuant to Rule 26(C6)? I believe the additional discovery is necessary inasmuch as there is a pending motion for a DCFS investigation and the answers will help aide the court with regard to the issue of what is in the best interest of the minor child.

Please let me know as soon as possible. Thank you, Nancy'

5. Intervenor never received an answer from the respondent, nor has respondent called or otherwise communicated with Intervenor regarding the request for discovery.

6. After the May 28, 2014, hearing before this Court, the Intervenor did not lodge further documents with the court; the Intervenor filed motions that are set to be heard by the court on July 15, 2014.

ARGUMENT I

The subject matter of the Request for Admissions is proper and necessary as it goes directly to the best interest of the child, PR. The pleadings filed in this matter, as well and pleading filed in the Juvenile court matters, indicate that at least eight (8) minor children are living in the respondent's household. Additionally, upon information and belief the respondent's girlfriend is residing in respondent's household.

The police reports indicate that domestic violence has occurred in the respondent's household. DCFS and Child Protective Services have likely become involved. The Request for Admissions are questions based on the police reports. Upon information and belief neither respondent nor petitioner has informed the court about the activities in respondent's home that have led to police investigations and subsequent involvement of DCFS and Child Protective Services. Intervenor's Request for Admissions are to illicit answers to determine the factual basis of the police reports and are not designed to smear the reputations and character of associates or relatives or respondent.

II

The Intervenor has requested that the respondent answer the first ten (10) Requests and stipulate to the remaining Requests inasmuch as the answers go directly to the issue of the best interest of the child PR and the Motion for DCFS Investigation. Although the Requests are more than ten, there is a need in this case for extraordinary discovery. The discovery is proportional given the importance of the discovery issues. The discovery is reasonable considering the needs of this case, the complexity of this case as it relates to the best interest of the minor child PR. The respondent has not alleged that answering the discovery requests will impose an undue burden or affect his resources.

The likely benefits of the proposed discovery outweigh any burden or expense that may be involved. The discovery will further the just and speedy determination of one of the issues in this case. The discovery is not cumulative or duplicative. The information sought cannot be obtained from another source that is more convenient, less burdensome or less expensive. The Intervenor does not have independent access to the information sought in the Requests for Admissions. Wherefore, Intervenor objects to the respondent's Statement of Discovery Issues.

JUNE 30TH, 2014: MOTION FOR ATTORNEYS FEES REGARDING REQUEST TO LODGE, MOTION AGAINST DCFS, filed by Connie C, Commissioner Bloom presiding

Comes now, Connie C, Attorney at Law, and on behalf of Kirk J, files the foregoing Motion that Intervenor, Jody Rhorer, pay attorney fees of Kirk J for all costs related to Mr. Rhorer's attempt to Lodge documents after the May 28th, 2014, hearing, at which the Commissioner struck other 'lodgings' finding them improperly filed.

Kirk J also requests attorney fees for all costs associated with the Motion filed by intervenor, Jody Rhorer, requesting a Court Order directing DCFS conduct an investigation. Kirk J filed a response to that motion which included what is inarguable, that this Court may not Order relief against a non-party who has not been served. When counsel for Kirk J was contacted by Nancy S's office regarding setting a hearing on that issue, Counsel told the staff member that hearing on the matter would be improper in that DCFS still has never been served with the Motion and the Motion purports to ask for the Court to Order DCFS to do something. The staff member told counsel she would check with Nancy S about that issue, but it was her understanding that Nancy S wished to get the Order and then let the Division object.

However, the staffer indicated she would check with Nancy S and call back. The staffer never called back. Instead, counsel received a voice mail on her office phone (counsel had been speaking to Nancy's Office on her cell) that a hearing had been set on the matter.

The Utah Supreme Court has described it as 'incontrovertible' that 'due process dictates and principles of fairness counsel that [a nonparty] be given an opportunity to challenge the district court's assertion of jurisdiction over it. Even if counsel could have been unaware of the inarguable point of law when the Motion asking for an Order against DCFS was filed, she was made aware of the principle by virtue of Kirk J's opposition. Instead of remedying the issue of service regarding DCFS, Nancy S simply filed a Notice to Submit. The Court indicated it would not sign the Order until the Commissioner held a hearing. When again reminded (through the Office staffer who indicated she would present the issues to Nancy) the Office instead caused a hearing to be set on the matter by calling the office phone instead of the cell phone the staffer had been speaking to the staffer on.

CONCUSION

Mr. Rhorer's attempt to get an Order against a non-party is clearly improper, and his failure to remedy the service defect, after having been reminded of it once in a court pleading and once informally suggests an attempt to 'get one over' on the Division of Child and Family Services. Kirk J suspects that the Motion is interposed for an improper purpose based on the history of filing in this matter. Instead of dealing with legal issues squarely presented, Mr. Rhorer has opted to file anything and everything designed to smear the character of Kirk J and Kelly H. Kirk J suspects that Mr. Rhorer filed the Motion related to DCFS not with a belief that he was entitled to the relief of the District Court 'ordering' the Division to perform a discretionary function (which would be a clear violation of the separation of powers doctrine) but rather, so he could rake more muck before the Court. Indeed, by filing the Motion, and presenting his opinion as to exactly what he thinks is going wrong, and how DCFS is 'falling down on the job' by failing/refusing to investigate, Mr. Rhorer is accomplishing a backhanded 'tattle-tale' of his gripes against Kirk J.

WHEREFORE, Kirk J prays the Court award reasonable attorney fees in favor of Kirk J for the cost of reviewing, responding to, and having heard the Motions related to lodging and the DCFS motion.

JULY 7TH, 2014: HEARING, Commissioner Bloom presiding

Journal Entry: Since the Commissioner still had not made a ruling, Nancy filed once again for action to be expedited on two of the counts: DCFS to conduct an immediate investigation of the home based upon the 9 visits by the police and a Guardian ad Litem to be appointed to represent the best interest of Payshence.

Judge Bloom's court room was not a place of order. Kelly could stand and blurt out ridiculous accusations about Jody any time she felt the urge because she was not represented by an attorney.

Kirk and Connie played the same game every time went go to court. "I'm hearing impaired and I need headphones."

"I'm sorry but you are supposed to make arrangements for that prior to the court date," the clerk states.

"My client needs headphones so he can hear," his attorney says.

"The court only has one set. We will have to see if we can find them," the commissioner replies.

It's the same stall tactic every time. Use up the little time we have to get Kirk J head phones so we don't have enough time to present our case. Once the headset is on, Kirk doesn't move, just stares down at his hands. The headset seems to block what everyone is saying more than amplify it as he rarely reacts or speaks. His attorney never takes a note or brings a file. She just wings it. I bet she was great in her high school debate class.

I remember when I was on the debate team and our topic was "International Human Rights." As a 17-year-old girl I was about as interested in that subject as I was in knowing what dirt was made of, but somehow, I managed to really kick some butt. Once I read a quote that had the acronym, GNP, in it. When my opponent was conducting his rebuttal against me, he asked what GNP stood for, I immediately blurted "General Net Purpose!" We won the match regardless of my blundering response. When I read the judge's note it said, "GNP is Gross National Product. Nice cover."

I recognize the same tactics in Connie and it seems to be working. She is a spineless weasel that will make up anything on the fly without preparation, conscious, or truth. What a schmuck! The amazing thing is, the commissioner doesn't seem to pick up on this.

It's all I can do not to pull Kelly's dentures right out of her filthy mouth. She is like a mechanical, spouting, tattooed crypt keeper with fake breasts. She yells things out about my husband like, "He stuck his daughter's face into a garbage can full of maggots" and "He beat me up 'cuz I stopped sucking his thing," - only she didn't say thing. The court allows this! She has no attorney so she can disrupt however she would like. This is how our judicial system works?

I don't get to sit up at the table with Jody because I am nothing in the court's eyes. I must sit back by Deanne and stay quiet. I guard the 5 wrapped gifts anticipating the joy the next day when Payshence opens the Karaoke Machine. Jody picked out a Cabbage Patch doll as he always bought these for his girls and hopes she will remember. We got her a princess outfit and a big doll that matches it and resembles Payshence with the same blue eyes and wavy blonde hair. I wrapped the gifts in cheerful yellow and pink paper with bows - hoping the love I put into it would carry to her.

Nancy mentioned the gifts to the Commissioner for us and the fact that the next week was Jody's daughter's birthday. Commissioner Bloom's reaction was unanticipated and apathetic. "I don't appreciate you making my courtroom a vehicle for your client's deliveries. I will not force the plaintiffs to bring her these gifts. Let's take a break and both sides need to discuss this."

Kirk, his attorney and Kelly exited the courtroom. When they returned, Connie began her impromptu speech. "My client does not want his daughter to have these presents as it will be very confusing for her. Like, what are they supposed to say? These are from some strange man?"

My head dropped between my legs and I began to sob - even though sobbing or any other form of emotion is not allowed in the court room and is addressed with swift dismissal from the bailiff. How can these people be so cruel? We never even asked that they tell her they are from her dad. We just wanted her to have birthday presents! Diane patted my back, trying to comfort me. I know I have to keep it together or I will be excused from the court room. The bailiff had already warned me that I was going to be removed for making a face. I'm not sure what the face was but apparently one is to remain expressionless in the court room or will be removed. I can attest to this though, the Commissioner has mastered the art of expressionlessness.

Of course, the whole idea behind going back to court was in hopes that the Commissioner would go ahead and render her ruling, but instead she stated that she had set everything aside until she heard what we were presenting today. Backfire! Next, she told us, "I should have a decision in the next couple weeks, however." HOPE!!! We would know something within 2 weeks. Years of waiting were about to come to an end.

With some relief that in two weeks at the most we would be able to watch Payshence open the presents with our own eyes, we gathered the gifts and headed for the parking garage. I do admit that I deliberately entered the elevator, gifts in hand, that Kirk, Kelly and Connie were on. I thought Jody, Nancy, and Deanne would follow behind me but when the doors closed, it was the four of us and a sweet little family.

I had noticed this family before as they had also been carrying a gift while they waited to enter another court room. The three little daughters were in matching white dresses. Their parents hovered over them in a protective manner. They no longer had their gift with them. There wasn't much room and I boldly went to the back of the elevator and stood by Kelly. I wanted her to see the presents in my hands. I wanted her heart to soften and for her to get them to her little girl. Instead, she confronted me. She had been going on about getting child support from Jody when I entered the elevator.

"You can't get child support from someone who is not able to see his child," I interrupted.

"Listen Bitch," she snarled, "don't get in my face! You don't know who you are messing with."

"Oh yeah?" I replied, remembering some of the things Jody had told me about her - how she had tried to run over him in a car; how she had run a car right through a house. She had thrown a giant candy cane through the front window of Kirk's house, causing glass to shatter on the kids inside. She had an extensive arrest record. She was downright crazy. I took a deep breath and stood up straight.

"You don't know who *you* are messing with!" I said, leaning toward her, trying to keep the presents balanced, and lowering the tone of my voice. "Just try me."

Connie was in another mental state and seemed oblivious to the whole thing. The family, on the other hand, had crowded as close together as possible in one corner and the parents were attempting to shelter the girls from scene. Deaf Kirk, who heard the whole thing, put his arm around Kelly and told her to not speak to me as he pulled her as far into the back corner as he could. It doesn't take long to go down 2 flights in an elevator and just in time, the door opened.

As I walked out it occurred to me, Kirk and Kelly want Jody to pay child support but want the court to name Kirk as the father and allow Jody absolutely no rights or visitation. Was this also happening with the other children?

JULY 7TH, 2014:   HEARING MINUTES, Commissioner Bloom

Hearing is held on the Intervenor's motion to amend order to include the CD recordings of Juvenile Court proceedings and to include in the Court's analysis a copy of Kirk J's deposition. Also, the motion for a Division of Child and Family Services investigation will be heard
*The Commissioner, after hearing argument, **RECOMMENDS** that:*
*1. Motion for attorney fees is **RESERVED**; counsel must submit an affidavit of fees.*
2. The Court previously took under advisement Mr. Rhorer's involvement as a party in this case. The request for a DCFS investigation will be ruled on with the under advisement, as well as the CD recordings and Kirk J's deposition.
*3. **The Court's under advisement decision will be forthcoming in the next couple of weeks**.*
4. The Court will NOT order Kirk J to accept gifts for the child from Mr. Rhorer. The Court encourages the parties to work together to decide on this issue.

So that was it? $1,000 in attorney fees to go to court and the ruling is we cannot have the gifts delivered and attorney fees would be reserved. What was the point? We were advised by Nancy that the court would be discussing a GAL for Payshence and a DCFS investigation. Those items weren't even addressed.

JULY 9TH, 2014:   OBJECTION TO MOTION FOR ATTORNEYS FEES RE: REQUEST TO LODGE MOTION AGAINST DCFS, filed by Nancy S, Commissioner Bloom presiding

Intervenor, by and through counsel Nancy S, hereby responds to the Motion for Attorneys Fee Regarding Request to Lodge and Motion Against DCFS.
STATEMENT OF FACTS

1. *On May 27, 2014, the Intervenor filed a Motion for Order for DCFS Investigation requesting that the court order a DCFS investigation or in the alternative for an evidentiary hearing that evidence may be submitted and testimony heard on the motion. Respondent was served by Greenfiling.* **Respondent has not filed a response to this motion.**

2. *On June 2, 2014, the Intervenor filed a Motion to Amend Order. Respondent was served by Greenfiling.* **Respondent has not filed a response to this motion.**

3. *On Tuesday, June 17, 2014, after the time had expired for respondent's replies to the motions, and respondent having failed to object or otherwise respond to the motions, the Intervenor filed a separate Request to Submit on the motions. Proposed Orders were filed concurrently.*

4. *On Wednesday, June 18, 2014, the respondent filed a Response to Notice to Submit Motion for Order for DCFS Investigation stating that DCFS required notice and service, and further that 'without proper service, the Division of Child and Family Services is not a party, this Court may not make Orders against them.'*

5. *On Thursday, June 19, 2014, Commissioner Bloom's clerk called counsel of Intervenor and advised counsel to notice the motions for hearing.*

6. *On Monday, June 23, 2014, the parties received notification via Greenfiling that the Proposed Order Amending Order and Proposed Order for DCFS Investigation were filed unsigned with a note stating, 'The motion must be scheduled for a hearing before the Commissioner, see Rule 101 regarding Practice before a Commissioner.'*

7. *During the week of June 23, through June 27, 2014, counsel for Intervenor was out of the office; but counsel communicated with her assistant by telephone regarding these matters.*

8. *Over the course of June 24, and June 25, 2014, legal assistant Deanna B, at the instruction of Nancy S, made attempts to communicate with Connie in order to set the hearing as ordered by the court. When calls and emails were not returned by Connie, Intervenor set the matter for hearing. An affidavit of Deanna B is attached which sets forth the communication between counsel for Intervenor and counsel for Respondent.*

9. *Neither Nancy S nor Deanna received a response from Connie. Connie did not call Nancy's Law Office, nor did she respond by email. Counsel for Intervenor assumes that Connie never returned the assistant's call inasmuch as Nancy's Law Firm never received a call from the commissioner's assistant attempting to set the motion for hearing. After waiting two days, and at the instruction of Nancy S, Deanna filed the Notice of Hearing on Friday, June 27, 2014.*

10. *On Monday, June 30, 2014, Connie filed a Motion for Attorney Fees Regarding Request to Lodge and Motion Against DCFS* **regardless of the fact that Intervenor has never filed a 'Request to Lodge' nor a 'Motion Against DCFS'** *and regardless of the fact that the court ordered the parties set the motion for hearing.*

11. *Respondent has failed to comply with Rule 11 requirements. With regard to Jody's Motion for DCFS Investigation, the respondent makes the vague statement that Kirk J suspects that the Motion is for an improper purpose based the history of filings in this matter.' If the respondent has filed the Motion for Attorney's Fees as a request for sanction pursuant to Rule 11 of the Utah Rules of Civil Procedure, the respondent's motion should be denied for failure to comply with the strict requirements of the rule.*

Rule 11 states in relevant part:

(c)(1)(A) By motion. A motion for sanctions under this rule shall be made separately from other motions or requests and shall describe the specific conduct alleged to violate subdivision (b). It shall be served as provided in Rule 5, but shall not be filed with the court unless, within 21 days after service of the motion (or such other period as the court may prescribe), the challenged paper, claim defense, contention, allegation, or denial is not withdrawn or appropriately corrected. If warranted, the court may award to the part prevailing on the motion the reasonable expenses and attorney fees incurred in presenting or opposing the motion.

Respondent's motion is deficient in several respects: (1) the motion fails to reference Rule 11 as the basis for the motion and fault to properly entitle the motion as a motion for sanctions; (2) the motion fails to describe the specific conduct for which the sanctions are sought; (3) the motion was filed with the court instead of being served upon the Intervenor first; (4) the motion was filed with the court prior to the expiration of 21 days after the Intervenor received the motion via e-filing.

Case law mandates the denial of a motion for attorney's fees when the procedural and substantive requirements are not met: In Dahl v. Harrison, 'Rule 11 sets forth a detailed procedure that a party seeking a sanction for violation of the rule must follow. We have stated that the motion must strictly comply with rule 11's requirements that the rule 11 motion be served on opposing counsel as a precondition to filing the motion with the court,' the Utah Court of Appeals states that the court cannot award attorney's fees using its equitable powers if there is statutory authority for an award. Respondent has alleged 'bad faith' and 'improper purpose' as a basis, both of which are addressed by statute.

WHEREFORE, *Intervenor prays that this court deny the respondent's motion for attorney's fees and for such other further relief as the court deems just.*

JULY 9TH, 2014: AFFIDAVIT OF DEANNA B, filed by Nancy S, Commissioner Bloom presiding

Deanna B, being first duly sworn upon her oath, deposes and states as follows:

1. *I am employed by Nancy S's Law Office as a Legal Assistant.*

2. *On June 24, 2014, I called Connie at her office and left a message asking her to call me back about the case.*

3. *One June 24, 2014, Connie returned my call at Nancy's Law Office. Pursuant to Nancy's instruction, I advised her that based upon a telephone call between Commissioner Bloom's clerk and Nancy S and the Commissioner's recent filing regarding our Motion for Order for DCFS Investigation and Motion to Amend Order, the Court was requiring that a hearing be scheduled on our motions. Since there were no responsive pleadings or objections to our motions filed with the Court, I asked Connie if she would stipulate to our motions. She said no, absolutely not. I then asked her if she wanted me to make a conference call with the Court to schedule a date for hearing. Ms. Connie said she did not want to do that. I then asked her if she would provide me with some dates that she was available to schedule a hearing on our motions. She told me that she just got into the office, received my message and called me. She stated that her calendar was still in her car. Ms. Connie told me to obtain her email address from the Utah State Bar website and email my request to her and she would respond. I told Ms. Connie that I would do that.*

4. *On June 24, 2014, I sent Connie an email asking her if she would provide us with some dates that she would be available for a hearing on our motions and advised her that I had left a message for Commissioner Bloom's clerk to try to obtain some dates that the Commissioner would be available. I have attached a copy of the email as Exhibit 1.*

5. *On June 24, 2014, Connie replied to my emails asking if DCFS and the attorney had been served and that this motion could not be heard without them. She stated that she didn't want to waste time setting the hearing if service had not been completed. I have attached a copy of Ms. C's email as Exhibit 2.*

6. *On June 24, 2014, I responded to Ms. Co's email and told her that DCFS and/or their attorney had not been served. I stated that it was my understanding that the Court needed to enter an order first and then the order was to be served. I told her I would check with Nancy S about service of DCFS and/or their attorney when she returned to the office and get back to her. Ms. Connie replied by email 'Okay.' Attached is a copy of both emails as Exhibit 3.*

7. *Ms. Connie states in her Motion for Attorney Fees Regarding Request to Lodge and Motion Against DCFS that when she spoke with the 'staff member' at Nancy's Office regarding setting a hearing on that issue, Counsel told the 'staff member' that hearing on the matter would be improper if the DCFS still has never been served with the Motion. This issue was not raised or discussed during our telephone conversation. Ms. Connie did ask about it in her responsive email which is attached hereto as Exhibit 2, and I did tell her that I would check with Nancy and get back to her. Ms. Connie was never told that it was my 'understanding that Nancy wished to get the Order and then let the Division Object' as stated in her motion.*

8. *On June 25, 2014, I spoke with Nancy regarding service upon DCFS and/or their attorney. She asked me to contact the Court and confirm whether or not service needed to be done prior to an order being entered. I spoke with Commissioner Bloom's clerk about service upon DCFS. I told her what Connie had stated in her email and asked her if we needed to serve DCFS prior to our motion being heard or if we need to schedule the hearing and see if the Commissioner was going to order an investigation or not and then serve DCFS. She told me that we needed to set it for hearing and then if an investigation was ordered, DCFS would need to be served. She indicated that she could make a conference call with Connie's office to schedule a date for hearing. She tried to reach Connie but was unable to do so. She told me she left a message for Connie telling her that she was giving me some dates the Commissioner was available and she was giving me the option of picking one of those dates and just setting the hearing in hopes that Connie would be available or that she could give me some dates and I could get back to her. She gave me some dates that were available for setting the hearing. Since the earliest date available was July 15, 2014, (and there was only one spot left on the calendar for that day) I asked Nancy if we set the hearing on that date if I was able to reach Connie and if, for some reason she was unavailable on that date, if I could call her back and set it for one of the other amiable dates. She said that would be fine. I let her know that I would not file the Notice of Hearing that day, that I was hoping to hear back from Connie first.*

9. *After speaking with Commissioner Bloom's assistant I attempted to contact Connie at her office telephone number and received her voice mail. I asked her to please call me back to discuss the information Commissioner Bloom's assistant had given me regarding service upon DCFS and scheduling the hearing on our motions.*

10. *I also sent Connie an email informing her what Commissioner Bloom's assistant had told me about service upon DCFS and explained what she and I had discussed regarding the hearing and asked her to please let me know if she was available on July, 15, 2014. I have attached a copy of the email as Exhibit 4.*

11. *I did not receive a response from Connie, either by telephone or email.*

12. *On June 26, 2014, I attempted to contact Connie again by telephone (at her office) and it went to her voice mail. I did not leave another message.*

13. *On June 27, 2014, after waiting two days for Connie to respond, and pursuant to Nancy's instruction, I E-filed the Notice of Hearing in this matter.*

14. *Connie stated in her Motion that I never called back. I did call her back as Connie admits in her next sentence: 'Instead, counsel received a voice mail on her office phone that a hearing had been set on the matter.' I do not have Connie's cell phone number, she has never provided me with that number and she did not tell me what telephone she was calling from, although she did tell me that she had just returned to her office, received my message and returned my call. In addition, Commissioner Bloom's assistant told me that she too had left a message for Connie advising her of the situation.*

15. *I have communicated with Connie regarding these issues both by telephone and by email. I tried to coordinate the hearing with her by offering to place a conference call with the Court and she declined to do so. I advised her of the information I was given by the Court's clerk regarding service upon DCFS and scheduling a hearing on our motion via email and by attempting to call her office number. I have never received a response from Connie.*

In frustration with the process and the back and forth bickering between the attorneys which seemed to be getting us nowhere, I wrote a letter to Payshence's school teacher in hopes of getting some sort of insight in to her present life.

WEDNESDAY, JULY 9TH, 2014

Dear Ms. Simpson,

I am the wife of Jody Rhorer, the father of Payshence Rhorer, although you may know her by a different name. I was reading the numerous pages of police reports from incidents that have happened in the home where she currently lives and your name was listed in a report where Payshence's mother, tried to take her from the school.

Three years ago, Payshence was taken from her father, who had raised her to that point, and given to the man that currently has her and 3 of her brothers. There is a law in the state of Utah where a man that is married to a woman will have custody over the biological father. That is the situation she and several of the brothers are in. They all have different fathers and a man that is not biologically related has the children.

I dated Payshence's dad for the past 2 years and we were married in June. He has been fighting for full custody since she was taken from him. He told me about her on our first date and his fight to get her back. He has 3 other daughters that are her sisters that he has custody of. He hasn't been able to see her or talk to her since her mom lost her rights. The man that has her uses her and Kelly's other children as pawns. I have been to court time and time again over the past 2 years and I know Jody has spent around $20,000 in attorney's fees so far fighting for his little girl. We finally got our hearing on May 29th, but the judge still has not rendered a decision.

The reason I am writing you (and no one, not even Jody knows I'm doing this) is because I have never met this precious little girl and I know that kindergarten is a tender time. I have only seen pictures of Payshence and if you saw her dad, you would have no doubt she is his (he also has 2 DNA tests to back this up). I'm just wondering if you can tell me a few things. Is she happy? Healthy? Can she read yet? Does she look clean and loved? I was told she doesn't have a bed and sleeps on the floor in the toy room. She has been molested at least 2 times and our attorney has obtained the medical records. I thought you should know this in case she acted out or was reclusive so you could understand her situation.

I decorated her room last year thinking we may get her. I bought her dress for the wedding in June and she wasn't able to wear it or be there with us. When school starts again, if we don't have her yet, please put in a word to her new teacher to watch over her and pay special attention to anything out of the ordinary. Thank you for taking the time to read this, and if you are not able to answer me, would you please just let me know you got my letter?

Thank you so much,
Deone Ehlers-Rhorer

JULY 13TH, 2014

Deone,

I understand your desire to know more about Payshence. However, as a teacher, it is my responsibility to protect the privacy of the children I teach. I do not feel comfortable going into any specifics. What I can do is assure you that she was loved while she was in my classroom. I have felt a continued desire to make sure that she is placed in loving classroom environments. I feel as though she and her brothers trust me and know that I am on their side.

I understand that her situation is rough and iI have dealt with some repercussions of this directly. That being said, she does have happiness and love in her life. Best of luck with what you're pursuing. I hope that what's best for Payshence happens.

Ms. Simpson

I had certainly wished for more information, but was actually surprised that the teacher responded to me at all! It did give me a small amount of comfort knowing that her school was aware of her situation and cared.

JULY 21ST, 2014: Silence. Maybe she meant by the end of the month.

JULY 31ST, 2014: Nothing.

In August a new ruling came out in a Cedar City, UT, court that was favorable towards our case. Nancy immediately took action and attached a brief to send to the Commissioner. Maybe this would jar her memory that a little girl sleeping on the floor of the toy room in a basement was waiting to be reunited with her daddy. That the 5 large binders bulging to capacity with evidence showing why this precious child should not be subject to the hell that she has been forced to endure by the State of Utah, collecting dust in the corner of her chambers, should demand immediate attention. But alas, nothing.

SEPTEMBER 20TH, 2014: JOURNAL ENTRY

Tomorrow will be two years since I met Jody. He told me about his daughters over dinner at a steak house. Our table was in a mock covered wagon and the lights were dimmed. It was very cozy, private, a place you could feel comfortable talking about your deepest hopes, sorrows, and accomplishments.

It was at this time that I knew that he held the attributes of a father that I had longed for my own son's father to have. He was devoted and had put aside his own dreams and education to care for his girls. This is when he first told me about Payshence.

Now I have had some long and miserable pregnancies. Four of them to be exact. 9 plus months of morning sickness, bed-ridden, sicker-than-a-dog-with-parvo type of pregnancies. But I must say, there has been nothing as emotional as what the past 2 years have brought. I literally feel like I have been expecting for 24 months.

I have decorated her room; bought her clothes (which she has probably grown out of but hang in her closet); purchased a dress for our wedding that she never got to wear; got presents for her 7th birthday that sit in a closet, still wrapped; framed her pictures and displayed them around the house; emailed her school teacher to see how she it doing - all for a little girl I have never met. It felt like she was mine since Jody first showed me her pictures and I have felt overwhelmed with expectations ever since.

Over four months have come and gone since we went to court. Every day we wake, we wonder if it's the day we get some news. Each milestone we come to - summer break, the wedding, her birthday, Jody's birthday, school starting again, false promises from the Commissioner - only bring deeper despair as we anticipate what could be happening to her. I know that we pray every night for angels to surround and protect her, and for the Commissioner' heart to be touched.

The first thing Nancy or Deanna did each morning was contact the Commissioner's secretary to see if a ruling had been made. Sometimes I called Nancy's office just for reassurance, but, of course, they couldn't really offer me much of anything.

"The good news is that she hasn't said, No." Deanna or Nance would say. "She is very thorough and backs up all her decision with case study. She is taking her time because this decision will create a precedence in the State of Utah. Nothing like this has been done before."

I know all of these statements are made to give us comfort, but in the back of my mind, I keep thinking, "What if she just doesn't want to deal with it? What if she never makes a decision? What do we do then?"

When I asked our attorney if there was anything we can do (besides the tactics she kept trying to bring the case to the forefront) - like tattle on her to someone higher up or call her up personally and ask her if she knew how many a couple equals - she told me, "No. She can take as long as she likes. There is nothing we can do and there are no rules that give a time frame that a judge has to abide by.' Of course, this was not the answer I was looking for. There must be a rule about this!

I had her entire school wardrobe picked out of the H & M magazine - each page folded on the outfits I wanted to buy her. Unfortunately, the deadline date for free shipping had since expired. Jody told me that Kelly's boys would always be dirty and have dried food stuck to their shirts. I wondered who combed Payshence's hair. Does Payshence take care of the other kids in the house? Does she feel like a little mama? Who picks out her clothes for school and makes her lunch?

I drove by the elementary that she should be going to. It's nearly brand new and state of the art. I was anticipating early registration and wondering if she would get any of the teachers that taught my boys when they went to the old school that had been torn down. Now I see the kids playing on the playground.

I've started to mentally work though my schedule: Who's going to pick her up from school? Do we alternate days between Jody and me? What if I have work appointments!?! Should I get her a little suit and she can go with me and start learning the business? What about putting a room together for her in the office where she can play when I'm working? My grandparents used to bring me to their paint store all the time when I was a little girl and I loved it. I entertained myself for hours and watched my Grandma Rose consult with ladies about wallpaper while Grandpa Fred made sure there was always fresh coffee for the painting contractors. There was a red toilet seat that said HOT SEAT in big black letters in the employee bathroom. While I learned a lot from my grandparents, I never learned what that meant.

I want to teach her everything. I hope she loves me. She doesn't even know I exist. Another confession. I have been looking at Halloween costumes in her size.

AUGUST 21ST, 2014: EMAILS from Nancy S's Office

Hi Jody and Deone, We still have not received a decision on your case. However, the Utah Court of Appeals issued a decision in a similar case addressing who may challenge paternity of a child born into a marriage. We think this case helps our case. We have made a motion to the court to take judicial notice of that case. I am attaching a copy of the motion and the court decision. I hope you both are doing well. Nancy

Good afternoon Deanna, Jody told me that we had a little movement from the commissioner. Would you please send me a copy of the brief and also any details on how long Connie has for a response? Also, can you let me know how much the cost of doing the brief and filing is so that we can send you a check. Hope you and Nancy are well! We so appreciate you, Deone Ehlers-Rhorer

AUGUST 21ST, 2014: MOTION FOR JUDICIAL NOTICE OF ADJUDICATIVE FACT, filed by Nancy S, Commissioner Bloom presiding

Intervenor, by and through counsel Nancy S, pursuant to Rule 201 of the Utah Rules of Evidence, hereby moves the court to take judicial notice of the following adjudicative fact:

Utah Court of Appeals Decision filed August 14, 2014: J.P.R. v. L.M. 2014 UT app 191. A copy of the Appellate Court decision is attached hereto.

This motion is based on the fact that this Appellate Court decision is recent and was not available at the time of the hearing on these matters.

AUGUST 21ST, 2014: OPPOSITION TO MOTION OF JODY RHORER REQUESTING "JUDICIAL NOTICE" OF ADJUDICATIVE FACT, filed by Connie C, Commissioner Bloom presiding

    Comes now, Connie C, on behalf of Kirk J, files the foregoing Opposition to Intervenor, Jody Rhorer's Motion that this Court take Judicial Notice of a case decided by the Court of Appeals as an "adjudicative fact" pursuant to Rule 201 of the Utah Rules of Evidence.

    The scope of the Rule is limited to 'adjudicative fact only.' The types of 'facts' which are subject to judicial notice include those which are generally known within the territorial jurisdiction of the court, and which can be 'accurately and readily determined from sources whose accuracy cannot be questioned.'

    While it may be a judicially noticeable fact that a case was decided, the same cannot be denied, that a case was decided is irrelevant, unless it applies to an issue in the case at bar. Even if the holding might be relevant to some issues pending in the case at bar, how it might impact any pending legal issue is a matter of law, and a matter of interpretation, not a 'fact'.

CONCLUSION

    If Mr. Rhorer believes the recently decided case should be considered by the Court in deciding any issues still under consideration, the proper vehicle is not to allege the deciding of the case as a judicially noticeable "fact" but rather to move for leave to be tried what impact the case might have on issues pending in the case. Should the Court grant that motion, Kirk J should be permitted to respond to any briefing/argument.

SEPTEMBER 20TH, 2014: INTERVENOR'S REPLY MEMORANDUM TO MEMORANDUM IN OPPOSITION, filed by Nancy S, Commissioner Bloom presiding

    The case of JPR v. LM. 2014 UT App 191 is limited to the issue of identifying the persons who have standing to assert parentage under the Utah Uniform Parentage Act, specifically under the provisions of UCA 78B-15-607. The respondent has set forth alleged facts in his oppositional memorandum, many of which are immaterial to the issues required in an analysis of the Utah Court of Appeals' recent decision, and most of which are inaccurate. Mr. Rhorer addresses the allegations as follows and sets forth the following facts:

    1. Kirk J and Kelly H were not cohabiting at the time PR was conceived or born. **In these proceedings** *the parties have admitted under oath that they had not cohabited since May 30, 2005, more than one year prior to the minor child's conception and more than two years prior to her birth:*

    a. Petition for Divorce filed by Kelly H in which she states, 'The parties separated on or about 05/30/2005.'

    b. The Vital Statistics Form filed in this matter listing May 2005, as the 'date couple last resided in same household.'

    c. Kirk J's Answer to Petition for Divorce in which he admitted the allegations in paragraph 2 of the Petition other than correcting the date of the marriage as having occurred on April 17, 2003. He did not deny that the parties separated on or about May 30, 2005.

    d. Kirk J, in a hearing before this court on December 20, 2012, stated to the court, 'We, we got married in 2003, and she left in 2003. I mean, we, we haven't even been together since then.' **In other proceedings** *Kirk J testified under oath that the parties were not cohabiting during the time PR was conceived or born. In his deposition taken December 15, 2011, Kirk J testified that he and Kelly H separated in 2004 or 2005. In that same deposition Kirk J testified that in 2006 he was living with Kim J, his girlfriend.*

    2. There were two Juvenile Court actions. The first action was initiated in 2008 and concerned PR and two male children of Kirk J and Kelly H. In those proceedings Kirk J appeared and accepted custody of the two male children, but did not assert his parental rights to PR. Kirk J abandoned PR in those proceedings. PR was placed in kinship placement with Mr. Rhorer's mother and later returned to Kelly H's custody. During that time PR lived with Kelly H and Jody Rhorer. Jody Rhorer held himself out to be the father of PR. Judge V ordered Mr. Rhorer to establish paternity. Mr. Rhorer followed the court's instructions by submitting to DNA testing and filing a paternity action in Third District Court. Neither Kirk J nor Kelly H informed the court of their marriage. Kirk J did not hold himself out to be the father of PR.

    3. Mr. Rhorer did not flee the State of Utah due to criminal charges and this allegation should be stricken as the parties have not provided any evidentiary support for the allegation. Mr. Rhorer was working at a construction job in Missouri; in fact, Kelly H left the State of Utah with PR to join Mr. Rhorer in Missouri. The Affidavit filed by the DCFS worker to retrieved Kelly H filed an Affidavit which she stated that Kelly H wanted to take PR to Missouri to be with 'her family.' This affidavit has been field in this case.

    4. *The allegations of paragraph 4 are untrue. Mr. Rhorer missed some hearings due to his job in Missouri; however, he always asserted his parental rights throughout those proceedings. Kirk J was absent throughout those proceedings.*

    5. *There is no evidentiary support for the allegations that Mr. Rhorer voluntarily absented himself from the 2008 proceedings; he was the only father asserting parental right to PR in those proceedings.*

    6. *The Juvenile Court did not find Kirk J to be PR's father in the 2008 proceedings. The minor child PR was never placed with Kirk J during the 2008 proceedings. PR was with Kelly H and Mr. Rhorer. A second Juvenile Court action was initiated on February 10, 2013, involving PR. In that action the State of Utah filed a petition to terminate Kelly H's parental rights. Because of the marriage, Mr. Rhorer was not involved in the proceedings. PR was placed in foster care. Kirk J was given extended visits with PR in April 2012, and was forced to accept custody of PR in July, 2012.*

    7. *The parties marriage prevented Mr. Rhorer to have standing to appeal any order concerning PR. Once the parties initiated their divorce action, Mr. Rhorer intervened to establish paternity of PR.*

    8. *Kirk J was not granted physical custody of PR in 2010. The Minutes and Order of the hearing on May 20, 2010, grants Kelly H custody of PR. Kirk J was involved in the second Juvenile Court proceedings because the parties had finally admitted that a marriage had existed and therefore Mr. Rhorer was not allowed to be a party to the action. The minutes and order of the hearing on July 31, 2012, show that PR was placed with Kirk J. Prior to that time Kirk J had only limited visitation with PR.*

    9. *Mr. Rhorer did not appeal the order because the parties had not yet filed for divorce.*

    10. *The paternity action was filed by Mr. Rhorer in 2009 before Mr. Rhorer learned that the parties were married and before the parties informed the court they were married. At that time the Juvenile Court was telling Mr. Rhorer to establish paternity of PR.*

    11. *Mr. Rhorer's attempt to establish paternity was in good faith and pursuant to court order. The DNA test results establish Mr. Rhorer as the father of PR and an order was entered on June 16, 2010. At the time neither Mr. Rhorer nor the Juvenile Court, nor the Attorney General, knew that Kirk J and Kelly H were married and that there was a presumed father.*

    12. *Mr. Rhorer's DNA testing was done on March 11, 2010, before Kirk J's involvement in Juvenile Court proceedings and before the court or Mr. Rhorer knew he was the presumed father.*

    13. *The order through ORS was later set aside on August 12, 2010, when Kirk J and Kelly H revealed their marriage.*

    14. and 15. **In this action** *both parties have raised the issue of paternity as to PR:*

    a. *Petition for Divorce filed by Kelly H wherein Kirk J's relation to PR is listed as 'other' rather than 'father,' then identified Kirk J as father to other children named in the Petition.*

    b. *Petition for Divorce filed by Kelly H which states:*

    'three of my children are not biologically his, one being my two-year-old.' PR's date of birth identifies her as the child referenced in this statement.

    c. *Answer to Petition filed by Kirk J in which he disagreed with the allegations in paragraph 9 only as to his statement that he had been awarded custody and guardianship of PR in the juvenile court proceedings. Kirk J did not deny that he was **not** the father of PR.*

    In other proceedings the parties have raised the issue of paternity as to PR:

    a. *Answer to Complaint filed by the Office of Recovery Services in which Kirk J denied that he was the presumed father of PR.*

    b. *Statement of Kirk J in his Answer to the ORS action in which he states that he previously denied the same allegations in the West Jordan, Utah Court.*

    16. *Both parties have raised the issue of legal paternity as set forth above and as reflected in the pleadings filed in these proceedings.*

    17. *The parties did not object to Mr. Rhorer's motion to intervene in order to establish paternity of PR, even though Kirk J was present at the hearing before the Honorable Stanley and had the opportunity to object. This shows Kirk J's intent that Mr. Rhorer be allowed to establish paternity. Further, in the ORS action Kirk J, as the presumed father of PR, could have admitted the allegations in the petition, avoiding the DNA test to disprove parentage of PR;*

    18. *A bifurcated decree of divorce was granted in this matter in September 2013.*

    19. *The allegation in paragraph 19 of Kirk J's memorandum is untrue. On May 10, 2013, four months prior to the entry of the Divorce Decree, Mr. Rhorer filed a Motion to Intervene in order to establish his paternity of PR. A hearing was held before the Honorable Stanley on June 25, 2013.*

OTHER RELEVANT FACTS

20.   Neither Kirk J nor Kelly H appealed the Order granting Mr. Rhorer's motion to intervene in order to establish paternity of PR.

21.   PR did not live with Kirk J until 2012. The Petition for Divorce filed by Kelly H alleges that PR began living with Kirk J on May 31, 2012.

22.   Mr. Rhorer has presented evidence to the court of his close and loving relationship with PR including photographs of her with Mr. Rhorer, her siblings, grandparents and other family members, and an Affidavit of Mona Rhorer. For the first five years of her life PR lived with and enjoyed a daughter-father relationship with Mr. Rhorer.

23.   Kirk J has never submitted any evidence whatsoever that he had a relationship at all with PR. Kirk J alleged in his Answer to the Petition for Divorce that PR began living in his residence on July 31, 2012. Thereafter, Mr. Rhorer continued to visit PR until 2013. Neither Kirk J nor Kelly H has refuted Mr. Rhorer's statements in this regard.

JODY RHORER HAS STANDING TO ASSERT PATERNITY

Mr. Rhorer's standing does not conflict with the provisions of 78B-15-607 which states:

(1) Paternity of a child conceived or born during a marriage with a
presumed father as described in Subsection 78B-15-2014(1)(a), (b), or (c),
may be raised by the presumed father or the mother at any time prior to
filing an action for divorce or in the pleadings at the time of the divorce.

In this action, both Kirk J and Kelly H raised the issue of paternity. Both parties alleged that Kirk J was not the father and neither objected to Mr. Rhorer's motion to intervene to establish his paternity of PR and to request custody of PR.

The Utah Court of Appeals restated the prior decision of the court that addresses when a third party may intervene to establish paternity when the child was born within a marriage. The language is clear and unambiguous:

'that section 607 reflects the Utah Legislature's intent to **encourage a presumed father to stay married to the mother and to raise the child in an intact marriage. Unless the couple decides to seek a divorce,** section 607 limits the persons with standing to raise the paternity of the child to the presumed father and mother.'

Because Kirk J and Kelly H divorced and did not raise PR within an intact marriage, Jody Rhorer is allowed to intervene. The Legislature's intent was to encourage a presumed father to stay married to the mother and to raise the child in an 'intact marriage.' While there is no definition of an 'intact marriage,' the case law and the legislature has given us guidance in the plain language of the decisions. An intact marriage is not a marriage in which the parties divorce. Social norms of an intact marriage include a couple cohabiting together. By their own admissions Kirk J and Kelly H did not cohabit during the majority of their marriage.

Our societal norms of an intact marriage would presume children whose biological fathers were their mother's husband. In this case, the parties had admitted that at least four of the five children, including PR, were fathered by men **other than** Kirk J. The parties had not presented any evidence whatsoever to show that their marriage was intact.

The respondent's characterization of the relationship between Mr. Rhorer and Kelly H is incorrect. Mr. Rhorer did not sleep with a married woman; rather, Mr. Rhorer and Kelly H lived together in a loving and committed relationship. Kelly did not tell Mr. Rhorer that she was married. This is not difficult to accept given that she did not tell the Juvenile Court that she was married until she was forced to do so when the State of Utah was attempted to terminate her parental rights.

Further, the proper forum in which to challenge the ruling of a state court is an appeal to the Utah State appellate courts. Neither Kirk J nor Kelly H appealed Judge Stanley's Order allowing Mr. Rhorer to intervene in order to establish his paternity of PR and to assert his parental rights to custody and related matters.

OCTOBER 1ST, 2014: EMAIL from Nancy S

Hi Jody and Deone, We called the Commissioner's clerk and she is going to confer with her about the status of her ruling and will call us back. I will let you know when that happens. Nancy

OCTOBER 7TH, 2014: Charge: Kirk J FAIL TO YIELD RIGHT OF WAY - Class C Misdemeanor. Attributes: Accident.

OCTOBER 23RD, 2014: MINUTE ENTRY by Commissioner Bloom

This court took under advisement several motions pending before it at hearings held May 28, 2014, July 15, 2014, and with supplemental relief requested on August 21, 2014. Present at the May 28, 2014, hearing: Petitioner Kelly H, Respondent Kirk J, represented by Connie, Brent N, GAL in juvenile court case, Nancy S, counsel for Intervenor Jody Rhorer.

Present at the August 21, 2014, hearing: Kelly H, Kirk J represented by Connie and Mr. Rhorer represented by Nancy S. Counsel for the ORS waived his appearance for the hearing.

Several motions are pending before the court which the court will address. The motions are as follows: Mr. Rhorer's Motion to Establish Jody Rhorer as the Natural and Biological father of PR; Motion for Determination of Parentage, Motion for Custody and in the Alternative an Evaluation and Motion for Interim Parent-Time, Kirk J's Motion to Disregard DNA Test, Motion to Reconsider Order Granting Intervention, Mr Rhorer's Motion to Strike Respondent's Motion to Reconsider Order Granting Intervention of Jody Rhorer and Motion to Strike Respondent's Motion to Disregard DNA Paternity Test Submitted by Intervenor, Motion for Appointment of a Guardian ad Litem, Motion to Strike Notices of Lodging, Motion for Order for DCFS to Conduct an Investigation of Motion to Submit Affidavit of Wendy C and Birth Certificate of PR, the Minor Child and Motion to Amend Order. On August 21, 2014, Mr. Rhorer filed a Motion for Judicial Notice of Adjudicative Fact which was not heard at the hearings listed; however, an Opposition to Motion Requesting Judicial Notice of Adjudicative Facts was filed on August 21, 2014. These motions address the issues the court took under advisement at the May 2014, and July 2014, hearings; the court shall also address those issues.

During the time this matter was taken under advisement, Intervenor Jody Rhorer filed a Motion for Judicial Adjudicative Fact. In the Motion, he asserts that the recent Utah Court of Appeals Decision field August 14, 2014, JPF v. LM, 2014 UT App. 191 should be considered by the court and take 'judicial notice' of the opinion. Counsel for Respondent, Kirk J, filed an Opposition to Motion of Jody Rhorer Requesting 'Judicial Notice' of Adjudicative Fact, asserting that this case is not subject to the doctrine of judicial notice. Respondent correctly asserts that the case should not be asserted to be a 'judicial fact' but that briefing the issue as to how this decision affects the court's application of the law to the facts of this case is appropriate.

Wherefore, the court recommends that Intervenor may brief the issue as to how JPR v. LM should be read and applied to the facts of this case. The court shall specifically adopt the timeliness under Rule 7 of the Utah Rules of Civil Procedure, allowing any motion to be filed within the next seven days, and response and reply times as articulated under Rule 7. The court shall then consider written argument of counsel, and apply the facts as appropriate. Upon review of this briefing, the court shall issue it recommendations.

Stalled yet again. The Commissioner had sat on our case for months and issued an order to "brief" a ruling from another court versus how it affected our case. Are you kidding me? Can't she just read the damn ruling? Why does the court insist on taking people's time, money and romp all over their emotions in this manner?

Do you, as the reader, really believe that having Nancy and Connie argue the JPR v. LM ruling will bring us closer to a decision by the judge and that the ruling will be expedited by them doing so? Or do you think the Commissioner could take it upon herself, in all her wisdom, to read the ruling that was already conveniently attached to the Motion for her?

OCTOBER 30TH, 2014: INTERVENOR'S SUPPLEMENTAL MEMORANDUM RE MOTIONS, submitted by Nancy S, Commissioner Bloom presiding

Intervenor, by and through counsel, Nancy S, submits this Supplemental Memorandum in support of Intervenor's motions before the Court, and specifically addresses the Utah Court of Appeals Decision filed August 14, 2014: JPR v. LM, 2014 UT App 191 ruled that:

*1. **The issue of paternity of a child can be raised by the presumed father or mother at any time prior to filing an action for divorce or in the pleadings at the time of the divorce of the party.** In the case at bar, Kelly H raised the issue of paternity in her Petition for Divorce. Kirk J raised the issue of paternity in his Answer to the Petition for Divorce. Bother parties raised the issue of paternity at the time they stipulated to allow Mr. Rhorer to intervene in their divorce action specifically to establish his paternity of the minor child and to seek custody of the minor child. Prior to the divorce action, Kirk J raised the issue of paternity of the child in the ORS action in which he voluntarily submitted to DNA testing in order to disestablish his parentage of the minor child. An Order was entered accordingly.*

*2. **The Utah Legislature's intent in enacting the Utah Uniform Parentage Act is to encourage a presumed father to stay married to the mother and to raise the child in an intact marriage.** The Court in JRP stated: 'that section 607 reflects the Utah Legislature's intent to **encourage a presumed father to stay married to the mother and to raise the child in an intact marriage. Unless the couple decides to seek a divorce,** section 607 limits the persons with standing to raise the paternity of the child to the presumed father and mother...'*

In the case at bar Kelly H and Kirk J had initiated divorce action and their bifurcated divorce has been granted. The working in the Court's decision is clear and unambiguous. The limitations in section 607 apply 'unless a couple decides to seek a divorce.' Since Kelly H and Kirk J have divorced, the limitations on Section 607 of the UUPA do not apply.

The Legislature's intent was to encourage a presumed father to stay married to the mother and to raise the child in an 'intact marriage.' The facts presented at the hearing of this matter show that the parties in this action never had an intact marriage. Kelly H alleged in her Petition for Divorce that Kirk J was not the biological father of four of the five children born in their marriage.

Brent N who acted as the GAL in the Juvenile Court action, stated at the hearing on May 29, 2014, that in his opinion it was clear that the parties never had an intact marriage. The parties presented no evidence to contradict these allegations...The Court stated:

> *"The district court's analysis of the relevant provisions of the UUPA is entirely consistent with our decision in RP. Because the mother and the presumed father have decided to raise the child as issue of the marriage, lack statutory authority to raise the child's paternity."*

CONCLUSION

The fact scenario in the case at bar is not consistent with the facts in these cases. Kirk J and Kelly H divorced, there is no intact marriage to preserve, they each have raised the issue of paternity of the child in the divorce action and in the ORS action prior to the divorce. The reasons for applying the limitations in sections 607 of the UUPA do not apply to the case at bar and thus Jody Rhorer should be allowed to proceed as Intervenor to establish his paternity.

NOVEMBER 5TH, 2014

Hi Deone:

Per our telephone conversation, I have attached a copy of the Opposition of the Supplemental Memorandum filed by Connie.

I have attached a copy of the entry from Commissioner Bloom, our Motion for Judicial Notice, and our Supplemental Memorandum which was filed on October 30, 2014. Opposing parties' responses are due on November 13, 2014, and our reply to that is due on November 20, 2014. Nancy would like you to send a check in the amount of $1,000.00.

Thank you.

Deanna B, Legal Assistant

When we received the email from Nancy's office with the following Memorandum, we were furious at the accusations put forth by Connie and her references as "Facts". A fact is something that is true and can be proven to be true. Her Memorandum was nothing more than thirteen pages of fabrication and falsehoods. We could not understand how a court could accept a Memorandum of Lies without any proof to back it up. But that is the way of Connie. Her baseless journals submitted to the court typically lacked any documentation. When court cases where referenced, she failed to provide the actual cases.

I printed it out and Jody and I wrote our side notes on the Memorandum as we read it. I then emailed it to Nancy the next day. By now we were getting very exhausted by the back and forth and lack of results. To make her job easier, we thought our written rebuttal would be helpful. Our responses are embolden in the brackets:

NOVEMBER 13TH, 2014:   KIRK J'S OPPOSITION TO JODY RHORER'S SUPPLEMENTAL MEMORANDUM, filed by Connie C, Commissioner Bloom presiding

Comes now, Connie, Attorney at Law, and on behalf of the Respondent, Kirk J, files the forgoing Opposition to Jody Rhorer's "Supplemental Memorandum" regarding Motions.

FACTS

(1) Kirk J and Kelly H were married and cohabiting at the time of conception and birth of PR in July of 2007.
{**NOT a fact - she lived in Oregon with Jody - proof of hospital medical bills for postpartum care provided.**}

(2) A child welfare action was brought by the Division of Child and Family Services when PR was an infant.
{**Provide the PROOF and documentation. PR lived with Jody - evidence to support has been provided by Jody.**}

(3) Though Mr. Rhorer was not initially personally present (having fled the jurisdiction because of a pending criminal matter) his mother appeared before the Juvenile Court asserting that she was 'grandmother' of PR.
{**Jody was not allowed in since he hadn't established paternity and did not FLEE.**}

(4) The Juvenile Court issued a warrant for Jody Rhorer due to the assertions that he was father, and because he did not appear at the shelter hearing.
{**Jody had no clue about the shelter hearing and was not served. Connie needs to provide documentation.**}

(5) Mr. Rhorer eventually did appear, but later voluntarily absented himself from the proceedings. {**Not true.**}

(6) The Juvenile Court was eventually made aware that PR's mother, Kelly H, was in fact married to Kirk J at the time of the conception and birth of PR, and the Juvenile Court issued an Order, that despite being titled a 'dispositional order,' specifically indicates that Kirk J was found to be father of PR by clear and convincing evidence.
{**Where is the order and what is that evidence?**}

(7) Jody Rhorer did not appeal that Order.
{**Once again, what Order does she refer to? He has never stopped fighting for his daughter.**}

(8) As part of the Juvenile Court proceeding, Respondent Kirk J was granted physical custody of PR in 2010, and sole legal and physical custody of PR in 2012.
{**No physical custody in 2010. No documentation provided by Connie.**}

(9) Mr. Rhorer did not appeal the Order granting Kirk J permanent legal and physical custody of PR. {**He wasn't a party to the action. He couldn't appeal it.**}

(10) Instead, Mr. Rhorer attempted to establish paternity of PR in a District Court action, in which he intentionally failed to inform the Court that the child had a presumed father, and that the Juvenile Court had jurisdiction and had made a finding related to paternity. He obtained a default order of parentage and the District Court then set it aside.
{**Jody was not aware of the "marriage" and had an attorney that filed and advised him.**}

(11) Mr. Rhorer also caused to have the Office of Recovery Services engage in biological testing without advising the Agency that PR had a presumed father due to marriage of the mother to another man at the time of the child's conception and birth.
{**The Court ordered the DNA testing as a way to assert his parentage**}

(12) Mr. Rhorer also failed to inform ORS about the Juvenile Court proceeding in which Kirk J was found to be father of PR.
{**False. The Court also ordered Kirk to take a DNA test.)**

(13) Mr. Rhorer's efforts through ORS to obtain an administrative Order of Paternity upon DNA testing also resulted in an Order of Child Support.
{**Where is the copy of the Order?)**

(14) At no time in this action has Respondent Kirk J 'raised the issue' of legal paternity of PR. {**Why would he?**}

(15) At no time in this action has Kelly H raised the issue of paternity of PR.
{**Yes, she has. She fluctuated back and forth depending on with whom she was on good terms with.**}

(16) Both Kirk J and Kelly H have acknowledged, having found out through the DNA testing, that Kirk J is not biological father of PR, however neither have raised the issue of legal paternity and in fact in all pleadings in the divorce, have averred that custody/child support determination of PR involved the two of them.
{**There was no way Kirk could have been Payshence's father as he hadn't been in a relationship with Kelly per his own testimony since 2005. Some of his testimony even states his relationship ended in 2003, shortly after their marriage.**}

(17) No request has been made by either Kelly H nor Kirk J to disestablish Kirk J's paternity.

{Kelly has testified in court in front of Commissioner Bloom that Kirk is not Payshence's father. It is on record.}

(18) A divorce decree was granted in this matter in September, 2013.

{Kirk and Kelly were ordered multiple times by the court to divorce and were legally separated prior to Kelly and Jody's relationship, per Kirk's own testimony. Jill has also been ordered by the courts to divorce Mr. C as she does not reside with him and allegedly has a child with Kirk.}

(19) Mr. Rhorer filed motions for the first time in this matter in December, 2013.

{Not so. Jody began his fight from the time Payshence was taken from him.)

Mr. Rhorer now argues that JPR v. LM. supports the proposition that he has standing to contest paternity of PR in this proceeding. To arrive at this conclusion, Mr. Rhorer ignores the clear working of statues which apply, and instead, latches onto something in the nature of a 'policy statement' contained in the decision.

JPR, specifically states that 79B-15-607 UCA applies in a circumstance when there is a 'presumed father,' meaning, the person married to the mother of the child at the time the child is conceived or born...(and) makes clear that only the presumed father, Kirk J, and the mother, Kelly H, have standing to raise the issue of paternity of PR. The clear wording of 78B-15-607 specifies that the paternity issue may be raised by the presumed father and mother at any time prior to filing an action for divorce or in the pleading at the time of the divorce of the party.

Mr. Rhorer ignores the wording of the statute, which JPR definitively finds is applicable, which specified that either Kirk J or Kelly H would have asked the Court to disturb the marital presumption of paternity before filing of the divorce action or in the pleadings, which was not done in this case. The pleadings merely acknowledge that Kirk J is not PR's biological father, but then both request that custody/visitation/support issues be determined as between them.

To overcome the clear direction that only presumed father or mother have standing to raise paternity, Mr. Rhorer latches onto a 'policy statement' in the case, 'that action 607 reflects the Utah Legislature's intent to encourage a presumed father to stay married to the mother and raise the child is an intact marriage.'

Counsel can find no statutory definition of 'intact marriage' either in the statutes or in the cases interpreting them. Mr. Rhorer has offered no definition of that phrase to guide this Court. However, Mr. Rhorer asserts that the marriage between Kelly H and Kirk J was 'never intact,' citing their long period of living apart, including that men other than Kirk J and Mr. Rhorer are biological fathers of other children (not PR) also born during the legal marriage of Kelly H and Kirk J.

It seems that Mr. Rhorer's interpretation of this concept of 'intact marriage' involves some qualitative analysis and inquiry into the happiness, harmony, cohesiveness, and co-habitation between the married couple. Mr. Rhorer asked the Court to conclude that because the marriage of Kelly H and Kirk J has not been that type of 'happy union' the Legislature envisioned, at least since the time Mr. Rhorer impregnated Kelly H, that the Court should find different rules should apply to him than are described in 78B-15-607.

Even if the Legislature would like to encourage parents to stay married and raise children as issue of the marriage, it is clear that the qualitative review of the 'happiness' and cohesiveness of the parties to a marriage cannot be the touchstone to contest paternity. 78B-15-607 states that either the presumed father (husband) or mother may challenge the marital presumption prior to filing of a divorce Petition.

Therefore, the statute allows either of those designated persons, the presumed father or the mother, to raise the challenge irrespective of whether there is a divorce, and before any divorce filing. Theoretically then, either husband (presumed father) or mother could file a paternity action asking to disestablish paternity, even if no divorce is ever filed. However, it does not allow the challenger in Mr. Rhorer's position to make the challenge. Therefore, irrespective of 'intactness' and whether a divorce would be filed, the only persons who may raise the issue is set by statute as mother and presumed father, not a putative father such as Mr. Rhorer. Mr. Rhorer's argument that he should be brought into the sphere of potential paternity challenges because the marriage wasn't viable or happy flies in the face of the terms of 78B-15-607, and the statement of JPR v. LM, that 78B-15-706 controls standing in such cases.

Nothing in JPR suggests that the scope of lawful challengers can be broadened in any way. In fact, the decision makes clear that common law has been abrogated by the adoption of the Utah Uniform Parentage Act, and that 78B-15-607 controls such challenges, including restricting who may bring such a challenge. Because the terms of the statute do no allow someone situated as Mr. Rhorer to bring such a challenge, and he is therefore prohibited.

Mr. Rhorer's reliance on the 'intact marriage' encouraging husband and wife to stay married' policy argument is odd in light of the factual underpinnings of this case. Mr. Rhorer slept with a married woman. In light of the fact that fornication and adultery are still crimes in the State of Utah, it is fair to conclude that the Legislature would not seek to encourage the behavior Mr. Rhorer engaged in with Kelly H. Instead of considering that his actions, which arguably significantly undermined the viability of Kirk and Kelly's marriage and increased the likelihood of severance of the legal bonds which ensured that both spouses would support the children of the marriage, Mr. Rhorer instead urges that since the marital home wasn't that great to start with, the Legislature must've invested that he be permitted to burn down the house. His interpretation of the 'intact marriage' concept would allow him to snatch his biological child from her home with her family, while leaving even her half siblings, who were also born of the same marriage, to perish in the flames. **(This is absurd! And what about the fact that Payshence had 3 sisters that the State 'left to perish in the flames' when they took her from her family?)**

Mr. Rhorer's arguments and position in this case elevate his desires to a preeminent over concerns of stability and support of the children. It is and has been his position that because he is biological father of PR, then he has some entitlement. A review of the historical underpinnings of the area of parentage law, which is not less relevant in this modern age where biological parentage can be scientifically determined is warranted, particularly where Mr. Rhorer asks this Court to strain to interpret a policy statement favoring 'intact marriage' to benefit someone who endeavored in every way possible to destroy a marriage.

At least as far back as the ancient Roman law **{Wasn't that 2000 years ago?}**, the rule has been quite general that a child born to a married woman is presumed to be the offspring of her husband and legitimate. This presumption is rooted in the realization of the importance of the integrity of the legally recognized family as the basic unit of society. It was endowed with such sanctity that deviations resulted in severe sanctions both social and legal. In former times, bearing a child out of wedlock visited disgrace not only upon the immediate parties and their families, but quite unreasoningly, extended to the innocent child and was actually intensified as to him by depriving him of practically all legal right. It was said that he was legally related to no one; had no rights as an heir; was not even entitled to a name, although he could gain one by reputation.

He was not denied the privilege of aspiring to positions of dignity and honor in either church or state; he could have no heirs except those of his body; and if he dies without descendants, his property escheated to the state. It was to avoid the dire consequences to the child involved, as well as to protect the family unit, that courts have always gone to extreme lengths to hold issue legitimate, and the presumption was practically absolute. <u>Holder vs. Holder</u> (Utah **1959)**.

Note that in discussing the practical and policy reasons underpinning the martial presumption of paternity in the husband, the Court specifically mentions preservation of the 'integrity' of the legally recognized family as the basic unit of society. The 'legal' family denoted the legal relationships which come from a 'legal' marriage. 'Legal marriages' begin with the issuance of license, and ceremony by a qualified officiant, or presence of certain prerequisites to common law marriage. Legal marriage ends upon dissolution; annulment, divorce, death of a spouse, as provided for the Code. There is no accepted view of legal marriage which recognizes 'happy, cohesive marriages in which spouses co-habit' versus marriages where one spouse is sleeping with someone like Mr. Rhorer. Both types of marriages, happy/cohesive and cohabiting, and nefarious, low-down, cheating marriages are provided the same legal protections where the children are concerned precisely because the focus is not about the adults who can make their own decision, good and bad, but because the children cannot and are brought into their situations for better and worse, innocently, but equally entitled to support.

The historical discussion in the <u>Holder</u> case reminds that the 'legal marriage' is supported, and the marital presumption of paternity in the husband exists because the innocent children of the marriage (particularly those who otherwise might bare the stigma of not being the biological child of the husband) ideally should be embraced, attached, accepted, incorporated, and in every way owned and identified as offering of the legal marriage. The development of DNA technology which allows people scientific near-certainty as to biological relation, which post-dates the decision in <u>Holder,</u> does nothing to disturb the emotional and societal reality that it is in the best interest of children to be claimed by both spouses of the marital union in existence at the time of the child's creation and birth.

That the Legislature intended that to continue to be the case is evident in the fact that the marital presumption of paternity felt biological paternity should trump, it could have said so. It did not. If the Legislature felt how happy a marriage was should determine whether a putative father has standing, it could have. It has not. Instead, in 78B-15-607, the Legislature has clearly indicated that a mother or presumed father are the only ones with standing to move to disturb the presumption of paternity in the husband. The history of the recognition and status of the legal family unit indicates that while the relationship between spouses is to be furthered and encouraged, the relationship between legal parents and children, and the support from legal parents to legal children is paramount.

Further, the legal issue of paternity has already been concluded by clear and convincing evidence by the Juvenile Court in a proceeding in which Mr. Rhorer participated, and then voluntary absented himself. He then opted instead to strategically select a District Court paternity action in which he did not properly notice Kirk J, and an ORS paternity action (also without notifying the parties of the parental presumption/Juvenile Court determination). After obtaining the DNA testing which concluded he was biological father of PR he had failed and refused to pay any support for the daughter he asserts is his legal child, despite the child support as part of that ORS action. The same amounts to legal abandonment.

{Clearly Jody would prefer to pay all of Payshence's expenses by being able to raise her. There is no order for Jody to pay child support because the state hasn't recognized him as the father. How can they expect him to pay support when he is not even allowed to see her or talk to her or even be recognized as any type of relative at all?}

Wherefore, for all the foregoing reasons, this Court's presumption, and because the Court must recognize the Order already issued by a Court of competent Jurisdiction, namely the Juvenile Court of the District, this Court must conclude that Mr. Rhorer has no standing, and reiterate that Kirk J is legal father pursuant to the Order of the Juvenile Court.

CHAPTER 15
TIME FOR CHANGE

Jody was having one of his long phone conversations with his mom.

"She's really bad and the doctors don't give her much time," George stressed.

Jody responded, "Well Mike says she's still pretty much workin every day. Why is she doing that if she's so sick?"

"I dunno, Jody! Why don't you just call her yourself if you don't believe me." George was getting emotional.

"Well if she's sick, Mom, you and Dad should drive out to Florida for Thanksgiving and Deone and I 'll meet ya there." Jody was testing to see how serious his grandma's condition really was. George could be a bit dramatic at times.

"Why don't you just drive out and pick us up on the way?"

Jody was starting to get irritated. "Deone and I will fly out and if you and Dad really wanna see your sister and Dad's brother then hop in your van and meet us there. Florida's not that far from Missouri, Mom. We can't take a week off work just for drive time. If we are goin out there, we're gonna make a vacation out of it."

A little genealogy on the family tree: Jody's grandma is also his mom's sister and his grandpa is his dad's brother. George was one of the youngest of about eight. Her mother was a raging alcoholic and when George was around four, the State of Missouri was going to put the children in foster care and break up the family. George's oldest sister, Arlene, had married at age 12 and already had two sons and a stable home. Her husband was much older and he agreed to adopt her siblings. Arlene became her brother and sister's legal mother when she was 16 years old.

When the older girls began to come of age, Arlene's husband started abusing them, so she took the kids and became a single mother of nearly a dozen children in her mid 20's. When George was 16, she married Terry, who was also in his 20's. Then Arlene met Ronnie, Terry's brother. They were married until she died of cancer at the beginning of 2015.

I know this story because Arlene told me during our 5 day stay with her and Ronnie and cousin Allen in Palmetto, Florida over Thanksgiving of 2014. I was glad to get to meet her. She was a gracious hostess and wonderful cook. Taking her and Ronnie to see some of the sites in Florida that surrounded them that they had never ventured out to was a welcome break from the stress going on back in Utah. We were tired of waiting and waiting and hearing nothing from Commissioner Bloom.

NOVEMBER 18TH, 2014: EMAILS from Nancy's office

When I sent the rebuttal notes on "KIRK J'S OPPOSITION TO JODY RHORER'S SUPPLEMENTAL MEMORANDUM" to Nancy, she shot back in anger. I tried an upbeat email to mend the bridge, but it was basically discarded. Jody's letter, however, was responded to with rage.

Hi Most Amazing Girls,

Jody and I agonized over this ridiculous pontificating response by Connie to your brief. We wrote our thoughts for a rebuttal in the margins. I don't know if this will help you or not and if this is actually a blessing that she brought these things up as it gives us a chance to set the record straight in the event Bloom's memory has faded or she didn't take the time to read all of your laborious documentation. Please excuse the hand writing and I hope you can make out the words as I was so upset and tired when we were going through it last night.

One thing that Jody wanted me to reiterate, he did not start a physical relationship with Kelly for months after they moved to Oregon. Kelly never lived with Kirk as long as Jody has known her. She always led him to believe she was unmarried. She conceived in Oregon. Connie's allegations are false, fabricated, and undocumented. There it not an ORS order for Jody to pay child support. It seems to me that they want money from Jody but want to give him no rights or contact with his daughter.

We are still praying hard. Thanks for all you do,
Deone (and Jody) Rhorer

And Jody sent a much more to-the-point email.

Dear Nancy,
I feel we are going in circles. Everything Connie wrote we already went through. I feel that time is wasted on this as well as money. If Connie can get away with what she has been pulling off we need to take this further to Judge Stanley. It's time to become more aggressive. Connie can draw this out by making up a bunch of lies and allegations. It's time to open up a can of WHOOP ASS. We spoke to someone today involved with the courts and were told that we are able to go to Judge Stanley since he is the one to hold Bloom accountable. What are we doing with her in the first place? She has wasted our time, not kept her word, and left my daughter to suffer another 6 months. We were told today that we could go above her head to Stanley. What proof do we have that she even read all the volumes of evidence you prepared for her? If she had she would have acted and stopped this nonsense.

Also, I want to know why Kelly is even part of this? They are no longer married and she has no custody. Connie needs to be put in her place and Bloom needs to take charge of her court room and do her job. Kirk needs to be painted as the felon kidnapper that he is. Connie paints me as a slimy uncaring flakey deadbeat. It's time to show the courts who I AM - Payshence's DADDY who will stop at nothing to get his baby girl back. The state of Utah is a hypocrite. Commissioner Bloom knows that Kirk has a kid with a married woman and Kelly's 5th kid was born when she was still married to Kirk but that boy was given to his biological daddy.

If the state refuses to give me my daughter then they need to take those kids and give them to the "Husbands" that Connie kept referring to. Then they can hurt like I have hurt. Demand those kids be taken into state custody until this is settled. Then let Connie run her mouth about "intact marriages."

We need a forceful plan of action now. DONE.
Jody Rhorer
cc: Steven K

NOVEMBER 19TH

Jody and Deone, I am very familiar with the facts as we have already presented them to the court. I have started preparing a brief countering their stated facts. Nancy S

Jody and Deone, Since you are complaining about me to Steven K, I strongly advise you to seek other representation. Nancy S

Jody and Deone, In your letter to me you state that time and money is being wasted. I am spending my time today and tomorrow answering the brief filed by Connie. Next week I will send to you a detailed Statement of Services rendered on your case to date showing you the time I have spent and the money owing for my services. Nancy S

NOVEMBER 20TH

Hi Nancy,

My heart sunk when I got to my emails last night and read yours. I'm so sorry that you were hurt by Jody's email. I know that his words were not directed "at" you but "to" you about his frustration with Connie and that he has a very explicit way of expressing himself. He, in no way, intended to diminish the job you have done for us. He has praised you and your efforts and staff countless times. He has always felt you were the one that would get his little girl back for him and still believes that.

We were caught off guard by Connie's response. I had no idea she could pontificate like that and thought her response should have only been limited to your brief. We didn't know what to do as there was no message from your office as to what would happen next; only a copy of the response.

I thought it would be beneficial to put in our side notes, but I wasn't sure if it was going to help or not - so I offered it and figured you knew best and would discard if it wasn't useful.

We have not spoken to any other attorneys about our case. I was training one of my part-time agents, he has worked in probation and parole for 20 years. He said he was taking his family to Disneyland and I told him that we wanted to take Jody's daughters there if we ever get his baby back. We started talking about Payshence and how the Commissioner hadn't ruled and it had been six months. He told me about the superior Judge and that the "squeaky wheel gets oiled" in the justice system as well as anywhere else. He said we needed to make as much noise as possible and contact Judge Stanley as he should be overseeing the case. I know he is not an attorney and was referencing his own experience but I'm sure after going through this for 3 1/2 years that you can understand how anxious we are.

I hope you can accept this sincere apology. We know how much of your heart, soul and time has been put into this and every blow we feel, every lapse of silence from the court, is felt by you as much as it is felt by us. I also know we will get Payshence back and it will be because of you and Deanna. I feel in my heart that she will be in our home on Christmas morning opening her presents from all the Christmases and birthdays missed - and for that we will thank God for you.

Sincerely,

Deone Ehlers-Rhorer

We, in turn, received this chilly response from Deanna:

Nancy asked me to send you a copy of the attached reply brief which was filed with the Court today. She instructed me to advise you that if you have any problems with the brief to call the office and make an appointment to meet with Nancy to discuss the issues.

Thank you.

Deanna B, Legal Assistant

No other responses were given to our letters.

NOVEMBER 21ST, 2014:　JOURNAL ENTRY

On our way to Florida for a visit with Jody's grandma who is dealing with cancer. We, of course, hoped to have our little girl with us, but alas, another month with no conclusion.

However, we finally got some movement and oh what drama that has caused. It began with a long-awaited call from Commissioner Bloom finally responding to the latest attachment Nancy S made to our case concerning another case that had been settled in Cedar City that showed promise in setting a precedence in ours. Why is our own team fighting now? Surely, we cannot move forward like this. Connie wanted to cause turmoil and it is working.

Once we arrived at Grandma Arlene's mobile home park, there was quiet and time to regroup. I spent many hours reading through the court case and trying to work through strategies in my head - trying to make sense of it. There is so much to get my mind around.

The serenity was broken by an email to Jody from Nancy's law office. It was a STATEMENT OF ACCOUNT - our first actual computer-generated invoice. The amount billed was $68,198.20!

Jody had been giving Nancy large sums of money since she took over his case. He typically gave her cash or a money order. Sometimes I would mail checks to her. We hadn't received an actual bill from her or signed a contract of expectations either. We estimated that Jody had been paying between $1,500 and $2,000 a month to Nancy and to say that Jody was quite upset over this surprise bill would be an understatement. Some odd things about the statement - there were dates and detailed description of action taken, but no time attached - just a whole number. For example:

11/18/2014 Meeting with Deanna to pull facts from file and continue
preparation of Reply Memorandum. NS $250.00

11/18/2014 Email from Deone telling me that they are dissatisfied with my
work and how the case has been going; response to email. NS $25.00

11/18/2014 Receipt and review of email from client with disparaging and
insulting opinion about how I have handled his case and telling me that I
have not been aggressive enough and that time and money has been
wasted on the case, and instructing me how to proceed on the case; email
response to client. NS $75.00

11/20/2014 Receipt and review of email from Deone. NS $25.00

11/20/2014 Call from client telling me that he is upset about what
opposing counsel had written in memorandum. NS $25.00

11/20/2104 Telephone call with Deanna asking her to send the client copy
of Memo and telling client that if he had a problem with it, to call me and
set appointment. NS $25.00

   And so on and so forth.

   To that point, Nancy and her office staff had been putting their energy and heart into our case and exploring every avenue to win. I even noticed that Deanna would call Jody after hours and on the weekends. Sometimes she would keep him on the phone for long periods of time. But there was something I didn't know about those conversations that came out when we received the bill - Deanna was interested in much more than Jody's case - she was interested in Jody.
   Apparently, she had been trying to get Jody to come to her house while her husband was out of town. He brushed it off and kept the focus on the case, but due to the change in events, it was time to reveal this to Nancy.
   We were still on vacation so I put my energy into research. Some things weren't adding up to me. Nancy was exceptional at research and putting together elaborate details, but she shut down in the court room and clearly let Connie push her around. It also didn't seem that the amount of time it was taking to get an answer to our hearing from last spring was normal. So, I did an internet search to find out what was a "normal" amount of time to wait for a verdict from a hearing. There's a plethora of free legal advice on the internet; it is followed by a lot of attorneys trying to get your business.

   QUESTIONS:

   We went to court in May and the commissioner still has not rendered a
   decision. What is the difference between a commissioner and a judge and
   why was our case assigned to a commissioner? She has told us on several
   occasions that she would make a decision but then months of silence go by.
   Is there something we can do or someone to contact to speed up the process?
   Does she answer to a "higher power"?

   Attorney **ANSWER:**

   Whenever a court takes a matter under advisement, it is supposed to render it's decision by no later than 30 days. I'm not sure why your situation is taking so long without having a lot more information about your case. A commissioner is a judicial officer who handles preliminary matters in domestic relations cases. They are not a judge but their rulings are of the court which are signed off on by the judge assigned to your case. In the Utah District Courts where there are commissioners, all cases are assigned both a judge and a commissioner. There are things you can do to move the matter along and yes, the commissioner does answer to a higher power. You can contact the judge assigned to your case and have the judge find out what's going on. I'm assuming you don't have an attorney? If not, you should get one.

Hmmm. If that wasn't a big waving red flag…

DECEMBER 1ST, 2014: EMAIL from Nancy S

Jody, Deanna has explained your conversation to me today. I think you and I should meet to discuss how to proceed on your case. Please call me so that we can make an appointment. Thanks, Nancy S

When Jody explained that Deanna had been coming on to him and calling him excessively, Nancy's tone changed completely. The STATEMENT OF ACCOUNT was dropped. Deanna was put on a short suspension and then terminated all together. It was back to business as usual.

DECEMBER 4TH, 2014: CRIMINAL MISCHIEF; INTENTIONAL DAMAGE, DEFACE, DESTROY PROPERTY Class B Misdemeanor - Shane S; This case involves domestic violence. Arraignment scheduled on February 13, 2015.

DECEMBER 4TH, 2014: ASSAULT, DOMESTIC VIOLENCE Class B Misdemeanor, Kelly H; 12-26-14 Warrant issued for Failure to Appear. Court finds defendant indigent and appoints Salt Lake Legal Defenders to represent the defendant. Appointed Counsel. Pretrial conference scheduled for March 13, 2015.

2015

Since we were making no progress, we decide to go viral. I spent days contacting the local, state, and national media. Every newspaper, news agency, television show, news source that was looking for a story - I sent them ours. I filmed Jody talking about his daughter and my son, Logan, made a little movie that we posted on Facebook and also a Go Fund Me account so we could raise more funds for attorney costs. My sister, Raelene had a connection with our local newspaper, The Standard Examiner, and an article was published on the front page of the Saturday edition. All this in hopes of some positive help, but instead all we got was rude troll remarks and Facebook riots from the other side. No help came.

FEBRUARY 1ST, 2015: STANDARD EXAMINER NEWSPAPER ARTICLE

"Jody Rhorer looks at the unoccupied bed as he and his wife, Deone, discuss the legal situation of his biological daughter, Payshence, in the room of their house they have set up for her in Eden on Tuesday, January 27, 2015. Due to Utah laws, Jody's biological daughter is in the legal custody of the daughter's mother's ex-husband. "She is thinking why don't you come see me anymore, Daddy?" Jody said about his daughter. "And I am trying to see her, love my daughter."

A 7-year-old girl nicknamed Payshence has a "presumed"' and "adjudicated" fat

her, as well as a separate "biological" and "social" father. That only begins to explain the complicated ordeal in which young Payshence is stuck. Eden resident Jody Rhorer, the biological father, is putting up the fight of his life to see his daughter again. He said the fight is being complicated by a state law, the Utah Uniform Parentage Act.

"It is legalized kidnapping," Rhorer said of the Act. "The courts are pushing this to extremes and shoving me out of my daughter's life."

It has been 18 months since Rhorer has seen his youngest child, he claims. He also says he has spent more than five years in and out of courtrooms, tens of thousands of dollars in legal fees, and many sleepless nights trying to get the state to recognize his parental rights.

Now Payshence remains with her birth mother's former husband. There is a beautiful canopied bed, still-wrapped birthday presents, and clothes waiting for Payshence in his Eden home. "I want my baby to know her dad hasn't given up," Rhorer said. "It is driving me crazy."

Rhorer said he wonders every day how his daughter, now in first grade, is doing; if she can read, if she is clean, if she is happy. For the first three years of her life, Payshence was raised by Rhorer, her biological father. His name was placed on her original birth certificate.

Payshence was born to Rhorer and Kelly H out of wedlock in 2007. The girl is Rhorer's fourth daughter. Rhorer had custody of his three oldest daughters before Payshence was born. The couple and his three daughters returned from Oregon to Utah a few months before the girl was born so her mother could be close to family.

At one point while Payshence was young, Rhorer and her mother were making wedding plans, purchasing wedding fanfare all the way down to the dress and napkins, until a kink was discovered. Kelly had not yet divorced Kirk J, her first husband, whom she had married four years earlier in 2003. Rhorer said Kelly intentionality hid her marriage from him and during other court cases, conduct which Rhorer's attorney said in court documents "constitutes fraud and fraudulent misrepresentations, as well as perjury upon the court."

Kirk J later told Utah Courts that he and Kelly H had not resided in the same household since 2005, two years before Payshence was born.

Under the Utah Uniform Parentage Act, which became law in 2005, Kirk J was the little girls "presumed" father because he was married to her mother at the time of the baby's conception. Although the couple contemplated divorce as early as 2003, Kelly H and Kirk J did not terminate their marriage until 2013, after a court ordered the two to file for divorce.

"The couple did not live together. Their marriage was never a functioning marriage," Rhorer said, adding that each of Kelly's five children has a different biological father. Attempts to reach Kirk J and Kelly H were not returned.

In a November 13, 2014, court document, Kirk J's attorney wrote, "…neither Kirk nor Kelly have raised the issue of legal paternity and in fact in all pleadings in the divorce have averred that custody/child support determinations involve the two of them. Only the presumed father and the mother have standing to raise the issue of paternity. No request has been made by either Kelly H nor Kirk J to disestablish Kirk J's paternity. It is and has been Rhorer's position that because he is the biological father, that he has some entitlement." The memo also refers to the Utah Uniform Parentage Act, saying it lacks statutory definition of an "intact marriage."

"Mr. Rhorer asks the Court to conclude that because the marriage of Kelly H and Kirk J has not been that type of 'happy union' the Legislature envisions, that the Court should find different rules apply to him," according to the memo. "Even if the Legislature would like to encourage parents to stay married and raise children as issue of the marriage, it is clear that the qualitative review of the 'happiness' and cohesiveness of the parties to a marriage cannot be the touchstone as to whether a challenger (aside from mother and husband) may have standing to contest paternity. There is no accepted view of legal marriage which recognizes 'happy, cohesive marriages in which spouses cohabit' versus marriage where one spouse is sleeping with someone else.

Both types of marriages, happy/cohesive and cohabiting, and nefarious, low-down, cheating marriages are provided the same legal protections" in order to protect innocent children entitled to support. Rhorer said despite this argument Kelly H and Kirk J were divorced more than a year before his attorney wrote the November memo.

"Martial presumption of paternity remains despite the ability to determine biological paternity," the memo goes on to state. "If the Legislature felt biological paternity should trump, it could have said so." The Utah Uniform Parentage Act, sponsored by Senator Lyle Hillyard, took effect January 1, 2005. According to media reports, the bill was originally meant to deal with surrogacy as well as demands for child support refunds when a man finds out he is not the biological father of a child.

"The premise of the Paternity Act, is that marriage means something and there needs to be a clear line for births that occur during a marriage," Hillyard said. "If a married woman has relations with someone other than her husband and she becomes pregnant, her husband is still responsible and has the right to raise that child unless he chooses to decline that right and opportunity and then the State looks for the biological father. I don't intend to try to amend the Paternity bill (during this session of Utah Legislature). I am sorry but I just don't have time this session to try to change the law but if I did, I cannot make the change retroactive so it would not impact Jody's case."

For the first few years of her life, Payshence stayed with Rhorer, being raised alongside her three half-sisters and near Rhorer's parents and sister. At one point, a juvenile court judge temporarily placed Payshence with Rhorer's mother. The grandmother became a licensed foster parent at the suggestion of the state to continue caring for the girl, but it was not to be.

Rhorer was court-ordered to establish paternity, which he successfully did via a DNA test in July of 2010. For six short months in 2010, Rhorer was given custody of his daughter until the courts discovered that Kirk J was still married to Kelly H. Despite the conclusive paternity test and years-worth of father-daughter interaction between Payshence and Rhorer, the Court deemed Kirk J the girl's "presumed" father and removed Rhorer from Payshence's birth certificate.

They "bastardized my daughter," Rhorer said. "I had three hours after court to hand over my child. My daughter never knew this guy and they just took her away." The court officially awarded custody of Payshence to Kirk J in 2012. For a while Rhorer was able to have limited visitation with his daughter. He even took her clothes shopping for her first day of kindergarten. But that ended in July 2013, when Kirk J stopped allowing visits.

Now, the case is in the hands of Salt Lake City Third District Court. According to court records, on July 15, 2014, the Commissioner said her decision on granting Rhorer parental rights would "be forthcoming in the next couple of weeks."

For several months, the court remained silent. Hoping to "wake" the commissioner, Rhorer's attorney filed information with the court showing the outcome of a similar case in Cedar City in August 2014. In October, the commissioner responded, asking Rhorer's attorney to file a case brief summarizing his evidence, as well as for a rebuttal from Kirk J. The brief and rebuttal were filed in November. Still, the waiting game continues. Rhorer holds out hope to soon see his daughter. In the meantime, Rhorer has contacted lawmakers about the unintended consequences of the Utah Uniform Parentage Act."

JANUARY 4TH, 2015: EMAILS to Nancy S

Happy New Year Nancy, My son made a video over Christmas about Payshence. Jody wanted it sent to you for feedback. We plan on sending it to the media. It was really hard not having her over another holiday. We are so disappointed in Commissioner Bloom. She just doesn't seem to have a heart or care at all. If she did, she would have made some sort of effort before now. Looking forward to your response, Deone

JANUARY 5th

Hi Deone, I received your gift and I hope you got my Christmas card. So sorry for not responding sooner. I was out of the office last week with the flu, but back this week. I am also disappointed in Commissioner Bloom and will look into requesting that she rule or turn it over to the Judge. Thanks, Nancy S

January marks an important time in Utah - State Legislature is in session. My sister Raelene was also connected with a State Representative in her area that thought she could get us a meeting with some of the seasoned state law makers. Since our letters to Congressman Bishop and Governor Herbert were brushed off, I left several messages for my State Representative Christensen, and once he finally answered the phone, found him to be nothing short of disinterested and apathetic.

Now a chance to sit down, face to face, and make a plea for help with the very person that assisted in drafting the Utah version of the UUPA - Senator Hilliard.

If we could get a sympathetic ear - someone that would help draft an amendment to the law that could help cases like ours and possibly save some people from suffering in the future; a law that would recognize fathers for how important they are and show that they have the capacity to love just as much as a mother, this could be our day!

Raelene had everything lined up. She presented the information to Nancy in a meeting we had set up but Nancy was still chilly towards us due to the Deanna incident. She said she couldn't come to the meeting so it was the three of us, myself, Jody and Raelene. I had put together packets of information for the three lawmakers that would be in attendance. We met at the Capitol cafeteria an hour in advance to prepare our presentation. Our meeting took place upstairs in Senator Hilliard's office.

We had 15 minutes to present our plea. Raelene, who had been by our side throughout the entire process and had a great understanding of the case, started the meeting. I filled in and then a few questions were asked of Jody. One profound statement was made by Hilliard: When the presumed father took a DNA test to prove he's not the father he automatically recused himself from being the father. The case should have ended there."

I then asked why it had been nine months and we still didn't have a ruling from our May court date. That's when I learned that there was a 60-day ruling period. Hilliard was a family law attorney by profession. Why had Commissioner Bloom held out for nine months?

The meeting seemed to go well and right after it ended Jody and I went to the court house to see if we could speak with the Commissioner. Once in her office, we were allowed to speak to an assistant on a phone that was in the reception area. I asked about our case and was told that they wouldn't talk to me since I was not a party so I put Jody on the phone and put my ear up to the receiver.

"We've been waiting nine months for an answer from Commissioner Bloom, can you tell us why?" Jody asked. "We just left Senator Hilliard's office and he told us she only had 60 days to make a ruling."

"It hasn't been 60 days," the assistant said.

"Our hearing was last May? It's January now!" Jody was doing his best to control his emotions.

"Just a second." The assistant put us on hold.

After a few minutes she came back on the line. "It looks like the last Lodging in this case was mid-October."

I was close enough to the phone to talk. "Are you telling me that every time our attorney lodged something with the court, she reset the clock?"

"That's correct," she responded.

"Well it's the end of January so it's been more than sixty days since the last lodging in October. Let Commissioner Bloom know that, I said, and hung up the phone.

Jody and I looked at each other in astonishment. What kind of attorney doesn't know the time frame of rulings? Every time Nancy made a new lodging to "draw attention to our case" she reset the 60-day ruling allotment. All this waiting was due to lack of knowledge on her part.

My gut told me something wasn't right all along and I had a feeling that there would be more, and there was.

Jody called Nancy to let her know how the meeting went. I was too upset to speak to her and really wanted her fired. After a few weeks I called Hilliard's law office where he practiced family law. I called several times until I was finally told that he wasn't practicing law any more. His law office was able to get my messages to him and he eventually called me back. He told me he couldn't do anything to help us. Personally, I think he could if he wanted to, he just didn't really care to. He said he would personally call Bloom and ask her to speed things up. I'm not sure what did it, if it was the meeting at the Capital or our visit to the Commissioner's office, but within a couple days, a phone conference was set up.

FEBRUARY 9TH, 2015: EMAIL from Nancy S

Hi Jody and Deone, The Commissioner has set February 20th at 10:00 to give her ruling. She said that she has read every document, but has not listened to the Juvenile Court CD that we lodged with the court, so she has given me until this Friday to file a transcript of the hearing. I will need to hire a court reporter to transcribe the hearing on an expedited basis. Connie brought up the subject of your You Tube video and that she received a call from the press. She made an oral motion that the You Tube video be taken down immediately because it identifies Payshence. I believe you should take it down. We need to talk about this further. She didn't bring up the subject of the press article that Deone sent to me this morning, but she may do that. I think we should meet about this ASAP. I am leaving the office for a meeting downtown, but will be in the office tomorrow. Please call me so we can arrange to meet.
Thanks, Nancy

FEBRUARY 9TH, 2015: MINUTES FROM PHONE CONFERENCE

Commissioner Bloom held a telephone conference to discuss issues involving the current under advisement work. The Court informs counsel the CD which is the subject of the 2/28/2012 notice of lodging has not been reviewed by the court. The Court requests a transcript of the CD.

*The Commissioner **RECOMMENDS** that:*

1. The State (representing the Office of Recovery Services) is recused from today's phone conference as well as the recommendation hearing.

2. Nancy S is directed to obtain a transcript of the juvenile court hearing on 2/28/2012, and deliver to opposing counsel and the court by the 13th. A Response will be provided by the 17th.

3. A recommendation hearing will be scheduled for 2/20/2015 at 10 AM.

Connie made an oral motion regarding Mr. Rhorer allegedly providing court documents to a reporter, and displaying the child and information on You Tube.

*After some discussion regarding this issue, it was agreed that if the information on You Tube has any image of the child, or personal information, that will be **REMOVED**.*

*The Commissioner further **RECOMMENDS** that:*

4. If Connie wishes to file a motion for temporary restraining order, to be heard on the 20th, that would be okay. If the issue is resolved, counsel may submit an order reflecting such, which the Court may sign.

FEBRUARY 13TH, 2015: FINANCIAL DECLARATION and it's 48-page counterpart filed by Jody Rhorer.

We were finally here! The end. The decision we had been waiting so long for. She could wear her outfits and I would be registering her in the new elementary school and my husband's pain and suffering would end and we would be a happy-ever-after family.   I had been thinking about it for so long; planning all the details and I could finally write the ending to this book.

FEBRUARY 20TH, 2015: DECISION OF MOTIONS, Transcript of Court Hearing

THE BALIFF: ...Bloom presiding. You may be seated.

THE COURT: Good morning. We're here in the matter of Kelly H versus Kirk J. I would ask that counsel and parties to please state your appearance.

NANCY S: Nancy S on behalf of the Intervenor, Jody Rhorer, and Mr Rhorer is here.

THE COURT: Thank you.

CONNIE: Connie on behalf of Kirk J. Could we have just a second while he can make sure that the hearing device works.

THE BAILIFF: All rise. Court is again in session. Please be seated.

THE COURT: Okay. We're back on the record in the matter of Kelly H versus Kirk J. I did take a brief recess to allow the IT people to assist us so that Mr. J's hearing device would be working. Mr. J, you can hear now, correct?   Okay. Do note that both councill are present for Mr. J and Mr. Rhorer. I will ask for the record as to whether Kelly H is present.

NANCY S: She isn't present, Your Honor. She did send someone along to say that she's ill. We'll just ask that you go ahead without her being here.

THE COURT: Okay. Thank you. I'll also note for the record that we do have another intervenor in this case, and that is the Office of Recovery Services. Counsel has informed the court that he is waving his appearance as well. This matter has been before the court for some time. I have now had the opportunity to review the lengthy file and documents that have been provided by the parties. Given this, I am prepared to give my ruling. I'll first indicate that this matter was taken under advisement with several motions pending before the court and several hearings that the court held in May, July, and August of 2014.

There were several motions that were pending before the court and additional information that has been provided during the course of this case. I do want to indicate some procedural history which is relevant to the court's ruling today.

First, Kelly H is the Petitioner in this action. She filed a verified petition for divorce on November 21, 2012. Kirk J is the Respondent in this action and filed a response to the petition for divorce on December 11, 2012. Kelly H and Kirk J were married as asserted by Kelly H on or about April 17, 2002. They separated on or about May 30, 2005, according to the verified petition.

Kelly H has had several children during the course of Kelly H's and Kirk J's relationship. The child who is the subject of those motions is Payshence Rhorer and I will refer to her as PR. I will not refer directly to any of the other children that are referred to in the divorce case given that these motions are relevant only to PR.

Kelly H requested temporary custody of PR and the other children at a hearing that was held December 20, 2012. At the hearing the court found that there were two juvenile court orders regarding the children which grant permanent custody of the children to Kirk J. The court found that Kelly H had not met her burden or satisfied the requirements to be awarded custody of the children at that hearing.

The district court indicated it would obtain copies of the court orders from the juvenile court case. Shortly thereafter this court conducted a Rule 100 conference, pursuant to Rule 100 of the Utah Rules of Civil Procedure, with Judge V. During this conference a commissioner and judge from Third District and juvenile courts agreed that Kelly H's request to modify custody and parent-time should be heard in juvenile court given the significant amount of litigation that had occurred there between those parties regarding the children.

The issues regarding custody and parent-time were referred to that court during the conference. Jody Rhorer filed a motion to intervene in this matter on May 10, 2013, alleging that he is the biological father of PR. The matters were submitted to the judge who granted his motion of intervention at a hearing held June 25, 2013. Kirk J was present at the hearing and did not object to the intervention motion. Kelly H was not present at the hearing. The court will note that Kelly H and Kirk J were still married at the time.

The Office of Recovery Services filed a Motion for Intervention on June 24, 2013. Their motion for intervention was granted on June 25, 2013. Kelly H filed a motion to bifurcate in March of 2013. Based on an agreement by Kelly H and Kirk J, the option to bifurcate was granted on September 27, 2013. The bifurcated decree of divorce was signed the same day.

Mr. Rhorer filed a motion to establish himself as the natural and biological father of PR. Motion of Determination of Parentage and a Motion for Custody or in the alternative for a Custody Evaluation and Motion for Interim Parent-Time on December 9th, 2013.

A hearing was held January 16, 2014, where the district court determined that the juvenile court continued to have jurisdiction over the subject child. The district court determined it would not proceed on any motion before it regarding PR until the juvenile court terminated its jurisdiction over her, given the juvenile court has exclusive and continuing jurisdiction until their jurisdiction is terminated. Otherwise, Mr. Rhorer was instructed to take his motion before the juvenile court. The district court held a hearing on several motions filed by the parties on May 28th, 2014. The four entered certain recommendations regarding procedural issues and took other issues presented under advisement. At a hearing on July 15, 2014, additional issues were presented to the court which the court will be addressing in its under-advisement ruling.

On August 21st, 2014, Mr Rhorer filed a Motion for Judicial Notice of Adjudicated Fact which was opposed by Kirk J in his Opposition to Motion Requesting Judicial Note of Adjudicated Fact filed August 21, 2014. The court requested the issues under the motions be briefed and considered by the court. The court received additional argument from counsel through the end of November, 2014. A Notice to Submit was interred shortly after the final documents were provided.

In February, 2015, this court did request a transcript of a CD recording that was provided by Mr. Rhorer. This court typically does not review those given the procedural issues with regard to that, and that transcript has been provided.

Upon review of the several orders provided by the Third District Juvenile Court and additional cases in the Third District Court that involve some or all of the parties, the court has determined the following:

On November 6, 2009, a child welfare hearing was held regarding PR in juvenile court. I will refer to that as the Child Welfare Case No. 1. In that hearing the court determined that there was no service on Jody Rhorer whom the court stated was, quote, "the biological father of PR," end of quote. On November 7, 2008, Kelly H, Kirk J, and Mr. Rhorer were present at a hearing in the Child Welfare Case No. 1. The order from the hearing indicates that, Kelly H, the mother; Kirk J, who is referred to as the stepfather; and Mr. Rhorer, who is referred to as the father; were present. The order indicates that Mr. Rhorer was served a copy of the juvenile court petition in open court. The juvenile court determined that DCFS may consider returning custody of PR to Kelly H, "if the father, Mr. Rhorer, moves out of her residence and there is verification to that effect." Other orders entered including an order that Mr. Rhorer have no contact with Kelly H directly or indirectly. The pleadings indicate allegations by Kelly H that Mr. Rhorer was very abusive to her and that he had been throughout the relationship.

On November 20, 2008, a child welfare hearing was held in the Child Welfare Case No. 1. Kelly H, Kirk J, and Mr. Rhorer were not present, but their counsel was present. Counsel for Mr. Rhorer was allowed to withdraw, "as the father is not proven to be the legal father."

The petition was amended to, "dismiss all references or allegations to Mr. Rhorer in that he had not establish paternity." Kelly H's counsel advised the court that he had moved out of state. No visitation was granted to Mr. Rhorer until he again appeared in court.

On February 12, 2009, a review hearing was held in the Child Welfare Case No. 1. Neither Kelly H, Mr. Rhorer, or Kirk J were present. The order indicates a report that Kelly H left the state with PR. On March 2, 2009, a shelter hearing was held in Child Welfare Case No. 1. In the hearing, the issue of paternity was addressed as well as visitation. In the order it indicates the following: "The court noted that paternity hasn't been established and addressed visitation."

On March 19, 2009, a child welfare proceeding was held in Child Welfare Case No. 1. In the hearing the attorney general is recorded to indicate that, "Mr. Rhorer never established paternity regarding the child."

On August 28, 2009. Mr. Rhorer filed a petition for decree of parentage in the West Jordan court. That case I will refer to as "the paternity case." In the petition he asserts that he is the father of PR and Kelly H is the mother. Based on the service of Kelly H and subsequent default, a Decree of Parentage was entered on January 25, 2010. The Decree of Parentage indicates that there was a case before the juvenile court regarding the child but does not indicate whether the juvenile court jurisdiction had been terminated.

Several court hearings in Child Welfare Case No. 1, subsequent to the March 19, 2009, hearing occurred, where the issue of the establishment of paternity were discussed. On August 14, 2009, Mr. Rhorer filed a motion for paternity.

In a juvenile court hearing in Child Welfare Case No. 1 held February 16, 2010, the permanency order indicates the following:

"The court received a court report and Decree of Parentage from Jody Rhorer. The assistant attorney general informed the court that Kirk J and Kelly H are still married. The petition filed by Mr. Rhorer in district court to establish paternity did not provide any notice to Kirk J." The court then appointed conflict counsel to Kirk J, the presumed father.

On April 17, 2010, an additional hearing was held in the Child Welfare Case No. 1 where Kirk J and Mr. Rhorer were present. At that hearing the parties were to discuss the paternity and parentage issues to address at the next hearing. At hearings held May 20, 2010, and July 20, 2010, in the child Welfare Case No. 1, the matters before the district court were discussed. The no-contact order was continued between Kelly H and Mr. Rhorer and ultimately the child was returned to the care and custody of Kelly H. Juvenile court jurisdiction was terminated.

(Page 13 is missing from the transcript.) ...an order was established, was dismissed and the order was stricken.

On February 14, 2012, a new shelter hearing was commenced and held in juvenile court. I will refer to this as the Child Welfare Case No. 2. In the hearing the court determined that the removal of PR was reasonable, and orders were entered regarding Kelly H's visitation including supervision orders and order regarding drug testing.

At all subsequent juvenile court proceedings prior to the permanent placement of PR with Kirk J in the Case No. 2, he is referred to as PR's father. In the disposition order for hearing held August 27, 2012, in the Child Welfare Case No. 2 the juvenile court made the following finding, "Kirk J, is the father of PR.". After several hearings addressing the issue of removal of PR in Case No. 2, on July 31, 2012, the juvenile court entered the following order, "Permanent custody and guardianship of PR is placed with Kirk J." PR was released from DCFS custody.

On February 11, 2014, Mr. Rhorer requested that the juvenile court release its jurisdiction in the Child Welfare Case No. 2, which motion was granted on February 25th, 2014.

The first issue I need to address is Mr. Rhorer's request that custody be established to him and that he be granted the right to say that he is the father of PR. He asserts that he resided with her for several years. He asserts he has a relationship with her and that the allegations of abuse and neglect against PR rise to the level he should be awarded custody. Mr. Rhorer, again, is requesting that the court adjudicate him to be the natural and biological father and be awarded custody or in the alternative that a custody evaluation should be performed and that he should be award interim parent-time.

Kirk J and Kelly H object, asserting that Kirk J was adjudicated to be the father of PR in juvenile court and that Mr. Rhorer does not have standing to seek such a request. Kirk J requests the court reconsider Mr. Rhorer's intervention given this argument regarding him not having standing. On the standing analysis, I must begin with the statute. The relevant statute that is Utah Code 78B-15-101. Referred to as the UUPA, Utah Uniform Parentage Act.

Standards maintaining proceedings is articulated under 78B-15-602. That statute says that persons with standing are the child, the mother, the man whose paternity of the child is to be adjudicated, any support enforcement agency, authorized adoption agency or child placement agency, representative to act in another capacity, and intended parent.

The statute does indicate several definitions. Under Section 102 it states that an "adjudicated father" means a man who had been adjudicated by a tribunal to be the father of the child. An "alleged father" means a man who alleges himself to be or is alleged to be the genetic father or possible genetic father of the child but whose paternity has not been determined. A "declarant father" means a male who along with the biological mother claims to be the genetic father of the child and signs a voluntary declaration of paternity to establish paternity. A "presumed father" means a man who, by operation of law, is recognized as the father of the child until that status is rebutted or confirmed as set forth in this chapter. It does indicate under this chapter under Section 104 that several courts have authority to adjudicate paternity. The two that are relevant to this proceeding are district court and juvenile court.

Establishment of parent/child relationship is clarified under Section 201. The first one I will address is if there's a declarant father where a father needs to file a declaration of paternity with the mother. What a man must show for there to be a valid declaration of paternity is that the declaration was signed or otherwise authenticated under the penalty of perjury with two witnesses stating there is no presumed father and no other exists consistent with the testing.

Subsection 3 of that statute states the declaration is void if it falsely denies the existence of a presumed, declarant, or adjudicated father of the child. In this case Mr. Rhorer asserts that he is a declarant father, given the child's name - - his name was on the child's birth certificate at one time. This statute does contemplate that once a declaration of paternity is signed by the father and mother, the father's name will be put on the birth certificate. However, I don't have the declaration of paternity which shows all of these elements being fulfilled, particularly given there was a presumed father, and I have no indication that it was declared that there was one or that there was not. At this point given the evidence that is before me, I cannot find that Mr. Rhorer is a declarant father. But he is an alleged father seeking to have his paternity established.

With regard to Kirk J, he is the presumed father. He was married to the mother at the time the child was born and is indeed the presumed father and has been found to be so by the juvenile court. Mr. J is also the adjudicated father, given the statute contemplates that juvenile court can establish this adjudication and we have a court order from the juvenile court that indicates that he is the father of PR.

There are three different factors that I must consider, whether we have a presumed father, we have an adjudicated father, we have an alleged father, and there's an assertion that Mr. Rhorer is a declarant father, but I don't have the elements before me to show that he has complied with all of the statutory requirements to prove that. I must examine if 602 gives standing to certain individuals to assert parentage. There's a statute of limitation of who can make assertions.

Under Subsection 1 of 78-B-15-607, it states, "Paternity of a child conceived or born during a marriage with the presumed father as described in Subsection 78-B-15-204 1, a, b, or c, may be raised by the presumed father or the mother at any time prior to filing of an action for divorce or in the pleadings at the time of the divorce of the parents."

This section also outlines when genetic testing may be done and what the presumed father and mother must seek to rebut presumption. There is no inclusion in the plain language of this statute of when any other person may come forward and assume paternity. This also asserts that **the presumption may be rebutted by certain information including genetic testing and evidence the presumed father and mother of the child neither cohabited nor engaged in sexual intercourse with each other during the probable time of conception.** Subparagraph 4 states the following, "There is no presumption to rebut if the presumed father was properly served and there has been a final adjudication on the issue."

We have some recent case law which have issues very similar to this case but with some significant differences that have been brought before the court of appeals. The case I refer to is RP versus KSW and DRW. The court read that to be that there is a limitation that only the mother or presumed father can challenge the paternity. This case, however, does assert certain distinctions from this present case. In this case it does indicate that there was no adjudication of parentage, which we have in this case, and there is no constitutional challenge.

The court also specifically stated under footnote 13, "We express no opinion on the issue of who has standing once petition for divorce has been filed."

In this case, the petition for divorce has been filed and has actually been granted, so this case is distinct from the RP versus KSW case. So, I must engage in the same analysis that the court of appeals did in considering the statute by already determining that the limitation was that only a married mother and presumed father could raise the issue of standing. This statute does in no way state that if a divorce case is final that some third party can come in and seek means to establish their parentage. The statute and all of its subparts outline the challenges that the mother or presumed father can bring and articulates no means for a third party to interject. Given that, I see the plain language of the statute specifically states that the mother and presumed father are the two individuals that can challenge the issue.

I'll also indicate as previously stated Kirk J is the presumed father, was married to Kelly H at the time the child was conceived and born. Kirk J is the adjudicated father. Juvenile court action states he is the father. Mr. Rhorer is an alleged father, and I do not have enough information to determine if Mr. Rhorer is the declarant father.

I find that under subparagraph one that only Kelly H and Mr. Rhorer can challenge the parentage. In examining Kelly H's request for a divorce in her original verified petition, her petition has much boilerplate in it. However, in the section where she has included her own provisions it refers to Kirk J as, quote, "other," instead of father.

Again, at other places in the petition it indicates him to be the father and parent. In another portion of the petition she asserts, "Three of my children are not biologically his." She also has a motion before the court that concedes that Kirk J should have custody of PR but asserts that Kirk J is not PR's biological father.

Under the statute it says the issue can be raised and then the presumption can be challenged. In her petition she raises the issue but she does not seek to rebut the presumption, but the issue is raised in her petition. Given that, I see that the issue with regard to Kirk J not being the biological father being raised but the challenge not being placed by Kelly H. I do not see in his answer Kirk J challenging his parentage.

We also have subparagraph four which states, "There is no presumption to rebut if the presumed father is properly served and there's been a final adjudication of the issue. This paragraph indicated that once the court adjudicates the presumed father to be the father there is no longer a presumption to rebut. Kirk J's parentage was adjudicated in juvenile court. There's no dispute that he was properly served and that that final adjudication did occur. So, under 78-B-15-607(4) this statute clearly states Kirk J has been adjudicated the father and that the limitation of challenging that from my read of this has been closed.

This does not complete the analysis, however. We have the RP versus KSW and DRW case where the court looked at the issue of constitutionality, specifically stating the following:

"Ultimately we conclude that the UUPA has preempted the common law on the issue of who has standing to challenge the presumed father's paternity. We also conclude that the UUPA limits standing here to husband and wife." Thus, the district court properly dismissed RP's petition. Although constitutional considerations might require further analysis in cases such as this where the alleged father has an established relationship with the child, RP has not raised a constitutional challenge in the district court or on appeal. Accordingly, we will leave for another day the issue of the constitutional implications of the UUPA standing limitation where the alleged father has an established relationship with the child.

Looking at the child's history in this case, I've now had the opportunity to review the pleading in the juvenile court Case No. 1, Case No. 2, the parentage case filed by Mr. Rhorer and the Office of Recovery Services case.

I see that the child has resided with Kelly H, with Mr. Rhorer, with Kirk J, and has been in DCFS custody and foster care. The factors that Mr. Rhorer asserts are that he lived with the child for several years. The juvenile court record confirms that for a time Mr. Rhorer and Kelly H were residing together. The orders also indicate restraints against Kelly H having contact with Mr. Rhorer. Again, Kelly H asserts in her petition that she and Kirk J were separated in 2005. The child was born in 2007. There is no evidence that is before me that the child lived with Kirk J until placed in his care and custody in 2012.

There are concerns regarding the safety of the child in the care of Kirk J that have been asserted by Mr. Rhorer. Some of those concerns were considered in the context of the juvenile court action, and there are additional concerns he articulates. I also see that Mr. Rhorer has no means to assert his paternity given he attempted to do so in the first juvenile court case. I have no indication that he was notified of the second juvenile court case. He filed a parentage petition which was later dismissed, and upon the parties filing for divorce, he's again asserted his parentage. Given this, this case specifically indicates that the court should consider the constitutionality issue if there is an established relationship with the child, but the question is what issues the court must consider in addressing this constitutional issue. In reviewing the statutes, I found one statute which I find to be persuasive of the court to consider certain factors to determine whether Mr. Rhorer should proceed with his standing.

Under 79-B-15-608 it articulates the authority to deny motion for genetic testing or disregard testing results. The factors are as follows: Under Subparagraph 1a, the court should consider the conduct of the mother or the presumed or declarant father and whether that estops the party from denying parentage. Subparagraph b, it would be inequitable to disrupt the father/child relationship between the child and the presumed or declarant father, also best interest factors of the child including the length of time between the proceeding to adjudicate parentage and the time that the presumed or declarant father was placed on notice that he might not be the genetic father; B, the length of time during which the presumed or declarant father has assumed the role of father of the child; C, the facts surrounding the presumed or declarant father's discovery of his possible non-paternity; D, the nature of the relationship between the child and the presumed or declarant father; E, the age of the child; F, the harm that may result to the child if presumed or declared paternity is successfully disestablished; G, the nature of the relationship between the child and any alleged father; H, consideration of whether there would be a custody evaluation.

The second issue is an evaluation. Mr. Rhorer has requested that there be a custody evaluation. However, we have several factors under this statute that I find to be appropriate for the court to consider in determining whether Mr. Rhorer has standing to proceed. There are certain factors specifically which I believe an evaluation would support. Those factors are, under 78-B-15-607 Subparagraph 1b, whether it would be inequitable to disrupt the father/child relationship between Kirk J and the child.

Other factors under Subsection 2, Subsection 2d, is the nature of the relationship between the child and the presumed or declarant father. Subsection F, the harm that may result to the child if presumed of declared paternity is successfully disestablished. G, the nature of the relationship between the child and any alleged father, and I, other factors. These issues are relevant to the issue as to whether I find it to be appropriate for Mr. Rhorer to assert these things.

So, I am going to recommend at this point that we have an evaluation of those issues. The person who performs the evaluation must have the qualifications that evaluators do have under the rules regarding custody evaluations which is Rule 493 of the Utah Rules of Judicial Administration.

I am going to ask counsel to contact evaluators who could perform the evaluation. Once I get that information, we'll rule on how that would be paid.

The second issue is the Guardian ad Litem. Before any of this commences, I'm recommending a GAL be appointed to talk to this child, and when we come back, I will get that input. Again, I think this is one of those cases where I see a child in so many different placements and so many different allegations that truly best interest should be focused on at this point. I will also specifically direct the GAL to communicate with the juvenile court GAL.

We do have an issue with regard to cost. There has been a time where the office of GAL would be available at low or no cost to the parties. Due to somewhat recent legislation, that is not a resource that I have the ability to appoint here, so we do need to look at a private GAL. I need significant financial information to make that determination, but what I will recommend at this point given this is Mr. Rhorer's request that he initially pay that cost and ultimately at the next hearing I do want financial information from both other parties to determine if that should be reallocated. I will indicate that there's a presumption that their hourly rate will be $150 per hour and that a $1,000 will be the retainer.

Mr. Rhorer, I'm asking that you address that issue first, and we'll come back and look whether you'll be reimbursed. I do want the GAL to interview this child and that no person discusses with the child that things might change for her until I hear from the Guardian. I'm including a specific restraining order that neither party discuss my ruling today. If she knows - and I hope she doesn't - but if she knows say, "That mean old judge says I can't talk to you. Don't worry about it. Go play with your friends. Go do your homework. Don't worry." Let the GAL start this discussion.

When we come back, I'll hear from the Guardian to see if there are any concerns that have not been raised yet. I was going to bring in the binder to show how much has been submitted to the court, but I think you're very aware what's been submitted to the court, but I do want this to be dealt with sensitively given this child has been involved in so many different court actions. We'll come back at the review hearing. I will hear from the Guardian and proposed evaluators. Typically, these evaluators don't look at these factors as I'm articulating under this statute.

What I've done is review the statute under the UUPA and found factors that seem relevant to the issue given it's in the 600 area where the court is looking at whether Mr. Rhorer even has standing. I will take the input of the GAL prior to making a ruling on how this child would be introduced to any evaluation and we will be treating this very carefully.

There is a request to strike notices of lodging. Some of those notices of lodging include certain court cases. Insofar as the court could review them, I will allow those to remain. There is an assertion by Mr. Rhorer that he is provided full review of all the cases of the parties. Anything outside of that I would grant. I'm also going to reserve the issue regarding rejecting the DNA test for future adjudication. Mr. Rhorer has also requested that DCFS conduct an investigation. Some of the allegations occurred during the pendency of the juvenile court action so may have already been investigated. Though there are other concerns here he articulates.

What I will recommend, first of all, is that Mr. Rhorer provide any assertions he has of concerns to the Division of Child and Family Services. Any adult who is aware of any abuse or neglect of a child that has not been reported has an obligation to report that. Also, under Utah Code 30-D3-5.2 it states, "When in any divorce proceeding or upon a request for modification of a Divorce Decree an allegation of child abuse or child sexual abuse is made implicating either party, the court, after making an inquiry, may order that an investigation be conducted by the DCFS within the Department of Human Services in accordance with Title 62A, Chapter 4A."

A final award of custody or parent-time may not be rendered until a report or investigation consistent with 62A, 4A, 412 is received by the court. That investigation shall be conducted by the Division of Child and Family Services within 30 days of the court's notice and request for an investigation. I am going to request that counsel for Mr. Rhorer contact them and indicate to them that I will be requesting their appearance at our next hearing to provide a report, given the statute does authorize that to occur.

Given that they have 30 days to complete their investigation, our review hearing will be heard not earlier than 45 days. I want them to have the time to finish the report and be here, so we will need to look at probably the last week of March for our review hearing. We'll come back at the review hearing, and each party is to give the following: **Financial Information** to allow the court to make a determination about the appointment of GAL; information about evaluators who would be able to perform this evaluation, and requests on how the costs would be allocated.

Custody evaluations typically take a cost and I do need to determine if the parties have that ability to pay for this type of evaluation. Mr. Rhorer is the one seeking this, but I do want to have that financial information before that determination is made. ***We will proceed quickly as soon as I get the information from DCFS and the GAL.*** *My clerk has provided to both counsel today a pink sheet. That is the form that the Office of Guardian Ad Litem has requested that we provide to the parties at the time of the hearing. They have also requested that the parties fill that in and provide it to us the same day of the hearing.*

We are now required to prepare findings and an order from the hearing and provide it to them. My intention is to get that to them today so they will put on notice that they have been appointed and that they need to identify an attorney that will be willing to proceed.

Kirk J, you have the child in your care. It will be your obligation to set up the appointment so the interview can occur. And, Mr. Rhorer, you're given the cost initially, subject to possible reapportionment when I have more financial information. Mr. Rhorer, if you could come up with that and then at the next hearing when I have additional financial information, I can make a determination as to whether there should be reimbursement.

Given this, we do have this one constitutional issue that RP versus KSW indicates is an issue that must be considered, and this case specifically indicated that Mr. Rhorer did have a relationship with the child at some point. That is the very issue mentioned in the opinion that the court could consider that issue. Given that ruling, I'm following the case law where it does indicate that the court must consider that issue.

Given that the DCFS will be given that hopefully today, we probably could have a hearing first week of April. And I also ask the attorney who will be preparing the order to indicate that some of these allegations may very well have already been investigated and, if they have been, that the report include those that have already been resolved because this child has been involved in so much juvenile court involvement where DCFS is directly involved.

As a concluding comment, I will indicate I have been doing this job for a significant period of time and nowhere have I seen facts and case involvement of such complexity and so many different analyses that must have occurred. Given the timing of all of those cases and the UUPA and its requirements, this was quite a complicated analysis. It did take some time. I apologize for that time, but at the same time I wanted to make sure that I was clear on all of the arguments on all of the cases, and there were quite a few. All of those interplay with this case and involve this child, and hopefully with this new evaluation I can address this constitutional issue.

My contemplation is I can evaluate whether Mr. Rhorer has a constitutional right to proceed despite my reading of 78B-15-607 that states that there is no presumption to rebut if presumed father is properly served and there's been an adjudication. I think it is clear, but this case does indicate there remains this constitutional issue that must be addressed.

So those are the recommendations of the court. I agree with assertions that this may be somewhat complicated. It was quite involved, and I wanted to make sure that specific issues were addressed. So, Counsel, are there any questions?

NANCY S: *Just procedurally you said you want to get something out today and you lost me there. What is it the court needs today?*

THE COURT: *The Guardian ad Litem order.*

NANCY S: *Okay. And it's related to this pink sheet, which I noticed says mother and father. We have three parties here. Kelly H is not present.*

THE COURT: *90-some-odd percent of cases do not have the complexity of a mother and two possible fathers. We have enough cases that I think they'll be clear if you just include in there that Mr. Rhorer is an intervenor and is requesting parentage be established.*

NANCY S: *This asks for the children to be listed. Does the court want any child listed other than PR?*

THE COURT: *And Kirk J is the one having this issue because Mr. Rhorer isn't involved with the other children. Oftentimes, the GAL may want to interview other children. They have the obligation to ensure that any parent who had rights also weigh in on whether they do so. I don't have enough information on any of those other children to make that determination, but if you want to indicate that those are individuals that the GAL may want to seek an interview with, you can include that in what you stated, but we will prepare the order today.*

So next time we'll come in and look at what type of mini evaluation focusing on those issues can be done. We will start with the GAL first. Until I hear from the Guardian PR will not be told or informed of anything regarding whether this reintroduction will occur. So, there's a restraining order on everyone to not discuss with her until I hear from the Guardian. The ruling was long but the actual orders are quite brief. I'll ask which attorney would be willing to prepare the order to follow these recommendations?

NANCY S: *I would be willing to do that.*

THE COURT: *Thank you, Counsel. I do want to indicate for the record that I was given more than sufficient information to evaluate all of this. The binder was quite large. I did review everything that I indicated I reviewed. And it's a complicated case, and I know a complicated case - but for the parties I understand this is about a child and we are going to proceed very carefully and delicately for her to ensure that when we're done, hopefully it's final and the child can simply proceed with her life and not have these concerns.*
Thank you all for your attendance today.

FEBRUARY 20TH, 2015: FINDINGS OF FACT AND CONCLUSIONS OF LAW REGARDING APPOINTMENT OF GUARDIAN AD LITEM, Commissioner Bloom

FINDINGS OF FACT
1. This case involves the following alleged issues in relation to the child.
a. _X_ child abuse, child sexual abuse and neglect.
b. _X_ child custody.
c. _X_ child parent-time.
d. _____child abuse, child sexual abuse and neglect that has been alleged in a complaint, petition or counterclaim, and reported to Child Protective Services.
e. _X_ paternity.
2. The court finds that in regard to indigentcy, as set forth in most recently revised poverty income guidelines that:
a. _X_ one adult party is not indigent.
b. _X_ both adult parties are indigent.
The finding of indigence is based on the following: _____.
3. The court has taken into consideration the limitations of involving a Guardian ad Litem and finds there is a need based on the following:
Allegation of abuse and neglect: challenge to parentage between presumed, adjudicated father and an alleged biological father. Significant Division of Child and Family Services involvement.
4. The parties have filed their financial declarations with the court or disclosed to the court their income and applicable expenses for the purpose of setting the amount that the parties will be required to pay toward GALs fees and expenses.

CONCLUSIONS OF LAW
1. Pursuant to UCA 78A-2-703(1),705(1), the court concludes that this case involves matters as indicated in the preceding Findings of Fact.
2. Pursuant to UCA 78A-2-703(1)(ii), the court has determined the issue of indigentcy and found that either one adult party is not indigent or that both adult parties are indigent.
3. Pursuant to UCA 78A-2-703(2), the court concludes that there is a high priority need and basis for the appointment of a GAL, and one should be appointed by the court.
4. Pursuant to UCA 78A-2-703(3),705(4), the specific issues relevant to those indicated in the Findings of Fact paragraph 1 have been identified by the court and should be bifurcated from the other issues in this case; and a final order should be issued within one year after the day on which a GAL is appointed, except as may be ordered prior to that time pursuant to UCA 78A--2-703(3)(5); and 705(5)(6).
5. Pursuant to UCA Sec. 78A-2-0705(9), the court concludes that the parties should pay for the Guardian's fees, court costs, and paralegal staff, and volunteer expenses in the proportion the court deems to be just and designate in the court's order herewith.
Signed by Judge Stanley and Commissioner Bloom

FEBRUARY 20TH, 2015: ORDER APPOINTING A PGAL, Commissioner Bloom

Pursuant to the Court's Finding of Fact and Conclusions of Law entered herewith, Utah Code Ann. 78A-2-705 (as amended), and Rule 9-906(8) of the Rules of Judicial Administration, the Court orders as follows:

1. The Court appoints a private Guardian ad Litem to be assigned by the Office of GAL and to represent the best interests of the minor child in this matter.

2. The clerk of the court shall provide a copy of this order forthwith to the Private Guardia ad Litem Program.

3. The private GAL shall be involved in resolving the following issues for the child:

Allegations of abuse and neglect; challenge to parentage between presumed, adjudicated father and an alleged biological father. Significant Division of Child and Family Services involvement.

4. The above-referenced issues shall be bifurcated from the other issues in order to minimize the time constraints placed upon the private GAL.

5. A final order will be issued within one year of the date of this order, except as may be ordered by the court prior to that time pursuant to UCA Sec. 78A-2-705(5)(6).

6. The parties shall pay the PGAL:

a.   X   an hourly rate of $150.00; pay for the other applicable PGAL fees, court costs, paralegal, staff, and volunteer expenses, if any; and pay and maintain a retainer in the amount of $1,000.00, to be proportionately paid by the parties as follows:

0% Petitioner(s)
0% Respondent(s)
100% Intervenor Jody Rhorer

7. The GAL shall file a notice of appearance with the court within five (5) business days of the day on which the attorney was assigned to the case, and represent the best interest of the child until released by the court.

8. The GAL is granted full access to any and all medical, psychological, or school records pertaining to the child. The parties are ordered to cooperate including signing any necessary releases and making the child available to the GAL. Any records obtained shall be protected by the GAL and maintained as confidential.

Signed by Judge Stanley and Commissioner Bloom

FEBRUARY 20TH, 2015: HEARING, Commissioner Bloom

Hearing is held for the Commissioner to present recommendations from issues taken under advisement. Prior to making recommendations, the Commissioner presented detailed historical facts, statutes, case law and constitutionality issues.

The Commissioner **RECOMMENDS** *that:*

1. The motion to set aside intervention of Mr. Rhorer is **RESERVED** *for now.*

2. The custody evaluation will be performed by a qualified evaluator on the issues identified on the record. Counsel are to provide information regarding evaluators at the next hearing.

3. A PRIVATE Guardian ad Litem will be appointed. The GAL will attempt to communicate with the GAL from the Juvenile Court. For now, Mr. Rhorer will pay the costs ($1,000) retainer and $150 per hour, subject to possible reallocation.

4. The parties are **RESTRAINED** *from discussing today's ruling with the child.*

5. A **REVIEW** *hearing to be scheduled no sooner than 45 days from now, to hear from the GAL and review the proposed evaluators - 4/16/15.*

6. Regarding the request to strike the notice of lodging, anything outside the full review of all the cases of the parties will be allowed to remain.

7. The request to reject the DNA testing is **RESERVED**.

8. Counsel for Mr. Rhorer will instruct him in providing any un-investigated assertions of abuse to the Division of Child and Family Services. Counsel will also inform the DCFS worker to be present at the review hearing.

9. All parties are to provide financial information, suggestions for evaluators, and a request for how costs should be allocated prior to the next hearing.

Nancy S is directed to prepare the order, and include that some allegations have already been investigated, and which ones have been resolved.

FEBRUARY 20TH, 2015: EMAIL from Nancy S

Hi Jody and Deone, I am attaching the Findings of Fact and Conclusions of Law regarding the appointment of a private Guardian Ad Litem, and the Order to appoint the PGAL. This Order has been transmitted to the Guardian Ad Litem's office. They have 5 days to make an appointment. As soon as one is appointed, the GAL will call me and I will pay him/her.

A GAL is an attorney who will represent Payshence. The GAL will act as an advocate on behalf of her, just as if Payshence hired the attorney to represent her in this matter. I will let you know as soon as I speak to the GAL and give you his/her information. Let me know if you have any questions. Thanks, Nancy S

FEBRUARY 23RD, 2015: EMAIL from Nancy S

Hi Deone, The GAL's office has appointed Mary C as PGAL. I am attaching a copy of the letter I received today. I called Mary and left a message for her to return my call. Also, I called DCFS Friday and talked to them about reporting. They requested that I email the info to them, but I am trying to set a meeting to talk to someone and go over the information and documentation I have. I will keep you apprised of things as they progress. Thank you for the additional $500 payment Friday. Nancy

FEBRUARY 25TH, 2015: LETTER from Guardian ad Litem

Dear Counsel:

Please be advised that I have been appointed as Guardian ad Litem to represent the best interest of the child in the above-entitled case. I will not be functioning as a custody evaluator, social worker or therapist, but only as an attorney in the best interests of the child involved.

I believe that it is important that I be brought current with developments in this matter, and would ask each of you to provide me with the following information:

a) current address and telephone numbers for your respective clients;

b) current placement orders regarding the parties' minor child;

c) names, addresses and telephone numbers for any therapists or counselors that the child is now seeing, or has seen during the pendency of these proceedings;

d) names, addresses and telephone numbers for any therapists or counselors that the parties are now seeing, or have seen during the pendency of these proceedings;

e) releases for all therapists and counselors so I may speak to them as part of performing my appointment and representation of the child;

f) copies of any documents you feel would be pertinent for me to review regarding the best interests of the minor child;

g) provide a short (2 pages) statement of concerns in this case;

h) any law enforcement and/or DCFS reports; and

i) notifications of any scheduled hearings, depositions, mediations, deadlines, motions, discovery, or otherwise.

I plan on reviewing this case file and the information provided to me. I would like meet with your client's child as soon as possible. Your assistance in facilitating this would be greatly appreciated. Please have your client contact my office to arrange for an appointment where I can meet the child in person.

I have enclosed a retainer agreement for Jody Rhorer. Please have him schedule an appointment as soon as possible and bring these documents with him and the required retainer. Please include me in your mailings and notifications of hearings, depositions, conferences, correspondences, etc. Please ensure that I have the chance to review orders prior to submitting to the court. If you have any questions or concerns, please do not hesitate to contact my office.

Sincerely,

Mary C, Attorney at Law

MARCH 2ND, 2015: LETTER to Guardian ad Litem from Nancy S

Dear Mary C:

Thank you for your letter. This is a complex case involving several court proceedings, two in Juvenile Court, a paternity case filed by my client in West Jordan Thirst District Court, and the current case before Commissioner Bloom and Judge Stanley. I am submitting the following information for your consideration:

1. <u>Background:</u> Kirk J and Kelly H married in 2003, but did not live together. Shortly after their marriage Kirk J served two years in prison on drug and arms convictions. Kelly's petition for divorce alleges they separated in 2005. During their marriage Kelly birthed five children. The paternity of four of the children are in question. Kelly and Jody Rhorer began a relationship in 2006. Rhorer did not know that Kelly was married. Payshence Rhorer was conceived when Kelly and Jody lived in Oregon and she was born on July 16, 2007, shortly after the couple returned to Utah. In 2008, a Juvenile Court action commenced due to domestic violence allegations against Rhorer. At that time Kirk J was given temporary custody of Kelly's sons, but did not take PR and did not assert that he was PR's presumed father. Neither Kirk nor Kelly told the Juvenile Court they were married. PR was placed temporarily with Georgia Rhorer, Jody's mother, and was later returned to Kelly. Jody was told by Judge V to establish paternity. Rhorer underwent a DNA test to establish that he was the biological father of PR and his petition establishing paternity in Third District Court in West Jordan was granted. In 2010 a second petition was filed against Kelly in Juvenile Court when she was driving erratically with PR and her son in the car. During those proceedings the Juvenile Court learned that Kelly had allowed her stepbrother, a sex offender, to babysit PR. The Court filed a petition to terminate Kelly's rights. She then told the DCFS worker that she was married to Kirk. Until then Mr. Rhorer did not know Kelly and Kirk were married. The Juvenile Court ordered Jody to dismiss the paternity action as Kirk was then known to be the presumed father of PR. Mr. Rhorer dismissed his action. PR was placed in DCFS custody and in February 2012, she began having overnight visitations with Kirk to determine placement. In a February 28, 2012 hearing a DCFS worker informed the Juvenile Court that PR had a vaginal fungus infection and was having trouble sleeping and was not adjusting to staying in Kirk's home. The Court was told that PR. had described a "peeking game" that she was forced to play with adults named "Mike" and "Anthony" and that PR didn't want to talk about it and she referenced to one of these men as her "boyfriend". <u>Mr. Rhorer is concerned that these troublesome findings were never again addressed by the court.</u>

The Juvenile Court was concerned about domestic violence in Kirk's home. Brent N, GAL, expressed concern that Kirk had eight children in his home and expressed concerns about the home environment.

Kirk was awarded custody of PR in July 2012 with conditions that he not consume alcohol and that he not have convicted criminals in his home, and that Kelly could have only supervised visitation. Mr. Rhorer is concerned because: (1) The sex offender has frequented Kirk's home with PR; (2) alcohol and domestic violence has continued in Kirk's home and elsewhere concerning PR, and (3) Kirk allows Kelly to visit PR without supervision and to have PR for extended periods of time;

(4) Kelly married Shane S in 2013 and they have had domestic violence charges against them: (5) Kelly's husband has a history of criminal charges including drugs and violence; (6) Kelly has a history of criminal charges including drugs and violence;

(7) Dan J, Kirk's father is a babysitter for PR and has sex offense charges against him and has been involved in domestic violence charges at Kirk's home; (8) Kirk's live-in girlfriend, Jill, has domestic violence charges against her and her Facebook page shows she associates with mothers supporting marijuana; Jill's husband, Ken C, has a sex offense charge.

The Juvenile Court ordered Kelly and Kirk to divorce. Rhorer intervened in the divorce proceedings. Kelly was not present at the hearing; Kirk did not object. Contemporaneous with this motion to intervene, Kirk denied paternity of PR in an ORS action in Third District Court and voluntarily took a DNA test to disprove his paternity.

Kelly and Kirk's divorce was bifurcated and a divorce was granted, however, issues of custody and visitation are still pending. Rhorer filed a motion for custody and visitation and a custody evaluation, a motion for DCFS investigation and motion to appoint a GAL. Kirk and Kelly have filed a motion to overturn Jody's intervention. Mr. Rhorer was ordered to contact DCFS about his concerns. The issue of Rhorer's intervention was reserved by the court pending the DCFS investigation and the GAL findings. Kirk has argued that the UUPA limits standing to challenge paternity of a child to the presumed father and mother. It was ruled that since Mr. Rhorer had an established relationship with PR prior to her placement with Kirk J, the constitutionality of the statute should be addressed. The court will address whether it's in the best interest of PR for Jody to intervene after analysis of the factors in U.C.A. 78B-15-608.

Mr. Rhorer's concerns include:

1. PR. has known Jody as her father. Kirk J allowed Mr. Rhorer to have visitation with PR until October 2012 when Mr. Rhorer appeared in court to support Kelly H. PR no longer has physical access to Jody.

2. Jody's older daughters have been allowed to visit PR by Kirk J and have seen Kelly's sex offender cousin in Kirk's home. They have seen Kirk and others in the home consuming alcohol and acting intoxicated. They have seen Kirk's J's home and PR in neglect. Mona Rhorer has filed an affidavit with the court. She believes that PR has not had a bed in Kirk J's home and has had to sleep on the floor or share a bed with other children.

3. Police have been called to the home on many occasions due to domestic violence. Kirk's live-in girlfriend has older children in the home. A police report was made by these children that Kirk was abusive and frequently drunk; the children ran out of the home, called the police and reported that they wanted to kill themselves because of Kirk and the conditions of the home.

4. Police have been on Kelly H, who has a long history of intravenous drug use and violence. Police have been called to Kelly and Shane's home because of domestic violence. Both Kelly and Shane have had domestic violence charges against them. Kirk has allowed Kelly to take PR without supervision. Kelly's Facebook shows PR with Kelly in her home.

5. Mr. Rhorer is concerned that PR is being abused by Kirk, Jill, or by others in Kirk's home or people who are allowed to come in to Kirk's home.

6. Mr. Rhorer is concerned that Kirk never got counseling for PR after the February 28, 2012, hearing at which time it became known about PR having to play the "peeking game" with adult men and having a "vaginal fungal infection.

7. Mr. Rhorer is concerned about PR's safety as Juvenile Court ordered that Kirk have no alcohol or domestic violence in the home and no people with criminal convictions when PR is present. Kirk has ignored these orders.

Neither Jody nor his wife, Deone, have had any counseling; nevertheless, I am attaching a Release for each of them for you to obtain information.

I am attaching: Motion for DCFS investigation with police reports, Affidavit of Mona Rhorer, Affidavit of Jody Rhorer, Notice of Lodging of Juvenile Court documents. Jody does not have access to DCFS reports; however, Kirk and Kelly have access to these documents and should submit them for your review.

Sincerely,
Nancy S

MARCH 2ND, 2015: ORDER REQUIRING DCFS INVESTIGATION, submitted by Nancy S, Commissioner Bloom presiding

Based upon Intervenor's Motion for Order for DCFS Investigation, the arguments of counsel having been heard before the Court on May 28, 2014, the petitioner having been present but not represented by counsel, the respondent having been present and represented by attorney Connie, the Intervenor having been present and represented by attorney Nancy S,

IT IS HEREBY ORDERED as follows:

1. Intervenor's Motion for DCFS Investigation is granted;

2. Counsel for Intervenor shall contact the DCFS and submit any concerns for an investigation;

3. DCFS shall conduct an investigation into the allegations contained in Intervenor's Motion and any concerns submitted by the Intervenor.

4. *DCFS shall obtain and investigate any other information relevant to the welfare and best interests of the minor child.*

5. *DCFS shall prepare a report as to their investigation and submit the same to the Court. The report shall include any resolution of any issues which have already been investigated by DCFS;*

6. *A representative of the Division of Family Services shall appear at the review hearing scheduled for April 16, 2015, to provide to the Court a report pursuant to the orders herein.*

MARCH 3RD, 2015: EMAILS from Nancy S

Mary, I received a call from DCFS, they have opened a CPS investigation of child endangerment and domestic violence, and also sex abuse allegations against one of the male children in the home. The supervisor's name is Amy O. She will be reviewing this information for assignment to a caseworker. Thanks, Nancy S

Hi Jody and Deone, The CPS caseworker assigned is Lindy S. I talked to the supervisor and she said Lindy will want to talk to you and will either contact you directly or through me. If we don't hear from her by tomorrow p.m. I think you should call. Let me know if she contacts you. Thanks, Nancy

MARCH 3RD, 2015: KIRK J'S OBJECTION TO ORDER REQUIRING DCFS INVESTIGATION, submitted by Connie C, Commissioner Bloom presiding

Comes now, Connie, Attorney at Law, and on behalf of Kirk J, files the foregoing Objection to the Proposed Order Requiring DCFS Investigation submitted by Mr. Rhorer. Grounds and reasons are that it is inaccurate and its terms exceed the scope of both the Court's authority to make Orders for DCFS Investigation and the Division of Child and Family Service's authority under its enabling legislation 62A-4a et seq., to conduct investigations.

The Court's Order

At hearing February 20th, 2015, the Court Ordered that DCFS was to conduct an investigation. Mr. Rhorer was ordered to report to DCFS any and all concerns that he had regarding treatment of the minor that the Division in turn was to examine their records to determine whether any of Mr. Rhorer's concerns had yet to be investigated, and then make a report to the Court at the next hearing.

The Proposed Order/Disputes

Paragraph three of the Proposed Order includes a directive that the Division "shall conduct an investigation into the allegations contained in Intervenor's Motion." Undersigned does not have the benefit of a recording of the hearing, however, her notes do not reflect that DCFS was to act on the pleadings, but rather, that Mr. Rhorer was personally directed to report to DCFS (which is required by law before asking the Court for an Order in any event).

Paragraph four of the Proposed Order includes a directive to the Division that it "shall obtain and investigate any other information relevant to the welfare and best interests of the minor child." Undersigned's notes of the hearing contain no indication the Court made such a sweeping and all-encompassing Order against the Division. Rather, the Division was Ordered to investigate any reports to Mr. Rhorer which it had already investigated previously.

Title 62A-4a et seq.

The section which addressees such "Child Protective Services" investigation states "the division shall make a thorough pre-removal investigation upon receiving either an oral or written report of alleged abuse neglect, fetal alcohol syndrome, or fetal drug dependency, when there is reasonable cause to suspect that such a situation exists. The division shall make a written report of its investigation that to include a determination regarding whether the alleged abuse or neglect is supported, unsupported, or without merit. Further, the Division is to notify the person making the report of the Division's conclusion upon completion of the investigation.

Therefore, the statute empowering the Division to investigation defines the investigation into allegation of abuse, neglect, and provides that such information is confidential. These are to be disclosed to a limited scope of persons which include a court.

Analysis

Mr. Rhorer expanded the scope of the oral pronouncement of the Commissioner to include a mandatory directive that it, "shall obtain an investigation of **any other information relevant to the welfare and best interests"** of the minor. The pronouncement of the Commissioner was not that sweeping. The Commissioner Ordered that Mr. Rhorer report any concerns to the Division, and the Division to investigate those matters if it had not done so. The Order did not purport to tell the Division to conduct any other or further investigation, let alone on requiring them to investigate "any other information relevant" to welfare and best interest. The statutory authority of the Division of Child and Family Services pursuant to the State's power is to investigate abuse and neglect for the protection of children. While the "best interest" of children may be an ultimate ideal of the Division, that does not empower the Division to act as a Government investigator, consultant and expert to the District Court on "any relevant matters" to "welfare and best interests."

The terms contained in the proposed Order requiring investigations of "any relevant matters" not only exceeds what was articulated by the Commissioner during the hearing, it places responsibility and authority on the Division that it does not possess. Pursuant to 42A-4a-412(f) makes clear that the Division is specifically **not** authorized or empowered to offer opinions on such matters to the District Court as part of their report into abuse and neglect.

WHEREFORE, because the proposed Order contains terms which were not articulated by the Commissioner, and even if they had been the expansion into anything "relevant" to "welfare and best interests" exceeds the statutory scope of a C.P.S. investigation and authority to report, the Court must strike those provisions from the order.

MARCH 3RD, 2015: RESPONSE TO JODY RHORER'S REPLY TO KIRK J'S OPPOSITION TO NOTICE TO SUBMIT AND MOTION FOR ATTORNEY'S FEES, submitted by Connie, Commissioner Bloom presiding

Connie, Attorney at Law, files the foregoing Response to Jody Rhorer's Reply to his Opposition to Notice to Submit and Motion for Attorney Fees.

(1) Nancy S, Counsel for Intervenor, Jody Rhorer, asserts she emailed a copy of a proposed "Recommendation and Order" along with a recording of the February 20th, 2015, hearing, and that undersigned did not respond.

(2) Undersigned counsel received no emails (with or without attachments) on February 23rd, 2015. In that no such email was received, no "response" would be possible.

(3) Nancy S's disposition of her version of events in paragraphs 3, 4, and 5 of her pleading contains no other references to dates on which events occurred such that this Court may evaluate her alleged time line in connection with her assertion in her Notice to Submit filed March 3rd, 2015, that undersigned provided the proposed orders "seven days ago of approval as to form."

(4) Undersigned Counsel has both searched her emails including junk and deleted folder for the entire period between February 20th and the day of the filing of this Petition several times in a concerted effort not to overlook any emails.

The following is reflected in Counsel's inbox, (a) February 24th, 2015, an email without attachments from Nancy S, (b) February 25th, 2015, an email from undersigned to Nancy S, (c) February 25th, 2015, two emails from undersigned to Nancy S, in the first, she states she "will draft," the DCFS order, and the later one containing an attachment which was the first draft of the proposed DCFS Order. (d) February 26th, 2015, an email from undersigned to Nancy S which for the first time, asserts, "I attached a recording of the hearing to the email previously sent to you," (f) February 27th, 2015, an email from Nancy S when she demands to know what counsel "wants to do," about the "orders" in the case.

APPLICABLE RULES

Rule 7(f)(2) of the Utah Rules of Civil Procedure provides, "objections to the proposed order shall be filed within 7 days after service." Rule 6(a) of the Utah Rules of Civil Procedure indicates that the day an event occurs should be excluded, and then all intermediate days, including weekends and holidays should be counted. Therefore, excluding February 27th, the date upon which Counsel for Mr. Rhorer served the documents, Mr. Rhorer filed his Notice to Submit and asserted seven days had elapsed on the **third** day since service. Utilizing the direction contained in Rule 6 for computing time, and the fact that counsel served the documents Friday February 27, 2015, the 7th day which Kirk J might still file a timely objection is Friday March 6th, 2015.

DISCUSSION

Nancy S's Reply sidesteps the precise issue which is the subject of both the Opposition to the Notice to Submit and the Motion for Attorney fees, specifically, that the explicit assertion that Nancy S provided the proposed Orders "seven days prior to March 2nd for approval," was a false statement.

Nancy S's February 25th, 2015, email indicates she "will" draft the DCFS Order and her first draft was emailed to Counsel that same day. She concedes that she changed that Order, and while not supplying a date herself, undersigned has attested the second draft came through by email, and was E-filed February 27th, which was the very first time undersigned was provided any version of any proposed "Recommendation and Order."

Instead of responding to the challenge that the Notice to Submit contains a false statement of fact, Nancy S seeks to deflect responsibility by asserting undersigned was uncommunicative and "still" hasn't filed an objection to the Orders. She further asserts that undersigned is attempting to delay. These arguments are attempts to confuse the issue before the Court. No matter how impatient Nancy S is to have signed Orders, she is not at liberty to make false statements to the Court as to how long an opposing party had to consider the proposed Orders. Neither is she at liberty to decide to "shorten" the period for objection. In a nutshell, Nancy S's position is that because counsel did not respond in a way and in time **she** felt was in order, Nancy S felt entitled to the Court's execution of the Orders irrespective of the fact that the objection period had not run, and even if it required a false statement to induce the execution of the Orders.

"Lawyers shall not send the court or its staff correspondence between counsel, unless such correspondence is relevant to an issue currently pending the court and the proper evidentiary foundations are met or as such correspondence is specifically invited by the court," Rule 14-301(12). Utah Standard of Professionalism and Civility. Counsel for Kirk J is not attaching copies of the described emails because of the foregoing Standard.

However, Counsel stands ready to provide copies of all email correspondence so the Court may more accurately determine the timing of service of the proposed Order on Counsel, and to evaluate the Motion for Attorney fees. (Counsel has expended an additional two hours in reviewing Nancy S's response, pouring over emails repeatedly, research, and drafting this Response. Therefore, the prior affidavit in which Counsel requested attorney fees should be updated to reflect three hours expended rather than two. Naturally, Counsel would welcome the Court's review of Nancy S's email records in this regard as well so that the messages might be compared as between sender and recipient.

MARCH 3RD, 2015: AFFIDAVIT OF Connie IN SUPPORT OF MOTION FOR ATTORNEY'S FEES, submitted by Connie, Commissioner Bloom presiding

I, Connie, being first duly sworn, depose and say:

1. I am over 18 years of age and a resident of the State of Utah and all statements made in this affidavit are true and based on my personal knowledge or belief.

2. I am a member in good standing in the Utah State Bar and officer of this Court.

3. I represent Kirk J, a party to this action, and as such, receive filing though the Court's email filing system when documents are filed via the internet.

4. I have emailed communication with Nancy S, counsel for Intervenor.

5. After Commissioner Bloom pronounced her oral ruling at a hearing February 20, 2015, Nancy S offered to draft the Orders.

6. Nancy S emailed a proposed Order regarding a DCFS investigation to undersigned on February 25, 2015.

7. Counsel wrote an email back disputing some provisions contained in the draft.

8. Friday, February 27, 2015, Nancy S emailed undersigned counsel, "What do you want to do about the proposed orders in this matter?"

9. Shortly thereafter Nancy S emailed that she was making some changes to the Order regarding the DCFS investigation.

10. Shortly thereafter Nancy S caused to be filed a second version of the DCFS investigation order and an additional order entitled "Recommendation and Order" via the Court's E-filing system on Friday, February 27, 2015.

11. Undersigned Counsel got those orders via email by the Court's E-filing system.

12. On the morning of March 2, 2015, the very next business day, and the third day of seven that Kirk J had to respond to the proposed order by rule, Nancy S caused to be filed a Notice to Submit the Orders filed the Friday before asserting in that filing that opposing counsel had had them seven days.

13. Counsel has had to reschedule other matters and take up time she would have endeavored to spend reviewing the orders and/or drafting an objection to respond to the notice to submit which contains a false statement as to how long undersigned had the Orders.

14. Kirk J does not have means to pay counsel to respond to pleadings which appear to be filed with disregard to demonstrable fact.

15. Counsel has expended 2 hours in researching this matter (which has never come up in counsel's twenty plus years plus in practice, in that blatant misstatements of fact are rare), drafting, and obtaining this affidavit and her hourly fee is $175.00. Therefore, Counsel prays that she be awarded $350.00 in fees.

MARCH 4TH, 2015:   REPLY TO OPPOSITION NOTICE TO SUBMIT AND MOTION FOR ATTORNEY'S FEES, submitted by Nancy S, Commissioner Bloom presiding

Intervenor hereby replies to the Respondent's Opposition to Notice to Submit and Motion for Attorney's Fees.

1. Counsel for Intervenor received the recording of the February, 20, 2015, hearing on the afternoon of Friday, February 20. On Monday, February 23, counsel for Intervenor emailed to Connie the proposed Recommendation and Order, together with the recording of the hearing.

2. Respondent did not acknowledge receipt and did not suggest any changes to the Recommendation and Order.

3. Counsel for Intervenor then emailed Respondent's counsel suggesting a separate order for the DCFS Investigation inasmuch as it needed to be completed by the next hearing scheduled on April 16, 2015. Respondent replied that she did not object. Counsel for Intervenor then emailed to Respondent's counsel the proposed Order Requiring DCFS Investigation; thereafter, Counsel for Intervenor noticed that the numbers identifying the statute and Rule in the first Recommendation and Order had typographical errors and brought the errors to the attention of the Respondent's counsel with a corrected Recommendation and Order. No substantive changes were made.

4. Counsel for Intervenor did not hear back from Respondent's counsel and sent emails requesting a response.

5. When counsel for Intervenor did not receive a response or any suggestions for changes to the Recommendation and Order and the Order Requiring DCFS Investigation within the allotted time, the proposed orders were submitted to the court.

ARGUMENT

Intervenor gave respondent the required time to suggest changes to the orders. Respondent's failure to acknowledge receipt of the proposed orders and recording of the hearing, and respondent's failure to make suggestions to change the orders, failure to approve the orders as to form, and failure to communicate with Intervenor's counsel regarding the proposed orders is an example of Respondent's willful effort to delay the DCFS Investigation and to delay the other matters addressed in the Recommendation and Order.

The Respondent's filing of the Opposition to Request to Submit and Motion for Attorney's Fees has no merit and is being used as a means to delay the furtherance and resolution of the matters before the court. The proposed Recommendation and Order is still before the court and the parties have not been notified of the court's approval. Nevertheless, Respondent still has not filed an objection thereto.

WHEREFORE, the Respondent's Opposition to Notice to Submit and Motion for Attorney Fees should be denied.

MARCH 4TH, 2015: CERTIFICATE OF SERVICE, by Nancy S, Commissioner Bloom presiding

I hereby certify that on this date I mailed a true and correct copy of Intervenor's Financial Declaration and supporting documents to: Connie C and J Hunt.

MARCH 4TH, 2015:   EMAIL from Nancy S

Hi Deone and Jody, I just had a long conversation with Mary C, the GAL, and described the history of this case and our concerns. She is going to go over to Kirk J's home and try to talk to Payshence. She will also talk to Kirk J, Kelly H and Jill C. She may contact you both directly, or she may call me to arrange to talk to you. I will let you know. If you hear from her, please let me know. Her first concern is meeting with Payshence. Nancy

MARCH 5TH, 2015: EMAILS Nancy S

Hi Jody and Deone, Yesterday I spoke at great length with Mary C., the GAL, about our case, Kirk and Kelly's history and the Juvenile Court case involving Payshence and I told her that one of your concerns was that Kirk and Kelly will not be honest about the DCFS investigation. I told her about you and your family's relationship with Payshence and that we are concerned for her safety and that your child needs to be protected. Mary said to me, "Well, now she has an attorney." I thanked her. I believe she is taking this very seriously. Today I emailed Mary the contact info for the new CPS worker, I received the following response from Mary: "Got it. Thanks. I'm still trying to get Kirk J and Payshence in to my office."

After I filed the Orders with the court for the Commissioner's and Judge's signatures, Connie sent me an email telling me I better withdraw the Orders or she would file papers against me. I ignored her and she filed an Opposition to the Orders. I prepared and filed our reply memorandum. Connie then filed an Objection to the DCFS Order requesting that the court limit the DCFS investigation into Kirk. Today I received the Order (without changes or limits) with the Judge's signature and sent it on to DCFS. Connie is fighting to keep DCFS from fully investigating Kirk, but the court is ruling against her. I am still speaking with custody evaluators to perform the study requested of Commissioner Bloom so that I can present the names of the proposed evaluators and their costs at the hearing in April.

I hope you get in touch with Emily, the new CPS worker, and that she can locate the papers you took to DCFS. Please let me know if you hear from Emily or Mary C and keep me advised. I will do the same with you both. Nancy

Hi Jody and Deone, I just received a call from the new CPS worker, her name is Emmy R. She wants the police reports and other documents and I told her you would deliver them to her. She is located on Fashion Blvd in SLC - it's a red brick building. Also, she will talk to you. Please call her. Thanks, Nancy

The following day I made copies of all the pertinent information and brought it to Emmy in Salt Lake. I also called her office in advance to make sure she would be there so I could speak to her. We had already made a trip to the DCFS office in West Valley with Nancy which resulted in nothing. We were put in a conference room for about thirty minutes before a sloppy looking, uninterested woman in her late thirties came in with a yellow legal pad. Nancy explained our case and the court order while the woman sat and stared wryly at us. She had no questions, jotted down a couple things on her paper, then excused us.

"What was that?" Jody asked Nancy.

"Well I gave her a copy of the order so they should start doing something - there isn't a whole lot of time before our next hearing."

I was speechless. My instinct and common sense told me nothing productive would be coming henceforth of that meeting. When I arrived at the red brick building, I was not able to meet with Emmy as I had hoped. The receptionist accepted the large bundle of documents through an opening in a security glass window. I looked around at the confined reception area - shabby plastic chairs, some little ones for children and larger for adults, kid's books, and a lot of literature on abuse filled the small, empty, waiting room.

I never heard a word from the Department of Child and Family Services, the shabby lady from West Valley, Emmy, or any CPS employee regarding the court ordered investigation.

MARCH 6TH, 2015: EMAIL from Nancy S to Private Investigator John B

Hi John, It was a pleasure speaking with you on this case. We won our Motion for DCFS investigation based on the police reports you obtained for us. I need to have copies of police reports since June 2014, on the following: Kirk J; Jill C; Kelly H; Shane S. I am attaching court dockets for charges against these people since June 2014, which may be of value to you. MY INTENT IS TO TURN ANY NEW REPORTS OVER TO DCFS AS SOON AS I GET THEM FROM YOU. THANKS FOR YOUR HELP ON THIS. Nancy

MARCH 6TH, 2015: EMAILS from Nancy S

12:52 PM

Hi Jody and Deone, I am attaching court documents filed by Connie today. She first filed an Objection to the Recommendation and Order I submitted to the court and then a motion for a hearing on her motion for attorney's fees and a proposed order setting a hearing on her motions. I prepared our reply memorandum and I am attaching it to this email. She has now filed other motions which I will send to you in another email. Nancy

12:57 PM

Jody and Deone, I am attaching more motions filed by Connie today. I will need to work on preparing our reply over the weekend. This is getting ridiculous and I am alleging in all our responses that Kirk J is filing these motions to delay the furtherance of the case and to delay a final resolution of the matters before the court. Nancy

MARCH 6TH, 2015: OBJECTION TO PROPOSED RECOMMENDATIONS AND ORDER, submitted by Connie C, Commissioner Bloom presiding

Comes now, Connie, on behalf or Kirk J, files the Objection to Recommendations and Order Proposed by counsel for Intervenor Jody Rhorer:

(1) Page one, Counsel for Kirk J's name is spelled incorrectly.

(2) Page one, it is asserted there is "evidence before the Court that Mr. Rhorer had an established relationship" with the minor, PR. There has been no evidentiary hearings in the case, and at best, there is an assertion or allegation by Mr. Rhorer he had a relationship with PR. The Court has not made findings by any standard of proof to that allegation.

(3) Page three, the Court has previously ruled on Motions to Strike documents Intervenor sought to lodge in the case and those were previously granted. As it relates to the transcript of the hearing, Counsel for Mr. Rhorer supplied in February 2015, and the Appellate cases supplied, those items are Ordered Lodged and made part of the record.

*(4) The Proposed Order contains none of the findings articulated by the Commissioner, which included (**Counsel apologizes that those notes regarding findings are not detailed as the Court articulated, and may be missing particulars. Counsel recreated those findings exclusively from the typewritten notes she took during the Commissioner's oral pronouncement from February 20th, 2015.**)*

Counsel for Mr. Rhorer asserted in her Reply for Motion for Attorney's fees that she had emailed undersigned Counsel a copy of the recording of the February hearing. Undersigned never got any such email, and therefore did not have the benefit of the recording in drafting this objection. Undersigned will obtain the recording and draft more precise findings if directed to do so by the court in that the very precise language of the Commissioner's oral pronouncement would likely aid the District Court in its evaluation of the Recommendations.

(a) The Court reviewed all the pending motions in the matter;

(b) The Court reviewed the Juvenile case files, which the Court denominated Juvenile cases "1" and "2."

(c) The Court reviewed all the pending motions in the matter.

(d) Intervenor asserted he was father of PR in the Juvenile court case "1" but ceased to appear in that case, which caused the Juvenile Court to note that Mr. Rhorer never established paternity.

(e) Mr. Rhorer has asserted he is "declarant father," due to his assertion that he was once on the birth certificate of PR, but a declaration of paternity requires a sworn oath that there is no presumed father, which could not have been done in this case by virtue of Kelly H having been married to Kirk J at the time of the birth of PR, he is presumed father of PR.

(f) In any event, Mr. Rhorer has provided no declaration of paternity of PR, and therefore, the Court finds he is not "declarant father" of PR.

(g) Mr. Rhorer thereafter filed a Paternity Court case in District Court, but didn't notice Kirk J of that proceeding, and though he managed to obtain an Order of Paternity of PR in that District Court proceeding, he thereafter agreed that Order be stricken, and the paternity action was dismissed.

(h) Though Mr. Rhorer was noticed of Juvenile Court case 1, he was not noticed of Juvenile Court case 2.

(i) In Juvenile Court case 1, he was not noticed of Juvenile Court case 2.

(j) That finding and Order was made in 2010, and was not appealed.

(k) Mr. Rhorer is an alleged father.

(l) In the divorce filing herein, Kelly H noted that Kirk J is not biological father to some of her children, and did not indicate Kirk J was biological father of PR, however, having noted that issue, she did nothing to "challenge" paternity, nor did Kirk J.

(m) *The Court findings that standing to challenge paternity by virtue of the applicable statute is limited to Kelly H, Kirk J as presumed father, and a "child support agency," and Mr. Rhorer, as an alleged father under the terms of the statute, does not have standing.*

(n) *However, the case of J.P.R. v. L.M., 2014 UT App. 191, which was decided during the pendency of the Commissioners deliberation and review of the pending motions expressly reserved decision as to whether an alleged father might bring a Constitutional challenge.*

(o) *The Court's Order regarding a limited evaluation by a custody evaluator is for the purpose of investigation into specific factors related to Mr. Rhorer's challenge in that regard, and there may be a Constitutional associational basis under which he might assert standing to contest paternity.*

Connie did not obtain the court CD's, transcripts, recordings, etc., on her own as is customary by attorneys. Instead, she ordered our attorney to do it for her - expecting her to pay the fees to obtain the documentation needed to prepare and respond to orders. She even expected our attorney to mail and pay postage for materials *she* was responsible for obtaining. And our attorney did just as Connie demanded.

And although we had removed all internet publication in January, Connie still filed a Motion to Cease, which was entirely contrary to her pleadings for attorney fees in which she claimed we cause her excessive and unnecessary work as she knew we had taken down the internet pleas.

MARCH 6TH, 2015: MOTION FOR ORDER INTERVENOR JODY RHORER CEASE PUBLISHING CONFIDENTIAL MATERIALS/MOTION FOR ATTORNEYS FEES, submitted by Connie C, Commissioner Bloom presiding

Comes now, Connie, Attorney at Law, and on behalf of Kirk J, files the foregoing Motion that Intervenor, Jody Rhorer, cease any and all publication of confidential information in this case, and Motion that he pay attorney fees of Kirk J for all costs related to the pursuit of the Motion. Grounds and reasons follow:

Kirk J's counsel brought to the attention of this Court that Mr. Rhorer caused to be posted on "Youtube" a fully public internet forum, a plea for money through a donation generating website called "GoFundMe" which included both the minor's name and photographs, which could cause her to be identified. The video, which contained the likeness of Mr. Rhorer speaking to the camera, also made a plea to the press to get involved.

Counsel also advised the Court at the same time the issue of the video was discussed, that she had been contacted via a voicemail from a reporter from the Ogden Standard Examiner. The voicemail advised that the reporter was writing an article about Mr. Rhorer and his efforts to get custody of "his" child, and asked for comment. Naturally, undersigned counsel did not respond to the voicemail.

When advised on the record of these problems regarding the disclosure of the information designated as confidential by the Courts, counsel for Mr. Rhorer indicated that she knew nothing about it, but indicated that she would review any link to the video on Youtube.

Undersigned emailed counsel a link, and while counsel for Mr. Rhorer did not respond within a few days, when undersigned attempted to view the video via that same link, the video indicated it "does not exist" in the Youtube platform. Counsel presumes that Mr. Rhorer removed the video, however, Counsel has been unable to determine whether the information or similar information is still up and active on the "GoFundMe" website which contained Mr. Rhorer's page soliciting funds by way of donation.

Counsel for Kirk J was provided a link to the Standard Examiner article which can be found on the internet at http://www.standard.net/Local/2015/02/06/Utah-Uniform-Parentage-Act *Eden Father: Utah Parentage Act is Legalized Kidnapping.*

The depiction of Mr. Rhorer in the published photographs makes clear that it was he who was the proponent of the article. Undersigned counsel never provided the pleading which the reporter extensively quotes, and therefore, counsel must assume that Mr. Rhorer supplied the reporter with that court filed pleading designated confidential. The article also publishes details of prior Juvenile Court proceedings, which are confidential.

The article which came into existence directly due to Mr. Rhorer's solicitations for donations and press attention, explicitly names himself, Kirk J, and Kelly H and uses the minor's first name, such that she would be easily and readily identified. Mr. Rhorer is quoted as stating, "they bastardized my daughter." Mr. Rhorer's use of this most heinous legal designation in reference to Kirk J's legal child is nothing short of an outrage.

Further, the statement is libelous, in that it is not factually accurate. The minor was not born out of wedlock. She was born during the marriage of Kelly H and Kirk J and therefore, is not and never was a "bastard." Mr. Rhorer's self-serving is harmful to the minor in publishing her in some of the most derogatory terms ever used, not only culturally, societally, and legally.

The phrase "bastard" is epitome of a characterization which would hold one up to public scorn and ridicule. One of the 59 published comments from readers even picked up and ran with Mr. Rhorer's comment, quipped that it was Mr. Rhorer who "made the child a bastard," or words to that effect. The comments then generally ridicule the adults in the child's life, her family system, and even make fun of her name. That the public would join in taking digs at the minor was entirely predictable and demonstrates that Mr. Rhorer has caused the minor to be held up to the glaring and corrosive light of public ridicule.

Mr. Rhorer participated in and caused to be brought about the identification of the minor, publication of materials designated as confidential under the Utah Rules of Judicial Administration 4-202.02(4)(B)(i) and 4-202.02(4)(B)(v)(viii) and characterization of the minor in the most offensive terms known in American Jurisprudence. His conduct must be swiftly and appropriately addressed by this Court.

MOTION FOR ATTORNEYS FEES

Mr. Rhorer should pay the cost of attorney fees to prepare the Motion, including the cost of any research, drafting, preparation of affidavits, hearings, and preparation of any Orders. The Court should also pay the costs of Kirk Js attorney to attempt to have the article removed from the Internet. Courts of general jurisdiction possess certain inherent power to impose monetary sanctions on attorneys who by their conduct thwart the court's scheduling and movement of cases through the court.

While undersigned unequivocally supports Mr. Rhorer (and any citizen's) right to disagree with any law and to speak, inform, or even publish such disagreement, Mr. Rhorer is not at liberty to break the law in doing so. In providing complete names of all participants, and the minor's first name, as well as providing court filed documents that are designated by law as confidential, Mr. Rhorer has exceeded his legal boundaries. Further, causing the derogatory and untrue designation "bastard" to be involved and published to describe the minor is nothing short of libel, which has never been considered protected speech under the First Amendment.

Wherefore, the Court should immediately Order Mr. Rhorer to stop making any public comment which identified the minor, stop making slanderous or libelous remarks about her, cease and desist any publication of remarks in any media which would tend to hold her up to public ridicule, and to pay fees for the prosecution of this motion and to pay any fees incurred by Kirk J in his efforts to have the article removed by the Standard Examiner.

***THIS MATTER** having come before the Court upon Motion of Kirk J against Mr. Rhorer directing him to cease further publication of confidential details of this case, and for attorney fees related to the same.*

***IT IS HEREBY ORDERED** that a hearing on this matter shall be scheduled.*

Certainly, Jody would not refer to his daughter as a bastard, and Connie knew that. The "bastardization" reference was used by Nancy in regards to the State of Utah removing Jody's name from Payshence's birth certificate. And her legal name was never used either - as Payshence is the name Jody gave her. We were careful not to name individuals but referred instead to the UUPA state law. Jody was being banned from having photos of his own child on line or referring to her at all as his daughter.

MARCH 6TH, 2015: EMAILS from Nancy S

8:47 PM

Guys, I'm attaching our Reply to Connie's motion to cease publication of protected information. She has been emailing me this afternoon, now she is saying that she never received my February 23, 2015, email with our proposed Recommendation and Order and she never received the recording of the hearing.

I've resent the email to her three times. She is calling me a liar and she wants to Subpoena my IT person to testify in court about my emails. I sent her an email stating that we should ask the court to designate a computer forensics expert to examine her computer and my computer and report the the court about the emails. I am going to ask Commissioner Bloom to meet with Connie and myself to try to resolve these issues. This is getting to be beyond ridiculous and I am getting to be beyond patient. I will keep you informed. Thanks, Nancy

8:51 PM

Nancy, Looks like Kelly H is going to court next week for assault. Do you think she didn't appear because of the 2 warrants out for her arrest? Deone

Your guess is a good one. I am hoping to get the most recent police reports from the investigator early next week and will send them to you, DCFS, and the GAL. This investigator is the former FBI guy who has done quite a bit of work on our case. I would like you and Jody to meet with him if he has the time next week. Nancy

MARCH 6TH, 2015: INTERVENOR'S REPLY TO RESPONDENT'S OBJECTIONS AND REQUEST FOR HEARING, filed by Nancy S, Commissioner Bloom presiding

Jody Rhorer, by and through counsel Nancy S, hereby replies to the Respondent's objection and request for hearing as follows:

FACTS

1. On February 23, 2015, at 1:44 p.m., counsel for Intervenor emailed to Respondent's counsel proposed order and attached a recording of the February 20, 2015, hearing. The email asked "Please let me know if you want any changes."

2. On February 25, 2015, the parties agreed to separate the ruling as to the DCFS investigation due to the timeliness of the investigation.

3. On February 26, 2015, counsel for Intervenor again emailed Respondent's counsel with a reminder that a recording of the hearing had been provided.

4. On February 27, 2015, counsel for Intervenor again emailed Respondent's counsel asking about the proposed order, but did not get a response or requests for changes.

5. On March 2, 2015, the proposed orders were filed with a Request to Submit.

6. The Order Required DCFS Investigation was signed by Commissioner Bloom on March 3, 2015, and by Judge Stanley on March 5, 2015.

7. Respondent filed objections on March 6, 2015, alleging that a recording of the hearing was not provided. Upon receipt of the objection counsel for Intervenor again emailed to Respondent's counsel a recording of the February 20, 2015, hearing.

ARGUMENT

At the hearing on February, 20, 2015, the court stated that although the hearing was lengthy, the ruling itself was short. The Recommendation and Order set forth the court's ruling. Respondent's objections are untimely inasmuch as they were not submitted within the required time allotted by Rule 7 of the Utah Rules of Civil Procedure. Respondent did not request changes to the orders despite repeated request for changes by the Intervenor. The Order Requiring DCFS Investigation was approved and by the Court and objections thereto are moot.

Respondent's motions filed since the court's ruling on February 20, 2015, have been made for improper purposes. Respondent's motions are made in a willful attempt to delay the furtherance of these proceedings and resolution of the matters before the court. Respondent could have communicated to the Intervenor and requests for changes after receipt of the proposed order; instead respondent waited until the matter had been submitted for approval by the court to file oppositions, motions for attorney's fees, all with the intent to impose further delays in the proceedings. Intervenor should be awarded attorney's fees for having to respond.

WHEREFORE, *Jody Rhorer respectfully requests that Respondent's objections and motion for hearing be denied.*

MARCH 6TH, 2015: RESPONSE TO NANCY S's REPLY TO THE OBJECTION TO PROPOSED RECOMMENDATIONS AND ORDER FOR FEES, submitted by Connie C, Commissioner Bloom presiding

Comes now, Connie C, and on behalf of Kirk J, files the foregoing Response to Nancy S's Reply to the Objection to the Recommendations and Order and request for fees.

FACTS

(1) The first time undersigned saw the proposed Order regarding the recommendations was Friday, February 27th, 2015, when the proposed Order E-filed by Nancy S was served via the Court's e-filing system. **(Narrators Comment: Notice the careful wording used by Connie "the first-time undersigned saw." She doesn't say she didn't receive it earlier, she alludes that she never read it as a way around the fact that she did receive it on time but hopes this detail will not be picked up by the court.)**

(2) At the same time, Nancy S e-filed a corrected version of the proposed DCFS Order, the first draft of which was emailed to counsel by Nancy S February 25th.

(3) February 27th was the first time undersigned saw the version of the DCFS Order summated to the Court for signature.

(4) Up to and including the time of filing of their pleading, counsel for Kirk J has not received a copy of the recording of February 20th, 2015, despite Nancy S's protestations that she has emailed it twice.

Counsel again reiterates her offer to supply any/all emails between counsel and indeed implore the Court to request counsel's email records. Not only will the email record inform and enlighten the Court as to what was sent and received on any given date, an email sent from undersigned to Nancy S on February 25th, 2015, refutes the accusation that Counsel for Kirk J hasn't in any way attempted to delay anything in this case or any DCFS investigations.

February 25th Counsel encouraged Nancy S to have her client report any allegations immediately, and not wait for a Court Order, because the Division starts counting its 30-day CPS investigation period upon referral. While not providing the exact citation, counsel informed Nancy S of the Division's requirement to finish investigating within 30 days of referral. Counsel has sought to move the matter forward, while at the same time exercising sound professional judgment related to review of and objections to proposed Orders. Counsel received both proposed Orders February 27th, 2015. As such, the seven days to respond included March 6th. Both objections were filed on or before March 6th.

Counsel cannot ascertain how the District Court can evaluate or review can be had on the Order proposed on the Recommendations because it is devoid of any findings. Undersigned assumed that the Court went through such a painstaking litany of the procedural history, the statutes, and the case law, because the Commissioner expected that the findings, basis and rationale supporting the Recommended Orders be included for the District Court's consideration and those aspects are a necessary part of the Proposed Order, which is the basis upon which Kirk J filed his Objection as he has an interest in the completeness of the form of the Order which reaches the District Judge. The Commissioner undertook a very detailed analysis of the applicable law and the relevant procedural history and facts, Kirk J feels that should be outlined for the District Court's evaluations, and any subsequent review.

MARCH 7TH, 2015: EMAILS from Nancy S

1:35 PM

Deone, I would like to file our Reply before Monday. Will you please check Facebook and let me know if Kirk J has a Facebook page and if he has posted photos and info about Payshence? I know Kelly has done that. If Kirk hasn't posted any info, but his girlfriend or someone else associated with Kirk has, will you let me know that, too? Thanks, Nancy

11:35 PM

Hi Nancy,

I've spent the last 2 hours on Kirk's, his girlfriend's, and Kelly's Facebook pages. Both Kirk and his girlfriend have posted photos of Payshence. Can you encourage the GAL to look at Kelly's FB very thoroughly? There are so many disgusting pictures that show what she is about.

There are pictures of her sucking on woman's breasts (and other private parts) and vice versa, French kissing women, and her husband, Shane, also doing things to other women. There are a lot of photos of her in stripper costumes and Shane laying on a bed with no clothes on covered in $20 bills (looks like the loot Kelly earned stripping). There is quite a bit of lewd dialog. It's really hard to follow what she is even saying as it is all gangster slang and swear words. She does have dialog with a 21-year-old girl in Dec. of last year and the girl says that she is pressing charges against her for hitting her. This may be the assault case from December. I'm not sure how much you are able to get involved with the GAL, but I hope the social media is part of their investigation. I am actually physically sick now after viewing such disgusting sights and knowing that Payshence endures that life daily. Deone

MARCH 7TH, 2015: RESPONSE TO JODY RHORER'S REPLY TO THE MOTION TO CEASE PUBLICATION AND FOR ATTORNEY FEES, submitted by Connie C, Commissioner Bloom presiding

Connie C, Attorney at Law, files the foregoing Response to Mr. Rhorer's Reply to the Motion that Intervenor cease any and all publication of confidential information in this case, and Motion that he pay attorney fees.

As an initial matter, Mr. Rhorer seems to fault Kirk J for not pursuing the issue of his publication on Youtube, a video depicting pictures of the minor and identifying her in a plea to raise funds for Mr. Rhorer's legal defense, and entreaty to the press to contact Mr. Rhorer. Kirk J had no need to pursue the matter of the Youtube video further, because within a couple days of sending the link to Mr. Rhorer's counsel, the video was removed.

In response to the issue of his publication of confidential details of this case. Mr. Rhorer complains the Petitioner and Respondent have pictures of the minor on their Facebook Accounts. The same reality constitutes a collateral attack about other behavior, presumably in the hope the Court will lose sight of the issue. Without averring to the truth or falsity of that allegation, the matter of sharing pictures of children on a Facebook account accessible only to invited "Facebook friends" is entirely different from publication in a newspaper of general circulation.

Mr. Rhorer responds that in characterizing the minor as a "bastard" in that publication of general circulation, he was merely using a "legal phrase." While the phrase is undoubtedly a legal one, it is also a resoundingly reprehensible one which casts the object of that classification into the decidedly inferior class compared to others.

The incendiary comments posted by readers establishes the effects of that characterization, and Mr. Rhorer brought that on PR after providing detailed information so that her identity was established.

It should be noted, since Mr. Rhorer wishes to rely on the status of the word as a "legal" one, that his invocation of the term was patently incorrect. The minor was born into a legal marriage, and as such had a presumed father by virtue of that marriage. Without disruption of that status or disestablishment of paternity, the Honorable Judge V then issued his Dispositional Order that by clear and convincing evidence, Kirk J was the child's father. Therefore, Mr. Rhorer's statement, which sets off negative public comment about the minor, does not describe the minor in the least. Rather, the term was wrongfully used to stir up sympathy among reader to Mr. Rhorer's position. The net effect of Mr. Rhorer's participation is public scorn for the minor.

ATTORNEY'S FEES

Since Kirk J's counsel brought to the Court's attention that Nancy S filed a Notice to Submit with an incorrect statement in it, attesting that seven days had elapsed since the proposed orders were provided to counsel, Nancy S, has repeatedly asserted "bad faith" and "improper purpose" for the sake of delay.

Counsel for Kirk J requests the Court disregard these assertions made in an attempt to obfuscate the issues before the Court. Just as Kirk J has a right to the time designated by law to review and object to proposed Orders, he has a right to ask the Court's assistance when private details of the case, including identification of his daughter, is made in the media.

This proceeding can in no way be "delayed" by Kirk J's pursuit of this Motion to protect his child's privacy. The issue regarding the Youtube video was presented to the Court as soon as counsel found out about it. Counsel for Kirk J did not pursue it further because the removal of the recording mooted the issue. Counsel then filed this Motion about publication as soon as she learned the article had been published. The Motion is not "delaying" any proceedings in that the matter is going to hearing April 16th as previously scheduled.

For Mr. Rhorer to assert that it constitutes "bad faith" for a parent to request the Court's intervention when private details of such a case are published in the newspaper is unfathomable. This case involves the most sensitive details of the minor's life and relationships, and Kirk's resort to the Court for assistance in protecting her from the harsh glare of the media and public ridicule is infinitely appropriate.

MARCH 9TH, 2015: INTERVENOR.S REPLY TO MOTION TO CEASE PUBLICATION AND FOR ATTORNEY FEES, submitted by Nancy S, Commissioner Bloom presiding

Intervenor Jody Rhorer, through counsel, Nancy S, hereby replies to the Respondent's "Motion of Order Intervenor Cease Publishing Confidential Materials/Motion for Attorney Fees":

PRELIMINARY STATEMENT

This motion, as well as all other motions filed by Respondent since the court's ruling on February 20, 2015, is being made in bad faith and is a deliberate attempt to divert the court's attentions away from the single issue which is most paramount in this case, the issue of the best interest of the minor child, PR.

The Respondent's flurry of motions is designed to cause more delay in these proceedings, to hinder the DCFS investigation, to obstruct the court's directives to the GAL appointed for PR, impede the Intervenor's ability to comply with the court's directives and timelines pursuant to the court's ruling of February 20, 2015, and to delay a final resolution of the matters before the court. Respondent will likely persist in filing motions and requests hearings as a means to ask for a continuance of the review hearing.

Respondent's abuse of the judicial process must be addressed by the court. Respondent has filed motions late and has then defended the late filing in further motions and filed multiple motions for attorney fees without complying with the prerequisites required for the motions under the Utah Rules of Civil Procedure. Respondent has filed motions for hearings on Respondent's motions and now files this motion asking the court for remedies which exceed the court's jurisdiction, and addresses issues previously resolved by the parties prior to the February 20, 2015, hearing. Sanctions are appropriate for both the Respondent and his attorney. Intervenor paid the GAL's fee of $1000 pursuant to the court's order. Intervenor has filed his Financial Declaration pursuant to the court's order, and the court's ruling addresses a possible custody evaluation and allocation of costs among the parties. Mr. and Mrs. Rhorer are working and saving money to pay for the costs. The Respondent is knowingly and intentionally imposing a great financial hardship on the Intervenor by the filing of these excessive motions requiring Intervenor to incur additional attorney's fees.

FACTS

1. During a telephone conference with the court on February 9, 2014, Respondent's counsel brought to the attention of the court a "Youtube" video of Intervenor Jody Rhorer. Respondent's counsel alleged that Mr. Rhorer had disclosed confidential information about the minor child by using the minor child's name and by showing photographs of the minor child, and alleged that Mr. Rhorer had criticized the State of Utah and the Parentage Act, and that Mr. Rhorer had solicited funds for his legal bills.

2. No evidence was submitted to the court to support the allegations.

3. Counsel for Intervenor informed the court that she had no personal knowledge of the video. Respondent's counsel offered to send a link via email to Intervenor's counsel.

4. At that time the Court ordered counsel to either resolve the issue of Mr. Rhorer's alleged dissemination of confidential information regarding PR prior to the upcoming hearing on February 20, or in the alternative the court would hear arguments on Respondent's oral motion for a restraining order at the hearing.

5. Counsel for Jody Rhorer, received a link via email to a "Youtube" video from Respondent's counsel and on the same day replied via email that she would confer with Mr. Rhorer and contact Respondent's counsel by telephone.

6. On February 11, counsel for Intervenor called Respondent's counsel and left a voicemail stating that in the video the minor child was not identified by the name used in the court documents, but that Mr. Rhorer had removed the video.

7. Respondent didn't renew his motion for a restraining order at the February 20, hearing.

8. In January, 2015, Mr. and Mrs. Rhorer were contacted by a reporter from the Ogden Standard Examiner and agreed to be interviewed.

9. The Facebook accounts of Petitioner and Respondent shows photographs of the minor child and references her with the same name used by Intervenor in the video, and the name used by the reporter in the newspaper article, and have posted references to those proceedings and to Intervener.

ARGUMENT

In a legal proceeding the identity of a minor child is confidential. In the video Mr. Rhorer was careful not to use the minor child's name as it appears on the legal documents. The identity of the Petitioner and Respondent, as well as the identity of the Intervenor in this action is not confidential information. Mr. Rhorer's criticism of the law and legal process is protected by the Constitution. Any plea for help in deferring legal cots is immaterial. Nevertheless, Mr. Rhorer removed the video out of an abundance of caution.

The Respondent now files this same motion concerning the video and a newspaper article published by the Ogden Standard Examiner and makes the same allegations, including allegations that are constitutionally protected and allegations that are immaterial. Mr. Rhorer is not the author of the newspaper article. He has not endorsed the article. He is not responsible for the language or information contained in the article. The newspaper article is hearsay. If Respondent wishes to pursue this matter, Respondent's remedy is to file suit against the newspaper and request an injunction.

The article contains language of a legal nature. The language that Respondent finds objectionable is a legal term to describe a very horrific and tragic situation. Sadly, it is the term used by the Guardian ad Litem in the Juvenile Court proceedings concerning PR and a term used in court pleadings in the case. The term is not slanderous or directed to anyone or to any party to those proceedings.

There is no evidence that Mr. Rhorer defamed, or caused to be defamed, the minor child or anyone else to these proceedings. If the Respondent believes he was slandered by Intervenor, the Respondent's remedy is to file a defamation suit.

Conversely, the Petitioner and Respondent over the past two years has consistently used Facebook to publish confidential information about the minor child by posting photographs of PR and identifying her by the name used in these proceedings. The Petitioner has at times published details about these court proceedings. The Petitioner has named Mr. Rhorer in her Facebook postings and her postings may amount to slander. Respondent's and Petitioner's Facebook postings are not hearsay. If anyone should be restrained from publishing identifying material about the minor child, it is the Petitioner and Respondent.

CONCLUSION

Respondent's motion is without merit and exceeds the issues before the court. Mr. Rhorer has not publishing information identifying the minor child. Respective counsel for Respondent and Intervenor resolved this issue and accordingly, the Respondent did not renew his motion for improper purposes as described above.

WHEREFORE, Intervenor prays that the court deny the Respondent's motion and for an award of attorney fees for having to respond to this motion.

MARCH 9TH, 2015: NOTICE OF HEARING, submitted by Nancy S, Commissioner Bloom presiding

YOU ARE HEREBY NOTIFIED that hearing on the following motions/issues will be heard on April 16th, 2015. Please conduct yourselves accordingly.
(1) Kirk J's Objections to proposed DCFS and Recommendations Orders.
(2) Kirk J's Opposition to the March 2nd Notice to Submit.
(3) Kirk J's Motion for Attorney fees for the Opposition to the Notice to Submit.
(4) Kirk J's Motion for Order to Cease Publication of Confidential Details.
(5) Kirk J's Motion for Attorney fees regarding Motion to Cease Publication.

MARCH 17TH, 2015: EMAILS from Nancy S

2:58 PM
Hi Mary, This email concerns Payshence Rhorer in the matter of Kelly H vs Kirk J, Jody Rhorer, Intervenor, Third District Court. Kelly H's stepbrother, RB, is a convicted sex offender. In the Juvenile Court proceedings Payshence was taken away from Kelly H and placed in DCFS custody because she allowed RB to babysit her. Kirk J was ordered by the Juvenile Court not to allow people with criminal convictions in his home or around PR after she was placed in his home in 2012.
Kirk J was ordered not to allow Kelly H to have visits with PR unless they were supervised visits. My client just sent to me the attached photograph of RB with Payshence sitting next to him and RB holding BS, another of Kelly H's children. This photograph is on Kelly H's Facebook page with the caption "Uncle R." I am also attaching a copy of the Utah Sex Offender Registry for him. My client is concerned that both Kirk J and Kelly H are allowing Payshence to be around the sex offender, RB. I have submitted this information to the CPS worker as well. Thank you, Nancy S

3:11 PM
Thank you for this information. I am copying Emmy R at DCFS on this email. We are meeting the children, Kirk, and his girlfriend this Thursday at 4. Mary

3:30 PM
Hi Jody and Deone, I received an email from Mary C, GAL. Please contact her to arrange to meet with her. She wants you to bring in all the police reports that pertain to Jody. If we need to meet about this, please let me know and we can schedule something. Nancy S

9:10 PM

We will call her to schedule a meeting. Jody doesn't have any police reports but he does have his background check. He hasn't had any type of trouble since he left Kelly. Deone

9:33 PM
Right, but since we have given DCFS and the GAL police reports about Kirk and Kelly that go years back, we need to be forthcoming about any police reports involving Jody. I have the court dockets for Protective Orders, etc., with Kelly and a few other minor things that may have resulted from police reports. I can meet with you guys and give you that information so that Jody can go around and request the police reports from the various police departments. We need to submit the reports to the GAL, regardless of how minor the infractions or how long ago the reports were made. I am working from home this evening drafting court pleadings on another case, but will be in the office tomorrow if you guys want to call. Nancy

We had already been through all this. Nancy was acting like Jody had something to hide and her request to take another day off work to run all over three counties to obtain police reports for minor tickets dating back to when he was a teenager was not necessarily out of a desire to be "forthcoming" but more than anything to satisfy herself. Nevertheless, he did as she asked and, to no surprise, there were no stunning revelations that came forth from his efforts. It was actually to the contrary. He was told at one police station that they didn't keep
these kinds of records for minor infractions from years ago.

We had another meeting with Nancy in her office. There were graphs and diagrams and white boards with far fetching ideas. She kept stressing to Jody and I that we needed to provide her with the "smoking gun" against Kirk. Her idea that Kirk and Kelly and their extended family were "breeding" children to become drug dealers for them was spiraling out into many corridors of her imagination but with no proof to back it up. She had become obsessed with the "WHY" and refused to accept that we were up solely against a law and the State and as horrible and absurd as she could possibly paint the situation with Kirk and Kelly, it just didn't seem to make a difference with the Court.

Nancy made a list of things she wanted John B to do. This list comprised focus on the KTB - Kearns Town Bloods and the SAC - Soldiers of the Arian Culture; interviewing school resource officers; looking up juvenile records against the other children in the home; finding and interviewing Shane S's parents; finding the pastor at the Baptist church that counseled Jody and Kelly; contacting the Unified Police Neighborhood Narcotics Force regarding the drug dealer, Henry, to establish a tie to Kelly and Kirk; contacting the Crimes Against Children Task Force and Attorney General's Office.

In my mind I was thinking, "Nancy has completely lost it!"

"This is going to take money," Nancy said, looking down at my purse on the floor of her office near the chair I was seated on. "John has put so much time into this case and we really need him going forward."

"I just don't think this is the direction we should be going. We have given you all the information we have and you want us to come up with more. I don't see how interviewing Shane's parents will get us anywhere. They aren't going to help us. They'll be on his side. We're out of resources, Nancy. We can't keep paying John. All I have seen is some photos of the kids standing in front of Kirk's house and pictures of his garbage. This isn't getting us anywhere," I directed.

I could see the disappointment stretch across Nancy's face. She had worked hard and gone down every possible avenue, but it didn't add up and she just couldn't accept the fact that Payshence was plucked away from Jody and her sisters and forced to live with Kirk J because of a law and a mother that knew Jody would protect Payshence from her negative influences. And that was all there was to it.

MARCH 24TH, 2015: JOURNAL ENTRY, Meeting with GAL

Feeling anxious and excited! We're at Nancy's office waiting to meet with Mary C, the Court Appointed Guardian ad Litem. Payshence will have her own attorney, her own voice, her own representation. Jody's parents and daughters will be there too. We wait with anticipation. Mary is late but it gives us time to talk with Nancy and prepare for what questions may be asked.

"Remember, Jody, be an open book," Nancy is saying, "If the GAL asks for anything, you just give it to her."

The door is opening. Bleach Blond Barbie just walked in pulling a small case with wheels, wearing red capris, matching stilettos, and a cardigan sweater. She looks like she's headed out for a lunch date on the Wharf in San Francisco. Feeling disappointed but should give her the benefit of the doubt.

Interviews are starting. She wants to speak with the extended family first. They've been waiting an hour so it's best she gets that out of the way so Jody's parents can take the girls home.

Now it's Mary, Nancy, Jody and me. Nancy's showing Mary recent risqué photos Kelly posted on Facebook. Mary is looking hard at a photo of Kelly in a two-piece lingerie set, standing outside in a campground during the Sturges motorcycle convention.

"She has a nice body," Mary says, out of the blue.

I can't believe she just said that out loud! "She's a meth addict," I remind her, "She doesn't eat."

"Oh, right," Mary replies still staring at the picture. "So, Jody, you have custody of your three older daughters, correct?"

"Yeah, I have had since they were little. In fact, Commissioner Bloom was my girl's Guardian ad Litem when I was in court getting 'em."

"Did you just say Commissioner Bloom was GAL for your other girls? Mary just woke up from her lusty daze!

"Ya, so?"

"Excuse me please." Mary's walking out into the hall with Nancy following. Jody and I are confused. Nancy's back now with a glum look on her face.

"Mary reported to the Office of Guardian ad Litem that Commissioner Bloom represented your girls in the past and thought it may be a conflict of interest." Nancy is tripping over her words.
"You said to be an open book - to, to tell her everything!" Jody's mad. "I've told you before about that and you never said anything about it being an issue."

"Don't get worked up, Jody. I didn't think it was an issue. Let's just wait this out and see what happens." Nancy's trying to smooth over.

"But we're almost there! We have a court date coming up in a few weeks. Comm Bloom is on our side and we need her." I have a really bad feeling. "What's the worst thing that could happen? We need to know."

"She could recuse herself." Nancy can barely speak. "But I don't think she will."

MARCH 25TH, 2015: FACEBOOK POST from Kelly H in response to Jody's Youtube post in January

"for all of you f****** idiots that are feeding into jodi Rhorer bullshit on youtube need to get a life K get over it you don't have a daughter with me never have never will and bringing other people into it all the kids and everything else grow up and get a life like I said and just like Jill C said praying for her home and for our kids that are in her home I think also more importantly we need to pray for the idiots trying to cause drama because unlike you "folks" were content and happy in our lives sorry about your punk ass oh and more importantly our kids are just fine you have your own kids to worry about so like I said we gone shine regardless of how much you try to take it away or hatn cuz you aint - One more little piece for all you b****** Big bitches or Sasquatch looking b****** jodi wife why be a punk about it you know where I be"

MARCH 26TH, 2015: EMAIL from Nancy S

Hi Deone, I talked to Emmy from DCFS late yesterday afternoon. She is out of town tomorrow and can't be at the meeting. I suggested that another DCFS worker be present and she said that if a DCFS worker came to the meeting then an attorney from The Attorney General's office would need to be present. I said, "Great, let's get someone here." She did not promise, but said she would work to see if someone from DCFS can be at the meeting.

She said she interviewed Kirk and Jill, but still is trying to interview Kelly. She said she could not give me information about the situation at their home due to DCFS policies, but that she would prepare and submit her report to the court and be at the court hearing in April. She said there's still a lot of work to do on the case before the hearing, particularly with Kelly. She received the most recent police reports that I sent regarding Kelly and Shane and she's investigating those incidents. She said that everything we reported to DCFS at their office had already been investigated by DCFS and that she would report on that to the court. Really, not much more than that. Nancy

MARCH 28TH, 2015: EMAIL CHAIN from Mary C, GAL, to Connie and Kirk

11:54 AM
Connie,
I was hoping you could provide or have your client give authorization for me to access to the following records:
1. Any and all juvenile records relating to Payshence.
2. Any and all criminal records of both Jill C and Kirk J.
3. Birth certificates of all the children living in Kirk's home;
Also, can you please provide the names of all the children living in Kirk's home and both the names of each child's legal parents, and biological parents if different. Thank you for your cooperation. Mary C, GAL

Mar. 30, 2015 1:14 PM
Connie, Additionally, I am requesting that your client provide me with the name of Payshence's current teacher and provide a release for me to speak with her former teacher. Kirk will need to contact the school to provide this release. Please advise as to when this is complete. I have also had my assistant trying to coordinate with Kirk so that I can speak with Jill's oldest two children.
I'd like to do a walk-through of the home this week if possible, as well. Maybe my conversation with them can happen on the same day before or after the walk through. Please have your client contact my office to schedule this time. Thank you for your cooperation, Mary C

Mar. 30, 2015 9:24 PM
Mary, Please see my prior email about being in Tucson. I return late in the week and I will be tending to emergencies at that point. If you still need information by next Monday (as I understand my client is aware of your request). I would suggest you call my cell at that point.

Mar. 30, 2015 10:00 PM
Connie, I do not have an email for your client to provide him with the list of requests below so I'm uncertain as to whether he's received this list. Have you forwarded my requests to him? Mary C, GAL

Mar. 31, 2015 1:16 PM
Kirk, As we discussed, I went through the items I needed from you as addressed in the emails below. Please get back to me once you have contacted Payshence's school so that I may speak with her teachers. You also stated you'd get me the DCFS reports regarding Jody and the placement of Payshence with you. Mary C, GAL

10:31 PM
Nancy, I was thinking that in the meantime it might be beneficial for Jody and Deone to do what is necessary to become foster parents in the event that Payshence is taken out of Kirk's home for any reason in the future. I think it would also be wise to ensure Jody's parents are current with their foster parent's status. This way they might be first in line to take Payshence if she were taken out of the home by the State. - Mary

May 29th, 1:20 PM
Jody and Deone,
PLEASE READ THE EMAIL FROM MARY!! Remember when Mary and I left my office together during our meeting Friday? I need to talk to you both about the conversation we had. I am doing everything in my power and trying to get Mary to exercise her power to get Payshence away from Kirk and in your custody. Please call me together Monday and get yourselves qualified as foster parents! Tell Jody's parents to get qualified as foster parents! ASAP! Nancy

When Jody's mom was awarded temporary custody when Payshence was taken from Kelly by DCFS, she and Terry got their Foster Parent Certification at the suggestion of the court so they could take care of Payshence instead of her being placed in a stranger's care. But instead of the court taking that into consideration, Payshence was placed in another foster home and random children began to be dropped off at George and Terry's home even though they had specified they only wished to have their granddaughter placed with them.

Needless to say, when I read the emails instructing us to become foster parents, I felt very skeptical based upon Jody's parents experience, but Jody called George anyway and asked her to look into what she needed to do to reactivate her license and I looked up the location of our local foster parent registry and printed the information from their website. When I went to their building, there was a "closed" sign on the door even though it was regular office hours, so I left and went back to work.

By now I was so weary of the constant runaround and the nearly daily demands by Nancy on pointless tasks that got us nowhere. My gut told me something was not right. My gut told me not to spend my time pursuing this. This was all part of the wild goose chase just like Jody running all over getting copies of old traffic tickets.

MARCH 29TH, 2015: EMAIL CHAIN from Nancy

1:11 PM
Jody and Deone, Forwarding this email to you showing that Mary C is asking John to get her in touch with the cop from the Gang and Narcotics unit to accompany her to Kirk's home. After you left Friday, Mary told me that John is going to be very important to our case and that she is glad he is working for us. She emphasized this several times. I think we should talk about John's continuing involvement and give him any information we can think of so that he can continue his investigation. He is going to cost money, but it's worth it. Nancy

ATTACHED EMAIL:
John, It was nice meeting you on Friday. Can you provide me with Lynn's number so I can schedule a time for him to do a walk-through of Kirk's home? Thank you, Mary

Mary, I just spoke with Lynn. He is either going to accompany you to Kirk's home on Friday at 4:00 pm OR he may assign one of his guys that actually works the Kearns area for the Metro Gang Unit and knows the lay of the land and which gangsters are active. You should be forewarned that if any of the officers who accompany you to the home find any contraband (drugs, firearms, etc. in plain sight) because Kirk is a convicted felon, they may decide to arrest him on the spot. Just be aware. Thanks - John

2:51 PM
Hi Nancy, Thank you for all the updates. Jody and I discussed the concern of still not having approval by the judge for him to intervene and we feel there is no point in continuing to pay for services, such as the Private Investigator, John, when he hasn't even been granted this yet. When we listened to the ruling, we were under the impression we could move forward and the Commissioner just wanted to get a clear picture of what was going on with Payshence to support her decision to reunite her with her father. Thanks for all you are doing, Deone

3:51 PM

Deone, I don't mean that Mary C and I talked about whether you understand the ruling. I mean that she and I talked about what the ruling was and what it means to our case. Commissioner Bloom does want to know about Payshence and what has been going on with her, but you need to understand the basis for her ruling. She does want Jody to have Payshence back and Mary and I discussed that in depth. The legal issues in this case are complex. We should set a time to meet so that I can discuss everything with you. Nancy

March 30th, 5:38 PM
Jody and Deone, I am concerned that I have not communicated sufficiently with you about the ruling. I will try to break it down for you as best I can:

1. Because we showed that Jody had an established relationship with Payshence it would be unconstitutional NOT to allow him to establish his paternity,

2. BUT, only if it is in the best interest of Payshence.

3. If the court finds that it is in the best interest of Payshence for Jody to establish his paternity, then Jody can proceed and the court will make orders regarding custody.

4. The court granted our motion for appointment of a GAL. Mary C will report to the Court whether she believes it is in Payshence's best interest for Jody to establish paternity. The Court is relying on her opinion.

5. The court granted our motion for DCFS Investigation because we alleged abuse in Kirk's home and with Kelly. DCFS is investigating and will report to the court about what has been happening with Payshence since she was placed in the home.

Mary C already believes it is in Payshence's best interest to be with Jody. She needs to document everything so that her opinion (which will favor Jody) holds up in court.
She told me that she is relying on John and his expertise to help her. She is asking that the former DCFS worker become involved in the DCFS investigation because she has more information than Emmy and is more willing to help her. Mary is working to document everything so that her opinion cannot be challenged successfully by Connie. Mary confided in me that she would like to ask the court to allow her to observe Jody and Payshence together, and she is considering how she can approach the court with this request. I hope this clarifies the order. Jody is still in. The only thing we need now is to show it is in Payshence's best interest to keep him in. It appears to me that we have that covered, but we need to remain a team, including Mary and John. Nancy

9:58 PM
I think the confusion lies in the term "standing." I interpret Standing to mean that Jody can go forward to establish parentage but then we are told he doesn't have Standing. When I read what you wrote in this email - I interpret it to mean he does have standing and that the GAL and DCFS will give evidence and their professional opinions to back up Bloom's decision. Is this correct or am I interpreting things wrong? Deone

March 31st, 9:25 PM
Standing means he can intervene to establish paternity. Who is telling you he doesn't have standing? The court has not dismissed him from the case.
Nancy

John was the third private investigator Nancy had hired without our consent and all he had done, besides looking up criminal records, was sit in front of Kirk's house and take some photos as well as pictures of alcohol bottles in Kirk's garbage can. While he was sitting in his vehicle across the street from Kirk's house, Jill walked right up to him and asked him what he was doing. What a great P.I. - sitting in broad daylight in plain view and getting busted while doing it! I was unsure why Nancy was so insistent that he stay on payroll.

2:05 PM
Jody, Emmy at DCFS sent the following info to Mary:

"A case in September, 2001, the allegation was physical abuse against Jody's daughter, Mia. The case was regarding Mia having severe dental abscess. The case was closed - unable to locate. The last case was a sexual abuse case. It was alleged that Jody had provided alcohol and had sexual contact with a 17-year- old female. This case was supported for Sexual abuse in November 2012. No charges were filed. Nancy

5:03 PM
I lived in Missouri with Mia, Tina, and Mona during that year. Jody

5:23 PM
Do you know Krista Rhorer?

5:25 PM
My x-wife.

5:32 PM
You filed for divorce in SLC on Nov. 19, 2012. This offense on Nov. 12, 2012, may be a different person with your name, but we need to prove it. Please get the report. Nancy

5:37 PM
What do I need to prove and how do I need to prove it when there was no case filed and I believe when there was no case filed there's my proof. Plain and simple not guilty of anything.

5:39 PM
Should we let Mary C believe it was you? OK by me. Nancy

5:45 PM
If she hasn't got the email where the case was closed, we can forward that to her. I'm leaving to go do donation work - won't be back until next week. Jody

6:41 PM
Just get the G__damn report, Jody. Do it when you get back in town.

April 9th, 10:40 AM
Nancy, Here's the police report you requested. As you can see, there were no charges - it was all made up by a 17-year-old. The report she made to the school officer admitting she fabricated the story is not included here so you would have to get that from the school. Deone

April 10th, 9:05 AM
Thanks for sending this. I believed Jody when he told me the story was not true, but we need to submit this to the GAL to prove it. I appreciate your getting this to me. Nancy

April 1st, 9:49 AM
Hi Deone and Jody, I copied you on this email between Mary and myself because I want you to see that she is on our side. Last Friday she asked me to update my research on Utah case law and to research decisions issued from the other 49 states that might support her conclusions and opinions in our favor. (Very unusual for a GAL to request this.) We have received info from DCFS that we need John to investigate for Mary. John generously wrote off about 50 hours of his time for the work he did on your case last year. I paid him from the fees you paid me but I can't afford to do that again. You wrote to me that you didn't want to pay for John, but he is vital to our case. I need Jody's and your permission to ask John to stay involved. Please confirm so that I can contact him today. I would like to meet with you and Jody as soon as you get back in town to go over the information provided by DCFS. Nancy

10:34 PM

Hi Nancy, We are ok with John going forward but we want details of what he is investigating and the time that he is estimating that each job will take as well as how much he makes per hour. We are trying to gauge our budget. If we know what to expect, we can be prepared for it, but to just say, "Yes, John can do whatever he thinks needs to be done," leaves us wide open for a huge bill that we may not be prepared for. We appreciate very much all you do and have done in the past. Every spare dime we have goes towards this. We just need to know in advance how much we have to set aside. Let us know what works for you next week as far as us coming to meet. HAVE A VERY NICE EASTER! Deone

April 2, 10:04 AM

Hi Deone, I understand. I am sensitive to what this is costing you and Jody. Even Mary C asked me how you guys are affording this and I told her that you are hard-working people and everything you have is going toward this effort. We all see how great Jody and you are, as people and parents. Mary told me she knows a lobbyist who may take this to the legislature next year. She wants the law changed so that men like Jody can have their children. You have a wonderful Easter, too. Thanks - Nancy

APRIL 3RD, 2015: POLICE REPORT

On Friday April 3rd, 2015, while working suppression in the Metro Gang Unit, I was requested by Sgt. Bell to accompany a Guardian ad Litem on a house visit in Kearns involving possibly a Kearns town Blood gang member. I was informed to meet with John B (Private Investigator) and the GAL at the Kearns substation. I met with both John and Mary C at the Welcker substation and they informed me on the case.

Mary informed me that she was the GAL for a 7-year-old female who was not his biological daughter. Mary said she had received information that Kirk was possibly a Kearns Town Blood gang member and wanted me to accompany her on this visit because she did not know what to look for to show any signs of gang affiliation that would put her client, Payshence, in danger.

Mary and I responded to the address...I followed Mary up to the door and stood by as she knocked. A female answered the door which was Jill C. Mary introduced me to Jill and informed her that I was going to accompany her on her house visit. Jill told her that was fine and invited us into the house. I stood in the living room as Mary spoke with Jill explaining to her about the visit. I could hear Jill consent and agree with Mary checking the entire house. All of the kids who lived in the house were in the front living room including Payshence.

*Jill and Kirk escorted Mary and I through the house while Mary searched through closets and dresser drawers. At times, Jill even opened up closets and rooms allowing Mary access to be searched. I followed Mary around from room to room ensuring her safety and also looking for any signs of gang affiliation. At times I looked in drawers and closets with Mary to see if there were any signs of gang affiliation. I did not see any. I asked Kirk if he was a member of Kearns Town Blood and he said no. I asked Kirk if he hung out with any of them and he said no. **Kirk said it has been a long time since he had seen anyone from KTB.** Mary wanted to speak with the two older siblings in private so I stayed with her and was present while she spoke with them. We left the house without incident. I didn't remove anything from the home and reported to Mary there were no signs of gang affliction.*

APRIL 3RD, 2015: LIMITED APPEARANCE, Assistant Attorney General, Commissioner Bloom presiding

Pursuant to Rule 75 of the Utah Rules of Civil Procedure and any other applicable provisions, the Assistant Attorney General hereby enters a Limited Appearance on behalf of the Attorney General's Office as attorney for the Division of Child and Family Services to object to the exercise of jurisdiction over the agency.

APRIL 6TH, 2015: RECUSAL OF COMMISSIONER, Submitted by Commissioner Bloom

On April 6, 2015, this court was informed that this commissioner was a Guardian ad Litem for and represented the children of the Intervenor in another matter. The court, upon review of the court files, has now identified the case where Commissioner Bloom was the GAL for the children in that case. Mr. Jody Rhorer, the intervener in this action, was a party in the case and the father of the children.

Based on this information, this commissioner hereby recuses herself from the present matter. This case shall be reassigned to a new commissioner as soon as possible. Any hearing that is scheduled to be heard before Commissioner Bloom is hereby stricken. A new hearing may be scheduled once a new commissioner is assigned.

APRIL 6TH, 2015: MOTION FOR DISCLOSURE REGARDING COMMUNICATIONS BETWEEN THE GUARDIAN AND COURT/MOTION FOR UNSEALING, Submitted by Connie C, Commissioner TBA

COMES NOW, _Kirk J, by and through Counsel, and moves the Court for disclosure regarding the Communications between the appointed GAL and the Court which led to the Commissioner's unilateral decision to recuse herself, and unsealing of the 2002 paternity case in which Commissioner acted as Guardian which led to recusal._

On April 6th, 2015, roughly 22 months after Mr. Rhorer's entry into this case, during which there were numerous hearings, Orders, and a detailed ruling including recommendations (which is still pending) Counsel was notified that the GAL had communicated with the Commissioner regarding how the Commissioner had represented the children in her prior capacity as a GAL in a paternity case in 2002, involving Mr. Rhorer as a party.

Kirk J was not provided a written Motion, and therefore, is unaware of what manner of communications between the GAL and the Commissioner could have occurred. Further, Kirk J avers that such a matter should've been handled by motion with notice to the parties, and that in light of the fact that the Commissioner now feels her prior involvement in Mr. Rhorer's family situation warrants immediate recusal, Kirk J feels that he should have information regarding the prior case involvement. Clearly, Mr. Rhorer has not found Commissioner Bloom's prior involvement as GAL in a paternity case significant enough to move to recuse the Commissioner, or even mention it. However, the Commissioner felt it significant enough to recuse herself without a motion by any party.

In that the Commissioner has undertaken to act in this case for almost two years, because Mr. Rhorer never moved her recusal, and no motion was filed, and indeed it is unclear how the Guardian could have had communications with the Commissioner, Kirk J prays for the Court's Order that he be provided all details regarding that communication as well as that Court Order of the 2002 paternity case resulting in the Commissioner's decision to recuse herself be unsealed.

APRIL 6TH, 2015: MOTION TO STAY PROCEEDINGS, Submitted by Connie C

Kirk J, by and through Counsel, moves the Court for its Order Staying these proceedings, including signature and entry of the proposed findings and ruling which are presently pending the District Court's signature.

Grounds and reasons are that on April 6th, 2015, approximately 22 months after Jody Rhorer first appeared in this case, the Commissioner recused herself due to prior representation of children when she was a GAL in a paternity case involving Mr. Rhorer. This recusal was done without a Motion by anyone, without hearing or knowledge of the prior case at all. Kirk J has no knowledge as to the history of the matter of the justification for immediate recusal.

Kirk J is concerned that the immediate and unilateral recusal of the Commissioner presiding over the case without a motion or hearing draws into question the fairness of the proceedings up to now. Kirk J believes he should have full information as to why the Commissioner recused herself without a motion or without the parties being made aware of the situation and that the Commissioner assigned in the stead of Commissioner Bloom should pass on whether the matter should be re-decided by a Commissioner who does not have a conflict. Parties are entitled to a Commissioner and Judge who are conflict free to ensure the fairness of the proceedings and, more than mere reassignment is called for under the circumstances.

**WHEREFORE**, Kirk J prays the proceedings be stayed, particularly related to the signature of the proposed findings and recommendation in that those were the result of actions of a Commissioner who now recognizes a conflict so significant she has recused herself without a motion, hearing, cause being stated, or an opportunity for consideration of a waiver. To ensure the viability and fairness of the matter, signature of the proposed Order would not be appropriate without further process.

So many sudden setbacks. Merely days until our hearing and now everything was off, the clock was set back, and we start all over again. What did Mary do? For someone who was "on our side," she sure messed this one up! And Connie putting up such a ruckus? Trying to get everything thrown out of court for bias! And DCFS only looking up bogus cases on Jody that were ancient history and never even substantiated - in fact, were proven fabrications in the first place when their court ordered assignment was to report on Kirk, Kelly, and Jill. None of this made any since at all. We were trying our best to find a silver lining in all the chaos but it didn't seem to exist.

APRIL 9TH, 2015: MOTION FOR REMOVAL AND MEMORANDUM FOR REMOVAL AND REAPPOINTMENT OF GAL, Submitted by Connie C, Commissioner TBA

Kirk J, by and through Counsel, moves the Court to remove appointed Guardian ad Litem, Mary C, and reappoint.

FACTS

(1) Commissioner Bloom issued an oral ruling on February 20th, 2015, that a GAL would be appointed, and that because at least one of the parties was not indigent, the GAL would be drawn from the list of private attorneys on the roster who serve in the capacity.

(2) On that same date, an appointment was made pursuant to 78A-2-705, U.C.A.

(3) Mary C entered appearance pursuant to that Order on February 25th, 2015.

(4) Mary C had incidental contacts with Kirk J and his co-habitant girlfriend, Jill C, to facilitate an interview of the minor subject, PR.

(5) Interview of PR occurred at the Office of Child and Family Services in mid-March.

(6) Later, Mary C's office requested other children residing in the home (who are not direct subjects of the paternity controversy) be made available for interview at her law office.

(7) The location of the interview was changed by Mary C to the home of Kirk J.

(8) The interviews of the children were scheduled for April 3rd, 2015, at 4:00 p.m.

(9) Mary C arrived in a vehicle driven by a very large imposing Polynesian male who was wearing clothing and a badge which identified him as a Gang Task Force Agent.

(10) Mary C introduced the man as her "friend," Ski, who has been identified as Unified Police, assigned to the Metro Gang Task Force.

(11) At the door, Mary C indicated an intent to search residence.

(12) Both Kirk J and Jill C felt they could not resist Mary C's demands regarding the search in that they knew that she would be making a recommendation about custody of PR, and they did not dare offend her or resist in any way.

(13) Neither Mary C nor Detective Ski ever advised that consent to the search could not be compelled, that a search of the home would need to be supported by probable cause upon a duly authorized and executed warrant, that no such warrant existed, and/or that the residents were at liberty to decline a search or call counsel about the matter.

(14) Mary conducted an exhaustive search of the including all drawers, closets, cabinets, a backpack, a locked cabinet in the garage, garbage inside the house, a boat in the backyard.

(15) The children were present, because Mary C had asked them to be for purposes of interviews she asserted she would be doing and were upset by the intrusion.

(16) The Detective actively participated in the search, including going out to "his truck" to get a flashlight when lighting was insufficient for her to see in an under-stairs closet/storage space, using his own flashlight to see in dark spaces, and standing on his tiptoes on a raised flowerbed to see inside a boat on a trailer in the backyard when he determined that his mounting the boat ladder might cause the boat to overturn.

(17) He also asked if a backpack in one of the children's rooms was an 18-year-old son of Jill C's, who is temporarily residing at the home, and started going through it.

(18) The Detective asked Kirk J specific questions about affiliation with a gang called Kearns Town Bloods and if he knew persons that the Officer identified as members of that gang.

(19) The vast majority of time spent by the Detective and Mary C at the home was dedicated to searching, not interviewing the children.

DISCUSSION

Utah Code provides that a private GAL shall "conduct or supervise an ongoing, independent investigation in order to obtain, first-hand, a clear understanding of the situation and needs of the minor." The Code specifically addresses that the "fundamental liberties" and "constitutional rights" of the parents are to be a matter of training, and observed when implemented into the practices of the GAL. The Utah State Constitution contains a parallel provision which provides "the right of the people to be secure in their persons, houses, papers and effects against unreasonable searches and seizures shall not be violated; and no warrant shall issue but upon probable cause supported by oath or affirmation, particularly describing the place to be searched and the person or thing to be seized."

Several factors demonstrated that what occurred at Kirk J's home was an unlawful search conducted by State actions color of law. First, it cannot be argued that Mary C's purported and asserted authority to act was conferred exclusively by the Order of the Court appointing her pursuant to State law. Detective Ski's actions were demonstrably State action due to his employment as a law enforcement office, and his exhibition of his uniform, badge, and identification as a law enforcement officer.

Mary C facilitated the search by use of a ruse, stating one purpose to interview the children, and then, only after arriving at the home with a law enforcement officer, indicating that she would search. That Mary C and the law enforcement officer were conducting a search/law enforcement type investigation is supported by the fact that he was a gang task force officer, attended a call which has been described as a civil assist/keep the peace. Mary C informed counsel for Kirk J after concerns about this event were raised, and Detective Ski was selected specifically because Mary C believed there was information of gang affiliation.

Therefore, the Detective's presence was not a generalized "keep the peace" function, but rather in furtherance of a law enforcement investigation related to what Mary C and the Detective apparently believed to be Kirk J's gang ties.

It is also apparent from the circumstances that the Detective and Guardian were working jointly to conduct a generalized investigation of possible criminal activity in that they looked into everything: panty drawers, closets, closed containers, garbage, without any regard to how such a search in any way advanced or expounded on PR's "best interests." It flies in the imagination how the Guardian's intimate knowledge of the contents of the locked cleaner cabinet, a sixteen-year old's underwear drawer, the adult's nightstand drawer and the bedroom garbage could add regarding PR's "situation and needs."

The Detective's interrogation of Kirk J also reveals that the purpose of the visit was a law enforcement-type investigation. The specific nature of his questioning related to gangs further demonstrates the classification of the event as "civil assist/keep the peace" was a pretext. Kirk J was never given the minor courtesy of being given any type of an advisement of his constitutional rights, of which he was being deprived. Rather, he was simply informed that the GAL appointed by the Court to make recommendations about custody of his daughter would be searching the home.

CONCLUSION

Though the Statutes allow a Guardian to conduct an "ongoing investigation" into the "situation and needs" of the minor, it also directs the GAL to be trained on and implement restrictions which recognize and respect the parent's fundamental liberties and constitutional rights. Among those rights include the right against unreasonable searches and seizures, and compelled self-incrimination. The Constitutional touchstone of these provisions is not whether something incriminating is found or used against the person, but rather the recognition that violation of these rights is a tangible harm in itself.

While such instructions are unjustifiable when committed by law enforcement, the situation here is even more severe. Knowing full well Kirk J would feel intimidated and coerced out of fear of a future negative recommendation, Mary C ran roughish over his household and its inhabitants. Employment of a ruse to execute a search of Kirk Js home, aiding police in extracting a statement from Kirk J he felt he could not refuse, and searching every nook and cranny of a home while children looked on constitutes abandonment of the role of GAL. The activities in no way further the best interest of PR, evidence that Mary C wishes to act as an agent of the police, for whatever reason.

Viewed in the most positive light, the events reflect a pronounced lack of training or understanding of fundamental constitutional rights which a GAL is statutorily required to respect. Viewed in the most negative light, the events constitute a civil rights violation. Either way, Mary C can no longer function in the role of GAL, and therefore, Kirk J prays the Court remove her and reappoint.

APRIL 9TH, 2015: AFFIDAVIT OF JILL C, Submitted by Connie C

I, Jill C, being first duly sworn, depose and say:

1. I am over 18 years of age, a resident of the State of Utah and all statements made in this affidavit are based on my personal knowledge or belief.

2. I am the girlfriend of Kirk J and we share a child in common and live together with PR, who is subject of this action, some of Kirk J's children, and some of mine.

3. I was present in Court February 20th, 2015, when Commissioner Bloom ordered that a GAL be appointed in the above-referenced case.

4. In due course, I learned that a person named Mary C was that appointed GAL.

5. I was informed by Kirk J that Mary C wished to come into our home to interview three of our children, and that she would come Friday, April 3rd, 2015, at 4:00 p.m.

6. I was willing to have Mary C in our home and speak to the children.

7. I was aware of no other purpose Mary C had in coming to my home other than to interview three other children she identified, however, in that the Division of Child and Family Services has come to my home before, I am aware of a practice whereby representatives walk through the house, look for obvious safety risks, ask children about their rooms, ask to see them, and even check the fridge and cupboards for adequate food supplies.

8. Even knowing of these types of practices, I was willing to have Mary C come to the home to discharge her duties as appointed GAL for PR.

9. I saw Mary C arrive in an SUV driven by a man.

10. When Mary C and the man arrived at the door, I saw the man with her was a very large Polynesian male whom I do not personally know, but recognized as a coach involved in the same football league as one of my sons.

11. The man, who Mary C called her "friend," and introduced as "Ski," was a police officer, which was obvious by the fact that he was wearing a badge and law enforcement garb which identified him as being assigned to the "Gang Task Force."

12. I could not see the typical side arm or taser worn by law enforcement officers on the person of the Officer, however, he was a very large individual who I would estimate to be five foot ten to five foot eleven inches and between 275-300 pounds.

13. I was completely surprised to see an Officer with Mary C.

14. At the door, Mary C stated she "forgot" to tell us that she intended to search my home then immediately stated something to the effect that in actuality, she intentionally did not tell us she was bringing the officer because she intended to search and didn't want us to know in advance.

15. I was not told we could refuse to allow the search, and in fact did not feel I dare offend Mary C or refuse anything she asked, for fear of a negative recommendation regarding Kirk J's daughter, PR, whom lives with us, and whom I dearly love.

16. I understood that Mary C's authority to be at my home came from the Court's Order appointing her as GAL in the case regarding PR, and that as such, she was acting under authority of the laws of the State of Utah when she said she was going to search my home.

17. I was never told by either Mary C or the Officer that I could decline the search, that I had any rights, that the officer lacked probable cause to search my home without a warrant, that in order to obtain legal authority to search my home a judge would have to find probable cause for the search, or that I could contact an attorney.

18. The children were present and the entire time Mary C and the Officer went through everything in the house, I was concerned for how they were being impacted by the goings on.

19. Mary C seemed unconcerned or unaware that a search of private areas of the house, including the children's rooms and effects, might be unsettling or unnerving.

20. Mary C searched my home in an intrusive and probing manner, including looking in all drawers in the bedrooms, all closets, cabinets, a backpack belonging to one of my children, a locked safe, a locking cabinet in the garage, the freezer in the garage, a boat parked in the backyard, and even the garbage still within the confines of the home.

21. I watched the reaction of my sixteen-year-old daughter as Mary C went through her underwear drawer, touching and moving the contents around, and felt powerless and unable to do anything to mitigate her embarrassment and sense of personal violation about the situation.

22. The Officer was actively involved including going out to his car to get a flashlight when Mary C had difficulty viewing a dark corner in my room and inside a closet and under a stairwell, being present when Mary C took two children in the backyard to question them, and searching, including discussing how he might overturn the boat in the backyard due to his size and weight in relation to the boat.

23. Mary C stayed in the house when the Officer went to his car to get his flashlight, and exhibited no indication whatsoever that she felt unsafe in our home.

24. *Because Mary C had set up the meeting to interview the children, the children were present, and following the adults around during this search, and Mary C suggested no measures to protect the children from observing the search.*

25. *Because the children were following along when Mary C was going through drawers and containers in the bedroom I share with Kirk, I discretely alerted Mary C to the fact that a satchel I expected she would search (based on the fact that she was searching everything) had "couples toys" in it and requested that she not take them out of the bag in front of the children.*

26. *Apparently unwilling to leave any stone unturned, Mary C palpated the bag and looked inside despite having been told of the private nature of the contents.*

27. *The search conducted by Mary C and her law enforcement "friend" was entirely different from the DCFS walk-through I have experienced in the past.*

28. *Mary C did not confine her search to items in plain view and issues of safety, but rather, conducted a detailed, exhaustive, and frankly humiliating search of each and every private and closed space within the house, not only belonging to Kirk J and myself, but also all of the children.*

29. *When I attempted to show Mary C photos I had compiled demonstrating how long PR had been with Kirk - which contradicts claims of Intervenor and alleged father of PR, Jody Rhorer, as to the extent and duration of his relationship with PR - Mary C seemed disinterested.*

30. *I finally gave her a disc of the pictures and asked her to take them with her in hopes she might view them later.*

31. *The time Mary C spent on her undisclosed purpose of searching dwarfed the time she spent on her disclosed purpose of interviewing, and in fact, I believe she only interviewed two of the three children she arranged to interview, though all were present and available to her.*

32. *Because Mary C admitted that she intended to search, and intentionally did not tell us the true purpose of her visit, and because she brought a Gang Task Force Officer, whom she called her "friend," to increase the intimidation we would naturally feel by her presence, I feel violated and do not feel Mary C is performing the function of a Court appointed GAL.*

Further, your affiant sayeth naught. Jill C.

I am 100 percent positive this "sworn affidavit" was written by Connie. As I am sure the following affidavit of Kirk was as well. I'm sure Jill does not use such words as "palpate." I only know that word from working for a time in the veterinary industry and reading in the pet histories that the doctor "palpated the dog's stomach to attempt to feel any obstructions." Neither Jill nor Kirk have vast or even moderate vocabulary and grammar skills. Reading this furthers my belief that this fight is not theirs, but Connie's.

APRIL 9TH, 2015: AFFIDAVIT OF KIRK J, Submitted by Connie C

I, Kirk J, being first duly sworn, depose and say:

1. *I am over 18 years of age and a resident of the State of Utah and all statements made in this affidavit are based on my personal knowledge or belief.*

2. *I was present in Court February 20th, 2015, when Commissioner Bloom ordered a GAL be appointed in this case.*

3. *In due course, I learned that a person named Mary C was the appointed GAL.*

4. *I cooperated with requests made by Mary C, including making my daughter, PR, available for interviews by Mary C at the DCFS office.*

5. *After that meeting, I was notified by a paralegal in Mary C's office she wanted to interview other children in my home, and was told the interviews would occur at her office.*

6. *Mary C later asked to come to my home instead.*

7. *Mary C stated that her purpose in coming to my home was to interview three other children who live in my home, and she told me which children she wished to speak with.*

8. *The appointment was scheduled to occur Friday, April 3rd, 2015, at 4:00 p.m., and I made sure the three children she wished to interview were present.*

9. *When Mary C arrived at the door, she had with her a very large and physically imposing Polynesian male, approximately six feet two inches tall, approximately 250 pounds, with a badge wearing clothing which identified him as a "Gang Task Force" officer.*

10. *I could not see a side arm or taser typically worn by law enforcement officers on his person.*

11. I was completely surprised to see a law enforcement officer with Mary C.

12. Mary C stated she "forgot" to tell me that she intended to search my home.

13. I was completely surprised by the presence of a law enforcement officer with Mary C and felt intimidated by their presence, not because anything illegal was going on in my home, but rather, because knowing that the GAL would be making recommendations in my case regarding my daughter, I did not feel I dare offend her or refuse anything she asked for fear of negative recommendation.

14. I understood that Mary C's authority to be at my home came from the Court's Order appointing her as GAL in my case, and that as such, she was acting under authority of the law.

15. I was never told by either Mary C or the Officer that I could decline the search, that I have any rights, that the officer lacked probable cause to search my home without a warrant, that a judge would have to find probable cause for the search, or I could contact my attorney.

16. Mary C searched my home in an intrusive and probing manner, including looking in all drawers in the bedrooms, all closets, cabinets, a backpack belonging to one of my children, a locked safe, a locking cabinet in the garage, the freezer in the garage, a boat parked in the backyard, and even the garbage in my bedroom.

17. The Officer was actively involved at my home including going out to his car to get a flashlight when Mary C had difficulty viewing inside a closet space under a stairwell, and in a dark corner in my room, being present when she took two children in the backyard to question them, and search, including discussing how he might overturn the boat in the backyard due to his size in relation to the boat.

18. Mary stayed in the house when the Officer went to his car to get his flashlight.

19. He also specifically questioned me about whether I knew people he asserted were gang members, such that I understood that what was occurring was not merely a cursory check on the safety, adequacy, or cleanliness of my home, but a law enforcement investigation.

20. I answered his questions because I felt under the circumstances, with Mary being in control of making recommendations about my daughter, if I didn't go along with whatever they wanted to do, she'd report negatively to the Court.

21. Because Mary C had set up the meeting to interview the children, the children were present and following the adults around during this search.

22. I perceived the sixteen-year-old girl residing in my home was upset while Mary C went through her panty drawer, touched the contents, but Mary seemed to have no cognizance whatsoever that her presence with a huge law enforcement officer going through private spots in the home unannounced might be disturbing and upsetting.

23. When I attempted to show her photos of me and PR at earlier times in her life which evidence that contrary to claims of Intervenor and alleged father of PR, Jody Rhorer, she has been with me, Mary C seemed disinterested to the point I insisted that she take a disc of the photographs in hope that she would look at them later.

24. I have no confidence that Mary C can act in the role of GAL in this case related to my daughter, PR, based on her action intentionally misleading me about the purpose of her visit to my home, and assisting and/or placing a law enforcement officer in a search of my home under circumstances the Officer would have had to ask for a search warrant.

Further, your affiant sayeth naught. Kirk J

APRIL 9TH, 2015: DECLARATION OF LEGAL ASSISTANT, Submitted by Mary C

I, M.S., hereby declares, states, and alleges as follows:

1. I am a Legal Assistant at Mary C's law firm.

2. I am 25 years old and competent to testify to the matters set forth in this Declaration.

3. This Declaration is based upon facts personally known to me based on information and belief as to matters I believe to be true.

4. On March 25, 2015, I personally called the Respondent in this matter. I indicated that the PGAL would like to speak with three of the children in the household at Respondent's residence so that she could do a walk-through inspection of the home at the same time.

5. Respondent was unable to schedule an appointment on my initial phone call as he had to make sure the children's schedules were clear. I spoke with the Respondent approximately 3 times regarding the visit; each time I spoke with the Respondent I reiterated what would be happening and who the GAL would be speaking to.

6. Respondent was not hesitant to have the GAL come to his home; in fact, the Respondent stated that it would be better for her to come to his home as his children are generally more comfortable talking to people inside the home versus outside.

7. *I hereby declare under criminal penalty of the State of Utah that the foregoing is true and correct. M.S.*

APRIL 9TH, 2015: EMAIL from Mary C

Deone, I spoke to the owner of the firm and he informs me that the March bills will be going out shortly and April bills will go out in May. However, I have estimated about $2,592.19 as due and owing as of approximately April 7th. We will need to get this taken care of before I can continue to do anymore work on this matter. As of yesterday, I've gone through the $1,000. I still need to do a walk-through of Kelly's home as well. Please let me know how you'd like to handle this. Mary C

I sent Mary a check right away, but we were told that all in all to expect around $3,000 for the entire GAL service. She had already exceeded that and we were just getting started. On top of that, most of her bill was coming from her defense of herself and her own actions. I was having a hard time biting my tongue but I didn't want her to get angry with us as Payshence's future was in her hands.

APRIL 9TH, 2015: MOTION TO SUBMIT TO JUDGE AND FOR ENTRY OF ORDER, Submitted by Nancy S, Commissioner TBD

The Intervenor, Jody Rhorer, by and through counsel Nancy S, hereby requests that his motion be made to the Honorable Judge Stanley. Intervenor moves the Court for the entry of an Order pursuant to the Amended Recommendation and Order filed in this matter.

FACTS

1. Motions in these proceedings were held before the Honorable Commissioner Bloom in May, July, and August, 2014, and were taken under advisement.

2. On February 20, 2015, the parties convened before Commissioner Bloom at which time an oral ruling was made.

3. The Respondent, nor any other party, objected to the Commissioner's ruling.

4. Intervenor, by and through counsel, prepared and filed a Recommendation and Order that was opposed by Respondent.

5. Thereafter, Intervenor, by and through counsel, submitted a transcript of the February 20, 2015, hearing to Respondent's counsel with an Amended Recommendation and Order.

6. Respondent's counsel, via email, indicated the Amended Recommendation and Order was substantively correct but requested minor changes thereto, specifically to grammatical and/or spelling errors. The requested changes were made and summated to Respondent's counsel.

7. Thereafter, Respondent's counsel refused to reply to numerous requests via email and telephone to approve the Amended Recommendation and Order.

8. Intervenor requested the Commissioner's Clerk substitute the original Recommend-ation and Order with the Amended Recommendation and Order to submit the same to the Commissioner.

9. Commissioner Bloom recused herself from these proceedings on April 6, 2015.

10. The Amended Recommendation and Order remains unsigned and requires an Order and entry upon the record.

ARGUMENT
This motion should be made to the Honorable Stanley

It is appropriate that this motion be made directly to the Honorable Stanley to avoid further delays and to promote a final resolution of the matters which have been pending before the court for almost one (1) year, and for purposes of judicial economy.

There were no objections to the Commissioner's ruling

The Amended Recommendation and Order conforms to the February 20, 2015, oral ruling by Commissioner Bloom. The Amended Recommendation and Order and copy of the transcript is attached hereto. Neither Respondent nor Petitioner, objected to the Ruling.

The parties have proceeded in compliance with the Commissioner's Ruling

1. *A private GAL was appointed and has performed extensive work in representing the interest of the minor child. Intervenor was ordered to pay the initial retainer of $1,000 with the condition that the cost thereof would be reapportioned among the parties at the review hearing scheduled for April 16, 2015. Intervenor paid the initial $1,000 and an additional $1,000 that was requested by the GAL. The GAL has requested an additional payment of approximately $3,000 in order to proceed.*

2. *The Intervenor's Motion for DCFS Investigation was granted and the Division has commenced an investigation.*

3. *Intervenor's counsel has contacted custody evaluators pursuant to the Ruling.*

4. *The Intervenor filed a Financial Declaration with the court pursuant to the Commissioner's ruling, although the Petitioner and Respondent have failed to do so.*

An Order should be entered to prevent prejudice to the Intervenor

The Intervenor, in reliance on the Commissioner's ruling and the failure of any party to object, has incurred substantial attorney's fees and costs. Intervenor's counsel has performed legal services pursuant to the ruling and in preparation for the review hearing which was schedule for April 16, 2015. Additionally, Intervenor has paid the GAL to date. The Intervenor cannot afford to continue to pay the GAL and the court should reapportion the costs and order the Petitioner and Respondent to share in the costs of the GAL. The failure of the court to enter an order in conformance with the Amended Recommendation and Order would substantially prejudice the Intervenor.

WHEREFORE the Intervenor respectfully requests this motion be submitted to the Honorable Judge Stanley and that the Court enter an order in conformance with the Amended Recommendation and Order filed in this matter.

APRIL 10TH, 2015: EMAIL from Nancy S to the GAL

Mary, Connie has filed a motion to have you removed as the GAL for Payshence. Will you be responding to the motion? Do you customarily respond to such a motion? Concurrently, I can prepare a motion and memo in opposition, but I will need your Affidavit responding to the allegations in her motion and the affidavits. I received a copy of your emails to Deone Rhorer regarding your bill. What will you charge to respond to the motion and prepare an affidavit? Nancy

3:32 PM
Mary, I note that Connie did not cite any law to support her allegation that you or the officer had a duty to inform Kirk J of his "constitutional rights." If she means a Miranda warning, it is not required unless there is an arrest, which there was not. And you are certainly not required to inform him. I will also need an affidavit from the officer to confirm that he did everything by the book. Will you please confirm for me his name and any contact info you have for him? Nancy

APRIL 10TH, 2015: EMAIL from Nancy S to Jody and myself

8:59 AM
Hi Jody and Deone, I have been out of town, but returned last night and I am in the office today. Commissioner Bloom has recused herself from the case and the April 16th hearing has been cancelled. The court is in the process of assigning a new commissioner to the case. DCFS has entered an appearance objecting to the court's jurisdiction over DCFS. I need to talk to the GAL to get more information about this.

Connie has filed a motion for discloser asking that the court release information about how it obtained information regarding her recusal and why Bloom recused herself, and a motion to stay the proceedings asking that the court NOT sign any order it entered of February 20th. I am attaching copies of the pleadings.

We need to talk together about this and discuss how this impacts our case, the work I need to perform to address these issues and payment for my services. Please give me a call as soon as possible. Nancy

11:02 AM
Deone, If we can prove Kelly is taking Payshence without supervision there is a chance we can get her out of Kirk's home because Kelly poses a danger. It's the weekend and I'm thinking that Kirk may let Payshence go with Kelly, so if you get this email and you know Kelly's address please email it to me. Nancy

4:41 PM

Jody and Deone, I would like to file a motion and memorandum asking that all motions be made directly to the Judge, and certify the issues for trial to get before the Judge. I need to prepare our objections to Connie's motions and prepare our own motions. _I am thinking of filing a motion with supporting memoranda asking the court to find that the Parentage Act discriminates between men and women_, but I need to do some research. Also, we need to find a "smoking gun" that will show Payshence may be in harm in Kirk's home and I need to ask John for his assistance. Have you and Jody worked on becoming foster parents? Please let me know if you want me to work on your case this weekend and if I have your permission to consult with John. Also, can Jody verify that he signed a Voluntary Declaration of Paternity after Payshence was born? This is important. Vital Statistics won't' give us the info because Jody's name was removed from the Birth Certificate after the West Jordan paternity case was dismissed. I am thinking of asking Mary C to see if she can get the document on behalf of Payshence, but I know you are trying to keep costs down. If Jody is sure he signed one, we really need a certified copy of it. Sorry for all the emails. I am sending them to you as I think of issues that need to be addressed or as they come up. Thanks, Nancy

11:55 PM

Hi Nancy, This form has a mailing address for Kelly. It's not one that we recognize from the past and Kelly's FB said she was getting moved into her new apartment. I think that may be it. Jody and I cannot drive down tomorrow because of our work commitments. He wants me to call you at 10:00. It's difficult for us to take time off work. I have to rearrange my client schedule every time. I also have a new employee starting in the morning. Jody has employee's also that count on him and when he takes off work, they aren't able to work.

I look forward to going over all the details with you tomorrow. We have many questions and feel we are at an impasse as to what to do until we know what is going to happen with the new judge. We are extremely disappointed in what has happened with Bloom as well as the fact that the GAL may end up being dismissed as well. We would like to know what John has accomplished since our last meeting before we move forward anymore with him. Also, we need to know what things costs prior to incurring charges. I said that before and then got a surprise bill from Mary C for another $2600. She needs to collect that from Kirk and Kelly as they were supposed to be paying 1/3 each of the financials deemed so. I look forward to talking tomorrow. Thanks again, Deone

April 13th, 2015 10:49 AM

Jody and Deone, I am attaching the Motion for Entry of Judgement if we want to ask Judge Stanley to enter the Order pursuant to Commissioner Bloom's ruling on February 20th. I'm also attaching the Amended Recommendation and Order. This needs to be filed asap. Nancy

April 14th, 2015 11:13 AM

Hi Mary, Jody was not able to meet with me yesterday, but I spoke to Deone by phone. I emailed Jody asking him to call me today, but I have not heard from him, so I don't know how they want to proceed. The Amended Recommendation and Order is scheduled to be signed by either Comm. Bloom or Comm. Kase today and then sent to the Judge for his signature. We can then request a hearing before the court at which time I will ask that the cost to you be allocated among the three parties. I appreciate your willingness to stay involved and help and I understand that you need to be compensated. Thanks, Nancy

11:22 AM

Nancy, I get that it's a financial burden that Jody is carrying alone, especially when there are numerous pleadings going back and forth. I will get the Affidavits to you today or tomorrow. Mary

4:54 PM

Mary, I am attaching the police report of the incident in October 2007, wherein a 13-year-old boy sexually abused J1, J2, and TJ, who is Kirk's ex-girlfriend, Kim's, son. Although this report is from 2007, it shows a pattern that is obvious when compared to subsequent police reports and the parties' behaviors. Kirk and Kelly have never held themselves out to be married. Their "marriage" was an arrangement for this group to collect children. Kirk has had other women doing the same for him - Kelly H, Kim J, Jill C. They intentionally confuse identities and relationships and this has been going on for several generations. I have documents to show this. Kirk and this group have sex offenders as members and as people surrounding them. They have all been convicted of drug possession/distribution, giving false identities. The children have been harmed, and there is a pattern of continuing harm.

The Report:

1. Kirk allowed the boys to go with Kelly. (This is still happening, and he is allowing Payshence to be with Kelly.)

2. Kirk and Kelly told the police that they were divorced, then she told another officer that Kirk J was her boyfriend. (There are numerous other documents in which they deny being married.) There is a pattern of fraud, and Jody and Payshence are victims of that fraud.

3. According to the police report, Kirk has another son whose name is TJ. TJ is not Kirk's son, and thank goodness Kim J had the presence of mind to file a paternity action in 2008 to name the biological father of her children before she escaped Kirk J. THIS GROUP intentionally gives false identities of themselves and the children. (There are numerous other documents in which the adult relationships and the relationships of the children to each other and to the adults are misrepresented.)

4. Both J1 and J2 have been sexually abused. There is evidence that Payshence was sexually abused in 2009. There is evidence that Jill C's daughter was sexually abused. What other children in the home have been sexually abused? Have any of them received counseling? Are the boys likely to behave inappropriately because of the abuse?

5. Kirk, Jill, and Kelly all have family members who have been convicted of sex crimes. Mona Rhorer has seen them at Kirk's home. They are Facebook friends with sex abusers and so are the children. Kirk allowed his father, a sex offender, to babysit Payshence. Payshence was a baby when this happened to these three boys in Kelly's care and with the permission of Kirk.

I am also attaching a drawing made by an investigator which shows links to the possible offenders concerning the "peeking game" Payshence talked about and she mentioned "Mike" and "Anthony". I'm just asking the questions: Were these men identified? Was there an investigation? Were charges filed against them? What happened? Did Kirk ever try to identify these offenders so they could be prosecuted? Why not? Were they his friends. – Nancy

5:19 PM

This is an example of how this group intentionally misrepresents their identity. In June 2010, B.W.L. died. His obituary states that Jill C is his daughter. Jill's Facebook names J.S.L., B.W.L.'s wife, as her mother. But in January 2015, when R.D.N. died, Jill filed a petition to be named Personal Representative alleging that she was the daughter of R.D.N., and she took over his estate. I hope Payshence will know her true heritage. Nancy

5:30 PM

I have documents that show Kelly H has named three different men as her father P.H., D.H., M.N. She has at times identified M.N. as her "stepfather." I have documents that show Kelly has named her mother as J.H., and sometime her mother is L.H. This Group intentionally misrepresents their relationships so they can collect children. Nancy

5:51 PM

Kelly's sister, T.A.H. died in 2005. Her obituary states she was born to J.H. and P.H. It lists M.N. as her stepfather and L.H. as her stepmother. It lists Kelly as her sister. The obituary omits the name of her husband. He is Jamey C. (also an a.k.a. for Kirk J). He left Utah after T.A.H. was murdered. Her estate was probated and D.H. petitioned the court alleging that he was T.A.H.'s father. He was appointed Personal Representative. This Group intentionally misrepresents their identities so they can confuse the public, the State, and biological fathers so that they can collect children. Nancy

5:58 PM

L.H. has also been known as Smith, Baggs and Roma. She has had children with Smith and Roman, and either or both D.H. and P.H. I don't know if she was ever married to R.B.'s father. (R.B. is a convicted sex offender and is a visitor at Kirk J's home.) But Kelly refers to R.B. as her "stepbrother." Nancy

7:15 PM

The Order was submitted to Comm. Bloom today for her signature and then will be submitted to Judge Stanley for his signature. He has no reason to not sign it since no objection was made to the order. The hearing will be on the same issues. I need to answer the pleadings Connie has filed. I will be notified electronically when Judge Stanley signs the Order. If that happens tomorrow, I will call the court and ask for a hearing date. The date depends on the court's schedule. I'll be in court on another matter in the morning, in the office around noon. Nancy

April 15, 7:45 AM

Deone, Do you, or your sister, etc., know anyone associated with the Sutherland Institute? It is a non-profit organization in Utah that promotes legislation. It may be a resource that could provide financial assistance and legal costs if we can get them to endorse your case.

Mary C told me about this organization when we spoke this afternoon. They are a conservative group and have lawyers working for them. They've intervened in other legal proceedings. Their main objective is to promote family values. If we can meet with a representative and tell them Jody's story and the conditions Payshence is living under because of the Parentage Act, perhaps they will intervene or help in telling the court that this was an unintended consequence of the UUPA and file a brief as to the unconstitutionality of the statute. They are powerful and we should try to get them on our side. Nancy

2:00 PM

Mary, Thanks for sending me the birth certificates. Kirk can't be the biological father of J1 because Kirk was incarcerated at the Utah State Prison from 12/15/1999 to 4/24/2001. In Kelly's divorce petition she listed only four children and failed to include DS as a child born during the marriage. She alleged that Kirk was not the biological father of 3 of her 4 children. As to BS, there were several paternity actions filed, one by Kelly, one by Bock S who was fighting for custody, and one by ORS. When Brock took the DNA test and learned he was not the biological father, the case was dismissed. ORS has confirmed that the biological father is T.T., a friend of Kirk J's. Without DNA testing, who knows the truth about the biological fathers of these children? Nancy

4:07 PM

The hearing is scheduled for May 11 at 9:00 a.m. Let's meet asap. Nancy

JOURNAL ENTRY

I think Nancy has gone bonkers. An entire section of her office has been turned into a make-shift-who-done-it-lab. She has white boards with timelines and has even put together an elaborate family tree consisting of all sorts of people I have never even heard of. She has convinced herself that there is a giant, decades long conspiracy of stealing children to use in drug sales so that Kirk can sell through minors without getting himself in to trouble.

She is so obsessed with finding the "why" and the motivation behind Kirk having so many children that are not biologically his that she has now fabricated a story that she actually believes. She is trying to get the FBI, the local police, and anyone else involved - but she has proof of none of this. I have tried to explain to her that this is all circumstantial but she cannot wrap her head around it.

She is going on long email rants which take me hours to decipher. I have to wait until evening when I am home from work to read through what she sent that day. She has had Jody and I come down to her office so often that we are not getting our work done at our jobs. When we go to her office, she looks at us and says, "So, what's up?" as if we were the ones that called the meeting - then she looks at my purse. I knew she wanted more money. We never get bills - she just calls meetings and say she needs more money to keep going. Jody and I are starting to think we may be her only clients. Her obsession has become unhealthy. The sad truth is, the children in that home were placed there by the State of Utah because of the Utah Parentage Act. Kirk went along with it because it serves him and he can control Kelly. He has different live-in girlfriends from time to time that take care of the details. It is not out of love any more than it is out of a preconceived child-stealing plan. It just happened and we just can't seem to get it undone.

APRIL 15TH, 2015:   DECLARATION OF MARY C, GAL, by Mary C, Commissioner Kase presiding

I, Mary C, hereby declare, state, and allege as follows:

1. I am the Private Guardian ad Litem in this matter and am competent to testify to the matters set forth in this Declaration.

2. This Declaration is based upon facts personally known to me except as to those matters based upon information and belief, and as to those matters, I believe them to be true.

Nancy3. In scheduling my visit at Kirk J's home, my assistant contacted Kirk numerous times and informed him that I would like to speak with 3 of the children and walk through the home.

4. I had my assistant disclose what I intended to have happen, but I do not make it a point to explain to the parents in detail everything I intend to do or how I intend to further the best interests of my client. This is attorney privileged information and not subject to disclosure.

5. As a PGAL, I am appointed to "represent the best interests of the minor" and to conduct or supervise an ongoing, independent investigation in order to obtain, first-hand, a clear understanding of the situation and needs of the minor.

6. It is common practice amongst GAL's to do home visits of the clients to obtain a "first-hand and clear understanding of the situation and needs of the minor child." There are no rules that prevent home visits. An extensive home investigation was necessary especially when my client is only 7 years old and there have been serious allegations of criminal activity. I was concerned about the safety of my client's environment based on these various allegations.

7. Prior to my visit at Kirk's home I had been informed by an FBI agent that Kirk J and Kelly H had criminal histories with weapons and drug use. In addition, I had reviewed several documents regarding Kirk and Kelly's criminal pasts.

The FBI agent also informed me of the potential of gang affiliation and underground system of using children to sell drugs with the intent of avoiding potential jail time for the adults based on the understanding that if the children were caught selling the drugs, they'd only be subject to the juvenile court system that has more lenient punishments.

8. On April 3, 2015, I did an investigation of Kirk J's home. Based on allegations of violence, drugs, abuse of alcohol, prior criminal convictions, criminal affiliations, gang affiliations, and weapons, I felt it imperative to ensure my safety during my investigation of the home and brought along Officer Ski for that purpose.

9. Upon my arrival I introduced Officer Ski and informed Kirk and Jill of what I would like to do. When I asked if this would be okay, they agreed and cooperated with my investigation even offering to have me look in certain places, take off boat covers, and empty out closets. I did not demand or require that they empty closets or remove boat covers.

10. I did not go through garbages or try to overturn a boat. Kirk and Jill offered to get the ladder down on the boat and take the tarps off to which I declined.

11. During the investigation Jill did alert me to a bag with "couples toys" to which I looked into, but I did not pull out the bag or empty its contents for all to view. The contents remained in the bag and I did not touch what was inside.

12. Officer Ski did not touch anything in the home. He was simply there to keep the peace.

13. During our visit it became apparent that Officer Ski and Kirk and Jill had seen each other at local little league sporting events. They struck up a friendly conversation about this and also talked about what Officer Ski does as a Gang Task Force Officer. Officer Ski was not questioning them, but rather engaging in normal conversation.

14. I spoke with all the children that day, but specifically with the two oldest children. I also viewed various pictures Jill tried to show me on a computer, but the images were coming up like the size of thumbnails, so I thought it would be better to view on my own computer. I took the CD Jill made containing family pictures for better viewing at a later time.

15. Kirk J is familiar with the justice system as he has a criminal record and is no doubt well aware of his rights, but failed to make any objection about my investigation of the home.

16. In past communications with Kirk, he has often questioned why I need to know certain information and wasn't afraid of voicing his opinions and concerns to me. For instance, when I asked Kirk about the family dynamics for each child living in the home as to who their biological parent was and whether there were different legal parents for each child, he became irritated and questioned me as to why I needed to know this information. However, neither Kirk nor Jill requested I stop so that they could call their attorney about my investigation.

17. Despite raising concerns about my investigation in the past, Kirk didn't once during my April 3rd investigation raise concerns or object to what I was doing. Kirk and Jill were very cooperative and willing to allow the investigation to occur even helping to facilitate it.

18. After visiting the home I am not concerned with the physical environment surrounding my client. The home is clean and organized despite being small and having approximately 8 people living in there. I didn't see any signs of violations of Kirk's parole with weapons or drugs. Had I not been able to perform an extensive investigation I would not have been as clear on this point and would still have lingering concerns in this regard. If there is any drug use, possession of weapons or gang affiliation, I did not see signs of such in the home.

19. As a PGAL, I'm not in a position of government authority and have no obligation to read Miranda Rights or warn of constitutional protections as they do not apply when I am an actor of the State. Although I have been appointed by the Court, I do not work for any government agency. Moreover, there was no arrest or criminal investigation going on that would even warrant Miranda Rights or constitutional protections.

20. I have not been able to coordinate a time to visit Kelly H's home as she was just evicted from her previous home and she has recently moved. DCFS has recently recommended that Kirk only allow Kelly supervised visitation at this time.

21. I was informed by Jody Rhorer's daughters that Kelly had solicited drugs and alcohol to them in the past while they were minors.

22. I notified DCFS and they are looking into these claims along with investigating a case of domestic violence witnessed by one of the children between Kelly and her current husband.

23. At this time, I also recommend supervised visitation with Kelly and my client.

24. My client appears to be happy and healthy in Kirk's home, although there are still some concerns, including but not limited to:

a. The constitutionality of certain statutes as applied to Jody Rhorer. Having the Court's input on this would be helpful in making my recommendations.

b. It doesn't appear that my client, PR, has developed appropriate attachments. PR easily attaches to new people she barely knows. Although this may be due to her friendly nature, I believe it's also indicative of an attachment disorder possibly due to various men and women coming in and out of her life and she doesn't differentiate between whom is mom and dad or understanding the sibling arrangement when there are various children in the house with different biological and legal fathers and mothers. This could lead to issues later in her adolescence where PR views all male peers as boyfriends and I recommend that PR have counseling with a therapist that works specifically with attachment disorders.

c. There are concerns of alcohol being consumed around PR. I recommend that PR not be in the presence of any adult with a blood alcohol level above the legal limit of .08.

d. There are concerns that people with criminal backgrounds are being allowed around my client. I recommend that no one with a criminal background that is not party to this case be allowed around PR.

25. In my capacity as the PGAL, I have spent hours working on this case and have done the following to date:

a. Spoke with former GAL.

b. Met with Kirk and Jill and have talked to Kirk on the phone.

c. I have met with all the children living in the home.

d. Visited Kirk's home.

e. Met with Jody and his new wife, Deone which took about 3 hours.

f. Met with Jody's parents.

h. Met with and spoke to FBI agent.

i. Met with and have communicated several times with DCFS caseworker.

j. Spoke with client's former teacher.

K. Spoke with DCFS caseworkers that went into Kirk's home for several months.

L. Reviewed: i. Police reports/court dockets pertaining to various criminal incidents re: Kelly, Kirk, and Jody; ii. Juvenile transcripts; iii. Pleadings; iv. Case law

26. *Thousands of dollars in legal fees have already been expended in this matter. Appointing a new PGAL would only increase the costs of this litigation and delay the final resolution of this matter. My efforts thus far are evidence that the best interests of this child are indeed being advocated. This matter has been an intense undertaking and the efforts made on behalf of PR have been taken seriously in light of the facts presented to me.*

27. *I hereby declare under criminal penalty of the State of Utah, pursuant to the Utah Code 78B -5-705, that the foregoing is true and correct.*

APRIL 17TH, 2015: AMENDED RECOMMENDATION AND ORDER OF COMMISSIONER BLOOM is signed and officially in effect.

On February 20, 2015, the Court having convened to address the following motions filed by the parties which were heard by the Court and taken under advisement: Intervenor's Motion to Establish Jody Rhorer as the Natural and Biological father of PR; Motion for Determination of Parentage, Motion for Custody and in the Alternative for Custody Evaluation and Motion for Interim Parent-Time, Kirk J's Motion to Disregard DNA Test, Motion to Reconsider Order Granting Intervention, Mr. Rhorer's Motion to strike Respondent's Motion to Reconsider Order Granting Intervention of Jody Rhorer and Motion to Strike Respondent's Motion to Disregard DNA Paternity Test Submitted by Intervenor, Motion for Order for DCFS to Conduct Investigation, Motion to Submit Affidavit of Wendy C. and Birth Certificate of PR, the minor child and Motion to Amend Order.

APRIL 20TH, 2015: EMAIL from Nancy S to Mr. Duncan

Mr. Duncan,

I am an attorney representing Jody Rhorer in a paternity action. I am attaching a brief explanation of the facts in this matter. This concerns the Utah Parentage Act, and in particular Section 78B-15-607 which limits challenge to paternity of a child born into a marriage to the mother and her husband. The facts of this case were not contemplated by the Utah legislature and I am asserting that the statute is unconstitutional as to my client and others similarly situated. I would appreciate your reading the attachment and calling me to discuss the case and the statute. We are hoping that you and your organization can help.

Thank you,

Nancy S

April 21, 11:31 AM

Dear Nancy,

Thank you for reaching out to the Sutherland Institute about this case. The situation you describe is terribly tragic. It is awful to think a child would have to endure these kinds of challenges.

You are no doubt correct that the legislature did not have in mind a scenario where a husband encourages his wife to have children with other men when it codified the very longstanding presumption of paternity. We can only pray that is a very rare situation (and I suspect it is extremely rare, if it has ever happened outside the people involved in your case). The legislature has enacted a number of laws that are directly on point, however: laws related to abuse and neglect of children. The facts you describe here are undoubtedly abuse.

You mention an investigation by a GAL in the second portion of the memo. It would seem more appropriate to involve law enforcement and the Department of Child and Family Services. In fact, depending on the knowledge that the various parties have of the drug abuse, crime, obscuring of family's ties, etc., some of the parties may even have a duty to report. Your client was wise to motion for DCFS investigation and appointment of a GAL in his own case.

There are a couple of reasons I would counsel the Sutherland Institute against involvement in the case. First, the Institute has taken the position as amicus in other litigation that Utah's

strong policy is, and should continue to be, that the only secure foundation of a biological father's parental rights is marriage to the mother. While a father cannot control the decisions the mother may make, he can control whether he has a sexual relationship with her that may result in a child. The Constitution, we have argued, is not meant to provide a backstop when that protection is not taken. Of course, we recognize that mothers as well as fathers, may act in despicable ways but that possibility does not justify courts creating new, broad constitutional rights that provide almost limitless discretion to judges to determine what is in the best interests of children.

Second, a constitutional claim that the presumption of paternity is unconstitutional faces the very significant hurdle that the U.S. Supreme Court has specifically rejected that claim in Michael H. v. Gerald D., 491 U.S. 110 (1989). Is your intention to ask the courts to reconsider that decision or are you making a state constitutional claim? I believe Utah courts have also been hesitant about overturning the presumption but I would need to conduct some research to ensure that is correct.

Third, since this appears to be a facial challenge rather than an as-applied challenge, I worry that there might be unintended consequences if the courts were to adopt a constitutional rule that courts cannot apply the presumption of paternity. I am aware of instances where the mother makes a terrible mistake and conceives a child with one man while married to another but reconciles with her husband who is more fit to act as a parent than the partner in adultery. It does not seem like good public policy to allow the latter to disrupt an ongoing marriage (the statute deals with situations where there has been a divorce and does not prevent the assertion of paternity by the alleged father in that case). Obviously, one question would be the nature of the new constitutional rule the courts would be asked to apply. Would it say that a man who has developed a parent-like relationship with a child can assert paternity as the Commissioner's findings suggest (#20)? That could be problematic. For instance, you note that there is another woman now living with the presumed father. If the courts were to strike down the presumption of paternity, wouldn't Mr. J have the ability to seek custody of those children based on his ongoing relationship with them?

Would the rule be that any man who claims to be the biological father can contest the paternity of the husband and have a blood test ordered? That would seem to be ripe for abuse by a vengeful ex-boyfriend or a mentally unstable person or really anyone. That is the concern addressed by the current law. I assume the rule sought here would be something more like: an asserted biological father who was defrauded by the mother in a sham marriage can challenge the paternity of the father's husband. That, however, doesn't avoid the problems raised by the previous rule. Who would determine whether the marriage is a sham or not? Would there be any protections against a person seeking paternity for inappropriate reasons? If the mother agrees the marriage is a sham, she can contest paternity under the terms of the current law.

Fourth, assuming that I am mistaken in my understanding of what is being sought in this case and that the claim is not open to the concerns outlined above, we would need to know more before determining that it is a suitable test case. For instance, it is not clear what grounds the husband has to object to the motion to establish paternity (#19) when he has already disclaimed paternity and has been established a non-parent (#14).

This seems important since 78B-15-607(4) says that there is no presumption if the question of paternity has already been adjudicated.

It is also not clear why the mother is contesting your client's paternity claim when she has disclaimed the husband's paternity. Wouldn't that end the presumption under 78B-15-607(1)?

Perhaps I am missing something but it seems the statute doesn't preclude your client's claim. I hope this response is not too disappointing. I will share it with my colleagues at the Sutherland Institute in case they feel my analysis is in error. I really do feel terrible about this situation. No child should be made to suffer because of the choices of adults but that unfortunately happens far too often. Creating new constitutional rules with potential unintended consequences just does not seem to be the answer to that problem, particularly where the statute or another statute might already offer the protection sought.

Best wishes,
The Sutherland Institute

This major shutdown by the Sutherland Institute didn't stop Nancy from reaching out to other entities, including the University of Utah, but to no avail. The "Best Interest of the Child" was really not the concern of the court. There really wasn't a concern of the court. They were just going through the motions as precious time ticked away.

APRIL 20TH, 2015: MEMORANDUM IN OPPOSITION TO RESPONDENT'S MOTION TO STAY PROCEEDINGS, submitted by Nancy S, Commissioner Kase presiding

Intervenor Jody Rhorer submits this Memorandum in Opposition to Respondent's Motion to Stay Proceedings.

FACTS

1. The Amended Recommendation and Order in this matter was signed by the Honorable Stanley on April 20, 2015.

2. Respondent filed his Motion to Stay Proceedings on April 6, 2015.

3. Respondent does not set forth the Rule pursuant to which Respondent is filing his motion pursuant to the Utah Rules of Civil Procedure.

4. Intervenor prepared a Recommendation and Order, to which Respondent objected.

5. Intervenor prepared an Amended Recommendation and Order with changes proposed by the Respondent.

6. Intervenor presented the Amended Recommendation and Order to the Respondent and requested a signature Approved as to Form; however, Respondent failed and refused to approve the Amended Recommendation and Order.

ARGUMENT 1.

The Respondent's Motion is Untimely and Insufficiently Pled

The Respondent's motion fails to state under which Rule Respondent is pleading for relief. Rule 62 of the Utah Rules of Civil Procedure governs stay of proceedings to enforce a judgment.

If Respondent is moving to stay the proceedings under Rule 59, Respondent's motion is untimely in that Rule 59(e) states, "A motion to alter or amend the judgment shall be served not later than 14 days after entry of the judgment." Respondent's motion was filed weeks prior to the entry of the Order in this matter and is untimely; further Rule 59 governs judgments made pursuant to trial, and not pursuant to order after hearing by a Commissioner. Respondent's motion does not present a sufficient reason for the court to stay the entry of the Amended Recommendation and Order. Respondent's motion is untimely and should be denied.

Respondent has waived an opposition to the entry of the Amended Recommendation and Order and is estopped from opposing the entry of the Amended Recommendation and Order II.

After Respondent objected to the first Recommendation and Order prepared by the Intervenor, the Intervenor submitted to Respondent a transcript of the February 20, 2015, hearing before the Honorable Commissioner Bloom and an Amended Recommendation and Order. Respondent requested minor spelling and grammatical changes. Intervenor made these changes and resubmitted the Amended Recommendation and Order to Respondent requesting a signature Approved as to Form. Respondent refused to sign the same. After the Amended Recommendation and Order. Respondent has waived any objection, and is now stopped from bringing an objection at this time.

There is no Compelling Reason to Stay these Proceedings III.

The motions in this matter have been pending before the court for a year, and any delay will prejudice the Intervenor and other parties to this action. Absent a compelling reason to stay the proceedings, the court must deny the Respondent's motion.

A stay in the Proceedings will Prejudice the Intervenor IV.

At the February 20, 2015, ruling, Commissioner Bloom ordered the Intervenor to pay the PGAL's initial retainer inasmuch as the order for an appointment of a PGAL was pursuant to the Intervenor's motion for the same. The ruling includes a provision that the cost of the PGAL may be reallocated among the Petitioner, Respondent, and Intervenor. Intervenor has paid the PGAL a total of $2,000 to date and there is an outstanding bill in the amount of approximately $3,000 for services performed by the PGAL on this case. This is a complex case involving the constitutionality of the Utah Parentage Act regarding standing to assert paternity. This case presents unique facts that if combined with the application of the Utah law have not been adjudicated in the State of Utah. Intervenor has paid tens of thousands of dollars in attorney fees related to the appointment and proceedings concerning the PGAL.

A stay in these proceedings would unduly burden the Intervenor by imposing additional financial hardship to him and would impede his ability to proceed in this matter.

The Respondent's Motion is Made for Improper Purposes V.

This motion, as well as all other motions filed by Respondent since the court's ruling on February 20, 2015, is being made in bad faith and is a deliberate attempt to divert the court's and the parties' attentions and efforts away from the single issue which is most paramount in this case, **the issue of the best interests of the minor child, PR.**

The Respondent has filed a flurry of motions since the February 20 ruling which are designed to cause more delay in these proceedings which have been ongoing for a year, and to delay a final resolution of the matters before the court. Respondent is abusing the judicial process. Respondent has filed motions which are untimely and late and has then defended the filings in further motions without evidentiary support for the allegations contained in the motions. Respondent has filed multiple motions for attorney fees without complying with the prerequisites required under the Utah Rules of Civil Procedures and motions for hearings on Respondent's motions. The court's ruling of February 20, 2015, addressed a possible custody evaluation. Mr. and Mrs. Rhorer are working to earn and save money to pay these costs. The Respondent is knowingly and intentionally imposing a great financial hardship on the Intervenor by the filing of these excessive motions requiring Intervenor to incur additional attorney fees.

WHEREFORE, the intervenor respectfully requests that the court deny the Respondent's motion to stay proceedings, for an award of attorney's fees in Intervenor's favor and for such other and further relief as the court deems just.

APRIL 21ST, 2015: Emails from Nancy S

April 21, 9:02 AM
Guys, I need to ask another attorney or a litigation support firm to help with the research on your case regarding the constitutionality issue. What amount can you pay to them? Please let me know asap. Thanks, Nancy

April 22, 1:42 PM
Jody and Deone, Unfortunately, due to time and budget restraints I can't put any more time into the investigation aspect of your case. I will be focusing my time and efforts on the legal issues and preparing for the upcoming hearing. I am concerned about our lack of conclusive evidence. I don't know what the GAL's report will say but I know the visit to Kirk's home was favorable to him. The attorney for DCFS has said that they do not have any recent reports of alleged harm or neglect of children in the home. Without something conclusive that we can submit to the court, things do not look favorable for us inasmuch as your ability to proceed is based on the "best interest of the child" standard. In the meantime, let me know if John or anyone else will be doing investigation work for you. We need to make sure it is done properly, and in a way that the results are admissible in court. Thanks, Nancy

5:27 PM
Jody, You had David B as your attorney in this matter first, and then Steve K. Do you remember either of them filing a Notice of Paternity Action with the Utah Vital Records Dept.? It occurs to me that we should probably do this and if it was already done, then Vital Records will let us know. I've asked my secretary to fill out the form for you to sign and we can file it with a copy of the petition Steve K filed for you. I'm suggesting this just in case something happens down the road where Kirk decides to give up his parental rights to some other man or his parental rights are taken from him, then you will be notified regarding Payshence. I'm not suggesting this to be negative, just to be safe. Thanks, Nancy

6:36 PM
If you want John to do any work, the best thing we could have at this point is surveillance video showing that Kirk allows Kelly to have Payshence unsupervised. Nancy

9:30 PM
Mary, I looked at Kirk J's Family Tree. I'm attaching my notes, just FYI. Kirk is choosing which children to legally claim and which children not to claim.
He put his name on the birth certificates of the 2 children born prior to his and Kelly's marriage; but he did not put his name on the birth certificates of the 3 children born while they were married. There is a pattern here, which is generational, albeit the motives are not obvious. In looking at the legal documents this Group files pro se, it is obvious that an attorney is advising them. I've contacted two investigative divisions of the Utah AG's office and have described what I've found and my suspicions that this Group is acting for improper purposes. Each division has told me that this situation is outside the scope of their investigative functions.

If Kirk J was adjudicated as Payshence's father as Connie and Ms. Nickle claims, his name should have been added to her birth certificate pursuant to the order, although I'm not going to bring this to Connie's attention. How can it be in a child's best interest for her presumed father to be unwilling to place his name on her birth certificate and allow her birth certificate to be absent a father's name? How can it be in a child's best interest that her presumed father deny his paternity in an ORS action? This whole situation doesn't pass the sniff test. By the way, I contacted the Sutherland Institute and they are not willing to get involved now, but they want to "reconnect" after the hearing. Thanks, Nancy

Notes on Kirk J's "Family Tree":

6-Year-old female child in home – According to state law, K.C. should be listed as father on this child's birth certificate. Jill C must have lied about her marital status at the time of the child's birth. Why wouldn't she want K.H.'s name on the child's birth certificate? He knows he's the father. Why hasn't Kirk J put his name on the birth certificate? (Certainly K.H. would have signed off on the birth certificate like he did for the child Kirk had with Jill 14 months later.)

Why would they want this child's birth certificate to be void of any father's name? I believe Jill was already living at Kirk's home when she gave birth to the little girl, now 6 years old. She started appearing in the Juvenile Court cases as the children's "stepmother" around that time, and this is when Kim left Kirk.

Youngest boy in home – Why would they want K.C. (Jill's legal husband) to "sign off" on this child's birth certificate to allow Kirk J to claim paternity, but not for the 6-year-old girl? I wonder why Kirk wants to be named the father of this child?

J1 and J2 – Kirk knows he and Kelly were not married when these children were conceived and born. J1 could possibly be his, but not due to any "presumed" status, as suggested. Kirk was in prison when J2 was conceived. Kirk knows this; he just doesn't know we know this. M.M. is J2's biological father. The birth certificate shows that it was amended a week after the birth, perhaps to add Kirk's name as the father. Apparently, any man can sign a voluntary declaration of paternity and have his name put on a child's birth certificate without proving a biological relationship to the child or marital relationship with the child's mother.

BS – Kirk's name should be on this child's birth certificate because he was married to Kelly when he was born. Why does this child have the last name "S_ _ _ _" when they know his biological father is T.T.? Why do they want this child's birth certificate to be void of any father's name?

Payshence – Kirk's name was never on the birth certificate. Jody's name used to be on it. *If Kirk has been adjudicated the father, as Connie and Ms. Nickel are arguing, then why hasn't he put his name on the birth certificate? Why do they want her birth certificate to be void of a father's name?*

DS - The other child born during the marriage whom Kelly accidentally forgot to tell the court about in her divorce petition and Kirk accidentally forgot to mention during the proceedings: I wonder what his birth certificate looks like? The court first learned about this child when I raised the issue in a hearing last year.

I am convinced that this Group is intentionally confusing the identities of these children by their acts and omissions. And the adults are confusing the identities of their parents – and maybe they really don't know. Just like Kelly is confused, like her sister was confused, just like Jill is confused, just like their parents and step-parents are confused. I hope someone is keeping an accurate log. It is unfortunate that children are not given a constitutional right to the truth, absent a legal adoption.

April 22, 9:37 AM
John, I included you on an email to Mary C. Two divisions of the AG's office have told me to report my concerns to the local police agency for them to investigate. Kirk J and this group are defrauding the government and the public, but we don't know why. Should I report this to the police? Do they investigate matters like this? is there a Federal agency who will investigate? I'm reaching a dead end. I'd like your advice. Thanks, Nancy

APRIL 21TH, 2015: MEMORANDUM IN OPPOSITION TO RESPONDENT'S MOTION FOR REMOVAL OF GAL, submitted by Nancy S, Commissioner Kase presiding

Intervenor by and through counsel, Nancy S, hereby submits this Memorandum in Opposition to Respondent's Motion for Removal of Guardian ad Litem, Mary C., the PGAL appointed in this matter, as well as her assistant has filed Declarations with the court. The Declarations set forth the following facts:

1. The Respondent had prior knowledge of the private GAL's intent to walk through the Respondent's home to speak to the children in the home.

2. A police officer accompanied Mary C to Kirk J's home to keep the peace.

3. Respondent and his live-in girlfriend were cooperative with Mary C, and neither of them objected to Mary's actions during her visit to the Respondent's home. The Respondent and girlfriend helped facilitate Mary C's visit to the home.

4. The Respondent and his girlfriend know the police officer who accompanied the PGAL and engaged in friendly conversation with him during the time he was at the home.

5. The police officer did not touch anything in the Respondent's home, nor did he search the home, nor did he search anyone in the home.

6. On prior occasions the Respondent has objected to Mary C's concerns and questions, but the Respondent did not object to her actions during the visit.

ARGUMENT I
The PGAL did not Violate Policy or Procedure

Mary C had authority to act as she deemed appropriate and in accordance with what she believed to be in the best interest of the minor child. Mary C's Declaration is clear about her beliefs and concerns as to the safety of the minor child which required her to act as escrowed in her Declaration. The PGAL's actions should be in favor of the minor child.

The Respondent's Constitutional Rights were not Violated II

Respondent and his girlfriend are familiar with the criminal justice system. Attached is a printout of the Respondent's criminal history and Jill C's criminal history. Their backgrounds suggest that they have been instructed as to their constitutional rights many times. If they had any concern using the PGAL's visit, they certainly would have denied entry to the Respondent's home or have called counsel for advice.

The PGAL was justified in asking a police officer to accompany her to the Respondent's home in order to keep the peace. The safety and concern in conducting an investigation, and possible repercussions in doing so, has been a topic of discussions among legal scholars and GAL's and was specifically addressed in The Journal of Law and Family Studies. A PGAL is not exempt from a law enforcement agency's duty to respond to a request to domestic violence. The Petitioner, Respondent, Jill C, and other's criminal records who do not reside at the Respondent's home is attached. The PGAL in this matter conducted her investigation to avoid harm to herself or anyone else.

Public Policy is Best Served by Denying Respondent's Motion III

The interests of public policy require that the Respondent's motion be denied. The Court must protect the PGAL as it protects a minor child inasmuch as the PGAL stands in the shoes of the minor child. The PGAL's concerns about reprisal or adverse personal consequences in the performance of her duties may impede the PGAL's candor and/or ability to be impartial and render an unbiased report.

The Granting of Respondent's Motion would Prejudice the Intervenor
The Respondent's Motion Should be Denied in the Interest of the Judicial Economy IV

Respondent objected to the Intervenor's motion to appoint a private GAL which required a hearing before the court. At the subsequent ruling the Court addressed and granted the Intervenor's motion. At the hearing the Court instructed the parties to file financial declarations to determine the apportionment of fees to the PGAL. Intervenor has complied by filing his financial declaration. The Respondent and Petitioner have failed to file their financial declaration to date. The Court has expended many hours in its analysis of the facts and law pertaining to the appointment of the PGAL and the best interest of the minor child.

Removing the current PGAL and requiring another to recommence a new investigation would impose an unnecessary burden on the court's resources.

The Respondent's Motion is Made for Improper Purposes VI

*This motion, as well as all other motions filed by Respondent since the court's ruling on February 20, 2015, is being made in bad faith and is a deliberate attempt to divert the court's and the parties' attentions and efforts away from the single issue which is most paramount in this case, **the issue of the best interest of the minor child, PR.***

***WHEREFORE**, the Intervenor respectfully request that the Court deny the Respondent's Motion for Removal and Reappointment of GAL and for an award of attorney's fees in favor of the Intervenor for having no response hereto.*

APRIL 24TH, 2015: EMAILS from Nancy S

Hi Jody and Deone, John called me yesterday and said he had talked to Deone. He suggested that he talk to Payshence's teacher and I told him the GAL has already done that. He mentioned that Connie was alleging that the police officer violated Kirk's constitutional rights and I let him know that I had addressed that issue. I am attaching to this email the Memorandum I filed Tuesday in your case. Connie also filed a motion to open Jody's paternity case where he got custody of his daughters. We would need to oppose that motion only if there is something in it that is unfavorable to you. I didn't represent you in that matter, so please let me know if we should oppose it. Please let me know today. Nancy

April 28, 3:43 PM
Hi Jody and Deone, I am attaching a motion filed by Connie today. It is a motion to strike the Declaration filed by Mary C. I need to prepare a memorandum opposing this motion, as well as the other memorandum and prepare for the hearing. Please call me to discuss payment. Nancy

10:08 PM
Nancy, Shouldn't Mary be the one to defend herself? This is all directed towards her. Is it true that the commissioner struck down 600 pages of attachments to our case? There is nothing in Jody's past custody case for his three older daughters that needs to be hidden. He was the one that was granted the custody. Can you write a brief response and then argue it on May 11th? Feel free to give Jody a call tomorrow. Deone

April 29, 6:59 AM
Deone, Mary is not a party to the lawsuit, Jody is. She can file a response, but the hearing is not hers to lose. You can talk to her if you want. The motion, as well as three other motions, require our immediate attention. The Commissioner ruled at the Feb. 20th hearing that the attachments would be allowed, but Connie has filed a motion to set aside her ruling. That is another motion we need to respond to. I don't understand what you are saying. I need to meet/speak with you and Jody before I do anything. You both need to call me so that we can go over everything only once and I can answer your questions. If we don't hurry there won't be time to respond to anything before the hearing. Nancy S

5:40 PM
Hi John, Connie is filing motions and making unfounded allegations about you, she is trying to remove Mary C and to Stay all Proceedings and has filed other motions. She has attached exhibits regarding you to her motions. Will you please send me your response as I am trying to prepare memorandums opposing her. Thanks, Nancy

6:16 PM
Jody and Deone, In thinking about these recent court filings, Connie just gave us a reason to submit to the court evidence of the criminal history of all the adults surrounding Payshence and the reasons why we believed there may be gang involvement and other irregularities involving this group. This needs to be done asap. But this will take time and I will need to ask John for his assistance. I don't want to be in a position where WE are asking the court to continue the hearing because we are not prepared. I really need to hear from you. Nancy

10:30 PM
Nancy, This is so ridiculous. We never hired anyone. They were hired by your office. You already submitted the criminal histories twice. We have asked several times for John to give us his plan and what it will cost but he hasn't responded. I, Jody Rhorer, put my trust in you with my life and my daughter's. Thank you.

April 29, 7:11 AM
Jody and Deone, Yes, it is ridiculous, but I still need to prepare responses to all the motions. If you don't want me to proceed, then I need to withdraw as your attorney. If you want me to proceed, then I need to clear my calendar and work on your case the rest of this week and into next week. But I need to talk to you and we need to talk about payment. Thanks, Nancy

7:32 AM

Jody and Deone, Connie has opened a dangerous door for her client. If you will call me, I can explain my strategy better to you. I would like to hear from both of you today. I am feeling like I'm alone in this monumental effort. Nancy

4:30 PM

Jody and Deone, I just received an email from Mary C, she is filing a response to Connie's motions, as well. I am working on our response. Nancy

Jody and I were feeling overwhelmed by the bickering between the three attorneys. None of this was moving us any closer to getting Payshence but we were caught in the middle regardless. Jody would call Nancy but never get any concrete answers. She just wanted us to come to her office so we could give her more money. Still, we had yet to see a statement of account or an invoice of any kind - moreover, any results. She was becoming more demanding and we were stuck in a game of chase-the-tail.

APRIL 25TH, 2015:   MEMORANDUM IN SUPPORT OF MOTION TO VACATE ORDER, submitted by Connie C, Commissioner Kase presiding

COMES NOW, Kirk J, by and through Counsel and files the foregoing Memorandum in Support of his Motion to Vacate the Order Signed by Commissioner Bloom, April 17th, 2015.
FACTS
(1). Commissioner Bloom was appointed to this matter fairly immediately after filing the case, with the first hearing occurring in front of her in December of 2012.

(2) Documents were filed on behalf of Intervenor, Jody Rhorer, December 9th, 2013.

(3) Commissioner Bloom conducted six hearings in the matter to the merits of the contentions raised by Intervenor in his quest to establish paternity and obtain custody of PR.

(4) The public docket entry states, "On April 6, 2015, this court was informed that this Commissioner was a GAL and represented the children of the Intervenor in another matter."

(5) The matter, a 2002 filing is mentioned, and Commissioner Bloom recused herself.

(6) Counsel for Kirk J was sent minutes of that ruling from appointed GAL, Mary C.

(7) Because there was no motion for recusal, Counsel filed a request for information as to how the recusal occurred.

(8) Undersigned got a voicemail from Commissioner Bloom's clerk to the effect that it was GAL Mary C who supplied the information which lead to her recusal. (Naturally, information supplied via voicemail is not part of the record, which is the rationale behind Kirk J's filing a written pleading asking for information which lead to the recusal in the first place. Response to a motion by phone does not suffice.)

(9) The hearing set in the matter was stricken pending reassignment to another Commissioner.

(10) Kirk J immediately filed a Motion to Stay proceedings, which specifically included the signing of the pending order based on Commissioner Bloom having declared her recusal was due to her conflict of having worked as GAL in a case involving Jody Rhorer as a party.

(11) There was no ruling on that Motion.

(12) Despite her recusal, Commissioner Bloom signed the Proposed Order and referred it for signature of the presiding Judge April 17th, 2015.

(13) Despite the pending Motion to Stay and Motion for Information about Declaration of the Conflict which lead to recusal, the District Court signed the Order April 21st, 2015.
Commissioner Bloom was Without Authority to Sign the Proposed Order
In this case, the only thing one can impart from Commissioner Bloom's self-recusal is that she found bias or prejudice which gave rise to a situation where her impartiality might reasonably be questioned. Then, nine days after declaring such situation, she signed the Proposed Order in the case which was the culmination of literally months of work, and purported to dispose of central legal issues in the case, and forwarded the same to the presiding Judge for signature.

After declaring a conflict which arose to the magnitude of immediate recusal without even an option on the part of the parties to consider waiving, the Commissioner cannot be said to have authority to sign an Order going to the merits of the case. She had only the authority requested to conduct "ministerial tasks" such as arranging for another Commissioner.

The Court did not Rule on the Motion to Stay

When the Commissioner recused herself, Kirk J immediately filed a Motion to Stay and that the Order not be signed.

The Court, in signing the Order, utterly disregarded the Motion. Rule 7 of the Utah Rules of Civil Procedure allows a litigant to file Motions and outline procedures for reply and the Court's ruling on Motions. This Court ignored the filings of the Motion to Stay in signing of the Order. Kirk J objects to procedures in this case which result in actions being taken based on phone calls, voice mails, et cetera, while proper written Motions are disregarded and ignored.

Procedural Due Process

The Due Process Clause of the Fourteenth Amendment to the United States Constitution, made applicable to the States, requires as a fundamental requirement that a litigant be supplied process before a neutral magistrate. A magistrate is not neutral if that magistrate has herself identified a conflict so severe it required recusal without any opportunity for notice or a hearing.

*The information contained in the Court minutes contains the only information we have as to the nature of the conflict which is the Commissioner's prior representation of children in a 2002 case in which Mr. Rhorer was a party. Given that is the origin of the conflict, it is clear that the Commissioner had the conflict all along. If the conflict is so severe the Commissioner can no longer act having been made aware of the conflict, then it is manifest that the Commissioner **never should have** acted in the matter at all. As such, the Order signed in the matter must be vacated. Kirk J acknowledges the issue which has arisen was attributable to an oversight on the part of Commissioner Bloom. But the existence of this conflict is not his doing.*

Commissioner Bloom, having identified for herself a reason she cannot act on the case, the burden should not shift to Kirk J to live with decisions made by a Judge with a conflict simply because it's inconvenient and time consuming to go back and start over. His fundamental rights should not be sacrificed for the sake of expedience, cost, or convenience.

APRIL 27TH, 2015:   REPLY TO "DECLARATION" OF MARY C, submitted by Connie C, Commissioner Kase presiding

COMES NOW, *Kirk J, by and through Counsel, files the foregoing Reply to the "Declaration" of private appointed Guardian ad Litem, Mary C. This pleading is offered in the event the Court does not Strike the "Declaration" as is prayed for in his Motion to Strike.*

FACTS

(1) April 6th, 2015, when asked via email about her search of Kirk J's home after having made an appointment to interview children, Mary responded "I did a home inspection. I always bring another person for my safety and so I can have a witness as to the walk through. I like bringing an officer when I do so."

(2) Also, April 6th, 2015, when asked for confirmation about the details Kirk J said occurred, including that Kirk J was not told in advance there would be a search, Mary C replied, "I do not make it a policy to tell the parents exactly what I'll be doing in advance. My role in this case is to look out for the best interest of PR and to ensure her living quarters are safe. There have been several allegations of drugs, weapons, gang affiliation, violent tendencies, etc. It was my intent to clear that concern up."

(3) The police report of Mary C's April 3rd, 2015, search of Kirk J's home is attached hereto and incorporated herein by this reference as Exhibit I.

(4) That incident report reflects that the Gang Task Force Officer who went with Mary C to Kirk J's house was told by his supervisor to meet with Mary C and John B (Private Investigator).

(5) The report then recites that Detective Ski, "met with both John and GAL Mary C and they informed me on the case."

(6) The report then goes into great detail about criminal activities suspected to be occurring at Kirk's home, including gang involvement, and that the reason Mr. Ski is needed is because Mary C does not know what to look for in the way of evidence of gang involvement.

    (7)   The report specifies that Mary C reported that she had received information that Kirk J was possibly a Kearns Town Blood member and she wanted Detective Ski to accompany her because she did not know what to look for and to show her signs of gang affiliation.

    (8)   The report then outlines details of the search, including that "closest and dresser drawers" were searched by Mary C and concludes no evidence of gang involvement was found.

    (9)   No mention is made as to what happened to private investigator, John B, after he met with the Detective and Mary C at the Welker substation and why he accompanied Mary C to Unified to speak to the Gang Task Force but not to Kirk's home for the search.

    (10)   John B is a private investigator and his employee biography which is available online touts that he is a "retired Special Agent with the FBI."

    (11)   Mary C's declaration mentions in two places that she has spoken to an FBI agent, and in fact, the FBI agent is the only person Mary C asserts she spoke to without expressly mentioning a name for the individual.

    (12)   Undersigned Counsel's requested the name of the FBI Agent from Mary C, but the request, which was made by email, has gone unanswered.

    (13)   In April, 2014, some ten months prior to the appointment of GAL, Kirk J and his live-in girlfriend noticed people watching their home.

    (14)   Two males were seen in the area in April of 2014, conducting surveillance.

    (15)   Kirk J called the police on one of the individuals who confirmed he was a private investigator watching and filming Kirk's home.

    (16)   The man confirmed he was a private investigator who asserted he had a right to conduct surveillance and film, but he was told to move along because he was illegally parked.

    (17)   Also, in April, 2015, a neighbor of Kirk's confronted a male who indicated he was a private investigator watching the home for alleged drinking and maltreatment of the children.

    (18)   The neighbor was given a business card which indicated the person was a private investigator named John B.

    (19)   Using the information from the business card given to the neighbor, the girlfriend, who resides with Kirk, was able to search the internet and find the employee profile of John B.

    (20)   The girlfriend was able to verify by looking at the employee profile of John B that he was one of the individuals seen in her neighborhood watching Kirk J's home in April of 2014.

    (21)   The time the girlfriend saw the individual she was able to identify as John B was ten months before the Unified Police Department incident from April 3rd, 2015.

    (22)   Nancy S has mentioned in Court prior to the appointment of Mary C that Mr. Rhorer hired a private investigator.

    (23)   After the Motion to Remove Mary C was filed, Mary C caused to be filed her "declaration" and an affidavit from an employee of hers to the effect that Kirk J was informed prior to the visit that the home would be searched.

    (24)   Kirk J was provided a copy of the employee affidavit reasserting that he was never told the home would be searched.

DISCUSSION

    The foregoing facts present a very troubling circumstance. If in fact Mr. Rhorer employed private investigators in 2014, and one of the individuals conducting surveillance of Kirk's home was John B, it would seem that Mary C was working with Mr. Rhorer's private investigator. It is problematic indeed that in "informing the Gang Detective" about the case, John B and Mary C provided the same scandalous accusations about criminal associations, Gang Involvement, et cetera, that Mr. Rhorer has been attempting to introduce in this case. Therefore, it seems logical to conclude that Mary C basically adopted the views of Mr. Rhorer, even to the point of utilizing his private investigator to "help her" to explain to the Gang Detective the kind of evidence they expected could be found in the house.

Mary C's omission of the name of the FBI Agent she says she's "met with" when she names everyone else begs the question as to whether the omission is intentional. The documents and information provided establish that Mary C has made inconsistent statements about the event. Mary C asserted at times the visit to the home was a "walk through." The police report clearly describes an exhaustive search. Further, the police report establishes that the police officer was not taken to ensure Mary C's safety. The "pre-meeting" between the Gang Task Force Officer, private investigator John B, and Mary C is all about evidence they wanted to find, not safety. Rather than searching, she was accompanied by the able and vigorous retired FBI Agent, John B. Instead, for reasons not disclosed, John B did not accompany her; the Gang Task Force Officer did, and they did an exhaustive search. Kirk J suspects that the reason John B was involved was because he was conversant in Mr. Rhorer's version of the events; that Mary C has adopted that version of events; that she wished to further Mr. Rhorer's investigation of Kirk J and his household; and that John B suspected that he would be identified and therefore that the search would not be successful.

CONCLUSION

What has occurred in this case is as shocking as it is sad. The initial Motion for removal establishes Mary C violated Kirk J's fundamental and constitutional rights and therefore should be removed. Her diametrically opposed assertions made through her emails and "declaration" that Kirk J was forewarned, and he wasn't, is disturbing.

Mary C's assertions that Kirk J "should've know better" and "could've refused consent" to search is offensive. The reason lawyers have special obligations to represented parties is because it is not a level playing field when one party's attorney communicates with another. It is very clear that Mary C consciously and premeditatedly colluded to obtain a strategic position to get into the home and search for information that John B informed would be present. A bigger question is why, if Mary C sincerely wished to search without unfairly posturing to overcome Kirk J's resistance, she didn't contact his counsel in advance. For a GAL to be able to function properly, a party like Kirk J has to be able to trust that she is truly working toward the best interest of the child, not as an arm of the opposing party.

Mary C's actions are a significant departure from the proper and lawful activities of a GAL. Mary C seems to sincerely believe that her role appropriately includes the types of "investigation" she has conducted here. Kirk J feels her behavior is unlawful, and represents a bias and lack of objectivity which render her incapable of functions in the role of GAL.

APRIL 27TH, 2015: MOTION TO STRIKE "DECLARATION" OF GAL MARY C, submitted by Connie C, Commissioner Kase presiding

COMES NOW, Kirk J and files the Motion to Strike the "Declaration" of PGAL Mary C.

FACTS

(1) On or about April 20th, 2015, Mary C caused to be filed a document entitled, Declaration of Mary C. Kirk J is unfamiliar with any procedure which allows an attorney to file a "declaration" instead of a proper pleading as described by Rule 7 of the Utah Rules of Civil Procedure, but it is clear that Mary C's pleading had a dual purpose of asserting her version of events of April 3rd in an attempt to counter the Motion to Remove her as well as attempting to provide substantive recommendations about the case. However, the pleading is styled as if the averments in the pleading are sworn "facts".

(2) The substance makes clear that the document purports to respond to Kirk J's Motion to remove Mary C for violating his rights by searching his home.

(3) The "declaration" purports that it is made under "criminal penalty" of perjury pursuant to 78B-5-705, U.C.S. which provides that, "if the Utah Rules of Criminal Procedure, Civil Procedure, or Evidence require or permit a written declaration upon oath" such may be made with a declaration if the information is true under criminal penalty.

(4) The propositions contained in the declaration, which are factual assertions, arguments, and/or recommendations are advanced in the same form, as if they are sworn facts.

(5) The basis of opinions or conclusions are not offered in the document.

FACTUAL ASSERTIONS

78B-5-705, U.C.A. provides that, "if the Utah Rules of Criminal Procedure, Civil Procedure, or Evidence require or permit a written declaration upon oath..."such a writing may be made with a declaration the information is true and correct under criminal penalty. Rule 11 of the Utah Rules of Civil Procedure has similar language, but refers to "a person," and state, if a rule requires an affidavit or a notarized, verified or acknowledged signature, the person may submit a declaration pursuant to the Utah Code Section 79B-5-705."

The Statute which allows for appointment of the Guardian ad Litem, 78A-2-705, describes activities to be undertaken by the GAL that are clearly attorney advocacy to represent the minor's best interest. To emphasize that the Guardian's assertions are not "facts" to be declared under penalty of perjury, 78A-2-705(14) expressly requires that "[i]n every court hearing where the private attorney guardian ad litem makes a recommendation regarding the best interest of the minor, the court shall require the private GAL to disclose the factors that for the basis of the recommendation." Therefore, GAL assertions are not meant to be viewed as facts, but rather opinions, positions, and recommendations which require verifiable factual support.

Where Mary C has asserted factual positions which are contrary to the factual assertions presented in the affidavits of Kirk J and Jill C about the search of their home, she is not in a position to merely override their assertions through filing of a "declaration" and have the contested matters concluded in her favor. The unfortunate situation is that Mary C caused the situation which gave rise to the factual dispute by deciding to go to Kirk J's house with a law enforcement officer, and then searching the home high and low. Considering the outrageous nature of the conduct, it is not surprising that Mary C endeavors to explain it away. Regarding disputed facts, the Court should not accept Mary C's version simply because she is an attorney.

OPINIONS AND RECOMMENDATIONS

It is Kirk J's position that due to the behaviors of Mary C in over-reaching and abandoning a proper role of GAL, that the Court should remove her and not consider any opinions or recommendations offered by her. However, if the Court is inclined to consider her "declaration" as offering opinions and recommendations, Kirk J avers that it is deficient and unreliable. Mary C speaks to "allegations" of criminal conduct, gang affiliation, consumption of alcohol, lack of bonding and attachment, the minor's identification of "her father", the minor being around people with criminal backgrounds, et cetera, all without stating any basis for any of these beliefs, opinions, and recommendations. Mary C does not even bother to note where she derived any of that information, let alone how it can reliably be viewed to support any opinions of recommendations. Where the "declaration" departs from its central mission of being a factual summary and attempts to make recommendations, the recommendations are unsupported with any factors which underlie the suggestions or recommendations.

CONCLUSION

A GAL is not witness or a special master qualified to summarily report "facts" to be accepted by the Court. The GAL occupies the position of attorney for the minor. As such, the GAL is entitled to access and avail herself of the Rules which govern attorneys, such as Rule 11. She is entitled to file pleadings in proper form, present arguments and respond to the arguments of others. Where the "declaration" departs from its central mission of being a factual summary and attempts to make recommendations, the recommendations are unsupported with and factors which underlie the suggestions or recommendation. Therefore, it doesn't comport with 78A-2-705(14), and the Court should disregard the recommendations as unsupported.

Connie was treading on thin ice by her attack of both Mary and Commissioner Bloom. When things weren't going the way Connie wanted, she would create ***drama motions*** packed with assumptions and conclusions without merit. Connie knows exactly where Mary got the information about Kirk - Nancy supplied it to her. But it's all public knowledge and Nancy had already supplied it to the court as well - at least three times.

APRIL 28TH and 29TH, 2015:   EMAILS from Nancy S

5:30 PM
Hi Jody and Deone, These are more filings by Connie which I need to answer. Nancy

10:19 PM
Nancy, Mary C brought this on. We shouldn't be left holding the bill for what has happened. Mary needs to respond. You were not there so you should not be responding. It needs to come directly from Mary C. Deone

April 29, 7:07 AM
Jody and Deone, Connie brought this on. If Jody doesn't want me to respond to the motions then he needs to tell me. Jody, if that is the case then, regretfully, I need to withdraw as your attorney. I was planning on working on your case today and the rest of the week, but I won't do anything until I hear from you. Nancy S

Suddenly I was not a decision maker anymore. My direction, which always came from my discussions with Jody, was no longer valid if Nancy didn't like the instructions I was sending her.

MAY 4TH, 2015:   COUNTER MOTION AND MEMORANDUM FOR ATTORNEY'S FEES AND OTHER SANCTIONS AS A RESULT OF VEXATIOUS LITIGANT AND RESPONSES TO REPLY TO DECLARATION OF MARY C; MOTION TO STRIKE DECLARATION OF MARY C; AND AFFIDAVIT OF KIRK J, submitted by Mary C, Commissioner Kase presiding

COMES NOW the PGAL, Mary C, and hereby respectfully submits this Motion and Memorandum for Attorney's Fees and Other Sanctions as a Result of Vexatious Litigant:

FACTS
Memorandum in Support of Motion to Vacate Order

1. On or about April 25, 2015, Respondent filed his Memorandum in Support of Motion to Vacate Order. At the very last paragraph on page 3, Respondent stated, "In that Commissioner Bloom recused herself without a Motion, without resort to providing information, and without allowing for the process of possible waiver by the parties, Kirk J **must conclude the recusal was for bias and prejudice."**

2. Page 4 states, "While there is a process articulated in Rule 63 of the Utah Rules of Civil Procedure regarding disqualification which would lead to a more developed record regarding the need for disqualification it was not utilized in this case. Rather, Commissioner Bloom's recusal of herself without a Motion leads to assumptions that have to be drawn."

3. The last paragraph on page 4 states, "In this case, the only thing one can impart from Commissioner Bloom's self-recusal is that she found bias or prejudice which gave rise to a situation where her impartiality might reasonably be questioned."

Reply to "Declaration" of Mary C

4. On or about April 27, 2015, Respondent filed his Reply to "Declaration" of Mary C.

5. On page 6 first paragraph Respondent states, "It seems logical to conclude that Mary C basically adopted the views of Mr. Rhorer, even to the point of utilizing his private investigator to help her."

6. On page 6 third paragraph Respondent states, "the police report establishes that the police officer was not taken to ensure Mary C's safety...[it] was all about evidence they wanted to find, not safety."

7. Page 7 first paragraph Respondent alleges, "Mary C has adopted that version of events, that she wished to further Mr. Rhorer's investigation of Kirk J and his household, and John B suspected...he would be identified, and therefore the search should not be successful."

8. Page 7 second paragraph states, "The initial Motion for removal establishes Mary C violated Kirk J's fundamental and constitutional rights...endeavoring not to disclose John B's name suggests that Mary C is well aware of the wrongfulness of incorporating Mr. Rhorer's private investigator, John B, into her activities."

9. Pages 7 last paragraph states, "It is very clear that Mary C consciously and premeditatedly colluded to obtain a strategic position to get into the home and search for information that John B informed her would be present."

10. Pages 8 second paragraph states, "This situation reflects that Mary C in fact used her position to coerce a search, and that the perimeters and object of the search were framed in conjunction with Mr. Rhorer's private investigator."

11. Page 8 last paragraph states, "Mary C's actions are a significant departure from the proper and lawful activities of a GAL...Kirk J feels her behavior is unlawful, and represents a bias and lack of objectivity which renders her incapable of functioning in the role of GAL."

12. Last paragraph states, "The documents and information provided establish that Mary C has made inconsistent statements about the event. When first asked, she advised counsel it is 'not her practice' to let parents know what she will be doing. Later, she caused to be filed an employee affidavit which asserts Kirk J was informed in advance."

Police Report

13. The police report from April 3, 2015, states Officer Ski 'followed Mary around from room to room ensuring her safety."

Motion and Memorandum for Removal and Reappointment of GAL

14. On or about April 10, 2015, Respondent filed his Motion and Memorandum for Removal and Reappointment of GAL.

15. Page 7, second paragraph, Respondent alleges the PGAL abandoned her role as the Guardian ad Litem and that "Mary C wanted to act as an agent of the police..."

Affidavit of Jill C. Regarding Private Investigator John B

16. On or about April 28, 2015, Respondent's girlfriend, Jill C, filed her Affidavit.

17. Paragraph 20 states, "Mary C had abandoned her role as GAL, and rather has taken up the role of Agent or assistant to Intervenor Jody Rhorer's attempt to project Kirk J and I in a bad light."

18. Paragraph 23 of the Affidavit states, "I must assume that the reason Mary C did not come to the home with private investigator, John B, was because she knew that Kirk J and I would recognize him on sight as the investigator employed by Jody Rhorer and would not let him in the home."

Affidavit of Kirk J

19. On or about April 28, 2015, Respondent filed the Declaration of Kirk J. Paragraph 8 states, "At no time was I told Mary C intended to search the home."

20. In an e-mail sent to Respondent's attorney, Connie, on March 30, 2015, the PGAL wrote:

"Connie,

Additionally, I am requesting that your client provide me with a release for me to speak with Payshence's former teacher and also to speak with her current teacher. Kirk will need to contact the schools to provide this release. Please advise as to when this is complete. I have also had my assistant trying to coordinate with Kirk so I can speak with other children in the home. I'd like to do a walk-through of the home this week if possible, as well. Please have your client contact my office to schedule this time. Thank you for your cooperation."

E-mail and Declaration of Mary C, PGAL

21. In an e-mail sent to Respondent's counsel on April 6. 2015, the PGAL states, "My role in this case is to look out for the best interest of PR and to ensure her living quarters are safe. There have been several allegations of drugs, weapons, gang affiliation, violent tendencies, etc. It was my intent to clear that concern up.

22. In paragraph 4 of the Declaration of Mary C, the PGAL states, "I had my assistant disclose what I intended to have happen, but I do not make it a point to explain to the parents in detail everything I intend to do or how I intent to further the best interests of my client."

23. Paragraph 6 of the Declaration of Mary C, PGAL, in Response to Motion and Memorandum for Removal and Reappointment of GAL ("Declaration of PGAL") states, "An extensive home investigation was necessary especially where my client is only 7 years old and there have been serious allegations of criminal activity. I was concerned about the safety of my client's home environment based on these various allegations.

24. Paragraph 7 of the Declaration of PGAL states, "Based on allegations of violence, drugs, abuse of alcohol, prior criminal convictions, criminal affiliations, gang affliction, and weapons, I felt it imperative to ensure my safety during my investigation of Kirk J's home and brought along Officer Ski for this purpose."

*25. Paragraph 18 of the Declaration of PGAL states, "After visiting Kirk J's home I am not concerned with the physical environment surrounding my client. The home is clean and organized despite being small and having approximately 8 people living in the home. I did not see any signs of violations of Kirk's parole with weapons or drugs. **Had I not been able to perform an exhaustive investigation I would not have been as clear on this point and would still have lingering concerns in this regard.** If there is any drug use, possession of weapons or gang affiliation, I did not see signs of such at the home."*

COUNTER MOTION ON VEXATIOUS LITIGANT
LEGAL STANDARDS
Rule 1 of the Utah Standards of Professionalism and Civility:

Provides, "Lawyers shall advance the legitimate interests of their clients, without reflecting any ill-will that clients may have for their adversaries, even if called upon to do so by another. Instead, lawyers shall treat all other counsel, parties, judges, witnesses, and other participants in all proceedings in a Courteous and dignified manner."

Rule 3 of the Utah Standards of Professionalism and Civility:

Provides that, "Lawyers shall not, without an adequate factual basis, attribute to other counsel or the Court improper motives, purpose, or conduct. Lawyers should avoid hostile, demeaning, or humiliating words in written and oral communications with adversaries. Neither written submissions nor oral presentations should disparage the integrity, intelligence, morals, ethics, or personal behavior of an adversary unless such matters are directly relevant under controlling substantive law."

The most frequent remedy used by trial Courts to address disrespectful or abusive pleadings is to strike objectionable language or the entire pleadings. Utah Courts are given explicit authority to 'strike and disregard all or any part of a pleading that contains redundant, immaterial, impertinent or scandalous matter. Where litigants demonstrate disregards for the judicial process by filing frivolous or disrespectful papers, they increase the costs of litigation, precious judicial resources, and insert an uncivil and unproductive tone into the proceedings.

ARGUMENT

All of the above quotes made by the Respondent are violations of Rule 1 of the Rules of Professionalism and Civility. Further, the language expressed in the above quotations are violations of Rule 3 of the Rules of Professionalism and Civility. Respondent automatically assumes there's "bias and prejudice" on the part of Commissioner Bloom attributing improper and unethical behavior on her part to the point of wanting to have the entire history of this case re-litigated. Respondent then tries to sugar coat the defamatory and derogatory statements about Commissioner Bloom by claiming that "Kirk J acknowledges the issue which has arisen was attributable to an oversight on the part of Commissioner Bloom." Respondent can't in good faith argue "bias and prejudice" on the part of Commissioner Bloom as a means to re-litigate everything and in the same breath also claims it was a mere oversight implying there's no reason to start from scratch in this matter.

All of the statements above were likely drafted by Respondent's counsel who is, or should be, well aware of the Rules of Professionalism and Civility. Respondent's counsel has alleged wrongdoing on the part of Commissioner Bloom and the PGAL without any evidence of such allegations and without any proof that there is some bias or prejudice against Respondent. Respondent's counsel has also explicitly accused the PGAL of colluding with the Intervenor.

What's interesting is that Respondent continually discusses how he's been wronged or doesn't trust the PGAL without mention of how the PGAL has failed to be a zealous advocate for her client, PR. The PGAL had no prior knowledge that Respondent and his girlfriend knew of John B until the girlfriend filed her Affidavit. Respondent claims in his Reply to "Declaration" of Mary C that "if Mary C was merely concerned about personal safety, rather than searching, she was accompanied by the able and vigorous FBI Agent, private investigator, John B. Yet, Respondent claims the PGAL was colluding with Mr. Rhorer and his investigator and is arguing out both sides of his mouth. Had the PGAL taken John B to Respondent's home, Respondent surely would have argued that the PGAL was in fact helping John B to further his investigation. The fact that the PGAL took a totally neutral third party should be evidence that the PGAL did not want there to be any cause for concern that she was in any way taking sides.

The Court possesses the power to maintain the orderly and productive manner in which this case is litigated. Respondent should not be allowed to file anything with the Court until he has received approval to file such pleadings to ensure the pleadings comply with the Rules of Professionalism and Civility...this court should award attorney's fees for the time the PGAL has expended in responding to Respondent's disrespectful commentary not only because they are improper, but because it has ultimately increased the costs of litigation, wasted precious judicial resources, and inserted an uncivil and unproductive tone into the proceedings. The court should also strike the pleadings recently filed to address the defamatory accusations of the Respondent.

CONCLUSION

In light of the totality of all the Respondent's vexatious behaviors in this case, this Court should prohibit the continuation of Respondent's inappropriate and improper actions by: (1) requiring Respondent to submit any subsequent pleadings in this matter to the Court for prior approval before actually filing to ensure that the Rules of Professionalism and Civility have been met; (2) require Respondent to pay the PGAL fees expended for the vexatious litigation tactics; (3) deny the Respondent's Motion to Strike Declaration of Mary C; (4) a finding that Respondent has perjured himself; and (5) entry of any other awards, orders, or sanctions as this Court deems reasonable and appropriate.

MAY 5TH, 2015: NOTICE OF INCOMPLETE FILING by Kelly H, Commissioner Kase presiding

1. According to the Court's docket, all parties (except the Petitioner, Kelly H) are represented by Counsel.
2. The Certificate of Service filed by the Petitioner does not reflect that the Petitioner's Motion or Statement Supporting the Motion were sent to all parties and or their attorneys.
3. Petitioner needs to contact and or send a copy of the Motion and Statement Supporting the Motion to all parties and or their attorneys.
4. A certificate of Service indicating that the above-mentioned matter has been satisfied must be filed with the Court.

MAY 6TH, 2015: MEMORANDUM OPPOSING MOTION TO STRIKE DECLARATION OF GAL, submitted by Nancy S, Commissioner Kase presiding

Intervenor, Jody Rhorer, by and through counsel, hereby submits this Memorandum Opposing Motion to Strike Declaration of GAL.

The Declaration of Mary C was filed in response to the motions filed by the respondent. Now the respondent seeks to strike the responsive pleading filed by the GAL. The Declaration is necessary for an adjudication of the matters brought before the court by the respondent.

Respondent presents no basis in law or in fact for the striking of a responsive pleading. Once again, respondent's motion is made of improper purposes, as set forth in Intervenor's prior memoranda opposing the respondent's numerous motions made after the February 20, 2015, ruling. Respondent's many motions are "smoke screens" designed to divert the Court's attention away from the single most important issue, **the best interests of the minor child.**

This motion is another meritless and bad faith attempt by the respondent to prevent full disclosure to the Court and to delay a final resolution of the matters before the court, which matters have been pending for well over a year.

Furthermore, the respondent filed this motion to strike the GAL's Declarations, and then filed a response to the Declaration, making the respondent's motion to strike the Declaration moot.

WHEREFORE, the Intervenor respectfully requests the court to deny the respondent's Motion to Strike the Declaration of the GAL and requests the court to award attorney's fees to the Intervenor for having to respond to the same.

MAY 6TH, 2015: MEMORANDUM OPPOSING MOTION TO VACATE ORDER, submitted by Nancy S, Commissioner Kase presiding

Intervenor Jody Rhorer, through counsel Nancy S, hereby submits this Memorandum Opposing Motion to Vacate Order filed by the Respondent.

Commissioner Bloom's ruling was made prior to the Commissioner's refusal and prior to her having received information which led to her recusal. The Respondent did not object to the ruling. There is no evidence before this court that the ruling was made improperly or that the ruling has resulted in prejudice to the respondent. Commissioner Bloom acted in her discretion and had the authority to sign the Recommendation and Order pursuant to her ruling.

The respondent has failed to state any controlling rule that would preclude Commissioner Bloom from signing the Recommendation and Order.

The written Recommendation and Order was filed by Intervenor. When the Respondent objected to the Order and Recommendation that it lacked findings for the ruling, the Intervenor ordered a recording of the February 20, 2015, ruling, had it transcribed, and submitted the same to Respondent's counsel together with an Amended Recommendation and Order. The Amended Recommendation and Order was filed with the court, and the respondent did not object. There is no evidence before this court that the Recommendation and Order or the Order for DCFS Investigation has resulted in prejudice to the respondent or any of the parties.

The record shows a history of the respondent's filing meritless and vexatious motions, which motions are rife with disrespectful allegations against the Court, Commissioner Bloom, opposing counsel, other parties to the litigation, and the private GAL. Respondent's motions filed after the February 20, 2015, hearing, include the most recent motions filed for improper purposes and with the intent to create a "smoke screen" to divert the Court's attention away from the single most important issue, **the best interests of the minor child.**

Vacating the court's order would not serve the best interest of the minor child nor would it serve the interest of any party to these proceedings, which proceedings have been ongoing for more than a year. Following the ruling of February 20, 2015, the respondent has flooded these proceeding with motions designed to cause unnecessary delays, to hinder the DCFS investigation and the performance of duties required by the PGAL, and further to impede the Intervenor's ability to comply with the Court's directives and timelines to the court's ruling of February 20, 2015, and to delay a final resolution of the matters before the court.

Intervenor has brought to the court's attention the respondents abuse of the judicial process. In his Reply to Respondent's Motion to Cease Publication filed on May 19, 2015, the Intervenor stated, "Respondent will likely persist in filing motions and requesting hearings as a means to ask for a continuance of the review hearing scheduled for April 16, 2015." Respondent's motion to vacate, as well as the other numerous motions filed by respondent including the most recent motions which are unnecessary and untimely, serve to illustrate and confirm the respondents abuse of process and the ultimate motivation of respondent's motions.

WHEREFORE, the Intervenor respectfully requests the court to deny the respondent's Motion to Vacate Order and requests the court to award attorney's fees to the Intervenor for having to respond to the same.

MAY 9TH, 2015: MOTION TO STRIKE GAL'S COUNTER-MOTION, submitted by Connie C, Commissioner Kase presiding

COMES NOW, Kirk J, through Counsel, and moves the Court to Strike the document filed by GAL, Mary C, entitled: COUNTER MOTION AND MEMORANDUM FOR ATTORNEY'S FEES AND OTHER SANCTIONS AS A RESULT OF VEXATIOUS LITIGANT AND RESPONSES TO REPLY TO STRIKE DECLARATION OF MARY C; AND AFFIDAVIT OF KIRK J.

Grounds and reasons include that the pleading is not an approved pleading under the rules of Civil Procedure, and is over-length (the caption on the document is too lengthy to reproduce).

Rules of Civil Procedure

Among appropriate pleadings are motions U.R. Civ.P.7(b)(1) which are to be filed with supporting memoranda. Response to a motion and supporting memorandum is to take the form of a memorandum in opposition. Mary C had styled her pleading as a "counter motion" which is not a pleading provide for by the Rules. Where there is a motion, a memorandum in opposition is the proper pleading, not another "motion" in "counter" as a response. Mary C's pleading seems to attempt to oppose Kirk J's Motions by interposing new issues, such as asking for attorney fees and sanctions for "vexatious" litigation.

Over-length

While it is difficult to tell where the "counter-motion" ends and any memorandum begins, let alone the perimeters of any "responses" which were intended to be included in the pleading, it is clear that the body of the pleading is twenty-one pages in length. Memorandum are limited to ten pages. Because the pleading is a conglomeration of so many things, it is impossible to distinguish which portion is purportedly a memorandum and the document is twenty-one pages in length; it should be stricken as over-length.

MAY 9TH, 2015: KIRK J'S MEMORANDUM IN OPPOSITION TO GAL'S MOTION FOR SANCTIONS AND FEES, submitted by Connie C, Commissioner Kase presiding

COMES NOW, Counsel Connie C, and files the foregoing Memorandum in Opposition to Mary C's Motion for Sanctions and Fees which were made as part of her pleading entitled:
COUNTER MOTION AND MEMORANDUM FOR ATTORNEY'S FEES AND OTHER SANCTIONS AS A RESULT OF VEXATIOUS LITIGANT AND RESPONSES TO REPLY TO STRIKE DECLARATION OF MARY C; AND AFFIDAVIT OF KIRK J

(This pleading is provided in the event the Court does not strike this pleading as requested in Kirk J's Motion to Strike filed May 9th, 2015.) Mary C's claim of entitlement for relief under the heading "counter motion on vexatious litigant" cites the Rules of Professionalism and Civility. The segment then cites case regarding the Court's authority to address violations of the Rules, and other standards of professional decorum.

Regarding Commissioner Bloom

Mary C takes up the issue that Kirk J has preponderance regarding Commissioner Bloom's recusal of herself and seems to characterize Kirk J's presentation of the issue as some kind of actionable violation of the Rules. Kirk J's presentation of that issue was offered with citation to Rules applicable to recusal, and an analysis based on the facts of the case. The Rules of Professionalism and Civility do not require a path to forego bringing as issue before the Court, even on topics which might be viewed as "sensitive" such as recusal.

Kirk J is unable to ascertain why his presentation of the issue that Commissioner Bloom recused herself under circumstances of this case would lead to a conclusion that Mary C is entitled to fees or sanctions. Mary C's characterization of Kirk J has alleged "wrongdoing" on the part of Commissioner Bloom is incorrect. Kirk J's pleading merely analyzed the Rule regarding recusal, and in absence of any record of the matter, determined that the recusal must have been for "bias" because there appeared to be no other justification for the recusal. "Bias" is not "wrongdoing" of any kind. It merely suggests a predisposition or affiliation of the variety that all humans, including judges, have. Mary C is at liberty to offer analysis or argument regarding the same Rules, or supply other authority and urge a different interpretation.

However, there is no basis to assert that because Kirk J objected to how the recusal occurred, and further objects to a recused Commissioner signing an Order after recusal, that Kirk J's counsel has been uncivil or unprofessional. Professionalism and civility do not require a litigant to forego properly presented legal issues.

Regarding Mary C

As it related to the recusal issue and Kirk J's assertions with regard to Mary C, the assertions were made properly, directly, professionally, and with appropriate support. It can be established that no proper motion was filed regarding the recusal. There was no hearing. It appears factually that it was the GAL who brought to the attention of Commissioner Bloom that the Commissioner had served as GAL in a case involving Mr. Rhorer in 2002. Mary C does not dispute these issues, she simply characterizes his presentation of the issue as some form of unprofessional attack. Kirk J avers that he is entitled to present the issue. Counsel cannot fathom why she should not be permitted to include in a pleading that by rule, motions are to be in writing, served on the parties, with opportunity to respond. He has adequately presented that that did not occur in this case.

Regarding Mary C's behaviors in aligning herself with Mr. Rhorer, Kirk J fully understands it has raised the ire of the GAL. However, simply because Mary C takes offense is not a reason for Kirk J to be precluded from bringing this very important issue before the Court. Kirk J has not presented the issue lightly, in an unsupported, uncivil or unprofessional manner. Kirk J has provided documentation in the form of affidavits, police reports, and emails, and offers analysis as to how the materials combine to lead to the conclusions asserted. Mary C does not dispute the factual matters Kirk J alleges. Rather, she simply states that her authority to "investigate" and her duty to further the child's "best interest" justify her actions in this case.

In presenting this very important issue to the Court, counsel for Kirk J has been direct and clear, but he has not been offensive or derogatory. Kirk J understands that it is difficult for a GAL to stomach challenges to her objectivity.

What is abundantly clear is that Kirk J feels there are boundaries to the scope of lawful activities of a PGAL. It is equally clear that "best interest" according to Mary C is what she says it is, and her interpretation of that phrase justified any action on her part without further inquiry into any other applicable provisions of law.

Mary C has not responded to the analysis offered by Kirk J. Kirk J provided citation to Utah law which requires her to protect a parent's fundamental and constitutional rights. He has further presented an analysis, supported by police reports and constitutional rights and affidavits which make out a violation of those duties.

He has alleged that Mary C affiliated with Mr. Rhorer's private investigator, and she has admitted the same. Kirk J has alleged, based on the material he presented, that Mary C adopted Mr. Rhorer's position and allegations about "gang activity" which lead her to take Mr. Rhorer's private investigator with her to obtain the assistance of a gang task force officer to go with her to search Kirk J's home.

Mary C has not made out any legal entitlement to attorney fees or sanctions, she has merely indicated she disagrees with his position. She is entitled to disagree with his potion, but Kirk J is entitled to bring his concerns to the Court by way of properly supported and properly drafted Motions, and he has done so. The diametrically opposed views are properly before the Court to decide. That Mary C disagrees, or even is offended by Kirk J's position is not a justification for her to obtain fees or sanctions. She is not "right" because she is GAL. Kirk J is not "wrong" because he is "merely" a party to this action.

WHEREFORE, Kirk J prays Mary C's Motion for Fees and Sanctions be denied.

MAY 9TH, 2015: MOTION FOR HEARING BEFORE DISTRICT JUDGE, submitted by Connie C

COMES NOW, Counsel Connie C, and moves the Court to issue an Order Setting Hearing in front of the District Judge. Grounds and reasons are that Kirk J has moved for an Order Vacating an Order signed by the District Judge due to the fact that it was recommended and signed by Commissioner Bloom who recused herself, and then signed the Order. A hearing to vacate an Order signed by the District Court is not properly to be heard before the Commissioner. Only the District Court should hear such a matter.

WHEREFORE, Counsel prays that the District Court issue its Order setting hearing on the Motion to Vacate and any other matters or issues related to the Order in question, and for such other and further relief as the Court deems appropriate in the premises.

MAY 12TH, 2015: MOTION TO DISQUALIFY ATTORNEY FOR DCFS And MEMORANDUM IN SUPPORT OF MOTION TO DISQUALIFY, submitted by Nancy S, Commissioner Kase presiding

Intervenor, through counsel Nancy S, hereby moves the court for an order disqualifying the Assistant Attorney General representing the Department of Children and Family Services in this matter for reasons of conflict of interest and bias.

PRELIMINARY STATEMENT

The court granted Mr. Rhorer leave to intervene in this matter in order to establish his paternity of the minor child, PR, which minor child has resided with the respondent only since 2012, and pursuant to the orders of the Juvenile Court. On February 20th, 2015, the court granted Intervenor's Motion for DCFS Investigation. The court ordered Intervenor and counsel for Intervenor to report any concerns to DCFS. The Order required DCFS to conduct and complete an investigation within 30 days of the Order and to thereafter appear at the review hearing to report to the court concerning the DCFS investigation. The court also granted Intervenor's Motion to Appoint PGAL.

As set forth in the Amended Recommendation and Order, the court found that given the facts in this case, the court must consider the constitutionality of 78B-15-607 which limits standing to challenge paternity of a child born within a marriage. The court ruled that an evaluation of the factors in 78B-15-608 will be undertaken by a custody evaluator to determine if Intervenor has a constitutional right to proceed. The Order provides that the court will hear reports and advice from the PGAL concerning how the minor child will be introduced to the evaluation process. The Order required DCFS to appear at the hearing to submit its report.

FACTS

1. Mary C was appointed PGAL for the minor child.

2. On February 25, 2015, the Intervenor and his counsel reported and informed the DCFS and gave to them the 30-day requirement for completion of the investigation and the court's order that DCFS be in attendance to report at the review hearing.

3. Intervenor and DCFS proceeded to exchange emails and telephone calls regarding information and the investigation.

4. On April 7, 2015, more than 30 days following the order requiring the DCFS investigation, Assistant Attorney General Ms. Nickel, filed a Notice of Limited Appearance for DCFS to "object to the exercise of jurisdiction over the agency."

5. No other motion has been filed by Ms. Nickel on behalf of DCFS.

6. On April 20, 2015, counsel for Intervenor received a phone call from Ms. Nickel, the contents of which is set forth in the accompanying Affidavit of Nancy S.

7. On April 30, 2015, counsel for Intervenor contacted the DCFS caseworker who had previously corresponded with counsel to inquire about reported matters. Ms. Nickel emailed counsel for Intervenor with instructions to not contact DCFS. Counsel for Intervenor responded asking to whom she should report further concerns to and that Ms. Nickel was incorrect and that she had a duty to report all concerns to DCFS and again asked who I should report to, Ms. Nickel responded via email stating, "All of your concerns have been noted." Copies of these email exchanges are attached.

8. On May 13, 2015, in response to an email from the PGAL requesting the DCFS report, Ms. Nickel responded that she reviewed documents given to DCFS by the Intervenor which included court proceedings and stated, "The court proceedings also included a review of the verified petition in the interest of PR, filed in November 2008, that made allegations of domestic violence against Mr. Rhorer and Kelly H and were later dropped when it was found out that Kelly H was married to Kirk J." A copy of the Minutes, Findings, and Order dated November 7, 2008, pertaining to that matter is attached as Exhibit 3.

9. The 2008 court proceeding referenced in Ms. Nickel's email was never provided to DCFS by Intervenor.

10. Ms. Nickel was the Assistant Attorney General representing DCFS in the 2008 court proceedings referenced by her.

11. Ms. Nickel has not acknowledged nor indicated that she has reviewed the numerous domestic violence charges against Kirk J, Kelly H, Shane S, Jill C, or any other person in Kirk J's home or Kelly H's home while the minor child was involved.

ARGUMENT

The Division of Child and Family services is meant to be an unbiased third party. The actions of the agency's attorney, Ms. Nickel, have shown bias and prejudice toward the Intervenor, Jody Rhorer. Ms. Nickel's limited Appearance is for the purpose of "objecting to the exercise of jurisdiction over the agency" only. She has never filed a motion on behalf of DCFS. However, in her April 20, 2015, telephone call to counsel for Intervenor, Ms. Nickel stated that Jody Rhorer did not have standing in this action and that he was not an Intervenor. Despite counsel's explanation and argument to the contrary, Ms. Nickel continued to argue on behalf of respondent and did not address the issue of her stated interest, i.e. to object to the court's jurisdiction over DCFS. When counsel for Intervenor stated that it was a matter before the court to decide, Ms. Nickel made what could be considered a threat, although the nature of the threat was not illuminated inasmuch as Ms. Nickel suddenly hung up on counsel for Intervenor.

Ms. Nickel acted improperly in arguing the Respondent's case to counsel attempting to influence counsel to dismiss the Intervenor's action. The Court has ordered that DCFS appear at the review hearing and to submit a report regarding their investigation. Ms. Nickel has refused to describe the nature of the report, nor has she confirmed whether DCFS will be at the review hearing. The bias and prejudice of Ms. Nickel in representing DCFS may affect the outcome of the case. She should be replaced with an attorney who does not have predetermined opinions with regard to Intervenor and Intervenor's right to proceed to establish paternity.

Ms. Nickel represented DCFS in the 2008 and 2012 court proceedings in Juvenile Court concerning the minor child. The court proceedings which Ms. Nickel referenced in her email addressed alleged wrongdoing on the part of Intervenor only.

She does not state whether DCFS, her client, has investigated the numerous domestic violence allegations against the other parties and their partners, although Intervenor supplied to DCFS court dockets and police reports evidencing an abundance of domestic violence charges against the other parties to the litigation and other individuals in Kirk J's home and in the presence of the minor child.

Kelly H and Kirk J married in 2003, but kept their marriage secret from Jody Rhorer and the State of Utah. Together, Kirk J and Kelly H have used the marital presumption to allow Kirk J to obtain physical custody of children fathered by other unsuspecting men, including PR, whose biological father is Jody Rhorer. In the 2007 Juvenile Court proceedings neither Kirk J nor Kelly H told the court that they were married or that the minor child, PR, was born during the marriage. Kirk J appeared in court as the father of the two older children, together with Kim J named in the court document as "stepmother" to the two older children, and Kirk J was awarded custody of those children, but he did not claim PR as his own. In those proceedings, PR was place with Jody Rhorer's mother in kinship placement and was eventually returned to Kelly H while she and Jody Rhorer continued their relationship. Jody Rhorer established his paternity of PR in District Court. Afterwards, Kelly H informed DCFS that she and Kirk J were married. That news was delivered to the court by Ms. Nickel.

As the attorney representing DCFS in the Juvenile Court proceedings, Ms. Nickel has information that may be vital to the determination of Intervenor's rights in the present matter. Ms. Nickel has misused her position to selectively disseminate information to her client in order to damage Mr. Rhorer's position in this litigation, and to favor the respondent. Her actions will likely prevent a complete and fair DCFS investigation and report of investigations to the court.

WHEREFORE, the Intervenor respectfully requests the court to disqualify Ms. Nickel as the attorney representing the Division of Child and Family Services and require that another attorney appear on the agency's behalf.

EXHIBIT 2

Emails from Ms. Nickel
 May 13, 2015
Counsel:

I think the court should hear the matters on #4 first, but I do not think that it is a best interest standard that applies. It is a statutory standard that indicates who can challenge a paternity finding.

If #4 is heard first, that may do away with the necessity of hearing anything that pertains to #1, 2, 3, and 5. As to Mary C's inquiry about DCFS: DCFS has investigated the items under the March 5, 2015, order. There are statutory issues about who can get the report, so I will not be disseminating anything in writing, nor will the Division disseminate anything in writing.

I will say that DCFS reviewed a large box of documents delivered to them from Nancy S. Those documents included past police reports, numerous court proceedings and affidavits dating back to the 1990's. The court proceedings also included a review of the verified petition in the interest of PR filed in November, 2007, that made allegations of domestic violence against Mr. Rhorer and Kelly H that were later dropped when it was found out that Kelly H was married to Kirk J. A home visit was done. PR and other children were interviewed. Under the facts of this case, DCFS is precluded from releasing anything, except to the court, and what is released cannot include conclusions drawn. I will indicate that from my review of the agencies' actions, the agency found nothing to dictate a threat to the child's immediate safety or welfare.

Ms. Nickel

April 29, 2015 12:21 PM
Nancy,
As the referent of the case involving the Kelly H/Kirk J I'm letting you know that it has been closed.

Emmy, DCFS

12:38 PM
Emmy,
Thank you for this information. Will you be appearing at the court hearing scheduled for May 11th?
Nancy

4:37 PM
Emmy,
What cases were closed? The case on Kelly H and Shane fighting? Or the case on Kelly smoking weed in front of Payshence? Or the case where Kelly offered alcohol and weed to Jody Rhorer's two youngest daughters? Have all of these been investigated?
Mary C, GAL

11:37 PM
Deone and Jody,
I was in the room when Tina told the GAL that she was offered alcohol and marijuana by Kelly, and that she saw Kelly using marijuana. She didn't mention anything about Kirk, his girlfriend or anyone else at the time. If she is saying that Kirk or his girlfriend, or anyone at Kirk's house offered her drugs and alcohol then that is something I need to talk to her about in your presence or by phone with you on the line. If Tina tells me something that hasn't been told before, then I want to report that to DCFS and the GAL and request an investigation.
We gave a copy of Mona's affidavit to DCFS, but I am going to email the caseworker and the GAL another copy of it tomorrow. Jody, can you talk to your daughters and ask questions about what they have seen or heard at Kirk's home? Ask if they were exposed to drug use, offered drugs or alcohol, or saw other inappropriate behavior or were treated inappropriately and who was involved? Have they seen R.B. with Payshence? Have they seen Payshence being mistreated by anyone? Please do this and let me know asap. If you can arrange a phone call tomorrow, I will make myself available. Please keep in touch with me about things.
Thanks,
Nancy

9:42 PM
Yes, I will. Tina told the GAL that she was offered drugs and alcohol in the presence of Shane, Kirk, and Kelly. If you want her statement, we will get it to you. Also, in the statement Mona's made it states R.B. was at Kirk's drinking liquor and it also describes her neglect.
Jody

April 30, 2015, 9:53 PM
Emmy and Mary,
Was this investigated: I submitted the attached Affidavit of Mona Rhorer to DCFS. In paragraph 12 Mona describes her having seen R.B. multiple times at Kirk J's home with Payshence and other children. He is a registered sex offender and cannot be around children. He is Kelly H's stepbrother. I am attaching the Affidavit, the sex offender registry for R.B., a photo on R.B.'s Facebook page, and a court docket on his sex offense case. I have other documents showing that Kelly was residing with R.B. in 2011 and 2012.
Also, has DCFS investigated the issues addressed by Judge V in 2012: Who were the offenders who forced Payshence to play the "peeking game" she told DCFS about in 2012? "Mike" and "Anthony"? Were they identified? Where charges brought? What happened to Payshence? How did she contract a vaginal infection? Was she treated? Was she provided counseling? I brought this matter to the attention of DCFS. I am attaching another copy of the Order requiring DCFS investigation.
Nancy S

11:24 AM
Nancy,

I have entered my appearance as of April 3. Please do not contact my client.
Ms. Nickel, Attorney for DCFS

11:31 AM
Ms. Nickel,
The court ordered that I report all my concerns to DCFS. To whom should I report my concerns?
Nancy S

11:32 AM
I think you have reported your concerns.
Ms. Nickel

11:42 AM
Ms. Nickel,
Your thoughts are incorrect. I have a right to report my concerns as is set forth in the Recommendation and Order and the Order requiring DCFS Investigation. To whom should I report my concerns without you obstructing the order?
Nancy S

12:52 PM
All of your concerns have been noted.
Ms. Nickel

May 11, 4:09 PM
Hi Jody and Deone,
Connie has filed more pleadings and I have responded. I am attaching them. I am also issuing a Subpoena for DCFS to attend the hearing and submit their report. Ms. Nickel at the AG's office is claiming that the court does not have jurisdiction over DCFS. I have asked her to confirm whether a DCFS representative will be at the hearing and whether DCFS is filing a report. I have not heard back from her. I will keep you updated.
Thanks,
Nancy

May 14, 5:39 PM
Jody and Deone,
I had an extensive conversation with Senator Hillyard this week. He is not willing to propose legislation to amend the Parentage Act. He conferred about your case with the Texas attorney who authored the Parentage Act and was advised against trying to carve out an exception to the law that would allow a biological father to assert paternity when the child is born to a married woman and the child has a presumed father, even under circumstances like yours. He said it would "open a can of worms." This means that you will need to find some other legislator to take up the cause. We can talk about this if you want to give me a call.
Nancy

Our conversations with Nancy had been going in circles for some time. We had met with Senator Hillyard ourselves in January and Nancy was invited to the meeting but did not attend. Hillyard had already told us he wouldn't help us. It seemed that she just kept bouncing in different directions but had no concrete legal plan to get Payshence back. With each motion made by Connie, Nancy would go into a full-on reactionary panic - but just stating the same things over and over again. Jody and I were feeling stretched in every way and exhausted by the constant back and forth bickering between all three attorneys and now the DCFS people too. Mostly though, I still carried feeling in my gut that something was not right. Nancy was forgetting things - things she had submitted to the court; things we had just discussed. The case was taking a toll on her too.

MAY 12TH, 2015: INTERVENOR'S MEMORANDUM OPPOSING RESPONDENT'S MOTION FOR HEARING BEFORE DISTRICT JUDGE AND RESPONDENT'S ORDER SETTING HEARING BEFORE DISTRICT JUDGE (Re: Respondent's Motion to Vacate), submitted by Nancy S, Commissioner Kase presiding

Intervenor, through counsel Nancy S, hereby submits this memorandum opposing the respondent's Motion for Hearing Before District Judge. The respondent's motion requests a hearing on respondent's motion to vacate the Amended Recommendation and Order.

FACTS

1. The respondent's Motion to Vacate Order and supporting memorandum were filed with the court on Saturday April 25, 2015, and Intervenor was served with the same on Monday, April 27, 2015.

2. The respondent's motion did not include a request for hearing.

3. The respondent's memorandum did not include a request for hearing.

4. Respondent didn't request the Motion to Vacate be submitted to the court for decision.

5. When respondent filed the Motion to Vacate, the hearing for the Recommendation and Order of the Honorable Commissioner Bloom was scheduled for May 11, 2015.

6. On May 6, 2015, the hearing was continued at the Petitioner's request. The court asked counsel for dates to re-set the hearing.

7. On May 7, 2015, counsel for Respondent agreed to re-set the hearing before the Honorable Commissioner Kase for May 18, 2015.

8. Respondent filed this Motion for Hearing Before District Judge on Saturday, May 9, 2015, and Intervenor was served with the same on May 11, 2015.

9. Respondent filed an "Order Setting Hearing Before District Judge" with the motion.

10. The Certificate of Service on Respondent's Motion and Order is incomplete as it doesn't contain the service information for all parties.

ARGUMENT I
Respondent's Motion is Contrary to the Best Interest of the Minor Child

The minor child has resided with the responded only since May 2012. The Amended Recommendation and Order provides that the Intervenor may be allowed to proceed to establish paternity of the minor child if the court finds it is in the best interest of the minor child for Intervenor to do so. One of the factors in consideration is the length of time the minor child has resided with the respondent. The respondent's motion is meant as a means to delay the court's findings and extend the time in which the minor child resides with the respondent, all to thwart the court's rulings as they pertain to the Intervenor and the best interest of the minor child.

The Respondent's Motion is Untimely and Does Not Comply with the Utah Rules of Civil Procedure II

Respondent's Motion for Hearing Before District Judge asks that the court rule on respondent's Motion to Vacate, and all other matters related to the Recommendation and Order signed by the Honorable Commissioner Bloom. The Recommendation and Order contains a provision that a review hearing be scheduled, which hearing is now set to be heard before the Honorable Kase on May 18, 2015.

The Respondent has failed to comply with the Utah Rules of Civil Procedure in the following respects:

1. Respondent has not filed the required memorandum with the Motion for Hearing Before District Judge.

Rule 7 (c)(1) states in relevant part: "all motions, except uncontested or ex-parte motions, shall be accompanied by a support memorandum." Respondent has failed to cite points and authorities in support of the motion.

2. Respondent's motion is untimely in that the filing thereof does not afford the Intervenor, or other parties, to respond to the motion in a manner set forth by Rule 7 which states in relevant part:

"Within 14 days after service of the motion and supporting memorandum, a party opposing the motion shall file a memorandum in opposition. Within 7 days after service of the memorandum in opposition, the moving party may file a reply memorandum in opposition."

Respondent filed this Motion only 5 business days prior to the upcoming review hearing before Commissioner Kase. The hearing is premised on the Recommendation and Order which respondent is attempting to vacate.

3. The respondent did not request a hearing on the Motion to Vacate. Neither the respondent's Motion to Vacate, nor the supporting memorandum, includes a request for hearing. A request to submit for decision could have included a request for hearing.

Respondent's Order setting Hearing Before District Judge is improper. Respondent does not cite any Rule whatsoever that allows such an order to be filed.

Respondent's Motion for Hearing Before District Judge is Improper And is Filed in Bad Faith III

The review hearing on the Recommendation and Order was schedule for May 11, 2015, however, on May 6, 2015, the hearing was continued at the petitioner's request. The court gave counsel specific dates and times to re-set the hearing. On May 7, counsel for respondent via email to Intervenor's counsel, agreed to re-set the date for May 18, 2015. Two days later the respondent filed the Motion for Hearing Before District Judge, asking that the court vacate the Recommendation and Order.

This Motion is an example of the bad faith attempts by respondent to delay a final resolution of these proceedings which have been pending before the court for more than one year. Respondent is attempting to undermine the court's prior ruling in this matter. Intervenor should be awarded attorney's fees for having to respond to this Motion, and respondent should be sanctioned for filing this Motion and prior motions which have been excessive, untimely, unnecessary and designed to delay these proceedings and to inflict undue hardship and financial hardship to Intervenor.

WHEREFORE, Intervenor respectfully requests that the Court deny the respondent's Motion for Hearing Before District Judge, for an award of attorneys' fees in favor of the Intervenor and against the respondent, for sanctions against the respondent, and for such other relief as the court deems just and proper.

MAY 12TH, 2015: SUBPOENA TO APPEAR AND TESTIFY AT A HEARING, submitted by Nancy S, Commissioner Kase presiding

TO: *State of Utah*
       Department of Child and Family Services
YOU ARE HEARBY COMMANDED to appear in the Third District Court for the State of Utah at the time, date, and place set forth to testify at a hearing in the above noted case. This Subpoena is being served on a governmental agency and the following describes the matters on which examination is requested: Any and all investigations pursuant to the attached Order Requiring DCFS Investigation dated March 5, 2015.

Under URCP 30, you are required to designate one or more persons who will testify on your behalf. You may set forth, for each person designated, the matters on which the person will testify. Those persons must testify to matters known or reasonably available to the Department of Child and Family Services.

You must also bring with you any and all written reports or investigations prepared by the Department of Child and Family Services pursuant to the Order Requiring DCFS Investigation dated March 5, 2015.

MAY 13TH, 2015: RESPONSE AND COUNTER MOTION TO MOTION TO STRIKE PGAL'S COUNTER MOTION ET CETERA, submitted by Mary C, PGAL, Commissioner Kase presiding

COMES NOW the PGAL, Mary C, and hereby respectfully submits this Response to Motion to Strike PGAL's Counter Motion, as follows:

1. This matter has been assigned to a Commissioner. Rule 101 governs the practice before Commissioners.

2. There are no page limits for pleadings when practicing before a Commissioner that are outlined in Rule 101 nor does Rule 101 reference Rule 7 for such limitations.

3. Rule 101 allows for counter motions. The PGAL's Counter Motion was properly filed pursuant to Rule 101. It is unclear why Respondent filed his Motion to Strike the PGAL's Counter Motion when it's clearly properly filed according to Rule 101.

4. This is one more unnecessary pleading field by Respondent requiring a response. The filing of unnecessary pleadings only wastes time and judicial resources and the PGAL should be awarded her fees for having to respond to Respondent's Motion to Strike the PGAL's Counter Motion and to deter future unnecessary and frivolous filings.

MAY 14TH, 2015: EMAILS from Nancy

Hi Jody and Deone, A lot has been happening on your case this week. I am attaching documents filed by the other parties and documents which I have prepared and filed with the court. I have filed a motion to disqualify Ms. Nickel as the attorney for DCFS with my Affidavit and supporting documents. I have issued three subpoenas for DCFS to appear at the hearing the AG for DCFS has objected to and I have filed a motion to compel their compliance with the Subpoenas. Connie filed a motion for hearing on her motion to stay proceedings and I filed a memorandum opposing the same. Connie filed a Motion to Strike the PGAL's counter motion and Mary C has filed a response and counter motion to Connie's Motion to Strike. Let me know if you have any questions, Nancy

Why is DCFS digging their heels in and refusing to cooperate? Jody said Kelly had struck up a friendship with Ms. I several years back during one of the neglect investigations. She was one of the social workers assigned to the case and her and Kelly became party buddies.

If there was a conflict of interest with Commissioner Bloom, why is there not a conflict of interest with Ms. Nickel who has been part of the case with Kirk J before Payshence even came into the picture? Connie is a juvenile court attorney. Does she and AG Nickel have some sort of relationship outside of the court room? The way she ignores all the evidence against Kirk and Kelly and only addresses the 2008 allegation against Jody for putting Kelly out in the street in her underwear when he found the nine needle marks in her arm leaves one to wonder.

Response from Mary C, 5:35 PM to the Court:

There seems to be an issue as to the topics that will be discussed at the upcoming hearing scheduled on May 19th. Would it be possible to set up a teleconference with Commissioner Kase to get clarification on the topics that will be argued? Thank you, Mary C, PGAL

From Commissioner Kase's Assistant to all parties May 15, 8:57 AM:

Good Morning, It is in the Commissioner's practice to hear the issues that have been properly and timely noticed up for hearing and or issues that have been previously discussed at hearing which then resulted in a recommendation that the matter be set for review.

Commissioner Kase has a full morning and afternoon calendar scheduled for today and tomorrow and thus is unable to entertain a Telephone Conference between now and Monday. Thank you, Judicial Assistant

MAY 14TH, 2015: AFFIDAVIT OF NANCY S IN SUPPORT OF MOTION TO DISQUALIFY ATTORNEY FOR DCFS, submitted by Nancy S, Commissioner Kase presiding

1. On April 20, 2015, I received a telephone call from Ms. Nickel, the Assistant Attorney General representing the Division of Child and Family Services.

2. She told me she wanted to continue the hearing. I told her that I would not agree to continue the hearing.

3. She told me that she was not a party to the litigation and that the Order Requiring DCFS Investigation was not proper.

4. I asked her if she was going to file a motion. She said she would if she "had to" and if I would not agree.

5. I asked what she wanted me to agree to.

6. Ms. Nickel started arguing the respondent's case and told me that she had appeared in the Juvenile Court actions and that Kirk J had been adjudicated the father of the minor child.

7. I explained to her Commissioner Bloom's ruling of February 20, 2015, that the statute can be challenged as unconstitutional since Mr. Rhorer had an established relationship with the minor child, and that it is my client's position that the petitioner raised the issue of paternity in her petition for divorce, and that the respondent could have refused to take the DNA test in the ORS action and could have acknowledged his paternity of the minor child, but he instead denied paternity and took the DNA test to disprove his paternity.

8. AG Nickel laughed at me and told me that I did not understand the law and I did not understand the ORS action.

9. I tried to explain the Commissioner's ruling regarding the appointment of the PGAL and DCFS investigation and the discussion in the ruling about the best interest of the child and the ruling with regard to an evaluation of the factors set forth in U.C.A. 78B-15-608.

10. She told me that she didn't "read it that way," that Mr. Rhorer "doesn't have standing," that he "is not an intervenor," and that I needed to "do something about it."

11. I told her that Mr. Rhorer is still in the position he was the day Judge Stanley granted him the right to intervene. Ms. Nickel continued to argue with me and repeated that Mr. Rhorer did not have standing and that I needed to "do something about it." I told her that I did not work for the court, that it is a matter for the court to decide. She said, "Nancy, you know better than that."
She told me that if I wasn't going to do something about it then she was going to do what she had "to do." She then hung up on me.

12. At some point during the conversation I asked her if she had talked to the private Guardian ad Litem and she told me "no" and that I was the first person she had called.

13. During this telephone call Ms. Nickel became angry and spoke to me in a demeaning manner, telling me that I did not understand the law.

14. During the phone call she did not argue her position regarding any objection to the court's jurisdiction over DCFS other than her statement as set forth in paragraph 3 above.

15. It is my impression that AG Nickel was calling me on behalf of Kirk J and that she was trying to influence me to dismiss my client's action.

MAY 14TH, 2015:   MOTION FOR ORDER TO COMPEL COMPLIANCE WITH SUBPOENA, submitted by Nancy S, Commissioner Kase presiding

The Intervenor by and through counsel hereby moves the court for an order compelling the Division of Child and Family Services to comply with the Subpoena issued in this matter and served upon the Attorney General for the State of Utah, the DCFS, and the Department of Human Services on May 13, 2015, and requiring that the agency designate one or more persons to appear at the hearing scheduled for May 18, 2015, to testify the investigation performed by DCFS pursuant to the Order Requiring DCFS Investigation by the Court and to submit reports of the investigation as ordered by the Court.

Ms. W, as executive director of the Department of Human Services has objected to the Subpoena for the reason that she is not available on the date of the hearing and that she lacks personal knowledge of the information requested. The Subpoena specifically requests the appearance of a person who has knowledge of the investigation. Further, the Order Requiring the DCFS Investigation was attached to the Subpoena which makes clear the subject of and the reason for the Subpoena. If Ms. W is not available and does not have personal knowledge, then another person with knowledge should be ordered to attend the hearing as ordered by the Court.

On March 25, 2015, DCFS was given a copy of the Order Requiring DCFS Investigation and informed about their duty to complete an investigation and their court ordered appearance at the hearing. DCFS has not made any objections to the Order Requiring DCFS Investigation and has had ample time to perform their investigation, prepare the report and prepare to attend the hearing. Ms. Nickel agreed via email for the date of the hearing.

Mr. Rhorer's status at the present is that of Intervenor. Any change in status at a future date which may or may not occur is not grounds for noncompliance with a Subpoena.

WHEREFORE, Intervenor respectfully requests that the Court enter an Order requiring DCFS and its agents to comply with the Subpoena and to attend the hearing scheduled for May 18, 2015, to report regarding their investigation as set forth in the Order Requiring DCFS Investigation and the Amended Recommendation and Order.

MAY 14TH, 2015: OBJECTION TO SUBPOENA TO APPEAR AND TESTIFY AT A HEARING, STATE OF UTAH, DEPARTMENT OF HUMAN SERVICES, submitted by Utah Attorney General's office, Commissioner Kase presiding

The Department of Human Services, by and through its counsel, Assistant Attorney General, herby makes this Objection to Subpoena to Appear and Testify at a Hearing State of Utah, Department of Human Services alleging as follows:

1. *Pursuant to Rule 45 of the Utah Rules of Civil Procedure, the subpoena fails to allow the Executive Director a "reasonable time for compliance." The Executive Director was served on May 12, 2015, to appear May 18, 2015.*

2. *Ms. W is unavailable on May 18, 2015, as she is scheduled to be in Denver, CO, from May 18-21, 2015.*

3. *According to the court clerk's office, this matter is scheduled at 9:00 a.m., along with three other matters. Presumably, it is not scheduled for evidentiary hearing, so Ms. W's requested attendance is suspect. Counsel who issued the Subpoena has not contacted Ms. W or the Office of the Utah Attorney General to indicate the nature of her testimony, or whether testimony is going to be taken at the hearing.*

4. *Although it is unclear what testimony Ms. W would be expected to provide, there is a reference to a DCFS case number on the Subpoena. Also, there are documents attached to the Subpoena that relate to a court-ordered investigation by DCFS, a division of the Department over which Ms. W is the Executive Director.*

5. *Ms. W does not have personal knowledge regarding the DCFS investigation or any of the matters that may purportedly relate to this case. The more appropriate representative from DCFS may be the investigator, caseworker, supervisor, program administrator or regional director who has actual knowledge of related cases or investigations.*

6. *Upon information and belief, it seems that the party issuing the Subpoena, Jody Rhorer, through counsel, is subject to having that party status revoked as a motion to that effect may also be before the Court. If that party status is revoked, the Subpoena may be invalidated.*

WHEREFORE, *the Division respectfully objects to the Subpoena and requests that the Subpoena be quashed as to Ms. W and the Department.*

Through the process I have come to this conclusion - Motions are the way that attorneys communicate with each other. During all this back and forth bickering between the attorneys, the court and commissioners never responded to any of it. It occurred to me when I read the email from Commissioner Kase's assistant that he would only address the motions that were "properly and timely noticed up" that all of these filings were just pontifications amounting to nothing more than an ego contest amongst the attorneys at our expense. I also made notice that on the rare occasions that we did go to court, many of the motions I read were never even discussed or addressed.

I was also very suspicious about the backlash we were getting from DCFS. What were they hiding? Why were they being so belligerent? Clearly there was copious amounts of evidence and past investigations of Kirk, his girlfriend, and Kelly. We had all the police reports to prove it. Why were they refusing to testify in our court hearing? It was a simple request that would not require an extreme amount of time or effort on the part of DCFS if they kept good records.

After all, we had prepared an entire box of evidence and I personally delivered it to Emmy's office. On three occasions we made phone reports to DCFS about the situation going on in Kirk's house and elaborated on the things Mona had told us about the kids breathing into the breathalyzer to start Kirk's vehicle as well as the condition of the house and the numerous violations of the court orders. Nothing. I also sent two emails to DCFS and was also told that they didn't think my concerns merited investigating. So, I ask this? What is their role anyway?

MAY 15TH, 2015: INTERVENOR'S NOTICE OF ELECTION OF CUSTODY EVALUATOR, submitted by Nancy S, Commissioner Kase presiding

Pursuant to this Court's Amended Order and Recommendation entered on April 20, 2015, the Intervenor submits his election of Dr. Natovich, PhD as the custody evaluator to undertake an evaluation of the factors set forth in U.C.A. 78B-15-608 to determine if Intervenor has standing to proceed to establish paternity of the minor child.

Ms. Natovich's fees are billed at the base rate of $4,000 with an additional $600 for each individual involved in the matter. Additional fees may be required. Intervenor requests that the costs be allocated equally among the Petitioner, Respondent, and Intervenor.

MAY 15TH, 2015: KIRK J'S RESPONSE REGARDING IDENTITY OF ANY CUSTODY EVALUATION, submitted by Connie, Commissioner Kase presiding

COMES NOW, Connie, on behalf of Kirk J, and files the forgoing Response Regarding the Identity of any Custody Evaluation. Kirk J has no objection to Dr. Natovich, PhD, per se. However, regarding the contract appended and scope, Kirk J wishes to provide the following excerpted comments from Commissioner Bloom regarding the function of the custody evaluator:

"Mr. Rhorer has requested a custody evaluation. We have several factors under this statute that I find to be appropriate to consider in determining whether Mr. Rhorer has standing to proceed. There are certain factors specifically which I believe an evaluation would support; whether it would be inequitable to disrupt the father/child relationship between Kirk J and the child; is the nature of the relationship between the child and the presumed or declarant father; the harm that may result to the child if presumed or declared paternity is successfully disestablished; the nature of the relationship between the child and any alleged father; other factors."

Accordingly, it is clear that the Commissioner was specifically declining to Order a custody evaluation, but rather, an analysis of the named factors, and how those might bear specifically on a later determination as to whether Mr. Rhorer should be found to have standing. (Therefore, any proposed contract for a custody evaluation would not be applicable to this situation, and presumably the cost for such a limited analysis should naturally be less than a full-blown custody evaluation.)

The Commission continued: "So I am going to recommend at this point that we have an evaluation on those issues. What I've done is reviewed the statute in the UUPA and found factors that seem relevant to the issue given it's in the 600 area where the court is looking at whether Mr. Rhorer even has standing."

Kirk J's only reservation in the selection of the candidate suggested by Mr. Rhorer is that the evaluator be specifically informed that this is **not** to be a custody evaluation or a report on the "relative worth of" Kirk J or Mr. Rhorer. It is to be an analysis of those specific features of the particular statute that the Commissioner felt somehow provided a proxy measure as to whether Mr. Rhorer could make out some "constitutional" argument that he should be given standing.

As it relates to payment, the Commissioner indicated she would address how the evaluator be paid at a later time. Naturally, Kirk J avers it is patently inequitable for him to be forced to pay any amount for Mr. Rhorer's efforts to obtain standing in this case in which the Commissioner has already found Kirk J both presumed and adjudicated father.

MAY 15TH, 2015: EMAIL from Nancy

9:53 AM

Jody and Deone, I have been in a War with Ms. Nickel, counsel for DCFS, for the past two weeks. There have been numerous emails going between and among the attorneys about the investigation and if DCFS will be at the hearing. She wrote in an email to Mary C that the DCFS Investigation did not show any immediate harm to Payshence. IMPORTANT: IS THERE ANYTHING ELSE THAT YOU, OR YOUR DAUGHTERS, OR ANYONE ELSE KNOWS ABOUT KIRK J OR THINGS GOING ON AT HIS HOUSE THAT NEEDS TO BE REPORTED? Ms. Nickel has told me that we can't contact her client, DCFS, directly because she is their attorney. This is contrary to the law and order of the court. If you know ANYTHING that I should report, I want to do that tomorrow. Please let me know one way or the other. They have investigated the information we gave them and the incidents related to the police reports. I need NEW information that has not been reported yet. Deone, you mentioned something about what Jody's daughters told you. Tina called me, but she is a minor and I should not be talking to her. If you have any information that has NOT been reported, please let me know today. For Instance, Jody's daughters told the PGAL about Kelly offering her drugs and alcohol, but was Kirk J involved? Did anything like that happen at his house with him present? What did he say or do? Things like that. Mary C was going to ask for the test at the hearing. But I don't know if her investigation showed enough evidence to warrant asking for a hair follicle test. Thanks, Nancy

12:23 PM

Jody and Deone, Just FYI, I'm forwarding to you these most recent email exchanges between Ms. Nickel and Mary C wherein Mary is trying to get the DCFS report before the hearing. Nancy

MAY 13, 2015 5:15 PM

Ms. Nickel, Because the investigation pertains to my client, I am entitled to any information that involves Payshence. Has a report been prepared regarding DCFS's investigation? If so, I need a copy of this report please. Thank you. Mary C, Attorney at Law

5:26 PM

Mary: While I am very familiar with the GAL's access and obligations in juvenile court where I know you are entitled to the materials, I am not so familiar with the access and obligations of the GAL in district court. I will look into the issues and get back to you. Ms. Nickel

7:40 PM

Ms. Nickel, I do not see that there is a difference in the role of a GAL whether it is in juvenile or district court. That would seem to suggest that any attorney's duties to their client changes depending on the court they are in. This is obviously not true. As Payshence's attorney, I would like to receive a copy of a report today regarding DCFS's investigation. There was an order from the court for DCFS to provide a report and the order has not been modified or changed and we have a review hearing on Monday.

It is imperative that I have as much information as possible to defend my client. I find it odd that I was allowed to work in tandem with DCFS in the questioning of the minor children living in Kirk J's home, but now I am possibly being prevented from obtaining information about such investigations. I am concerned about our past conversation wherein you called me and proceeded to scoff and scorn my investigation claiming Jody doesn't have standing in the case.

Based upon Nancy's recent filing, it appears she had the same conversation with you. I'm troubled that there might be a delay or refusal to provide this because of your position regarding Jody's standing. First, there has been no ruling stating Jody does not have standing. However, this is beside the point, regardless of whether Jody has standing or not, I am entitled to a copy of DCFS's report and to continue my investigation. More importantly, I do not represent Jody, I represent Payshence and am entitled to have access to any investigation pertaining to her. I stand in her shoes. Please help me understand why DCFS would not be required to provide me with the report. If there is no reason I should not have access to the report, I would like one today. I don't believe this is an unreasonable request in light of the fact that there has been a standing order regarding the production of a report from DCFS. Thank you for your prompt attention to this matter. Mary C, Attorney at Law

MAY 16th, 2015

Jody and Deone, I am forwarding this email to you so that you will know my position regarding what should be done at the Monday hearing. This is an email I sent to Mary C two days ago. Since this is the first hearing before Commissioner Kase, it's anyone's guess what he will want to do at the hearing. There have been numerous exhaustive emails between everyone about what should be done at the hearing. Connie filed a Motion for Clarification and Mary wrote the Commissioner's clerk asking for clarification. The answer was not determinative. Nancy

EMAIL forwarded to Mary from Nancy on May 14th:

Mary, Now we know. I'm glad you asked the question. We filed Jody's Financial Declaration with the court shortly after the February 20th hearing. I haven't seen any Financial information filed by Kirk or Kelly.

I've reviewed the Amended Recommendation and Order. It sets forth Commissioner Bloom's finding that because Jody had an established relationship with the child, the court MUST consider the constitutionality of the statute which limits challenge to a child born during the marriage. Also, the court will take input from you as the PGAL as to how Payshence will be introduced to the evaluation. I am revising my approach to the Monday hearing. I will be arguing that the court has ruled that Jody's constitutional right to proceed must be evaluated given the facts in this case and prior case law. And pursuant to the Amended Recommendation and Order the court should proceed as follows:

1. The court should appoint a custody evaluator to undertake the evaluation of the factors in 78B -15-608 to determine if Jody has a constitutional right to proceed;

2. The parties should submit names of custody evaluators to the court (I have spoken with several and Dr. Natovich has agreed to allow me to submit her name);

3. The court should hear your report as the PGAL and will take your input as to how Payshence shall be introduced to the evaluation;

4. The court should hear a report from DCFS as to information about Payshence's welfare since 2012 when she was placed with Kirk J;

5. The court should review financial information submitted by the parties to determine an allocation of fees to you as the PGAL;

6. The court should review the parties' financial information to determine how the costs of the evaluator should be paid.

Paragraph 14: "The court has reviewed the statute under the UUPA and found factors that seem relevant to the issue given the court is looking at whether Mr. Rhorer has standing, and the court will take the input of the Guardian prior to making a ruling on how PR would be introduced to any evaluation and will treat this very carefully." Mary, I apologize for the confusion surrounding these issues. This has been a tough one to deal with for a number of reasons. Nancy

12:12 PM

Mary, If things go sour for Jody, I can request additional briefing and can use the dissenting opinion in Pearson. The RP v. KSW case was published two days before our first hearing in this case in March 2014, when we asked the court to take jurisdiction from the Juvenile Court. I had read the opinion that morning. (Ms. Nickel was at that hearing and when I walked in the courtroom, she showed me the opinion and told me that Jody didn't have a chance.) Afterward I briefed the case and the constitutionality of the statute as it applies to Jody. We then briefed the JPR case that was published while waiting for the Commissioner's ruling.

I have spoken with Senator Hillyard several times, the last time this past week. He discussed Jody's case with the Texas attorney who authored the Uniform Parentage Act and was advised that making any exceptions legislatively to the limitation in 78B-15-607 would "open a can of worms". So, he is not willing to sponsor any reform legislation. However, he again told me that the facts in Jody's case were never contemplated by the legislature. I again asked him for his help. He told me that many attorneys have asked him to testify and he has declined and that he's telling me the same thing: that if I can get a court order saying that the court will listen to him that he would make the trip from Logan to SLC. I wonder if I could get a court order? Nancy

12:27 PM

Jody and Deone, I just included you on emails between Mary C and myself. I have spent 22 hours this past week working on your case. So far today I have spent 4 hours working on your case. Yesterday I filed a Request for Hearing on our Motion to Compel Compliance with the Subpoena. I also filed our Notification of Election for Custody Evaluation. Connie filed her response. I'm attaching those. Nancy

MAY 18TH, 2015: MINUTES FOR REVIEW AND MOTION, Commissioner Kase presiding

The parties discussed the issues to be addressed at the hearing. The Commissioner continues the hearing to May 27, 2015, at 2:00 p.m. for reasons as stated on the record. **All parties are to bring their income verification to the hearing.** The Motion to Vacate the prior order is to be heard first, then the Motion to Vacate/Replace the GAL, then the Motion to Cease Publication and then the review of the order will be addressed.

The State and DCFS counsel present today who explained the restraints on pro-action of documents as stated on the record. The Commissioner finds that the state has complied with the court's order and is not required to attend any further hearing.

MAY 20TH, 2015: EMAILS from Nancy

2:32 PM

Hi Jody and Deone, I received a call today from a DCFS worker about our Subpoena. I talked to her about a records request under the GRAMA laws. She told me that the records can only be given to a perpetrator and that the PGAL is not even entitled to them. This is due to a change in the law that limits access to DCFS records. I told her about the 2012 Juvenile Court proceedings and the "peeking game" described by Payshence. She looked that up and told me said that the report was deemed "unsupported" because they could not locate the alleged perpetrators. At least that answers what became of those allegations. We could file a motion with the court asking for an order that the DCFS records be reviewed "in camera" which means only the Commissioner would be able to look at the records; but all the many reports regarding Kirk, his girlfriend, etc. were deemed "unsupported." It may show a pattern of reports, but I don't know if it will help our case. Nancy

6:48 PM
I'll call you tomorrow and I'm going to send you a payment. Deone

8:18 PM
The hearing is on the 27th at 2:00 p.m. William H is an attorney in SLC who has filed a lawsuit in Federal Court representing unmarried biological fathers against the State of Utah. I think you both should make an appointment to see him and ask if Jody can join the lawsuit as a plaintiff. I've emailed him about your case and have placed several calls to him. He returned my call but I was in court. I placed another call to him today. Also, Connie alleged that John was doing surveillance of Kirk J's home and attached a police report to her motion. I believe Jills affidavit includes a statement that the person she saw doing surveillance was John. That was not a part of his investigation. It was not him or anyone associated with him. The only way to clear that up is to have him testify.

The Court will hear Connie's motion to cease publication of Jody's Youtube video. In my response I said that Kelly, Jill and/or Kirk publish on Facebook photos identifying Payshence and at the same time identify Jody by name.

Will you please go through the Facebook pages, including anyone close to them, and download and send to me anything you see where Payshence is mentioned or shown and the page also mentions Jody or the court action? Please email them to me as soon as possible. This will save me time so that I don't have to do this. Jody, you mentioned you wanted to listen to this again, so I am forwarding you the Juvenile Court audio recording in which Judge V was told about Payshence having a fungal infection while at the Christmas Box house. A woman in the courtroom started crying. It's hard to hear, but I think she told the Judge that "Anthony" is a friend of the sex offender (R.B.). Do you recognize the voice of the woman? Who is Anthony? Nancy

JOURNAL ENTRY:

Another trip to Nancy's office. She called an urgent meeting again. We took off from work with anticipation that she would have some news to reveal that was best done in person. We sat across from her as she rested her hands on her desk, her fingers interlocked. "So, what's up guys?" she said as she glanced down at my purse sitting on the floor by my chair.

So that's what this meeting is about. Why doesn't she send us a monthly bill like most attorneys? I have asked and asked that she discusses her strategies and plans of action with us before she banks so many hours - especially since so much of what she has put on herself has been redundant. We truly appreciate the passion she has for our case, but it has been ineffective and so many mistakes have been made that have cost us precious time and our resources.

Nancy stressed that we needed a "smoking gun" to incriminate Kirk. She asked again about Facebook postings - which I had already sent to her twice. She then brought up finances with Jody.

"I can't keep doing all this. I have to pay my staff and keep the lights on."

"I'm doing all I can, Nancy. I've been sending you money every month. I just sent money last week." Jody said.

Nancy's eyes darted toward me. "Well maybe it's time for your family to help you out."

This enraged Jody. "This isn't my wife's fight. This was my issue before I married her. I don't expect my wife to pay my bills."

Nancy shot back. "This is all of our fight, Jody! We are all in this so you need to figure this out or I can't be your attorney anymore."

The truth is, I tried to help financially as much as I could. It is my fight too because it is the only thing that stands in the way of my husband's complete and total happiness. I opened my pocketbook and wrote Nancy a check.

MAY 20TH, 2015:   RESPONSE TO INTERVENOR'S MOTION TO DISQUALIFY ATTORNEY FOR DCFS, submitted by Assistant AG Ms. Nickel, commissioner Kase presiding

Comes now, State of Utah, Division of Child and Family Services through its counsel, Assistant Attorney General, and hereby submits this Response in Opposition to Intervenor Jody Rhorer's Motion to Disqualify Attorney of DCFS filed May 14, 2015.

The State opposes the motion and respectfully requests the Honorable Court to deny said Motion.

PRELIMINARY STATEMENT

Assistant Attorney General entered a special limited appearance as counsel to the DCFS on April 3, 2015. Intervenor became aware of Ms. Nickel's involvement in the case or before April 3, 2015, where she filed a Notice of Limited Appearance. On April 3, 2015, she contacted counsel for the Intervenor and asked the Intervenor to cease communications with DCFS. Both Intervenor and his counsel had been in contact with DCFS beginning February 25, 2015, and had multiple contacts until Ms. Nickel requested the communication end.

LEGAL ARGUMENT

1. Intervenor has failed to provide any authority to support this argument.

Intervenor's motion makes numerous allegations and assertions against Ms. Nickel without any authoritative support. Under the Utah Rules of Civil Procedure, motions must include "grounds for the relief sought." There is not a single authoritative citation in Intervenor's motion.

11. Assistant Attorney General is statutorily responsible for representing the Division of Child and Family Services for this case.

Ms. Nickel acted within the scope of her statutory responsibility in representing DCFS in this case. Pursuant to Section 62A-41-113 of the Utah Code, the Attorney General's Office is statutorily responsible for enforcing the provisions of the Child and Family Services Act, which mandates the Attorney General represent DCFS "in all Court and administrate proceedings related to abuse, neglect, and dependency including shelter hearings, dispositional hearings, dispositional and periodic review hearings, and petitions for termination of parental rights." The AG's Office must be available to and advise DCFS caseworkers on an ongoing basis.

111. AG Nickel appropriately established herself as liaison between her client and opposing counsel.

Ms. Nickel's role in this case is advocate for DCFS; her actions have been and will continue to be within her statutory responsibility and authority. Intervenor's memorandum states that "Intervenor and his counsel" had contact with DCFS from February 25, 2015, until she noted her involvement with the case on April 3, 2015. Intervenor suggests that AG requested Intervenor's counsel stop contacting DCFS, AG Nickel was "attempting to thwart" Intervenor's compliance with a Court ordered investigation.

This is a mischaracterization of her legal obligations as counsel for DCFS. Utah Rules mandate when "representing a client, a lawyer shall not communicate about the subject of the representation with a person the lawyer knows to be represented by another lawyer in the matter, unless the lawyer has the consent of the other lawyer." Any continued unauthorized communication among Intervenor or his counsel and DCFS would violate Rule 4.2.

IV. Intervenor's Concerns Regarding DCFS are Moot Based on the May 18, 2015, Court Order.

Intervenor's concerns regarding DCFS compliance with the Court Ordered report and Ms. Nickel's potential bias are now moot pursuant to the May 18, 2015, Court Order which found DCFS "fully satisfied" the March 3, 2015, Order.

CONCLUSION

In conclusion, the State urges the Court to deny Intervenor's Motion to Disqualify Attorney for DCFS. Intervenor does not support his argument with authority. Ms. Nickel acts within her statutory authority and responsibility in representing DCFS. Therefore, the State respectfully requests that Intervenor's Motion to Disqualify Attorney for DCFS be denied.

MAY 21ST, 2015: ORDER submitted by Utah AG's Office, Commissioner Kase

This matter came on for hearing on May 18, 2015. The parties and persons present were: Kelly H, Petitioner; Kirk J, Respondent; Connie, Attorney for Respondent; Jody Rhorer, Intervenor; Nancy S, Attorney for Intervenor; Mary C, PGAL; Ms. Nickel, Assistant Attorney General for the Division of Child and Family Services; Assistant Attorney General for the Department of Human Services.

The Department appeared pursuant to a Subpoena to Appear and Testify at a Hearing State of Utah, Department of Human Services issued by counsel Nancy S on behalf of Intervenor, Jody Rhorer. The Department, through its counsel, filed an Objection to Subpoena to Appear and Testify at a Hearing State of Utah, Department of Human Services. Nancy S also filed a Motion to Order to Compel Compliance with Subpoena, directed at the DHS.

Ms. Nickel appeared on behalf of the Director of the Division, who received a Subpoena to Appear and Testify at a hearing served on the Office of the Attorney General issued by counsel Nancy S on behalf of Intervenor, Jody Rhorer.

The Court heard from Ms. Nickel regarding the three subpoenas received by the State. The Court explained that this hearing is not for the taking of evidence and that no appearance or testimony are expected from the Department, the Division, the Office of the Attorney General or their representatives. The appearances today of counsel for the State entities satisfies any legal requirement that may exist pursuant to the subpoenas.

The Court heard from Ms. Nickel regarding the March 3, 2015, Order for the Division to conduct an investigation and provide a report to the Court. The Court, having heard from the parties and receiving no objections, hereby makes the following Order:

ORDER

1. The Subpoenas received by the Department of Human Services and the Division of Child and Family Services are satisfied and no further appearances are required.

2. The March 3, 2015, Order for DCFS to report to the court has been fully satisfied.

3. A records request must be made by any parties for the DCGS report. The Court can hear further facts and arguments from the parties with respect to any request, upon proper pleading, notice and scheduling of a hearing at that time. The Court is not ordering the Division to share its report at this time.

4. Intervenor's Motion for Order to Compel Compliance with Subpoena is denied.

The May 18th hearing was the only one I was not able to attend. My sister, Jennifer, went for me and took these notes:

Two astute and brittle women came to represent DCFS and the AG's office. There was a lot of back and forth between Jody's attorney and the Judge and the two women. The Judge overlooked Commissioner Bloom's order to have DCFS conduct an investigation. The AG said there was a report but that she didn't have to turn it over to anyone. She said there were no findings of abuse or neglect. The GAL said she had a right to the report but the AG shot back that she didn't have to give it to her. The Judge recommended the AG's office get on the same page with the GAL. He seems to want everyone to work it out without him becoming too involved. He said he didn't have enough information but that the State doesn't have to come to the next hearing.

Kelly H was still unemployed and didn't have her financial declaration completed. She stated she was not seeking custody of Payshence but she didn't want Jody to have custody of her daughter. Connie argued that her client shouldn't have to pay anything to the GAL. Kirk has not filed his financial declaration because he is also unemployed. Nancy confirmed Jody had filed his financial declaration.

Commissioner Kase reiterated that he had spoken personally to Commissioner Bloom and she ensured him that there was no conflict of interest that caused her to recuse herself - she just felt it was best to not cause a reason for a future appeal.

MAY 22ND, 2015: EMAILS from Nancy S to William H

2:45 PM

Will, It was a pleasure speaking with you today. I am forwarding to you my previous email. My client has authorized me to provide you the attached Order on his case. It was drafted verbatim from the hearing transcripts. The next hearing is before Commissioner Kase next week. Commissioner Bloom recused herself when it became known that she had been the GAL on my client's prior case years ago when he was awarded custody of his three older daughters. Please let me know if you want further information. I am certain that the constitutionality issues need further briefing. I appreciate your help. Thanks, Nancy

MAY 23RD, 12:03 PM
Thanks. Got it. Looking through it now. Best regards, William

MAY 22ND, 2015: EMAILS from Nancy

Jody and Deone, Following up on my previous email to you. I spoke with attorney William H today. I went over the facts of your case with him, but did not disclose your identity. I explained the court's ruling that the constitutionality of the statute may be challenged in Jody's case because we proved his established relationship to Payshence. William is interested in your case. He has an extensive background in paternity law and representing unmarried biological fathers, and said he has never heard of a case similar to yours. He has vast knowledge in the constitutional aspect of paternity law. We need his help on this issue. I should be hearing from him in the next couple of days and will keep you posted. Nancy

May 23, 8:44 AM
Hi Jody and Deone,

Mary C has subpoenaed two witnesses associated with the PGAL program to be at the hearing next week, including the Director of the GAL program. Mary wrote me the following: "It's my understating from the GAL office that I didn't do anything wrong and they intend on being present at the hearing to support me. They have continuously informed me that I will stay on the PGAL roster and that they don't find anything wrong with my investigation. They're actually frustrated with Connie and don't like her tactics. I don't think Commissioner Kase was pleased with her either."

It was clear to me from the hearing that Commissioner Kase was not pleased with Connie. I think this reassignment of your case to Commissioner Kase may be a good thing. John has agreed to be at the hearing at no cost to you, which is very generous on his part. I will proffer his testimony at the hearing if necessary. I am meeting with him Tuesday at noon.

Nancy

MAY 27TH, 2015: COURT HEARING TRANSCRIPT

THE COURT: All right. We have the matter of Kelly H vs. Kirk J and Jody Rhorer as an intervenor. I think we discussed the order of the motions to be heard, to start with the motion to vacate the previous order. Is that right?

CONNIE: Yes. If you have any questions, I'd be happy to answer them, but I think that it's fully briefed the way I see it. My take on it is that is he's looking at the face of the rules and the - the Rule 63 and then the Rule of Judicial Administration, there doesn't really seem to be a provision for self-recusal for no reason, and because there wasn't a motion and there's just the minute entry, it basically says because the commissioner previously served as GAL. That kind of speaks to an association. It doesn't readily say much more than that. The rule envisions that even - you know, that people don't live in a vacuum, that there are associations, and that there's even a procedure to ask for waivers of any potential conflict. That didn't happen. So, I'm trying to get a ruling from you, which you're not the one that recused yourself, as to --

THE COURT: I can only infer from the record what the reasoning was. I'm not going to ask her to tell me privately what - but my inference is - and I - because I've been working with Commissioner Bloom since she's been on the bench - anytime anything associated with her involvement as the GAL comes up where she - there's any concern at all that she might have some private reason to favor one party or other or might have some impressions of the parties - I mean she wouldn't have remembered this because she wouldn't have gotten this far into in without recusing herself, but she probably sometimes wishes she wouldn't - but a hard and fast rule that anytime she was involved with the parties or a case as a GAL, to avoid any appearance of impropriety, she just automatically recuses herself. As I understand the rule and the statute, if a commissioner decides that she isn't comfortable continuing to hear the case because of a past association or current familiarity with the parties. I mean if she recuses herself from a case in which one of the lawyers has a child that attends the same school she does - we fortunately in Salt Lake have the luxury of being able to be extremely rigid about that. If whoever the judge is in Richfield sees somebody in the grocery store every time they go to the store they can't very well recuse themselves because there's nobody else to hear the cases. As far as I can tell, this is no different than any other case that she's ever recused herself on in which she's simply become aware of a past association. So as far as signing the order, I think that is a ministerial act. I think she had already made the decision substantively before she became aware of the - did you notify her that she had been the Guardian before, Mary? Is that how that came about?

MARY C: Yeah. So, when I met with Jody, he had mentioned that the commissioner had been the former GAL in his previous case regarding his other children. At that point bells went off, and so I didn't want to cause any issue, and I just felt like it would be better if we all got on the phone, so I called the court clerk –
and when Connie actually filed her motion regarding what had occurred, I immediately sent her an email explaining what had happened, and that was that I called the clerk to just advise that there was a possible conflict but I wanted to see if we could get everybody on the phone to see if we could stipulate to keeping Commissioner Bloom on the case, but I guess Commissioner Bloom had a full day of cases and I think she was going out of town the next day or something.

THE COURT: I think this would have been waivable, if it's a conflict at all. I mean I think if she had simply made a record that although she was a Guardian in a prior case, she wouldn't have any recollection of the parties or anything, and therefore it wouldn't influence her judgement. I'm sort of tipping my hand a little bit, but is there anything more that you have to say about this?

CONNIE: Just to say that that really is the conundrum in that you're talking about the Commission's - what you know to be her practices across various cases, just from dealing with her cases, and I'm dealing with one case and trying to make a record and to decide what happened. I think your presumptions about what the commissioner thought and whether she remembers or anything like that, that's reasonable, but you are forced to make the assumptions because there isn't a record.

THE COURT: But even if she - I mean if that were the case, she clearly would have had to recuse herself, but if the reverse is true, I think that again we're very cautious about avoiding the appearance of impropriety in terms of being involved in cases where we may have some reason to favor one party or the other, even if we don't actually. I read the order.
I can't see anything - there's one thing that I might have done differently, but frankly, it would have probably favored the other side even more in one analytical point only, but I think that that order was based on written record and her understanding of the law and I don't know that I could have come up with a different conclusion, because she's not really resolving factual disputes, and she's simply attempting to recognize that there's some case law there that opens the door for a person in Mr. Rhorer's position to at least seek to establish legal parentage. So, my recommendation on that is going to be that the motion to vacate the previous order be denied. I think we need to go forward with the orders -- the motions as they are now before us. If you'd like to proceed, I think your next one is to replace the GAL. I know we have other guardians here, so it would probably be a good idea if we can get that issue addressed.

CONNIE: Okay. You asked me when we were here previously to proffer, and as if I could I'll tell you the information from the persons that would testify if we were going to have testimony. Kirk J, his girlfriend, Kelly H, Sargent Bell of the Unified PD, Detective Ski, John B, private investigator, director of the GAL's office, Mr. Newt of the GAL's office, and Mary C. So, some of this is background. I will try to make it as concise as possible, your Honor, but I appreciate the Court's indulgence on this, since it a fairly kind of protracted tale.

Connie then proceeded to explain in detail every component of Mary C's expedition to Kirk J's home previously mentioned in her complaints filed with the court. About twenty minutes into the accounting of events a cell phone rang.

CONNIE: Sorry. My client's hearing impaired. I guess he left his phone on.

KIRK J: Sorry.

THE COURT: Is that ring tone like a foghorn or something?

CONNIE: Sounds like it. Yeah. But that's my concern about it. I think it was a series of really unfortunate decisions, but what I think it leads me to is how can I encourage my client to cooperate with Mary C specifically after these things had occurred. I think she's required by obligation to have an objective and open investigation, and she certainly isn't authorized to, you know, mislead and not authorized to interview a represented party or have someone do that on her behalf.

THE COURT: You had not given her permission to interview your client during the course of this?

CONNIE: No. You know, I don't know what I would have done had I been asked if that - I mean I've been told there's this concern, you know, would you mind me - I - you know, I wasn't asked, and that's kind of wherein lies the problem, because I really - I really honestly believe that Mary C's heart was in the right place. I think she was - felt like she was doing the right thing for her client, and I don't detract from her ability to do that.

I'm just looking at a client who I can't in good conscious ask him wholeheartedly embrace the notion of cooperating with - and I think he needs to be able to. He needs to be able to for her to be able to function, and frankly, sadly, I - I - when I'm told, you know, I did something other than what I told you I was going to do I don't feel like I have a responsibility to be forthright with you. I, as a practitioner, don't feel like that I can - that I can cooperate and - you know, in my role as advocate for him. So, I just think the whole thing is a sad state of affairs. Like I said, I think it was a series of judgements that - I know Unified wishes that they - I spoke to Sergeant Bell today, and he told me it never would have went down that way if he had, you know, looked into it further. You know, I don't want this to turn into something where then it is an undercurrent of something where we can't - that we can't cooperate, because that's not my client and that's not what I want to do.

THE COURT: I think I understand your point of view. I'm not sure who I need to hear from next. I don't know if Nancy wants to comment first and then Mary, and then it's unclear to me.

NANCY S: Yes, your Honor. I would like to shed some light on John B's involvement in this. Jody told me at the beginning of this case that during his relationship with Kelly H, he became aware of possible gang associations involving the parties, and I had a duty to investigate that. I can't just make those allegations. I have a duty to perform a due diligence investigation. In doing so, we employed the services of John B. He is a former FBI agent and has worked with the Metro Gang Unit. He was the agent in charge of an investigation that led to the first RICO prosecution of violent street gangs here in Utah in federal court, so he is an expert in this matter.

We asked him to do an investigation independently and give us his opinion. John B is here today and he can tell you that he looked at the social media accounts of the parties and some of their associations and he looked at the criminal records of the parties, and they do have vast criminal records, including felonies. He saw gang signs being flashed by people on Facebook pages or signs by individuals associated with the parties, including Kirk J, who wanted to be identified, perhaps, as part of gangs, and this concerned him.

He has told us that Kelly H's husband was at one time associated with a gang, and that he included that in his report to us. When Mary C, as PTAL asked us for our concerns, we told her of our concerns in that regard. Mary C's investigation was not a part of our investigation. Ours had been completed at that time. John B also saw Facebook pages with children shooting guns, and Kirk being a convicted felon would not necessarily be able to have guns, and that was a concern as well. Again, we gave these concerns to Mary and she followed through with the investigation. It was not a part of our report. We never received a report from Mary or from the police officer who accompanied her. In fact, if the police report had not been attached to a memorandum filed by the respondent, we wouldn't have known that he stated that he -- at one point he had been associated with a gang.

Also, the officer being Polynesian, I think that is not - I would object to that. I don't think there's any reason to be afraid of another person based on the color of their skin or their ethnicity or their race, and that's - I'd like to go on record as saying that, your Honor. Mary C did what she needed to do in order to be safe and in order to look for things, but John did not ask anybody to look for gang signs anything related to gangs.

I would like to say that Mr. Rhorer has paid the GAL a total of $2,000 today, and granting this motion to remove her would be prejudicial to Mr. Rhorer. It would delay the proceedings unnecessarily, and certainly it is not in the best interests of the child, or in the best interests of the judicial economy.

I would just like to emphasize - oh, also the report attached to I think Kirk's girlfriend's affidavit of an investigation in 2014, John does not know that individual -- he doesn't know anything about him. John's investigation was completed many months before our meeting with Mary and giving her our concerns as she asked for. Thank you.

THE COURT: Thank you. Did you want to say something Kelly?

KELLY H: Yes, I do. Just when it comes to the private investigator that Mr. Rhorer paid for, which my kids called me several times upset, crying. They went to his car taking pictures of him, waving to him, and the way they came of knowing of this individual is because he knocked on neighbor's doors asking questions, and that's how my kids became aware of him. I feel 100 percent that the private investigator obviously is paid individually or for Mr. Rhorer's - for his benefit, which that's where the Guardian ad Litem comes in and where they all work together. The gang affiliation, I feel that you should know that of course anything that Mr. Rhorer can use or say, whether it's false or true, which he knows there's no gang affiliation, never has been between me, my ex-husband Kirk, nor Mr. Rhorer. He's going to say things or anything he can to try to use that in his benefits.

Also, the - Kirk is a fe - an ex-felon or a felon, so the pictures of me and my children where there's things that you can teach your kids to shoot guns, he was never there, and also that my husband - current husband, Shane, has never been nor is he a known gang member. Mostly just like I said, the personal - the private investigator, of course they're going to pay high amounts of money to try to do what they can to try take my daughter from where she is very well cared for and where she's been for the last six-and-a-half years. That's just really all I have to say right now.

NANCY S: Your Honor, I'm sorry, may I - I have something I forgot to tell the Court. John never told anybody that he was working for DCFS or that he was an FBI agent. He was a former FBI agent, but I believe he identified himself only as in investigator.

THE COURT: I think that's what Connie also indicated when he called there.

CONNIE: Exactly.

MARY C: I think first and foremost, I have to point out that Connie has not cited any rule that I have violated. She's just made arguments that maybe they didn't like the way the investigation went down, but she hasn't cited any specific rule that I have violated, and I think that's profound and very important. It appears that she's also changed her tone quite possibly from the pleadings. They seemed fairly accusatory in the pleadings, and now I believe that may be because she's actually talked to the Office of the GAL. The case of Schoolcraft says, "When a child needs a Guardian, he needs an advocate, someone who will plead his cause as forcefully as the attorneys for each competing custody claimant pleads theirs. The basic premise of the adversary system is that the best decision will be reached if each interested person has his case presented by Counsel of unquestionably undivided loyalty. No person is more interested in a child custody dispute than the child and representation should be set accordingly."

I am not neutral. I represent the child, and I am an adversary to Jody, Kelly, and Kirk. I do not represent them, and I conducted my investigation as such. I don't know too many opposing Counsel that would actually share and divulge to the opposing party their strategies or their technique or their efforts. That's just not the way that the adversarial system works. They were informed that I would be there. I intentionally didn't give them the details of how that would occur - and I don't know about this forgetting or not telling them. That is just inaccurate. I sent a letter to Connie when I first was assigned to the case, this is what I do with all of my PGAL cases. I send a letter to opposing Counsel letting them know that I have been appointed and that I need information, and that I'm going to need to be able to interview their client. I did interview Kirk and his live-in girlfriend with my client and some of the children that live in the home at DCFS with one of the DCFS caseworkers because we didn't feel like it would be very beneficial to have two interviews of the children and having them reiterate twice. So, we kind of did it in conjunction. At that time, I spoke with Kirk, and Connie was - should have been aware of that. If she wasn't - but I also sent her an email informing her that I would be going to the house. Surely, she would realize that I'm not going to just not say anything to her client, that there'll be some discussion at that time.

I am charged to be objective, but that doesn't mean I don't look at all the negative and all the positive facts. To suggest that I'm biased in pleadings without one shred of evidence besides blanket allegations is unprofessional, uncivil and unethical, and puts a foul tone into the proceedings of this case when the Court should be focused on the best interest of the child, not my investigation.

In Schoolcraft it states the GAL has "a duty to investigate the case and present to the Court what those best interests might be. It is the GAL's duty to stand in the shoes of the child and to weigh the factors as the child would weigh them if his judgment were mature as though he was not of tender years." I am appointed to represent the best interest of the minor and to conduct or supervise an ongoing, independent investigation in order to obtain firsthand understanding of the situation and needs of the minor. There is nothing that says what constitutes what an independent investigation entails. I was to look at the allegations of abuse and neglect, challenge to parentage between presumed adjudicated father and the alleged biological father, and significant division of family services involvements.

My assistant contacted Kirk on numerous occasions and informed him that I would like to speak with some of the children and also do a walkthrough of the home. I also sent an email on March 30th, telling Connie that I would be doing the walkthrough. I believe Kirk's credibility is at issue when he claims in paragraph 8 of his declaration that, quote, "at no time was I told the GAL intended to search the home." I told him numerous times that I was going to be going through the home. In this case an extensive home investigation was necessary, especially when my client is only 7-years-old, and there have been serious allegations of criminal actively. I did my investigation based on allegations of violence, drugs, abuse of alcohol, prior criminal convictions, criminal and gang affiliations, and weapons. It wasn't just few things. There was a stack of police reports and things. The juveniles in the home have some records as well.

I specifically did not take John on my investigation because he did work for Jody, and I made that very clear to him, but because he knew of my concerns about my safety, he helped me facilitate that. I didn't realize that Kirk already knew about John. So that was - to suggest that I'm hiding something or not divulging that, it was simply because I thought that there was some attorney work product that was privileged, and I didn't feel like I could breach that.

THE COURT: What - you mean - so John has been retained by Mr. Rhorer, and their communications and his work would be work product, but why are you bound by that if you're an adversary?

MARY C: Well, I didn't know if -

THE COURT: But I mean if you're an adversary, you just went to great lengths to point out that you don't -

MARY C: Sure, but I wasn't - I wasn't sure, but if - I didn't know that they had known that, and I didn't feel like I needed that - I was a - I was a -

THE COURT: It's a fine point, but I'm not sure why you would be bound by any kind of privilege they gave you - information, then it seems to me it's information that's been disclosed to somebody outside of the attorney's office and employees.

MARY C: But needless to say, if the Court was going to require me to disclose that, I would have. I would need to base my opinions and recommendations somehow, and I would probably have to disclose it at that point, but I wasn't trying to hide anything. Okay? Connie seems to suggest that I didn't take Officer Ski with me because there weren't any safety concerns because he went out to get a flashlight. We had been there for quite some time and there wasn't any issues at that point when he did go out there.

THE COURT: By that point you were comfortable enough being alone in the house?

MARY C: Yeah. Yeah. Upon my arrival I did introduce the officer and told Kirk and his girlfriend what I wanted to do, and they did give their consent. I didn't hide the fact that it was an officer. He's not much larger than Kirk. I don't know why he's saying that he's this huge officer. I think the primary thing here is that consent was given, and they didn't tell me to stop. In past communications with Kirk, he's often questioned why I needed to know certain information. I was on the phone with him one time and I was asking him about the parentage of several of the kids in the home. There are six kids in the home with different parents, different biological parents, different legal parents of both mothers and fathers. It's kind of confusing. So, he - he kind of pushed back and questioned me and got a little bit aggressive because he wanted to understand why I needed to know that.

After visiting the home I'm not concerned with the physical home environment surrounding my client. Had I not been able to perform that extensive investigation, I don't think I could say that honestly to this court. She's a happy, sweet, beautiful, darling little girl. The kids were bouncing off the walls, as kids do. They were running around. I talked with Kirk's girlfriend and my client's little sister about Easter. None of the children were crying.

When I was interviewing my little 7-year-old client at DCFS she said that she had seen her mother smoking weed. It's disconcerting that a 7-year-old knows what the word weed is. Just recently Kelly was arrested for assault, and it seems to be a pattern of some violent and aggressive behavior, and so of course it was worth doing that to see the true nature of the environment at this home.

For how many kids are living in that home, one of my concerns is that there's six children living in the home, and it was well kept for how small the home was. The one thing that I'm concerned about is there's six children, all of which have different legal fathers, different biological fathers, different legal and biological mothers, and it's extremely confusing.

Your Honor, the whole thing with Commissioner Bloom, trying to get that taken - you know, starting from scratch and then with the defamatory accusations against me in the pleadings. Frankly, I believe it's just become a witch hunt with all efforts aimed at trying to divert attention away from the facts, and laser beam focus on placing officers of the court and opposing Counsel in a false light, all of which are irrelevant to the to the best interests of my clients, and it's just simply wasting time. In fact, I think your Honor had stated at the last hearing that - and it was directed at Connie, and I quote, "This is an incredibly aggressive and litigious position you and your client are taking in this case."

We're wasting time. My client is being prejudiced every day that we don't get this resolved, because she - we can't give her back this lost time. We can't. It's imperative we get the constitutional issue addressed and out of the way and stop messing around with this witch hunt.

As I said, I'm an adversary. It doesn't matter whether Kirk and Jody or Kelly like me. I have done extensive research in this case and it's cost a lot of money. There's one thing that I wanted to say regarding the backpack, because the other children do have a little juvenile history -- it had some gang marks on it. It was tagged like -

THE COURT: Like you'd see taggers do on an overpass? Hmm.

MARY C: I'm concerned about those children being in the home with my client. At the last hearing Kelly got up and was a little bit upset and said that her daughter had called her crying. The person Connie said called crying was the oldest daughter, who is not legally or biologically Kelly's daughter. So there seems to be some serious confusion as to who's mom, who's dad. Even after this, my assistant contacted Kelly several times because we were still trying to set a time to meet with her, and Kelly had been evicted and was trying to find a new place.

Your Honor, my client is in this situation through no fault of her own. She's the product of these parties, and unfortunately, she's kind of been caught in the middle, and I don't believe her rights are being considered. A custody evaluator needs to be secured here. We need to work closely with the custody evaluator to secure that proper introduction. She's going to get information from me, and to start this all over again and start the process over again when I - when I'm literally at $9,000 in the hole, and to go through all of this investigation with a new PGAL is going to be expensive. If in fact Jody does have standing, my client should be able to immediately start building that relationship. No one in this room can give her back that time that she's missed.

I'm also concerned about they're possibly being a sexual discrimination claim in regards to the statute as it applies to Jody, and we can discuss that hopefully sooner than later, but I believe that the best interests of the child should be an overriding concern in this situation, and right now as time goes by, as we're wasting this time arguing about Commissioner Bloom and my investigation, my client needs to be seeking therapy.

I feel that there may be a detachment disorder - this is what I have noticed in the time that I have spent with her, and I think with the parents, various males and females coming in and out of her life, I think it's extremely confusing for her, especially when Kelly at the last hearing claimed that one of the children that's not her child is her daughter. So, I think that there's not lines drawn for these children. I do believe that Payshence needs to be getting some counseling, and believe that the attachment issue may become an issue when she's an adolescent where she meets boys and every boy is her boyfriend. I'm concerned about that. She needs to be able to differentiate relationships, who is mom, who is dad, who is cousin, who is aunt, who is uncle, who is a friend and who is a boyfriend.

I would like all the parties to take a hair follicle drug test immediately, like tomorrow. I don't think anyone should be drinking above the alcohol legal limit when - in the presence of this child. I know that DCFS in the past had required that Kelly only have supervised visitation while they were pending their investigation. I don't know - do you know what has happened with that? Do you know, Connie?

CONNIE: Oh, I didn't know you were looking at me. I'm not privy to their records. I understood there was a CPS investigation, but I - she's not my client and I wouldn't have access to that.

MARY C: Do you know, Kirk? About the supervised visitation?

CONNIE: Well, you don't know.

KIRK J: About the supervised -

CONNIE: They - DCFS asked my client during the pendency of the CPS investigation not to allow unsupervised contact between Kelly and the child, and he has not allowed that. That's as far as he knows.

THE COURT: You don't know if they have any protocol?

CONNIE: I wouldn't know. Those records are - you know, she would maybe - do a - Kelly could maybe do a GRAMA request since it's her record.

MARY C: I would recommend that supervised parent-time continue for Kelly until there's a pos - you know, a negative hair follicle test. I am concerned that she did - that there's some allegations about soliciting drugs to minors, and that my client saw her mom smoking weed. So those would be the recommendations at this point. I would like to recommend that we get into a hearing sooner than later to address the constitutionality of Jody's position. Like I said, the more time we waste on this issue -- whether I'm the GAL or not, that needs to be addressed pronto.

THE COURT: Well, I mean if it turns out that he's not, it certainly ends an awful lot of litigation right there. If his standing is denied - you know, it - well it won't because there will probably be an appeal and stuff, but at least in terms of ongoing active litigation here, it would cease for a time.

MARY C: Yeah. But your Honor, one more thing, as I've stated, I have spent a ton of time in this matter. I don't - the - Kirk was ordered to provide some financial information. I have not seen that forthcoming. My fees are extensive. To spend hours and pleadings upon pleadings, and we've had two hearings on this case, and now we're going on, you know, an hour-and-a-half here on this hearing to defend the representation of my client without one citation to a rule governing the GAL that's been violated.

I'm asking that respondent and his Counsel should be solely responsible for the fees attributable to my defense in continuing to defend my client. I think that would only be fair because it seems to have turned into a little bit of a witch hunt and diversion of the true issues before this Court and Mr. Rhorer is on the hook for everything, and it would seem only fair that as we're trying to get this child representation that her representation is being paid, and like I said, Kirk hasn't filed any declaration with this Court regarding his financials despite the Court requiring him to do so.

THE COURT: So, I'm - the representative of the GAL's office, whichever of you feels more comfortable. Ms. K, since you're kind of the boss, since I'm not familiar with the actual protocols that you expect the Guardians to follow in some of their investigatory practices, do you have anything to say about that that I might want to consider?

MS. K: Sure. So, I think it's clear that my interpretation and what the actual practice was very different, that PGAL's are often asked to witness - to observe visitation, to observe kids in the home with different parties, and that has raised concerns for me. I think the statute is vague. It does say that a Guardian is to conduct an independent investigation, and what does that mean?

Does that mean that you're supposed to go out and do that all yourself? I would argue that you wouldn't. I would argue that an independent investigation, you're an attorney, you rely on other people to engage in that type of conduct. However, that has not been the practice.

So, what we have done since this issue has been brought to our attention is we have best practice guidelines. We are in the process of redoing those practice guidelines because I believe our GAL's need better direction - it hasn't been clear. Our viewpoint of this case is that we believe that we need to do better training. I think it's appropriate to be a zealous advocate, but I think that attorney GAL's have to be cautious about the activities they're engaging in in order to limit them being witnesses, to limit their exposure in terms of safety. I don't want people going into homes where they're not feeling safe. I think it's a training issue so that would be my perspective. I think in this case, the relationship that I would focus on is the relationship that Mary has with her client. That's the most important factor. I don't think that whatever occurred has changed the relationship she has with her client.

THE COURT: Okay. You have not heard anything here that would lead you to conclude that Mary grossly deviated from accept - sort of the standards that private Guardians have generally been following up to this point?

MS. K: I would say that PGAL's have been engaging in all kinds of behavior that they wouldn't do on a case if they were representing an adult, and that's been my concern. We're not investigators. We're not therapists or caseworkers or police officers. We gather information from those sources. I don't think that what occurred is so far off from what other PGAL's have done, and what frankly we've seen ordered to do in the past. I think we need to change that, and that's what I want to work on.

THE COURT: Thank you. Connie, anything more? It's your motion.

CONNIE: Just briefly, your Honor. You know, the fact of the matter is, if Mary didn't feel comfortable at the house, if she didn't feel safe, the easier answer is stay away. The - it is very clear that the purpose in going over there was to search for evidence of crime. They - the three words in the police report amongst the 250 words about searching the house to ensure safety don't change the fact that it was for a search for evidence of crime. Mary saying she interviewed my client before this event is a surprise to me. I didn't know that, and that is an ethical violation. An attorney's not allowed to speak to a represented party without permission of Counsel. I reviewed the letter that was emailed to me while we were sitting there. It talks about interviewing the children, not my client.

I understand that they're going to say yeah, consent was granted. My client says he didn't stop them from doing that. It was coerced consent, and coerced consent is no consent at all under the law. Here's the thing, I feel like I'm being vilified for bringing these issues before the Court. The fact of the matter is, this is my client's little girl by virtue of an order in the juvenile court. He is here because Mr. Rhorer wants to assert paternity. Okay. That doesn't mean that he has to basically bear every intrusion, and he has a right to Counsel too. I'm an advocate. Yes, I'm an advocate, and I think I have every right to come in here and say you know, his house got searched illegally, and I got told there was going to be a walkthrough when there wound up being a full-blown law enforcement supported search that was occasioned by information given by party's private investigator.

So, I keep hearing delay, delay, delay, delay. I don't see how bringing these issues to the Court causes any delay. There has been delay, yeah. We changed commissioners. It took the other commissioner five months to rule, but she outlined it in the ruling. I'm not seeing the things that my client is doing. He was cooperative. He's turned himself inside out. He's done absolutely everything he was asked, and then - and then to find out afterward, oh, guess what, that walkthrough was a search. Guess what, that FBI agent mentioned in the declaration was actually Mr. Rhorer's private investigator. I am concerned when the GAL says, "I'll do whatever I think I should do," and then Ms. K very politically correctly comes up here and says it's a training issue.

THE COURT: I think this is an issue that I haven't ever been asked to even consider, much less rule on, so I'll do the best I can here with this. Also, I don't have the same history with the case that my predecessor would have had. So, this is the way I view this. Although it's been characterized as an illegal search, I'm not sure that's the standard. I mean clearly a coerced search would lead to the exclusion of evidence in a criminal matter, and the allegation is at least that this was done in such a way that the parties right here - Kirk felt like he had no choice but to let the GAL into the home with a police officer.

The other part of it is the sort of not being fully candid about what was going to happen in advance. While that might not be illegal, it - I mean it reminds me a little bit of somebody who records phone calls between themselves and other people and doesn't say that they're doing it. It's not illegal under Utah law to do that. It's a manipulative practice that I frown upon, unless the law has changed, and I don't think it has.

Ms. K's observation that the GAL's have to be careful not to make themselves into witnesses I think is a legitimate concern as well.

I think this case is going to continue to be a very, very difficult and contested and disputed case, and you know, frankly, short of just being Draconian and saying you're going to trial next week and just forget about doing anything else, which isn't - can't do that, obviously, I'm not sure that there's anything that the Court can do to fix that problem. This is a can of worms that the parties have grown that is going to take a while to get sorted out, and I hope it doesn't take the entire next seven years or something for this thing finally to be put to rest. So, in considering the request to replace the Guardian - I certainly am not disregarding the impact of having to have someone else somewhat start over.

At the same time, I - I think that the process - and as difficult as this case has been, and from what I can tell, it's been in juvenile court a bunch. I mean this thing has just been all over the place. Rather than have one more thing to complain about and - for there to be sort of a motivation for somebody to not cooperate and to not feel good about the process, I think applying kind of the same standard that I think Commissioner Bloom may have applied by avoiding the appearance of impropriety. I think the better course of action is to appoint a new GAL, ask Mary to turn over all the information that she has so they don't have to come back and reinvent the wheel on things that she's done.

They don't need to do a separate additional investigation. Mary has already reported to the Court that there's not a current safety issue that she was able to identify, so the new GAL doesn't have to go back out to the house. So, the new GAL is going to probably need whatever the retainer was previously ordered.

CONNIE: Because the issue basically was raised by Mr. Rhorer in the first place, Commissioner Bloom required a $1,000 retainer to be paid by Mr. Rhorer to the GAL.

THE COURT: Right, and he's now paid the GAL some money --

CONNIR: The thousand.

THE COURT: - so - so there may be some time before he's able to -

CONNIE: And as it relates to the -- as it relates to the financial situation, I thought we had that resolved last time. My client is unemployed. I could have sworn that you had indicated that there would be no reason for him to file a financial declaration if in fact he is unemployed. He'd be willing to swear that - that he's unemployed or whatever you would like, but he has no income.

THE COURT: He can file a -- all right. How does he support himself?

CONNIE: He had unemployment, and he does live with his girlfriend. They are not married. She is employed at the present moment.

THE COURT: She's supporting basically the entire household?

CONNIE: Basically, she is supporting the household.

NANCY S: Your Honor, at the last hearing your Honor stated that Kirk should file a full financial declaration. Mr. Rhorer has complied with that. I believe the parties should be required to do that as well.

THE COURT: Okay. Well, I still would like that to be done. I mean I think it's important for the Court to have that full-blown financial declaration with whatever income verifications may exist so it's in the Court's file in case I get hit by a truck tomorrow and somebody else has to take over this. So, in any event, the same orders will apply with regards to the new GAL as applied to the previous one. I understand Mr. Rhorer isn't immediately able to produce a retainer for the Guardian, that it would be appropriate maybe to negotiate that in terms of the timing, at least of advancing any additional costs.

NANCY S: Excuse me, your Honor, could you clarify? Are you ordering that Mr. Rhorer pay more money to the new GAL?

THE COURT: If there's another retainer that the Guardian wants, then he'll be responsible for it. If it's - if they can't get somebody to take this case on at this point pro bono or something, I don't know. The evidence that we do have is that neither Kelly or Kirk have anything. They are clearly indigent. I don't know if there's a PGAL who could step in and pick this case up at this point in time hoping that their involvement doesn't need to be as extensive as Mary's has up to this point in time.

NANCY S: Your Honor, one of the things we were going to cover in this hearing was an apportionment of costs to the GAL, and an apportionment of costs to the evaluator to undertake the evaluation pursuant to the factors in 78B-15-608. Mr. Rhorer should not have to bear the totality of those costs. He's unable to do that.

THE COURT: Right. Okay. Well, we'll address that in conjunction with the custody evaluation, but I want to go back and look. Somewhere in here I did see a financial declaration. When there are this many entries into the docket, I mean literally hundreds at this point in time, sometimes it's hard to spot things on the screen, so if you'll give me just a moment here.

NANCY S: Are you looking for Mr. Rhorer's? That was filed on March 4th.

THE COURT: That helps. There it is.

NANCY S: Your Honor, also since it's been brought to the Court's attention that many of the children in the home have different father's, perhaps those fathers are contributing to the household financially. I think that should be taken into consideration as well if that is actually happening. Kirk's girlfriend, who is still married to the father of some of her children, and if she's getting any income from him or any child support for the children that needs to be taken into consideration as well, if he is in fact living off her income.

THE COURT: We haven't gotten to the custody evaluation, but I'm not deviating from the order with respect to the GAL. I think that Mr. Rhorer bears a very, very heavy burden of going forward here in intervening in a case and seeking to establish parentage in a case where the child was born during marriage. I understand that there's nothing wrong with him asserting his rights and he's got a constitutional right to do it, but he - you know, it's - at least as far as the GAL is concerned, I think that it's an unfair order.

However, I would - and Mr. Rhorer is - by his financial declaration, he is not indigent, so I'm not sure that we have the ability to appoint a pro bono guardian.

NANCY S: Your Honor, I would also like to point out that he was awarded custody of his three minor children some years ago. I think there are two children that are still minors.

THE COURT: There are two children living in the home, and so there are four people, and is his wife working?

NANCY S: Yes. What I would like to point out, your Honor, is that yes, the reason we're here is that Mr. Rhorer is attempting to establish paternity, but also Kirk and Kelly allowed him to do so. There was a hearing before Judge Stanley. Kirk appeared there and did not object to Mr. Rhorer intervening in this matter in order to establish paternity.

At the time Mr. Rhorer was still in a relationship - quasi relationship with Kelly. Kelly did not appear, but did not object to his establishing paternity at that time. So, the petitioner and the respondent do bear some responsibility for where we're at now with regard to Mr. Rhorer going forward. They did not object to his participation in these proceedings. So, it's not just Mr. Rhorer who brings us here today. It's the Petitioner and the Respondent as well. It would be unfair for Mr. Rhorer to have to bear all of those expenses. He works. He earns income. He provides for his family. He provides for the two daughters he has at home. There's just so much he can do, and this should be fair and equal among the parties.

THE COURT: One of the things that I'm unclear on, did - as I understand it, that Commissioner Bloom's order was that parties contact evaluators and basically determine who would be willing and able to do this particularly focused kind of custody evaluation. Do you have that information?

NANCY S: Yes, your Honor. I actually contacted six different evaluators, and I submitted the name of Dr. Natovich who agreed to undertake this evaluation. This was dated May 15th, this year that I submitted her name together with her costs, which is just an estimation of her curriculum vitae.

THE COURT: I'm familiar with Dr. Natovich. What did she indicate she would - is that in here somewhere?

NANCY S: I have a copy of what I submitted to the Court, your Honor. I told her what the requirements would be, the specific statute she would have to evaluate. I told her that we were challenging the constitutionality of the statute, and she said that she would be able to perform that.

Her retainer is a base rate of $4,000, with an additional $600 for each individual involved. This includes parents, step-parents, or significant others, and all children named in the court action. For example, the standard fee for an evaluation involving two parents and one child would be $5,800.

CONNIE: Your Honor, I don't have a problem with that particular doctor, but my concern, and I attempted to contact her, she - she was out of town. She called me back, and then I called her back but we haven't actually spoken, is my concern is that - that paperwork pertains to a custody evaluation, and all those details pertain to a custody evaluation, and that's not what we even need here. We need a very specific evaluation of very limited factors not a full-blown custody evaluation and that price structure to me doesn't seem right anyway. So, I don't think that information could possibly be accurate based on the limited nature of the analysis here.

NANCY S: Well, your Honor, I did speak to her, and this is the information she gave to me. I had to speak with a half dozen evaluators who turned it down because they did not want to undertake it. Ms. Natovich did understand what her duties would be, and this is what she gave to me as her fees.

THE COURT: Okay. Well, she's not here, so if she truly is intending to charge that much for what should be a more limited scope evaluation - maybe it isn't. I mean maybe she's basically looking at the same things, figures, it's going to take about the same amount of work no matter what - even if her recommendation is detracted at a different set of facts than simply the best interests of the child. So, the language of the order Connie quoted that's a provision in this order specifies the things to be addressed, but it's - includes the nature of the relationship between the child and any alleged father, other factors. If it's going to cost over $6,000 even prior to participating in any mediation or writing up a final report, where is that money going to come from?

CONNIE: See, and that's -- that's my concern. My client is unemployed. I know how custody evaluators work their business. You give them money, then they put you on a calendar, then you get some work product out of them. My concern is if my client doesn't have money and the Court orders him to pay any portion of it, then he's going to get blamed because of delay - because he doesn't have money.

THE COURT: Sure. So why -- why is he currently unemployed?

KIRK J: Just got out of school.

CONNIE: He was - he was employed, I believe, as an electrician and then went back to school and had just recently gotten out of school and has not secured employment yet.

THE COURT: What was the schooling?

KIRK J: Heating and air.

CONNIE: Heating and air conditioning, so maybe with - if it ever gets hot, maybe he will get a job, but right at this moment he doesn't have money. And I for - and then the other thing is just an equitable thing. I want to point out to the Court that this is not an issue that my client sought out. I mean he was simply trying to get divorced from Kelly under circumstances where he has permanent custody and guardianship of this child that was born of his marriage. He was not represented when Mr. Rhorer showed up and intervened. Just because Mr. Rhorer was permitted to intervene doesn't - doesn't - it doesn't follow that my client invited, you know, I'll pay your costs. I mean that doesn't follow - it's inequitable to ask Kelly and Kirk to pay for it.

NANCY S: Your Honor, the Court is supposed to treat unrepresented persons the same as represented persons. They're held to the same standard. Kirk did appear at the hearing. He was given notice, and he agreed to allow Mr. Rhorer to establish paternity. Prior to that time there was an ORS action in which he said he was not the child's father, and Kirk volunteered to take a DNA test to prove he wasn't the child's father. This child has been with Kirk only since the end of 2012. Prior to that, the child was with Mr. Rhorer. Kirk absolutely knew what he was doing at the end of the hearing. He even asked Judge Stanley if he needed to sign anything, you know, to put a rubber-stamp on allowing Mr. Rhorer to intervene.

CONNIE: Your Honor, I - I have to respectfully disagree with counsel. My client has never in this action said it would be okay for Mr. Rhorer to establish paternity. He simply did not object when he came in and tried to intervene.
NANCY S: In order to establish paternity.

CONNIE: Well -

KELLY H: Your Honor, if I may just - sorry - interrupt just a little tiny bit, I'm sorry. The day that I had my daughter, Mr. Rhorer told me on the phone, he was in Missouri, "I hope you die, you B, while you're having her." He spent very, very little time with her off and on from the time she was born until maybe 17 months is - that he may have pictures of her. Other than that, she has resided in a very - in a very nice like - I can't think of the word I'm trying to say, but has resided with Kirk, because of my mistakes and my involvement with the Court. He had very, very little to do with her from the time she was born until she was maybe 17 months old.

THE COURT: Okay. I gather nobody is paying anybody any child support?

CONNIE: No. Because -- because Mr. Rhorer was attempting to seek a forum where he could get the paternity established, he did get a biological test. That's how we know he's biologically dad, and - because ORS, that's what they do. They're all about child support. They established a child support obligation on Mr. Rhorer. He's never paid it. My client has never asked him to pay it because my client has acted as dad all this time.

NANCY S: Your Honor, my client would gladly pay child support. What actually happened was Judge V in juvenile court told Mr. Rhorer to go establish paternity because Kirk never stepped forward to say he was married to Kelly or that he was the biological father of this child. Mr. Rhorer then had an attorney, Mr. Nem. He went in, established his paternity, and then at that point in time, Kelly told a DCFS worker she was married. Kirk was brought in as the presumed father.

Judge V instructed Mr. Rhorer to dismiss that action. Mr. Rhorer's name is the only name that's been on this child's birth certificate as the father. When he was ordered by Judge V to dismiss this paternity action because the presumed father suddenly appeared, his name was taken off the child's birth certificate, and that's how Judge V ordered him to take the DNA test and it showed in fact he was the biological father. He had voluntarily taken a DNA test when he was working in Missouri. **He's the only man who has wanted to be this child's father and has established that he is this child's father.**

THE COURT: All right. Well, again, this is - I - these parties have put themselves in a position of engaging in a very difficult and expensive process without really having the resources to do it. You know, I mean at some point in time if you're going to try to litigate something, then you need to expect that it's going to cost you a lot of money, and - whether you have the resources to pay for that or not, you're going to be on the hook for it. I don't think this is a situation that's just created by the acts or decisions of one party or the other.

I don't see how I can find with the indications that I have right now as to Kirk's employment status that he's got significant ability to pay, but goodness, he was an electrician. He's now trained to work in the heating and air conditioning industry. Why that hasn't resulted in a job I guess is not easy for me to evaluate, but it seems to me that we'll go ahead and appoint Dr. Natovich, ask her to relook at the factors that she's being asked to actually focus on, and determine if she can accept, perhaps, at least a smaller retainer to get started, because what I anticipate is this is not going to be a protracted custody evaluation, but rather a relatively quick look at the factors that are outlined there and some sort of summary report to the Court that maybe will require her to attend a hearing, and I'm guessing that hearing is ultimately going to need to be in front of Judge Stanley. It seems to me that with Mr. Rhorer already having the entire cost of the GAL it is not inequitable to require that Kirk and/or Kelly in whatever manner they divide it up be responsible for half of the cost of Dr. Natovich's fees, and that you work to limit those fees.

I also want you to meet with the new GAL and ask to set up a plan that will not cause unlimited fees to be billed. I mean there should be a couple of things they need to do. I'll recommend that the order show that the parties share the cost of the custody evaluator, understanding that I want to make clear to the evaluator that her role should be limited to focusing on those specific factors. I think the idea of maybe getting some drug testing makes sense. I would like each party to provide a hair follicle drug test within the next week.

Kirk needs to investigate getting the child at least evaluated by a therapist to determine if she's got any sort of - this whole life that she's lived and the confusion that she's lived in has resulted in her needing any kind of therapy, and if she is, then hopefully you can find some means to get some assistance and get her into therapy. Again, the costs - even wealthy people run out of resources at some point, and these parties don't have those kind of resources so - and I don't know how attorneys are getting paid here, but that will - I'll recommend those orders.

I think it's appropriate for Kirk to be making efforts to obtain some appropriate employment, and I think until - unless he does that, or until the Judge tries this case, I don't believe I have enough basis - I'm already making him pay for part of this custody evaluation, so I'm not going to recommend at this point in time the other costs be reallocated, but I think that should still be treated as a reserved issue. Respondent and Defendant are to have their financial declarations filed in the next 20 days.

I would ask to have Connie prepare an order from this hearing reflecting my rulings with respect to the various things, the custody evaluation order such as it is prepared. So, if you wouldn't mind doing that?

CONNIE: May I get a CD, or will I have to go down to the clerks and ask for it?

THE COURT: You need to go downstairs and do that. I haven't been given a good explanation for why Kirk couldn't be working at this point other than he just hasn't found the right job yet, but he certainly seems to have plenty of qualifications so I would think and hope that that will be the case at some point in the near future.

CONNIE: May we be excused?

THE COURT: Yes. Absolutely.

MAY 27TH, 2015: COURT HEARING, personal notes

I got the normal "stare down" from Kelly. I never broke gaze however, and after so many seconds, she looked away. One for me! Kelly also stomped in and out of the court room, making an excessive amount of noise and disruption. She seemed to do this in reaction to Mary's long and incriminating verbal report.

As Payshence's attorney, Mary said that if Jody is granted standing, Payshence should immediately be able to reestablish her relationship with Jody and that a significant amount of time had been lost with Payshence that she cannot get back. Payshence needs to be in therapy as well and is suffering from "detachment disorder." The first time she met with Payshence was for 20 minutes and the second time she saw her, Payshence was crawling all over her and Officer Ski as well. Payshence cannot differentiate relationships.

Connie was not her normal annoying self. She was cooperative, soft spoken, with a smidgeon of humility for a change. I did notice, however, that she had an excessive amount of stammering and stalling in her speech pattern. I looked this up on the internet and found the following:

1. They repeat themselves. If someone begins to stammer, repeating words or phrases, it is a sign that they are trying to think of what to say next. This may indicate that they are concocting a story to tell. Again, compare their nervous speech to their normal speech.

2. They pause before answering. A long or abnormal pause before someone answers a question may be a tip-off that they are lying. This is especially true if the answer should be simple and obvious. A pause before answering a seemingly easy question may mean that they are trying to keep track of what they've already said and how to keep the lie going.

Mary wanted to reiterate that she was not being removed due to violation of any rules. Kase said Mary was not in violation of rules but wanted to bring in a fresh face so as to not "complicate things." As far as Mary's fees were concerned, once Kirk and Kelly turned in their financials, he would be able to reallocate.

Connie was ordered to prepare the Order for the hearing. Connie was not pleased that she had to be the one doing this. She asked the court if they would give her the CD from the hearing or if she would have to purchase it. The Commissioner said she would need to buy it, the same as everyone else did. It was a long but productive hearing. I feel happy.

MAY 27TH, 2015: MINUTES FOR REVIEW AND MOTION, Commissioner Kase

The Motion to Vacate the previous order is addressed. The Commissioner recommends: that the Motion to Vacate be denied. The parties argued the remaining issues. The Office of GAL proffers information for the record regarding the practices of their office.

The Commissioner recommends:

1. That a new Private Guardian ad Litem be appointed; Mary C to provide all her documents and other information to the new PGAL; the scope of the new PGAL should be limited as stated on the records. A PGAL who is willing to reduce their retainer should also be sought as stated on the record. Intervenor is still to pay the initial costs for the PGAL;

2. All parties to provide complete financial declarations in the next 20 days;

3. Dr. Natovich is appointed as custody evaluator, parties to explore the possibility of her accepting a smaller retainer; the Petitioner and Respondent are to bear one-half of the fees and the Intervenor Jody Rhorer to bear the other half;

4. The child is to be made available by Respondent to be evaluated by a therapist.

MAY 27TH, 2015: EMAILS from Nancy

6:09 PM

Hi Jody and Deone, This is a summary of the court's decision:

1. The motion to vacate Commissioner Bloom's order was denied. The Order remains as-is.

2. The motion was granted to remove Mary C as the PGAL. The GAL's office was advised to appoint a new PGAL who will either serve pro bono or significantly reduce his or her costs. Mary C will turn over her investigation and findings to the new PGAL which should keep the costs down. Jody will pay the initial cost of the new PGAL. The apportionment of costs for the new PGAL is reserved (which means the court will review the issue and make orders at a future hearing). However, the court did not find that Mary C violated any rules or did anything wrong in her investigation. His ruling was to avoid the appearance of any impropriety.

3. Kirk and Kelly are to file complete Financial Declarations with supporting documentation with the court.

4. Dr. Natovich is appointed to perform an evaluation of the factors in the statute so the court may resolve the constitutionality issue. I will contact Dr. Natovich and will talk to her about lowering her costs to start the evaluation. Apportionment of the costs will be determined by the court. Commissioner Kase agreed that it wouldn't be fair for Jody bear the entire costs.

5. All parties, Kirk, Kelly and Jody, are to have a hair follicle tests done in the next 7 days.

Connie was ordered to prepare the Commissioner's Recommendations and Order. I will review it and either approve it before it is submitted or submit my objections to it. We have the option to object to the Commissioner's ruling today – and ask that Judge Stanley hold an evidentiary hearing on the issue of removing Mary C. I don't know if this will really help us since the majority of the PGAL's work is complete. The new PGAL will need to speak with Payshence and help introduce her to Dr. Natovich and represent her through the evaluation process. I can make the argument that Mary C is best to do this and it may be detrimental to have a new PGAL appointed. You guys tell me what you want me to do in this regard. We have only 10 days to object. Although I would have preferred to have Mary stay as the PGAL, there is a silver lining: removing her is one less issue Connie can raise on appeal, and it gives us an issue that we can raise on appeal.

One note – you guys are sooooo much better than Kirk and Kelly or Kirk and Jill in every way. The court sees this. Our filing your financial declaration on time and Kirk and Kelly not filing theirs is a problem for them, not for us. It makes you look even better to the court. Kirk making the excuse that he is "unemployed" at this crucial time just makes him look bad. Since Commissioner Kase is new on the case I tried to get in everything I could about the background of the case and Jody's actions in being Payshence's Dad. I'm surprised Connie didn't make any objections. And Kirk is to have Payshence see someone for counseling as recommended by Mary C. If he doesn't follow through with this, I will raise the issue with Dr. Natovich and argue that he is not acting in the child's best interest. If I think of anything else that I forgot in this summary, I'll let you know. Thanks, Nancy

Time and time again Nancy offered up the services of others "free, pro bon, reduced rates, etc.," but not only have we paid the full fees for all the services rendered, we paid many of the fees that Kirk and Kelly were ordered to pay so we could move forward with the case. As much of a financial strain as this has been, we never had expectations of others to work for our cause for nothing. Everyone deserves to make a living.

We thought it was best to not object to the Ruling to remove the PGAL. It was a battle that just didn't need to be fought and we hoped the case would now focus on Payshence.

MAY 28, 8:15 AM: Emails from Nancy

Good Morning Mary, I had a few questions: My clients have decided we should not object to Commissioner Kase's ruling regarding your removal just to save time and money. And you have done most of the work already. We appreciate your report to the court and that the court order included everything you recommended. I am going to order a CD of the hearing to make sure Connie is drafting the language of the order correctly. Do you need/want to review the Recommendation and Order that Connie is preparing, particularly since it will reference you?

Are we entitled to a copy of your report or information? I still want to get the DCFS records or have them reviewed in camera by the court, particularly if the older children in Kirk's home are now going through the Juvenile Court system. I'm not sure how that's done, but I'm sure Connie and Ms. Nickel will kick up a fuss about it. What do you want to do about the billing to you on this case? I want the court to order that you be paid in full by all three parties. Who should I talk to about getting a new PGAL appointed ASAP? Im not sure how the program works, but Commissioner Kase suggested that the GAL's office find someone to work on a reduced fee basis? Any advice or suggestions about that?

I am glad you asked Commissioner Kase to clarify that you were not being removed for any wrongdoing. He certainly would not have made orders based on your recommendations if he believed your investigation was improper. And I don't believe that Connie found out for the first time yesterday that you interviewed her client at DCFS; if that's the case there are communication problems between herself and her client. If she files a Bar complaint against you for any reason to this case, please let me know if I can help in any way. Ms. Nickel may file a Bar complaint against me, and frankly I don't' care. In my opinion both Connie and Nickel's motivations and actions in this case are questionable. Thank you for everything you have done to help Payshence – Nancy

8:47 PM
Jody and Deone, Mary C called me. She wants to object to Commissioner Kase's ruling to remove her as Payshence's attorney. The GAL's office is going to assist her. She is concerned that another PGAL will not take this case as seriously as she is doing. She wants me to enter an objection on Jody's behalf. If she is allowed to remain as the PGAL she will work on the case pro bono and will not charge you. Nancy

MAY 29TH - JUNE 3RD, 2015

2:40 PM
Jody and Deone, Below is my email exchange with the Office of GAL. I'll be speaking with them tomorrow and will let you know what they suggest.

Hi J, I represent Jody Rhorer in a matter which Mary C was appointed PGAL for the minor child, PR. I would like to object to the Court's removal of Mary C in this matter. I believe it is in the best interest of the child for her to remain a PGAL in order to prevent the child from having yet another person introduced to her during this process. The court did not find her investigation was improper and adopted her recommendations in his order. I don't know if the Court has authority to remove her from this case. I would appreciate any input you can give. Nancy

Response from the Office of GAL:
Nancy, I cannot agree with you more. I would like to discuss this with you either over the phone or in person. After yesterday's hearing, the attorney in our office who handles appeals and I discussed this case. I have several thoughts about this. Is there a time you are going to be at the courthouse in the next couple of days? Maybe you could come by my office on the 2nd floor, and we can discuss this? If you aren't going to be around here the next couple of days, we could schedule a time to discuss this over the phone. J

Will, Our hearing before Commission Kase was this past week. Dr. Natovich was appointed to perform an evaluation of the factors in 78B-15-608 to determine if my client, Jody Rhorer, can go forward to establish paternity of his child. The GAL reported to the court that the older boys in Kirk's home, ages 13 and 14, are already going through the Juvenile Court system and she is concerned about the impact on my client's daughter. She said that PR, age 7, shows signs of an associate disorder and recommended she enter counseling, and the court ordered counseling for the child and that the parties have hair follicle tests done for drugs and the court ordered them. I am trying to arrange a meeting with my client and his wife for next week. Are you interested in speaking with us? Would you be willing to take on the constitutionality issues? I look forward to hearing from you. Nancy

Nancy,
Frankly, these father's rights cases are largely a "labor of love" for me too, but you can pass on to them that as a solo practitioner, I've gotten involved in so many of these that it is very difficult at times to just meet overhead. (I know you are no stranger to this concept.) One of the advantages of having me involved is that he's not starting from ground zero, meaning I'm not having to "re-invent the wheel" on the constitutional issues (sorry for barrage of metaphors).
I think the client will have a huge let up, and what would cost him tens of thousands with another attorney will be a fraction with me. When I was with a downtown firm for 18 years, we required a $5,000 retainer on all new cases - one reason (among many) why I left. I could move forward on a $2,500 retainer, with a promise to pay a minimum of $500 a month after that is exhausted, however, there is a good chance that most of my involvement (at least at trial court level) could be done within the initial $2,500. It's hard to estimate overall fees/costs, as you know, because so much of this kind of litigation is reactionary - we respond to what they do, and that can be unpredictable at times, and be more expensive than initially predicted. My best estimate would be that beyond the $2,500, it would most likely be another $3,000 at the trial court level. If there is an appeal, it would likely be an additional $5,000, leaving aside costs (filing fees, costs for transcripts, etc.). I hope this helps. Let me know. William

11:23 AM
Jody and Deone, William H asked me about your ability to pay and I told him about your situation and what you've been required to pay so far. He sent me an email which I am attaching. Basically, he will need a retainer of $2,500 and then if he exhausts that amount, a payment of $500 monthly. I can tell you, his fees are extremely reasonable given his constitutionality argument, but we need his help. He is willing to meet with us next week. Please let me know when we can set a time to sit down with him at my office and at least we can have him explain our position. Thanks, Nancy

May 30, 7:15 PM
Hello Nancy, I just realized in this pursuit of my baby daughter I have given everything to it and I have neglected my own family. I am broke and....sad to say, I bail out. I thank you for the experience of Connie kicking everybody's ass. I will not continue more court dates and will not spend another dime. This is just a leech pool. It's pretty bad that a free attorney and people that don't even have jobs can rule the court when God himself knows where my daughter belongs. Jody

June 1, 9:57 AM
Jody, The proper response to me would have been "Thank you." Connie has not kicked anyone's ass, we have kicked hers because you are still in the lawsuit. I have convinced the court that your rights under the Constitution of the United States of America have been violated. This is a big win for you, and I'm sorry you can't see it. That's why I wanted to meet with you to explain this. I have worked my fingers to the bone for you and have not demanded payment for all the work I've done. My law firm has suffered financially because I have given your case priority over my other clients. I have gotten the PGAL to work for you for free. I have spent 20 hours finding an expert in Constitutional Law to work for you at a discounted rate for nearly nothing given the job he has agreed to do for you. I would expect you to as least show some gratitude for what I've done and for what everyone has done, and is willing to do, for you. Nancy

10:34 AM

I have a telephone conference scheduled for today at 11:30 with the Utah State Office of GAL because they want to fight for you and have asked me to join them. Should I cancel that call and not give a damn? Nancy

June 3, 8:44 PM

Jody and Deone, Regrettably, this is notice that I will be filing a Withdrawal of Counsel on Monday and will no longer represent Jody. I am required to inform you that you have 14 days from the date of the last hearing to file an objection to the Commissioner's ruling. The only ruling that may be adverse to you is the recommendation to replace Mary C as PGAL. You will need to retain other counsel to proceed or to dismiss your court actions. I'll have your file in my office. In the meantime, if I receive any further information or notifications on your case, I will forward that information to you. Nancy

Prior to Jody's email, he had received a phone call demanding about $25,00 from Nancy to move forward with the case; to hire an advisor, William H, to help her with the constitutional aspect of the case; to continue payment to the GAL that Nancy wanted to fight to keep in place even though we requested she not spend our money doing so; to pay for the private investigator who still had not told us what he had done or what he planned to do; and to pay for Dr. Natovich's evaluation. He felt so discouraged by the financial burden that he just didn't know how we could keep moving forward.

He told Nancy to throw in the towel - we were done. She reacted with anger and threats to withdraw as counsel. Then she called and asked us to meet at her office - stating that she had found a way for us to move forward without the huge financial burden.

Again, we took off work and went to see her in Salt Lake. And again, we sat across from her, hands clutched tightly on her desk. And again, this happened:

"So, guys, what's up?"

"Are you kidding me?" Jody got up and left the room.

"What's wrong with him?" Nancy asked.

"I'll tell you what is wrong with him! For years he has been fighting for his daughter and for years he has gotten nowhere. He works six or seven days a week - long, hard hours and nearly every dime he makes goes to this case. We have to pay the GAL who caused Commissioner Bloom to recuse herself when we could have had a ruling by now - but instead we have to start all over again! You have made blunder after blunder while each day that goes by without his daughter is a day he will never get back. Instead of focusing on what is real, you have gone on these crazy witch hunts trying to figure out WHY Kirk wants a bunch of other guy's bastard children. You have become obsessed with the WHY and lost focus of HOW we can get her back. I'll tell you WHY! Because he had to. The state forced Kirk to take them because of this ridiculous law. He doesn't want those kids. He doesn't love those kids. It just gives him power over Kelly. It gives him control. We are not made of money, Nancy. We want this more than anything but if we are going to keep running into issue after issue I don't know how long we can hold on!" Finally, everything I had been feeling came out. And with that, I walked out of her office too.

What Nancy didn't know was that Jody had with him $13,000 in cash that he planned on giving her to move forward. He had a Jeep Wrangler that he had sold just a couple days before our meeting for the sole purpose of funding the next several months of the case. Now we would be looking for a new attorney - our fourth.

JUNE 3RD, 2015: LETTER from Nancy

Deone and Jody,

You both should know this:

1. FEES: I have worked 25 hours a month and have been paid for less than 4 hours per month. Jody owes me over $80,000 and I have not bugged Jody about paying me. He has paid me a total of $18,850 since January 2014, and out of that I have paid costs of $4,500. Net fees paid to me have been $14,350. This case has been a labor of love for me because I have cared about Payshence, and I know Kirk J is engaged in some kind of enterprise involving the children he has collected in his home. Connie has made this personal for me. I have been the "free attorney." Kirk J has probably paid more fees.

2. <u>COSTS:</u> I have absorbed most of the costs. You paid $400 for a transcript.

3. <u>PRIVATE INVESTIGATORS:</u> The private investigators have worked pro bono or I paid them out of my pocket. John B was in court pro-bono. You paid him $500 for his work that exceed $5,000. He has written the balance off.

4. <u>PRIVATE GUARDIAN AD LITEM:</u> You paid Mary C $2,000. Payment of her bill was reserved by the court based on my motion to allocate the costs equally among the three parties.

5. <u>OFFICE OF GAL:</u> The Office of GAL is objecting to Mary C's removal at no cost to Jody.

6. <u>FUTURE PGAL:</u> Mary C wants to stay on the case because she is emotionally invested in this case. I am not supposed to let anyone know this, but she is leaving her current firm so that she can work on the case pro-bono. If she can't remain on the case, she will have another PGAL appointed who will work pro-bono for Jody.

7. <u>OTHER ATTORNEY:</u> William H has agreed to help Jody and to reduce his fees substantially. This is a gift.

8. <u>EVALUATOR:</u> The court appointed Dr. Natovich. I believe she is willing to reduce her fees. I am supposed to call her back today.

Hopefully some day you can acknowledge the many hours of work and care others have given both of you and Payshence.

Nancy

I don't know what she was trying to do offering other's services again for nothing or next to nothing and none of this was true or accurate anyway - just another ploy to try to keep us going in her direction, and clearly she was still delusional - bringing up her "child collection" theory again; Stating that Kirk had paid more in fees than Jody had while having full knowledge that Connie was working one hundred percent for free. Her numbers didn't add up either, and since Jody had given her mostly cash and she had only sent us the one statement out of anger during Thanksgiving, there was no way for us to prove otherwise. I would no longer be manipulated by this woman. This would be a very bad breakup.

JUNE 4TH, 2015: EMAIL from Nancy

Today I prepared and filed an Objection to the Commissioner's ruling to remove Mary C. I promised to do that in order to support the office of GAL and Mary C, and wanted to follow through with my promise. Nancy

What about her promise to us? What about Jody's request as her client to not pursue keeping the GAL? And the Objection was written as if it was from Jody himself…

JUNE 4TH, 2015: OBJECTION TO COMMISSIONER'S RECOMMENDATION, submitted by Nancy S, Commissioner Kase presiding

The Intervenor, by and through counsel Nancy S, hereby objects to the recommendation of the Honorable Kase made on the 18th day of May, 2015, removing the PGAL, Mary C, and ordering the appointment of a new PGAL for the minor child, and ordering Intervenor pay the initial fees of the new PGAL. The objection is on the following grounds:

1. The best interest of the minor child is to allow Mary C to continue as PGAL.

2. The Commissioner stated on the record that he did not find any wrongdoing on the part of Mary C in her investigation and while acting in her capacity as PGAL.

3. After hearing her report, the commissioner adopted her recommendations to his ruling.

4. The removal of Mary C and the appointment of a new PGAL will substantially prejudice the intervenor.

5. The Rules of Civil Procedure do not provide for the removal of a PGAL by the court at this juncture in the litigation.

6. The intervener incorporates herein his arguments set forth in his Memorandum in Opposition to Respondent's Motion to Remove the GAL filed by the Intervenor, attached thereto.

ARGUMENT I

The Best interest of the Minor Child

Mary C has developed a relationship of trust with the minor child. Removing her from this case, appointing a new PGAL, and causing yet another person to be introduced to the minor child is contrary to the child's best interests.

The minor child is a 7 year-old-girl. At the hearing on May 18, 2015, Mary C reports that the child exhibited signs and symptoms of an associative disorder and recommended that the respondent immediately obtain psychological counseling for the child. The Court ordered that the child be placed in counseling. Mary C reported that the child appears confused about the identities and familial connections between herself and others in the respondent's home.

The court records show that the child has been placed in the care and custody of many people during her young life, including the Intervenor Jody Rhorer, the petitioner Kelly H, and more recently with the respondent Kirk J in August 2012. Additionally, in 2008 Juvenile Court action the child was ordered in kinship placement with Jody Rhorer's parents.

In a subsequent 2012 Juvenile Court action, about which Mr. Rhorer was not given notice, the child was placed in the custody of the DCFS. Mary C reported that while in the custody of the respondent, the minor child has had a succession of women living in this home who have either brought children into the home or who had children by other men while residing in Kirk J's home. She opined that this may be a contributing factor to the minor child's disorder.

There was No Finding of Wrongdoing on the Part of Mary C II

The Commissioner specifically stated that he did not find any wrongdoing on the part of Mary C while in the course of her duties or otherwise. The Commissioner's ruling was to avoid any appearance of impropriety and to avoid any unnecessary litigation among the parties. The parties have been litigating this matter for 18 months, well before the appointment of a PGAL. The docket shows thirty-three court filings by the Respondent since the February 20, 2015, hearing at which time the court granted Intervenor's motion to appoint a PGAL. The removal of Mary C will likely not stop the respondent's pattern of vexatious litigation.

The Removal of Mary C and the Appointment of a New PGAL Will Substantially Prejudice the Intervenor III

Mr. Rhorer was ordered to pay the PGAL the initial fee inasmuch as her appointment was pursuant to Mr. Rhorer's motion. He has paid to Mary C the amount of $2,000 to date and there is a substantial amount owing. The court reserved the issue of apportionment of future payments. The appointment of a new GAL would necessitate Mr. Rhorer's payment of additional amounts. Mr. Rhorer would be prejudiced by an order which will impose so great financial hardship that it will prevent his ability to continue the litigation.

The Rule of Civil Procedures do Not Provide for the Removal of a PGAL V

UCA 78A-2-705 governs the appointment of a PGAL. Subparagraph (8) provides that a party may object to the assigned private attorney GAL within seven days after a party discovers that the PGAL presents an adverse party in a separate matter. Neither of these circumstances exist in the case at bar. The statute does not provide for the removal of a PGAL merely because a party disagrees with the GAL's investigation methods or recommendations.

__WHEREFORE__, the Intervenor Jody Rhorer respectfully requests a rehearing before the Honorable Stanley, for introduction of evidence related to the best interest of the child in support of Intervenor's objection, that the Intervenor's objection be sustained, and for the award of attorney's fees and costs against the respondent and in favor of the Intervenor, and for such other and further relief as the court deems just.

JUNE 5TH, 2015: CUSTODY EVALUATION ORDER, Commissioner Kase

The Court, having found that it is in the child's best interests that a custody evaluation be performed and that all parties cooperate to insure the custody evaluation be timely concluded, __ORDERS:__

1. Dr. Natovich, PhD is appointed to perform a custody evaluation pursuant to Utah Code of Judicial Administration (UCJA) Rule 4-903 and shall execute and file with the Court an Acceptance of Appointment within 15 days of the date of this Order, or a written statement declining the appointment.

2. Parties and counsel shall cooperate as reasonably requested by the evaluator including:

(a) Payment of the initial retainers two week prior to the commencement date;

(b) Payment of subsequent retainers during the evaluation and report-writing within two weeks of these being requested by the evaluator;

(c) Submission of signed evaluation agreements from the parties and their spouses/partners with the evaluator two weeks prior to the commencement date;

(d) Participation in appointments during regular working hours and as needed during the evaluation period; and,

(e) Submission of any documents, names of collateral, contacts, and other pertinent material for review during the first months of the evaluation process.

3. *Petitioner and respondent shall pay* **50%** *and intervenor shall pay* **50%** *of all evaluation costs incurred through completion of the written evaluation.*

4. *The custody evaluation shall comment no later than 30 days from the date of this order.* **If the commencement or any delay in the evaluation process is caused by failure of the parties and/or counsel to cooperate as noted in paragraph 2, the evaluator shall give prompt written notification to the Court.**

5. *If an evaluator declines an appointment, the Court shall consider appointment of an alternate evaluator or termination of the evaluator.*

6. *Prior to the completion date, the evaluator shall provide written notice to the Court, with copies to counsel, of the completion, and that the case is ready for a Custody Evaluation Settlement Conference.*

7. *It is anticipated the data-gathering will be completed within* **120 days of this Order.** *The Court shall schedule a status conference approximately 120 days from the date of this Order unless the Court is earlier notified by the evaluator that data-gathering is complete and a Custody Evaluation Settlement Conference may be scheduled. The Court shall provide notice of the status conference to the parties and counsel.*

8. *Upon receipt of the evaluator's written notice of data-gathering completion, the Court shall promptly schedule a CESC, unless the Court otherwise directs.* **The notice completion may include suggestions or requests regarding the manner in which the CESC is conducted, including alternatives to a CESC.**

9. *The findings and recommendations of the evaluator and any privileged information obtained by the evaluator shall not be disclosed to any person except the GAL for the child, a medical or mental health professional for treatment, therapy or counseling for the parties or their children, or a parent coordinator appointed by the Court.*

10. *The evaluator shall consider those factors specified in UCJA Rule 4-903.*

11. **If a party fails to comply with the terms of the Custody Evaluation Order, in addition to other sanctions, the Court may strike said party's pleadings and enter his/her default regarding the custody issue.**

12. *A party requesting a written custody evaluation report shall provide written notice to the evaluator within 30 days of completion of the CESC. The parties shall submit retainers for the writing of the report within one week of the request for a written report.*

JUNE 10TH, 2015: NOTICE OF DECLINATION, submitted by the GAL's office, Commissioner Kase presiding

The Office of GAL respectfully submits this Notice of Declination pursuant to a recommendation made by Commissioner Kase on May 27, 2015. At that hearing, the Office of GAL was ordered to reassign a new PGAL after Commissioner Kase granted the Respondent's Motion to Remove and Reappoint PGAL.

FACTS

1. On February 20, 2015, the Court appointed a PGAL to represent the minor child, PR.

2. On February 23, 2015, the Office of GAL received the Order Appointing PGAL from the court, and assigned the case to Mary C.

3. On February 25, 2015, Mary C entered her appearance as PGAL for the minor child.

4. On March 9, 2015, a Notice of Hearing was filed, advising the parties and counsel that five different issues were calendared for April 15, 2015. Those issues involved objections to proposed orders, an opposition to a Notice to Submit which was filed by the Intervenor, a Motion for Attorney's Fees and a Motion to Cease Publication of Confidential Details.

5. On April 6, 2015, Commissioner Bloom recused herself from this case, as it was discovered that over twelve years earlier, she represented the children of the intervener in another matter. The hearing scheduled for April 16, 2015, was stricken, pending reassignment of the case to another commissioner.

6. The case was re-assigned to Commissioner Kase and a Review and Motion Hearing was set for May 11, 2015.

7. On May 4, 2015, the Petitioner requested a continuance of the May 11, 2015, hearing, and on May 7, 2015, the Court ordered the Review and Motion Hearing be continued to May 18, 2015.

8. However, on May 10, 2015, the Respondent filed a Motion to Remove Appointed PGAL and Reappointment of PGAL.

9. At the May 18, 2015, hearing before Commissioner Kase, the Respondent's Motion to Remove PGAL was scheduled to be heard, along with the issues referenced in the May 9, 2015, Notice to Submit.

10. The May 18, 2015, Review and Motion Hearing was continued to May 27, 2015, because, the parties disagree about the position the office of GAL was taking regarding the Respondent's Motion to Remove PGAL, Mary C.

11. The Director of the Office of GAL and the Program Coordinator for the PGAL Program were subpoenaed to appear, and both appeared at the May 27, 2015, hearing.

12. At that hearing, the Commissioner heard proffers from the Petitioner, Kelly H, counsel for the Respondent, counsel for the Intervenor, the current PGAL, Mary C, and the Director of the Office of GAL.

13. At the May 27, 2015, hearing, after hearing the proffers of counsel and the Petitioner, Commissioner Kase stated that, "this case, no matter what we do, will continue to be contentious. There's nothing the Court can do to fix that problem." Commissioner Kase recommended that, "rather than having one more thing to complain about...and having a motivation for someone to not cooperate, I think to avoid the appearance of impropriety, I am going to appoint a new PGAL."

14. Commissioner Kase ordered the Office of GAL to re-assign a PGAL to this case. Commissioner Kase indicated that the Order Appointing PGAL that was previously entered by the Court on February 20, 2015, was still valid, and was to be used by the Office of GAL in determining the most appropriate PGAL to represent the minor child in this case.

15. On June 4, 2015, counsel for the Intervenor filed an Objection to the Commissioner's Recommendation.

ARGUMENT
THE LAW DOES NOT PROVIDE FOR MIDCASE SUBSTITUTION OF A PGAL FOR ANYTHING LESS THAN A LEGAL CONFLICT OF INTEREST OR INABILITY TO PRACTICE LAW

1. A private attorney GAL is an attorney designated by the Office of GAL, who is not an employee of the office. The Director of the Office of GAL is required by rule to coordinate the appointments of GAL's among different levels of courts.

2. A court may appoint a PGAL in district court cases involving abuse, neglect or issues of custody and parent-time. The court is to "consider the limited number of eligible PGALs when making an appointment" and to make findings justifying the appointment.

3. While the law allows for the court to make a general appointment of a PGAL, both the statute and the rule specify that selection of the particular PGAL is left to the Office of GAL.

4. The Director then "shall contact and assign the case to an eligible attorney, if available." The Director maintains a list of PGALs and uses a method of selection developed by the Director and the GAL Oversight Committee.

5. The statute provides that a party may object to a PGAL's appointment, but must do so within seven days after receipt of the assignment. A party may object at any time based on a legal conflict of interest but must do so within seven days of discovery of the conflict. If the court determines the party has grounds to object to the assignment, the court may order the Office to assign a new PGAL. Even then, the Office of GAL may notify the court that no alternative PGAL is available.

6. Once the seven days to object has passed, the statute provides that complaints about a PGAL are to be filed with the Director. "The decision of the Director regarding the complaint is final and not subject to appeal."

7. The law provides for the court to terminate a PGAL's appointment, but not to terminate the assignment of the particular PGAL. Thus, the court may terminate the appointment (1) once the specified issues requiring the PGAL are resolved; (2) once the court determines that the minor no longer requires the services of the PGAL; or (3) when there has been no activity on the case for six consecutive months.

8. The fact that practitioners have preferences for different counsel does not justify a court to order a law firm, a legal defender agency, or a legal services agency to switch out counsel. A court would not order such a substitution for anything less than a legal conflict of interest or a matter affecting counsel's ability to practice law. To do otherwise would be unfair to the represented client and to counsel.

JUNE 10TH, 2015: KIRK J'S MOTION TO STRIKE "NOTICE OF DECLINATION" BY THE GAL'S OFFICE, submitted by Connie C, Commissioner Kase presiding

COMES NOW, Kirk J, by and through Counsel, and files the foregoing Motion to Strike the "Declination" filed by the Office of the GAL on June 10th, 2015.

Facts
1. As a courtesy, and pursuant to that Office's statutory duty of selection and oversight of qualified PGAL, counsel for Kirk J informed the Office of the GAL of an illegal search of Kirk J's home made by the PGAL, Mary C.

2. The Office of the GAL was made aware that Mary C gained access to Kirk J's home by asserting she wished to interview children, and asserting she wished to do a "walkthrough."

3. *The Office of the GAL was specifically made aware of concerns that Mary C had misstated her intention regarding a visit to Kirk J's home, and then conducting a full-blown law enforcement assisted search.*

4. *The Office of the GAL was further informed of concerns that Mary C misstated in a Court filed pleading that she had met with an "FBI Agent" when in fact, she has garnered the assistance of, and was working at the direction of a **former** FBI Agent, who was working as private investigator for Jody Rhorer.*

5. *The Office of GAL was made aware that Kirk J's concern regarding the misidentification of Mr. Rhorer's private investigator as an "FBI Agent" was specifically for the purpose of imparting some measure of credibility to accusations or suspicions of criminal activity articulated in Mary C's report which would have not existed had Mary C been forthcoming about the true identity of the individual, and his alignment with Mr. Rhorer.*

6. *The Office of the GAL was implored to take action regarding these concerns with Mary C **before** this matter went to hearing May 27, 2015.*

7. *Instead of taking action regarding the concerns related to Mary C's's conduct, the Office of GAL did not act, specifically indicating it would wait for the Court to act.*

8. *At no time did the Office of GAL move to intervene in this proceeding, or enter limited appearance on behalf of their office as a whole or as an administrative body charged with maintaining the system of PGAL via its education, certification, roster program.*

9. *At no time did the Office of PGAL file any pleading asserting that the Court had lacked authority to remove a GAL, or that the Court had authority under certain circumstances.*

10. *The GAL Attorney and Director were subpoenaed to the May 27, 2015, hearing.*

11. *Both spoke at some point during the hearing.*

12. *Neither asked to intervene on behalf of the Office of GAL, neither offered any argument or authority for the proposition that the Court would lack authority to remove a PGAL in a particular case for any reason.*

13. *At least one representative of the Office of GAL was present in the Court hearing, having heard Mary C inform the Court that not only had she caused Kirk J to be interviewed without consent of his counsel at the time of the search, but that she had personally interviewed him in a prior occasion, and that his counsel "should have known" she was going to do that.*

14. *That representative was present when counsel for Kirk J informed the Court she was never asked for permission to speak to Kirk J and that representative was present to hear the Commissioner indicate that that issue was one "for the bar."*

15. *On June 10, 2015, the GAL's Office filed a document entitled "Notice of Declination" in which it argued for the first time that the Court lacks authority to remove a particular PGAL from a case "for anything less than a legal conflict of interest or a matter affecting counsel's ability to practice law."*

DISCUSSION
Lack of Intervention/Limited Appearance

The GAL's Office as an entity is not a party to this proceeding. Its involvement is tangential, and occasioned its statutory duty to devise a system of educating, certifying and maintaining a roster of qualified attorneys eligible for appointment as PGAL. The administrative workings of the GAL's Office as a whole led to Mary C's placement on the roster, and in due course, her assignment to this particular case. If the GAL's Office as an administrative body wished to obtain standing to make legal arguments, file pleadings, and urge any particular legal position, it should have moved to intervene or file a limited appearance for that purpose. It did not do so.

Having failed to enter this case for the purpose of litigating the issue of removal of Mary C when the issue was placed before them, and having failed to timely intervene or enter appearance, this Court cannot recognize the "Notice of Declination" which is nothing more than a post-hoc attempt to "join the fray" after the argument regarding the issue is over. It very well may be that the Court may have found the GAL's position interesting, enlightening, and worthy of consideration.

Presumably the next PGAL will be competent to advance the best interests of the child, undeterred over-reaching by any of the parties. Certainly, if Mr. Rhorer is concerned with the minor's best interest, it is impossible to argue somehow that is 'unfair.' In fact, he was the one who asked for appointment of the GAL. As to "unfairness" to the PGAL's client, Kirk J's daughter, the Commissioner specifically found that there would not be disruption in representation to the minor under the circumstances of this case.

Mary C was involved in the matter six weeks to the day from the date of her February 20th appointment to April 3rd, the day she tossed Kirk J's home. Mary C was invading the quiet enjoyment of the home. Such an "attorney-client" relationship can easily be supplanted with a new GAL, as the Commissioner appropriately found.

CONCLUSION

Having opted not to pursue an appropriate legal avenue to be recognized as a person or entity with a proper interest in the controversy regarding the removal of Mary C as PGAL in this case, the Office of the GAL has missed its chance. The Court must strike the pleading entitled "Notice of Declination" filed by the GAL.

Even if the Court were to view the pleading and the Guardian's Office attempt to advance a legal argument about the matter as procedurally appropriate under the circumstances, the authority offered by the Office does not support the conclusion it asks the Court to reach. Just because the statutes provide for objection to a particular Guardian early in the proceedings, it does not follow that the Court has no authority to remove a Guardian later in the proceedings. The Court always retains general supervisory authority to administer matters before it. Accepting the logic offered by the Office of the GAL would lead to ludicrous results, and the Court is not at liberty to interpret legislation such that it leads to absurd results.

WHEREFORE, Kirk J prays the Court strike the pleading entitled "Notice of Declination" filed by the Office of GAL, and for such other relief as the Court deems appropriate in the premises.

JUNE 11TH, 2015: EMAILS from Nancy

I am filing a withdrawal of counsel, or in the alternative a Motion to Withdraw. It would look better for you to file a Substitution of Counsel. Nancy

3:31 PM
We are working on it. Deone

3:45 PM
(Withdrawal of Counsel Notice attached)
I have dated this to be filed Monday. Nancy

9:24 PM
There are several dates in your attachment that have passed in May. I am wondering if those are actually supposed to say June? Deone

9:54 PM
Your new attorney can clear that up for you.

JUNE 15th, 1:21 PM
As stated, I will be filing my withdrawal today and will send to you the court accepted Notice of Withdrawal of Counsel. Nancy

4:03 PM
Have your new attorney file a Notice of Appearance. Nancy

I realized Nancy was giving us every chance to change our minds and keep her as counsel and I knew her heart was in the right place but there were just too many issues and her inability to stand up to Connie and perform in court let alone lack of knowledge of constitutionality was not something we could deal with any longer.

We had been working on finding new counsel. I had requested all our records from Nancy but she wanted several days to get everything together. When I picked up the boxes from her office, it felt awkward and uncomfortable. I signed for the materials with the receptionist. William H's number was written on a message pad.

I had a client that was an attorney that had been following our case. He had a lot of interest and had expressed a desire to take on the case on multiple occasions. I drove to his office and let him know we were considering making a change of attorneys. He, in turn, referred our case to another attorney in his office, Seth, that he felt was more qualified to handle it as Seth had a current custody case that they thought had some similarities to ours. I left two boxes of records for Seth to review.

After two weeks we were informed that Seth was not interested in the case but they recommended Brad K in Salt Lake City. We then received a bill in the mail for $1,500 for looking at our case just to tell us they were not interested in taking it.

I pulled out the note with William H's number on it and gave him a call, but he never called back. We had lost precious time so decided to take the recommendation of Brad K.

JUNE 15TH, 2015: WITHDRAWAL OF COUNSEL, submitted by Nancy S, Commissioner Kase presiding

Nancy S hereby withdraws as counsel for Intervenor Jody Rhorer. No motion is pending and no hearing or trial has been set. Intervenor has filed an Objection to the Commissioner's Recommendation on May 27, 2015.

JUNE 15TH, 2015: EMAILS between Nancy and Mary

3:28 PM
What happened? Mary

June 16, 8:48 AM
Mary, I hated to do that and I am agonizing over it. You and I have discussed the need to brief the constitutional issues in this case. I wanted Jody to hire another attorney to co-counsel with me on the constitutional issues, but I know he can't afford two attorneys. I am bowing out and hoping that he will hire William H. I've talked to Will and he is willing to reduce his fees substantially to work on Jody's case. Will has represented unmarried biological fathers in adoption matters.

He told me there are 9 constitutional issues that apply to Jody's case. Last year he filed a Federal Court action for unmarried biological fathers alleging RICO violations. He is THE expert in the application of constitutional law to paternity cases. And Will knows Connie and her tactics very well and has been up against her in court many times and won!

The way I see things, it is a miracle that the court has allowed a constitutional challenge in Jody's case. Since I don't specialize in constitutional law, Jody needs to hire an expert to have any hope of winning. I have given Jody and Deone the contact information for Will and I'm copying them on this email. Nancy

JUNE 15TH, 2015: ACCEPTANCE OF APPOINTMENT

I, Doctor Natovich, hereby confirm that I have received and reviewed the Custody Evaluation Order in the above-entitled case, that I am qualified to perform this evaluation consistent with the provisions of Utah Code of Judicial Administration Rule 4-903, that I submit to the jurisdiction of the Court and agree to comply with the provisions of the Custody Evaluation Order, assuming full cooperation of the parties and counsel.

I hereby accept my appointment as custody evaluator.

BRAD K

JUNE 16TH, 2015:

We met with Brad. He was tall, thin, soft spoken, with studious glasses, in his mid 50's. He was a family law attorney and seemed to know what he was talking about. What we did not know about Nancy when we inherited her from Steve K was that she was NOT a family law attorney - she was an attorney that negotiated with insurance companies.

We gave Brad the retainer and left his Salt Lake downtown high-rise office and waited to see what he would do. The next several months consisted of Connie objecting to everything. Apparently, Nancy had filed the wrong form for the custody evaluation and Connie was all over that. It had to be refiled which meant more lost time.

We also learned about a father's rights group in Ogden, close to where we lived - so we decided to go. The group that gathered was very small. The man that was heading it up had a book he had written and was hoping to sell it. We sat and listened to several men complain about their exes and how their custody arrangements weren't fair. We knew quite early in the meeting that this was not a group that could help us but rather a support group consisting of fathers that needed to air their gripes to others in similar situations. Needless to say, we didn't go back.

JUNE 18TH, 2015: EMAILS from Nancy

1:14 PM

Jody and Deone, Dr. Natovich called me today. She knows I have withdrawn as your attorney but is starting her evaluation and wanted information. I told her to contact you directly to see if you had hired a new attorney. I told her that with your permission I would release information to her and discuss your case with her. You need to address this issue as soon as possible. Nancy

4:43 PM

Nancy, You may release information and discuss with her. We are in the interview process right now with attorneys. Dr. Natovich's fee has been paid so she can move forward. Both Jody and I spoke to her assistant yesterday. Deone

5:23 PM

Dr. Natovich, It was a pleasure speaking with you today. I received the attached email authorizing me to release information to you regarding this matter. Please call me at your earliest convenience so that we can arrange a time to meet. The file is still at my office. Thank you, Nancy

June 19, 2:21 PM

Dr. Natovich has not responded to my email or the phone call I placed to her. I will not be able to meet with her next week because of my schedule. Please have your new attorney arrange to meet with her. Nancy

AUGUST 18TH - 25TH, 2015: EMAILS from Brad K

11:33 AM

Hi Brad, Can I get a copy of the order Connie drew up for the May hearing and also your rebuttal? Deone

6:34 PM

Hi Deone, I am sorry I missed you yesterday - I was in a mediation until 9:00 last night. I have attached a copy of my draft of the Order from the May 27 hearing.

Connie had not drafted one - the only order she drafted was the proposed evaluator order that I sent you. The GAL, Mary C, withdrew from the case yesterday. I will be in the office tomorrow if you have any questions. Thanks, Brad K

10:45 PM

If Mary C was ordered off the case, why did she just withdraw yesterday? How does the court go about hiring a new GAL? When will that take place? Deone

August 19th, 10:44 PM

Hi Deone, Let me address each of your questions. Yes, we can still add those items in on the proposed order. I did have my assistant listen to the portion of the hearing where the Commissioner makes his recommendation, and compare it to the minute entry that the Court included in the docket. But it sounds like we need to be more specific about the counseling part, so I can review that tomorrow and make the changes. Aside from the counseling, was there anything else from the proposed order that you saw that either needs to be added or made more specific? Connie does have until Thursday to respond - she sent me an email complaining about the orders that I drafted, and said she was going to call me. I never heard from her and sent her an email today telling her that I am available tomorrow if she wants to discuss it.

Finally, I am not sure why it took Mary C so long to withdraw. I know that the office of the GAL initially objected to her removal, and she may have been waiting to sees the result from that. If that is the case, Mary probably gave up and decided not to fight to stay in the case. Now the office of the GAL will appoint a new private GAL, which should happen in the next couple of weeks. If I missed anything, let me know. I will be in touch on Friday if I don't hear from Connie before then. Thanks, Brad

August 25th, 12:50 PM

Any updates? Deone

5:45 PM

Hi Deone, We are moving forward with the objection to Connie's orders - in response she sent me the two draft orders that I have attached. At this point, the limited evaluation order is the priority - I want to talk with you or Jody about the differences in the order that I drafted, and this most recent one from Connie, and decide if there are enough differences to justify the cost and time. Are you available for a call tomorrow? The order from the May 27 hearing is extremely long - she does include part of the items that you wanted to add, but leaves other items out. I suspect this one will probably end up in another hearing. Let me know what time you are available tomorrow. Brad

AUGUST 18TH, 2015: AMENDED ORDER RE: LIMITED PURPOSE EVALUATION, Submitted by Brad K, Commissioner Kase presiding

This matter came before the Honorable Commissioner Kase for a telephone conference. The Petitioner was present. The Respondent was represented by counsel of record, Connie. The Intervenor was represented by counsel of record, Brad K, The GAL, Mary C, was also present.

THE COURT, *having determined that Intervenor Jody Rhorer has an alleged relationship with the minor child, PR, and finding that Mr. Rhorer has no means to assert his paternity pursuant to Utah Uniform Parentage Act, and further finding that Mr. Rhorer's alleged relationship with the minor child PR therefore raises issues regarding the constitutionality of the Utah Uniform Parentage Act's standing limitations, now hereby* **ORDERS, ADJUDGES,** *and* **DECREES:**

1. Dr. Natovich, PhD, is appointed to perform a limited purpose valuation to determine whether Intervenor has standing to proceed to establish his paternity of the minor child, PR.

2. In performing this limited purpose evaluation, Dr. Natovich shall consider the following factors from Utah Code 78B-15-608.

a. whether it would be inequitable to disrupt the father-child relationship between the Respondent and the minor child;

b. the nature of the relationship between Respondent, Kirk J, and the minor child, PR;

c. the harm that may result to the child if the presumed paternity is successfully disestablished;

d. the nature of the relationship between the minor child and Intervenor Jody Rhorer; and

e. any other factors. When considering any factors not specified in this order, Dr. Natovich shall consult with counsel.

3. Parties and counsel shall cooperate as reasonably requested by the evaluator, including:

(a) Payment of the initial retainers two week prior to the commencement date;

(b) Payment of subsequent retainers during the evaluation and report-writing within two weeks of those being requested by the evaluator;

(c) Submission of signed evaluation agreements from all parties and their spouses/partners with the evaluator two weeks prior to the commencement date;

(d) Participation in appointments during regular working hours and as needed during the evaluation period; and

(e) Submission of any documents, names of collateral contracts, and other pertinent material for review during the first month of the evaluation process.

4. The Intervenor, Jody Rhorer, shall pay the retainer requested by Dr. Natovich. The Court may consider reappointment of said costs at trial.

5. This limited purpose evaluation shall commence no later than 14 days from the date of this Order. If the commencement or any delay in the evaluation process is caused by the failure of any of the parties or counsel to cooperate as required by this Order, the evaluator shall give prompt written notification to the Court.

6. If a party fails to comply with the terms of this Order, in addition to other sanctions, the Court may strike said party's pleadings and enter his or her default.

7. The Petitioner, the Respondent, and the Intervenor are to file updated Financial Declarations with the Court within 10 days of the telephone conference held on September 16, 2015.

AUGUST 18TH, 2015: ORDER FROM HEARING (May 27, 2015), submitted by Brad K, Commissioner Kase presiding

*A review hearing was held before the Court on May 27, 2015. The Petitioner was present. The Respondent was present, and represented by his attorney. Intervenor Jody Rhorer was present, and represented by his attorney, Nancy S. The PGAL, Mary C, was present. The Court, having reviewed the documents on file, having heard argument from counsel and the parties, and having been fully informed in the premises, hereby **ORDERS** and **DECREES**:*

1. The Respondent's Motion to Vacate the Order of April 20 is denied.

2. A new private GAL shall be appointed. The February 20, 2015, Order of Appointment and Findings shall remain effective for this appointment. The scope of the new private GAL shall be limited as stated on the record. Mary C shall provide all of her documents and other information to the new PGAL. A PGAL who is willing to reduce his or her retainer should be sought. Intervenor shall pay the initial costs associated with the PGAL.

3. All parties shall provide complete financial declarations within twenty days.

4. Dr. Natovich, PhD, is appointed to perform a limited purpose evaluation. The parties shall explore the possibility of the Doctor accepting a smaller retainer. The Petitioner and the Respondent shall bear one-half of the costs of the fees for the evaluation. Intervenor Jody Rhorer shall pay one-half of the costs of the fees for the evaluation.

5. The child shall be made available by the Respondent to be evaluated by a therapist.

6. The parties are mutually restrained from publication of the issues in this case.

7. Each party shall provide a hair follicle drug test to the new PGAL within two weeks.

AUGUST 18TH - 25TH, 2015: OBJECTION TO ORDERS/REQUEST FOR HEARING, submitted by Connie C, Commissioner Kase presiding

*Comes now, Connie C, Attorney at Law, and on behalf of the Respondent, informs the Court that counsel for Mr. Rhorer and Kirk J have been unable to agree on form of Orders from the May 27th, 2015, hearing, as well as a correct form of Order for the limited scope evaluation Ordered previously by Commissioner Bloom, and the subject of an Order which has been signed by the Court, but which is incorrect. It describes a "custody evaluation" rather than the limited scope evaluation described by Commissioner Bloom. A portion of the dispute includes particulars related to payment for the evaluation and it would be of assistance to counsel to have further discussion and direction from the Court regarding that matter. **WHEREFORE**, Kirk J prays the Court set a hearing on the matter, and for such other and further relief as the Court deems appropriate in the premise.*

SEPTEMBER 10TH, 2015: MEMORANDUM RESPONDING IN PART TO RESPONDENT'S OBJECTION TO ORDERS, submitted by Brad K, Commissioner Kase

INTERVENOR, *Jody Rhorer, by and through his attorney, Brad K, and pursuant to Rules 7 and 101 of the Utah Rules of Civil Procedure, hereby submits his Memorandum Responding in Part to Respondent's Objection to Orders as follows: There are two orders at issue in the Respondent's Objection to Orders: (1) the proposed order from the hearing held by the Court on May 27, 2015, and (2) the Court's Custody Evaluation Order entered on June 5, 2015. This Memorandum only addresses the Court's Custody Evaluation Order, and is therefore a partial response. In the event the parties and counsel are unable to resolve their dispute over the Order from the May 27, 2015. hearing, Intervenor, Jody Rhorer, will file a memorandum addressing the issues with that proposed Order.*

STATEMENT OF FACTS:

1. At a hearing held on February 20, 2015, in response to Jody Rhorer's request for a custody evaluation, Commissioner Bloom ordered a limited evaluation on several factors contained in Utah Code § 78B-15-608.

2. At a hearing on May 27, the Court appointed Dr. Natovich to conduct this limited evaluation.

3. As a part of its order relating to this limited evaluation, the Court: a. Ordered the Petitioner and the Respondent to bear one-half of the cost of this evaluation, and Intervenor to bear the other one-half of the cost; b. Asked the parties to explore the possibility of Dr. Natovich accepting a smaller retainer; and. c. Indicated that the Court would prepare the order.

4. On June 2, 2015, the Court signed a Custody Evaluation Order.

5. Pursuant to the Court's Custody Evaluation Order: a. The parties were required to cooperate as requested by the evaluator, including: paying the initial retainer two weeks prior to the commencement date; signing evaluation agreements from the parties and their spouses two weeks prior to the commencement date; participating in appointments as needed; and submitting documents and other pertinent material for review. b. The evaluation was to commence no later than 30 days from the date of the Order; and c. The evaluator was ordered to give the Court prompt written notice of any delays in the commencement of the evaluation caused by the parties and/or counsel.

6. On July 1, 2015, Dr. Natovich filed a letter with the Court asking the Court for clarification on the Court's order before proceeding.

7. In a minute entry dated July 1, 2015, the Court indicated that if the parties and counsel were unable to agree upon the scope of the evaluation, a telephone conference could be scheduled, and the parties were to submit clarifying language to the Court.

8. Counsel for the Respondent and Intervenor, Jody Rhorer, have communicated regarding the scope of the evaluation and generally agree on what the scope should be, including the following: a. whether it would be inequitable to disrupt the father-child relationship between the Respondent, Kirk J, and the minor child, PR; b. the nature of the relationship between Respondent, Kirk J, and the minor child, PR; c. the harm that may result to the child if the presumed paternity is successfully disestablished; d. the nature of the relationship between the minor child, PR, and Intervenor Jody Rhorer; and. e. any other factors.

9. The points of the order that are disputed, and therefore in need of further clarification from the Court, are as follows: a. How much of the one-half of the evaluation fee are the Petitioner and the Respondent each responsible for; and b. Whether the language included in the Court's Custody Evaluation Order, and paraphrased in paragraph 5 above, should be included in the Order appointing Dr. Natovich.

10. In accordance with the Court's minute entry dated July 1, 2015, Intervenor, Jody Rhorer, submits herewith a proposed order including the requested clarifying language as Exhibit A.

WHEREFORE, Intervenor Jody Rhorer requests that the Court review the proposed order attached as Exhibit A, and if it finds that the proposed order meets with its approval, sign the order. In the alternative, Intervenor Jody Rhorer requests that the Court schedule a telephone conference to address the evaluation order. DATED this 4th day of September, 2015

SEPTEMBER 11TH, 2015: EMAILS from Brad K

Hi Deone, We followed up with the Commissioner's clerk yesterday – she said that the Commissioner has a hard copy of our objection and order, and will make a decision. We asked if we could expedite the process by filing a request to submit, and she said no – the Commissioner will let us know as soon as he has made a decision. I will let you know as soon as we hear from him. Has Jody completed the drug test yet? Brad K

September 14th, 3:29 PM
Deone and Jody, Commissioner Kase scheduled a telephone conference on the proposed custody evaluation orders for Wednesday afternoon. I will give you a call afterwards to let you know what happens. If you have any questions, or want to talk before the telephone conference, let me know. Thanks, Brad K

September 22nd, 4:35 PM
Hi Deone, I spoke with Lynn in Dr. Natovich's office – she was planning on calling Jody today to get things scheduled. If you don't hear from her, let me know and I will call again. BK

September 23rd, 3:34 PM
Jody got everything signed today and we are meeting at Dr. Natovich's office on Tuesday at 12:00 for the initial interview. Deone

September 24th, 11:53 AM
Excellent – let's talk on Monday or Tuesday morning before you meet with Dr. Natovich. Based on the nature of the evaluation, I think it will be helpful to give Jody a little direction relating to that interview. I am going to send a copy of the revised financial declaration for you and Jody's review – if the information is accurate, I just need authorization to sign it on Jody's behalf. I will send it this afternoon. Thanks, Brad

September 25th, 11:40 AM
Do you know if Kirk and Kelly got their financials in? Deone

3:44 PM
No, neither have filed them yet. But they are not technically due until Monday. I have attached an updated declaration with the changes on Jody's income. I also changed the way the expenses show, since Jody is now paying the mortgage on the home his parents were living in. Will you have him confirm that I have his permission to sign this electronically on his behalf? Brad

It seemed like this day would never get here! Dr. Natovich was exactly like I pictured her - upper-middle aged, white sleek hair all one length stopping at her shoulders, slender build, classy and organic. She invited Jody and I in together and spent the first quarter of an hour discussing how we met and then sharing with us how she had met her husband while in college. I found it interesting that she shared some of her personal experiences with us; I also found it a little odd as our interview time was limited.

We proceeded to tell the Doctor about Jody's relationship with Payshence and how she was plucked away from him by the State and made to live with Kirk J. There were tears and a lot of emotion as Jody expressed to her how hard each day was without the knowledge that Payshence was healthy and happy and even more so, what she was thinking happened to her daddy. How could she not feel abandoned by her father and sisters? What was that doing to her as a human being? It was clear that Dr. Natovich had empathy for our situation. She also spent some time explaining the process to us and what her plan was for interviewing Payshence, Kelly, and Kirk. We finished our interview and she said she would be in touch.

OCTOBER 4TH, 2015: FINANCIAL DECLARATION Submitted by Kirk J
Although mostly incomplete and with no documentation for verification as required. Kirk's Financial Declaration was finally submitted to the Court.

OCTOBER 4TH, 2015: EMAILS to Brad K

Hi Brad, I have some questions. What recourse is there against Kelly where she has not complied to the Financial Declaration? Also, was there attached documentation that substantiates everything on Kirk's declaration? I know when Jody did his, we turned in all the documentation to validate it. It is not really a financial declaration without paycheck stubs, tax returns, etc.

Third, I notice that Kirk put his monthly mortgage payment under "rental income" and therefore it is a credit, not a debit. If all of his bills are added up and weighed out against the income he is claiming, he is substantially in the negative on debt vs. income. I don't see how he could realistically have the bills he has with the income he is claiming. Everything needs to be documented or thrown out. I would also like to know what utility companies he's using - I would like to sign up for those myself if he is getting water, sewer, garbage, gas and power for $115 a month. And an extremely important note: is he getting any government financial services because he has 8 kids in that house? Food stamps, utility assistance...??? If so, this needs to be disclosed as well. Will you please find out on all of these things?

You left a long voicemail on the cell phone of one of the realtors that works for me about Jody's drug test. She wasn't sure what you needed if you could please clarify. Also, only use my private cell number or Jody's. I'm easier to reach during the day as Jody is usually on a job site. Please take care not to leave our private information on the cell phones of other people. That was awkward for both me and my agent as I really didn't want to get into a full explanation of what is going on and she is probably wondering why my husband is taking a drug test for an attorney.

Thank you for your assistance and have a blessed day, Deone

NOVEMBER 2ND, 7:35 AM

Hi Brad, I was wondering if you were able to send the court C/D's to Dr. Natovich as we had discussed. Have you heard anything? Other than being told that Kirk J was meeting with her the week before last and that Kelly hadn't responded, we haven't heard from her. Deone

November 3rd, 5:10 PM
Hi Deone,
We did send the CDs to Dr. Natovich's office. I tried to follow up with her assistant today, and she left me a voicemail saying that she thought you might be sending her some of the pleadings from the case. Were you planning on sending any documents over, or would like my office to do that? Let me know. If you want to call, I will be in the office tomorrow afternoon. Thanks, Brad

I had already mailed off the package of documents Dr. Natovich had requested. Brad K was certainly not as quick at responding as Nancy was to my emails and phone calls. He had a more passive and "wait and see" approach. I found out he was teaching at a college which probably explained the time gaps between responses.

DECEMBER 6TH, 7:51 PM

Hi Brad, I sent a couple emails last week and left a couple voice mail messages. Can you let us know what you found out about Jody's next meeting with Dr. Natovich? If I don't hear back from you on Monday I'll go ahead and call her directly. Thank you, Deone

10:55 PM
Hi Deone, I apologize for not getting back to you – I was hoping to hear back from Dr. Natovich before I called you back. I have not heard anything yet. I will email and call her again tomorrow – but if you don't hear anything from me, then assume I've not had any luck, and feel free to reach out to her yourself! I will be in touch with any news – thanks! Brad

December 7th, 2:32 PM

Hi Brad, I left a message at Dr. Natovich's office as well. I am attaching photos that were just posted with Payshence shown with her mother over Thanksgiving without the court ordered supervision. Also, it appears that Kelly has a new boyfriend according to her Facebook status. Her husband, Shayne S, may end up being able to help in our case in some way. I think Dr. Natovich needs to know this was well. Can you forward this email on to her? I don't have an email address for her. So, what can be done about this since Kelly and Kirk are not following the orders for the court? Deone

5:47 PM

Deone, I forwarded the pictures to Dr. Natovich. I will let you know when I hear back from her. I am interested in the potential for using her husband to help with the case – what kinds of information do you think he may be willing to provide to us. As for the violation of the court's order, that will need to be addressed by filing an order to show cause with the court. Before we do that, I would like to see if Dr. Natovich will find that information useful, or if she will provide that information to the court. There are a handful of advantages of having that information come from her, rather than us. Brad

DECEMBER 9TH, 2015: VOICEMAIL FROM Mike L at NBC Television

"Hi Deone, I'm trying to reach you and Jody. I'm a producer with a new NBC show. Please give me a call back. Again, I'm a producer with a new NBC show and I want to speak to you and Jody. Thank you so much."

I wasted no time calling Mike back. We spoke for about twenty minutes and I choked back tears of hope believing our story would finally be heard and maybe get in front of the right person that could do something for us. Apparently, NBC was producing a series on father's rights and our article from the Standard Examiner had caught the eye of one of the producers on the internet. Utah apparently had several interesting cases that profiled on the internet giving up rights to children by their mothers and circumventing the rights of the fathers.

An appointment for screen testing on Skype was set up and Mike also planned on coming out to Utah from Los Angeles to meet us.

DECEMBER 9TH, 2015: EMAIL from NBC Television

Hey Deone, It was very nice chatting with you. Here are the confirmed details for Tomorrow, December 10 @ 2:05 PM MST. You'll be chatting with Sammy Jo. She's very nice. Please reply back with your Skype name when you can. And again, please dress business causal. Solid color would be best, black or white if possible. Let me know if anything comes up! Best, Erica

We held the screen test at my office. Before NBC began taping our interview, we were prompted on what to expect and then they asked us a series of questions regarding Payshence and our case. It lasted about thirty minutes.

Mike flew out just as he had indicated in our conversation. We met him at a hotel in Salt Lake. There was a film camera set up to record our interview. He seemed genuine and concerned about our situation. Mia came with us and he ask her questions as well. He explained that nothing is for sure in television and that our case was so unique and complex that it may take more than just a one- hour show. We didn't want to get our hopes up, but the thought of telling our story to the world sounded so promising.

Mike also told us about this attorney, William H, the same William H that Nancy tried to introduce us to. This attorney had met with NBC on several occasions already and was supposedly the premier expert on father's rights. NBC planned on hiring him for the show. With two positive endorsements we thought it may be a good idea to meet this man. Mike shared Will's phone number with us and we began a dialogue. We scheduled an appointment for December 22nd with William and he also requested we "friend" him on Facebook and join his Facebook father's rights page.

DECEMBER 11TH, 2015: GROUP TEXTS from William H to Jody and Deone

William H: William H here. Feel free to call me and set an appointment for when it works for you guys. There is no area of the law about which I am more passionate, personally or professionally. I have lots of help from numerous sources. Some FB groups: Birthfathers United, The William H Law firm, William H (my personal page).

Us: *We will join these tonight.*

William H: Okay. I will get on FB later tonight and accept your requests to join.

December 12, William H: Did Nancy ever raise constitutionality issues, such as under Troxel v. Granville (a US Supreme Court case) a biological father is PRESUMED to know what is in the best interest of his/her child, and can only be rebutted if the parent is shown to be unfit or incompetent by CLEAR AND CONVINCING evidence? Them keeping/taking Payshence from you violates that constitutionally guaranteed right as upheld in Troxel.

Us: *Nancy wrote up a lot of paperwork that she lodged with the court but when it came down to presenting things she sat there and figured that the commissioner would just read it all. We will email you more documents tomorrow.*

William H: Okay. So you don't know if she raised Troxel or DUE PROCESS constitutional issues or not? It's okay. I wouldn't necessarily expect you to, just wondered.
Us: *That does not sound familiar.*

William H: You assume that she would actually do her job…like most normal people expect of professionals they hire.

Us: *Exactly. For a year and a half she led us to believe she knew what she was doing. We honestly believe if she hadn't been our attorney we would probably be finished right now.*

William H: Man. I am so sorry it is not my style to criticize or sue other lawyers…I do so very judicially, but in her case, it is sounding like the criticism and a possible lawsuit for malpractice is deserved…she earned it.

Us: *Yes, we found out that she's not a family law attorney she is an accident injury attorney.*

William H: Oh, my hell…I am too a personal injury lawyer, but my main area of expertise is the stuff we are talking about…and have put this specialization together over more than two decades, with five out of six cases won before appellate courts. (83% success rate, when statistically, only 7% of all cases appealed are overturned.)
These are the kinds of cases that I eat, drink, and literally sleep…I've had dreams that have given me some pretty amazing insights into these cases. It is the area of the law about which I am most passionate. How much of a retainer do you have coming back to you, if you don't mind me asking?

Us: *About $1,500 out of $5,500. And not one damn thing has happened.*

William H: Roger that. Sad, so sad. It is that kind of no-real-result that gives lawyers a bad reputation overall and it just ticks me off. My dad (died in 1999) always taught me (he was 30 years in USAF full bird colonel) always taught me to do what is right (no matter how unpopular it may be) and let the chips fall where they may. A malpractice claim against Nancy is not a priority right now, but something to keep in the back of our minds.

Us: *We will contact our current attorney, Brad, and let him know that we are switching to you and to send the balance of the retainer to your office.*

William H: Thank you. I appreciate that. As for me, the money is secondary to me, especially right now. I want to hit the ground running on this thing. We can sort out any money issues later. Do you mind me asking what Nancy charged you as an hourly rate? I'm really pumped to meet you guys. I get pretty wound up about these cases. You probably won't be able to get me to shut up. Add to that by definition, lawyers are in love with the sound of their own voice…

Us: *She didn't bill like that. She would just tell us she needed money and we would wire it or drop cash off to her office.*

William H: FYI, I DO NOT bill you for the vast majority of texts messages...especially when just chit chat.

Us: *She got angry at us for questioning some of her tactics and sent us a bill for $78,000.*

William H: Okay. You never saw a bill from her? She didn't ever tell you what her hourly rate was?

Us: *I don't recall her ever going over a contract like most attorneys do - it started with $500 for her to go to a hearing for Steve K and then she just ended up taking over. I really think she shoots from the hip and makes it up as she goes along. It was a bad and really weird experience. We respect your expertise and professionalism and we know you have bills to pay like everyone else does.*

William H: This is a very dangerous lawyer who does that. I have sued other lawyers for malpractice, including other Utah lawyers. There is an unwritten code of "don't sue one in your own profession..." Many lawyers follow it. I don't. Oh my hell!!!! You can't script this stuff. **Truth is (sadly) stranger than fiction.**

Us: *As you will find out as you delve into this case - I'm sure it will be the most bizarre yet.*

William H: When you get $$$ back from her, be very careful about signing anything. Some lawyers try to put in a "release of all claims" against the lawyer in exchange for getting your refund. So wrong to do that and it's unethical. Most bizarre yet...well I will owe you some thanks for yet again, making the practice of law interesting.

Us: *We never signed parting paperwork or got money back from Nancy. Our current attorney is Brad K who we recently found out is a teacher - which explains why it takes him so long to get back to us if he does at all.*

William H: Oh okay. I wondered who Brad was. Makes sense now. How long did he represent you?

Us: *Since June.*

December 13, William H: I'm getting your emails. Thanks! Right on!!! I eat these legal documents for breakfast!!!

Us: *Hope you are hungry then.*

William H: Lol. At least five squares a day, but trying to lose weight to not fall so fast when skydiving.

Us: *There is good wisdom in that.*

William H: You're kind to say that, but conventional wisdom would sternly suggest that I not jump out of a perfectly good airplane to begin with.

Us: *Good point.*

December 18th, William H: I just sent this text to the supervising producer at NBC:

Good afternoon Gentlemen. Just wanted to give you a quick heads up. Not trying to be a pest, but thought you should know my schedule in January and February is filling up quickly. Obviously, if the show is approved and we have limited windows of time, I will reschedule everything I can to make room for taping the show. I have little control, however, when it comes to rescheduling court hearings and trials - judges aren't typically too sympathetic to the schedules of the lawyers. You guys have any update on where we are at? Thanks!! Well, here is some good news...I just got this text back:

"Hi William, I appreciate your time constraints. We are moving forward, and your case has been approved. Let me try to get you some specific information. I will try to get you as much info as I can, but network productions are always subject to change. So sit tight. I will get back to you ASAP."

My reply:
Thanks for the quick response. That is great news. More details coming in from Supervising producer…we can talk more on Tuesday but they are starting to pull together their filming schedule (February) and whether your show will premier, and contract being draft up by NBC lawyers. You have a lawyer you want to look at yours?

Jody: *You if you're OK with it.*

William H: Haha. Yes. I hoped you would see I was joking. I will do the best I possibly can.
Hey this is CRITICAL: FYI, I just got this text from the Supervising Producer of the show:
"Hey William, FYI, you can't speak to anyone about the show yet, media or social media. If NBC sees it, they'll pull it." Hopefully you guys are keeping this under wraps.

Deone: *We are - plus we are private people anyway.*

William H:
Haha. Very well. I gotta tell you, Jody, and don't' take this the wrong way, please, I'm a happily married man (28 years today, it's our Anniversary today), and love my wife like no other, but Deone is CRAZY gorgeous!! Maybe she should be my paralegal and sit next to us on the show because I think her insane good looks will make your strong case even stronger!!! Her pic on her email should inspire any man (and probably women as well) to want to do some real estate business with her. I have you on my calendar for 3:00 PM on Tuesday, December 22nd.

(When I read this text I got a sour taste in my mouth and a creepy chill went through my body. I felt it was extremely inappropriate that he should bring my appearance into the conversation. This man seemed very chatty for being a professional attorney and I had never seen anyone so proper in their punctuation using text messaging. What was all the "…" about? It was also odd that he didn't remember anything about our case or Nancy and was even ready to sue her in spite of the fact Nancy had been such an advocate of him.
At that point, I didn't want to meet with William at all. I wanted Jody to go by himself but he was equally upset by William's comments. After several days of discussion we decided to set the comments aside, attend the meeting, and put out trust in the fact that NBC television was giving him such a high endorsement. I went on line and researched William. I found he had been on several prominent national television shows as a father's rights expert and I also contacted three of the past fathers that were on his Facebook page that Will had represented and got good feedback.)

December 21, William H:
Sorry for this question but wanted to confirm…we have to do some year-end accounting and closing some books…were you guys planning on paying the $2,500 retainer tomorrow?

Jody: *We sure are.*

William H: Thanks so much. That helps with our year end stuff. Really appreciate it.

Jody: *Just thank God someone cares.*

William H: Well, dads are the part of my practice I care THE MOST about.

DECEMBER 22ND, 2015: INITIAL MEETING with William H

William's office was in the basement of his house in West Jordan, Utah. We were greeted at the door by three or four indoor dogs jumping and licking. William ushered us through the house; there was a quick introduction to his wife who was in the kitchen, then down the stairs to a very cramped and cluttered office with bookshelves that were full of memorabilia and law volumes. The house was average and in a bit of disrepair. Jody and I sat on low chairs in one corner while William sat on a stool looking down at us. He then began an hour and a half of pontificating about how great he was. We spent a little bit of time discussing our case and I mentioned I had called him before at the urging of Nancy S but had never heard back. He didn't recollect anything about Nancy or our case or acknowledge my phone call. I agreed to email over the pertinent documents he would need to bring him up to speed.

There are a few things in hindsight I have learned that seem to be consistently true:

An honest man doesn't have to tell you he is honest and an attorney shouldn't have to spend ninety minutes convincing himself out loud that he is awesome. Nevertheless, we gave him the $2,500 retainer in cash and he wrote us out a receipt. We then left to get our Christmas shopping done.

DECEMBER 28TH, 2015: EMAIL to William H

William, I'm sending you over multiple communications...there are also documents I have sent you regarding Kirk and Kelly from the past that state that they cannot consume alcohol; that the children cannot have any sex offenders around; that they need to get employment - these have all been and continue to be violated.

THIS IS FROM THE FEBRUARY ORDER FROM COMMISSIONER BLOOM AND INCLUDES ITEMS IN CONTEMPT:

1. The respondent's Motion to Vacate the Order of April 20 is denied.

2. A new PGAL shall be appointed. The February 20, 2015, Order of Appointment and Findings shall remain effective for this appointment. The scope of the new PGAL shall be limited as stated on the record. Mary C shall provide all of her documents and other information to the new PGAL. A PGAL who is willing to reduce his or her retainer should be sought. Intervenor, Jody Rhorer, shall pay the initial costs associated with the PGAL.

3. All parties shall provide complete financial declarations within twenty days. (Jody Completed his in February and updated it a few months ago.)

4. Dr. Natovich is appointed to perform a limited purpose evaluation. The parties shall explore the possibility of Dr. Natovich accepting a smaller retainer. The Petitioner and the Respondent shall bear one-half of the costs of the fees for the evaluation. Intervenor Jody Rhorer shall pay one-half of the costs of the fee for the evaluation.

5. The child shall be made available by the Respondent to be evaluated by a therapist.

6. Each party shall provide a hair follicle/strand drug test to the new PGAL within one week. (Jody completed a drug test months ago.)

It was further ordered that Mary C's recommendations regarding hair testing for drugs be granted and that those tests occur within a week of May 27th, 2015, and the tests were to be forwarded to the new GAL when appointed. Kirk J was further ordered to arrange for Payshence to see a counselor to determine if counseling is recommended, and if so, arrange to meet the child's counseling needs. No visitation without supervision by Kelly H and she is not to have visitation at Kirk J's home. Payshence is to be put in counseling immediately. Deone

DECEMBER 29TH, 2015: GROUP TEXTS from William H

William H: Continuing to get your emails and immersing myself in the case. My intern is finishing up the pagination of the two boxes of documents.

Us: *Great - when will you notify the court that you are taking over?*

William H: Probably this week. Just looking at some documents to make sure I have "ducks in a row" first, because that will likely be the first of a **"shock and awe"** series of filings.

<u>2016</u>

<u>JANUARY 6TH, 2016:</u> GROUP TEXTS to William H

Jody: Hello William, this is Jody. Just checking to see if you have any news. Thank you.

William H: Plowing through the documents. Intriguing!!! Looking forward to nailing this one. I MEAN NAILING IT BIG TIME.

Texting was William's preferred method of communication. His voicemail box on his phone usually said "The voicemail box is full," and he rarely responded to emails. Brad was no longer representing us so it was imperative that William file his notification to the court that he was our new attorney.

<u>JANUARY 15TH, 2016:</u> GROUP TEXTS to William H

Us: *Wondering if we could get an idea of timeline and when you plan to have something filed on Jody's case?*

William H: <u>It will be this next week because I am stacking up multiple documents, one to file right after the other for about five to six days,</u> depending on how the next couple documents and my research of the facts and law on them go.

Us: *Ok. Have you heard from NBC?*

William H:
Yes. Mike tells me that the lawyers are behind on everyone's contracts for all NBC shows because of the holidays.

January 30, Us: *Jody said you were going to call me with an update today.*

William H: Yes, In and out of service…traveling in this mess but I will call later in the PM.

4:04 PM, William H: Now a good time?

My conversation with William consisted of a handful of excuses followed up by promises that he would have his "shock and awe" motions done and filed soon. He stated that everything was pretty much ready to go, he was just putting on some finishing touches and would get them over to me for review. I was also concerned about the letter that was supposed to be coming from Dr. Natovich's office. She had sent an email stating that she planned on conducting a home evaluation and would be sending out a letter of instruction.

<u>FEBRUARY 1ST, 2016:</u> EMAILS to William H

Good Evening William, Just checking in to see if you are going to send over the 3 motions we discussed on Sat. I don't have anything in my email. We have scheduled the custody evaluator, Dr. Natovich, to do our home evaluation on Monday, February 10th, at 5:00 PM. It appears from the letter she sent that the visit to our home and to Kirk J's will complete her evaluation. We need to be ready to present findings in court. I would like to get the docs reviewed you have drawn up ASAP so you can get them filed. Please text Jody when you have sent the email so I can get the review done. If you have too many other cases going and you cannot make this a priority, please let us know so we can seek alternative council. We can't put this off any longer as 5 weeks have already passed since we met with you and there still has not been a formal Notice of Appearance or notification made by you to Dr. Natovich. Kind regards, Jody and Deone Rhorer

February 2

I'm working on finishing those up. I don't know if Jody told you, but I've been having some serious fatigue and mental acuity issues from the meds following my fall down the stairs. I'm getting better and stronger each day, and tapering off the meds, and will get everything to you ASAP. William H

FEBRUARY 5th, 2016: GROUP TEXTS to William H

William H: My mother-in-law died this morning. Will be a working weekend for me to get your matters and those of others done. Which is no problem.

Us: *So Sorry.*

February 8, Us: *Can you give Jody a call?*

William H: I'm on my way to the airport. I have him on the calendar for Monday.

Us: *Custody evaluation is on Monday.*

FEBRUARY 11TH, 2016: HOME EVALUATION by Dr. Natovich

The custody evaluator showed up promptly at 5:00 and brought with her a friend of similar age and stature. I had taken special measures to ensure the house was shown in its best light. Our home is in the woods and very much like a storybook house with cedar shakes and cobblestone exterior and a white slatted fence surrounding our nearly three acres of trees. We have a beautiful view of the mountain which hosts a small ski resort that can be viewed from our back deck. At the center of our home is a great room with a large stone fireplace reaching up to the second story of the vaulted ceiling. I fell in love with this cottage nearly fifteen years earlier and raised my four boys here.

On this particular day, I had the fire blazing in the fireplace, candles burning, relaxing music playing, and I had cookies and tea ready for Dr. Natovich, which she and her friend enjoyed before we did a walk about of the house. Mia was home and she asked if she could speak with her alone for a few minutes - which she did. As we walked room by room, the doctor mainly wanted to talk about the home decor and how she appreciated my style of mixing antiques, art, and modern together. I really don't think the evaluation could have gone any more perfect than it did.

FEBRUARY 11TH, 2016: DECLARATION OF PROBABLE CAUSE: STATE OF UTAH vs. Kirk J
THIS INFORMATION IS BASED ON EVIDENCE OBTAINED FROM (5) WITNESSES

Your declarant bases this information upon the following: The statement of 7-year-old "A" that she lives with her mom and stepdad, defendant Kirk J. "A" states that on or about September 13, 2015, defendant Kirk J spanked her on her butt twice and smacked her. "A" states she was scared and looked away when Kirk demanded her to look at him. When she wouldn't look at him, he smacked her on the face. "A" stated her stepdad used an open hand when he smacked her. Pursuant to Utah Code 78B-5-705 I declare under criminal penalty of the State of Utah that the forgoing is true and correct to the best of my belief and knowledge. Detective D.D.

FEBRUARY 11TH, 2016: WARRANT OF ARREST: State of Utah vs. Kirk J
THE STATE OF UTAH:
*To any Peace Officer in the State of Utah, Greetings: Any information, based upon a written declaration having been declared by **UNIFIED POLICE DEPARTMENT** Agency and it appears from the Information or Declaration filed with Information, that there is probable cause to believe the public offense of: **CHILD ABUSE**. Class A Misdemeanor, has been committed, and **KIRK J** has committed them.*

*　　**YOU ARE THEREFORE COMMANDED** to arrest the above-named defendant forthwith and bring the defendant before this Court, or before the nearest or most accessible magistrate for setting bail. If the defendant has fled justice, you shall pursue the defendant into any other county of this state and there arrest the defendant. The Court finds reasonable ground to believe defendant will not appear upon a summons.*

FEBRUARY 16TH, 2016: GROUP TEXTS to William

Us: *Custody evaluation was done and went well. When will you have the court docs filed for contempt? Could you get in touch with us regarding our case and the status?*

February 17, William H: Have you guys sent me a copy of the custody evaluation?

Us: *The evaluator has not completed it. She just did the home evaluation on Monday.*

William H: Did she give you some indication when it would be done?

Us: *She's going to Kirk J's house next. That's why we need to get a hearing scheduled for the contempt of court. She's probably going to ask for more money and Kirk and Kelly have never paid their portion. Jody had to pay the entire amount to get the process started. Can you contact her and see when she thinks she will have it done? Her contract said three to four months and we are at five months now.*

William H: I'm filing the notice of appearance in the custody matter today, and will be starting the series of filings over the next few days. (I got Deone's voice mail message.)

I had left an ultimatum voice mail stating that we needed to see some action or we were going to have to seek other counsel. It had now been two months since our initial contact with William and not one smidgeon of work had been done, just fast-talking empty promises.

February 19, William H: Just emailed you the Notice of Appearance I'm filing today.

Us: *Thank you.*

FEBRUARY 19TH, 2016: NOTICE OF APPEARANCE by William H, Commissioner Kase presiding
The above-referenced counsel, William H, hereby enters his appearance for and on behalf of Intervenor, Jody Rhorer, in this matter. He hereby requests that all notices, pleadings, correspondence, and other matters pertaining to this case be directed to him at the above-stated address and other contact information.

Seven weeks after we hired him, William H finally filed his notice with the court that he was our attorney. It took seven weeks for him to file two sentences. Once again, my instincts were telling me to run - but he had our money.

FEBRUARY 26TH, 2016: GROUP TEXTS to William H

Us: *When should we expect to see the two motions we discussed filed?*

William H: Monday or Tuesday.

Us: *Super.*

March 1, Us: *I haven't seen anything come over on my email pertaining to the motions you were going to have filed by today. Are those forthcoming later?*

William H: Media frenzy again yesterday. I haven't' forgotten about you guys. Documents coming soon.

March 3, Us: *So are the motions done then?*

No response. "WHAT THE HELL IS A MEDIA FRENZY?" I was thinking

March 5, Us: *So are the motions done then?*

William H: Nearly completed. I anticipate having them tomorrow. I'm in office all day thankfully, no court for once.

March 7, Us: *Please let me know when it's on my email so I can review it before you file.*

William H: Will do.

March 8, Us: *How is it going William?*

William H: Hiccup with my son. Up most of the night and he went into the hospital today. You are next on my list. I'm going to be working late tonight to try and finish up your motions.

Jody: *Hope your son gets well. We would like to kick Kirk and Kelly's ass. Dr. Natovich is overdue on her timeframe. We want this to get done ASAP.*

William H: Of course. I am truly sorry for delays. <u>You will see my claws come out very soon.</u>

Deone: *I see it this way. You had one turbulent night with your son - Jody's had four turbulent years without his daughter. Every moment lost will never be recovered. You were hired in December and its now March. If you can't do this, please just let us know so we can make other arrangements. Thank you.*

William H: Understood. Moving forward.

March 14, Us: *We need someone who is fired up about our case. In December you said you were but inactions have shown otherwise. Another week has passed and your promise to have the motions done has not come to fruition. If you cannot do this please just tell us and we will come and pick up our money and find another attorney.*

William H: I'm doing it later this week.

March 16, William H: Further review of documents. I noticed that there was an Amended Recommendation and Order entered on 4/20/15. Connie brought motion to vacate that order on 4/25/15. Nancy filed opposition to motion to vacate on 5/6/15. I don't see on the document or in the documents I'ver reviewed where Connie filed any reply on the motion to vacate, or that there was ever a ruling on that motion. Do you guys recall if either of those things ever happened.

Us: *We went to court in May about all of that. It should be in the ruling.* (I had emailed William that information in December.)

William H: I will look again.

<u>MARCH 18TH, 2016:</u> EMAILS from Dr. Natovich's office

Hello, Could you please update us as to who is currently representing you? Dr. Natovich is sending out a letter and we have a couple of different people listed. Best regards, Lynn

Dear Jody and Deone, I am in the process of completing the evaluation you have been involved with. I am requesting that all adult parties provide me with a current criminal background check as part of this process. You can obtain this at the Utah Bureau of Criminal Investigation in Salt Lake City. I would appreciate it if you would both obtain this and deliver the reports to my office as soon as possible, and by April 8 at the latest. Thank you for your assistance. Sincerely, Dr. Natovich

Hmm. Interesting request to be made on me. I wrote back that I had no criminal history and there would be nothing but a blank paper to send them. Regardless, I was told I needed to do it anyway so I spent half a day driving to Salt Lake City and obtaining a sheet of paper that stated "No Criminal Record Found." The request, being on all parties, was timely though considering Kirk J had yet another child abuse charge against him that would surely show up on his report - if he indeed provided one.

MARCH 22ND, 2016: GROUP TEXTS to William H

Deone: *William, you clearly have no interest in taking our case. I will be in your area today around 3:00. Please have a check ready for the $2,500 Jody gave you as a retainer made out to Jody Rhorer so I can pick it up. Thank you, Deone Rhorer.*

William H: I have considerable interest and have kept you in the loop. I've spent an enormous amount of time preparing for filings. I'm offended that after all I have done…that you would suggest that I have no interest.

Us: *You never even notified the custody evaluator that you were our attorney nor have you responded to the emails that were sent several days ago from her office.*

William H: Jody's is not a simple case. The record is thousands of pages long filing two boxes. I am the best qualified to handle this case, and as indicated last week I'm committed to moving it forward expeditiously. If you decide to go with other counsel, this is fine, but there will be no refund. In fact, you will see upon generation of an invoice that you owe me more money.

Us: *I have promise after promise from you that you would have motions filed. You have given us zero updates.*

William H: That is not true at all. I have updated you numerous times by text.

Deone: *I want copies of all of your updates as well as what you have done on the case. Please send copies of the motion you have prepared as you said they were nearly completed on several occasions. We have wasted another three months. Last December you rolled out a plan with us and none of it has been executed. You do have plenty of time, however, to promote yourself on Facebook. I expect you to do what you promised and treat my husband fairly or I will be posting about our experience of many promises and no delivery.*

William H: When was the last time you saw any such "promotion" on Facebook? That's fine. You can post whatever you like. Those who know me know my reputation and know the quality of my work.

Deone: *Well we have seen none of that - only excuses. What have you done?? I want copies. Did you notify Dr. Natovich? Did you even read the email I forwarded you? You never responded.*

William H: You can't even imagine what goes on behind the scenes in a case of this magnitude. Drafts shall be provided to you and I will have motions filed by no later than one week from today. **If I don't, I'm fine to give you a full refund of the $2,500 and to waive any additional fees that have been incurred**.

Deone: *Please answer my question regarding Dr. Natovich. Did you notify her that you were the attorney? Did you receive the email I sent and why did we not get a response?*

William H: You are not my client, Jody is. Whatever demands or agreements or withdrawals as counsel are going to come from him. There are numerous emails I have reviewed and responded to. I will double check when I'm back in the office and get an answer to your question.

Jody: *It's just this - you promised I would have visitations with my daughter - you promised there would be prosecution of contempt of court on Kirk and Kelly. You said that would happen immediately when we first met with you. We put our faith in you, William. All we need is to get you and Dr. Natovich in court. I've been at this since 2007. I'd like to see an end to this with me and my daughter back together. Me and Deone have no problem with help drafting or going over any documents and putting our thoughts together to help out on costs. The bottom line is when we met you in your office the things you said gave us hope.*

You were the pit bull we needed. When we get emails from Dr. Natovich, she doesn't even know you are our attorney. It raises some concerns - I hope you understand that. Remember you said that you eat cases like this for breakfast? That's what you told us. My wife is as equal as I am in this case if not more. She's put countless hours and time in to this case and knows it better than the back of her hand. Wish y'all could put your heads together and champion this cause.

And on another note, just think of the publicity that an attorney would get if this case was exposed to the public for what the State of Utah has done and with all the other adoptions and children that the state kidnaps and steals from fathers and to be the lawyer that champions and shows the world what this state does would make your Facebook page blowup. We need the most ruthless Constitutionalist attorney to present this case and stand by us.

MARCH 21ST, 2016:   LETTER TO COURT FROM DR. NATOVICH

Dear Commissioner Kase,

I am writing to update you regarding the evaluation involving the matter of Kelly H vs. Kirk J, (Jody Rhorer, Intervenor). At this point in time I have completed all necessary appointments and am reviewing materials. In light of the atypical nature of this case, along with dynamics between the parties, I believe it would be appropriate to forgo conducting a Settlement Conference as a forum in which to share my input. Instead, I think it would be more helpful to prepare a written summary of my findings to share with counsel and the Court. It might then be productive to meet in the context of a dedicated Settlement Conference to explore whether a settlement can be reached, provided that both parties and counsel are amendable to this.

Please advise me if you would prefer that I proceed otherwise. I would be happy to participate in a telephone conference with the Court and counsel if requested. Thank you for your consideration.

Respectfully,
Dr. Natovich

MARCH 24TH, 2016:   GROUP TEXTS to William H

Jody: *Hello William, this is Jody. We were wondering if you got that letter from Dr. Natovich. We do not want a mediation. We want to go to court and get my daughter ASAP. Let Dr. Natovich know to present her findings to the commissioner. That way we can have our hearing and a decision to have him get my daughter. No mediation at all. Won't even consider it.*

William H: Will do.

March 29, William H: Please confirm email addresses for me to send court filings to. They will come to you before my head hits the pillow tonight. Do you have an email address for Dr. Natovich?

Deone: *I'll forward it to your email.*

William H: My response to her letter coming to your email soon. It is a fairly "generic" response.

MARCH 25TH, 2016:   CHILD ABUSE INVOLVING PHYSICAL INJURY - Class A Misdemeanor, Outstanding Warrant, Kirk J

The records of the court indicate there is now an outstanding warrant for the arrest of Kirk J referred to as "Defendant." A corresponding amount of bail was set at the time the arrest warrant was issued.
Date of Warrant 2/11/2016   Bail $1,500.00

Pursuant to Section 59-10-529 Utah Code, $1,066.00 has been deducted from your state income tax refund and has been sent to the court to be considered as bail to guarantee the defendant's appearance in court. An administrative fee of $15.00 has also been deducted from your state income tax refund. Any refund balance is being returned to you.

The defendant must therefore appear in court within 40 days from the date of this notice. At the time of that appearance, the defendant will be given the opportunity to understand and exercise the constitutional and statutory rights including the right to be heard. If the defendant fails to appear within that 40-day period, the defendant's arrest may be issued.

MARCH 29TH, 2016: LETTER from William H to Dr. Natovich

Dear Dr. Natovich,

Thank you for a copy of your letter to Commissioner Kase dated 3/21/2016. As I'm relatively new to the case, I'm working to come up to speed on this unique and document-intensive matter, as well as the multiplicity of factual and legal considerations involved.

My initial reaction to your letter is very positive, insofar as we look forward to seeing your recommendations, and considering the potential for a global, or at least, partial resolution through a mediated settlement conference. We want to give any such efforts the greatest potential for success. I will discuss your letter further with my client, Mr. Rhorer, and advise him as appropriate.

Generally, I'm very much in favor of mediated resolutions, as opposed to battling it out in the courtroom, though I must admit that I enjoy, as an attorney/litigator, the courtroom/trial experiences. By the same token, I have some reservations, simply given the history of this case, and some of the very unique facts and circumstances. In short, I remain "guardedly optimistic" that we may be able to find considerable mutually-beneficial advantages to mediating this case.

Please let me know if you have any questions, comments, or concerns at this time, or if you need any additional information. You will notice my cell/text number is listed at the top of this letter. Text is the quickest and easiest way to get a response from me, especially as a solo practitioner, often away from the office. I look forward to working with you on this case,

Sincerely,

William H, WH Law Firm

What a bunch of hogwash! All he was supposed to do is notify the Doctor that he was our attorney - not apply for a job! They would not be "working together" she would merely be sending him the report from her evaluation as our representative. I was beginning to wonder if this guy knew anything at all. Jody was clear there would be no mediation, however, William jumped right into agreement of a mediation meeting.

MARCH 29TH, 2016, GROUP TEXTS to William H

Jody: *She says she's turning in her findings to the court and then she says she suggests that we mediate. We're not going to mediate. It's a waste of time and money. We need a court date in contempt of court - charges filed on Kirk and Kelly.*

William H: Understood. The letter was intended as a first contact with Dr. Natovich. The commissioner may request the parties to attempt mediation as a condition to certifying the case for trial. We will have to see how that shakes out. You haven't seen any report or letter with her recommendations yet, have you? If the court mandates mediation over Dr. Natovich's statement that "parties willing…" You won't have a choice.

I'm finalizing the other documents, including a request for a scheduling/status conference where we can discuss feasibility of mediation, and other deadlines in the case to get things moving along expeditiously.

Jody: *Nope I want a trial. I wave it. I won't show up. I don't mediate with kidnappers. It's like what Regan said - do not negotiate with terrorists. The state of Utah and Kirk and Kelly kidnapped my kid.*

William H: Jody you are not listening to me. If the court mandates it, you have to show up or you will NEVER be given a trial date. You can show up at mediation and say "Give me my child back. I don't negotiate with kidnappers," but you have to at least show up at mediation.

Jody: *I don't know what to say. You just sent that letter to Dr. Natovich saying you want your clients to mediate. Are you on Kirk and Kelly's side? Your letter has not one thing that I asked plus if you read her letter, it says if both parties are agreeable and I told you from the beginning I would not negotiate.*

William H: Jody you are not reading the letter correctly. Also, you are not understanding the larger strategy involved here, that 23 years of litigating these types of matters has given me. We need to have trust between you and me, and some confidence that I can guide you in the best route to achieve the desired result: GETTING YOUR DAUGHTER BACK TO YOU!!! No need to mediate. There is a huge strategic advantage to them thinking I am supportive of it, but you are dead set against it. Also, look at the fourth paragraph discussing my "reservations" about mediation. I'm nearly through drafting the formal "objection to mediation recommendation," for your review and approval, but I need the letter to Dr. Natovich to sink in for a day or two. There are litigation nuances that are at play that you may not fully understand or appreciate. It is the use of those nuances and strategies that I have used successfully to win four out of five cases with the Supreme Court, that strikes fear into those opposing Father's rights - - a reputation I have worked hard to develop over two decades -- an approach to these cases that has reunited many fathers with their children when naysayers have said they didn't have a snowball's chance. We've lost the trust and confidence between us for some reason, in part due to some circumstances that have led to delays. I've resolved several matters and have time opening up to pull the trigger on several things: (1) motion of order to show cause for contempt of court; (2) written discovery including request for admissions that will likely support a motion for summary judgment; (3) a motion for a declaratory order that 78B-15-607 is unconstitutional (4) the fraud, and tortious interference with custodial rights lawsuit; and (5) other strategies that I wish to discuss with you in detail now that I have immersed myself more in your case, 80% of which have been drafted. I feel I am the most qualified in all those areas and can give you the best chance of success. However, if you and I cannot use trust and a good working relationship, I feel it is better I withdraw from your case and you take your best shot with someone else. I'm tired and I feel like I'm hitting my head against a brick wall. I do not want to invest any of my time or your money in these things if you and I can't get on the same page.

I t was well past 10:00 PM and William H continued his rambling text messages. We had gone to bed and to sleep. When I read through the texts the next day it was like reliving the very first meeting we had in December and I knew this was his way of trying to buy more time and that he didn't have the motions completed as promised.

March 30, Deone: *As per the agreement you made on March 22nd to return the entire retainer of $2,500 to Jody Rhorer if you failed to deliver the agreed upon motions by end of day on March 29th, please have the check ready and all materials we delivered to you for pickup at your home between 10:00 and 10:30 tomorrow.*

William H: No that was not the agreement because he changed his mind and decided not to cooperate with the prosecution of the cases. There will be no refund. In fact, he owes me more for all the hours spent to get to this point. Once again, Deone, on these types of issues I must hear from Jody. He is my client not you. As to getting you all your files I can have them for you by next Wednesday. I'm out of town tomorrow through Tuesday of next week. I put in considerable work to get this case where it is and you (and Jody supposedly) are pulling the plug. Besides, if Jody had responded last night to my text messages (which he never did) I could have and would have finished and forwarded all documents to you as previously promised. Frankly I have my doubts that Jody was sober during the text exchanges. Much of his texts were incoherent.

Deone: *Jody doesn't even drink! We went to bed at 10:00. We have everything in writing and I will be posting all over the internet that you are a pompous fraud and a liar. I'm letting NBC know as well.*

Jody: *You are a joke, William. How many people put their trust in you and you gave them false hope? All you have done is lie to us - one lie after another.*

William: Clients that have trust in me have that trust because they have confidence in my abilities and the advice I give them. You REJECTED that last night repeatedly and would not respond to my pleas to get on the same page. That failure to have this case move forward now lies squarely on your shoulders, not mine.

Deone: *You have done NOTHING!! You are a joke and lazy - just full of excuses and I have already documented all of this to take to the Bar.*

Jody: *I don't need to argue with people that accuse me of things that I don't do. You said when we first met you that you were going to get me visitation with my daughter. You said you were going to file the contempt of court charges. You gave us hope. We thought you were the best there is. I guess this is what we get for putting our hope in you.*

William: I don't care. Do whatever you have to do. I don't care about you saying whatever you want. Make sure you tell the truth, including the exchange of texts last night or I will sue you for defamation and any and all causes of action that are appropriate. You should think about all the men I have helped, including Jody. I can't believe it has come to this. Fine he doesn't drink. You should have told me you were going to bed. You had to know that I was preparing a response to you.

Deone: *You have not kept your word a single time and people with jobs go to bed at reasonable hours. We only tell the truth and we have all your words documented including the promise to return Jody's money. We will see you in small claims court.*

William: All of those things can still happen, Jody. Just as I texted you last night. Lawsuits are living breathing animals, that change and develop over time. I also told you I am a solo practitioner and you are not the only client I have. Also, I can't help that some delays resulted from my mother-in-law being in hospice, then dying and then a family member attempting suicide in my home. Go for it. I will cross claim for all the other time and expenses I've incurred representing Jody. I have everything documented as well. It is a shame that we can't bury the hatchet and get on with the business of getting Jody's sweet daughter back where she belongs. Which I am still very much prepared to do. It takes a willing client, however, and one willing to take my advice and trust in my years of training, knowledge, and experience. Last night you were refusing to do that - repeatedly in your responses to my earlier texts. Why would I continue to work on your case if you do not listen to me and do not acknowledge what I'm saying and do not accept my advice. It would be absurd for me to continue doing so under such circumstances.

Jody: *Feel sorry for you William. Sorry I ever met you. I'll pray for you William.*

William: Sure, Thanks. I appreciate all prayers but don't feel sorry for me. I don't need your pity. My grandfather always taught me when you point the finger at someone, there are always three fingers pointing back at you. I will pray for you and your daughter as well, and that you find someone to help you in the manner you deem appropriate, though if contrary to proven track record, and contrary to and in the absence of sage advice, God help you. I will pray for that. You still haven't responded to my myriad of questions I've raised and I can only reasonably assume it is because you have no good answers. If you have a change of heart and want to move forward with guns blazing, I'm ready for that.

I don't know how Jody stayed so composed through all this. William clearly had mental issues and must have thought we were stupid to keep making his empty offers after all the insults he had flung our way. Now we were on the hunt again for competent counsel. We probably should have gone back to Brad since he was up to par on the case, but his style was that of a turtle - slow and steady. We wanted fast and furious.

MARCH 29TH, 2016: EMAILS to Dr. Natovich

Dear Dr. Natovich, Please, disregard the letter that was sent to you, without our approval, by attorney William H. We have no intention to mediate as there is no possible way mediation could have any fruitful results and would be a waste of time and money. We wish to proceed to court with Commissioner Kase immediately. We will be seeking counsel that listens to and abides by our wishes. Thank you, Jody and Deone Rhorer

March 30, 2:47 PM

Hi Deone and Jody, Just to be clear, I referred to the possibility of having a settlement conference with Commissioner Kase subsequent to my preparing a written summary. This is part of the usual procedure, and is typically conducted as a "mediated settlement conference." I believe that this meeting is what William H was referring to, not the option of pursuing mediation rather than a hearing with the commissioner. I hope this clarification is helpful. Sincerely, Dr. Natovich,

6:32 PM

Thank you Dr. Natovich, If you saw all the bizarre texts William H sent us late last night then you would know that he has no idea what he is referring to and does not appear to be a stable human being at this time in his career. Please do not include him in anything else. We are seeking other counsel and until that happens, we will handle things on our own as we feel we are the most prepared to do so. Please let us know when you have scheduled the conference with Commissioner Kase as we are most anxious. Jody and Deone Rhorer

CHAPTER 16
DEVIN C

We were at a loss for who to turn to for advice now on obtaining new counsel. We just kept striking out. We needed a home run. I went back to where we started - Stephen K.

"Hi Stephen. How are you doing down there in the land of warm?" I asked.

"I'm liking it. How are you and Jody? How is your case going?"

"Well, that's actually why we are calling. We need another Stephen K and we are hoping you may be able to refer us to someone."

"Nancy didn't work out for you?" Steve asked.

"No. She ended up going a little crazy and we had to let her go."

"I'm sorry. I really didn't know her well. I thought she would do okay standing in on the hearing."

"We are hoping you can point us to an attorney that would be the most like you - since we can't have you do it."

"Okay. Hmm. If I was to suggest an attorney that was similar to me, not me, but as close as you can get, I would suggest Devin C." He answered.

And that is how we came about hiring our next attorney. We had a meeting in his high-rise downtown Salt Lake City office building. It was similar to Stephen K's in that it had not been updated in about 20 or more years and contained just the basic necessities.

Devin C resembled the older gentleman character from the monopoly game. He was very to the point, much like Stephen K, and very budget conscious. We signed his contract and gave him the retainer to get started. Unfortunately, a majority of our documents were still in William H's basement so Devin would have to press on with what he had - and he did so promptly and without excuses.

GROUP TEXTS to William H

Deone: *Our attorney is Devin C as you should know as he noticed you on his filings. All communication should run through him. May I suggest that you send in your withdrawal in a speedy fashion as the more you badger us while we are still supposed to be under your representation the worse it will look for you in front of the judge.*

William: Send communication through your attorney as you requested.

Deone: *Please drop our materials off at Devin's office. He is expecting them. It is a real office with real hours.*

William: As you requested, send communication through your attorney.

APRIL 5TH, 2016: APPEARANCE OF COUNSEL, submitted by Devin C, Commissioner Kase presiding

COMES NOW *Devin C and hereby enters his appearance as counsel for Jody Rhorer, an Intervenor in the above-captioned matter.*

　　1. It is my understanding that William H, Mr. Rhorer's prior attorney, should soon be withdrawing.

APRIL 5TH, 2016: SUBMISSION OF LETTER FROM DR. NATOVICH AND REQUEST FOR CUSTODY EVALUATION SETTLEMENT CONFERENCE, submitted by Devin C, Commissioner Kase presiding

  COMES NOW *the intervener, Jody Rhorer, by and through his attorney of record, Devin C; and hereby submits the letter from Dr. Natovich dated March 21, 2016, indicating the custody evaluation has been completed and requests that the Honorable Commissioner's Office set a Scheduling Conference to set a Custody Evaluation Settlement Conference.*

  1. Dr. Natovich has indicated that it would only be appropriate to have a Mediated Settlement Conference after she provides a written summary of her findings to share with counsel and the Court prior to the Settlement Conference. It is the intervenor's suggestions that this approach be followed.

  Devin C explained to us that the Mediated Settlement Conference was not a mediation at all in the way that we understood mediations. It was more of an explanation of findings by the custody evaluator. Thus, all the confusion caused by William H just verified that he really did not know what he was doing but thought he could talk himself through anything.

  APRIL 6TH, 2016: APPEARANCE OF COUNSEL AND DEMAND FOR TRIAL BY JURY; THE STATE OF UTAH vs. Kirk J, Judge PP presiding

  TMH, Salt Lake Legal Defender Association, on appointment of the above entitled court, herewith enters an Appearance of Counsel of record for the above-named defendant and demands a trial by jury.

  APRIL 5TH, 2016: APPEARANCE OF COUNSEL FOR THE STATE OF UTAH vs. Kirk J, Judge PP presiding

  A ROSS, Deputy District Attorney, Salt Lake County District Attorney's Office, herewith enters an Appearance of Counsel of record for the above-named plaintiff.

  APRIL 21ST, 2016: NOTICE OF TELEPHONE CONFERENCE, Report Dr. Natovich

  After six pages of emails going round and round for days amongst the attorneys and associated parties, a time was finally established for a TELEPHONE CONFERENCE scheduled for May 2nd, 2016.

  JUNE 1ST, 2016: LETTER FROM DOCTOR NATOVICH

  Dear Counsel,
  I am enclosing my written report in the matter of Kelly H v. Kirk J, with Jody Rhorer as Intervenor. I will provide a courtesy copy to the Court, but will defer to you to formally file it as part of trial preparation if needed. Please feel free to review the contents of the report with your clients, but do not provide them with a copy. Thank you for your consideration.
  Sincerely,
  Dr. Natovich, PhD

  JUNE 1ST, 2016: LIMITED PURPOSE EVALUATION, by Dr. Natovich, Commissioner Kase presiding

CASE BACKGROUND INFORMATION

A. Case Summary:
  Kelly H was married to Kirk J in April 2002, and, according to verified petition, they separated on approximately May 2005. Kelly H gave birth to Payshence Rhorer, now age eight, in 2007, with her biological father being Jody Rhorer, intervenor in the present case. In 2010, Payshence was removed from Kelly H's care by the Division of Child and Family Services. Mr. Rhorer contends that she was placed in his care for approximately seven months during that year, and was then returned to her mother.

A second child welfare case was initiated in early 2012, and, during a related psychological evaluation, Kelly disclosed that she had never divorced Kirk J. This resulted in him being identified as Payshence's presumed father as a function of the Utah Parentage Act. Kelly's parental rights were ultimately terminated by Third District Juvenile Court, and subsequent Juvenile Court findings identified Kirk J as being Payshence's legal father. Kirk J was awarded permanent custody and guardianship of Payshence on July 31, 2012, when she was released from DCFS custody.

Mr. Rhorer filed a motion to intervene in this matter in May 2013, and his motion for intervention was granted the following month. In a hearing on February 20, 2015, the Court determine that Utah Statute 78-B-15-608 was most appropriate to consider in determining whether Mr. Rhorer has standing to proceed. The Court, therefore, ordered that the parties participate in a "Limited Purpose Evaluation" to assess the factors delineated by this Statute.

B. Current Living Arrangements:

Kirk J resides with his significant other in a home in Kearns, Utah. The residence is appropriately furnished, but shows signs of deferred maintenance and is limited in terms of space given the size of the family. At the time of the Examiner's visit Payshence had her own bedroom that contained a bed and dresser, as well as her clothing and a number of toys. In addition to Payshence, the following children resided in the home at that time:

Boy, age five - son of Kelly H and a former paramour (Kirk J is his legal father.)

Boy, age six - son of Kirk J and current girlfriend

Girl, age seven - daughter of Kirk's girlfriend and a former paramour

Boy, age twelve - son of Kelly H and an unknown paramour

Boy, age thirteen - son of Kelly H and Kirk J

Girl, age seventeen - daughter of Kirk's girlfriend and her estranged husband.

The Examiner was informed that, during the evaluation process, the seventeen your old left the home to reside with the family's pastor.

Mr. Rhorer resides with his wife, Deone Rhorer, in a home they own in Eden, Utah. Their residence is spacious and well cared for, and includes a dedicated bedroom for Payshence that has been established in the hope she will one day spend time there. Mr. Rhorer's fourteen-year-old daughter spends regular parent-time with the Rhorer family and was present during the Examiner's visit to the home. Mr. Rhorer also has two adult daughters whom he sees on a regular basis. Mrs. Rhorer has four adult sons ranging in age from nineteen to twenty-seven. They live in their own residences and spend time with her and Mr. Rhorer on holidays and other family occasions.

C. Summary of Procedures:

The present evaluation was completed between September 2015, and February 2016. This process included conjoint and individual interview with Kirk and his partner; Mr. Rhorer and his wife Deone; and a conjoint meeting with Kelly and her current live-in partner. Payshence met with the Examiner in an office setting, having been transported there by Kirk J. The Examiner also conducted a home visit at both Kirk's and Mr. Rhorer's residences. Payshence, as well as the rest of the children who reside there were present during the visit to Kirk J's home. Mr. Rhorer's daughter was present during the Examiner's visit to his residence.

The Examiner reviewed a large number of documents provided by the parties and/or counsel, as well as Utah Criminal History Reports for Kirk J, his girlfriend, Jody Rhorer, and Deone Rhorer.

CONCLUSIONS

A. Results of Clinical Interviews and Observations:

Kirk J was cooperative with the Examiner and completed all requested appointments, but was clearly quite frustrated by the evaluation process. In this regard he demonstrated a low level of investment in "impression management," for example, being difficult to schedule with and sometime demonstrating an overly irritable manner when interacting with the Examiner. Kirk J stated that the Court had determined that he is Payshence's legal father, and expressed the opinion that, as a result, Mr. Rhorer's efforts to become involved as Intervenor should have been disallowed. Kirk stated that it does not matter to him whether or not Payshence is his biological child, he considers her to be his daughter.

Kirk J maintains that Mr. Rhorer has misrepresented the degree to which he has been involved in Payshence's life, and he believes that they have had minimal interaction since she was an infant. In this regard, he states, "I've always been her dad since she was born." Mr. Rhorer maintains that he cared for Payshence much of the time even when he and Kelly were not together. It is Kirk J's opinion that Payshence has no recollection of Mr. Rhorer and that it would be traumatic for her to be reintroduced to him. He describes Payshence as being well adjusted at this point, and attributes this as being largely due to the fact that he has assured her that she is in her "forever home" with him and his girlfriend.

Kirk J indicated that Payshence enjoys spending time with her natural mother a great deal, and he has no concerns about this. He reports the Kelly routinely cares for Payshence every other weekend, in addition to occasional weekday visits.

Jody Rhorer approached the assessment process in an interested and cooperative manner. He demonstrated a high level of motivation and readily completed all tasks required of him. Mr. Rhorer indicates that he has been involved in a lengthy court process in an attempt to be able to re-establish a relationship with his daughter, Payshence. Mr. Rhorer indicates that she was in his physical custody during much of the first three years of her life, as well as for a period of approximately seven months in 2010. He reports that he saw Payshence on an intermittent basis after this, including a period in 2012 in which he resumed a relationship with her natural mother, Kelly. However, it was subsequently established that Kirk J was Payshence's presumed father, due to the fact that he had been legally married to Kelly H at the time of her birth.

Mr. Rhorer discussed his relationship with Payshence in an emotional manner often becoming tearful. He related a wide range of concern about her emotional and physical well-being, most resulting from what he describes as a complicated and chaotic family life. Mr. Rhorer expressed particular concern about Kirk J's criminal history, and the large number of children in his care under what appears to be questionable circumstances. He also believes that Kelly H continues to engage in inappropriate, if not criminal behavior, and questions Kirk J's judgement in allowing her to regularly care for Payshence, despite having had her custodial rights terminated.

All parties concur that Mr. Rhorer's older daughters were allowed to maintain contact with her after his contact was discontinued. These visits were facilitated by Kelly H during times that she spent weekends with Payshence after she had been placed in Kirk J's permanent custody. The parties disagree as to when and why Kelly stopped allowing this contact.

Payshence The Examiner met with Payshence in an office setting, as well as in the context of a home visit to Kirk J's residence. Her behavior was noteworthy in that she related to the Examiner in an inappropriately familiar manner, hugging her at the end of the office appointment, despite having been introduced to her less that an hour prior. This was even more pronounced during the Examiner's visit to Kirk's home. Payshence greeted the Examiner with a tight hug, and sat very close to the her on the couch shortly after her arrival, leaning into her and even put her head on the Examiner's shoulder. This behavior continued throughout the visit, to the point the Examiner had to re-direct Payshence when she persisted in stroking the Examiner's hair and arm. She was unusually interactive with the Examiner in both the office and home setting, eagerly seeking out one-on-one attention and exhibiting disappointment at the end of these visits.

This style of relating, marked by poor boundaries and excessive attention seeking, is characteristic of indiscriminate sociability, and is very concerning in that it is most often seen in children with attachment disorders. Difficulties of this type usually result from a child having inconsistent and/or multiple caretakers at an early age, preventing them from forming strong, secure attachments. Both Kirk J and his girlfriend noted that Payshence has had recurrent difficulty with stealing and lying, behaviors that are also consistent with problems of attachment. Her tousling behavior, along with her difficult history, point to a need for on-going counseling, however, this has not been pursued by her primary caretakers.

Concerns around attachment issues were further supported by her unusual response to the Examiner when asked to draw a picture of her family. After some hesitation to this typically easy task, Payshence announced that the request was "too confusing" and asked if she could make a list of her family members instead. She proceeded to do so, with entries such as "Moms -2; Dads - 3" and so on. When asked to identify who she meant by these entries, she described her "moms" as including Kelly H and Kirk's current live-in girlfriend.

She indicated that her "three dads" refer to Kirk J, Kelly's former spouse, Shayne S, and Kelly's current partner. In sharing this information, Payshence stressed that Kirk is her "real dad, but not adopted."

The Examiner then conversationally inquired, "Oh, I see, so you were born as a baby to your dad Kirk and your mom Kelly?" In response Payshence became visibly anxious and, in a very quiet voice, stated that she has "another dad" but added, "I'm not to talk about him." She confirmed with a nod that this individual is, in fact, named "Jody," adding that she believes that she lived with him for "awhile" but does not remember him. While it appears that Kirk J has actually prohibited conversation about Mr. Rhorer, it is evident that Kelly H has talked about him with Payshence at some length.

In this regard, Payshence shared the opinion that Mr. Rhorer is a "scary" person based on stories she has heard about him being physically abusive toward Kelly H and his older children. It was clear that she had heard about these alleged incidents in great detail, as she described them in a in a dramatic manner, as if she had actually been present at the time of their occurrence. It is my impression that Payshence's feelings about Mr. Rhorer have been greatly influenced by input she has heard from Kelly H, and that these stories contribute to a general sense of anxiety at the prospect of seeing him.

It was further noted that Payshence has an inappropriate range of knowledge about adult topics for her age. For example, she spoke at some length about her prior GAL, repeating Kirk's complaints about her almost verbatim. She also shared details about her biological mother's personal life, including Kelly's distress about having had her tubes tied because she would like to have a baby with her current boyfriend.

B. Consideration of Factors Included in 78-15-608:

The Statute indicates that the Court shall consider the best interest of the child, including a number of specific factors described below. A number of additional factors are included in Statute that are based on factual variables, such as length of time, as opposed to clinical judgement. The Examiner has, therefore, focused this analysis on the factors that are based on clinical expertise and judgment as they relate to the child's best interest.

1. The nature of the relationship between the child and the presumed or declarant father:

Payshence identifies Kirk J as her "real father" although she is aware that he is not actually her biological parent. She relates to him as a significant caretaker, turning to him for assistance and demonstrating spontaneous physical affection toward him. During her visit to the Examiner's office it was noted that she was quite concerned about the timeframe of the appointment, explaining that Kirk J had indicated to her that she "needed to make it quick." Approximately forty-five minutes into the visit Kirk J, in fact, knocked loudly on the Examiner's door, and stated that he needed to leave in order to meet family members for dinner. Payshence appeared apologetic in response, immediately cleaning up craft materials that she had been using and assuring the Examiner that she did not need to finish the project they were working on. The Examiner encouraged her to take the necessary materials with her so that she could finish the activity at home. Payshence was quick to show these to Kirk, assuring him that she had not stolen the items, but rather, that they had been given to her. Her response to Kirk, along with her concern that he would think she had stolen items from the Examiner's office, were more anxious than normal as she appeared visibly fearful of making Kirk J angry.

2. The age of the child:

At eight years of age, Payshence is capable of understanding the intricacies of her family of origin if they are explained to her in a factual and age appropriate manner. Further, she is young enough to develop a meaningful emotional connection to Mr. Rhorer and his wife if given the opportunity to do so.

3. The harm that may result to the child if presumed or declared paternity is successfully disestablished:

As noted above, Payshence is very aware that Kirk J is not her biological father. Her comment to the Examiner that he is her "real father" and not "adopted," suggests that this has been said to her in an effort to minimize any connection she may feel with Mr. Rhorer, whether the result of memory or the sense of identification with the natural parent commonly experienced by an adopted child. As such, it is the Examiner's opinion that there would be no harm to Payshence if the fact that Mr. Rhorer as her biological parent was acknowledged to her underlying concerns about her parentage and confusing family history.

4. The nature of the relationship between the child and any alleged father:

Payshence has no on-going relationship with Mr. Rhorer and it is unclear how much time has elapsed since they have had contact with one another. Despite input from Kirk J and his girlfriend to the contrary, Payshence is quite aware that Mr. Rhorer is her biological parent. However, she has been greatly influenced by negative input about his past alleged behavior, as well as Kirk J's prohibition against talking about Mr. Rhorer.

5. Other factors that may affect the equities arising from the disruption of the father-child relationship between the child and the presumed or declarant father or the chance of other harm to the child:

In considering Payshence's best interest there are a number of other factors related to her current family situation that are of concern to the Examiner. Both Mr. Rhorer and Kirk J have a significant criminal history that bear incidents occurring between 1999 and 2010. The most recent of these consisted of several misdemeanor charges including: intoxication; disorderly conduct; and wrongful appropriation.

Kirk J's Criminal History Report contains eighteen incidents occurring between 1997 and 2016. The most recent of these is a misdemeanor charge of child abuse with physical injury occurring on April 4, 2016. It appears that this charge has not yet been adjudicated. In March 2015, Kirk J was cited for having an open container while a passenger in a vehicle driven by his girlfriend, who was stopped for speeding. Kirk J was also charged with domestic assault in September of 2013, but was acquitted.

The fact that Kirk J has faced criminal charges in the past several years is concerning, especially the most recent events suggest that he remains at risk for future criminal behavior which could, potentially, result in his being unavailable to care for Payshence. Moreover, it is concerning that Payshence could potentially be the victim of future child abuse if this charge is found to have merit.

The Examiner also has concerns regarding Payshence's on-going contact with her biological mother, Kelly H. Direct observation of Payshence, her input about her relationship with her mother, and social media posts indicate that <u>Kelly H maintains poor boundaries and has questionable judgement. Kirk J and his girlfriend are well aware of Kelly H's history of drug abuse, as well as her unstable relationships that have often included domestic violence.</u> Despite this, they appear largely unconcerned about the possibility that she may be exposed to inappropriate situations and adult information when she's in Kelly's care.

SUMMARY AND RECOMMENDATIONS

A. Case Summary:

In summary, it is likely that Payshence will experience stress at the prospect of becoming reacquainted with her biological father, and she is unlikely to express any interest in doing so. At the same time, it is important that her stance in this regard appears to be the direct result of negative input about Mr. Rhorer that she has received from Kirk J and Kelly H. Payshence's comment to the Examiner that Mr. Rhorer is "not to be spoken of" clearly reflects Kirk J's negative view of Mr. Rhorer and his implicit communication to Payshence that she should not express any interest in him. In light of these observations, it is the Examiner's opinion that Payshence has been unable to form an independent opinion about Mr. Rhorer or the prospect of having contact with him.

At the same time, Payshence is well aware that Kirk is not her biological father, and likely experiences some confusion about the chain of events that led to Mr. Rhorer's absence from her life. Furthermore, a child identifies with their natural parent even if he or she is absent, and criticism of a biological parent is, in effect, experienced as criticism of the child. It appears that Kirk J and Kelly H's intent has been to influence Payshence in such a manner that she will have no interests in having contact with her biological father. Their efforts to accomplish this are likely to result in greater difficulties for this child who, in light of her difficult history, and my direct observation, likely struggles with issues of abandonment, identity, and self-esteem.

As a result, the Examiner can find no compelling reason to conclude that it is in Payshence's best interest to maintain the status quo in regard to her biological father. If anything, her family's effort to portray Mr. Rhorer as a frightening or, at best, inconsequential figure in her life, will likely add to her difficulties over time. Further, regardless of his past history, Mr. Rhorer now maintains a stable, responsible lifestyle, and demonstrates a consistent and long-term interest in being part of his daughter's life. Given her chaotic early life and the on-going family stress that she is faced with, <u>the Examiner cannot help but believe that it would benefit her to have as many caring and reliable adults in her life as possible.</u>

B. Recommendations:

Based on the present evaluation, it is the Examiner's opinion that it would be in Payshence's best interest to become reacquainted with her biological father, Jody Rhorer, and for her to be allowed to maintain an on-going relationship with him. A significant amount of time has passed since she has had contact with Mr. Rhorer. In addition, as discussed above, Payshence has been subject to significant negative input about him from her current caretakers. As a result, this will need to occur in the context of a formal reunification process designed to ensure that Payshence's emotional well-being is paramount.

It is, therefore, recommended that the parties immediately begin working with a qualified therapist to begin the process of reunification between Payshence and Mr. Rhorer. This will require the cooperation and participation by all adults involved in her care, as both sets of potential caretakers - Kirk J and his girlfriend, as well as Jody and Deone Rhorer - will need guidance as to how to best support Payshence in this process. All parties should participate in treatment as requested by the designated therapist, including facilitating her attendance when it is deemed appropriate.

Once Payshence is reacquainted with Mr. Rhorer, it is recommended that the GAL provide input to the Court as to whether or not regular parent-time should be instituted. This should take into account input from from the reunification therapist, as well as any other treatment provided working with Payshence or any of the adult parties involved. In lieu of the GAL, it would be appropriate for a Special Master to be assigned with specified decision-making power in regard to Payshence having on-going contact with Mr. Rhorer, including the frequency and length of such contact, as well as the logistics of how this would occur.

Respectfully submitted, Dr. Natovich

Amen! And there you have it. The GAL said the best interest of Payshence Rhorer is to be with her dad, Jody, and now a trained PhD backed that up in no uncertain terms - with a sense of urgency even! Oh happiness! Everyone we had spoken to had told us the Judge relies on the Evaluator to tell him what to do and nearly always, ALWAYS, rules with those recommendations. Let's go to court!

JUNE 1ST, 2016: EMAILS FROM DOCTOR NATOVICH

6:54 PM
Dear Counsel, I am attaching a copy of my report in the matter of Kelly H v. Kirk J (Intervenor Jody Rhorer) for your convenience. A signed hard copy will be sent by mail as well. Sincerely, Dr. Natovich
June 2nd, 2015 10:19 AM
There is no section regarding an interview with Kelly H, and her input as to the actual time Mr. Rhorer spent with the child at times she had the child with her. It was my understanding that after some confusion, and Kelly H not being called back, she persisted wanting to be interviewed. Did that interview not occur? Connie

5:30 PM
I did meet with Kelly H, and will provide an addendum with a summary of her input. I am out of town until next Monday but will do this upon my return. Dr. Natovich, PhD

JUNE 8TH, 2016: LETTER FROM Devin C to Dr. Natovich

Dear Dr. Natovich,
I received your report by email on June 2nd. There was no cover letter. On June 7th I received a hard copy in the mail and a copy of the letter requesting that the report not be disseminated to the parties. However, I had already sent a copy to my client before I received you letter. Because it appears inevitable that this case will proceed to trial, and the parties will be arguing the contents of your report to the Commissioner and to the Court, and that you will be called as an expert witness at trial, it was probably inevitable that the report would have to be released. I also note one of the parties is Pro Se. I apologize for any problems this has caused. Thank you for your attention and anticipated cooperation in this matter.
Respectfully,
Devin C

JUNE 16TH, 2016: VERIFIED MOTION FOR ORDERS AND NOTICE OF HEARING, submitted by Devin C, Commissioner Kase presiding

COMES NOW *the intervener, Jody Rhorer, by and through his attorney of record; and hereby moves the Court for entry of the following and gives Notice of hearing as follows:*
1. That the court grant Jody Rhorer standing to pursue a claim for time-sharing with the minor child at time of trial.
2. This Motion is supported by the recommendations of Dr. Natovich.
3. The Court should implement the recommendations of the Dr. as to reunification therapy. The Court should appoint one of the reunification therapists recommend by the Dr. in her report. The parties should be ordered to share the cost of this reunification therapy such that Jody Rhorer is responsible for 50% and Kelly H and Kirk J are responsible for the other 50% of the cost. All parties should be ordered to promptly cooperate in effectuating this reunification therapy including taking the child to appointments, and attending appointments themselves as recommended by the therapist.
4. Dr. Natovich should conduct a custody evaluation. This custody evaluation should not commence until the child has been in reunification therapy for a period of 90 days. The parties should share the cost of the custody evaluation pursuant to the same formula that her standing evaluation was allocated, and the same formula which is set forth above.
5. Time-sharing with the minor child after the conclusion of the reunification therapy should be subject to further Order of the Court at that time wherein the Court can consider the recommendations of the GAL, whether or not to appoint a Special Master, and what effect the custody evaluation and the findings therein should have upon time-sharing.
6. This Motion shall be heard before the Honorable Commissioner Kase on July 8, 2016.

We were absolutely elated. Justice for Payshence was soon to come. The recent child abuse report against Kirk J mentioned in the evaluation would certainly help seal the deal and we were sure the court would expedite things in light of the fact that Kirk continued his path of violence. Kelly was also aware that the pendulum was swinging in Jody's favor so she made a desperate attempt to discredit him to the court.

JUNE 16TH, 2016: HAND WRITTEN LETTER to Commissioner Kase from Kelly H

Honorable Judge Kase,
Judge I have included with this letter police reports some that I can remember, and summarized police reports of some of the DV cases with Teri, Jody's ex-wife. Judge its very concerning to me that Jody has never done or complied with completing DV classes and anger management groups. Jody has in the past chose to do jail rather than treatment because he denied having a very dangerous abusive problem. Its normal and ok in his eyes to behave in this manner. Judge please I'm very scared and worried of the treatment of my daughter would get from him. He was very abusive to his 3 other daughters mentally, emotionally, physically, and verbally.
I ask the court to order him complete anger management, DV treatment if allowed any contact with my baby girl. PLEASE JUDGE take a few minutes to review these police reports and records that show Jody's involvement with Domestic Violence.
Thank you, Kelly H

JUNE 20TH, 2016: KIRK J'S MOTION TO STRIKE REPORT OF DR. NATOVICH, submitted by Connie C, Commissioner Kase presiding

Comes now, Connie C, and on behalf of Kirk J, files the foregoing Motion to Strike the Report of Dr. Natovich, which was submitted by Mr. Rhorer's counsel to the Court June 12th, 2016. Counsel for Mr. Rhorer was copied in an email undersigned sent to Dr. Natovich on June 2nd, 2016, which addressed a concern that the report did not include information from Kelly H. Dr. Natovich responded by email that she did interview Kelly H and would provide an addendum after she returned from a vacation. The addendum has never been provided to counsel. Additionally, the Court previously had a deadline for Counsel to object to the report, which was May 23rd, 2016. However, that deadline was before Dr. Natovich provided any report to Counsel.
Counsel for Kirk J intended to file a pleading regarding the report, but naturally was waiting for the addendum which Dr. Natovich indicated she was sending. As such, the report filed by opposing counsel should be stricken. Counsel should be given reasonable time after receipt of the addendum to file any response or objection, and for such other and further relief as the Court deems appropriate in the premises.

JUNE 27TH, 2016: ADDENDUM TO CUSTODY EVALUATION, submitted by Devin C, Commissioner Kase presiding

COMES NOW *the intervenor, Jody Rhorer, by and through his attorney of record; and hereby submits the attached Addendum to Dr. Natovich's evaluation:*

ADDENDUM TO SUMMARY LIMITED PURPOSE EVALUATION

Background Information:
A written Summary of Limited Purpose Evaluation completed in this matter was submitted on May 30, 2016. The Examiner subsequently received communication from counsel for Kirk J inquiring as to why the summary report did not include information obtained from Kelly H. The Examiner, therefore, has prepared an addendum to address this concern.

Results of Interview with Kelly H:

Kelly H was interviewed by the Examiner on April 11, 2016. Her live-in partner accompanied her to the appointment. Kelly H reports that she spends time with Payshence on a regular basis, picking her up from Kirk J's residence every other Friday and returning her on Sunday. She indicates that she often spends additional time with her as well, for example, taking her to dinner after work, and sharing time with Kirk for birthdays and holidays. Kelly H states that she and Kirk J get along very well, and she reports no disagreements regarding her requests to spend time with Payshence.

Kelly H provided a detailed, but somewhat confusing timeline regarding Payshence's early years and history. For example, she initially stated that Payshence has been in Kirk J's care since age three-and-a-half. Upon further discussion, however, she corrected this estimate, stating that Kirk J has "probably had custody of her since she was four or four-and-a-half." The Examiner inquired about Payshence's early years in an effort to clarify the level of involvement by Jody Rhorer, Payshence's biological father. Kelly H describes her and Mr. Rhorer as having had a very inconsistent relationship, marked by frequent breakups and absences. She reports that Mr. Rhorer sometimes worked in Missouri during her pregnancy, and that he was not present for Payshence's birth, but did spend five days with her when she was two weeks of age. Kelly H indicates that when Payshence was approximately four months of age, she and Mr. Rhorer "were together" for a year, but notes that he was not present on a consistent basis.

Kelly H reports that she was the victim of recurrent domestic violence during her relationship with Mr. Rhorer, and that this ultimately led to involvement by the DCFS, and their break-up. She states, however, that prior to Payshence turning eighteen months of age, she took her to Missouri to be with Mr. Rhorer. This led to Kelly's extradition by the State of Utah, and Payshence's first placement in foster care. Kelly H believes that Payshence was in the State's custody for nine months, and that she was "almost three" when she was returned to her care. She reports that Kirk J was present throughout this time, however, the timeframe and nature of their relationship was unclear. Kelly H indicates that when Payshence was "about age three" she allowed Mr. Rhorer to spend time with her for "an hour or two a few times." She stated that, upon returning home from these visits, Payshence would say "scary things" such as "My daddy's gonna stab Kirk in the neck".   Kelly H reports that she discontinued Payshence's contact with Mr. Rhorer in response to this.

When discussing this chapter in Payshence's life, Kelly H appeared somewhat confused about the timeline, noting that Payshence was three-and-a-half when she was again removed from her care. This caused her to review her original estimate of how long Payshence has been in Kirk J's care. Kelly H had quite a difficult time delineating a clear chain of events around this period. She stated, however, that she is sure that Mr. Rhorer "hasn't seen her at all" since her second placement in foster care.

Conclusion:

It is evident that Kelly H cares about Payshence and greatly values the time she spends with her. She expresses serious concern at the prospect of Payshence becoming reacquainted with her biological father, Jody Rhorer, and believes that this would be very disruptive to her. While Kelly's opinions in this regard appear heartfelt, the fact remains that her ability to spend time with her her daughter is dependent upon the goodwill of Kirk J. As such, her input cannot be weighted as that of an unbiased party. As noted in the original written summary, Payshence has had a chaotic and unstable early childhood. The details of this remain confusing in that the timeframes described by Kirk J, Kelly H, and Mr. Rhorer are quite disparate. This makes it extremely difficult to ascertain who and when each may have cared for Payshence during the first four years of her life.

Respectfully Submitted,
Dr. Natovich

JUNE 20TH, 2016:   LETTER TO GAL from Devin C

Dear Mary,
Enclosed please find a copy of a redacted police report. It is my understanding that you may obtain an un-redacted copy. After you have received it, I believe it would be appropriate for all counsel to discuss the impact of this document upon our case. Thank you for your attention and cooperation in this matter.

Respectfully,
Devin C

JUNE 28TH, 2016:   EMAILS regarding Kirk's arrest

Hi Mary, As you saw in the evaluation report, Kirk J was arrested for child abuse on April 4th of this year. Jody went to the Unified Sheriff's office today to see if he could find out which child had been abused. The Sheriff's office is preparing the report for him to pick up but he was told that the GAL could obtain an un-redacted copy. I believe Payshence is in danger in that house and should be removed. I hope you are able to present this information to Commissioner Kase on July 8th. Thank you, Deone Rhorer

2:44 PM
Oh dear! I will request a copy. Do you know any details? Mary

3:25 PM
Unified Police Dept at 3375 S 900 W, SLC. Deone

3:38 PM
I called and left a message. Mary

She "called and left a message." Hmm. How protective of her. Mary C was back as PGAL. We had never been informed that she was reappointed to the case - she just resurfaced at a different law firm and, contrary to what Nancy has said, her bills began coming again.

JULY 1ST, 2016:   POLICE REPORTS REGARDING KIRK J, submitted by Devin C, Commissioner Kase presiding

COMES NOW *Jody Rhorer, by and through his attorney; and hereby submits the attached police reports regarding Kirk J: The undersigned Detective -* **UNIFIED POICE DEPARTMENT**, *upon a written declaration state on information and belief that the defendant, Kirk J, committed the crime of:* **COUNT 1 CHILD ABUSE**, *Class A Misdemeanor, as follows: That on or about September 13, 2105, in Salt Lake County, Utah, the defendant did intentionally or knowingly inflict physical injury upon a child.*
THIS INFORMATION IS BASED ON EVIDENCE OBTAINED FROM THE   FOLLOWING WITNESSES: *Detective D.A., Jill C (girlfriend), PR, M.M.*
DECLARATION OF PROBABLE CAUSE: *Your declaration based this information upon the following: The statement of 7-year-old "A" that she lives with her mom and stepdad, defendant Kirk J. "A" states that on or about September 13, 2015, defendant Kirk J spanked her on the butt twice and smacker her. "A" states she was scared and looked away when Kirk demanded her to look at him. When she wouldn't look at him, he smacked her on the face. "A" states her stepdad used an open hand when he smacked her.*
Pursuant to Utah Code I declare under criminal penalty of the State of Utah that the foregoing is true and correct to the best of my belief and knowledge. Detective D.A.
INITIAL R/O: *While on patrol I was dispatched to a child abuse investigation. According to the details I was to meet with a DCFS worker at an elementary school. Upon arrival, I met with the DCFS worker and Jill C, who is the mother of "A." According to DCFS, "A" came to school today with some marks she stated were consistent with being slapped. Jill then began to tell me what had happened last night between her daughter and husband.*
According to Jill, "A" was acting out of control and Kirk J asked "A" several times to calm down. Even brothers and sister told "A" to calm down but she would not. When asked why "A" was upset, Kirk told me "She was told she couldn't play with an electronic tablet, so she started to throw a fit." After several attempts of being told to calm down, Kirk went over to "A" and picked her up and took her to her room. "A" was screaming and kicking at her dad as he put her down on the floor. Kirk spun around and spanked her on the backside 2 times. "A," still screaming, turned back around and kicked Kirk in the legs.
Kirk admitted to me that he swatted "A" across the face, but not hard enough to leave marks. He then picked up "A" and put her on her bed where she stopped screaming and backed into the corner of the bed. The DCFS worker showed Kirk a picture she took of "A" which showed some petechial forming around her left eye, and what she described as slap marks across her face. I noticed the marks on "A" as well, but that the "slap marks" were vertical, not horizontal. When Kirk saw the picture, he stated "A" had been wrestling all day with her brothers and sisters, and that they are all physical with each other.

The DCFS worker and Kirk made out a safety plan for future reference and then left to go over to the house, while I stayed at the school with Jill and had "A" come down to the office so I could document the incident as well. When "A" arrived, I made sure she understood the difference between a lie and the truth, and then gave examples of each. Once she answered the questions to assure me she understood the differences, I asked her if I could take her picture. She allowed me to do so. I then asked her about the marks on her face and she told me she did not remember how she got them, but thought maybe her dad might have given them to her. I asked her what she meant by this, and she could not elaborate. I asked if she had been playing roughly with her brothers and sisters, to which she told me she has not. "A" also stated she never knew about the marks on her face until someone at the school had mentioned it to her. She stated they did not hurt, and that she could not feel them. She stated, "nothing hurt 'til I saw the polka dots."

I provided Jill and Kirk with a referral phone number to the Children Center to receive parenting classes and more resources to help with the kids. I also gave Jill a business card with the case number, for reference.

INVESTIGATOR FOLLOW UP: On September 16, 2015, I was assigned as the lead investigator for this case. I reviewed the information documented by the initial officer and the photographs taken at the scene. I contacted the DCFS case worker via email and inquired what the safety plan set up was and told her I would like to do a forensic interview with the victim.

I received an email back and she told me both the mother and alleged perpetrator are very cooperative and the safety plan put in place was that the AP would take time outs and not use any physical punishments. I was advised this was an isolated incident and she feels the children in the home are not at risk.

I contacted the mother at the phone number listed in the police report. The message identifier was not Jill's however, I left a message anyway requesting contact. I then attempted to call the second phone number provided, it went to Jill's place of employment. I called the number listed as a cell phone. The message indicated it was someone else. I didn't leave a message. I emailed DCFS and requested she contact the mother to set up an interview for Monday. I received contact from DCFS advising the family could only do Wednesday, September 23, 2015, at 5:30. I advised that would be fine and scheduled the interview. Upon speaking with the Children's Justice Center, I learned the time slot was not available. I contacted DCFS and asked if the family could do 4:00 instead. I received confirmation from DCFS a short time later that the time change would work.

INVESTIGATOR FOLLOW UP: On September 23, 2015, after my interview with "A" was complete, DCFS and I met with the mother to discuss the details of "A's" disclosure. Jill advised she wasn't there so she didn't know what had happened but what her daughter told me was the same as what she had told her mother. Jill said the night it happened "A" asked for an ice pack to take to bed with her, but she always asked for an ice pack because it gets hot in their house and she didn't find it suspicious.

I asked Jill if Kirk has told her what happened. Kirk told me he wasn't angry or upset with "A" at the time he smacker her and he didn't hit her hard. Jill told me she is really upset about it and has been cross with Kirk since the incident. Kirk has told her numerous times that he wouldn't ever hurt "A". I told Jill that "A" had disclosed her sister, Payshence, saw the whole thing as it was happening, she was in the room with them. I asked Jill if she could bring Payshence in for an interview next week sometime. Jill agreed and we scheduled an interview for her on Wednesday. Jill did mention that all the kids were wrestling around the night before the incident was reported by the school and "A" was standing on one of the boy's heads and fell. I confirmed with Jill that they are abiding by the safety plan set up by DCFS, she advised they were.

On September 30, 2015, I received a call from DCFS who told me Jill was sick and couldn't bring Payshence to the interview. She asked that I contact Jill to reschedule the interview. I called Jill and we rescheduled the interview for Thursday.

On October 8, 2015, after my interview with Payshence was completed I met with Jill and told her what Payshence disclosed. I explained that I was concerned that Payshence told me she didn't see her dad slap "A" on the face, just the butt. Jill told me they have been working hard with Payshence on just telling what she sees and not what she heard about. They have had issues with her lying lately. Jill told me she still believes Kirk slapped "A" even though Payshence didn't say she saw anything happen, and I reiterated that "A" may have just perceived Payshence saw what happened because she was in the room when it happened. I confirmed Kirk's phone number so I could call him and set up an interview.

INVESTIGATOR FOLLOW UP: On October 12, 2015, I attempted to contact Kirk J by telephone at the number given to me by Jill. I was able to speak with Kirk and he agreed to come to my office for an interview regarding what happened with "A." Kirk told me he could be at my office on October 14.

INVESTIGATOR FOLLOW UP: On October 28, 2015, I screened this case with the Deputy District Attorney at the Avenues Children's Justice Center during a Multi-Disciplinary Team staffing. The DCFS case worker was also available by phone and advised she supported the case against Kirk J. I was given a verbal confirmation by the DDA that charges of Child Abuse would be filed against Kirk J. This case will be closed pending formal information from the DA's office. I will make notification to the victim's mother at that time.

JULY 8TH, 2016:   KIRK J'S SECOND MOTION TO STRIKE REPORT OF DR. NATOVICH, submitted by Connie C, Commissioner Kase presiding

Comes now, Connie C, and on behalf of Kirk J, files the foregoing Motion to Strike the Report of Dr. Natovich, which was submitted by Mr. Rhorer's counsel to the Court June 29th, 2016, after the Doctor provided an addendum regarding information from Kelly H.

Dr. Natovich responded by email that she did interview Kelly H, and would provide an addendum after she returned from a vacation. In a nutshell, the report should be stricken because it does not conform to the Court's direction to evaluate the statutory factors found in 78B-15-608, UCA, and it is abundantly obvious that despite assurances she understood the "limited purpose" of the evaluation, the purpose was misunderstood by the evaluator.

After concluding that Mr. Rhorer had no basis for standing under any applicable statute, Commissioner Bloom theorized that Mr. Rhorer could potentially pursue a Constitutional argument that he could still request an order that he had standing. The Commissioner specifically listed factors, taken from a statute, she felt should be evaluated for a possible Constitutional argument for standing. The perimeters were provided to Dr. Natovich and she indicated that she understood the "limited purpose" of the evaluation.

Those factors include: conduct of the mother of the presumed or declarant father and whether that estops the party from denying parentage; whether it would be inequitable to disrupt the father child relationship between the child and the presumed or declarant father; also the length of time between the proceeding to adjudicate parentage and the time that the presumed or declarant father was placed on notice that he might not be the genetic father; the length of time during which the presumed or declarant father has assumed the role of father of the child; the facts surrounding the presumed or declarant father's discord of his possible non-paternity; the nature of the relationship between the child and the presumed or declarant father; the age of the child; the harm that may result to the child if presumed or declared paternity is successfully disestablished; the nature of the relationship between the child and any alleged father; the extent to which the passage of time recuses the changes of establishing paternity of another man in the child support obligation in the factor of a child; and other factors that may affect the equities arising from the disruption of the father/child relationship between the child and the presumed or declarant father or the chance of harm to the child.

Instead of addressing those ten statutory subparts as directed by the Court's oral ruling, the following categories were addressed as numbered paragraphs in the report: (1) The nature of the relationship between the child and the presumed or declarant father (2) The age of the child (3) The harm that may result to the child if presumed or declared paternity is successfully disestablished (4) The nature of the relationship between the child and any alleged father (5) Other factors that may affect the equities arising from the disruption of the father-child relationship between the child and the presumed or declarant father or the chance of other harm to the child. The "other factors" the evaluator noted as significant were criminal history on the part of Mr. Rhorer and Kirk J, and Kirk J allowing the child to visit with her mother, Kelly H.

None of the paragraphs following the above sub-headings address the ultimate matter before the Court, which is **disestablishment of paternity** of Kirk J. The evaluators comments do not address that issue. Rather, the report is a garden variety "best interest" custody-style evaluation, which talks about the minor being "reintroduced" or "having contact" with Mr. Rhorer. The issue before the Court is whether Mr. Rhorer should be given a "place at the table" to try to further assert he should be declared father (unseating Kirk J) on Constitutional grounds, this obliterating and destroying the legal and emotional relationship she has with Kirk J. It isn't whether it would be bad if the minor met or spent time with Mr. Rhorer, the evaluator completely failed to address that what Mr. Rhorer seeks to do is uproot the child from the father she knows and destroy the relationship entirely.

The Court's call for the evaluation per the transcripts never called for "best interest" opinions, but rather an evaluation of the listed statutory factors and the report and addendum utterly fails in offering assistance to the Court on evaluation of the statutory grounds.

The Report is Significantly Factually Inaccurate

Assertions that Kelly H had lost her parental rights as part of the juvenile case is inaccurate. This averment is stated as fact in the original version of the report and not corrected by the addendum. The examiner emphasized how "concerning" it is that Kirk J would allow visitation to Kelly H under such circumstances. The evaluator then focuses on Kirk J's opinions and attitudes about the litigation. It is concerning that a verifiable fact that the Court has recognized Kirk J was adjudicated father was treated as a mere opinion, and not verified. The evaluator's assertions that "it is confusing" as to where the minor lived is also problematic. Even for time periods that the custody could be verified by Juvenile Court documents were not outlined. No calls were made by the evaluator for additional information, to clarify the matter. If the evaluator was confused on the matter, it is more appropriate the matter go to hearing such that the Court might make a factual determination based on testimony and exhibits how long the minor has been with Kirk J, and what contact Mr. Rhorer might've had with the minor.

The Evaluation is Lacking in Significant Information

The report focuses on factual data which is functionally irrelevant to the Court's call of revaluation of the statutory factors in 78B-15-608. The report starts with a recitation regarding the evaluator's meeting with Mr. Rhorer, his wife and Mr. Rhorer's daughter's. The age of the daughters is not listed. The fine condition of Mr. Rhorer's home is mentioned, including that there is room for the minor.

*On the other side of the equation, the evaluator notes that Kirk J's home is smaller and crowded. The evaluation contains no detail regarding Kirk J's significant other who lives with the minor, cares for her as a mother would care for a child, and has a significant emotional bond with the child. The evaluator simply mentions there are other children in the home, but the sibling bond between the other children in the home is completely ignored. Those matters are significant "other factors" that bear on the equities of whether Mr. Rhorer should be permitted to proceed with his challenge to destroy those relationships. The evaluator summarily advises based on her brief meeting with her, that the minor has "boundary issues" and the minor should have therapy. Missing from the evaluation is that issue was already brought up in hearing by the GAL and the minor has been evaluated by a therapist and the therapist recommended that no therapy is necessary. The inclusion of this observation and recommendation for treatment made not in a clinical therapeutic session, but just from a meeting is misleading in light of the missing information that an evaluation has already been undertaken by a qualified professional, and treatment **not** recommended.*

That the ultimate recommendation includes "reintroduction" with Mr. Rhorer, and then work toward an agreement regarding "parent-time" illustrates that while evaluating this matter, the evaluator had no concept about the legal issues at hand, and therefore incorrectly assessed the potential harm to the minor. Mr. Rhorer does not want "reintroduction" and the matter is not headed to a "parent-time" order between Kirk J and Intervenor. Before the Court is an issue where Mr. Rhorer statutorily foreclosed from even asserting a paternity challenge, wishes to etch out an avenue to continue his fight on Constitutional grounds. His ultimate goal isn't to "share" the minor with Kirk J, but to disestablish Kirk's paternity, to remove him and all the minor's significant familial relationships, and basically "starting" in capacity of father.

Because the evaluator completely misunderstood that posture, and instead simply assumed the two legal challengers would "share" the minor somehow, the opinions and assessments in the report are functionally worthless, because they do not accurately state the harm to the minor of being uprooted and "starting over" with a new father, and being ripped from the father and family she knows entirely as Mr. Rhorer seeks. Because the evaluation was not conducted as outlined in the Court order, because it is basically a "best interest" custom comparison, because the evaluator completely misunderstood the proceeding, and therefore, did not offer accurate analysis of the potential effect on the minor, the Court should strike the report.

JULY 8TH, 2016: COURT HEARING TRANSCRIPT

COURT BAILIFF: All rise. Third District Court is now in session, the honorable Kase presiding.

THE COURT: Good morning. We have the matter of Kelly H and Kirk J and Jody Rhorer as an intervenor. This was set as a review hearing. I had asked the parties to brief the issues that I was going to be expected to consider today, and the only thing I have are Connie's motions regarding Dr. Natovich's report and this motion for temporary orders that Steven C has filed. I mean I'm not clear that we've even gotten past the step of determining whether Mr. Rhorer has standing to participate in the proceedings.

CONNIE: May I, your honor? I think kind of what has contributed to the problem is if the Court recalls, we got the deadline to file something. It was clear back on May 23rd, I want to say, and that is - I think the situation has been complicated by the fact that the report came in later than usual, and then there was the issue about the expectation that Kelly's information would be included. So, I agree with the Court completely, and I almost filed a motion to continue, but I figured in light of everybody's difficult schedule and that the Court had set this time aside, we would be better off getting here for further discussion. It's too complicated an issue for us not to submit full briefing on.

THE COURT: Isn't that really the threshold that we have to get past before anything else happens is to determine whether Mr. Rhorer has standing?

CONNIE: I think that raises constitutional issues that really cry out for adequate briefing and we just haven't gotten there.

THE COURT: I mean that's how this report or this evaluation from Dr. Natovich was recommended, and I've read, you know, the objections to the report in terms of whether it adequately addresses the factors that were supposed to be addressed.

DEVIN C: Well, paragraph 1 of my motion is that Mr. Rhorer be granted standing. If he is not granted standing and the Court were to boot him out of the case, everything else would be moot. If the Court does grant him standing, we're here. Then the next step would be what do we do, and that's my request for the other two requests, which is for introductory counseling with the minor child, reunification therapy as well as a custody evaluation. I agree the first step is to determine whether or not he has standing. I filed the other two motions because if he has standing it would make sense to come back for another hearing.

THE COURT: Well, I can appreciate wanting to use the opportunity to accomplish something today because it was so difficult getting everybody here. The other thing is Kelly delivered something to the Court. It doesn't appear it's been supplied to anybody else, a handwritten document with some police reports attached. There's no mailing certificate or certificate of service or anything. I don't know if you're aware of this.

DEVIN C: It was in my email this morning.

CONNIE: I got it by email this morning. I know the Court frequently deals with pro se parties, and Kelly doesn't apparently know what she's supposed to do, but –

THE COURT: Right. So, the handwritten document, probably is appropriate to include in the Court's record. I'm not sure the copies of the police reports - well, there were some police reports that were filed, I think, by your office, Devin, is that right, regarding the child abuse incident with Kirk J? This is a lot of material. I don't know if you've had a chance to go through these reports.

CONNIE: I haven't. As a matter of fact, I am not really sure why this happened, but I did not - if it came into my email through the e-filing system, I didn't see that police reports were filed by Counsel a couple of days ago. I only noticed it looking at Court XChange this morning. It could have been something that just missed my - that evaded my notice, but I haven't looked at that document yet, so there's a significant amount of material that we need to review.

THE COURT: Connie, are you up to speed on all these things that have been filed?

CONNIE: Not - I've actually not had time to review the things that were filed this morning. I am aware of everything that was filed on behalf of Mr. Rhorer.

THE COURT: Okay. Well, so what we have right now is we have a - some facts that are I think reflected in various things that have been filed with the Court - police reports and so forth. I don't recall there being - and I may be wrong. This case has been - it's so out of sort of the normal range of things that happened, but I don't recall if there has even been just any sort of basic factual affidavits that were filed at some point in the past regarding the chronology of events.

I know Dr. Natovich's report I think attempts to identify some of the chronological events when the - Kelly H and Kirk J were together and then not, and Mr. Rhorer's involvement with Kelly H is a little bit vague in the report as to when they were actually residing together, and the extent to which Mr. Rhorer might have had contact with the child apart from that time frame. It appeared to be a little bit vague in terms of the -- Kelly H and Jody Rhorer apparently reported slightly different chronologies.

Some of the factors that were referred to in Commissioner Bloom's prior order that were to be addressed, I'm not sure there's any evidence in the file pertaining to, so what - what I would like to do here, I hate to kick this can any further down the road, I honestly do, but what I would like to do it to give the parties an opportunity to file a written briefing regarding any factors that pertain to this constitutional claim that Mr. Rhorer has. I think it's already been established, or at least the law of this case is that he wouldn't have standing under the statute were it not for concerns about, you know, protecting his constitutional rights, and so I'd like to have something that actually states the parties' positions in writing with - referring to any facts that are in the file. I'd be okay with any party filing a supplemental affidavit that addresses any of those issues so that I can make a ruling, and then somebody can object and ask the judge to have probably a more formal hearing on it, because I think that's the process that's going to need to happen.

DEVIN C: Well, your honor, with all due respect, that's not how I see this. I see that as that battle has already been fought, and Judge Stanley has already ruled, and they said that the Court would consider standing based upon findings from Dr. Natovich or referring to her findings, but whether or not he pursued standing - that battle is already over. The constitutional issues have already been fully briefed, and Commissioner Bloom made the initial ruling, and Judge Stanley made the order, and that was the order that said Dr. Natovich will do her report, address the factors, and then based on that we'll decide whether or not he has standing. So, it seems to me we're reinventing the wheel. That's already been - I don't know what else I can submit to the Court –

THE COURT: Well, I don't think anyone has - for instance, Connie has concerns about the adequacy of Dr. Natovich's report. I share some of those concerns. I would like the parties to be able - and I have a really hard time with, you know, being asked to walk into court and just sort of get stuff verbally, particularly as complicated and unusual as this issue is, without giving me something to - you know, to sort of think about. I mean I think in - the indication when we scheduled this was I asked to have the issues that were going to be before me briefed, and they haven't been, not for - not post Dr. Natovich's report. The report is what it is. It is not binding on the Court, and it is a - you know, a report of an investigation of fact issues that are significant to the Court's determination, but I think the Court has to make a determination as to standing. So - I mean if you - if you want to make some oral argument about that and not brief it, understand the quality of my ruling may not be as great as if you had actually taken the information that we - we have - I mean you got Dr. Natovich's supplemental report just days ago. The other was a week or two ago, right?

CONNIE: Your Honor. I - I absolutely share the Court's concerns, and this is a matter of first impression. Commissioner Bloom thoughtfully outlined the way that she saw it, and actually it's - it's a novel expansion into a constitutional standing issue based on a couple of cases that came out during this case. So, I absolutely believe that it demands proper, thoughtful briefing, and not just oral argument. So, I would rest the idea of trying to feed you constitutional law on the fly and not give you an opportunity to read it, digest it, check into citations and analyze because this is actually not an easy question, and the Court would have to extrapolate from some different constitutional principles.

THE COURT: And I do not - I do not understand there to be - have - to have been a ruling by Judge Stanley that Mr. Rhorer has standing. The Judge just left open the question so the Dr. Natovich could address this in her report, and then the Court could make a determination as to whether he has standing. He's allowed to pursue standing. That's not the question. He's been allowed to intervene, I believe, but that doesn't mean that he's been determined to have standing to assert parental rights. Kelly H's parental rights were terminated, as I recall.

KELLY H: No, they weren't.

CONNIE: They never were and that's one of my concerns with the report. I followed up with Dr. Natovich asking for her - her fact, the basis for stating that.

THE COURT: Okay. Well, there was - I know there was a lot of activity in juvenile court, and there may have been something that she interpreted as having the effect of terminating Kelly's parental rights.

CONNIE: It appeared to me she got that information from Mr. Rhorer. That is absolutely incorrect.

DEVIN C: Well, that's disputed, but I guess what I struggle with is citations and constitutional law and case law. I think that battle is already over in this case. That's already been done in this case. Whether or not he is barred under the statute or whether or not he has constitutional rights, there's already an order that says that the Court would consider standing after input from Dr. Natovich. So, we have that. I don't know of any cases I could cite or any constitutional law I could argue that hasn't already been presented to the Court and already been ruled on. I would just argue - the next step is - now we're at the point that we have Dr. Natovich's input. Let's see if based on that, Mr. Rhorer should be given standing.

THE COURT: It's a matter of marshaling the evidence to analyze whether under the cases that were cited - the one that was referred to primarily by - I think it was mainly one, the RH or something like that case that came out. The factors that were identified by Commissioner Bloom in this order, I think that they're listed here in this order. The - you know, whether it would be inequitable to disrupt the father/child relationship between the respondent, the nature of the relationship between the child and presumed or declarant father, the harm that might result from the child if presumed or declared paternity is successfully disestablished. I think Connie referred to some other factors as well, the circumstances under which paternity was discovered and –

DEVIN C: Your Honor, I don't' know what to think. We have an order that the Court would consider standing after Dr. Natovich completed her report. She's completed her report. We have a disagreement about whether or not that report is sufficient to support standing, but I'm finding that conceptually different than briefing constitutional law, which I don't' see - there's nothing I would know to brief that hasn't already been ruled on by the provisional recommendation by Commissioner Bloom and ruling by Judge Stanley. I think where we're at now in this case procedurally is let's look at Dr. Natovich's report and is it sufficient to grant Mr. Rhorer standing. I don't' know what there is too brief about that.

THE COURT: I asked for written briefs on the issues that were supposed to be before me. I don't know how else I can say this. I'm not trying to make this more difficult than it needs to be. I can appreciate it's a little bit time consuming and expensive to set out in writing your reasoning as to why based on the information in Dr. Natovich's report and any other information that is available for - properly available to the Court whether Mr. Rhorer satisfies the standard for standing. To have to receive that information, this is - as Connie says, this is a case of first impression. This isn't the sort of thing that we just think about on a daily basis, so I've got everything kind of compartmentalized, and people can give me facts and I can plug them in. Frankly, the other part of it is, because of Rule 108, you know, when I make a ruling, it's going to be objected to by somebody, and Judge Stanley is going to have to hear it, and then you're going to have the argument about well, was this presented to the commissioner or not, and I want to make sure the record is very clear on this. I wouldn't be surprised if this case ended up being appealed at some point, and I want to make sure everything is properly addressed.

So, what I would like to have happen, and I don't know, Mary, do you really have an argument about standing? Do you - is that something that you believe is part of your charge? You're really more concerned with representing the child's best interests, which there is I guess some, you know, fact information there.

MARY C: Yeah, I agree. I mean that is my charge to look at the child's best interests. Obviously, I don't represent Mr. Rhorer, Kirk or Kelly, but I agree with Devin in the fact that I think those issues were already ruled on, but I understand the Court's desire to have that –

THE COURT: Where is there something that goes through the factors and says this is the evidence and this is the Court's determination? There isn't a ruling to that effect.

MARY C: Well, that's what I'm saying. I think that there is maybe confusion, and I'd rather have it on the record than not have it on the record.

DEVIN C: So, what I got - if I were to brief this, your Honor, I would say this is what Commissioner Bloom said the factors should be addressed for, this is what the factors that were addressed by Dr. Natovich, and they support standing. That would be my brief, which is the same evidence we have before the Court today.

THE COURT: Well, I - first of all, I don't think we're limited to Dr. Natovich's report. I think there may be issues - there may be facts, for instance, and this issue of Kelly's parental right being terminated, that's apparently incorrect. I think the record needs to be complete, and I don't think that simply proceeding - this is - you know, I mean it - in some respects, I almost think that we're - you know, Judge Stanley is going to end up hearing this anyway, and it might make more sense for him to, but I'm not going to ask him to do that without at least making an effort to a complete analysis of the standing issue. I - you know, honesty, Dr. Natovich's report doesn't cover a bunch of the issues that were supposed to be covered, and if there is not evidence on those issues, then I don't know how the Court can make a full determination as to that, but there may be affidavits in the file somewhere back there or the parties may need to supplement the record with their own affidavits establishing what facts are and are not disputed so that I can make that determination. I don't even know for sure if we know when Mr. Rhorer and Kelly H were residing together.

DEVIN C: We'll never know that because it's a he said she said. And so I'm just thinking out loud, but maybe it would make sense to use our time today to say what did Dr. Natovich not address that she should have, and issue an order that she address these factors in a supplemental report, and that that be submitted to the Court, or in conjunction with an order that this - to kill two birds with one stone since we're going to - we all know we're going to end up before Judge Stanley anyway is to say Dr. Natovich, you didn't address these issues, address them, and then set the matter for an evidentiary hearing with Judge Stanley.

THE COURT: Well, what I would anticipate, I don't know that I necessarily want to try to schedule you all to come back another time for another hearing on this subject. I think it would be more appropriate to get the information. I agree, Dr. Natovich probably ought to supplement the report one more time and address the factors that are missing, but then I think I need to be in the position fairly quickly to simply rule on it and let someone object to it and take it to the judge.

KELLY H: Your Honor, can I just say that Dr. Natovich, her only like reason for being involved in this case was to decide whether or not they have a relationship or a bond to know each other. She went into this full on like inspecting his house and like trying to decide whether or not it would be beneficial or not to my daughter to be reintroduced to Jody. I think that going back to her is just going to have her add in more stuff that –

THE COURT: Well, if you read her report, she does indicate that number 1, the child doesn't have a relationship with Mr. Rhorer. Number 2, that's partly as a result of a designed effort by Kirk and Kelly to try to block a relationship and to alienate her from him and tell him that he's a scary guy and all sorts of stuff. So, I mean there's - you know, that's a difficult situation to ferret out, but certainly as I'm reading this report, I'm thinking well, what she's saying is there's no relationship but a relationship would - she could have one. She's old enough that she can understand. And she's young enough that she's not, you know –

KELLY H: I told her and she knows that - I even - there was times that Kirk didn't want her to see Jody anymore, and I still allowed her to, and the reason I quit is because she would come home saying things like, "My daddy is going to stab Kirk in the neck."

CONNIE: Your Honor, may I? I want to say that I agree with the Court's analysis that Commissioner Bloom in the February 20th transcript did decide that statutorily Mr. Rhorer did not have standing to pursue this paternity issue, but she chiseled out a rather novel - and I don't think it's ever been used - idea that constitutionally based on the recent case law that had come up, she thought there might be a way he could assert standing and she suggested those factors from a different statute that Dr. Natovich eventually employed to submit that report. I disagree with both Counsel that the standing issue has been decided. It was simply that the evaluation could be made and that the Court would take standing up again. I ask the Court to do what you initially said, to allow additional submissions and require briefing.

THE COURT: Let me do this, then. You're here. I'd like you to make any argument that you think pertains to his issue of standing. I'm not going to consider the request for temporary orders until I've ruled on the standing issue, but I will ask you to make any oral argument that you'd like to make with respect to standing. I will then grant all three parties leave to supplement the record with any further briefing that you think needs to be had regarding those issues and once that information is submitted, then I will rule on that issue, and then you can object and take it to the judge or whoever.

CONNIE: Your Honor, I'm not comfortable making oral argument on a constitutional issue without having the opportunity to brief it, and with having this report for the minimal amount of time that we have had. I filed something just because we had a hearing. But there has been insufficient time to properly address constitutional issues.

THE COURT: Okay, but you're identified some defects in Dr. Natovich's report - a number of them, bunch of them - in terms of things that just aren't addressed, and so I think you're certainly prepared to at least indicate what things that are missing are important to this case. In other words, there might be some factors that don't pertain to this case. For instance, Mr. Rhorer has known of the child since birth, and the fact that he and Kelly H were living together as I recall, during a portion of that early time of the child's life. So, the discovery or parentage is - that's not an issue. It's not a situation, and I think the reason that can be a factor is - and I think we actually just even more recently had another Court of Appeals or Supreme Court case dealing with a kind of situation like this in which the father was precluded from taking the steps necessary to declare himself the father because the child was born prematurely or something, and then the time period lapsed before he was even notified of the child's birth. I think that's what the factor is about.

CONNIE: Well, here's the way I see it. As Commissioner Bloom outlined the way she saw the statute - and that was not objected to, that he doesn't have a statutory basis to assert a standing - she chiseled out this idea that perhaps he could establish constitutional standing, and she outlined those factors, but she wanted to see the evaluation. The way I see it, it is still Mr. Rhorer's burden to outline to this Court the various equities about standing, including the fundamental right of parentage. My client is legal father, and none of that has been briefed. None of it. I was going to bring up that recent case to the Court because I don't know how it applies, and I think it was - but none of these cases squarely fit the circumstances, and so the Court might be assisted by briefing or analogy of that case, but none has been filed.

THE COURT: All right. Well, Devin apparently doesn't believe that it's worth - or that there's any point in filing a written brief, but I - you're at least in a positions to make your argument as to why under the evidence that we do have before us why Mr. Rhorer should have standing, and then I will allow you to respond to that appropriately with a written brief, and allow Devin C as well to supplement if he needs to, since you're all here. I don't want to have your all come back for another set of hearings.

DEVIN C: Your honor, I think maybe - I'm going to start off by - if I could? I don't know what's missing from the report. So, I'm looking at Commissioner Bloom's order, and it would seem to me that Dr. Natovich already covered everything she was asked to cover so I'll just go through them.

The length of time during which the presumed or declarant father has assumed the role of father of the child, that was addressed. The facts surrounding the presumed or declarant father's discovery as possible non-paternity, I think that's on record. The nature of the relationship between the child and the presumed or declarant father, that's addressed. The age of the child, that's addressed. The harm that may result to the child if presumed or declared paternity is successfully disestablished, that's addressed. The nature of the relationship between the child and any alleged father, that's addressed. The extent to which the passage of time reduces the chance of establishing the paternity of another man and the child support obligation in favor of a child, that's addressed. Other factors that may affect the equities arising from the disruption of the father/child relationship between the child and the presumed or declarant father or the chance of harm to the child, that's addressed. All of those things are discussed by Dr. Natovich, every single one of them.

Commissioner Bloom goes on in her order and says, "Mr Rhorer has requested there be a custody evaluation. We have several factors to consider under the statute that the Court finds to be appropriate for the Court to consider in determining whether Mr. Rhorer has standing to proceed. There are certain factors specifically which I believe an evaluation would support." Whether it would be inequitable to disrupt the father/child relationship between respondent and the child, that's addressed.

Other factors, the nature of the relationship between the child and the presumed or declarant father, that's addressed. Subsection (f), the harm that may result to the child if presumed or declared paternity is successfully disestablished, that's addressed. The nature of the relationship between the child and any alleged father, that's addressed, and other factors are also addressed by Dr. Natovich. So, I guess I'm disputing that there's anything that Dr. Natovich should have addressed that she didn't. The Court says well, there's thing that she missed, so I would appreciate as we go through today, we have a common understanding of what is it Dr. Natovich should have examined that she didn't.

I'm looking at what I got this morning from Connie about missing evidence, okay. What's there. She lists - and I'm looking on page 2, conduct of the mother or presumed or declarant father and whether that estops the party. Whether it would be inequitable to disrupt the father/child relationship between the child and the presumed or declarant father, the length of time between the proceeding to adjudicate parentage and the time that the presumed or declarant father was placed on notice that he might not be the genetic father, that's addressed.

The amount of time during which the presumed or declarant father has assumed the rule of the child. While we have differences of which month or which year or how many days, there's no - that's a factual dispute that we have no choice but to say Dr. Natovich did her best job of determining that. The natural mother says one thing, natural father another thing. Dr. Natovich made every best shot, okay. The nature of the relationship between the child and the presumed or declarant father, that's in there. The age of the child, that's in there. The harm that may result to the child if presumed or declared paternity is successfully established, that's in there. The nature of the relationship between the child and any alleged father, that's in there. The extent to which the passage of time recused the changes of establishing paternity of another man in the child support obligation in favor of a child. I really don't know what that means. Other factors that may affect the equities arising from the disruption of the father/child relationship.

THE COURT: Well, I think what that means is where there's - probably where there's a missing parent. I don't think that has anything to do with this case.

DEVIN C: I'm happy to hear if there's any factor that Dr. Natovich didn't address that when you read her report isn't already in there. I don't see one. I think Dr. Natovich covered everything she was asked to cover, so what is it she didn't cover? So, let's talk about what she said. I'm not going to - I mean the Court has read the report. You don't need me to go over the report. Connie says well, there's factual disparity about whether or not mother's rights were terminated in juvenile court. Well, first of all, let me say that's a red harding. I don't think that goes to whether or not Mr. Rhorer has standing. I just - okay. I think it's a red herring. It may very well - if he does have standing and we have a custody evaluation and Judge Stanley ultimately at trial says this is who should get how much time with the child, whether or not her rights are terminated is obviously an issue. I mean until this morning I thought it was undisputed that her rights were terminated by the juvenile court.

THE COURT: Well, the reason I think that it is relevant is I think that Dr. Natovich looked at Kirk J's conduct in continuing to allow Kelly H to care for the child and to be involved in the child's life after she understood her parental rights had been terminated. I think that is a fact that she looked at that may be incorrect and that may have had some bearing on her consideration.

DEVIN C: So, my argument, your Honor, is I don't think it does have any. I mean for our purposes it shouldn't if Mr. Rhorer has standing. I don't see any purpose in sending this back to Dr. Natovich.

THE COURT: Okay. Well, you're - you had suggested that, so why don't you just address the factors as you think that they're covered in Dr. Natovich's report, and then - I mean you're right, I'ver read it, but I - but it –

DEVIN C: All right. Let's not take our eyes off the bright star of the child's best interest in all of this. The nature of the relationship between the child and the father, you have - it's undisputed that this little girl knows that Jody is her real father. There is strong evidence of alienation that we find. I mean Dr. Natovich had concerns about this child and this child't well being. The Court previously ordered this child into counseling. Connie made a representation in her motion that the child was evaluated and so therapy was deemed necessary. There's no factual allegation of that. We have no evidence at any point this child has ever seen a therapist. This child was ordered into therapy but never put into therapy.

The age of the child. Dr. Natovich said, "At 8 years of age, Payshence is capable of understanding the intricacies of her family origin if they are explained to her in an appropriate manner. She is young enough to develop a meaningful emotional connection to Mr. Rhorer and his wife if given an opportunity to do so." She found that as a factor in my client's favor.

The relationship between the child and the presumed or declarant father, she identifies Kirk J as her quote, "real father," but then they talk about Kirk J's and Kelly H's alienation of the child from Mr. Rhorer. Also, your Honor, if your one factor here in the nature of the relationship is Kirk J has multiple charges of child abuse. He has a pending case set for trial right now for physically abusing the 8-year-old half sister of this child. There's substantial evidence that his relationship with this child may not be healthy. Now this goes all different ways, okay. Kelly H has said well, Mr. Rhorer has his criminal convictions. Kirk J has a rap sheet. There's a dispute about whether or not in juvenile court Kelly H's rights were terminated. This child is in a dysfunctional family. This child is in a situation where her relationship with the parents she has is troubled. I don't think there's any doubt about that. So, if we look at the best interests of the child and how that affects standing, should Mr. Rhorer have a right to come in and say what's in the best interests of the child? Should I have custody? Should I have visitation? Is it okay for me to be a part of this child's life? So that factor was covered.

The harm that may result to the child if presumed or declared paternity is disestablished, and I quote, "It is the examiner's opinion that there would be no harm to Payshence if the fact that Mr. Rhorer is her biological parent was acknowledged by her current family. If anything, in fact, this would likely allay some of her confusing family history." Later on, Dr. Natovich recommends reunification therapy.

The nature of the relationship between the child and the alleged father. Payshence has no ongoing relationship with Mr. Rhorer. It's unclear how much time has lapsed. Payshence is quite aware that Mr. Rhorer is her biological parent. She's been greatly influenced by negative input about his past alleged behavior, as well as Kirk J's prohibition against talking about Mr. Rhorer. Jumping ahead, Dr. Natovich says it would be better if this child could have a positive view of Mr. Rhorer, thus relationship would benefit the minor child.

Then she talks about the other factors, and she talks about all of the criminal histories and the allegation, cross allegations against each other. To me, what struck me was the statement from Dr. Natovich, "The nature of these events suggests that he" - talking about Kirk J - "that he remains at risk for future criminal behavior, which could potentially result in his being unavailable to care for Payshence. Moreover, it is concerning that she could potentially be the victim of future child abuse if this charge is found to have merit." She specifically talks about Kirk J and his child abuse charges and the condition of his household and his criminal history as a reason as other factors and harm to the child, which is, I think, very important to the Court, your Honor.

The examiner had concerns regarding Payshence's ongoing contact with her mother. Kelly maintains poor boundaries and questionable judgement, history of drug abuse, unstable relationships. Despite this, they appear largely unconcerned about the possibility that Payshence may be exposed to inappropriate situations and adult information when she's in her natural mother's care. If the Court looks at this holistically, part of what I'm asking for when the Court issues its ruling is a custody evaluation to straighten all this out. If in fact Kelly H's rights have not been terminated by the juvenile court, then that would be a factor. If they have been terminated by the juvenile court, and whether or not there should be restraining orders issued or orders about her contact, that could be something Judge Stanley could do at trial, and that could be something the custody evaluation could recommend. It won't happen if the Court does not grant standing to my client.

The summary and recommendations talked about how she would have some stress, and then it talks about that it would be over weighted by the benefit of allowing Mr. Rhorer to become part of her life. A child identifies with their natural parent, even if he or she is absent, and criticism of the biological parent is in effect criticism of the child. It appears that Kirk J and Kelly H intended to influence Payshence in such a manner that she would have no interest in having contact with her biological father. Their efforts to accomplish this, however, are likely to result in greater difficulties for this child, who in light of her difficult history, likely struggles with issues of abandonment, identity and self esteem which completely contradicts the statement of Connie that this child doesn't need any therapy.

Again, I point out, this child has been ordered into therapy, and that order has never been followed by the Court. This child has never been placed into therapy, despite having been ordered to do so. I think the failure of Kirk J to enroll this child in therapy when he was court ordered to is also a factor that should be taken into account by the Court. I'm quoting again, "The examiner can find no compelling reason to conclude that it is in Payshence's best interest to maintain the status quo in regard to the biological father. If anything, her family's effort to portray Mr. Rhorer as frightening, or at best an inconsequential figure in her life, will likely add to Payshence's difficulties over time." Then it talks about how he has - now has a stable responsible lifestyle, and then it talks about his long- term interests in pursuing his daughter.

He has brought to this battle, thousands and thousands and thousands and thousands of dollars of lawyer fees, months after months after months in fighting. Fighting a paternity action in the West Jordan court, fighting in the juvenile court, fighting in this court. He has fought a never ending and unyielding battle to pursue his relationship with his child, which is the stability and the sincerity and duration of his desire for custody.

I look at all of Dr. Natovich's report, and I look at this - the recommendation as Commissioner Bloom and Judge Stanley adopted, and I'm still left with what could we ask that - what factor is there that Dr. Natovich didn't consider that when you read the report isn't already in there? If there is such a factor, my request would be that the Court identify it, and we issue a supplemental order to her saying please consider this factor or these two factors, but when the Court said that Dr. Natovich didn't consider some factors, I don't know what they are, your Honor. They may not be numbered, but I've read through them. I don't see a single factor that isn't considered.

The other thing, and I don't want to beat a dead horse, but I'm really disturbed about briefing constitutional law. That's res judicata of this case. The Court said Mr, Rhorer had a right to pursue standing, and that there would be factors that would be considered under the statute, and that those factors would be addressed as an investigation by Dr. Natovich. She's done the investigation. We have the factors. There's no more constitutional law to - that legal issue has been ruled upon in this case. So that's my position, your Honor.

THE COURT: I guess I want to make sure that we're clear. I think that the issue has been addressed in terms of there is a possibility that Mr. Rhorer, because of constitutional considerations, may be able to intervene, depending on the factors that have been identified. That doesn't have to be rebriefed. I understand that. It's marshaling - as I said, marshaling the evidence that's available to the Court in addressing those factors that I think is going to be very important that it's clear what is and is not addressed, and if there's something that's material, because frankly, some things probably aren't material because they don't apply in this case.

DEVIN C: I always appreciate guidance from the Court, but I honestly don't know what else I could brief or I could tell the Court any differently that I've told the court this morning or what's already in the recommendations.

THE COURT: Okay, Thank you. Connie, did you want to reply orally first?

CONNIE: Just really briefly to the oral arguments, because I - this is too important and too novel an issue not to have it down on paper with some coaching argument as to how some other legal principles might apply in this case, because it is a case of first impression. I would just point out that Counsel's argument is to the effect to that this Court should absolutely and unequivocally defer to Dr. Natovich simply because she filed a report, and that is never done. It's not appropriate. It basically renders your position and Judge Stanley's unnecessary. Counsel's argument was that Commissioner Bloom's ruling was if - if a report was filed, I will find standing, boom. That is not what was ruled on, and then Counsel contended with his argument just saying let's look at best interest, and this Court well knows that you cannot just under circumstances where some party has not demonstrated standing just say well, I'm going to ignore all that and just say I think - King Solomon lies - that this is where the child should be.

One of the most problematic things about the report is, and the thing that makes it very evident that Dr. Natovich did not understand the purpose of this report is that she did make recommendations about best interest. She was never asked to do that. She was asked to evaluate factual standards and provide information to the Court. She was never asked to provide a best interest analysis as to contact of reintroduction, and it's very troubling to me that she clearly does not understand what's going on in this case. It is absolutely unworkable under circumstances where we're talking about disestablishment of paternity on Kirk J's part and establishment on Mr. Rhorer and pretend like it's a custody fight. It isn't. It is tantamount to an execution of a parent and is clear that she didn't understand what was going on. I'm also perplexed by Counsel's argument that having abstained this custody evaluation is all it is. It's a custody evaluation that makes custody and visitation recommendations and how that should be facilitated, that we should also have another one.

I wanted to just alert the Court to my concerns about those arguments. The rest, what I will advise the Court is, I do think the rest of the parties disagree - we don't defer to the report, and they have a right to disagree, and to have this report in a timely fashion and submit additional factors to the court, as you have outlined, and I will submit full briefing as it relates to the standing issue. If Counsel feels like he doesn't know what else to say, the answer is say nothing, but you know, he could just submit to the Court I've said everything I want to say, but I disagree, respectfully. I think the Court needs a list of guidance as it relates to the extension of this constitutional issue of standing in this case where statutory standing regarding paternity has been excluded, and I agree that the Court deserves the benefit of that briefing.

THE COURT: Kelly, I think I'll ask you, do you have any further argument?

KELLY H: Jody's lawyer brought up that - well, when Dr. Natovich interviewed with all of us, when I went in she - I asked her did she want police reports, did she want this and that, and she didn't even want to see all that. Well, it's obvious that Jody took in police reports and stuff like that, so she used that against - you know, said that I have drug history, this and that, that it's been well over five years, and I've done all the treatment for any domestic violence, drug, anything that I was supposed to do I've done. I just wanted to point that out. The abuse that - let's see, sorry. Dr. Natovich reported that Payshence has attachment disorders. Yes, I'm sure she does, and she had a terrible first four years until she was about 4-years-old and placed with Kirk for good. We have had two different evaluations done with Payshence with Valley Medical Children's Health, who is specially taught to deal with children and they say that she is now a happy, healthy 9-year-old since she has been with Kirk for about five years.

DEVIN C: Well, your Honor, I'm going to object to that as hearsay since much of that is disputed. Those documents could have been provided to the Court - so we're not going to talk about those reports. I do however stipulate that that could be a supplemental briefing. If there are medical records or counselor's records that have seen the child, I think the record should be submitted.

THE COURT: Well, she's responding to - I think to your argument that Kirk J has ignored the Court's directive to get the child in counseling, and I think she can make that argument. If - since she would be aware of the child having been evaluated, certainly, and if she understands that result of the evaluation to be that the child doesn't require counseling, she and Kirk J will have acted on that, so it's not a hearsay in terms of a fact.

KELLY H: Yeah, she had two different evaluations at two different times of - I don't know if they were a year apart. I think they were a year apart, two different times, and you know, they both reflect the same thing that she's - she's a normal happy little girl and doesn't - doesn't need counseling, she's been with Kirk for about five years. What does the Court think will happen to my baby if she now after six years she has to be reintroduced to this stranger that all of the sudden wants to be known as daddy? What attachment disorders that she has or may have left will now be a hundred times worse.
I also have to bring up the conflicting information about the - I don't know if I need to right now, the - about the Guardian ad Litem and Dr. Natovich, the disagreement of whether or not Kirk's house is suitable for their family. When the Guardian went there, she said that the house was well put together and was fine for the family. At that time there was two more children living in the house. Then Dr. Natovich comes in and says that the house ain't big enough. They all have their own rooms for one - the two 5-year-olds share a room. This order was to decide whether my daughter and Jody had any relationship or bond. She clearly states in the report that she has no real knowledge of Jody, only remembers him by what - hearsay. She wouldn't know him is she sat next to him. She's just going to be traumatized. I can understand how people can be deceived by Jody's lies and charm. I was for four years every time he abused us and came back from whatever state he left to, and the things that - the times he says that he was in con - had contact with my daughter, there's a period of like nine moths where there was a no-contact order between him and me and my daughter, and during that period of time and some of the time that he told Dr. Natovich that he was with her was a lie, and he's - that's all I have to say.

MARY C: I think there was a misstatement in Kelly's argument about what I said in relation to the home that I just want to clarify. The home was clean, but there were a significant amount of people living in it for such a small house. It was, based on how many people were there, very clean, but that doesn't mean that there's enough living space. I don't' think that I ever said anything about that, but I don't know that that's relevant at this point in time. I would just like to ask, since it's Connie's motion to strike, and she's the one that's having the issues with Dr. Natovich's report, I would like to ask Connie what it is that she feels is lacking in the report. I don't want to come back another time so let's get it in writing on the record what it is that we need to do to update this report.

THE COURT: I guess part of the conflict or difficulty here is it's not clear to me if Mr. Rhorer is declared to be the father now and granted standing as the legal father of the child, if that doesn't disestablish Kirk J from being the father. And maybe it's because we have a situation that doesn't lend itself well to the normal paradigm of a father and a mother. This isn't a new development in society. This is not something that's never happened before, but it is something that doesn't fit within the typical analysis of custody determinations, because in those circumstances you're deciding the custodial issues between the father, whoever the father is, the legal father, and the mother, and - if there's an adoptive parent or - you know, something like that. I guess I'm not entirely clear that the Court wouldn't have some authority to order continued contact with everybody in some fashion equitably based upon something that Dr. Natovich or someone - you know, might recommend or what the judge thinks is appropriate based on the evidence before him.

I don't think that we have to cross that bridge now, but that does color how we look at this issue, because if the issue is, she gets one father, that's it, it's either Mr. Rhorer or Kirk J, whoever is not established as the father is out and he can only have contact through the mother, for instance. If that's ultimately the result, then that makes the issue a lot more difficult to decide. If it's - sure we can allow Mr. Rhorer to be involved as well, and so she'll have two fathers and a mother and two mothers really, and legally whether that's possible, I guess it's not something that I'm prepared to conclude, but I do think that does have some bearing on what the Court's needing to do here, because Connie's argument is look, if Mr. Rhorer is granted standing then Kirk J is out, and you're taking - you're disestablishing him as a father, even though the child has been living with him for most of her life. I'd be happy to have you include any commentary on that issue in your briefing as well.

The request Connie has to be allowed to supplement with some briefing will be granted and she has until August 8th to complete that. Devin, your role is more in terms of responding to her argument. You've made your argument and you think there's enough there. Dr. Natovich certainly is, I think, recommending essentially that Mr. Rhorer be granted standing based upon the factors that she's considered. I appreciate that, she's made a recommendation, and the Court should consider that recommendation.

DEVIN C: Your Honor, if I could say two things I would like the Court to rule on - because first of all, if we can find a juvenile court order that terminated Kelly's rights, it's a non-issue. Here's my point. Let's assume for the sake of argument that her rights have not been terminated by the juvenile court. I do not believe that would be grounds for the cost and delay to ask Dr. Natovich to do another report because I think it's a red herring. It's not directly relevant. The other thing - we're not her saying that Kirk J should never have a role in this child's life or he - who knows - if ultimately there's a custody evaluation that recommends that Kirk J retain custody of this child and Mr. Rhorer have some kind of time sharing or vice versa - what I want the Court to know today is it is not our position that Kirk should have no role in this child's life, and that if Mr. Rhorer is granted standing, that that means Kirk will never be a part of this child's life. I think when the Court makes it's ruling, I don't need to brief that, I can let the Court know that now.

CONNIE: And you know, it's somewhat frustrating to be here listening to these assertions that I should prove that there wasn't an order terminating Kelly's rights. Counsel wants to argue that Dr. Natovich's report is fantastic and the Court should accept everything in it. It's his motion for standing. I was in the juvenile court for all those years. My client was in juvenile court for all those years. Kelly H was in juvenile court for all those years. This divorce was filed listing the children and talking about how visitation should be arranged and that could not happen if her rights were terminated. She would't have a right to visitation. Devin C doesn't know the juvenile history of the matter and Rhorer wasn't there.

DEVIN C: Your Honor, this is easily done. The hearing was July 3rd to 31st, 2012, when the juvenile court granted permanent custody of the child with Kirk J and Connie can do something I can't - get a copy of that order.

CONNIE: That's been filed with the Court previously. It is the order of permanent custody and it doesn't say termination. It gave Kirk the right to determine Kelly's visitation through discretion.

DEVIN C: If it gives the mother visitation to be determined by Kirk J, then her rights would not have been terminated. So that order speaks for itself one way or another. If the Court will look at my motion, what I've asked for is that the first step - let's assume that he had standing for the sake of argument. I haven't asked for any time sharing. I haven't asked for custody. All I've asked for is the first step, that we get reunification therapy going. Then let's have a custody evaluation which wouldn't benign until after 90 days of reunification therapy so that we'd have that input, and then let's take a broader context look at this. For the purposes of what's before the Court today, I don't think it's directly relevant about whether or not her rights were terminated.

THE COURT: I wasn't really, you know, clear on what I was going to be hearing today, you know, I may - I may simply indicate I need further - you know, briefing on such and such, or I may indicate that you know, yes, I don think I need something else from Dr. Natovich on some factor. I don't' think the issue of Kelly's standing here really is driving anything. I was interested in reading her concerns about her behavior that seemed to be usual and to indicate an attachment disorder - the real clingy, you know, physical way the child even approached Dr. Natovich.

KELLY H: Your Honor, that's what I'm saying. If she's reintroduced to Jody and he all of a sudden wants to be this guy that's daddy and should be called daddy how that's going to affect her.

JODY: Your Honor.

DEVIN C: You're not allowed to address the Court. You can tell me and I'll address it.

JODY: Okay. Well, prior to this hearing they were ordered two times already to turn in things to the Court. I've turned in everything every time to show my background, to show everything. These people are standing here lying to your face. Everything you recommended they haven't done.

DEVIN C: I think what I would say is if we get to the point of standing and we have a custody evaluation, all of these allegations by each party and whether or not they should have to go to counseling - those would all be things taken into account by the custody evaluator. I'm anticipating that at some point the Court would issue a minute entry with its decision. Would the Court enter my request for the custody evaluation and reunification therapy as part of its minute entry?

THE COURT: I will. Just a second there.

JODY: I'd like to know who is going to be responsible for the safety of my daughter, Payshence, if he abuses her again? She's already been sexually assaulted. A boy was strangled last year, and this year there's been child abuse again. This is three times.

CONNIE: Your Honor! I would ask that the record - that the Court order that the speech by Mr. Rhorer be stricken from the record!

THE COURT: Thank you. What I'm looking for is the document that you've referred to, so that we can just get that cleared up. It's probably something you can refer to through XChange. When was juvenile court case 1 and juvenile court case 2 originally briefed? I'm thinking it might be in the - that was 2008. Well, it's not going to be easy to request and it wouldn't be a bad idea to have the GAL's input on that.

CONNIE: Im sure it would clear it up, but there's - there's - I know way more than 600 pages of documents that have been summated in this case, and I'm not sure that the Court wants to sit here all morning while I try to find it.

MARY C: Well, I think that the custody evaluation of Dr. Natovich was at a disadvantage to really evaluate Mr. Rhorer's relationship because she couldn't see that happening. I think that if there's a possibility that Mr. Rhorer will have standing, I think it only behooves the minor child in her interest to start establishing that relationship and seeing what that looks like so that we can more accurately give some kind of input on what's in the best interest of the child.

CONNIE: I object to the Court making any such ruling on such a temporary order related to custody or visitation when Counsel hasn't persuaded the Court that Mr. Rhorer even has standing.

THE COURT: So, what I would like then, is once you file your responses to Connie's submission then I want Connie to file a notice to submit saying it's ready and I'll know to look at it. I'd like to confer because I don't want this to be you file something, then you file something, then you file something, then so on. Thank you everybody. Enjoy the weekend.

I ask you, the reader, this, if a child is abducted and ten years later, the child is found to be living with people - a supposed mother and father and siblings - and that child has been incorporated into the life of her abductor to the point that she thinks they are her family; should she just be left there because she has become acclimated to the situation? We all know the answer to this question.

What if the family that legally adopted her didn't know she had been kidnapped? Does the state still leave the child with the innocent adoptive family or do they rightfully return her to her real, biological family? They take her and return her to her rightful family, of course. So how does the State of Utah justify what they have done to Payshence Rhorer thus far?

Another observation, it is brought up that Payshence has two "mommies' and that is certainly fine with the court. But if it's suggested that Jody be considered Payshence's father and be allowed to see her, then it's an absolute "NO." How can that possibly *NOT BE* a violation of his constitutional rights for *EUQAL PROTECTION*?

And lastly, the notorious Order to solve the mystery of whether Kelly lost her parental rights was sitting in the box he refused to return to us at William H's house. But alas, I was not allowed to speak or be part of the hearing. It was clear, however, that even Kelly and Kirk didn't seem to have the answer on this issue either or certainly they would have spoken up. Kelly had lost her custody to all her children, and the court had recommended terminating her rights - they even proposed to adopt Payshence out at one point - but in the end, the custody was given to Kirk for four of her kids and the order for supervised visitation, which had never been enforced, continued in effect.

JULY 20TH, 2016: LETTER to Assistant District Attorney

Dear Ms. R,

Please see the attached motion regarding my husband's daughter, Payshence Rhorer.

My husband had custody of his daughter until she was 3 1/2 and then the State found out her mother never completed her divorce and took his daughter and 3 half-brothers and gave them to Kirk J because of the fact he was the "presumed" father and the mother's custody had been terminated. The law that put this in effect is the Utah Parentage Act. My husband has been in court ever since trying to get his little girl back. We just finished an evaluation and went before Commissioner Kase on July 8th. My concern now if for her safety. Kirk J has several child abuse cases against him. Payshence was also molested and hospitalized when she was 5 and Kirk refused to cooperate with DCFS to prosecute as it was his friend that molested her. He's also harbored convicted child molesters in his home. I have court documents and records that document this.

If Kirk goes to jail or prison, we want you to know that Payshence's daddy and her 3 sisters and myself are here waiting for her to come home. We beg you not to put her in foster care. She has been so traumatized because of her drug addicted mother and this man she's been forced to live with along with 7 other kids. Please advise us if there is anything we can do.

Kind Regards.

Deone Rhorer

AUGUST 5TH, 2016: EMAILS to Department of Child and Family Services

Per our conversation, here are court documents regarding Kirk J and child abuse.
Thank you, Deone Rhorer

August 13th, 3:29 PM

Thank you for the information. We are still not able to open an investigation on this at this time as it does not meet the criteria for abuse or neglect. If you are ever concerned for the child's immediate safety, you can always call law enforcement and ask them to do a welfare check on the child. Thanks, DCFS Intake

6:58 PM

It's a law suit against Kirk J for child abuse by the State of Utah. How can that NOT BE Abuse and Neglect?

August 29, 6:46 AM

The information reported does not meet State legal definitions of abuse or neglect at this time. Even if there is a law suit against Kirk, it does not mean that it is a legal prosecution against him. A welfare check on the child, or a child protective order will be the best options at this time.
Thank you,
DCFS Central Intake

10:49 AM

DCFS came to the school and was part of this case. The court hearing is on Sept. 12 and 13. Why are there still children residing in that house while he keeps getting arrested for child abuse? There is something very wrong going on here. Deone Rhorer

September 10, 12:17 PM

At this time there is no open investigation. If there is an allegation of abuse or neglect you would like to report, please feel free to call us. We are open 24/7. Thank you, DCFS Central Intake office

AUGUST 8TH, 2016: MOTION FOR EXTENSION, submitted by Connie C, Commissioner Kase presiding

Comes now, Connie C, Attorney at Law, and on behalf of Kirk J, files the foregoing Motion for Extension of ten days in which to file a brief due August 8th, 2016. Grounds and reasons are as follows: Since the filing deadline was set, counsel's mother was moved from Wisconsin to Wyoming to an assisted living facility due to progressive complications of senile dementia. Because such a transition is particularly difficult for a person suffering from dementia, staff requested a family member attend counsel's mother as much as possible. Accordingly, counsel has made three trips to Wyoming, which the travel time alone is over 40 hours for the trips.
Additionally, counsel's work schedule remains the same, and has been more brisk than usual, with three arguments in the Court of Appeals, a brief, and a "memo" due before then. Counsel requested stipulation from counsel for the other parties. She has not received word back from them, although Devin C may be on vacation, and counsel may have an incorrect email for the GAL. Despite lack of stipulation, counsel prays the Court grant the extension due to circumstances beyond counsel's control in her family life and for other good cause stated.

AUGUST 9TH, 2016: INTERVENOR'S RESPONSE TO RESPONDENT'S MOTION FOR EXTENSION TO FILE BRIEF, submitted by Devin C, Commissioner Kase presiding

COMES NOW *the intervenor, Jody Rhorer, by and through his attorney of record, Devin C, and hereby responds to Kirk J's Motion for Extension to File Brief as follows:*
1. The intervenor will not object to a ten-day extension. However, the intervener reminds the Court that every day that he does not see his child is a day that is precious and irretrievably lost. Therefore, time is obviously important to the intervenor, nevertheless in consideration of counsel's personal concerns a ten- day extension is reasonable.

Of course, we did object but had no real say in the matter. We were told that the court would issue the extension regardless of our objection and we were therefore forced to accept another ten days of waiting.

AUGUST 17TH, 2016: TEXT from William

Good morning. I am out of the office for my son's wedding and don't have the small claims file with me. Could you please email me a copy of the small claims affidavit (complaint) and a copy of the return of service showing when it was served and the date of the small claims hearing? Thanks.

We did not answer.

AUGUST 17TH, 2016: KIRK J'S MEMORANDUM REGARDING STANDING & CONSTITUTIONALITY, submitted by Connie C, Commissioner Kase presiding

Comes now, Connie C, Attorney at Law, and on behalf of Kirk J, files the foregoing Memorandum regarding Standing, including Constitutional Issues.

Procedural History

The case arrived at this point when in February 20th, 2013, then Commissioner Bloom analyzed the case, and specifically observed that Kirk J is both presumed father due to his marriage to Kelly H at the time of the child's birth, and adjudicated father, due to an Order out of the Juvenile Court, which by clear and convincing evidence, adjudicated him father. The Commissioner correctly observed that the only persons with standing are the mother and the "presumed father," Kirk J. Additionally, there is "no presumption to rebut" because "presumed father" was served, and there has been an adjudication of paternity.

The Commissioner therefore concluded that according to the Utah Code, Mr. Rhorer is foreclosed from asserting a claim of paternity, and has no standing. However, due to a footnote in a then recent case, which indicated there might be a basis for standing in paternity cases under the Constitution, Commissioner Bloom configured a possible "standard" on which standing conferred by the Constitution might be evaluated. The outline of the standard is based on a different statute, 78B-15-608, U.C.A., regarding the Court's authority to ignore DNA testing.

The Court then Ordered a "limited purpose" evaluation to be conducted by a person qualified as a custody evaluator, Mr. Rhorer paid Dr. Natovich for such report. While Dr. Natovich was provided the verbiage of the Court's direction, and articulated repeatedly she understood the limited purpose for the report, the report filed does not conform to the Court's direction. It is also substantially inaccurate in stating as fact assertions which were made by Mr. Rhorer, and which were not verified. For example, the report was written as if Kelly H's parental rights had been terminated. New Counsel for Mr. Rhorer states at hearing he understood that proposition had never been open to question.

At hearing on the matter, in discussing the absence of Memorandum by the parities it acknowledged that the lateness of the filing of the report made drafting of the memoranda before the hearing impossible, deficiencies in the report were discussed, and Mr. Rhorer states in his position that he felt the issue of standing had already been decided based on Dr. Natovich's report. While the Court acknowledged Mr. Rhorer's counsel's statement that he really had nothing else to say regarding the standing/constitutional issues than had been said, the Court set the matter for submission of memorandum.

While Mr. Rhorer has passionately advanced his position of biological paternity, he has not offered any analysis to the Court regarding the fact that Kirk J is legal father of Payshence, and that as such, he is the holder of "fundamental" rights which cannot be deprived without due process. After establishment of parentage unless parental rights are terminated, a parent-child relationship established under this chapter applies for all purposes, except as otherwise specifically provided by other law of this state. Kirk J's Constitutionality protected parental rights are the elephant in the room Mr. Rhorer has never addressed, and which Commissioner Bloom's admittedly novel suggestion that a statute might be used as a proxy for a Constitutional analysis of standing fails to take into account.

Mr. Rhorer's argument regarding paternity is nothing more than an unabashed declaration that he slept with another man's wife, and that because he happens to be biological father of the child, he demands paternity rights. The Utah State Code soundly rebukes this type of demand in giving a paternity presumption to the woman's husband, and limited standing to contest paternity to the mother and husband, not the married woman's extra-marital sexual partner.

Since the case is strictly down to Constitutional standpoint, the Court must Order that from a Constitutional standpoint, Mr. Rhorer has no standing. First, in challenging Constitutionality, it is Mr. Rhorer's burden, and he has utterly failed to provide any analysis as to why the federal or state Constitutions recognized a claim of paternity in him, a man who slept with another man's wife. Ultimately, it is up to him to establish that legal paternity rights are a Constitutionally protected when he slept with Kirk J's wife, and Payshence resulted. To even attempt to establish this heretofore unknown sphere on Constitutional protection for men siring children within the confines of someone else's marriage, Mr. Rhorer is the one tasked to offer authority, analysis and argument which convinces the Court that despite a two hundred and thirty plus year acknowledged value in the stability provided by paternity findings based on marriage, that somehow that should be abandoned and a "new Constitutional order" recognizing value in siring children within someone else's marriage should be adopted.

While Commissioner Bloom was obviously trying to deal with a hard-fought matter, and a footnote suggesting there might be a zone of standing based on the Constitution, the framework draftee itself does not address fundamental Constitutional rights. It doesn't address that Kirk J is the holder of those rights as Payshence's presumed and adjudicated father. Nor do the factors she suggested the evaluator analyze have any demonstrated Constitutional protection.

While Kirk J feels the ordering of the limited purpose evaluation by Dr. Natovich was a mistake, and that the standard suggested by Commissioner Bloom is not an adequate proxy for actual Constitutional analysis, the report should be ignored by the Court. It is of serious concern that no efforts are made to verify information, and that so much of the report was based on self-report by Mr. Rhorer. It is also gravely concerning that in making "recommendations" Dr. Natovich assumed that Kelly H's parental rights were terminated.

Counsel for Kirk J repeatedly voiced to Dr. Natovich that based on what the Commissioner expected the report to contain, contact with Kelly H was absolutely vital so a time line of Mr. Rhorer's involvement including periods in which he ignored or did not pursue his parental rights, be accurately portrayed. Instead, the Doctor filed a report without even talking to Kelly H and then simply articulated that what she said was confusing.

Exacerbating that lapse in the report, it appears that the evaluator did not view Kirk J as a resource as to informing on his longstanding relationship with the child. The biggest and fatal flaw in the report, though, is that it's wholly deviated from its purpose. It was not a limited purpose analysis of the listed factors at all. Rather, it reads as a garden variety, albeit shorter, version of a custody evaluation, which the evaluator was told was specifically not what was requested. The recommendations are nothing more than a "best interest" conclusion, made worse by inaccurate information, and insufficient investigation. The document reveals that the evaluator did not have a grasp on the issues before the Court. Before the Court isn't an issue regarding whether she was able to verity facts going to the statutory factors she was asked to report on, so that the Court could analyze whether they could be utilized on ay Constitutional analysis of standing.

Conclusion

Because Mr. Rhorer has utterly failed to provide cogent analysis, support, authority or argument as to why the Constitution of the federal government or the State would provide him protection as biological father of a married man's presumed and adjudicated daughter, and because he has likewise failed to offer any support for the proposition that the Constitution would support vitiation of Kirk J's established parental rights, in addition to the issues outlined with the analysis/Evaluator's report, this Court must find that Mr. Rhorer has failed to demonstrate he has any Constitutionality protected standing to advance his claim of paternity.

Wherefore, Kirk J prays the Court find that Mr. Rhorer has no standing and dismiss his paternity claims, and vacate the Order which allowed him to Intervene in this matter.

AUGUST 23RD, 2016: SMALL CLAIMS COURT against William H, filed by Jody

PREPARED STATEMENT:
In December of 2015 we were referred to William H by NBC Television to represent us in the custody case for Jody's small daughter. They had contacted us after reading about our case on the internet. They also found William H on the internet as there are copious postings of him as a father's rights advocate. Upon further observation, it is clear that William H created an internet facade to get business.

Soon after giving William H a $2,500 retainer in the basement of his home where he keeps his law office, the inappropriate and odd behavior of what would become the equivalent of a train wreck and waste of four months that could have been used to further the case of returning my husband's little girl began.

After receiving some court materials I emailed him, William H sent a very unprofessional text to Jody and myself. My inclination at that time was to cancel all further contact with this man and we wish we would have done so, as things just got worse from there. However, we did meet, and a plan was made to move forward swiftly with a list of motions that were to be filed expeditiously. Weeks passed and we did not hear from William unless we prodded for an update. Each time we were promised action, none was provided, instead we received numerous excuses. It took two months for William H to file his Notice of Appearance with the court. He also failed to notify the custody evaluator that he was our new attorney, even though he was asked to several times - causing a delay in receiving the report as it was sent to the wrong attorney.

On March 23, 2016, we had had enough and requested the return of our $2,500 retainer. We had never received a bill showing any service rendered nor was there ever a service contract provided to us by William H. He then offered to return the retainer if he did not get the motions filed within "one week." On March 30th we requested the retainer to be returned as agreed after being badgered by William H until after we had gone to bed the night previous via text messages with crazy rhetoric.

In our first conversation William H requested we "friend" him on Facebook - which we did. His Facebook posts showed during the time he was claiming to be working on our motions, he was actually in another state visiting friends. We requested return of our two boxes of records as our new attorney needed them to move forward with our case. William H said he was out of town and would return them the next week. The following week, Jody tried contacting William H, but he did not respond. Jody and our son, Tanner, went to William's home to get the records since that is where his office is located. William H was there but refused to return the records, and instead, pulled up his shirt and gestured at a gun he was carrying. Jody left and contacted the police. The report testified that William H was contacted by the police but refused to respond. At this time, he was still the appointed attorney and flashed a gun at his own client.

On April 13th we requested our records be turned over to our new attorney and that William H withdraw as our legal counsel. Again, on May 24th, our new attorney sent a letter to William H requesting he withdraw as counsel and return our records - which he ignored. Our court filings continue to be shared with William H, and to our knowledge, he still has not withdrawn from counsel.

On August 17th, William H texted us requesting we send him the information on today's Small Claims Court Hearing - which further shows the disorganization and ineptness of this person that probably should not be practicing law. We have also filed a complaint with the BAR Association.

Your Honor, please return our retainer and order our records be returned in full as this man has put us through agony in addition to what we are already suffering due to the case with Jody's daughter.

We took the afternoon off work and went to the West Jordan court house for our hearing at 3:30. I had spent hours preparing everything to a tee, including printing out all the texts from William and supporting documentation. At 3:15 there was no sign of him. I really didn't expect him to show up but I never expected that when we stepped up to the podium to present our case and addressed the judge that he would dismiss our claim. Approximately fifteen minutes before the hearing, William emailed a counter suit to the judge which stated that he was suing us for ten thousand dollars.

The judge refused to hear our case stating that the amount William was suing us for took us out of his jurisdiction. I argued that we had never received an answer to our suite and that William had missed the response period and this was merely a ploy on his part as he was just trying to get out of appearing. I also argued that we had never been served a counter suit. The judge didn't care. He refused to hear our case. We were out the $100 filing fee plus the time away from work and our $2,500. We never got served the "counter claim." I was right in assuming it was just William's way of getting out of appearing. We would later be called to a hearing by the Utah BAR Association to testify against him. Once again, he was a no show. His Father's Rights Facebook page had posted that he was no longer practicing law and was seeking mental health assistance.

AUGUST 25TH, 2016: INTERVENOR'S REPLY BRIEF, submitted by Devin C, Commissioner Kase presiding

COMES NOW *Jody Rhorer, by and through his attorney of record, and hereby replies to the brief by the respondent dated July, 2016.*

1. On 7 July, 2016, the Honorable Commissioner Kase took this matter under advisement and invited the parties to brief this matter. The Respondent has filed his reply and the Intervener hereby replies.

2. The question before the Court is whether or not the Intervenor should be granted standing. The factors the Court can consider in granting the Intervener standing have already been ruled on by the Court based upon the recommendations of Commissioner Bloom, reflecting the hearing on 20 February, 2015, and subsequent Order which was executed by Judge Stanley. The Order is the law of the case. It should not be re-litigated. The constitutional rights of the parties have already been fully briefed and argued with reference to case law and statute and the Court has already ordered the process the Court would follow and the factors to determine. However, the Intervenor addresses the constitutional concerns once again in this Memorandum.

3. Commissioner Bloom recommended that the Court found one statute which would be persuasive for the Court to consider creating factors to determine whether Mr. Rhorer should proceed with his standing. Utah Code Ann. 78-B-15-608 was cited by the Court for the factors which should be considered. The Court ordered that Dr. Natovich do an evaluation taking into account the factual circumstances of the parties and the child and these factors. This brief will show how each of the factors were considered by Dr. Natovich and recommended in factors of finding standing.

4. The Court indicated it should first consider the conduct of the mother or the presumed or declarant father and whether that has estopped the party from denying parentage. Dr. Natovich found that the mother and respondent have alienated the child from Mr. Rhorer. It was found that Kirk J actually prohibited conversation about Mr. Rhorer with the minor child although the mother has talked with her at some length.

The minor child is of the opinion that Mr. Rhorer is a "scary" person based upon stories she has heard. It was found that it was clear that the minor child had heard about these alleged incidents in great detail and that the minor child's feelings about Mr. Rhorer were greatly influenced by input she had from Kelly H and she had a general sense of anxiety at the prospect of seeing him. It was found that the minor child was visibly fearful of making Kirk J angry. The Doctor's findings clearly show that the minor child has been distressed about this entire matter and the things she has been told about Mr. Rhorer and this has caused her anxiety.

5. The Court found that Dr. Natovich should consider whether or not it would be inequitable to disrupt the father-child relationship between the child and the presumed father. It is true that Dr. Natovich did not address this. However, this is a red herring. Mr. Rhorer has never taken the position that the Respondent should not have a relationship with the minor child or that the relationship would be disrupted. Instead, Mr. Rhorer has simply asked that as a beginning point, he have reunification therapy with the minor child to get to know the minor child and the minor child get to know him. He has asked for a custody evaluation where the Court could consider expert input as to what time-sharing arrangement between all of the parties would make sense and be in the best interest of the minor child. Since there is no request before the Court that the minor child's relationship with Kirk J be disrupted or terminated, such an inquiry would be premature at this point, and probably not at any point and may never be a factor in this case. Any investigation by Dr. Natovich would be purely hypothetical and is not an appropriate factor to consider at this point, and probably not at any point.

6. The Court then ordered that Dr. Natovich should consider the best interest factors of the minor child. This would include the length of time between the proceedings to adjudicate parentage and the time that the presumed father was placed on notice that he might not be the genetic father. Dr. Natovich found that the minor child was born in 2007 and was removed from her mother's care in 2010 by DCFS. Mr. Rhorer indicates that the minor child was in his care for approximately seven months during that year. Mr. Rhorer also indicated that the minor child was in his physical custody during much of the first three years of her life in addition to the approximately seven months in 2010. He also indicated seeing the minor child on an intermittent basis including a period in 2012 in which he resumed a relationship with the natural mother. While the natural mother disrupted this, there was an inherent necessity for Dr. Natovich to make judgements of credibility. Dr. Natovich found that the minor child and the natural father had established a significant relationship. As counsel pointed out in oral argument Mr. Rhorer has spent enormous sums on attorney's fees and emotional efforts pursuing a relationship with the minor child including throughout the Juvenile Court actions, this action, as well as a paternity action he filed in West Jordan that was later dismissed.

7. The next factor Dr Natovich was asked to consider was the length of time during which the presumed father has assumed his role with the minor child. Kirk J indicated he had a role in the minor child's life since she was an infant, while there are periods of time that he was not in the minor child's life when he and the mother were separated. Mr. Rhorer does not dispute that Kirk J has had a long-term relationship with the minor child and that he has acted as the minor child's primary care giver and sole custodian for a substantial period of time.

8. The next factor the Court was asked to consider was the facts surrounding the presumed father's discovery of his possible non-paternity. There is no indication and no claim has been made by any party that Kirk J ever believed he was the true biological father of the minor child, although it is undisputed, he has acted as her father figure.

9. The next factor the Court was asked to consider was the nature of the relationship between the child and the presumed father. As pointed out above the evaluator found the minor child was fearful of Kirk J. Furthermore, the evaluator noted the child abuse charges that have been filed against the respondent as well as the respondent's criminal history. The evaluator found that the minor child had poor boundaries and excessive attention seeking which is characteristic of indiscriminate sociability and very concerning and it is most often seen in children with attachment disorders. The minor child had recurrent difficulty with stealing and lying behaviors. There is a conflict about whether or not the respondent ever obtained the Court order counseling which Dr. Natovich found was appropriate. A summary of the report can be said to indicate that the minor child is not doing well in her relationship with the Respondent.

10. *The next factor was the age of the child. Dr. Natovich did address this indicating that at eight years of age she was capable of understanding the intricacies of her family origin and was young enough to develop a meaningful and emotional connection to the Intervenor and his wife if given the opportunity to do so.*

11. *The next factor indicated was the harm which may result to the child if the presumed paternity is successfully disestablished. That is addressed above. The evaluator specifically found that the child would not incur harm by being reintroduced to Mr. Rhorer, but in fact it would be in her best interest and help her deal with her attachment disorder. An axiom of family law is that the more adults in a child's life to love the child, the better off the child is.*

12. *The next factor was the nature of the relationship between the child and any alleged father. This is analyzed above, as Dr. Natovich talked about the minor child's relationship with both Kirk J and Mr. Rhorer and the minor child's feelings.*

13. *The next factor was the extent to which the passage of time reduces the chances of establishing the paternity of another man and the child support obligation in favor of a child. This was not addressed by Dr. Natovich. It is unclear how this factor would affect this case in any event. The passage of time has not reduced the chances of establishing the paternity of Mr. Rhorer, and in fact his biological paternity is undisputed. There are no issues regarding child support before the court. If Mr. Rhorer is granted standing and given a relationship with the minor child, whatever the nature of that relationship, the Court would retain powers to order child support obligations upon parties based upon the final time-sharing awarded by the Court.*

14. *Finally, other factors that may affect the equity arising from the disruption of the father-child relationship between the child and the presumed father or the chance of harm to the child. This is perhaps the most important factor as it implicates the best interests of the minor child. Dr. Natovich respectfully found that "there would be no harm to Payshence if the fact that Mr. Rhorer is her biological parent was acknowledged by her current family. If anything, this would likely alleviate some of her underlying concerns about her parentage and confusing family history." In considering the minor child's best interests there are a number of factors related to her current family situation that were of concern. There are the criminal histories of both parties, including the prior child abuse charges against the respondent and the most recent child abuse charges against the respondent which are pending wherein it is indicated that he physically abused the minor child's eight-year-old stepsister. The evaluator pointed out the recent nature of these events suggest that Kirk J remains at risk for future criminal behavior which could potentially result in his being unavailable to care for the minor child and that the minor child could potentially be the victim of future child abuse.*

The evaluator also found concerns regarding the minor child's ongoing contact with her mother whom maintains poor boundaries and questionable judgement, with reference to her history of drug abuse and unstable relationships involving domestic violence. The evaluator found that the mother and Kirk J appear largely unconcerned that the minor child may be exposed to inappropriate situations and adult information when in her natural mother's care. Dr. Natovich also referred at numerous times in her report to the negative statements made about Mr. Rhorer to the minor child by both the mother and Kirk J. While the evaluator acknowledged that the minor child would experience some stress at the prospect of being reacquainted with her biological father, that stance is the direct result of the negative input from her mother and Kirk J. It was found that a child identifies with a natural parent even if the natural parent is absent, and criticism of a biological parent is in effect experienced as criticism of the child. The evaluator found that the mother's and Kirk J's intent to influence the minor child negatively towards her father is likely to result in greater difficulties for the child who likely struggles with issues of abandonment, identity and self-esteem.

*Dr. Natovich found no compelling reason to conclude that it is in the minor child's best interests to maintain the **status quo** in regard to her biological father and that the current situation portraying Mr. Rhorer as frightening will likely add to the minor child's difficulties over time. Mr. Rhorer, despite his past history, now maintains a stable, responsible lifestyle and demonstrates a consistent and long-term interest in being part of his child's life.*

The evaluator specifically found that the minor child would benefit by having as many caring and reliable adults in her life as possible. It was found in the child's best interest for her to become reacquainted with her biological father and maintain an ongoing relationship with him and her three biological sisters whom Mr. Rhorer was granted full custody of.

15. *In the Memorandum filed by Kirk J, he raises two issues which the Intervenor believes are "red herrings" and do not impart the final ruling of the Court. First, Kirk J indicates that Dr. Natovich found out the mother's rights had been terminated. The Doctor later acknowledged that she was informed that she was incorrect but that she had relied on Kirk J's representations. Since the Juvenile Court Records are sealed, the Intervenor does not know whether or not the natural mother's rights were terminated. Neither the natural mother nor Kirk J have provided documentation one way or the other, although it was undisputed a proceeding was brought in Juvenile Court against the natural mother. This is not germane to the ultimate issue, and whether or not the natural mother's rights were terminated has no direct bearing on the intervener's standing.* **Kirk J also makes a great deal out of the issue that he also has rights. As noted above, it has never been the position of Mr. Rhorer that Kirk J's rights should be terminated and Kirk J may very well have rights to the minor child and a right to a relationship with the minor child. A finding that the Intervenor has standing does not automatically equate to a finding that Kirk J does not have any rights. The court may ultimately award a time-sharing schedule which involves all three parties.** (This section was not in the original draft that was given to us to review July 13th and Jody certainly would never agree to this. It was and is always his intent to have full custody of his daughter where he can protect her and raise her with integrity.)

16. *The Court should consider the issue of standing in conjunction with Mr. Rhorer's request that there be a custody evaluation so that the Court could fully address the harm to the child and the best interests of the child in a possible time-sharing schedule between all parents and an order of standing and a custody evaluation would grant the Court this information to be heard at time of trial.*

17. *At oral argument the Honorable Commissioner indicated that he may wish other factors to be addressed by Dr. Natovich but the position of Mr. Rhorer is that all relevant factors have been adequately considered and a further referral to Dr. Natovich would be a further delay. If Mr. Rhorer is found to have standing, and a constitutional right to a relationship with his minor child, every day that passes that he does not have a relationship with his child is an irretrievable and invaluable day that is lost forever.*

18. *Finally, Mr. Rhorer points out that since Dr. Natovich is already well acquainted with the background facts of this case it would be most cost efficient, effective and timely to have her be the evaluator who is appointed to conduct the custody evaluation in this matter.*

19. *Mr. Rhorer's modest request is that the Court at this point only order reunification therapy and that a custody evaluation begin after the reunification has been in place for some time and that the child's relationship with Mr. Rhorer be allowed to move forward.*

CONSTITUTIONAL LAW

20. *As indicated above, the law of this case has already been established and the Court has already given the Intervenor the opportunity to pursue standing based upon the factors to be addressed by Dr. Natovich. The respondent, Kirk J, has recently filed his Memorandum regarding standing and constitutionality. However, these grounds have already been covered by the Court. In March 2014, Kirk J filed his Opposition to Jody Rhorer's Motions to Establish him as the Natural and Biological Father of Payshence Rhorer and for Determination of Parentage.*

The most recent Memorandum filed by Kirk J brings up the same constitutional arguments that he brought up before, except that he brings up the issue of whether or not his rights would be automatically terminated if the Court grants Mr. Rhorer standing, and that his own constitutional rights are implicated. However, as set forth above, the intervenor is not taking that position. The arguments are simply rehashed. Attached as Exhibit "A" is Jody Rhorer's Reply Memorandum to Opposition to the Motions to Establish him as the natural, biological father which is dated 23 April, 2014, and filed with the Court. Attached as Exhibit "B" is Intervenor's Reply Memorandum to Memorandum in Opposition dated 20 September, 2014. Here again the constitutional issues were additionally argued and briefed. Attached as Exhibit "C" is the Intervenor's Supplemental Memorandum Re Motions dated 30 October, 2014, where again the constitutional, state case law and statutory issues have already been addressed and argued.

21. *Except for the brief supplemental analysis set forth below the Intervenor believes all the constitutional, statutory, and case law arguments have already been made in this case and were fully considered by Commissioner Bloom in her recommendation which was adopted in the Order signed by Judge Stanley. Kirk J is attempting to re-litigate issues which have already been decided.*

22. *In Jody Rhorer's Reply Memorandum in opposition to his Motion to establish him as the natural and biological father, he cites on several occasions the case of R.P. vs. K.S.W. and D.R.W. (2014). However, there is a provision in that case which was not quoted previously by Mr. Rhorer's prior counsel that Mr. Rhorer believes is important that the Court Consider. In Paragraph 7 of the ruling it states:*

"Ultimately, we conclude that the UUPA has pre-empted the common law in the issue of standing to challenge presumed father's paternity. We also conclude that the UUPA limits standing here to husband and wife. The District Court properly dismissed R.P.'s Petition.

> ***Although constitutional considerations might require fourth analysis in a case such as this - where the alleged father has an established relationship with the child - R.P. has not raised a constitutional challenge in the District Court on appeal. Accordingly, we leave for another day the issue of the constitutional implications of the UUPA's standing limitations which the alleged father has an established relationship with the child."***

In this case, these constitutional considerations are squarely before the Court and the Court of Appeals has said that persons in the same position as Mr. Rhorer can raise constitutional issues as to the statute. Also, as indicated in the prior Memorandums R.P. vs. K.S.W. was a case where the presumed father and the mother were still married and no divorce proceedings had been filed, unlike this case.

23. The Intervenor submits additional case law which supports his position, which has not been previously submitted to the Court. In Teece vs. Teece (Utah 1986) the Court held that while the principle that children born in wedlock are presumed to be legitimate is universally recognized, it is generally held that the presumption of legitimacy is rebuttable. This principle is again affirmed by the Court in J.W.F. vs. Schoolcraft (Utah 1988) where the Court again indicated that the presumption of paternity of a child born as issue of the marriage is rebuttable. In that case the Court held that if the presumption of paternity is rebuttable, the non-biological father has no responsibilities toward the child. "If that non-biological father has no responsibilities, then, as a corollary, he also has no rights with respect to that child, including custody rights." This is the line of reasoning Kirk J is afraid the Court will adopt, and that he will lose any rights to the child. However, the Intervenor acknowledges that there may be constitutional rights that also extend to Kirk J and he may have his own rights to a relationship with the child even if the presumption of paternity is rebuted.

24. The findings from Dr. Natovich fully support the granting of standing to the Intervenor due to the factors set forth by Commissioner Bloom and adopted by Judge Stanley.

SEPTEMBER 2, 2016:   REQUEST FOR RULING & NOTICE TO SUBMIT, submitted by Devin C, Commissioner Kase presiding

COMES NOW the intervenor, Jody Rhorer, by and through his attorney of record, Devin C, and hereby moves the Honorable Commissioner Kase to rule upon intervenor's Verified Motion for Orders dated 16 June, 2016, asking the Commissioner to recommend the intervenor have standing to pursue a claim for time-sharing with the minor child, for a custody evaluation, and for re-unification therapy.

After months of effort to get our documents back, William H was notified by the Utah Bar Association that he must return the materials to us immediately. The Bar also informed him that he needed to withdraw from the case as he still had not done so.

SEPTEMBER 8TH, 2016: LETTER from William H to Devin C

Re: Case files (two boxes) in Kelly H vs. Kirk J/Jody Rhorer Intervenor
Dear Devin:
Hand-delivered to you herewith are the two boxes in the above-referenced matter in which you are substitute counsel for Jody Rhorer. Please sign below confirming receipt of the boxes.
Best Regards,
William H

SEPTEMBER 8TH, 2016:   NOTICE OF WITHDRAWAL OF COUNSEL FOR INTERVENOR JODY RHORER, Submitted by William H

The above-referenced counsel, William H of The William H Law Firm, P.C. hereby withdraws as counsel on behalf of Intervenor, Jody Rhorer, in this matter. He hereby requests that all notices, pleadings, correspondence, and other matters pertaining to this case be directed to his substitute counsel, Devin C.

So once again, the waiting began again. Waiting, waiting, for the court to issue a decision on our case. Six weeks passed…

OCTOBER 23RD, 2016: LETTER from Devin C to Commissioner Case

Your Honor:
This letter will convey to the Court the Intervenor's desire to have the Court issue a ruling on the Intervenor's pending motion which was submitted to the Court for decision on September 8th, 2016. This is complicated and the Intervenor appreciates the Commissioner's attention to the issues and the complexities that are involved. Thank you for your attention to this matter.
Respectfully,
Devin C, Attorney at Law

NOVEMBER 15TH, 2016: MINUTE ENTRY, by Commissioner Kase

This matter came before the Commissioner on July 8th, 2016, on the Motion of Jody Rhorer, for an Order granting him standing to pursue a claim for time-sharing with the minor child in this matter and implementing an Order of Therapeutic Reunification between the Intervenor and the minor child. Although Mr. Rhorer had been granted leave to intervene in this matter, the issue of his standing to assert a claim based upon his biological parentage of the child had never been adjudicated. The Commissioner instructed the parties to brief the standing issue and any constitutional issues and notify the Court when the matter was ready for decision.

By letter dated October 23, 2016, the Intervenor's attorney indicated that the matter was ready for decision and requested a ruling on the standing issues. Having reviewed the Memorandum filed on behalf of Respondent, as well as the various other materials submitted in conjunction with these issues previously, the Commissioner finds and recommends as follows:

Background

This matter is before the Commissioner in a somewhat complicated procedural posture. In February of 2015, Commissioner Bloom, was presented with a number of motions, primarily following from the Motion of the Intervenor in this matter for various Orders and challenges to the Intervenor's standing to assert a claim for custody or parent-time.

In the Amended Recommendation and Order, dated March 31, 2015, the Commissioner reserved ruling on the issue of whether the Intervenor in this matter has standing to assert a claim for parentage or parent-time based upon the fact that he is the undisputed biological father of the child at issue, a 9-year-old girl born during the marriage between the Petitioner and the Respondent. The Commissioner determined that, because the Respondent is the presumed (and adjudicated) father, having been legally married to Petitioner when the child was conceived and born, the Intervenor would not be permitted to assert his claim for parentage based upon a strict application of the Utah Parentage Act. Due to a concern as to the constitutionality of the statute as applied in this matter if it operated to deny Intervenor the opportunity to assert his claim, the Commissioner ordered that a limited purpose evaluation be conducted by Dr. Natovich to assess factors listed in Utah Code 78B-15-608.

The intervenor had, at one time, filed a parentage action and, in fact, obtained an Order adjudicating him as the father of the child. However, because that Order was obtained without notice to the Respondent, who was the presumed father under the Parentage Act, that Order was set aside and that parentage action was dismissed. In a subsequent proceeding in Juvenile Court, the Respondent was adjudicated to be the father of the child and permanent custody and "guardianship" of the child was placed with the Respondent. The procedural history of this matter, including other cases filed in the Juvenile Court pertaining to this child, is set forth in detail in that Amended Recommendation and Order. That history of this matter is, as best the Commissioner can determine, at least a part of the reason for the constitutional concern raised by Commissioner Bloom about strict application of Section 607 of the Parentage Act.

Findings

The Amended Order Re: Limited Purpose Evaluation entered in this matter in October of 2015, specifies that the evaluator is to consider set forth factors from Utah Code 78B-15-608: (a) whether it would be inequitable to disrupt the father-child relationship between the Respondent and the child; (b) the nature of the relationship between the Respondent and the child; (c) the harm that may result to the child if the presumed paternity is successfully disestablished; (d) the nature of the relationship between the child and the Intervenor; and (e) any other factors. In a document submitted under cover dated June 7, 2015, Dr. Natovich summarized her evaluation and conclusions. The Doctor interviewed the Respondent, the Intervenor, the child, and the Petitioner in this matter.

The child has resided with the Respondent together with his current wife, the child's half-brothers, and several other related children, since she was placed in the Respondent's care by the Juvenile Court. According to Dr. Natovich's observations, the child appears to be displaying symptoms of an attachment disorder due to multiple caretakers at an early age, preventing them from forming strong, secure attachments. Dr. Natovich indicated that the child had a need for ongoing counseling to address her attachment disorder, and expressed concern that the Respondent and his wife have not effectively addressed that need at this point.

Dr. Natovich also indicated that, upon initial inquiry, the child did not identify the Intervenor as her father, although she was aware of his existence. She expressed concerns that the child's image of and attitude towards the Intervenor appeared to have been negatively influenced by the Petitioner and the Respondent, and that they had apparently described the Intervenor to the child as a bad and scary person. The child also related to Dr. Natovich that she did not actually remember the Intervenor, although she believes that she had lived with him at some point in the past. Dr. Natovich reiterates at several points in her report that the child views the Respondent as her "real" father, although she is aware she has a biological father, and that she "has no on-going relationship with (the Intervenor) and it is unclear how much time has lapsed since they have had contact with one another."

Next, Dr. Natovich referred to the criminal histories of the Respondent and the Intervenor, and noted that, while both the Respondent and the Intervenor had a criminal history, the Respondent's criminal history was much more recent, and included an un-adjudicated charge of Child Abuse with Physical Injury involving another child in the Respondent's home. The Intervenor's most recent criminal charges were in 2010.

The Doctor then expressed concerns about the fact that the child has ongoing contact with her biological mother while in the custody of the Respondent. She indicated that the Petitioner "maintains poor boundaries and has questionable judgment" based upon her history of drug abuse, unstable relationships, social media posts and willingness to expose the child to "inappropriate situations and adult information when she is in her natural mother's care." These concerns appear to be colored by the misapprehension that the mother's parental rights had been terminated and should not be in the child's life at all. In a case such as this, in which the mother's parental rights have not been terminated, the Respondent's willingness to work with the Petitioner and make sure that the Petitioner continue to have ongoing contact with her daughter would appear to be a positive, not a negative in this equation. The Petitioner and Respondent both report that they have a fairly good working co-parent relationship, and this is further supported by the fact that four other of the Petitioner's children, including 2 children by other fathers, continue to reside with the Respondent. The inference here is that the Petitioner recognized her own inadequacies as a primary caregiver and has entrusted those responsibilities to the Respondent who has willingly assumed those responsibilities and attempted to provide a home for the children.

There are some concerns reflected in Dr. Natovich's report that the sheer number of children in the Respondents home may make for a less than ideal living arrangement for the child while living with the Respondent. In contrast, Dr. Natovich has indicated that the Intervenor and his current wife have a very appropriate residence for the child in Eden, and that they have even prepared and preserved a bedroom for the child's use if and when she is allowed to spend time with the Intervenor.

Based upon the above information, Dr. Natovich concluded that, while the child "will experience some stress at the prospect of becoming reacquainted with her biological father and she is unlikely to express any interest in doing so, "that situation is more the result of the deliberate efforts by the Petitioner and Respondent to portray the Intervenor in a negative light to the child. Dr. Natovich also commented that the child 'likely struggles with issues of abandonment, identity and self-esteem," and that she "can find no compelling reason to conclude that it is in the child's best interest to maintain the status quo in regard to her biological father" and recommended a therapeutic process be initiated to reestablish some level of contact between the child and the Intervenor, review the matter, perhaps with the assistance of a Special Master, to determine on what terms regular parent-time should be instated. It doesn't appear that she is suggesting the child should be placed in the Intervenor's custody.

Analysis

The starting point of this analysis under Utah Code, when a child has a presumed father under the statute, only the presumed father or the mother can challenge the paternity of the child. Utah Code 78B-15-608 outlines factors for the court to determine if a challenge is properly before the court based upon paternity testing. It does not, in the Commissioner's view, expand who may challenge paternity, but indicates, if a challenge is made, factors to be considered in deciding whether to deny a request for genetic testing or disregard the test results.

*It's clear that the Intervenor has, fairly consistently, attempted to assert his claim based upon his biological parentage of the child, so this is not a case where the Intervenor has simply been voluntarily absent and uninvolved until recently. Is also appears to be the case that the Petitioner and Respondent are aligned against the Intervenor in seeking to prevent him from establishing a relationship with the child, likely for their own individual reason. It's not entirely clear to the Commissioner the extent to which the Intervenor was a part or allowed to participate in the Juvenile Court proceedings which resulted in an adjudication the Respondent was the child's legal father. **Had he been an active party in the litigation, the issue would be res judicata and there would be no further inquiry.** But, even if that is not the case, it isn't the adjudication of the Respondent's parentage that is the critical factor here, but rather the fact that Respondent was and is the presumed father. It's Respondent's presumed parentage which bars the Intervenor pursuant to the Parentage Act from seeking to establish himself as the father over and against the Respondent.*

*A fair reading of Dr. Natovich's report is that she focused to a large degree on factors enumerated in Utah Code, but more generally on what would be in the child's best interest. She concluded that reunification with the Intervenor <u>would not be harmful to the child</u> (although identifying an apparent attachment disorder which, it would seem, might be affected by introducing additional caregivers into her life). She also seemed to concluded that, **as between the Respondent and the Intervenor, the Intervenor would be a more stable parent, have a more appropriate living environment, and be less subject to concerns about criminal conduct. The fact that the Respondent was charged which Child Abuse in the very recent past also seems to have played into her conclusions.***

However, the factors in the statue are primarily oriented towards the relationship between the child and the presumed father and the disruption to that relationship that may occur if another father is allowed to intervene in her life as a parent figure. Certainly, if the Intervenor is in fact only seeking some limited parent-time, the disruption to the existing parent relationship between the Respondent and the child would presumably not be as great as an actual change of custody. However, although the living arrangements of the Respondent may be less than ideal and there may even be some concerns about his parenting, it is undisputed that the child has been placed by the Juvenile Court in the custody of the Respondent and has been living exclusively in his care for a number of years, that the child is not at this point the subject of any investigation with respect to any abuse of neglect toward her, and that the Respondent is maintaining a co-parenting relationship with the child's mother. Beyond those factors, there is no current ongoing relationship between the child and the Intervenor and, whether her attitudes towards the Intervenor have been colored by efforts by the Petitioner and Respondent to demonize the Intervenor, the child has no current attachment to the Intervenor, the preservation of which would be an important consideration.

Were the sole issue before the Court whether it would be in the child's best interest to have her biological father reintroduced into her life, Dr. Natovich's report might well be persuasive that would be a positive development for her. However, the inquiry is much more limited than that. Inasmuch as the issue before the Court, at its core, is whether the strict application of the Utah Parentage Act is unconstitutional as applied to the facts of this case.

Taking into account all of the factors discussed above, the Commissioner cannot conclude that there exists a compelling reason to grant standing to the Intervenor to assert his claim of parentage contrary to the provisions of Utah Code, and to enter Orders for the purpose of reintroducing him into this child's life.

Recommendations

For the foregoing reasons, the Commissioner finds that Intervenor lacks standing to assert his parentage claim, and recommends that the Intervenor's Verified Motion for Orders be denied. Counsel for Respondent is requested to prepare and submit an Order.

<u>**NOVEMBER 16TH, 2016:**</u> JOURNAL ENTRY

Devastation. Three years to get a decision and we are dismissed like a sudden sneeze! How could the Commissioner not see that plainly, her biological family wants her back and is the best place and only place she should be? That she is in danger both physically as well as the sheer jeopardy of her future existence and success. My father told me, "There is the Spirit of the Law and there is the Letter of the Law." The Letter of the Law is what is in writing to the very letter of what is written. The Spirit of the Law is the basis of what is written, but with moral intent. The Court and the Commissioner clearly have no Spirit.

My heart is hurting so bad. We are meeting with Devin C to discuss the next step of filing an appeal to go to Judge Stanley. Last night I was up until 2 a.m. dissecting the boxes of documents Nancy had put together when she was our attorney.

I actually found quite a bit of information that Nancy had not shared with us and that would have been great ammunition had she actually brought it up in court instead of just submitting copies of everything and hoping it would get read - which most likely did not happen. The biggest Ah ha was that Commissioner Kase resided over the custody appointment of Kelly's 5th child with Shayne S and GAVE Shayne joint custody of his child. This boy was conceived and born while Kirk was still married to Kelly AND the court hearings were also BEFORE Kelly and Kirk divorced. SO - Kase ruled based on the very law he quoted with two of the 3 exact same parties involved in favor of Shayne S.

We are meeting with Devin on Saturday and I will present all my findings and we will come up with a new game plan to go straight to Judge Stanley. This is *Jody's* daughter and he will never stop fighting for her.

NOVEMBER 21ST, 2016: INTERVENOR'S OBJECTION TO COMMISSIONER'S RECOMMENDATION, submitted by Devin C, Commissioner Kase presiding

COMES NOW the Intervenor, Jody Rhorer, by and through his attorney of record, Devin C, and hereby objects to the Commissioner's Recommendation handed down via the minute entry dated 15 November, 2016, that denied the Intervenor's Motion for Standing.

1. The Court previously ordered an evaluation to be done by Dr. Natovich to determine factors to aid the Court in determining whether or not the intervenor should have standing.

The Court ordered that Dr. Natovich consider certain factors.

2. The Court indicated it should first consider the conduct of the mother or the presumed or declarant father and whether that has stopped the party from denying parentage. Dr. Natovich found that the mother and the Respondent have alienated the child from Mr. Rhorer. The Court found that the minor child became visibly anxious when talking about Mr. Rhorer. It was found that Kirk J actually prohibited conversation about Mr. Rhorer with the minor child although the mother has talked with her at some length. The child had the opinion that Mr. Rhorer is a "scary" person based upon stories she has heard. Dr. Natovich found that it was clear that the minor child had heard about these alleged incidents in great detail. Dr. Natovich found that the child's feelings about Mr. Rhorer were greatly influenced by input she had heard from Kelly H and that she had a general sense of anxiety at the prospect of seeing him. Dr. Natovich found that the minor child was fearful of making Kirk J angry. An overall summary of Dr. Natovich's findings is clearly that the minor child has been distressed about this entire matter and the things she has been told about Mr. Rhorer cause her anxiety.

3. The Court found that Dr. Natovich should consider whether or not it would be inequitable to disrupt the father-child relationship between the child and the presumed father. It is true that the Doctor did not address this. However, this is a red herring. Mr. Rhorer has never taken the position that the respondent should have no relationship with the child or that the relationship should be disrupted. Instead, Mr. Rhorer has simply asked that as a beginning point, he have reunification therapy with the minor child to get to know the minor child and the minor child get to know him.

He has asked for a custody evaluation where the Court could consider expert input as to what time-sharing arrangement between all of the parties would make sense and be in the best interested of the minor child.

Since there is no request before the Court that the minor child's relationship with Kirk J be disrupted or terminated, such an inquiry would be premature at this point and may never be a factor in this case. Any investigation by Dr. Natovich would be purely hypothetical and is not an appropriate factor to consider at this point, and probably not at any point.

4. The Court then ordered that Dr. Natovich should consider the best interest factors of the minor child. This would include the length of time between the proceeding to adjudicate parentage and the time that the presumed father was placed on notice that he might not be the genetic father. Dr. Natovich found that the minor child was born in 2007, and that the minor child was removed from her mother's care in 2010 by DCFS. Mr. Rhorer indicated that the minor child was in his care for approximately seven months during that year. Mr. Rhorer also indicated that the minor child was in his physical custody during much of the first three years of her life in addition to the seven months in 2010. He also indicated seeing the minor child on an intermittent basis including a period in 2012 in which he resumed a relationship with the natural mother. While the natural mother disputed this, there was an inherent necessity for Dr. Natovich to make judgements of credibility. Dr. Natovich found that the child and the natural father had established a significant relationship. As counsel pointed out, Mr. Rhorer has spent enormous sums on attorney fees and emotional efforts pursuing a relationship with Payshence.

5. *The next factor that Dr. Natovich was asked to consider was the length of time during which the presumed father has assumed the role of the minor child. That was referred to Dr. Natovich indicating that Kirk J indicated he had a role in the minor child's life since she was an infant, while there are periods of time that he was not in the minor child's life when he and the mother were separated. Mr. Rhorer doesn't dispute that Kirk J has had a long-term relationship with PR and that he has acted as the minor child's primary care giver and custodian for a substantial period of time.*

6. *The next factor the Court was asked to consider was the facts surrounding the presumed father's discovery of his possible non-paternity. There is no indication and no claim has been made by any party that Kirk J ever believed he was the true biological father of the minor child, although it is undisputed he has acted as her father figure.*

7. *The next factor the Court was asked to consider was the nature of the relationship between the child and the presumed father. As pointed out above the evaluator found the minor child was fearful of Kirk J. Furthermore, the evaluator noted the child abuse charges that have been filed against the respondent as well as the respondent's criminal history. The evaluator found the child had poor boundaries and excessive attention seeking which is characteristic of indiscriminate sociability and very concerning and is most often seen in children with attachment disorders. The minor child had recurrent difficulty with stealing and lying behaviors. There is a conflict about whether or not the respondent ever obtained the Court ordered counseling which Dr. Natovich found was appropriate. A summary of the report can be said to indicate that the minor child is not doing well in her relationship with the respondent.*

8. *The next factor was the age of the child. Dr. Natovich did address this indicating that at eight years of age she was capable of understanding the intricacies of her family origin and was young enough to develop a meaningful and emotional connection to the intervener and his wife if given the opportunity to do so.*

9. *The next factor indicated was the harm which may result to the child if the presumed paternity is successfully disestablished. That is addressed above. Also, the evaluator specifically found that the child would not incur harm by being reintroduced to Mr. Rhorer, but it would be in her best interest and would help deal with her attachment disorder. An axiom of family law is that the more adults that are in a child's life to love the child, the better off the child is.*

10. *The next factor was the nature of the relationship between the child and any alleged father. This is analyzed above, as Dr. Natovich talked about the minor child's relationship with both Kirk J and the minor child's feelings.*

11. *The next factor to be addressed was the extent to which the passage of time reduces the chances of establishing the paternity of another man and the child support obligation in favor of a child. This was not addressed by the Doctor. It is unclear how this factor would affect this case in any event. The passage of time has not reduced the chances of establishing the paternity of Mr. Rhorer, and in fact his biological paternity is undisputed. There are no issues regarding child support before Court. If Mr. Rhorer is granted standing and is given a relationship with the minor child, whatever the nature of that relationship, the Court would retain powers to order child support obligations based upon the final time-sharing schedule ultimately awarded by the Court.*

12. *Finally, Commissioner Bloom recommends that the Court should consider other factors that may affect the equity arising from the disruption of the father-child relationship between the child and the presumed father or the chance of harm to the child. This is perhaps the most important factor as it implicates the best interests of the minor child. Dr. Natovich specifically found that "there would be no harm to Payshence if the fact that Mr. Rhorer is her biological parent was acknowledged by her current family. If anything, in fact, this would likely alleviate some of her underlying concerns about her parentage and confusing family history."*

Dr. Natovich found that in considering the minor child's best interests there are a number of factors related to her current family situation that were in concern.

These are the criminal histories of both parties, including the prior child abuse charges against the respondent and should include the most recent child abuse charge against the respondent which are pending wherein it is indicated that he physically abused the minor child's younger stepsister. The evaluator pointed out Kirk J's criminal history of eighteen incidents occurring between 1997 and 2016, which does not include the most recent child abuse charge which is pending. The evaluator found the recent nature of these events suggest Kirk J remains at risk for future criminal behavior which could potentially result in his being unavailable to care for the minor child and that the minor child could potentially be the victim of future child abuse. The evaluator also found concerns regarding the minor child's ongoing contact with her mother and that her mother maintains poor boundaries and questionable judgement, with reference to her history of drug abuse and unstable relationships involving domestic violence. The evaluator found that the mother and Kirk J appear largely unconcerned about the possibility the minor child may be exposed to inappropriate situations and adult information when in her natural mother's care. Dr. Natovich also referred at numerous times in her report to the negative statements made about Mr. Rhorer to the minor child by both the mother and Kirk J. While the evaluator acknowledged that the minor child would experience some stress at the prospect of being reacquainted with her biological parent, the evaluator found that the mother's and Kirk J's intent to influence the minor child negatively towards her father is likely to result in greater difficulties for the child who likely struggles with issues of abandonment, identity, and self-esteem. Dr. Natovich found no compelling reason to conclude that it is in the child's best interest to maintain the status quo in regard to her biological father and that the current situation portraying Mr. Rhorer as frightening will likely add to the minor child's difficulties over time. The evaluator found that Mr. Rhorer, despite his past history, now maintains a stable, responsible lifestyle and demonstrates a consistent and long-term interest in being part of his child's life. The evaluator specifically found that the minor child would benefit by having as many caring and reliable adults in her life as possible. The evaluator found it was in the child's best interest for the minor child to become reacquainted with her biological father and to maintain an ongoing relationship with him and her three biological sisters whom Mr. Rhorer was granted full custody of.

13. The Court made much of the fact that the respondent has an established relationship with the minor child. The intervenor would like to point out that the Respondent at first denied paternity when he filed his Answer. Because of his denial the Court ordered him to undergo genetic testing. The respondent did not comply and obviously wouldn't have been proven the biological father, and because of this the Court in 2012, ordered that he was not the biological father of the child and the Office of Recovery Services Complaint was dismissed. The Intervenor thinks it is also important that the Court be aware that it is no fault of the Intervener that there has been a relationship with the minor child develop with the Respondent over years despite the fact the Intervenor has been fighting since 2009 to have a relationship with the child. The original motion filed in the original Juvenile Court ultimately did not allow the intervenor to have rights to the minor child in Juvenile Court. The intervenor also brought a paternity action in the West Jordan District Court which was dismissed because of this action. Finally, the intervenor has been vigorously pursuing a relationship with the minor child in this action for years.

The intervenor has spent many, many thousands of dollars in attorney fees and years of heartache and struggle to have a relationship with his child and only because of the barriers placed by the court system, and the respondent and the child's mother, the Intervenor has not been able to have a relationship. The Intervenor reminds the Court that he had a deep and meaningful relationship with the minor child for several years before the child was taken from him. The respondent should not be rewarded for blocking the intervenor's relationship with the child and the inherent slowness of the court system which has given the respondent an opportunity to develop a relationship with the child.

14. Despite all of the above the Commissioner determined the inquiry of the Court should be very limited and only to determine and focus on the analysis of the child's relationship with the presumed father and the disruption of the relationship that may occur if another father is allowed to intervene in her life as a parent figure. The Commissioner believed that the best interest of the child is a factor that should be ignored, although Dr. Natovich found it would be in the best interest of the child to have a relationship between the respondent and the child would not be as great as an actual change of custody. By denying standing, the Commissioner did not even allow the Intervenor to seek a limited claim for parent-time short of custody.

15. The Intervenor respectfully disagrees with the Commissioner that there are not constitutional rights that attach to the intervenor as the child's biological parent who had a significant relationship with the minor child for years before the child was taken away from the Intervenor over the objection to the Intervenor.

16. The issues before the Court have been abundantly briefed with case law submitted upon multiple occasions by the parties. The Intervenor does not at this time re-submit all of the case law, as that is part of the Court's file. However, the Court in Teece vs. Teece and J.W.F. vs. Schoolcraft held that the presumptions of paternity of the child born of a marriage is rebuttable. The recommendation of the Commissioner indicates that there must exist a compelling reason for the Court to grant standing to the Intervenor.

It's unclear what compelling is. If the presumption is rebuttable, and Dr. Natovich's findings support rebutting the presumption, then the overcoming of the presumption shouldn't require a "compelling" reason. Is it not compelling that the intervenor loves his child and desires a relationship with her and has always sought that relationship? The Intervenor submits that the minor child's relationship with the presumptive father doesn't need to be disrupted, and the minor child would clearly benefit from a relationship with the Intervenor, that it would request a compelling reason to overcome the constitutional presumption that a natural father has a right to a relationship with his daughter when that relationship has been preserved to the utmost extent possible by the natural father.

17. The Commissioner's recommendations seem to be in conflict with the Court's prior order which appointed Dr. Natovich to conduct the evaluation. If it was a forgone conclusion that the only factor that the Court should consider is the disruption of the relationship between the child and the presumed father, then the Court would not have opened up the examination and directed Dr. Natovich to explore the other issues. The Court should not simply ignore the findings of the Doctor that it would not be disruptive to the child to have a relationship with the Intervenor, and it would be clearly in the child's best interest to do so. The Intervenor does not dispute that the preservation of the child's relationship with the presumed father would be an important consideration and is not taking the position that the presumed father's rights should be terminated, or that the Court must grant the Intervenor custody if the Court grants the Intervenor standing. That is what the purpose of a trial would be, to determine what should be the ultimate disposition in this case.

Terminating the Intervenor's rights with the minor child through no fault of the Intervenor, and when such a determination would be contrary to the best interest of the minor child, violates the constitutional rights of the parent and the child to have a relationship with each other that is positive for all concerned. The intervenor asks the Court not uphold the recommendation of the Commissioner and order instead that the Intervenor has standing and remand the matter to the Commissioner for determination of the Motion for a time-sharing evaluation and reunification counseling.

Devin's rebuttal was practically a repeat of his previous pleading with little added regarding the constitutional issue of our case. At our first meeting with Devin, he told us he would, "...have your daughter back to you by Christmas." Now Christmas was less than a month away and our odds weren't looking good.

DECEMBER 5TH, 2016: REQUEST FOR RULING & NOTICE TO SUBMIT, Submitted by Devin C, Commissioner Kase, Judge Stanley presiding

COMES NOW the Intervenor, Jody Rhorer, by and through his attorney of record pursuant to Rule 4-501(D) of Utah Code of Judicial Administration, requests the Honorable Judge Stanley to rule on the Intervenor's Objection to Commissioner Kase's Recommendation dated 21 November, 2016 filed with the Court.

DECEMBER 7TH, 2016: ORDER ON STANDING OF INTERVENOR & DENYING MOTOIN FOR ORDERS, Summarized by Connie, Commissioner Kase, Judge Stanley presiding

THIS MATTER came before the Court upon Intervenor, Jody Rhorer's, Motion that the Court grant him standing to further pursue a claim for time sharing with the minor child, and an Order of therapeutic reunification between himself and the minor. The Commissioner reviewed the pleadings in the matter, and recommends the following findings and Order:

FACTS/PROCEDURAL HISTORY

In February, 2015, then acting Commissioner Bloom was presented with a number of motions which resulted in a reservation of an issue regarding whether Intervenor has standing to assert a claim of parentage and/or parent-time with Payshence Rhorer. Commissioner Bloom had previously ruled that Respondent, Kirk J, was presumed father, by virtue of his marriage to Petitioner at the time of Payshence's birth, as well as being adjudicated father by Order issued by the Juvenile Court in a previous child welfare action. Accordingly, Commissioner Bloom ruled that Intervenor lacked statutory standing to assert a claim of paternity.

Having ruled Intervenor was not one of the persons described by the statutes as having standing to challenge paternity, and having reserved a ruling on whether Intervenor could make a showing of standing as a constitutional matter, Commissioner Bloom ordered a "limited purpose evaluation" to assess the factors listed in 78B-15-608. Dr. Natovich's evaluations and conclusions submitted June 7th, 2016, include that Payshence has resided with Respondent, Kirk J, and his current wife, the child's half-brother, and several other related children, and has consistently resided in like matter since being placed there by the Juvenile Court.

The Doctor observed that the child appears to be displaying symptoms of an attachment disorder which she notes, "usually result from a child having inconsistent and/or multiple caretakers at an early age, preventing them from forming strong, secure attachments." She noted that ongoing counseling is needed to address this concern, and noted she found Respondent and his wife have not effectively addressed the issue. Interviewing Payshence, Dr. Natovich learned that the minor knows Respondent is not her natural father, but that she does not know her natural father. The minor's image of her biological father appears to have been negatively influenced by the parties. Payshence expressed that he has been described as a bad or scary person. While she doesn't remember Intervenor, she believes she lived with him at some point.

Dr. Natovich reported concerns regarding Respondent and Intervenor's criminal history. At the time of the limited purpose evaluation, Respondent had pending charges of child abuse with physical injury with the victim being another child in the home. Intervenor's criminal history was less recent, with the last entry being 2010. She also expressed concerns that Kirk J allows contact with Petitioner, the child's mother, Kelly H. The report expresses that this is concerning in light of termination of Kelly H's parental rights. It is incorrect that Kelly H's parental rights have been terminated, and Respondent's activities in allowing Payshence visitation with Petitioner, and presumably successfully co-parenting Payshence with Kelly H are actually positives. Petitioner and Respondent also co-parent four other children, which bespeaks of Petitioner's recognition of her own parenting inadequacies, and Respondent's willingness to assume responsibility to provide a home for the children. It was pointed out the sheer number of children in Respondent's home may make it less than ideal as a living arrangement for Payshence, while Intervenor Mr. Rhorer and his wife occupy a large home with a room already made up for Payshence.

Dr. Natovich's conclusions, which are based on more of a "best interest analysis than application of the listed factors, include the child "likely suffers with issues of abandonment, identity and self-esteem" and will likely not express an interest in interacting with Intervenor, probably due to efforts on the part of Petitioner and Respondent to portray him in a negative light. However, Dr. Natovich opined that she "can find no compelling reason to conclude that it is in "the child's best interest to maintain the status quo in regard to her biological father" and recommended a therapeutic process, perhaps aided by a special master, to reintroduce Intervenor with the child. Nothing reported suggested that Intervenor be granted custody.

ANALYSIS

78B-15-204 and 607 provide that when a child is born to a married woman, and husband of the mother is presumed legal father, only presumed father and mother can challenge the presumption of paternity. It outlines factors to consider whether paternity testing establishing biological paternity in another should be disregarded when a challenge is properly before the Court. While Commissioner Bloom cited the suggestion in R.P. vs. K.S.W. (Utah 2014) that there might be a constitutionally based argument for standing, 78B-15-608 was not intended to expand standing to persons other than mother and presumed father. This is not a case where Intervenor has been voluntarily absent and uninvolved until recently. He has fairly consistently attempted to assert his claim of paternity, including having obtained an order of Paternity in District Court, which was then stricken for failure to notice Respondent, Kirk J. It is unclear how active Intervenor was in the prior Juvenile Court matters. Had Intervenor been an active litigant in Juvenile Court, the Court would find the issue of adjudication of paternity res judicata as to Intervenor. However, the lack of clarity on that point is not central to the analysis. It isn't the Juvenile Court adjudication of paternity which is the salient feature in the Court's analysis. Rather, the Parentage Act precludes Intervenor from asserting a claim of paternity over and against Respondent.

While Dr. Natovich's report seems to focus on best interest, and Intervenor possibly could be a more stable parent with a better environment, and less criminal history, the statutory factors she was asked to evaluate had more to do with the relationship between the child and presumed father, Kirk J. The minor has been in care of Respondent for years, he isn't under any current investigation for neglect or abuse of the minor and successfully co-parents with the child's mother. Contrast that Intervenor has no relationship with the minor.

If the issue before the Court was whether it would be in the minor's best interest to introduce the minor to Intervenor, the Court might be persuaded by Dr. Natovich's report. However, the issue is whether strict application of the UUPA is Unconstitutional as applied to these facts. Taking into account the factors above, the Court cannot make that conclusion.

CONCLUSION

*WHEREFORE, the Court cannot conclude a compelling reason exists to grant standing to Intervenor, Jody Rhorer, to assert his claim of parentage contrary to the provisions of 78B-15-607, and to enter Orders for the purpose of reintroducing him into this child's life.   Accordingly, Jody Rhorer lacks standing to assert he parentage claim and Intervenor's Verified Motion for Orders is therefore, **DENIED.***

At what point do you throw your hands in the air and shout, "I surrender?" There would be no white flag raised by Jody though; as long as another step in the judicial process existed, he was willing to take it. Jody was sure of one thing, if Payshence was allowed to see him, she would know exactly who her Daddy was. I have visualized that moment in my mind so many times - the look of shock and relief on her beautiful little face. It had only been a year in a half since she had called Tina and asked, "What happened to Daddy? I want to talk to Dad."

I knew when I read the evaluator's report referencing Payshence's voice dropping to a whisper when asked about Jody that she had been threatened and coached on what she was allowed to say. Dr. Natovich could see it. Mary the GAL could see it. Commissioner Bloom knew it. Why could the Court not see it?

DECEMBER 23RD, 2016: VERIFIED MOTION TO SET ASIDE COURT ORDER, submitted by Devin C, Judge Stanley presiding

COMES NOW Jody Rhorer, by and through his attorney of record and hereby moves the Court to set aside the Court Order denying the Intervenor standing until the Court has ruled on the Objection to the Commissioner's Recommendation.

1. If the Court allows the Order to stand, it could be construed to trigger the Intervenor's right to appeal to the Court of Appeals. If the Court is going to overturn the Commissioner's Recommendation then such an appeal would not be appropriate. However, if the Order is allowed to stand and the time to appeal is triggered, the Intervenor and the other parties are in a position where they may be spending resources toward an appeal which may not be necessary. Furthermore, it is not clear whether or not the Judge intended the signing of the Order to be a ruling on the merits of the Objection to the Commissioner's Recommendation.

2017

JANUARY 4TH, 2017: REQUEST FOR RULING & NOTICE TO SUBMIT, submitted by Devin C, Judge Stanley presiding

COMES NOW *Jody Rhorer, by and through his attorney of record, pursuant to Rule 4-501(D) of* Utah Code of Judicial Administration, and *requests the Honorable Judge Stanley to rule on the Intervenor's Verified Motion to Set Aside Court Order dated 26 December, 2016, filed with the Court.*

FEBRUARY 3RD, 2017: APPEAL HEARING, Judge Stanley presiding

Present: Jody and Deone Rhorer; attorney, Devin C; Mary C, GAL; attorney, Connie.

My notes:
Connie said she was confused because she didn't see an objection filed. Devin C said it was filed on November 23rd. Judge Stanley said this hearing was about setting the time for the appeal. Both Connie and the Judge say there was no objection filed in November. Connie said she asked Devin C for it twice. Devin C said Connie never asked him for anything. Connie said the objection was never filed so she wants to argue that we never got the objection filed in time so the judge needs to dismiss it. The judge continued the matter to March 7th.

FEBRUARY 4TH, 2017: JOURNAL ENTRY

Yesterday was another huge set back. Five years of this fight and I am becoming weary. I'm still not sure what all parties present thought the hearing was for, but we were under the impression it was to get a ruling on our appeal. Our attorney was ready with his argument, if needed, but really expected the judge to have reviewed the case and be ready to renew his decision. INSTEAD, the judge said, "What are we here for today? I have nothing in the system that has been filed on this case."
Our attorney's secretary somehow got distracted on November 23rd (maybe rushing out the door to prepare for Thanksgiving?) and failed to hit the SUBMIT button when she downloaded our appeal. She stamped it as "COMPLETE" and mailed us a copy, but no one else involved received it and in the passing several months of waiting, no one checked to make sure everything had been property lodged. SO - we missed our 30-day appeal window. Of course, Kirk's free attorney was drooling all over herself because of this idiotic mistake and I'm sure she has already filed a Motion to Dismiss our case. Now our attorney has to go in on his hands and knees and beg the Judge to hear our appeal. It was another heartbreaking day. Jody cried. I cried - multiple times - still am. I don't know what will happen now. Years of fighting may have been wiped away by a simple task uncompleted - the pressing of a button.

FEBRUARY 10TH, 2017: AFFIDAVIT OF JADE C, submitted by Devin C, Judge Stanley presiding

COMES NOW *Jody Rhorer, by and through his attorney of record and hereby submits the attached Affidavit of Jade C:*
My name is Jade C. I am employed by Devin C. I am writing this Affidavit because I made a mistake. On November 23rd, I was doing my work as normal. I had some other work besides Jody Rhorer's that I was doing. I was e-filing documents with copies mailed out to the parties listed on the mailing certificates, as is usual procedure. When it came to Jody Rhorer's turn, I opened the document "Objection" and prepared it for e-filing and mailed it to the people on the mailing certificate. Attached are screen shots of the steps I took to prepare the document.

I opened the Objection. I filled out and then signed the mailing Certificate. I saved the document as a pdf file so it would be accepted in e-filing. I made all necessary copies and sent them to the parties on the Mailing Certificate. I had written on the original "e-filed/cc: both parties/11-23-16." I left my desk at this point. I may have been distracted by answering my phone, leaving going to the restroom, or another personal activity. When I came back to my desk, I finished my work on the remaining documents. I thought I had finished the Objection so I placed it in the pile of finished documents. I didn't actually e-file the Objection. I put it in Devin's inbox without e-filing it. I assumed that I had e-filed it, because all of the steps were completed.

I have never made this kind of mistake before. E-filing has been in operation since 2013. My work demands attention to detail and this was an uncharacteristic error. Devin had no indication that the document had not gone through e-filing. Instead, he received confirmation it had been e-filed and copies mailed out. Devin counts on the staff hand writing the code at the bottom of a document. It is our system.

Once a document has been successfully e-filed, three emails come in per document reflecting a successful filing. I wait for ALL of the bounce-back emails from Greenfiling to be in the Inbox together so I can delete them all at once. The Rhorer Objection would have been mixed in with the other emails. I did not notice it was missing.

*   **SUBSCRIBED AND SWORN** to before a Notary Public.*

Of course, Devin C was very apologetic and embarrassed. He assured us that the judge would most likely allow our appeal and that he would not charge us for any work related to the mistake. All his sincerity and concern could not chase away the cloud looming over us that reminded us of the worse-case possibility.

FEBRUARY 10TH, 2017:   MEMORANDUM OF JODY RHORER IN SUPPORT OF INTERVENOR'S OBJECTION TO COMMISSIONER'S RECOMMENDATION, submitted by Devin C, Judge Stanley presiding

COMES NOW *Jody Rhorer, by and through his attorney of record and hereby provides the following Memorandum in support of the Court hearing the Objection to the Commissioner's Recommendation.*

1. The Intervenor filed a Verified Motion to Set Aside Court Order dated 26 December, 2016. Therefore, the Order which implemented the Commissioner's Recommendation has not yet become a final Order.

2. Because of clerical error while the intervenor prepared an Objection in a timely manner and believed the Objection had been e-filed, it was error on the part of Devin C's legal assistant which lead to the Objection not being filed.

3. The Intervenor suggests in the interests of justice that since the Motion to set aside the order was filed in a timely manner, the Court could hear the merits of the Objection to the Commissioner's Recommendation on a Motion to Set Aside Court Order.

4. Rule 108 provides that a party may file a written objection to the recommendation within fourteen days after the recommendation has been made in open Court or, within fourteen days after the Minute Entry of the recommendation is served. While it was counsel's intent to have this filed within fourteen days, and indeed based upon his communications with his staff counsel believed it had been done within fourteen days; the fact that it was not done should not defeat the Court hearing the merits of the matter. Such a hearing is in the interest of justice. Rule 108 doesn't indicate a remedy if the objection wasn't filed within fourteen days and doesn't prevent the Court hearing the merits of the matter after fourteen days if there was an inadvertent error.

FEBRUARY 14TH, 2017: JOURNAL ENTRY

Today is Valentines Day. This morning I made a trip to Payshence's school. I brought I large stuffed dog holding a stuffed hart, a bracelet, a hart shaped box of chocolates, and a card containing photos of Payshence with her sisters and with Jody. In the card I wrote, "*Your Daddy and Sisters love you and miss you.*"

I didn't let Jody know I was doing this until I had completed the task. It was my Valentines gift to him and I didn't want him to be implicated as a co-conspirator. I also filmed the entire event incase I was accused of something other than dropping off this gift of love. The whole mission took under 2 minutes.

There was one elderly woman working the front desk in the office. There were several children in front of me needing assistance. There was a pile of valentine related objects on a side counter. My turn came. I had tied everything to the stuffed dog with a big ribbon to ensure nothing would get lost or separated.

"Could you give this to Payshence Rhorer please?"

"Sure will." And the elderly lady plopped the dog down on top of the pile of valentines waiting to be delivered to children.

As I exited the school, I noticed my heart pounding hard in my chest. I hope Payshence feels the love that I sent with her gifts. I hope she is able to keep the dog and eat the chocolate and wear the bracelet. And I mostly hope that she is able to hide those pictures in a place that she can see often and remember.

MARCH 7TH, 2017: COURT HEARING, Judge Stanley presiding

My notes from court:

JUDGE STANLEY: Procedurally, where are we at at this point?

: (

DEVIN C: Did you read the Motion for Appeal?

JUDGE STANLEY: Was there a counter motion?

CONNIE: Your Honor, we oppose amending the judgement.

JUDGE STANLEY: Do you wish to brief the motion before I rule?

CONNIE: If the court doesn't want to accept my argument that you don't have jurisdiction over that then I want to argue.

JUDGE STANLEY: I'm concerned with over 500 pages in this case that I need time to be brought up to speed. I want to get up to speed quickly if you can point me in the right direction on what I should know.

DEVIN C: Both sides have briefed this case to death before I got the case. Everything is included in my brief.

JUDGE STANLEY: Can you point me to a docket number?

DEVIN C: If we have to have another court date, I would like to be able to wrap this up. We need to decide on the Motion to Amend.

CONNIE: My client is indigent. I picked him up on a child welfare case in juvenile court and he's pro bono.

JUDGE STANLEY: I'm not going to read the 500 pages. You have until April 3rd to argue the Motion to Amend.

Oh! WOW! What just happened? That was it? We waited months again just to have the unprepared judge refuse to read the case? He didn't even read Devin's motion! Connie missed the response period for a counter motion and he just ignored it.

The hearing, while brief, quickly turned the light on me. Connie had fabricated a huge story about my trip to the school. I was behind the main bench sitting in the spectator area, taking notes, and was not even able to speak and defend myself. She told the judge that I had gone to the school and represented to the secretary that I was Payshence's mother and then tracked down Payshence within the school and personally handed her the Valentines gifts and this was extremely traumatizing for Payshence.

Every part of me wanted to leap over the small wooden wall that separated the spectators from the participants, grab Connie by the nap of hair at the back of her neck - the way I had seen my grandma do to my Uncle Jeff when he was acting up - and make her eat the microphone that she spoke the lies about me in to. The one thing I was so grateful was not brought up was the photos of Jody and the sisters. It gave me hope that somehow, she was able to hide them and keep them.

We pushed and pushed to get our case in front of Judge Stanley just to have him treat it with disinterest and apathy. Devin tried, once again, to get the judge to make a decision and move forward but Connie, in turn, would object to every thing he said. Now we wait again - two more months. Who came up with this system? It is broken!! Sad, sad, sad.

APRIL 2ND, 2017: COURT ORDER, Judge Stanley presiding

THIS MATTER came on for hearing before the Honorable Stanley on the 7th day of March, 2017. The Petitioner **was not** present, nor was she represented by counsel. The Respondent **was not** present, but was represented by his counsel, Connie. The Intervenor, Jody Rhorer, was present with his counsel, Devin C. The State of Utah was not represented. Mary C, the GAL, appeared telephonically. Based upon the representations of counsel, the pleadings on file herein and good cause appearing therefore:
IT IS HEREBY ORDERED, ADJUDGED AND DECREED:
1. That this matter is set for a Review and Hearing on Objection to Commissioner's Recommendation if the Court allows the matter to go forward on 10 May, 2017.
2. That the Intervenor has filed a Motion for Amendment of Judgement and Relief from Judgment or Order pursuant to Rule 59-A3 and Rule 60 of the Utah Rules of Civil Procedure. The respondent may file any brief regarding this Motion and should do so no later than 3 April, 2017. The Intervenor has already filed a Memorandum in support of his Motion, but may have until 10 April, 2017, to respond to any pleadings filed by the respondent. The Court shall then, by Minute Entry, make a decision on whether or not the Intervenor's Motion for Amendment of Judgement and Relief from Judgement Order shall be granted. If the Court grants the Motion then the matter shall be heard, as set forth above, for hearing on the Objection to the Commissioner's Recommendation.
*3. **That the Intervenor shall take no steps to contact the minor child, nor shall he ask or encourage any third parties to do so.***

APRIL 3RD, 2017: KIRK J'S RESPONSE TO PROCEDURAL ISSUES REGARDING FAILURE/NEGLECT TO FILE OBJECTION/RULES 108/60/and 59, dubmitted by Connie C, Judge Stanley presiding

Connie C, Attorney at Law, on behalf of Kirk J, files the Response regarding procedural issues regarding failure/neglect of Mr. Rhorer to file an Objection to Commissioner's finding, and his "Verified Motion to Set Aside Court Order" filed the 23rd day of December, 2016, and his "Motion for Amendment of Judgment and Entry of Judgment" filed the same day.
Procedural History
On November 15, 2016, after more than two months of deliberation, and an October 31st, 2016, letter from Intervenor Rhorer, urging the Commissioner to decide the pending issues, Commissioner Kase issued a ten-page minute entry detailing recommendations for a finding that Mr. Rhorer lacks standing to assert a claim of paternity to RP.
On December 7th, 2016, Mr. Rhorer's attorney filed a "Request for Ruling and Notice to Submit," in which he asserted that an Objection had been filed November 21st, 2016, to the Commissioner's recommendation of November 15th, 2016.

Also, on December 7th, 2016, undersigned counsel for Kirk J sent an email to the address known to be used by Devin C, counsel for Mr. Rhorer. The email read, "I just got a court filing regarding a notice to submit regarding an objection which says it was filed with the Court November 21st. I didn't get that document, and unless I'm blind, I don't see it filed with the court. Devin, since this notice to submit says it was generated by you, could you please check in to it and get back to me?" (The email was also sent to the GAL.) Devin C did not respond.

The proposed Order that was submitted by undersigned counsel for Kirk J, ultimately resulted in the December 21st, 2016, entry of an Order Denying Standing to Intervenor Mr. Rhorer. On December 27th, 2016, counsel for Kirk J sent the following text to Mr. Cook, "I noticed that you filed something yesterday referring to an objection which you have indicated to the court you filed. When you emailed something about that before I wrote back promptly and said I never got an objection, my Judicial-link account shows no filing of an objection, and I believe I checked Court exchange at the time with the same result. Kindly send me a copy of the objection that you say you filed, because I am going to have to file a response, and it requires me to see this objection you say was filed. If you have a receipt from your electronic filing system showing when it was filed, it would be helpful as well." Again, Devin C did not respond.

The "Motion for Amendment of Judgment and Entry of New Judgment, purports to be filed pursuant to Rule 59, U.R. Civ.P., and asserts that it constitutes an "irregularity" in the proceedings that the Commissioner signed the Order, with an Objection and Request to Submit (on that Objection) pending. Intervenor concluded the Commissioner's signing of the Order with out the Judge considering the merits "prevented Intervenor from having a fair trial."

The "Verified Motion to Set Aside Court Order," attests that there was an Objection pending that the Order was signed over, and that, "it is not clear whether or not the Judge intended the signing of the Order to be a ruling on the merits of the Objection to the Commissioner's Recommendation." No rule or case was cited in support of the "Verified Motion to Set Aside Court Order."

At hearing February 3rd, 2017, Devin C addressed the Court as if an Objection had been filed. He affirmatively asserted it had, although both the Court and Counsel for Kirk J indicated that he had looked and could not find such a filing. Devin C then clarified that he had a handwritten note of a staff member on a hard copy of an Objection which indicated the document had been filed.

On February 3rd, 2017, an Objection was filed. The Objection purports to have been signed and certified to counsel November 23rd, 2016. An "affidavit" which purports to be information from a Jade C, but signed by counsel Devin C, asserting that Jade C works for Devin C, and that while she intended to and thought she e-filed the Objections in November, 2016, she did not accomplish the task.

Mr. Rhorer filed a Memorandum in Support of his Objection on February 10th, 2017. The Memorandum outlines that the Motion to Set Aside the Order was filed December 26th, 2016, and that the Court should consider the Objection despite the fact that it was not timely filed, because the Motion to Set Aside the Order was filed. The Memorandum merely asserts that Rule 108 "does not provide a remedy" if an Objection is not timely filed, but provides no analysis as to why timely filing should be excused.

Rule 108

A recommendation of a court commissioner is the order of the court until modified by the court. A party may file a written objection to the recommendation within 14 days after the recommendation is made in open court, or, if the court commissioner takes the matter under advisement, within 14 days after the minute entry of the recommendation is served. A judge's counter-signature on the commissioner's recommendation does not affect the review of an objection.

The Rule doesn't articulate a consequence for failure to file in a timely fashion, or any saving provisions for "excusable neglect." In addition to the Rule, counsel perused the Rule of Judicial Administration for guidance as to more particular requirements of filing, or savings provisions for inadvertence in the filing of electronic copies since "hard copies" are not required.

Kirk J has some concern that his two email communications in December regarding the fact that the Objection could not be verified as being found went unheeded, particularly when Mr. Rhorer has made repeated complaints as to the time being expended in this matter. Notwithstanding, Counsel for Kirk J would encourage the Court when interpreting the applicable rules, to consider the matter as one of simple inadvertence, oversight, or neglect.

Rule 59

Mr. Rhorer's reliance on Rule 59(a)(1) is interesting in the sense that his Motion is not entitled a Motion for a New Trial. The relief sought by Mr. Rhorer is simply a review of the facts found below, with a concomitant request that the Court find for Mr. Rhorer instead. Mr. Rhorer doesn't stop in simply asking the Court to find he has standing (based on the late filed objection) but that the Court Order "reintroduction" of the child to Mr. Rhorer to boot.

Evaluating the matter on it's face, the court must determine whether Mr. Rhorer was denied a "fair trial" simply by virtue of the Commissioner's recommendation becoming an Order of the Court due to inadvertent failure to file an Objection. Kirk J avers Mr. Rhorer was not denied a fair trial. This matter has gone on literally for years, with Mr. Rhorer having submitted volumes of material, and having at least three lengthy hearings in front of two different commissioners, culminating in Commissioner Kase and finding that Mr. Rhorer lacks standing. That Mr. Rhorer disagrees with the conclusion doesn't necessarily mean that the process was unfair.

Mr. Rhorer asserts that perhaps appeal can be avoided if the Court undertakes analysis of the late filed Objection. This argument, while compelling on its face, is fallacious. The Court must consider that either party has a right to appeal, and reversal of the ruling would simply change the identity of the Appellant.

Though the title of the Rule includes, "altering or amending a judgment" it does not seem to provide any standards upon which alternation or amendment can be granted. In this case, Mr. Rhorer essentially asks the Court to see the same evidence as the Commissioner, only see it differently, and arrive at the result he initially requested.

Rule 60

Mistakes; inadvertence; excusable neglect; newly discovered evidence; fraud, etc. On motion and upon just terms, the court may relieve a party or its legal representative from a judgment, order, or proceeding for the following reasons: (b)(1) mistake, inadvertence, surprise, or excusable neglect.

While Rule 60(b) speaks to "mistake, inadvertence...or excusable neglect" which might be viewed as having occurred here, it is not clear that it should be extended to failure to file an Objection to Commissioner's recommendation. Mr. Rhorer had fair proceedings before the Commissioner, and the procedure resulting in the Order was in accord with the law and procedures. He has a right to appeal, which provides further appropriate procedure and redress.

Rule 108 contemplates that if an Objection is not filed, the matter then proceeds to the "appellate track" with the Court of Appeals reviewing the legal ruling, rather than the District Court reviewing the Commissioner. In light of the fact that Mr. Rhorer has not briefed this particular rule to explain why it would be "just" for the Court to allow relief from the Order denying him Standing and taking up his Objection, Kirk J prays the Court not reach it.

Conclusion

While it appears that it was a simple mistake that an Objection was not timely filed in this matter, the foregoing discussion establishes that Mr. Rhorer had full and fair opportunity to litigate the matter of whether he has standing to assert a paternity right to the minor child. That he disagrees with the Court's Order and wishes for the relief he requested does not make the proceeding "unfair" or of the variety that the Court should grant the extraordinary relief as to be relieved of the Judgment and Order of the Court. Additionally, Mr. Rhorer has properly identified that he has a right to appeal. Kirk J prays that the Court deny Mr. Rhorer's Motions, and for such other and further relief as the Court deems appropriate in the premises.

APRIL 4TH, 2017: EMAIL to Devin C

My blood boils when I read Connie's rantings. I'm sure you are in the process of doing your response but it's clear that she sent her emails - if she really sent them - to the wrong Steve Cook. And she didn't provide them as attachments nor did she provide a copy of the text or number she sent it to. I doubt she has a cell phone number for you and if she texted a land line, she would have received a message back indicating it was a land line. Why didn't she pick up the phone and call.? Be careful - she lies a lot and you have to make her prove everything. Also, she had 14 days to respond and DIDN'T and then the judge gives her another 30 to write up her objection!!!! How is that fair? I don't get it. We look forward to seeing your rebuttal. Thanks! Jody and Deone

APRIL 4TH, 2017: INTERVENOR'S MEMORANDUM IN SUPPORT OF RULE 60(b) MOTION & REPLY MEMORANDUM, dubmitted by Devin C, Judge Stanley presiding

COMES NOW *Jody Rhorer, by and through his attorney of record, and hereby provides the following Memorandum in support of his Motion to Set Aside the Court's prior Order which was based upon the Commissioner's Recommendation.*

1. It is not disputed that the Rule 60(b) Motion was filed in a timely manner. It should also be undisputed that the Objection to the Commissioner's Recommendation was prepared and sent for e-filing in a timely manner, but it was error on the part of the Intervenor's counsel's paralegal to begin the e-filing, but not to complete the process. Counsel for Intervenor at all times believed the Objection had been filed with the Court, and only found out at the first hearing after the Commissioner handed down the Recommendation that the Court hadn't received the Objection.

2. Rule 60(b) is an equitable rule that allows Courts to balance competing concerns that final judgement shouldn't be lightly disturbed and that unjust judgment shouldn't be allowed to stand. It allows a Court to grant relief from judgment in circumstances in which the need for truth outweighs the value of finality in litigation. A liberal standard for application is justified in divorce cases...a court should modify a prior decree when the interests of equity require.

3. Here the Intervenor is raising the equitable claim that his constitutional right to a relationship with his daughter, and his daughter's constitutional right for a relationship with her father, are clearly equitable. The Court should seek truth. When excusable neglect is raised, the Court must consider whether conduct is excusable as an equitable issue and such a determination should take into account all relevant circumstances.

4. To be entitled to relief under Rule 60(b), excusable neglect, a party must show that the emotion is timely, there is a basis for granting relief under one of the subsections of 60(b) and the movement has alleged a meritorious defense. In the case the Intervenor's motion was timely, he has alleged that the Commissioner's Recommendation should be overturned on its merits to honor the constitutional rights of the parties and the best interests of the child, and his claims constitute and merits defense. The party seeking relief must show they did due diligence. Due diligence is established where the failure to act was the result of the neglect one would expect from a reasonable prudent person under similar circumstances.

Counsel relied upon the notation upon the pleading from his paralegal indicating the pleading had been filed and his reliance was reasonably prudent. It is of note that since the electronic filing rule has been instituted into the Court system, this is the only circumstance where this has happened to counsel for the Intervenor.

5. It is of note that there is a general doctrine that Courts should be liberal in granting relief against Judgments taken by default to the end that the controversies may be tried on the merits. "In making a determination of due diligence, a District Court is free to consider all relevant factors, including the prejudice either party will experience as a result of a grant or denial, the good faith of the moving party, and the level of control, if any, the moving party had over the circumstances that resulted in the neglect. In this case the Intervenor would be prejudiced without the Court hearing his claims upon the merit, but the Petitioner, the Respondent and the minor child would not be prejudiced by having the matter heard on the merits. Counsel acted in good faith at all times. "A trial court's discretion should be exercised in the furtherance of justice and should incline toward granting relief in a doubtful case to the end that the party may have a hearing. The court held "if the attorney exercised due diligence, defined as conduct that is consistent with the manner in which a reasonable prudent attorney under similar circumstances would have acted, a judgment may be set aside under Rule 60(b)(1). Counsel for the respondent humbly proffers that this pattern and practice of relying upon his paralegal's representations that pleadings have been e-filed, with those representations being made in writing on every single pleading, was reasonably prudent judgment, in retrospect in this case it was insufficient to ascertain the error that occurred. The Court should allow the Intervenor to seek fulfillment of his and his child's rights and consider the Objection to the Commissioner's Recommendation upon the merits.

REPLY MEMORANDUM

1. The Respondent's counsel claims that she sent an e-mail to counsel for Intervenor indicating that she received a Court filing regarding a Notice to Submit on the Commissioner's Recommendation that she didn't received. However, counsel for Intervenor never received that email and has no knowledge of the email ever having been sent. There is also a claim that a text was sent to counsel for Intervenor. However, counsel has a land line, does not have a cell phone, and cannot receive texts. Therefore, this text could not and was not received by him.

2. If counsel for Intervenor had received these informal communications from counsel for the respondent, then the matter would have been brought to his attention and presumably this matter would have been cleared up.

3. In her response to the Motion to Set Aside counsel for Respondent indicated that there has been no analysis as to why a timely filing should be excused. However, that analysis is set forth in great detail above. While counsel for the respondent points out that there is no rule regarding failing to object to a Commissioner's Recommendation in a timely manner, Rule 60(b) applies to circumstances similar to this one, and that rule is briefed above.

4. *Counsel for Intervenor fully briefs Rule 60(b). Counsel of Respondent points out an analysis of Rule 59 which grants a new trial for irregularity in the proceedings. The irregularity was the mistake and inadvertence which is otherwise briefed pursuant to the analysis of Rule 60(b) above. In her analysis of Rule 60(b) counsel for the respondent offers no case law of any kind and the case law is fully briefed in the Memorandum herein.*

APRIL 6TH, 2017: REQUEST FOR RULING & NOTICE TO SUBMIT, submitted by Devin C, Judge Stanley presiding

COMES NOW *the Intervenor, Jody Rhorer, by and through his attorney of record, pursuant to Rule 4-501(D) of Utah Code of Judicial Administration, and requests the Honorable Judge Stanley to rule on the Intervenor's Motion for Amendment of Judgement and Relief from Judgement or Order filed with the Court.*

APRIL 26TH, 2017: KIRK J'S OPPOSITION TO INTERVENOR'S MOTION TO AMEND JUDGEMENT, submitted by Connie, Judge Stanley presiding

Comes now, Connie, and on behalf of Kirk J, files the foregoing Opposition to Intervenor Jody Rhorer's Motion to Amend Judgment.

BACKGROUND

Mr. Rhorer was aware of the birth of Payshence, and the existence of a child welfare matter in front of Judge V when the child was an infant. Kelly H, mother, has stated on the record several times that Mr. Rhorer left the state of Utah when that case was filed to avoid a prosecution for domestic violence against her. The domestic violence perpetrated by Mr. Rhorer were included in the child welfare petition as well.

Mr. Rhorer's mother appeared in Juvenile Court at the shelter hearing in Child Welfare Case number one, and when asked about contact with the child, Judge V indicated that no order of visitation for Mr. Rhorer would be considered until he surrendered himself to the Jurisdiction of the Court. He never did. Instead Kelly H completed her service plan, and regained custody of the child, and Mr. Rhorer continued to see her through Kelly H without taking any measures to establish legal paternity. Kirk J was present and a part of that child welfare case, and throughout had a relationship with the child and integrated her as a sibling of he and Kelly H's other children.

Later in February 2012, another child welfare case was filed. During that case, Judge V was officially informed that Payshence was the legal child of Kirk J due to the presumption of paternity which arises by virtue of his marriage to Kelly H. While Kelly H worked her service plan in Child welfare case two, Kirk J was given first temporary custody of the child, and July 31st, 2012, permanent custody and guardianship of the child. Judge V issued an Order in which he legally adjudicated Kirk J father of the child. (Though Mr. Rhorer asserts to still have been visiting her, Mr. Rhorer did nothing to intervene in the second child welfare case, or ask the Juvenile Court to establish paternity.)

Based on the foregoing, on February 20th, 2015, Commissioner Bloom ruled that Kirk J was both adjudicated (from the Juvenile Court Order) and presumed father (by virtue of marriage) of the child. She further ruled that pursuant to 78B-15-608(1), only Kelly H and Kirk J had standing to challenge paternity. (In that they are mother and presumed father by virtue of marriage.) Neither were raising paternity of Payshence, so the Court indicated Mr. Rhorer did not have standing.

Commissioner Bloom noted that in a footnote of a recent case, the Appellate Court indicated it was not decided whether standing could derive from the Constitution. To fashion an "analysis" for whether standing has been made out Constitutionally. Commissioner Bloom "borrowed" the statute regarding whether DNA testing can be ignored.

In a hearing following the filing of the evaluation, Counsel for Mr. Rhorer argued that standing had been established upon the filing of the evaluation. Counsel for Kirk J disagreed, and pointed out that the Court intended to consider that report (and presumably other information already known) to attempt to discern whether there was a Constitutional basis for standing of a putative father who had produced a child with another man's wife during their marriage. Argument was had in front of the Commissioner regarding the particulars of the report, the deficiencies in the report, and how any particularly factual conclusions might weigh in the framework the Court adopted from the afore-mentioned statute. The Commissioner exhaustively reviewed the record and the evaluation, and found there was no Constitutional basis for standing.

MOTION TO AMEND

Mr. Rhorer's Motion to Amend (and underlying Objection to the Commissioner's Recommendation) in large measure simply reiterates his argument below. Contrary to Commissioner Bloom's novel and trailblazing attempt at fashioning a Constitutional framework for analysis for potential standing in this area, Mr. Rhorer's analysis of the issue is nothing more than a "best interest" argument. In fact, he leaps right over the standing issue, and attempts to persuade the Court that he should have visitation or reintroduction. This view ignores the applicable statutes, and accepted legal principles that a parent (a legal parent) is the one with the Constitutional right to determine with whom their minor child might associate.

While Payshence is the biological issue of Mr. Rhorer, biological paternity is not the panacea he seemed to believe. The ability to ascertain biological paternity through DNA is in its infancy relative to the principles of family and parent/child relationships firmly entrenched in our society at the time of the adoption of both the Federal and State Constitutions.

The marital presumption of paternity was, and is not now the embodiment of guess as to who the biological father of a married woman's child probably is. To the contrary, it is a societal restatement of the expectation and American value that a married man is to assume responsibility for the upbringings of the children of his wife, see to the bonding and cohesion between all of the children born of the marriage, and a father directive that such a man's devotion, and dedication to all the children born of his marriage is not subject to any condition.

Kirk J wishes to remind the Court that the counterpoint to the fact of Mr. Rhorer's biological paternity, that he incorporated the child into his family, the collective of children born to he and Kelly H during their marriage, that she calls him father, that he treats her, and has always treated her as his child. His other children claim her as their sister, and she see herself as their sister. Kirk J, not Mr. Rhorer, has finically supported the child all these years, and has had temporary or full custody of her for over five years. Before that, he shared time with the child with Kelly, and the only time Mr. Rhorer would have seen the child was when allowed by Kelly.

While Kirk J acknowledges that Commissioner Bloom felt that she should allow Mr. Rhorer opportunity to persuade her, absent a basis for statutory standing, that he has standing under the Constitution, he disagrees that an "evaluation" of any factors can dislodge Kirk J's parental right to decide with whom his legal child might associate.

Further, while this litigation has been permeated by Mr. Rhorer's attempts to fortify this standing argument by slinging mud at Kirk J, the Juvenile Court found fit to give Kirk J custody in 2012, and despite Mr. Rhorer's insistence DCFS be brought in again, Kirk J still effectively parents the child.

CONCLUSION

Mr. Rhorer's position is essentially that because he impregnated Kirk J's spouse, and the same had visited upon him a situation where he does not have rights to the child, the Court should carve out a special niche under Constitutional Law to permit him to fight for parental rights, custody and visitation when the statutes foreclose the same. In support of that proportion, Mr. Rhorer offers no analysis as to why the Constitution should provide him standing under the circumstances, where here, he claims to have spent very little time with Payshence when she was an infant or toddler. Instead, he attempts to malign Kirk J, as if attacking the child's legal father, the man who stepped up and parented the child day to day (and has for more than five years) changes or enlarges Constitutional protections. While faced with new technology which allows the Court to know who biologically is the father of a child, Mr. Rhorer has failed to persuade that he should be given Constitutional protection. Historically and presently, the societal and cultural norms embraced generally do not favor the man who impregnates another man's wife, thus fracturing the insular family. Despite Mr. Rhorer's vigorous litigation, including casting shade Kirk J's way, it has been Kirk J's supporting and fathering the child, parenting her in the same home as her siblings and half-siblings. Mr. Rhorer has pointed out that he has children and that Payshence has siblings on "his side" as well. However, Mr. Rhorer's children are adults, and essentially unknown to Payshence. Additionally, Mr. Rhorer's wife has never met the child.

Accordingly, Kirk J prays the Court approve and reenter the Order previously entered upon the Commissioner's recommendations.

MAY 10TH, 2017:   HEARING BEFORE JUDGE STANLEY, present Connie, Devin C, Jody, myself, Mary C. Kirk and Kelly did not show up.

THE COURT: All right. Kirk J vs. Kelly H, Intervenor Jody Rhorer. Those that are here, please state your appearance.

DEVIN C: Devin C with Jody Rhorer, your Honor.

CONNIE: Connie on behalf of Kirk J.

MARY C: Mary C, the GAL for the minor child.

THE COURT: All right. We're here on Intervenor's objection to the commissioner's recommendation; is that right? Are you ready to begin? Go ahead Devin.

DEVIN C: Your Honor, as I waded through all of the case law and have thought about this case a lot, I think the essence of this case comes down to two things, and they're both the same issue from different fathers. The little girl's relationship with her biological father and the little girl's relationship with Kirk J, and what kind of rights and duties and implications arise from those two relationships. If Mr. Rhorer had no relationship with this child, and he sought to assert paternity and rights, clearly he would be barred by the statute.

If Mr. Rhorer were seeking to take this little girl and terminate her relationship with Kirk J and say I don't care that she's integrated in your family, and I don't care that she's part of your life, I want to take her away from you, I think that's a common thread and holding in more than one appellate court decision that says no, you can't disrupt and take away the child's relationship with the man she sees as her father today. Despite Commissioner Kase's indication in his minute entry that says I have to weigh terminating Kirk's rights or the Court of Appeals decision that say you shouldn't terminate rights, and the pleading in fact that was last filed by Kirk J saying well, you can't take away his rights, to me that's all a red herring. My client is not trying to take this little girl away from Kirk J. He's asking the Court to give him a relationship with the child.

THE COURT: Ordinarily, among the bundle of parental rights is that a parent has the right to determine who, but for another parent, that minor associates with. Aren't you seeking to take away that right from Kirk J?

DEVIN C: So, we're not, because - your Honor, if I sought that, then I think that the Court of Appeals would tie this Court's hands, and I think the Court of Appeals would direct us that you must rule in Kirk J's favor. This is a unique case. I have not found a case with fact pattern like this case. I don't think Commissioner Bloom or Kase have ever been assigned a case like this. The reason Commissioner Bloom recommended and the Court ordered Dr. Natovich to do this is because of the unique circumstances in this case. What I'm asking the Court to do is to craft in what my experience would be a unique order different from any order that's been ruled upon by any court - any higher court ever, to my knowledge, in the United States - certainly not in the State of Utah - because that's a pivotal factor. I'm not asking this Court to give my client the right as a parent to terminate or dictate any relationship with Kirk J. I'm asking the Court to say we're not deciding today what that relationship would be. That's premature. We're giving him standing to seek a relationship. We know what the recommendations are and the preliminary steps.

The Court could go as far as to say based on the record, I'm going to rule that the scope of any evaluation and the scope of trial would be only to determine visitation rights, that it's going to keep custody with Kirk J, or the court could say I'm not going to make a decision about ultimate custody, but I'm going to rule that no matter what, this little girl is going to have a relationship with both dads. What that relationship looks like, I could use the help of an expert to determine that, but I'm not asking the Court to give my client the constitutional right as a parent. I'm asking this court to admittedly break new ground - to say no, why can't you have two fathers? We do this with divorces. We have mothers and fathers. We have two parents who often are hostile and angry, can't' stand each other. We give both parents rights. With that comes responsibilities, child support, duties, but also rights. Why can't this little girl have more than one dad in her life. There's no such thing as having too many people to love you or take care of you. I'm not asking for anything other than that, and I think that's really important. So that's only one phase of this, Kirk J's rights.

The other part, and what Commissioner Bloom looked at and the reason we're standing here is she made recommendations that this Court ordered because of the relationship my client had with this child. For almost three years Jody was in the home with this little girl - for the first three years of this girl's life my client was her daddy.

THE COURT: Natovich wasn't really able to pin that down, was she?

DEVIN C: Well we do know. We know that DCFS took the child from the home in 2010. We know that there is a dispute on whether my client had a relationship with the child in 2012. He said he did. The self-serving statements of the petitioner, the mother, when she talked to Natovich, well, he didn't see the child in 2012. That would be a credibly issue I suppose, but what's not disputed is that for the first three years he had that child, and for seven months of those first three years, mother took off. My client's proffer that I don't think is disputed, mom has a drug - mom hasn't taken part in these proceedings, at least as far as I know, from day one. Mom had serious drug issues. Mom disappeared and my client had the sole care of this child for seven months of those first three years.

If this Court thinks - and Dr. Natovich specifically found that my client had the care of the child and developed a long, strong relationship with the child. As far as exactly which months in 2012 he did or didn't see her, Dr. Natovich didn't make a factual finding. She just said it's undisputed that he had a relationship with the child the first three years. So, I'm asking the Court to take judicial notice of the kind of bonding that happens psychologically for the child, as well as the parent, during those formative years. Dr. Natovich touched on that, and she talked about how with therapy and how this child knows she has two daddies. This little girl - it is not a surprise to her. This little girl knows that Mr. Rhorer is her dad. She knows that, and that causes confusion. That's what this Court can do. We can go heal that little girl. We can put that little girl into therapy to help heal her. We can take my client's constitutional rights into account. That's what Commissioner Bloom said. When you have a relationship with the child, you're the father and you have a long-term relationship with the child, that vests in you the rights of a parent that we don't take away lightly. That's why the Court has to have balance.

Your honor, I think those are the two key issues. Does Mr. Rhorer have enough of a bond with this child to give him a constitutional right to a relationship with this child, and how does Kirk J's constitutional rights and case law guide us in crafting a decision? All the remarks about Commissioner Kase, about terminating Kirk J's rights or his brief about that are a red herring. As I struggled with this, because we had two different commissioners, if in fact when the Court signed the order that said that Dr. Natovich was to do her evaluation, if the end result was going to be nope, it doesn't matter what the facts are, you have zero percent chance, the Court has to rule as a matter of law that you have no rights, and you cannot assert your rights, and that's the law, period, black and white, end of it, then why did we have a - why did we go through and bother having an evaluation from Dr. Natovich if we weren't going to ever get to the point where we are today? That would be inconsistent.

I think that's the function of having two different commissioners, because if Commissioner Bloom would have followed Commissioner Kase's reasoning, we would have never had an evaluation. Commissioner Kase in essence said it doesn't matter what the evaluator said. The case law tells us if we're going to take away Kirk J, there's a relationship there we can't disrupt. That's not what I'm asking to do. That's why that's a red herring. Your Honor, I have in some great detail in my objection talked about the facts and the findings of Dr. Natovich, and so I'm happy to highlight those briefly. The Court said consider the conduct of the parties, and does that estop the party from denying parentage. Mr. Rhorer filed a petition for paternity in the West Jordan Court which was granted and was later overturned and dismissed because of this action. Mr. Rhorer tried to proceed in the juvenile court with Judge V, who shut him out and wouldn't let him take part. Mr. Rhorer has paid multiple attorneys thousands of dollars and fought years to have a relationship with this child. So certainly, his conduct has been consistent from day one and has never strayed, but he loves this little girl and wants a relationship with her.

Dr. Natovich did not make a finding about what the effect on this little girl would be upon losing her relationship with Kirk J. If that's what we're asking the Court to do, I don't think it would make any difference. I think I have to grant, and I will grant, Kirk J has a long-term relationship. She's in that family with other children.

She views him as her father, and she's scared of my client. It would be disruptive to just yank her out and say you're not going to see your brothers and sister ever again, and you're never going to see this man you call father ever again, you're with this person. While Dr. Natovich didn't make a specific finding on that, I think as she just assumed it would be - she talked about reunification therapy in her recommendation and starting off by just getting them to know each other, she didn't make any recommendations that the little girl be taken away from - and we never asked her to. The evaluator talked about the nature of the relationships with everyone. Kirk J doesn't want the Court to consider best interests of the child. He wants the Court to ignore his criminal history and his deficiencies and the effect on the child of all the bad things that he tells this child about my client. He wants this Court to ignore all that and say it's irrelevant.

I think it is relevant. I think if you find that my client has a constitutional relationship with this child, and you make a second finding that this child's relationship with Kirk J shall not be terminated, that it will not be the order of the Court, we're not seeking that, and that would be clear from day one, if we crossed those two bridges, I think we've established standing - then we can look at all of these allegations that fly back and forth. I think it's important for the Court to be aware that Kirk J entered a plea in abeyance to a charge of child abuse of an elementary aged child. Kirk J has his issues. So if you are weighing the harm and the benefit to society as a whole because you're making constitutional findings here, in this life, in this family and for society as a whole, is it a bad thing to have a child to have lots of people love her and have a relationship with her and find out what's in her best interest and not infringing on anybody's constitutional rights as well. That's how you do that, your Honor. You acknowledge Kirk J has constitutional rights to this child as well as Mr. Rhorer. Then this other stuff does become relevant, but I do agree that you have to cross those two bridges first.

Dr. Natovich, I think it's important that she did not make any negative findings. If my client were reintroduced into the life of this child, not only did she say that would help the child with the attachment disorder, and help her emotionally, but she didn't say there would be any harm at all to the child from having a relationship with my client. Only good, no bad. So, the child would be better served by having a relationship with her biological father. The child would still be served by having a relationship with Kirk J. The child is served. My client is served. Mother doesn't appear to care, so what does that leave us with? It leaves us with Kirk J saying I don't want you to have anything to do with this little girl. I don't want it. I don't want you to. Well, why? Why? Where's the harm? We know the benefit. Dr. Natovich gave us the benefit. Where's the harm? To this day I haven't seen any words spoken or any argument made that the child would be harmed by Jody having a relationship with his child and I quote, "There would be not harm to Payshence if the fact that Mr. Rhorer as her biological parent was acknowledged by her current family. If anything, in fact, this would likely allay some of her underlying concerns about her parenting and confusing family history." Then she went through all the findings and facts, and she made recommendations about reunification therapy. That's how I see this case. Does the Court have any questions?

THE COURT: No. Thank you. Connie?

CONNIE: Thank you, your Honor. One thing that strikes me about the law in the area - in this area, your Honor, is that you can't tell what it is. The case law doesn't help you. The analysis fashioned by Commissioner Bloom was in response to a foot note in another case where the Court said we're specifically not deciding whether there could be a constitutional right for standing. They didn't say but if we were going to do that, here's an outline that you might could use, and so Judge Bloom thought well, here's something that you might try. You know, I don't fault her for trying to find some kind of rubric where the Court might analyze potential constitutional standing in this area.

However, it isn't authoritative on this Court. It hasn't been accepted by any of the appellate courts, and Counsel said, if the statute forecloses standing in this case, that's not even in question. The statutory law forecloses standing. That starts us back on the idea can there even be under the constitution, which the way I read it, First Amendment, that's association rights for a man who has slept with another man's wife during their marriage, does the constitution provide standing for him to come in and challenge paternity rights, and let's make no mistake, you cannot have two fathers. You can have parents, and you can have a court order for parents who have standing, but what Counsel is asking for is the law of this - the State of Utah recognizes one man as the legal father of this child. That's my client, because there was a presumption of parentage due to the marriage, and he was adjudicated a parent in front of the juvenile court. Counsel wasn't here at that time, so I don't fault him for, you know, not being conversant with the record. It has been a long haul. It's going on a decade we've been involved in this case, but Mr. Rhorer did not avail himself of the juvenile court in the first proceeding, and that's because at that time when Kelly could get physical possession of the child, she voluntarily allowed contact, so he had no reason because he was getting the contact he wanted, to do the things Judge V of all people would want him to do in the child welfare action, so he laid back. It wasn't until she didn't like him anymore that - and you know, there was another juvenile court action and he couldn't have access to the child that he actually did anything

The paternity action where he got an order of paternity in district wasn't stricken because of the juvenile court case. It was because he didn't give my client notice. He was trying to finagle every wishy-washy way to get paternity rights without actually coming before the juvenile court, surrendering himself to the jurisdiction of that court in a child welfare action and doing what he needed to do. So, this is very much late action. Basically, if you're looking at constitutional law in the area of association, this is the way I see it. You're supposed to look to what would be the intent of the framers of the constitution in this area - would they recognize the right of a man who sleeps with another man's wife and produces a child to disrupt that family. With all due respect to Counsel, he's coming in late. This is a difficult case. I just heard nothing but a best interest argument, and my notes setting this hearing was we weren't arguing best interests. I could stand up here all day long and throw shade at Mr. Rhorer, because he is not a clean one owner either, but you don't need to know any of that to decide the standing question.

Make no mistake, the bundle of rights a parent has to raise their child the way they want to, to send a child to school where they want to, to determine who can visit with the child because they have that right, Counsel absolutely would be chipping away at that. To say here well, we don't want to try to get custody, we don't' want to enforce a visitant right, we don't want to try to take a child away, we don't want to try to terminate parental rights, bollocks. That's absolute legal fiction. If he gets standing, he's already got a motion for custody pending. That impairs my client's parental rights to say I'm dad. I've been dad by virtue of that marriage, by virtue of that order, and not only that, by virtue of his conduct. This isn't Mr. Rhorer has a relationship with the child. He doesn't. This child doesn't remember him. My client is dad, she calls my client dad. The other kids in the house are her siblings. That is her family. For the Court to look at that under a constitutional rubric that values the insular family - and by the way, values a dad who actually shows up to parent. My client has had that child by court order since 2012, has paid every bit of support, and has been the one she runs to when she scrapes her knee, and the one that she runs to if she wakes up at night and has a bad dream. This idea of well, can't we share her is absolutely legally and constitutionally untenable, your Honor.

The analysis of the evaluation done is sound. It is very clear that both of the commissioners who have been struggling with the issue of first impression thought it out very, very well, and the commissioner took months to consider this, and a huge record, even though some of it has been ignored. There are 600 pages filed by Mr. Rhorer that were stricken that are basically mud-slinging. Even so, the case file was gigantic. The commissioners gave a lot of thoughtful consideration to this issue, and frankly, the commissioner's recommendation is absolutely sound. Counsel hasn't provided any analysis under the constitutional rubric as to why the federal or state constitution would recognize any right on the part of some man to get some other man's wife pregnant and then step in and break up the family.

He's offered no analysis, simply just said what's the harm? What harm is that my client is legal father. My client is emotional father. The harm is that girl has a right to her family. My client has a right to his child, and this Court should not provide him standing. My client has fought for years and years and years and years to get the right that he has had all along, which is his legal right to parentage to the little girl that came out of his wife during their marriage, and furthermore, a right recognized by adjudication when Judge V presided over the juvenile court actions. So, your Honor, I would ask the Court to adopt the recommendation, to deny the objection, and certainly kick it up to the Court of Appeals or the Supreme Court, if they want to transfer it to the Supreme Court, and then they can determine it, but the analysis was sound and well supported. Do you have any questions?

THE COURT: No, thanks. Reply?

DEVIN C: Your Honor, if I could just very briefly? Connie referenced the framers to the constitution if you sleep with another man's wife. My client didn't just sleep with another man's wife. They fell in love, moved in together, they established a family, and they had a baby and lived together for three years, except for the seven months when Kelly left. That's not just sleeping with another man's wife. Why didn't Kirk J, if he wanted to be the father, say hey, this is a baby born of the marriage, it's my baby. Did he sue for custody? Did he serve the mother with divorce papers and ask for custody? Did he assert any visitation rights with this little girl, or custodial rights? No. He sat and let the matter sit until Judge V kind of took the bull by the horns and the child was removed, and then everybody got drug into the court system. My client is the only one that from day one has pursued a relationship with this child, and I think it's of note if we're going to talk about establishing a family and sleeping with another man's wife, that's why we're here is because it's not just that. If it were just that, we - this decade long battle wouldn't have gone on, but - so we're kind of saying the same thing over and over again.

Counsel said one thing that I strongly disagree with. Make no mistake, the law recognizes one man as the father. Who says? What law? There was a time when a man couldn't marry another man and a woman couldn't marry another woman. You have a unique situation, your Honor, and time is precious. We can't just say well, let's let the supreme Court decide this one day. Eery day is precious - every day my client doesn't see his little girl is a day that's lost forever and gone. So that's why the impetus is on you to make a decision about what's in this child's best interest right now. Who says you can't have two fathers? Who says you can't say this father has custody and this father has visitation, let's craft a support award and let's talk about attendance at parent/teacher conference and extracurricular activities, and let's talk about going to therapy. If you can have two mommies or two daddies, why can't you have two daddies and a mommy? Why not?

THE COURT: All right. Anything else from either side? Anything by case of evidence or anything –

MARY C: If I may speak as well, there was some talk about being able to decide which parent gets to see the child, and you know, as a family law practitioner, I've seen plenty of people go through divorce and want the ex-spouse completely out of the children's lives, whether that's wrong or right, it happens. There is no dispute that Mr. Rhorer has been constantly asserting his rights as the child's father from the beginning as has spent thousands of dollars doing so. I think that there's something else that hasn't been mentioned to this Court is that Mr. Rhorer has daughters from a prior relationship, and even Kirk J was allowing those girls to see the child up until this case started heating up. There was even a time where Mr. Rhorer was possibly seeing this child at that time.

As soon as this case started heating up, Kirk J and Kelly H have prevented Mr. Rhorer from seeing the child, through no fault of Mr. Rhorer's, and this case has just dragged on for a long time. So, if there's any reason why Mr. Rhorer hasn't been able to see this child, it's not because of his lack of trying. This child does know Mr. Rhorer, contrary to what Connie stated, and even Dr. Natovich mentioned this. She is well aware of who Mr. Rhorer is. If there's any question as to what Dr. Natovich was supposed to be finding that she perhaps didn't understand she was supposed to make some findings on, then the Court should endeavor to have her update those recommendations or give testimony on those questions she might not have understood, because this is a serious issue. This is a little girl's life, and she has a right to have as many people love her as possible. You know, we do a lot of talking about the rights of the parents, but what about the rights of this little child? Doesn't she deserve to be loved by as many people as possible? Dr. Natovich said it would be beneficial for the child to be reunited with Mr. Rhorer.

There's also something inherently discriminatory about the statute. The husband is presumed to be the father of the wife's child, but it doesn't go the other way. If Kirk J had an affair and had a child with another woman, that child would not be presumed to be Kelly H's child. It's discriminatory, and I understand why they did it back in the day because the framers of the constitution didn't have DNA testing to determine the paternity, but we have that today. We have that ability. There is no question that Mr. Rhorer is the father, and that he has had some relationship with the child. So as far as my recommendation would go is that I would recommend that Mr. Rhorer has some standing to assert his parental rights.

THE COURT: I'm going to take the matter under advisement, get something out promptly. I know how urgent this is to all concerned. It's pended long enough, so we'll get something out. Thanks.

<u>JUNE 1ST, 2017:</u>   MEMORANDUM DECISION, Judge Stanley

This matter came before the Court for a hearing on May 10, 2017, in connection with Intervenor Jody Rhorer's Objections to Commissioner's Recommendation. Mr. Rhorer filed his Objection at the same time as filing a Motion for Amendment of Judgment and Entry of New Judgment. In a Ruling on this Motion, dated April 12, 2017, the Court accepted Mr. Rhorer's Objection and directed the remaining parties to respond to the same. Respondent filed an Opposition to Intervenor's Motion to Amend Judgment which is a response to the Objection.

At the conclusion of the May 10th hearing, the Court took the matter under advisement to further consider the parties' written submissions, the Amended Recommendation and Order, entered by Commissioner Bloom on April 20, 2015, the Minute Entry, entered by Commissioner Kase on November 15, 2016, the relevant legal authorities and counsel's oral argument. Being now fully informed, the Court rules as stated herein.

At the outset, the Court notes that Mr. Rhorer's Objection to Commissioner Kase's November 15, 2016, Minute Entry recommendation. Commissioner Kase recommended the denial of Mr. Rhorer's Motion to grant him standing in order to pursue a time-sharing arrangement with the minor child, based upon his biological parentage of Payshence. Both in his Objection and through his counsel's oral argument, Mr. Rhorer has asked this Court to craft a remedy whereby he is ultimately granted limited parent-time with Payshence, while not actually seeking custody of the child or challenging Kirk J's status as Payshence's presumed father.

On the one hand, Mr. Rhorer indicates that he "respectfully disagrees with the Commissioner that there are not constitutional rights that attach to the Intervenor as the child's biological parent who had a significant relationship with the minor child for years before the child was taken away from the Intervenor over the objection of the Intervenor. At the same time, however, Mr. Rhorer asserts that "the minor child's relationship with the presumptive father does not need to be disrupted." Therefore, while alluding to his constitutional rights as a biological father, Mr. Rhorer is not actually seeking to assert these rights or to otherwise rebut Kirk J's presumed father status. More importantly, Mr. Rhorer is seeking to "disrupt" Kirk J's legal relationship with Payshence by establishing himself as the child's legal parent.

The Utah Court of Appeals in the case of R.P. v. K.S.W. concluded that the trial court properly dismissed a biological father's petition to establish paternity. The court concluded that the biological father lacked standing to challenge the paternity of the biological mother's husband, who was the presumed father under the Utah Uniform Parentage Act. Interpreting Section 607 of the UUPA, the court held that this statute "limits the persons with standing to raise the paternity of the child to the presumed father and the mother".

In contrast to the biological father in R.P., Mr. Rhorer is not seeking standing to challenge the paternity of the child. Instead, he is seeking to depart from the legal framework altogether. This framework permits only two people to be legally recognized as parents. While expressly disclaiming his right to assume the role of parent, Mr. Rhorer asks this Court to fashion a hybrid mold for him, one where he exercises-parent time, without full parental rights or any mention of parental obligations.

Under the statutory framework of the UUPA, "[a] man with an unrebutted presumption of paternity is the legal father of the child." Citing Utah Code Ann. 78B-15-102(18), defining the parent-child relation to mean "the legal relationship between a child and a parent of the child. The term includes the mother-child relationship and the father-child relationship - defining the father-child relationship as being 'established between a man and a child by...an unrebutted presumption of the man's paternity of the child under Section 78B-15-204." This statutory framework is intended to create an all or nothing proposition in terms of establishing a defined, legal parenting relationship based on a mother-child relationship and father-child relationship. Plainly, the Legislature has an interest in identifying up to two legal parents and has clearly done so. This enables society to specifically identify who may make decisions for the child, as well as those who are responsible for the child's support. The law clearly does not recognize the hybrid role proposed by Mr. Rhorer, particularly where **he has expressly abandoned his challenge to Kirk J's presumption of paternity, thereby confirming Kirk J's father-child relationship with the child.**

Ultimately, while Mr. Rhorer may have had a right at the time the biological mother and Kirk J sought a divorce to assert standing to challenge the child's paternity and to rebut Kirk J's paternity (assuming that Mr. Rhorer could mount a constitutional challenge to Section 607 as applied to him), he has plainly abandoned such a claim at this point. Mr. Rhorer has failed to give the Attorney General notice of any constitutional challenge to the statute's limited on who may rebut presumptive paternity. "If a party challenges the constitutionality of a statute in an action in which the Attorney General has not appeared, the party raising the question of constitutionality shall notify the Attorney General of such fact. The court shall permit the state to be heard upon timely application.

Mr. Rhorer has also failed to brief his theories of why Section 607 is unconstitutional as applied to him with adequate specificity to permit intelligent analysis. The mere mention of an issue without introducing support evidence or relevant legal authority does not preserve that issue of appeal. "Appellants' passing argument, without legal reasoning or case law support, primarily concerns Appellant's entitlement to notice of the competing adoption petition, and is not sufficient to have preserved in the juvenile court the latter two constitutional issues they now wish to raise on appeal. Because legislative enactments are presumed to be constitutional, those who challenge a statute or ordinance as unconstitutional bear the burden of demonstrating its unconstitutionality." Mr. Rhorer's mere mention of his constitutional rights in the Objection and his passing argument that Section 607 could be subject to a constitutional challenge, in the absence of any legal analysis or case law support, is not sufficient for the Court to consider and rule on these issues. Further, having failed to identify any basis for challenging Section 607 on constitutional grounds, Mr. Rhorer cannot meet his burden in demonstrating the statute's unconstitutionality.

Most importantly, as discussed above, Mr. Rhorer does not seek to rebut Kirk J's paternity and does not seek to establish himself as the legal father for Payshence. Absent a present willingness to do so, Mr. Rhorer has no standing to challenge Kirk J's status as presumed father under the UUPA. Accordingly, Mr. Rhorer's Objection to Commissioner's Recommendation is denied. The Memorandum Decision will stand as the Order of the Court and so further Order is required.

We were livid upon reading the judge's decision! On three separate occasions we sat in Devin's office and told him in person that we would only settle for full custody but he kept insisting his "trojan horse" theory was the only way that the judge would consider reuniting Payshence with Jody. His plan completely backfired and made Jody out to be the equivalent of an uncommitted uncle-type that just wanted an occasional visit.

Furthermore, for as many years as he had been practicing family law (he was pretty much at retirement age) and in his own words had litigated "over 2,000 cases," wouldn't he know that if he was going to argue constitutional rights that he would need to notice up the AG's office? Wouldn't he also know that he had to provide support for the allegations through case law? Personally, I felt Devin was tired and really had no passion for the practice any more. He just wanted to argue that Commission Bloom had already ruled and that is that, but no one else agreed with him.

JUNE 7TH, 2017: EMAIL to Devin C

Devin, Last night Jody and I finally read Judge Stanley's decision as it has taken us several days to absorb the fact that we lost. We were both surprised and upset by what we read. From the very beginning of this case we have insisted that we are seeking full custody and you said we had to ease our way in and just try for visitation - custody was discussed multiple times and Jody was very insistent about it. We trusted in your expertise and advise and it appears that our strategy painted Jody as a guy that just wanted to visit her and not take responsibility for her and her livelihood. We are crushed and we don't know where to turn now. Another year gone and no way to replace this time Jody is missing with his daughter. We would like a written clarification from you that Jody always had every intention of seeking full custody of Payshence. But that YOU thought that asking for parent-time would be the best way to try to get that. Thank you, Deone

Dear Mr. Rhorer:

Mr. Rhorer,

You have sent me correspondence asking that I set forth my explanation for why we took the position before the Court of why we were not asking for one hundred percent parental rights and to terminate Kirk J's rights. The reason for that is because all of the case law indicates very clearly that the Courts would not give Jody any rights at all if it meant terminating Kirk J's relationship with the child. That was the weakness in your case. Your only hope to prevail, and I am convinced of this, was that you had to concede that Kirk J could continue to have a relationship with the child. If you would have taken the position that you wanted full rights with Kirk J's right being terminated then you would have been asking the Court to go against all of the precedent and the case law.

Furthermore, I sent you case law that I told you was very dangerous and I believe that if the Court followed the case law your rights would have been terminated because the Court cases indicated this if Kirk J had a long-term relationship with the child that the Court could not disrupt that under any circumstances, and without regard to the best interest of the child. The petitioner's counsel, referred to this at the evidentiary hearing when she said "there could only be one father." Both the GAL and I said no to that and asked the Judge to forge new ground and rule that the child could have more than one father. It is true that when you first came into my office you took the position that you wished Kirk J to have no rights and you wished to take the child away from him. However, such a position was doomed to failure and you could not take that position and have any chance of winning an appeal. I understand the Judge in his Memorandum decision appeared to paint you as a person that did not want to assume full control of your daughter. However, he would be bound to follow the law, and if he did not, when Kirk J appealed, the Court of Appeals and the Supreme Court would follow the law. I cannot make it any more clear to you that I believe you were doomed to failure if you attempted to terminate Kirk J's right. The consequence of terminating his rights if you were granted standing is why Commissioner Kase ruled against you.

I would ask you to feel free to contact the GAL to see if she agrees with the approach which I took. I believe that she did. From the very beginning you knew that you were asking the Court to change the Constitutional Law of the State of Utah. From the very beginning I think you knew you were headed towards the Court of Appeal. The Judges's decision does not prevent you from appealing. Your time to Appeal ran thirty days from June 1, 2017, and you are still under that time deadline. If you are still seeking an appeal, I have told you that I would not charge you to help transfer any information to your Appellate lawyer.

   Sincerely,
   Devin C, Attorney at Law

JUNE 15TH, 2017:   WITHDRAWAL OF COUNSEL

   COMES NOW *Devin C, and hereby withdraws as counsel for the Intervenor, Jody Rhorer in the above-captioned matter.*

CHAPTER 17
CAM C

JUNE 23RD, 2017:   REFLECTING ON THE PAST SEVERAL MONTHS

2017 has been a hard one. I have been having health problems for much of the year - first being told in the emergency room that I had suffered a heart attack, then finding out that it was just high blood pressure.

In January, my arms began to be very painful at night, affecting my sleep. I went from doctor to doctor trying to find out what was wrong but to no avail. Through self-observation I determined that my pain was being caused by two to four hours a night of typing this book. It was at this time that I had been to see an internist and we had discussed a plan to observe my actions to make certain it was the typing that was causing it. But before my follow-up appointment in May, I had an accident on my horse and broke both arms and severed my liver. It is only now, six weeks later, that I am able to type again; but so much has happened.

I cannot understand how we can keep losing. Why? How? If it is clearly about "what is best for the child," why does she stay in a dangerous household amongst people that do not love her, are not her relatives, and are merely using her for their own gain? How can they leave her in harms way? Is it apathy? Laziness? Lack of interest? I know they say, "That's the law, sorry!"

What would this world look like if people really had heart? If every soul put one hundred percent effort in to their jobs? If each human being's work involved complete devotion to giving their very best effort? How would that change the world? Is it because so many people lack the ability to truly feel another person's anguish that our case has failed and failed and failed? When does one give up? When does one throw in the towel?

After losing the appeal Devin C recommended an appellate attorney, Jared J. We met with him. He was a good listener, compassionate and knowledgeable, he looked like Jesus and he was $350.00 an hour. His retainer - $10,000. Gulp. But he looked us in the eye with sincere compassion and an aggressive plan to back it up.

Prior to meeting with Jared, we seriously considered having me write up the appeal and represent us. How could I do any worse than our last series of attorneys? They all lost. They all took our money and didn't perform. They all claimed we had a case, but once they lost our case, their tone changed and they suddenly felt we never stood a chance. What did we have to lose that we hadn't already? At least Jody would be heard for a change instead of having to sit mute while Kelly blurted out absurdities or Connie spewed lies from the pulpit. But during our meeting, Jared brought up options, ideas, and legal references that were way over my head. He also clued us in on the fact that I would not be able to represent Jody as choosing to go Pro Se would mean that Jody would have to speak for himself and present the facts himself, and while that could be effective, the emotional side of things may take hold and prevail in his presentation. It was with some relief that we made a deposit towards the retainer with someone with much confidence and only two and a half weeks to complete the appeal. We left Jared's office with hope.

Two days later, Jared called with bad news. His partner had represented Kelly a number of years ago in juvenile court as her public appointed attorney and that was a conflict of interest. He would have to decline our case. He recommended his partner's wife who worked for another law firm and had spent years as an attorney in the juvenile court system. A meeting was set up several days later.

We drove to yet another fancy high-rise building in Salt Lake City to meet the partner's wife, Cam. Jared came to make the pass off of the materials we had given him. She was a very small woman in her 30's. She looked delicate and breakable - not the tall commanding Jesus figure that seemed like he would pull off a miracle for us. She began by telling us how things are and how the law works versus asking us about our case.

CAM: "So the way the Utah Parentage Act is written always gives custody to the presumed father who is the husband of the mother and without the presumed father or the mother agreeing to allow another father to interfere, there is really not a chance for a biological father to gain custody."

ME: "We know what the law says. Trust me, I have read it and every other case and document pertaining to it. We have been going through this for five years."

CAM: "Well I just want to be clear…"

ME: "Do you know anything at all about our case?"

CAM: "Sure I do."

ME: "What do you know?"

CAM, fumbling with the pages of the last court order issued from the appeal: "There is this order…"

ME: "So you don't really know anything about our case."

I proceeded to give her a brief rundown of how Jody had custody and how Payshence was taken from him and his daughters and what she had suffered and continued to suffer and about how the free attorney and her lies was the only reason why we were still in our present situation. She was expressionless other than a hint of ego and boredom.

ME: "Do you know Connie?"

CAM: "As a matter of fact, she's a friend of ours," gesturing towards her husband who had accompanied Jared to the meeting.

I must have turned multiple shades of anger as I could feel the increase in my heart rate and my impulse was to get up and leave. Jared picked up on this and took the opportunity to excuse himself and his partner.

ME: "She is our arch enemy. She is the only reason Jody's daughter isn't with us now."

Cam didn't even blink.

CAM: "I'm not scared of her. We work together in different capacities all the time. I've even worked with her on cases."

ME: "But we want someone that will annihilate her. I don't see how someone that is her buddy could do that."

We went back and forth about this for some time while Cam ensured us that she could handle Connie and give her everything she deserved and more while still maintaining their camaraderie. I maintained my skepticism. There were two reasons I didn't leave right then; 1. We were out of time and 2. She had an idea I had not heard before - going to the Juvenile Court for a welfare case to prove Payshence was neglected and that Jody and I should be able to adopt her. I don't know how feasible this was, but at least it was something different than the insanity we had been living for the past five years.

She didn't ask us more questions about our case. I suppose she was going to absorb everything through osmosis. She said to just email her all the documents I have. When I explained that there were over 3,000 pages, she remained stone faced and said, "I can get through that really fast." I hope she can get through them faster than the three full days it took my secretary to scan them to her.

JUNE 29TH, 2017: EMAIL from Cam

Hi Jody and Deone, Thank you for providing all of the documents, they are providing an excellent picture of what has happened in this case. I am nearly finished reviewing all of the documents uploaded to our system. Today is the final day to file a post-judgment motion pursuant to Rule 52. I will not be able to file a post-judgment motion by close of business and I am not certain whether Rule 52 is the correct rule to file under. I will be filing a motion for enlargement of time to allow me to determine whether a post-judgment motion in the district court case is appropriate. Please let me know if you have any questions. Cam

JUNE 29TH, 2017: APPEARANCE OF COUNSEL, ORDER OF INTERVENOR'S MOTION TO ENLARGE FILING DEADLINE, Submitted by Cam H, Judge Stanley presiding

Cam H hereby enters her appearance as counsel on behalf of Intervenor Jody Rhorer effective the date hereof. Intervenor hereby moves the Court for an enlargement of time to file a post-judgement motion in the above-captioned case. The Honorable Judge Stanley's Memorandum Decision was entered in on June 1, 2017. Mr. Rhorer's new counsel was retained on June 20th, 2017. Mr. Rhorer's counsel received a copy of the file on June 26th, 2017, and his case file contains approximately 3,000 pages of documents that are currently being reviewed and processed by his newly retained counsel. Today, Thursday, June 29, 2017, is the 28th day of the allotted time period. Mr. Rhorer's counsel has had three days to review this voluminous file and requests a 28-day enlargement of time to file.
*   WHEREFORE, Intervenor respectfully requests the Court to enlarge the time to file a post-judgment motion through July 5, 2017,* (this was only 6 days and should have said July 26th) *to allow adequate time to properly evaluate Mr. Rhorer's file and complete a post-judgment motion if deemed necessary.*

Thankfully, the Court granted the Motion. Had they denied it, we would have missed our chance to appeal to the Appellate Court.
    It was without so much as a word from Cam for the five weeks she had our case that another Request for Expansion was emailed to us from her office petitioning the Court to give her thirty additional days in which to prepare a motion.   The thing that really terrified me was the fact that the court could deny her request and she could miss the deadline all together. But worse than that was the fact she teamed up with Connie and her motion stated that both of them requested more time as a dual effort. My hunch that she could not separate her friendly relations with her buddy from our case appeared to be correct.

JULY 26TH, 2017: EMAILS from Cam's office

Jody,
Attached are the following documents filed today: 1. Stipulated Motion to Further Enlarge Motion Filing Deadline; 2. Request to Submit for Decision; and; 3. [Proposed] Order on Stipulated Motion to Further Enlarge Motion Filing Deadline.
*   Legal Assistant for Cam*

JULY 26TH, 2017:   STIPULATED MOTION TO FURTHER ENLARGE MOTION FILING DEADLINE, Submitted by Cam H, Judge Stanley presiding

*   Intervenor, Jody Rhorer, and Respondent, Kirk J, by and through their respective counsel of record hereby move the Court for a further enlargement of time to file a post-judgement motion in the above-captioned case. Mr. Rhorer's counsel needs additional time to review the pleadings on file and requests an additional 30-day enlargement of time to file a post-judgement motion if necessary.*
*   WHEREFORE, Intervenor and Respondent respectfully requests the Court to enlarge the time to file a post-judgment motion and an additional 30 days from the day of the signing of the order, filed concurrently herewith, to allow adequate time to properly evaluate Mr. Rhorer's file and complete a post-judgement motion if deemed necessary.*

Deone Ehlers-Rhorer   **358**

JULY 26TH, 2017: EMAILS to Cam

Cam, We do not hear a word from you and then, without even consulting us, you ask for another month? You clearly lack the compassion of a person that understands what it is like to live a day without your child. You had a month. You did nothing.

Now you ask for another, not even knowing if you will get it; not even consulting with us about it. We needed a raging bull and you show no interest in our case whatsoever. We no longer want any association with you. You have wasted our time. We want a full refund of our deposit. How unprofessional of you to send this via your secretary and never even discuss with us; never even ask us a single question about this case. You have failed us. You are terminated immediately. Jody and Deone Rhorer.

Jody A. Rhorer, Enclosed, you will find your invoice(s) for 7/27/2017. Please note if you have any trust funds with us, information regarding any application is reflected on the attached invoice. Please remit payments either by credit card or by mail. Thank you for your prompt attention to this matter. Cam

Cam, You are charging us $3,000 to do absolutely nothing!!!! Why should WE have to pay for you to do another extension when you had the file for FIVE WEEKS and you didn't even get one motion completed? We never got a single phone call or email from you about our case. It is YOUR FAULT you didn't get it done in time and you want to CHARGE US because YOU FAILED to do your job??? You want to CHARGE US to call Connie and ask her if YOU can have more time? NO WAY. You never consulted with us once. This is a joke. We expect to be refunded this money or we will take this to the Bar. Deone Rhorer

No response.

July 31st
Cam, $3,000 to file an extension and then not get your job done and file another exertion without even consulting us, without so much as a word over the whole period of time that you had to work on our case - no questions, no communication - plus we were clear that nothing was to be filed without our review first - is flat out robbery. To charge us for yet another extension is pathetic. We expect to be refunded our money. You wasted our time, made false promises, and failed to keep your commitment. I am giving you this opportunity to rectify this before I go to the Bar, to your Firm, and also to social media for on-line reviews. You should do the right thing. You have cost us so much time where we could have found someone that actually cares.   Jody and Deone Rhorer

JULY 26TH, 2017: WITHDRAWAL OF COUNSEL, Submitted by Cam H, Judge Stanley presiding

Notice is given that Cam H hereby withdraws as counsel for Intervenor, Jody Rhorer, effective the date hereof. This withdrawal is based on Mr. Rhorer's request. Intervenor is aware of the outstanding Stipulated Motion to Further Enlarge Motion Filing Deadline.

CHAPTER 18
DANNY P

$\mathbf{N}$ow we really had to hustle. Searching for a competent attorney has proven to be extremely difficult. All our attorneys came recommended and yet, they all had weaknesses - some more than others - but none had been able to win.

Jody called the attorney that had helped him out previous to our relationship, Joseph O. He, unfortunately didn't do appeals so I asked him who he hated to go up against more than any other attorney and if he was going to hire someone, who would it be. Joseph gave us three names. At the top of the list was Danny P. We called him first and got an appointment right away.

Danny's office was a modest older home on a busy road in Salt Lake City converted to a commercial building. He was relatively young and very to the point. The main thing we wanted to know was, could he win? Danny took a couple days to review the case and give it some thought before he decided to go ahead and accept it. We mailed him a retainer and he started work immediately.

AUGUST 15TH, 2017: EMAIL from Cam

Jody, This e-mail is in response to the e-mails dated July 27, 2017, July 31, 2017, and August 15, 2017. I diligently worked on your case as evidenced by the attached invoices detailing my work completed on your case from June 20, 2017, through July 25, 2017. I advised you at our initial client meeting that we were facing novel issues of standing, the constitutionality of Utah's paternity code, and a possible juvenile court petition. I advised you that I would need to review your file before determining whether we should challenge Judge Stanley's Memorandum Decision, file an abuse/neglect petition in the juvenile court, or both.

I also advised you that I would need to secure an extension on the time to file a post-judgment motion in the district court case. At no time did I promise any outcome or result. The work I have completed on your case included reviewing thousands of pages of pleadings and exhibits filed in your case, speaking with the attorneys on the case regarding abuse and neglect of the minor child and the constitutionality of the paternity code in preparation for filing a constitutional challenge to the same, and securing a post-judgment motion deadline of August 30, 2017. I did not bill you for the case law research and multiple conversations I had with several experienced family law attorneys regarding the novel idea of challenging the constitutionality of the paternity code. With that said, my firm has authorized to reimburse to you $1,500, one-half of the amount paid to the firm from your retainer. A check will be forwarded to you accordingly. Regards, Cam

AUGUST 26TH, 2017: APPEARANCE OF COUNSEL filed by Danny P

AUGUST 27TH, 2017: EMAIL from Danny P

Here is the Motion that I drafted. After reading through all of the pleadings, I determined that the Commissioner and ultimately the judge believed that Jody was merely seeking a timesharing arrangement, and no more. It appears the pleadings were poorly drafted and may have even been poorly argued. Certainly, the Judge in his ruling took the easy out, by finding that Jody was seeking a timesharing arrangement and nothing more. Therefore, he found Jody lacked standing. The Court never addressed rebutting Kirk's parental rights, which was before the Court and is in my motion. I do believe these are the issues and, other than that, I don't believe there is an error of law. Danny P, PLLC

AUGUST 28TH, 2017:   MOTION FOR AMENDED FINDINGS & FOR A NEW TRIAL, filed by Danny P, Judge Stanley presiding

Intervenor, Jody Rhorer, by and through counsel of record, hereby files their Motion for Amended Finding and for a new Trial.

(1-42 of the argument was a redundant repeat of what has already been presented to the court so that was eliminated from the re-account of this motion as it has been brought up so many times in this book already.)

ARGUMENT

It is apparent that the Intervenor's Verified Motion for Orders and Objection to Commissioner's Recommendation were poorly written and did not represents the intent of the Intervenor in this matter. The Court refers to page 9 that the Intervenor was only seeking a time-sharing arrangement. However, on the top of 10, the Intervenor's Objection alludes to the fact the Court would untimely determine Paternity and Custody at trial. The Verified Motion for Order and Objection was seeking a temporary order of reunification in order for the Custody Evaluation to proceed. It has always been the intent of the Intervenor to establish paternity and to seek custody of the minor child. (See December 9, 2013, Motion to Establish Himself as The Natural and Biological Father of PR, Motion for Determination of Parentage and A Motion for Custody or In the Alternative for A Custody Evaluation and Motion for Interim Parent-Time.) It appears Intervenor's prior counsel was merely trying to establish reunification as part of temporary orders, then a full custody evaluation to support the Intervenor's ultimate request for custody.

Pursuant to Rule 52, of the Utah Rules of Civil Procedure, Petitioner files his request to amend Findings entered on June 1, 2017. Pursuant to Rule 52(b):

(b) Amended or additional findings. Upon motion of a party filed no later than 28 days after entry of judgment the court may amend its finding or make additiona findings and may amend the judgment accordingly. The motion may accompany motion for a new trial under Rule 59.

Pursuant to Rule 59(a) of the Utah Rule of Civil Procedure, Petitioner filed his request for a New Trial, Pursuant to Rule 59(a):

[a] new trial may be granted to all or any of the parties on all or part of the issues, for any of the following causes; provided, however, that on a motion for a new trial in an action tried without a jury, the court may open the judgement if one has been entered, take additional testimony, amend finding of fact and conclusions of law or make new findings and conclusions, and direct the entry of a new judgment...

(a)(1) irregularity in the proceedings of the court, jury or opposing party, or any order of the court, or abuse of discretion by which a party was prevented from having a fair trial; (a)(6) insufficiency of the evidence to justify the verdict or other decision; or (a)(7) that the verdict or decision is contrary to law or based on an error in law.

The Intervenor believes there was an error by the Commissioner and the Court that led to the Intervenor's Motion being denied and the Court findings that the Intervenor lacked standing. As indicated, the Verified Motion for Orders and Objection was only intended to be temporary until Custody Evaluation based upon Dr. Natovich's recommendation. It is apparent that the Commissioner and Court deemed the Verified Motion for Orders and Objection as a permanent request and not a temporary request. Therefore, the Intervenor requests the Court Amend its findings and requests a New Trial in this matter. Furthermore, it is apparent that the Court has overlooked the ability of the Intervenor to rebut the Respondent's parental presumption in this matter.

1. The Commissioner found that the Intervenor lived with the minor child for a period of time. Intervenor asserts before this court that he lived with the child for the first 3 years.   2. The Petitioner and Respondent separated on or about May 30, 2005.   3. The Child was born in July 2007.
4. The Respondent has been excluded as the biological father of the minor child.   5. The Intervenor has tested with 99.99% certainty as biological father of the child.   6. The ORS by Administrative Order excluded the Respondent as the father of the child and found that the Intervenor was indeed the biological father of the minor child.

Pursuant to Utah Code Ann. 78B-15-607

(2) For the presumption outside of marriage described in Subsection 78B-15-204(1)(d), <u>the presumption may be rebutted at any time if the tribunal determines that the presumed father and the mother of the child neither cohabited nor engaged in sexual intercourse with each other during the probable time of conception.</u>

(3) <u>The presumption may be rebutted by; (a) genetic test results that exclude the presumed father; (b) genetic test results that reputably identify another man as the father in accordance with Section 78-B-15-505; (c) evidence that the presumed father and the mother of the child neither cohabited nor engaged in sexual intercourse with each other during the probable time of conception; (d) an adjudication under this part.</u>

Clearly, the Intervenor has the ability to rebut the parental presumption in this matter. It is clear that the parties separated in May of 2005 and the minor child was born 2 years later. The Petitioner and Respondent were not cohabiting nor engaged in sexual intercourse at the time the minor child was conceived. The Respondent has been excluded as the biological father of the minor child and the Intervenor has been determined to be father of the child with 99.99% certainty. The Intervenor has not abandoned his claim to rebut Respondent's paternity in this matter and seek custody of the minor child as the Court found on June 1, 2017.

Instead, the Intervenor was merely attempting to establish reunification and temporary parent-time until a custody evaluation could be completed in this matter. Based upon the foregoing, the Intervenor requests the Court Amend its Findings and/or grant a New Trial (hearing) in this matter to determine that the Intervenor has standing to rebut the Respondent's parental presumption and to seek custody of the minor child.

SEPTEMBER 8TH, 2017: KIRK J'S RESPONSE TO MOTION TO AMEND & FOR A NEW TRIAL, submitted by Connie C, Judge Stanley presiding

Comes now, Connie C, Attorney at Law, on behalf of Kirk J, and files the foregoing Response to the "Motion to Amend Findings and for a New Trial" filed by Danny P on August 29th, 2017. Danny P is Mr. Rhorer's eighth attorney in this matter. David B filed a Motion to Intervene in May, 2013. Steven K filed an entry of Appearance in August, 2013. Nancy S filed an entry of Appearance in December of 2013, Brad K filed an entry of Appearance in July of 2015. William H filed an entry of Appearance in February of 2016, Cam H filed an entry of Appearance in June 2017. Danny P filed his entry of Appearance in August, 2017.

MOTION TO AMEND FINDING

The Motion does not specify what amendments or additional findings Mr. Rhorer believes the Court should or could make. The "argument" section directly proceeding the text of Rule 52 criticizes prior counsel, Devin C's drafting, and asserts he "did not represent the intent of Mr. Rhorer." The "intent" alleged to be misrepresented is Mr. Rhorer's desire to establish legal paternity and obtain custody of the minor. Mr. Rhorer was present and sitting at counsel table at all hearings, including the ones attended by Devin C, who Mr. Rhorer now derides. If Mr. Rhorer disagreed with Devin C's recitation of his desires, or the strategy Devin C elected to advance before the Court, he sat silently by. Devin C served as Counsel for Mr. Rhorer after that time as well, ushering the initial objection and motion for new trial through the Court. It seems that Mr. Rhorer simply requests that the Court undo the work of his counsel because he didn't prevail.

Based on the time elapsed and number of attorney's representing Mr. Rhorer, he parts ways with counsel every six months or so. If this Court were to "amend findings," to correct things Mr. Rhorer wishes his attorney hadn't said at prior hearings, the decision of the Court in this case would never achieve finality. Aside from Mr. Rhorer's post hoc dissatisfaction with Devin C's approach, which may well have been strategic, he states no basis for amendment of the findings and order. Kirk J prays the Motion to Amend be denied due to the fact that it fails to state what Amendments Mr. Rhorer prays for, and fails to cogently analyze proper grounds for amendment.

Moreover, even if the Court wanted to "amend" to essentially undo Devin C's work, Mr. Rhorer still does not have standing, pursuit to 78B-150607 to assert a claim of paternity as properly decided by the Court, nor did Mr. Rhorer notify the Attorney General of any Constitutional challenge to the Statute, nor did he provide an adequate argument for the Court to consider the Constitutional Issue. If Mr. Rhorer has no standing, it does not matter what he wishes to argue before the Court.

MOTION FOR NEW TRIAL

Mr. Rhorer asserts he "believes there was an error" leading to the Motion being denied and ruling that he lacked standing. He asserted that the Court misperceived the motion and that it really was for a finding of legal paternity and order of custody which the "sharing" of the child as an intermediate temporary step toward Mr. Rhorer's ultimate goal of custody change. Mr. Rhorer's assertions that he can establish paternity under 789B-150607 ignores 78B-15-607(I), which makes clear the only person who may challenge paternity of "a child conceived or born during a marriage with a presumed father...is the presumed father, the mother, or a support enforcement agency."

Counsel acknowledges that Mr. Rhorer's latest counsel entered appearance only a couple days before the expiration of the extension period to file motions obtained by Cam H before her hasty exit from the representation of Mr. Rhorer.

Accordingly, she might not have had the time or opportunity to study the years of litigation, the pleadings, do the hundreds of hours of research which ultimately culminated in the legal finding that Mr. Rhorer lacks standing. The Commissioner and this Court read the provision in its entirety and came to the inescapable conclusion that Kirk J is the presumed father. Neither he, Kelly H, nor a "child support agency" have challenged Kirk J's presumption of paternity, and they are the only actors who can. While there might be a different result if 607(I) were to be ignored, the Court didn't ignore that provision in making its ruling, and it is not at liberty to ignore it now.

CONCLUSION

*The basis supplied by Mr. Rhorer does not support his motion to Amend, nor does the motion make clear what he seeks to have Amended. Mr. Rhorer's dissatisfaction with the result achieved by Counsel does not support his Motion for a new trial. Kirk J also observes that this is the second round of "post-trial" motions. While Mr. Rhorer has made repeated emotional pleas here to the effect that he is being deprived of "his" child, and on the internet via "go fund me" and a news article solicited by him and published by the Standard Examiner in Ogden, Kirk J, the minor, and her siblings suffer with the lack of peace finality of this case would bring. Kirk J has been the beneficiary of over four years worth of process when the ultimate conclusion of the Court is that he has no standing and therefore, is due **no** process at all. Even so, Mr. Rhorer has direct appeal as a remedy, and without a truly final decision in this case, Kirk J can't achieve the minor consolation that this process is actually moving forward. Because no just cause for amendment or new trial has been provided, Kirk J prays that the Court deny the motions, and for such other and further relief as the Court deems appropriate in the premises.*

We actually had nine attorneys if you count the Jesus look-a-like. Connie only started emphasizing the number of attorneys we had "gone through" when we fired her friend, Cam. She apparently took this personally enough to address it in her motion and even put a good word in in Cam's defense. Certainly, if we had a free attorney we would have to pause twice before switching, but instead, we had many non-productive and ineffective attorneys. Certainly not the desired outcome we wished for but, nevertheless, a very important part of the injustice of this book.

SEPTEMBER 8TH, 2017:   MOTION FOR ATTORNEYS FEES, submitted by Connie C, Judge Stanley presiding

Comes now, Connie, Attorney at Law, and moves for the Court's order for Attorney's fees to be paid by Mr. Rhorer. Grounds and reasons for the award of attorney fees are as follows:

Mr. Rhorer intervened in the divorce action between Kirk J and Kelly H to attempt to assert paternity on a child born during their marriage. His intervention in this case followed (1) his walking away from Juvenile Court proceedings before Judge V when the minor child was an infant; (2) his attempt to have paternity established through ORS which did not include informing them of Kirk J's parental presumption through marriage to Kelly H; and (3) his wrongful attempt to obtain an Order of Paternity in a District Court action by failing to notify Kirk J as a necessary party.

After institution of these proceedings, his conduct has been outrageous, and increased the amount of time and effort needed to litigate this matter. Mr. Rhorer caused to be lodged over 600 pages of basically defamatory material designated to prejudice the Court against Kirk J substantively without first establishing standing procedurally. Mr. Rhorer publicized the case, including the minor's identity on a web funding site called "go fund me" and caused a news article to be published in the Ogden Standard Examiner. Motions had to be filed, and hearings held to get Mr. Rhorer to agree to remove the funding site, and agree to stop bringing the identity of the minor into the public sphere. His publication caused comments to be filed with the Ogden Standard Examiner characterizing the minor as a "bastard".

Mr. Rhorer's false and defamatory reports that Kirk J is some kind of a "gang member" lead him to hire a private investigator to accompany the GAL to a police agency. After providing the false information regarding gang involvement, the GAL then went with law enforcement resulting in a search of Kirk J's home. That outrageous conduct, which had at its center Mr. Rhorer's false report of gang involvement, and his private investigator's purloining a law enforcement search spawned an extensive and unnecessary "layer" of proceedings. However, Kirk J was forced to file pleadings to ensure that Mr. Rhorer would be foreclosed from misusing law enforcement to attempt to discover materials in this case, and to establish limits to the proper role of the GAL in this matter.

*Mr. Rhorer's wife, **ever present in these proceedings**, has inappropriately contacted family members of undersigned counsel, asking for details about the location and condition of undersigned's mother. Mr. Rhorer has ratified those actions by failing to take appropriate action to correct them. Accordingly, counsel has had to expend effort at investigation and communication with appropriate persons to ensure personal information related to the location and condition of counsel's family members are held confidential.*

Mr. Rhorer's wife went to the minor's school and gave her gifts, misrepresenting her reason for being there, and misstating her association to the child. This disturbing conduct ultimately had to be brought up at hearing. Mr. Rhorer's repeated and chronic changes in Counsel have increased the effort toward concluding limitations immeasurably in that every single change of counsel has been a step back in "explaining" the case, communicating status, helping new counsel get "up to speed" and frequently file essentially the same motions that had already been heard over and over again. Based on current events with Mr. Rhorer's eight counsel having entered at the eleventh hour to file post-trial motions for the second time illustrates the extreme level of litigiousness that he has brought to bare on Kirk J. The level of limitation has bordered on vexatious, and current events reflect that Mr. Rhorer has no intention of accepting a duly issued ruling of this court. Rather, he clearly intends to attempt to achieve "do overs" rather than accepting the ruling and moving on with accepted appellate process.

*Kirk J, a man with many children in addition to the one at issue here, is all but indigent, and **undersigned, unwilling to step away and leave him to be "outgunned" by Mr. Rhorer's superior financial position, has essentially been working for free.** Respect is due to all litigants seeking their day in Court, and undersigned respects the process that brings contested matters to the appropriate forum. However, the actions of Mr. Rhorer and his incessant litigiousness leads counsel to believe that perhaps the only motivation Mr. Rhorer may have to ever allow finality in this case is to have to pay for both sides of the war he wages. Accordingly, undersigned prays the Court issue its Order that Mr. Rhorer pay Kirk J's reasonable attorney's fees, and for such other and further relief as the court deems appropriate in the premises.*

I believe this motion was designed for the sole purpose of attempting to discourage and intimidate us from moving forward. Filling the motion with disparaging and tainted details also served to influence David to think less of us as well. All Connie's efforts to get attorney fees awarded had, for the most part, been completely ignored by the Court.

SEPTEMBER 8TH, 2017: REPLY MEMORANDUM IN SUPPORT OF MOTION FOR AMENDED FINDINGS & NEW TRIAL, submitted by Danny P, Judge Stanley presiding

Intervenor, Jody Rhorer, by and through counsel of record, hereby files this Reply Memorandum in Support of Motion for Amended Findings and for a New Trial.

ARGUMENT

Respondent in his response appeared to only make derogatory remarks about Intervenor and his counsel, instead of simply focusing on the law and legal arguments. The Intervenor believes there was an error by the Commissioner and the Court that led to the Intervenor's Motion being denied and the Court findings that the Intervenor lacked standing. As indicated, the Verified Motion of Orders and Objection was only intended to be temporary to establish parent-time and to re-establish a relationship with the minor child for the custody evaluation based upon Dr. Natovich's recommendation. It is apparent the Commissioner and Court deemed the Verified Motion for Orders as a permanent request and not a temporary request. Therefore, the Intervenor requests that the Court Amend its findings and a New Trial in this matter.

Furthermore, the Respondent fails to acknowledge the undisputed facts in the case:

1. The Commissioner found that the Intervenor lived with the child for a period of time. Intervenor asserts before this court that he lived with the child for the first 3 years of her life.

2. The Petitioner and Respondent separated on or about May 30, 2005.

3. The child was born in July, 2007.

4. The Respondent has been excluded as the biological father of the minor child.
5. The Intervenor has tested with 99.99% certainty as the biological father of the child.
6. The ORS by Administrative Order excluded the Respondent as the father of the child, and found that the Intervenor was indeed the biological father of the minor child.
7. The parties have admitted under oath that they had not cohabited since May 30, 2005, more than one year prior to PR's conception and more than two years prior to her birth: a. Petition for Divorce, paragraph 2 filed by Kelly H in which she states, "The parties separated on or about 05/30/2005." b. The Vital Statistics Form filed in this matter listing May 2005, as the "date couple last resided in same household. c. Respondent's Answer to Petition for Divorce in which he admitted the allegations in paragraph 2 of the Petition other than correcting the date of the marriage as having occurred on April 27, 2003. He did not deny that the parties separated on or about May 30, 2005. d. Respondent, in a hearing before this court on December 20, 2012, stated to the court, "We, we got married in 2003, and she left in 2003. I mean, we, we haven't even been together since then.

Pursuant to Utah Code Ann. 78B-15-607
(2) For the presumption outside of marriage described in subsection 78B-15-204 (1)(d), <u>the presumption may be disputed at any time if the tribunal determines that the presumed father and the mother of the child neither cohabited nor engaged in sexual intercourse with each other during the probable time of conception. (3) The presumption may be rebutted by: (a) genetic test results that exclude the presumed father; (b) genetic test results that rebuttabley identify another man as the father in accordance with Section 78B-15-505; (c) evidence that the presumed father and the mother of the child neither cohabited nor engaged in sexual intercourse with each other during the probable time of conception; (d) an adjudication under this part.</u>

Clearly, the Intervenor has the ability to rebut the parental presumption in this matter. It is clear that the parties separated in May of 2005 and the minor child was born 2 years later. The Petitioner and Respondent were not cohabiting nor engaged in sexual intercourse at the time the minor child was conceived. The Respondent has been excluded as the biological father of the minor child and the Intervenor has been determined to be the father of the child with 99.99% certainty. The Intervenor has not abandoned his claim to rebut Respondent's paternity in this matter and to seek custody of the minor child as the Court found on June 1, 2017. Instead, the Intervenor was merely attempting to establish reunification and temporary parent-time until a custody evaluation could be completed in this matter. Based upon the foregoing, the Intervenor requests that the Court Amend its Findings and/or grant a New Trial in this matter to determine that the Intervenor has standing to rebut the Respondent's parental presumption and to seek custody of the minor child.

There you have it! Cut and dry. Clear as a bell. It's right there in plain ink in Rule 78B-15-607 - spelled out for the court to see dozens of times over the years; for the judge to read; for the justice to prevail - but no! Why? It says so, so why can't the judge make it so? I don't understand this. What is really going on here? Why does the State of Utah through it's elected and appointed judiciary want to deprive this little girl from her family? What are they afraid of?

<u>SEPTEMBER 20TH, 2017:</u> COURT HEARING

This was the third court hearing in a row where Kirk J was not in attendance. It's clear that this is the fight of Connie. Kelly was there but was quiet and sober for a change. Connie's main objective was requesting attorney fees. Danny argued that Commissioner Bloom had made many rulings in Jody's favor including the custody evaluation of Dr. Natovich. He went over the recommendations and what is in the best interest of the child.

"Jody has always had standing as the biological father and has met all of the factors in Rule 78B-15-607," Danny pressed.

Connie rebutted by stating, "The three persons that can bring up parentage is the mother, the presumed father, or the child." She said David is "ignoring this and is full of jibbity, jib, jib, jib." I found her comments to be very odd. She looked peaked and tired and was acting irrationally. Connie then stated to the court regarding Jody, "Don't give him the right to go to court again!"

Mary, the GAL, did speak up for a moment but could have certainly been more powerful in her presentation. "In my opinion, Jody has the right to assert his parentage."

Judge Stanley appeared a bit more attentive than in the past, but of course, didn't render a decision as that would come later. The big shocker of the hearing though, was a statement made by Connie that solidified my belief that she was pursuing this case for her own merits and ego.

"If it wasn't for the fact I don't walk away from a good fight, they would have won a long time ago."

I gasped under my breath when Connie made that statement on record! What could she possibly have against Jody to compel her to do this to him? She reviles him. This is personal to her. She is a complete stranger but has chosen to give her own precious time and resources to ruin a little child's life so she can ruin Jody's.

OCTOBER 1ST, 2017: MEMORANDUM IN OPPOSITION OF MOTION FOR ATTORNEY FEES, submitted by Danny P, Judge Stanley presiding

Intervenor, Jody Rhorer, by and through counsel of record, hereby files this Memorandum in Opposition to Motion for Attorney Fees. Respondent requests attorney fees in this matter. However, if the Court's ruling on June 1, 2017, was to remain as the Order of the Court, the Respondent lacks standing in this matter.

As a result, the Respondent is nonparty to this Case. Certainly, the Respondent submits over 4 pages of defamatory statements and factual disputes that are simply untrue. Intervenor doesn't believe it is productive or helpful to unnecessarily increase attorney fees by arguing over defamatory accusations which are irrelevant. At the end of the day, it is undisputed that the Intervenor is the biological father in this matter. The Intervenor is merely seeking to protect his Constitutional rights to have a relationship with his biological daughter. It appears the Respondent fails to recognize that as a biological father, the Intervenor does have Constitutional rights. It is also in the child's best interest for this Court to make a fair determination as to whether it is recognizing the Intervenor's relationship with his daughter. There is absolutely no basis for the Court to award attorney fees.

The Respondent fails to cite any statute or case law in the Motion to suggest he is entitled to attorney fees. Furthermore, the Court has scheduled a hearing to address the merits of the Intervenor's Motion and standing in this matter. Therefore, it would also be premature to rule the Motion for attorney fees prior to the hearing.

OCTOBER 2ND, 2017: JOURNAL ENTRY

A few observations. Connie has CHOSEN to work for free and she even brought this up at least twice in our last court proceeding - telling Judge Stanley that this was becoming exhausting for her since she was not being paid. How can a free attorney request fees?

Why does Connie keep bringing me into these proceedings when I am not a party? I think she may feel threatened by me, but in a different way than Kelly does. Is she trying to get me barred from the hearings? She definitely wants me out of the picture.

This Thursday there will be a reprimand hearing at the State Bar against William H in which Jody and I have been asked to testify. I bet William is a no-show.

OCTOBER 5TH, 2017: LETTER from the Utah State Bar

Re: Complaint Against William H
Dear Jody Rhorer:
At the conclusion of the hearing on October 5, 2017, the Screening Panel of the Ethics and Discipline Committee of the Utah Supreme Court voted to direct the Office of Professional Conduct to file a formal Complaint against William H in District Court (who did not show up for the proceeding).

Because you may be an important witness at the District Court proceedings, we ask that you keep the OPC informed of your current address and telephone number.

Sincerely,
Clerk of the Ethics and Discipline Committee

NOVEMBER 6TH, 2017: COURT HEARING TRANSCRIPT, Judge Stanley presiding; present Jody and Deone Rhorer, Danny P, Connie, Kelly H, Mary C. Kirk J did not attend.

THE COURT: All right. This is the case between Kelly H vs. Kirk J. Could I have Counsel's appearance, please?

DANNY P: Danny P for Intervenor, Jody Rhorer, who is present.

CONNIE: Connie for Kirk J, and your Honor, this is Kelly H. She's pro se party. This is the first time she's appeared in front of you.

THE COURT: Welcome, Kelly. So, this is intervenor's motion to amend findings, motion for a new trail, and then there's a motion for attorney fees. Danny P, it's your client's motion on the first matter.

DANNY P: Obviously I wasn't part of the original proceedings, but nonetheless, I was hired to file a motion to at least amend this Court's minute entry that was entered on June 1st of this year. Primarily what I was focused on is pretty much when I looked at Commissioner Blomquist's findings, and I think it was the order that was actually signed by this Court as well, that on February 20th of 2015, it was, subsequently entered by this Court on April 20th, 2015 - the commissioner at the time made several findings which of course, when I review the statute in this case, it's clear to me that the Intervenor has rebutted the presumption of father in this case, and he should have parental rights.

When I read the Court's June 1st minute entry, it seemed to me that the Court clearly found that the Intervenor didn't have standing, primarily based upon the fact that he was looking for limited parent-time, and he wasn't wanting to exclude the Respondent in this case, and quite honestly, when I reviewed the pleadings and so forth, it looked like to me that as I even indicted in my motion, that prior Counsel either just poorly drafted his previous motion, and certainly his objection to the Commissioner's recommendation, but even more so I think going back to his original motion that was filed in June of 2016, he clearly was just asking for parent-time pursuant to Dr. Natovich's recommendation. What she was doing, of course, is Dr. Natovich certainly was just trying to put a band-aid on the situation and say well, the Intervenor should have reintroduction and so forth, and she certainly found that it was in the best interest of the child to at least have a relationship with the Intervenor, which is her biological father, and I think that's undisputed in all the pleadings.

Then even in his original motion he asked as well if Dr. Natovich should conduct the custody evaluation. The new custody evaluation should not commence until the child has been in reunification therapy for a period of 90 days, which I think was consistent with Dr. Natovich's recommendation. When I read the June 1st minute entry it seemed to me that there was the Court's belief that all he wanted was limited visitation, and that's all he was requesting, and that was just on a temporary basis. That was never on a permanent basis, because as I pointed out in my motion, which appears to me that was overlooked by the Court, was certainly going back to December of 2013, where he clearly had filed his motion for custody and in the alternative a custody evaluation, was granted by Commissioner Bloom. Then he also filed a motion of determination of parentage.

I don't need to rehash, but I certainly have listed all of Commissioner Bloom's findings. What is more interesting is when there's a presumption, of course, that the Respondent at the time was the father, because clearly the Petitioner and the Respondent were married, but even in their own pleading that was filed by the Petitioner in this case, she never indicated that the Respondent was the father. Actually, it was to the contrary where she even pled in her pleadings, and even going back to the original petition that was filed in this case that essentially the Respondent was not the father, but essentially, she was saying that he should be awarded custody.

So even in going back to the original decree it was never established that the Respondent was the father, but what we clearly do have in the history of this case, even with Commissioner Bloom, because it was the finding of the Court ultimately that it was the Intervenor that is the biological father of this child.

Respondent was actually excluded from being the father of this child pursuant to genetic testing by the Office of Recovery Services, and ultimately, they closed their case against the Respondent for paying child support because he was not the biological father. Certainly, the Intervenor in this case had done what was ordered by this Court. Originally there was that limited custody or parent-time evaluation, and then all he was doing was requesting reintroduction or reunification therapy with the child so ultimately he could have custody, and that was what was being asked for by his prior counsel - even in his filed objection.

What was even more important that I point out in my motion that certainly he was just asking for it on a temporary basis, because on page 10 of his conclusion, he says that isn't what the purpose of a trial would be to determine what should be the ultimate disposition in this case, terminating the Intervener's rights with the minor child would be contrary to the best interest of the child, violates the constitution, and so forth. What he was really asking was that he just wanted to preserve the parent/child relationship, and ultimately, he did want custody of the child because that's what's been constant with all of the pleadings.

Once again, I'll admit that prior Counsel's objection and even his motion was poorly written, but that's what he was wanting on a temporary basis, and that was what the recommendation of the custody evaluator was. When I go so far to look at the statute which - and forgive me, your Honor, but I wasn't part of it, but I didn't see it in the Court's ruling, is if you look at the statute, which I've pointed out before this Court, is pursuant to 78B-15-607, referring to 204 that talks about the presumption when the parties are married, but 607 states, "Presumption may be refuted at any time that the tribunal determines that the presumed father and the mother of the child neither cohabited nor engaged in sexual intercourse with each other during the probable time of conception."

Certainly, we can go through the facts of the case. That's very clear wherein the petition for divorce, paragraph 2, said the parties had separated on or about May 3rd of 2005, and then of course the statute further talks about the fact that the presumption may be rebutted by genetic tests that exclude the presumed father, which clearly has been the finding of this Court, which has been submitted, and then of course genetic tests that reputedly identify another man as the father in accordance with 505, which we clearly have, which is clearly the findings before this Court as well that the Intervenor is the biological father.

Then furthermore as well in subparagraph (c) of that statute, it talks about evidence that the presumed father and the mother of the child neither cohabited nor engaged in sexual intercourse with each other during the probable time of conception. Once again, we do have that. That is actually the findings of this Court. It's consistent with all of the pleadings. So, when we look at this case, I think we've met all of the factors in 607, and certainly I think in the minute entry that was filed before this Court, I don't' think the Court did address the rebutted presumption.

THE COURT: Well, I mean ins't that what it's all about is whether he has standing to rebut the presumption? I mean you're jumping over the standing issue, which is really the only issue, not temporary visitation, not permanent visitation or parentage. The only issue at the last hearing before this Court was - the threshold issue was standing, and that's when both in the written materials, and as I recall the oral presentation, Counsel for Intervenor conceded that they were not seeking parentage at the time, that the remedy they were seeking at that time was visitation, and I didn't see at the time, and I don't see presently how that gets around the problem of standing.

DANNY P: Well, I think the motions were filed, as I pointed out. My client filed a motion for termination of parentage back before this Court on December 9th of 2013. At the same time when he filed that motion, he had also filed a motion for custody, and in the alternative for custody evaluation and motion for interment parent-time. Those were both filed subsequently I think on the same day, both on December 9th of 2013. So, he did establish a standing, and clearly even in his own motion of determination of parentage, he attached a copy of the genetic report indicating by 99.99 percent that he was the father of this child. That has never been rebutted or proven incorrect by the Petitioner or even the Respondent himself, and furthermore, that it was ORS that actually closed the case as well because it was the Respondent that submitted to a genetic test.

So, all along, I believe under the statue he has been asking for custody to be determined to be the father. I don't - unless I'm missing something, and you can correct me if I'm wrong, your Honor, I just don't' see where he didn't have standing. He's always had standing. He's always maintained that he was the father, and he's never waived from that. He's never backed away from any of his obligations in this case. I think the only conclusion that at least I can see from looking at the pleadings themselves is - and once again, I wasn't here at the last hearing, so I can only take the word of the Court as to what prior Counsel said, but at least when I look at the pleadings, what I see is confusion, maybe even on the part of prior Counsel.

It looks like to me that at the time he was only asking of reunification therapy pursuant to Dr. Natovich's recommendation. She certainly found that it would be in the child's best interest to have a relationship with her father, and so I think - and quite honestly, given the history of this case, I can't find too much fault in starting out with reunification therapy so that we can go ahead and establish custody and ultimately, that the child would be placed in his custody.

I don't necessarily think that that's not in the child's best interest, given the history of this case. I think if this Court was to make a ruling today that my client was to have custody, I would be first to say, and I think even my client would say that there needs to be some type of transition. That's all he was asking for, and maybe it was poorly written by prior Counsel, but I just don't see how he didn't have standing when he's always maintained it and he's already requested it from this Court. The only thing I can see that he could have done differently in this case is maybe filed the petition, but certainly I don't think that that was ever alluded, and certainly, at least as I've found by the commissioner's recommendation - she never required that a petition be filed. He's filed his motions. I think he has standing. If I'm missing something, your Honor, please tell me because I haven't been part of this case, and it's a long history, but when it goes to standing, I think he's always remained consistent and his ultimate goal was being the father of this child and having custody of his child.

When I look at 607, he's met every one of those factors on rebutting the presumption, and even more interesting as well is the fact that this child was born and conceived long after the Petitioner and the Respondent were separated, and under the statute itself it talks about whether or not they were cohabiting or having sexual intercourse. I've seen nobody rebut that fact in itself, and so clearly he does have standing.

I think certainly we're asking this Court for at least for a new trial, but certainly we're either asking for a new hearing, or that my client is deemed to have standing so that we can proceed on a trial and requesting custody, and we ultimately were requesting in our motion, most certainly that a custody evaluation be completed. It's obvious that the biological mother has not had custody.

The child is residing with the Respondent, who is not a biological father. I just can't see under the circumstances how that's in the child's best interest. Even noted, I think in even Commissioner Kase's minute entry or ruling he talked about the fact that he had concerns as to how many children were living with the respondent and whether or not that was a suitable living arrangement, and that certainly Dr. Natovich found that the proper living arrangements would be found with the Intervenor. It's just been unfortunate this case has dragged on for so long. I think it's best that either this Court give Mr. Rhorer standing so that we can have a custody evaluation or ultimately a trial. Does the Court have any further questions?

THE COURT: No, thanks. Connie?

CONNIE: Okay. So the thing the Counsel is missing is sub(1) under 78B-15-607. It lists the persons who have standing to challenge paternity when there is a presumed father by virtue of marriage, and those three persons are the mother, the presumed father, who is Kirk, and a child support agency, period. So I could see how Counsel would get confused about the rest of the subsection having ignored sub(1), but statutory standing is limited to those three individuals. Commissioner Bloom - we probably had two years of proceedings before she ruled on that issue, including finding that neither Kelly H or Kirk J raised those issues in the divorce. It's in her minute entry that yes, she acknowledges that Kelly stated that the child is not biologically Kirk J's, but she didn't ask for any determination of paternity otherwise, and in fact, asked for custody to be in him. The Commissioner, having had a couple of years to consider it and many hearings, wrote that very detailed finding that the problem with Mr. Rhorer's analysis about anything in which he has always mixed up the issues of, do I even have a right to be here to ask for any legal remedy with the remedy he's asking for, and the Court is absolutely right that the only issue that has to be determined ultimately before any of that other stuff - are you better, should we have reintroduction, how many kids are in the house, what's in the best interest, jibbity, jibb, jibb, jibb, jibb - we can't reach any of that until this Court can find he has standing.

Commissioner Bloom wrote that detailed findings after those years of studying this and many hearings saying you know what, you don't have a statutory right to standing. When that was coming out, the Court of Appeals filed a decision where in a footnote they stated perhaps somebody like Mr. Rhorer could establish constitutional standing, so then they're like oh, good. Well, we're dead in the water on the statutory issue, let's try to breathe some life in the constitutional issue. They utterly failed, and now this is our third hearing where a judicial officer is saying you failed, and yet we're back here saying well, we always have said we're biological father. You know what, that doesn't make any difference. You look at the Uniform Parentage Act, it doesn't say **hey, guess what, if it turns out that your DNA is in some kid, you have standing.** That's not what it says. There are many subsections that say this is adjudicated father, this is declarant father, this is presumed father, this is biological father, and guess what?

He has no in to say that hey, I happen to have produced this kid genetically, give the kid to me. He doesn't even have a seat at the table. Every one of those decisions has been correct.

Now we're on eight attorneys here, and there are probably 7,000 more attorneys that do family law, and I just wonder how many of them we're going to go through that are going to come in here and criticize prior Counsel and oh, it must be - it must be Devin C's fault as to how this didn't go right for me. No, Mr. Rhorer, it's not Devin C, it's not Steven K, it's not Nancy whatever, it's not the other four people that you hired. It's that the statute doesn't give you a right to standing when the parents are married, mom doesn't raise it, presumed father doesn't raise it, and the child support agency doesn't raise it as party to the divorce. You are foreclosed. He hasn't established constitutional standing. That's what you found last time, and it doesn't matter what he was asking for. He could have been asking for custody. He could have been asking for visitation. He could have been asking to change the kid's name. He could have been asking to direct her religious life. He could have been asking for a walk in the park hand in hand. He doesn't have a right to ask for anything. He is a legal stranger to this child. Statutorily he has no more right to stand in the Court and talk to this Court about a paternity finding of any kind or any of the things that might flow from it than I do.

So, I would ask mercifully, this child is 10 years old and has been with my client since 2012 under a final order of the juvenile court. He's presumed father. He's known to her as father. We could fight forever over who might be a better - better father, but this Court would be absolutely committing error to even engage in that kind of analysis. The Court has to find he doesn't have standing, he doesn't have a right, and I would ask the Court to finally order that no more new attorneys asking for a rehearing. This process has turned abusive at this point with eight attorneys. You know, it's a final order. They can appeal if they want to, but at some point, it has to end, and it's ended numerous times, and yet we keep coming back and coming back and coming back. He's never had standing. He hasn't made it today. The Court can't talk about visitation, reunification, custody, any of that because he does not have legal standing. I would ask the Court for its final order. I don't even know if you have to issue an order, strike the motion, deny the motion once and for all.

We have to be able to end this proceeding. Unless you have questions for me, your Honor. Thank you.

THE COURT: Kelly, do you have anything to say?

KELLY H: No.

THE COURT: Does the GAL have a position?

MARY C: Mary C on behalf of the minor child. I am concerned that it's been extended out. I haven't met with my client since probably about a year ago or something, because I don't want to expend resources if it's not necessary. However, it's my opinion based on the pleadings and all the hearings that Mr. Rhorer has been trying to assert his parentage over the minor child since - as far as I am aware of. With that, even reviewing the code, and maybe I'm just looking at the plain language of the statute - it says that the paternity of the child may be raised by the presumed father or the mother or support enforcement. It doesn't say shall only be raised by these people. The very plain language of the statute provides an open door for Mr. Rhorer.

DANNY P: Yes, your Honor. When I look at 607 as Counsel had pointed out, when I looked at subparagraph (1), basically it talks about if the issues are raised prior to adjudication and so forth, and in this case, at least the way I review these pleadings, in parentage petition that was filed, she actually states that the Respondent is not the father. I know that there's a bifurcated divorce decree, and I just reviewed it and it doesn't even adjudicate the Respondent as the father or anybody as the father. To me, when you look at it in conjunction with 607, and it talks about the presumption may be rebutted, the child was born in 2007, the parties separated in 2005. Under all of the facts that have been admitted to this Court by the Petitioner herself and even the Respondent, it's clearly obvious that under 78B-15-607 subparagraph (2), the presumption has been rebutted.

THE COURT: It's just not helpful to argue the merits. We really are talking about the issue of standing. And we were talking about the issue of standing when Devin C appeared here, and we had - the case had developed to the point where frankly, it was acknowledged by everyone in the room that he didn't have statutory standing. The issue was constitutional standing. So rather than argue the merits of a paternity claim, I really need to hear why you think Devin C did not concede the constitutional standing issue when he conceded he wasn't seeking paternity in that context.

DANNY P: Honestly, I don't know, your Honor. I wasn't at the last hearing, so I don't' know why - what the issue was regarding the standing. When I read the current case law, it talks about that - I do understand that the current case law talks about the fact that if mother and I guess in this case the Respondent do not rebut the presumption, then I do understand that there's case law out there that says that he doesn't have standing, but in this case, I think he does. The clear reason is because from the very get go in the petition it says the Respondent is not the father. We have ORS documents that say he's not the father. We have a court order that they've dismissed the case against him. The ORS opened up a case against the Respondent and it was dismissed, because they did a genetic test and he wasn't the father. So, when you look at the basis –

THE COURT: He was adjudicated to be father in the juvenile court. I mean you can talk all you want, we're talking about biological father standing to challenge the legal father of the child, because there really isn't any argument that Respondent in this case is the legal father. This is a paternity action. You're seeking to establish biological parent. To rebut the legal presumption, you have to have standing. The statute specifies who has standing. You're left then with constitutional standing, and that's where we were. That's how far we've gotten. We were all on the same page up to that point at the last hearing. It took a long time, as Counsel indicated, to get everybody on the page there, but that was where we were. At that point we are arguing constitutional standing whether or not Intervener meets these constitutional requirements, and that's where - and it was in that context, and I submit - I think it was clearly for tactical reasons that Intervenor made the argument that he wasn't seeking to establish paternity, only seeking parent-time.

DANNY P: Okay, but there is a dispute as to whether or not the Respondent - if you look at the original petition, it says he's not the father. All I can say is that pleading says differently in this case, because I think from the very get-go he's always asked for custody. He asked to be determined to be the father. He's never wanted just limited parent-time. I don't' know what happened at the last hearing, and I apologize, I really do. The way that I look at it, I don't see how he doesn't have standing, because he's clearly from day one since 2013 has asked for it. He never asked for just limited - he always wanted full custody.

When I go back to the petition, if I read that - I mean I'm more than happy to brief the current cases on this, because I have briefed these type of issues in other cases. Clearly when we have a situation where mom from the very get go said that the Respondent wasn't the father, to me that opens the door that my client does have standing to file a petition because if she was from the very get go saying that by virtue of the fact that they were married, or whatever language she wanted to use that the Respondent was the father, then I might say okay, I agree with that, because if she was always saying that he was the father in all the legal proceeding, then you're probably right, your Honor, that he didn't have standing. But the fact that she filed the petition in this case saying that the Respondent was not the father, and even all the subsequent pleadings that were filed have always said that he's not the father, and I'm more than happy to brief that one specific subject because I was more focused on the statute, that does open the door to him being - to have standing to file a motion of paternity. If you look at the petition itself, who is the father?

I can also point out, at no time has the responded in this case ever filed a counter petition claiming that he is the father of this child. So, if you're looking at standing, and you're looking at it in terms of subsection 607, even subparagraph (1), please show me a pleading where the respondent has pled before this Court that he is the father of this child. The fact is there in none. There's none because it - he's not the father. I'm challenging everybody in this Court to show me in any pleading at any given time that it's been pled that the respondent is the father.

THE COURT: Why does the Respondent have to plead when he has the legal presumption?

DANNY P: Well, because if you look at current case law, it says if there's a decree or there's a finding of this Court that the Respondent is the father, then yes, I think the Court is correct, at least based upon the Court of Appeal cases that talk about the fact that my client doesn't have standing. I'm very well aware of those cases before the Utah Court of Appeals, and I'm more than happy to cite those cases. I this case where 1) there is not a decree that indicates that the Respondent is the father, and at no time even going back to the petition was the Respondent alleged to be the father, it was actually alluded to be the opposite, it was alleged that he wasn't the father. To me those facts alone say the simple fact is that my client does have standing.

The cases I'm referring to are JLC vs. KAA, 2014 UT APP 245. In that case the father had filed an action against the mother claiming to be the biological father. The Court found that the father didn't have standing since KAA's husband was presumed to be the father. As the Court had indicated in that case that they remained married and continued to be together. In our case we do have a divorce action.

Then Reller vs. Reller which is also important, because the language of that statute talked about no - and that was an interesting case, because in that case the husband and wife were divorced, the husband was adjudicated as the father pursuant to the decree of divorce. Then at Court in that case, mother tried to file a paternity action against the biological father. What the Court had found in that case was that until such time the decree of divorce was set aside and a final adjudication that the husband is not the father of the child, but the wife was precluded, and so why I think that's important is we don't have a decree of divorce. We do have a bifurcated one, but we don't have a final adjudication in this case that talks about that the Respondent is the biological father. He had yet to be adjudicated before this Court to be the father.

If anything, we have the opposite in this case. We have mom that alleged from the very get go that the Respondent was not the father. So, if you compare the facts in Reller where it talks about that man didn't even have standing because there was a decree that said in that case that the Respondent or the husband, was the father, we don't have a final adjudication in that case, and from the very get go mom was saying he's not the father. I struggle with this Court saying that my client does't have standing when even mom had maintained through all of these proceedings that the Respondent is not the father, and I'm more than happy to further brief that one issue because –

THE COURT: Really, we have been through the round on briefing, so I'm not going to do another in this case, so –

DANNY P: Right. But nonetheless, I just don't see anywhere in the statute, and I apologize, your Honor, if I'm missing the boat on that one, but I just don't see how this Court can say he doesn't have standing when all of the pleadings all along seem to indicate that the Respondent is not the father.

MARY C: Your Honor, if I may also add onto that even if the Court isn't looking at the plain language of the statute, that it only shall be those certain individuals, I would suggest and assert that the mother actually did challenge the paternity and the presumption of the father being Mr. Rhorer by asserting that Kirk J wasn't the biological father, thereby complying with provision of 76, 78B-15-607(1). So even if the Court is considering saying well, it was only Kirk J or Kelly H that had the opportunity to do that, I would asset that Kelly H did that by claiming that Kirk J wasn't the father, thereby opening the door for Mr. Rhorer to assert that.

CONNIE: Your Honor, perhaps I can remind Counsel that Commissioner Bloom decided this issue four Intervenor's attorneys ago, and Mary C was there during that proceeding. Commissioner Bloom ruled that simply because Kelly H was honest, as she's required to be in her pleadings before the Court in stating that Kirk J wasn't biological father, that it didn't constitute her raising the issue of paternity because she wasn't saying hey, I want to settle paternity in someone else, I want to raise the issue. She in fact was simply saying yeah, I'm married to presumed dad, and I want him to have custody, and that's been decided.

You know, again, I also never filed a pleading that, you know, is a motion for the Court to find that the sun rises, either, but you know, my - it's - my client is presumed father. If you want pleadings that say that, I went back through my little data bank, I found 20 of them just by searching related to Kirk J by putting the phrase presumed father. There are others about adjudicated father because as the Court correctly notes, he was also adjudicated father in a prior proceeding before the juvenile court. You Honor, I - I would ask the Court to entertain my motion for attorney's fees, simply because - and I - I don't - you know, I do a lot of child welfare. I don't do a whole lot of family law. I know that attorney's fees are more prevalent in family law. I am hesitant to ask for them, but this -- as I said to the Court before, this proceeding has gone so far into the abusive level that I think it's warranted.

My client takes care of Mr. - the biological child of the Intervenor, and he has loved her as - absolutely as his daughter, raises her, financially pays for her and tries to, you know, gratis, because I'm not going to walk away from this when he's basically being - you know, they're trying to overrun him financially by getting attorney after attorney after attorney after attorney, and then, you know, keeping it going. I think that an award of attorney's fees under these circumstances are appropriate. It's - it was - I don't blame him for bringing it in the first instance, but it also has been misguided in the since of always trying to turn it into a best interest fight. You know, it's been a mud-slinging contest, and just getting down to the - can we focus on the issue of standing, it has long since gotten abusive, and I interpose, for the purpose of basically trying to break my client financially. **If it wasn't because of the fact that I can't walk away from a good fight, they would have won a long time ago,** but it doesn't make it right. I'm asking the Court to for fees.

MARY C: Your Honor, if I may just read the code and what it says –

THE COURT: No, we're done arguing that motion. If you've got something to respond to on the motion for attorney fees, you can respond. I have a hard time wondering why the Guardian ad Litem would have a position on the attorney's fees motion.

MARY C: No. I just didn't feel like that she had quoted or at least the party –

THE COURT: And I'm well aware of the statute, and we just - we do this in an orderly manner. It's not an ad hoc we stand up and argue when we feel like it, so I'll ask you to sit down, please. Danny P, do you want to respond to the motion for attorney's fees?

DANNY P: Yes, your Honor. You can't have it both ways before this Court. As I pointed out in our memorandum in oppositions, I begged and she didn't even file a response, please show me specifically somewhere in the statute or case law where it allows this Court to enter attorney's fees in this matter. Technically your've already ruled that he doesn't have standing, so technically he's not a party to this action, and so certainly at this point I don't know what reference to any statute that allows this court to award attorney's fees.

I don't think his pleadings are in bad faith. From the very get go, the way I see it is he's always maintained he's the father of this child, and so what father wouldn't fight to have his visitation and custody rights of his child? None. I don't see how he's acted in bad faith whatsoever. He's done everything possible. Even the pleadings speak for themselves, because even the Petitioner doesn't allege that the Respondent is the father. Certainly, even in Dr. Natovich's report it talks about the fact that the living situation with the Intervenor would be a much better living situation than the child is currently in. Certainly Dr. Natovich even pointed to the fact of the Respondent's criminal history. Given all that, I don't' see what reasonable person in Intervenor's position wouldn't have done what is possible, but I think what is clear, and it's a very interesting legal question I have, is if this Court finds that my client doesn't have standing, where in the statute does it allow this Court to award attorney's fees to a non-party? To me, I think that's it and I would submit on that, your Honor.

THE COURT: Okay. Connie, you get the last word on fees.

CONNIE: I can't do it, your Honor. I'm sorry, I'm done. I can't say another word.

THE COURT: All right. I'll take this matter under advisement.

Connie was so insensitive and frantic during the hearing. The way she directly addressed Jody with stabbing insults and kept referring to Payshence as the "kid" crushed my heart. The demands on the court to disallow us our rights to be in the court room and to hire attorneys and to keep fighting was over the edge of professionalism. She is tired of doing this and it's showing up in her presentation. All I can say is *the Bi-otch has no class.*

NOVEMBER 17TH, 2017:   MEMORANDUM DECISION, Submitted by Judge Stanley

This matter came before the Court on November 6, 2017, in connection with intervenor Jody Rhorer's Motion for Amended Findings and for a New Trial and Kirk J's Motion for Attorney's Fees. On June 1, 2017, the Court issued a Memorandum Decision regarding Mr. Rhorer's Objection to Commissioner's Recommendation. The Decision was issued following a hearing held before the Court on May 10, 2017. Mr. Rhorer was represented at that hearing by counsel, Devin C. Kirk J was represented by counsel, Connie. Mr. Rhorer is now represented by new counsel, Danny P.

Mr. Rhorer's Motion for Amended Findings and for a New Trial asserts that his Objection to Commissioner's Recommendation and Verified Motion for Orders were "poorly written" and didn't represent his intent. According to Mr. Rhorer, contrary to the indications in the Court's Decision, he is not seeking a time-sharing arrangement with the minor child, but rather he is seeking to establish paternity and custody of PR. Mr. Rhorer asserts his belief that both the Commissioner and the Court have erred in determining that he lacked standing or that he desired to fully assert his parental rights. He reiterates that he has proceeded thus far with the intent of merely establishing parent-time in order to re-establish a relationship with PR until custody could be fully determined. Ultimately, Mr. Rhorer is asking this Court to reconsider its Decision, to permit him to rebut Kirk J's parental presumption and to move forward with a custody evaluation.

On April 17, 2015, Commissioner Bloom, the prior Commissioner in this matter, issued an Amended Recommendation and Order. In addressing the various Motions before her, she noted in Paragraph 23 that:

Intervenor is requesting that custody be established to him and that he be granted the right to say that he is the father of PR. Intervenor is seeking that he be re-established with PR. He asserts that he resided with PR for several years. He asserts he has a relationship with her and that the allegations of abuse and neglect against PR rise to the level he should be awarded the custody. Intervenor, again, is requesting that the court adjudicate him to be the natural and biological father of PR, that he be awarded custody or in the alternative that a custody evaluation should be performed and that he should be awarded interim parent-time.

Commissioner Bloom noted that both Kelly H and Kirk J objected to Mr. Rhorer's position, "asserting that Kirk J was adjudicated to be the father of PR in juvenile court and Mr. Rhorer doesn't have standing to seek this request. Commissioner Bloom undertook a standing analysis:

On the standing analysis, the court begins with the relevant statute Utah Code Annotated 78B-15-101 UUPA. That statute says that persons with standing are the child, the mother, the man whose paternity of the child is to be adjudicated, any support enforcement agency, authorized adoption agency or child placement agency, representative to act in another capacity, and intended parent.

Commissioner Bloom determined under the statute, only Kelly H and Kirk J can challenge parentage. Further, the Amended Recommendation states that while Kelly H had indicated in her Verified Petition for divorce that Kirk J was not the biological father of three of her children, she did not seek to rebut the presumption. Commissioner Bloom concluded that under the UUPA Kirk J has been adjudicated father and that the limitation of challenging the same from the court's read is closed. However, Commissioner Bloom indicated that this did not end her analysis because of the decision in R.P. c. K.S. In light of the potential constitutional implications raised in R.P., Commissioner Bloom reserved further consideration of the constitutionality issue if Mr. Rhorer could demonstrate an established relationship with the child.

Following Commissioner Bloom's recommendation, Commissioner Kase was assigned to the matter and addressed Mr. Rhorer's Motion seeking standing to pursue reunification with PR. In his Order on Standing of Intervenor and Denying Motion for Orders on December 21, 2016, Commissioner Kase effectively rejected the concept that a strict application of the UUPA, one which limits standing to husband and wife to the facts in this case, would be unconstitutional.

Although Mr. Rhorer's Objection to Commissioner Kase's Order was not timely filed, the Court entertained his Motion for Amendment of Judgement and Relief and accepted his Objection. To be clear, when this matter came before the Court for hearing on May 10, 2017, the only issue was Mr. Rhorer's challenge to Commissioner Kase's conclusion regarding the constitutional implications of the UUPA's standing limitations where Mr. Rhorer has alleged an established relationship with PR. Absent these constitutional considerations, the law of this case and the law in Utah has settled that the UUPA limits standing in this case to Kelly H and Kirk J.

Yet, neither Mr. Rhorer's written briefing nor his counsel's oral argument focused on this constitutional challenge. Instead, the Court finds that Mr. Rhorer accepted Kirk J's parental rights and reiterated that he was merely asking this Court to take judicial notice of the bond he had formed with PR and find it sufficient to enter into a "multiple relationship" of fathering.

Notably, Devin C's oral argument recognized that absent an established relationship which could have constitutional implications, Mr. Rhorer was barred by the statute from gaining standing. Nevertheless, Devin C did not mount a constitutional challenge to rebut Kirk J's parentage, but instead asked this Court to create a unique Order, different from any other, wherein Kirk J would remain the legal father of PR, and Mr. Rhorer would be able to develop a relationship with the child. Now, with different counsel, Mr. Rhorer shifts from the dual parentage model and instead seeks to revisit the statutory framework on the issue of who has standing to challenge a presumed father's paternity. He asserts that "the Court has overlooked the ability of the Intervenor to rebut the Respondent's parental presumption. Yet, as the foregoing procedural history of this case demonstrates, this issue has been repeatedly examined and Mr. Rhorer has been found to not have standing to seek to rebut the presumption of Kirk J's paternity. The Court sees no legal or factual basis to revisit or reconsider these decisions, particularly since Mr. Rhorer's current arguments were not the subject of his Objection to Commissioner Kase's recommendation and were not before the Court at the May 10th hearing.

Based on the foregoing, the Court concludes that Mr. Rhorer has not provided any legal or factual grounds for the Court to amend its Decision or to grant him a new hearing. Therefore, his Motion for Amended Findings and for a New Trial is denied. Next, the Court has considered Kirk J's Motion for attorney's fees. The Court determines that Mr. Rhorer's filings thus far do not evidence bad faith sufficient to award fees. However, going forward, the Court may be inclined to award fees if it finds repeated efforts to advance a meritless position. At this juncture, however, Kirk J's Motion for fees is denied.

When it comes to attorneys, they have their own ideas and strategies, and while you may think you are in charge, you really aren't. All you can do is trust that they really know their craft and the law. But in the end, they are just people and they make plenty of mistakes. But their mistakes are costly and can change the course of your life. Now, our only option was to file another objection to the Judge's ruling.

DECEMBER 4TH, 2017: MOTION TO SET ASIDE MEMORANDUM DECISION ENTERED ON NOVEMBER 14, 2017, & CONSTITUTIONAL CHALLENGE PURSUANT TO RULE 24(d), Filed by Danny P, Judge Stanley presiding

Intervenor, Jody Rhorer, by and through counsel of record, hereby files this Motion to Set Aside Memorandum Decision entered on November 14, 2017, and Constitutional Challenge pursuant to Rule 24(d). Intervenor files his Motion to Set Aside pursuant to Utah Rules 60(b)(6) of the Utah Rules of Civil Procedures.

FACTS

1. Kelly H and Kirk J separated in 2005. Amended Recommendation and Order Findings (Feb. 20, 2015): Motion for Amended Findings, p. 14.
2. PR was born in 2007. Amended Recommendation and Order Findings (Feb. 20, 2015).
3. Intervenor has tested with 99.99% certainty to be the biological father of the child.
4. Intervenor and Kelly H lived together for a time. Amended Recommendation and Order Findings (Feb. 20, 2015).
5. Intervenor lived with PR from the time she was born until she was approximately 3 years old. Affidavit in support of motions filed on December 9, 2013.
6. Intervenor lived with PR for several years. Amended Recommendation and Order Findings (Feb. 20, 2015).
7. PR was taken away from Intervenor over his objection. Objection to Commissioner's Recommendation at p. 8.
8. On August 28th, 2009, Intervenor filed a motion for a decree of parentage in the West Jordan Court. Amended Recommendation and Order Findings 22(d)(Feb. 20, 2015).
9. There is no evidence that is before the court that PR lived with Kirk J until 2012.
10. An ORS complaint for child support against Kirk J was dismissed because genetic testing revealed he is not the biological father of PR. Amended Recommendation and Order Findings 22(g) (Feb. 20, 2015).

ARGUMENT

Pursuant to Rule 60(b)(6) of the Utah Rules of Civil Procedure, Intervenor requested that the Memorandum Decision entered on November 14, 2017, be set aside.

The Memorandum Decision entered on November 14, 2017, rules that the Intervenor had no standing to intervene in the present action based upon Utah Code 78B-15-607 based upon the fact that Petitioner was married at the time she became pregnant with the minor child in this matter. However, the statute is unconstitutional as it violates the Equal Protection Clause of the United States Constitution.

1. The Equal Protection Clause of United States Constitution Requires that Intervenor Have the Same Right as Kelly H to Establish the Paternity of PR because He Has an Established Relationship with PR and Because Kelly H Is Divorced from PR's Presumed Father.

As applied to Intervenor under the facts of this case, Utah Code Ann. Sec. 78B-15-607 (that "Statute") violates the Equal Protection Clause of the United State Constitution for two reasons. First, Kelly H's and Kirk J's divorce has frustrated the purpose of the Statute. Second, Intervenor and Kelly H are similarly situated with respect to PR. The United State Supreme Court recently had cause to explain the essence of the Equal Protection Clause in the context of gender-discriminatory laws:

For close to a half century, this Court has viewed with suspicion laws that rely   on over-broad generalizations about the different talents, capacities, or preference   of males and females. In particular, we have recognized that if a statutory objective is to exclude or protect members of one gender in reliance on fixed notions concerning [that gender's] roles and abilities, the objective itself is illegitimate. In accord with this eventual understanding, the Court has held that no important [governmental] interest is served by laws grounded...in the obsolescing view that unwed fathers [are] invariably less qualified and entitled than mothers to take responsibility of non-marital children. Overbroad generalizations of that order, the Court has come to comprehend, have a constraining impact, descriptive though they may be, of the way many people still order their lives. Laws according or denying benefits in reliance on stereotypes about woman's domestic roles, the Court has observed, may create a self-fulfilling cycle of discrimination that forces women to continue to assume the role of primary family caregiver. Correspondingly, such laws may dis-serve men who exercise responsibility for raising their children.

Sessions v. Morales-Santana, No. 15-1191, slip op. at 13-14 (U.S. June 12, 2017). This case squares with that final statement: Intervenor has exercised responsibility for raising his daughter. As will be explained below, (A) the Statute discriminates based on gender. Therefore, (B) the Statute is subject to heightened scrutiny, which requires the state to show that it has an important objective and that the means are substantially related to achieving that objective. (C) Because Kelly H and Kirk J are divorced, the State cannot show that Statute has an important objective in this case. Moreover, even if the State posts an important objective, (D) the Statute applied to Intervenor is not substantially related to achieving that objective because he and Kelly H are similarly situated in that they both have an established relationship with PR.

A. The Statute Contains Gender-Based Discrimination Because It Sets Forth Separate Rules for Mothers and Fathers.

The Statute prescribes one rule for mothers and another for fathers. Paternity of a child   conceived or born during a marriage with a presumed father, the mother, or a support enforcement agency at any time before filing an action for divorce or in the pleadings at the time of the divorce of the parents.

Utah Code Ann. 78B-15-601(1). Thus, when a child is born to a married mother, the Statute permits <u>every</u> mother to establish the paternity of her child. In contrast, the Statute <u>does not</u> permit every father to establish the paternity of his child. Namely, it only permits a "presumed father" to establish the paternity of his child:

A man is presumed to be the father of a child if: (a) he and the mother of the child are married to each other and the child is born during the marriage;

(b) he and the mother of the child were married to each other and the child is born within 300 days after the marriage is terminated by death, annulment, declaration of invalidity, or divorce, or after a decree of separate.

(c) before the birth of the child, he and the mother of the child's marriage to each other is declared invalid, and the child is born during the invalid marriage or within 300 days after its termination by death, annulment, declaration of invalidity, or divorce, or after a decree of separation....

B. Because it Discriminates Based on Gender, The Statute Is Subject to Heightened Scrutiny

The standard for analyzing whether a gender-discriminatory statute violates the Equal Protection Clause of the Constitution is settled: it is subject to "heightened scrutiny." This means that "the defender of legislation that differentiates on the basis of gender must show 'at least that the challenged classification serves important governmental objectives and that the discriminatory means employed are substantially related to the achievement of those objectives."

Moreover, "successful defense of legislation that differentiates on the basis of gender…requires an exceedingly persuasive justification." As applied to Intervenor, the Statute does not serve an important governmental objective because Kelly H and Kirk J are divorced. Moreover, even if the State could identify an important governmental objective existed, the gender-based discrimination is not related to achieving such objective because Intervenor and Kelly H are similarly situated in that they both have an established relationship with PR.

C. Because Kelly H and Kirk J Are Divorced, the State Does Not Have an Important Interest in Encouraging Them to Stay Married and Raise PR in an Intact Marriage.

In Caban v. Mohammed, the US Supreme Court determined a statute's governmental objective to relying on a New York Court of Appeals decision interpreted the New York statute. Therefore, it is appropriate to rely on the Utah Code of Appeals' interpretation of the Statute to determine its governmental objective. The Utah Court of Appeals had occasion to determine the Utah Legislature's intent in drafting the Statute in the 2014 case R.P. v. K.S.W. The court concluded that the Statute "reflects the Utah Legislature's intent to encourage a presumed father to stay married to the mother and to raise the child in an intact marriage. However, that intent is frustrated when a divorce has occurred, as an "intact marriage" no longer exists. Indeed, the Utah Court of Appeals appeared to recognize this discrepancy when it stated (in the very next sentence, no less) that "<u>unless the couple decides to seek a divorce,</u> section 607 limited the persons with standing to raise the paternity of the child to the presumed father and mother." ("We express no opinion on the issue of who has standing once a petition for divorce has been filed.") "Conferring standing to challenge the child's paternity only on the presumed father and the mother, <u>so long as they are committed to remaining married,</u> protects the marriage, the child, and the child's relationship with the presumed father from disruptive attacks by third parties."

Here, Kelly H and Kirk J are divorced, so the purpose of the Statute has been frustrated. Therefore, the gender discrimination contained serves no "important governmental objective" whatsoever in this set of facts. As a result, the Statute as applied to Intervenor violates the Equal Protection Clause by failing to satisfy the first prong of heightened scrutiny.

D. Even if the State Can Identify an Important Governmental Objective, the Statute Will Not Be Substantially Related to that Objective Because the Statute Ignores the Fact that Intervenor Has an Established Relationship with PR.

For the sake of argument, if the State is able to identify an alternative, "important governmental objective," the Statute as applied to Intervenor will still violate the Equal Protection Clause because it ignores the fact that he and Kelly are similarly situated in that they both have an established relationship with PR. The State will likely argue that the Statute's alternative "important governmental objective" is to ensure the welfare of children born out of wedlock to married mothers. If the state success in establishing this (or a similar) "important governmental objective," then the Statute applied to Intervenor violates the Equal Protection Clause because it substitutes gender for a fact-based determination of which parent will bear more love, affection, and concern toward the child.

In Caban v. Mohammed and Lehr v. Robertson, the United States Supreme Court outlined the boundaries of the Equal Protection Clause with respect to adoption statutes treatment of unwed fathers: "Statutes may not constitutionally be applied in that class of cases where the mother and father are in fact similarly situated with regards to their relationship to the child." In Caban, the statute at issue granted an unwed mother (but not an unwed father) the right to withhold consent to an adoption. In that case, the father, mother and two children had lived together as a family for two years, and both the father and mother participated in the care and support of their children. Thus, the Court determined that there was no reason to believe that the mother's relationship with the children involved more affection or concern than the father's relationship with the children. As a result, the Court held that the statute did not bear a substantial relationship to an important state interest because it "both excluded some loving fathers from full participation in the decision whether their children will be adopted and, **enabled some alienated mothers arbitrarily to cut off the paternal rights of fathers.**

In contrast, the mother and father in Lehr were not similarly situated, as the father "never established any custodial, personal, or financial relationship" with his daughter. Thus, because the parents in Lehr were not similarly situated, the Court held that "the Equal Protection Clause does not prevent a State from according the two parents different legal rights. In this case, the only distinction between Intervenor and Kelly H is their gender. Like the father and mother in Caban, they both lived together with PR as a family unit for three years. Like the father and mother in Caban, Intervenor and Kelly H both participated in the care and support of their children. Moreover, unlike the father in Lehr, Intervenor has an established personal and financial relationship with PR, and he has attempted to establish custody of her, too. Thus, Intervenor and Kelly H are similarly situated, so the Equal Protection Clause prevents the state from distinguishing who can and cannot establish paternity based on gender.

CONCLUSION

The Statute discriminates based on gender because when a child is born to a married mother it permits every mother - but only some fathers - to establish the paternity of the child. Gender-based discrimination is subject to heightened scrutiny. The Statute failed the first prong of the heightened scrutiny inquiry because its judicially determined purpose of preserving the marriage is frustrated because Kelly H and Kirk J are divorced. Moreover, even if the State establishes an alternative important state objective for the Statute, the statute's discriminatory means cannot be substantially related to that objective because Intervenor and Kelly H are similarly situated in that they both have an established relationship with PR. Therefore, as applied to Intervenor here, the Statute violates the Equal Protection Clause.

DECEMBER 13TH, 2017: KIRK J'S OPPOSITION TO MOTION TO SET ASIDE MEMORANDUM DECISION/AND "CONSTITUTIONAL CHALLENGE" PURSUANT TO RULE 24(d), Filed by Connie C, Judge Stanley presiding

Comes now, Connie C, on behalf of Kirk J, and files the foregoing Opposition to Mr. Rhorer's Motion to Set Aside Memorandum Decision on November 14th, 2017, and "Constitutional Challenge Pursuant to Rule 24(d). Grounds and reasons are as follows:

Before outlining his "Constitutional Challenge" Intervenor invokes Rule 60(b)(6) of the Utah Rules of Civil Procedure in support of his Motion to Set Aside the Memorandum Decision entered by this Court. Intervenor fails to advance any argument or offer any analysis as to how Rule 60(b)(6) would permit the Motion to Set Aside. It is important to note the preface to the Rule is, "Mistakes, inadvertence, excusable neglect, newly discovered evidence, fraud, etc." Rule 60(b), U.R.Civ.P.

"On motion and upon just arms, the court may relieve a party or its legal representative from a judgment, order, or preceding for the following reasons: any other reason that justified relief." Rule 60(b)(6). The Motion supplies **no** reason to set aside the Memorandum Decision, let alone one that justifies setting aside the Memorandum Decision. Intervenor simply interposes an argument that for the most part, has never been raised, a Constitutional challenge to the statute.

Interestingly, while present counsel for Mr. Rhorer approached his "last bite" at this apple by suggesting prior counsel, Devin C, was incompetent for not having presented proper arguments or advancing Mr. Rhorer's interests, no excuse is given in the present iteration of the Motion to Set Aside as to why present counsel didn't raise this "Constitutional Challenge" before the last hearing. The Utah Uniform Parentage Act is not new. The cases cited by Mr. Rhorer are not new. Certainly, the Equal Protection Clause is not new. Counsel would've known that Kelly H and Mr. Rhorer were of different genders before the hearing that resulted in the Memorandum Decision. There presumably is no excuse for not having raised this "Constitutional Challenge" until after the issuance of the Memorandum Decision.

*In any event, Rule 60(b)(6) places the burden on the Intervenor to demonstrate "any other reason that justifies" setting aside the Memorandum Decision. Because Mr. Rhorer has failed to advance **any reason** to justify setting aside the Memorandum Decision, this Court must deny the Motion.*

Connie was losing steam. This was, by far, the shortest memorandum she had written - far from the lengthy animated motions full of far-fetched exaggerations. She didn't even touch on the subjects of Equal Protection and Constitutional Rights, other than to say it was too late to bring it up now and we should have thought that one out long ago. Ah, but we had. Nancy S brought this up in many of her motions from the very beginning of the case. Devin C referenced it but never expanded on it because he already felt Commissioner Bloom had ruled on it in Jody's favor - he just couldn't get Kase or Stanley to see it that way, and, since they refused to review the important details of the case in it's entirety and instead requested to be merely being "brought up to speed," these very important claims were ignored.

And oddly enough, Connie brought up her buddy, Cam, once again in her motion for attorney fees - a completely irrelevant detail that lead to nothing, other than her anger that a chance to insert yet more control in this case through her friend was lost. She also bashed Danny for filing his motion to appeal on the final day of the deadline - something she is notorious for doing. You can count on Connie waiting to file nearly every response on the latest date to do so, and also requesting extensions when she did not get her work done timely. She also employed numerous stall tactics by simply ignoring our counsel's phone calls, emails, requests, etc., or inferring she had never received any of these communications. Connie is so quick to point out the very deeds she is most guilty of conducting.

DECEMBER 13TH, 2017: MOTION FOR ATTORNEYS FEES, filed by Connie C, Judge Stanley presiding
Comes now, Connie C, Attorney at Law, and files the foregoing Motion for Attorney's Fees.

Counsel filed a Motion for attorney's fees related to Mr. Rhorer's last pleading, which was a Motion to amend Findings and for a New Trial, which was filed August 29th, 2017. That pleading was filed by Danny P on behalf of Mr. Rhorer. Before that filing, another attorney had entered appearance for Mr. Rhorer June 29th, 2017, and immediately filed a Motion to Enlarge the time for filing a "post judgement motion." A stipulation to that enlargement of time was provided as a courtesy to that attorney. However, she was replaced, and the Motion filed by Danny P, as outlined above.

Before that attorney entered for Mr. Rhorer, Devin C filed a motion to Amend the Commissioner's Order, February 10th, 2017, and objections to the Commissioner's Order, which was allowed despite the fact that it was untimely filed. Therefore, Mr. Rhorer has had three bites at the apple regarding post-judgement motions. Each filing has caused delay as well, with another attorney entering appearance, then Danny P filing on what appears to undersigned to be the deadline for filing a Notice of Appeal, thus interjecting delay in the finality of this Court's Judgement.

The Memorandum Decision Order filed November 14th, 2017, denied undersigned's Motion for Attorney's Fees, but indicated the Court would consider it for any subsequent filing by Mr. Rhorer. Accordingly, Mr. Rhorer was on notice that the Court would consider such a Motion pertaining to post-judgement relief. It is procedurally deficient in that it does not articulate any cause as to why this Court should Set Aside the Memorandum Decision to permit a Constitutional Challenge which could have been filed before.

As undersigned argued at the hearing related to the last post-judgement Motion, it appears Mr. Rhorer will never stop filing such motions. The record of this matter in 2017 alone demonstrates that his filings are so numerous as to suggest vexatious litigation. Additionally, as outlined at the hearing, Kirk J believes that these constant challenges in the trial Court are interposed in an attempt to "out gun" him by superior financial resources. The number, timing, and procedural deficiencies in the pleadings suggest improper purpose, and constitute bad faith, thus justifying an award of attorney's fees. Counsel has intentionally not responded to the substance of the Constitutional Challenge in a deliberate attempt to mitigate the amount of fees. However, because there is no justification for interposition of a Constitutional Challenge post-judgement, and because this is now a third post-judgement motion in the past year, the award of fees is not only appropriate, but in counsel's view, necessary as a remedial measure.

WHEREFORE, Counsel prays the Court issue it's Order that the award of attorney fees is granted, and that the Court accept an affidavit of fees, and that Judgement be issued for a reasonable amount of fees to respond to this Motion.

2018

Another Christmas has come and gone. Before that, another Thanksgiving, and before that another Halloween. I often check Facebook to see if Kelly or any of her family members or Payshence's captors have posted photos of her - alas nothing. But Payshence has started her own profile. In fact, she has started four. She doesn't seem to know how to get back to her profile so she starts a new one. All her posts have been of her pretty little face and the caption says "me." She looks so sad. There was one post of a very scary looking dark monster-like face. It was set as her profile picture and the caption said "My Daddy." I presume this references Kirk J.

David said instead of moving on to the court of appeals that he needed to focus more on the Constitutional side of the case. Apparently, you cannot bring up new information at the appellate level, he needed to brief the Constitutional challenge first in front of Judge Stanley or he would not be able to bring it up in appellate court. He said that the judge was basically "winking" at him in his rulings and begging for the Constitutional argument to be presented.

In an article I read, it said the court of appeals has yet to have a father's rights case be presented in the State of Utah. I hope we are not the first. I pray Judge Stanley really is begging for the Constitutional challenge in our case and upon reading over his rulings, I do see many references to it. We now wait for the decision.

JANUARY 3RD, 2018: MEMORANDUM IN OPPOSITION OF MOTION FOR ATTORNEY FEES, submitted by Danny P, Judge Stanley presiding

Intervenor, Jody Rhorer, by and through counsel of record, hereby files this Memorandum in Opposition of Motion for Attorney Fees. Respondent requests attorney fees in this matter. However, if the Court's ruling on June 1, 2017, and on November 14, 2017, was to remain as the Order of the Court, the Respondent lacks standing in this matter. As a result, the Respondent is nonparty to this Case. Certainly, the Respondent submits over 4 pages of defamatory statements and factual disputes that are simply untrue. Intervenor doesn't believe it is productive and/or helpful to unnecessarily increase attorney fees by arguing over defamatory accusations which are irrelevant. At the end of the day, it is undisputed that the Intervenor is the biological father in this matter. The Intervenor is merely seeking to protect his Constitutional rights. Furthermore, it is also in the child's best interest of this Court to make a fair determination as to whether it is recognizing the Intervenor's relationship with his daughter. Therefore, there is absolutely no basis of this Court to award attorney fees.

Furthermore, the Respondent's Counsel stated to the Court that she is not charging the Respondent attorney fees in this matter. Utah Rules of Civil Procedure 73 requires that a party submit an affidavit that outlines the following:

(b) An affidavit supporting a request for or augmentation of attorney fees shall set forth; (b)(1) the basis for the award; (b)(2) a reasonably detailed description of the time spent and work performed, including for each item of work the name, position (such as attorney, paralegal, administrative assistant, etc.) and hourly rate of the work performed; (b)(3) factors showing the reasonableness of the fees; (b)(4) the amount of attorney fees previously awarded; and (b)(5) if the affidavit is in support of attorney fees for services rendered an assignee or a debt collector, the terms of any agreement for sharing the fee and a statement that the attorney is not sharing the fee or any portion there of in violation of Rule of Professional Conduct 5.4.UT R. Civ. P. 73

The Respondent fails to cite a need for the Intervenor to pay his attorney fees and simply suggests that attorney fees be granted as a sanction and not as a need pursuant to Utah Rules of Civil Procedure 73. Based upon the foregoing, the Motion for Attorney fees should be denied.

JANUARY 3RD, 2018: REPLY MEMORANDUM IN SUPPORT OF MOTION TO SET ASIDE MEMORANDUM DECISION ENTERED ON NOVEMBER 14, 2017, & CONSTITUTIONAL CHALLENGE PURSUANT TO RULE 24(d), submitted by Danny P, Judge Stanley presiding

Intervenor, Jody Rhorer, by and through counsel of record, hereby files this Reply Memorandum in Support of Motion to Set Aside Memorandum Decision entered on November 14, 2017, and Constitutional Challenge pursuant to Rule 24(d). Intervenor filed his Motion to Set Aside pursuant to Utah Rules 60(b)(6) of the Utah Rules of Civil Procedure.

Pursuant to Rule 60(b)(6), "On motion and upon just terms, the court may relieve a party or its legal representative from a judgment, order, or proceeding for the following reasons…(b)(6) any other reason that justifies relief." The reason as to why the Intervenor filed the Motion to Set Aside as the Court based its decision from Utah Code Ann. 78B-15-607, which is unconstitutional as it violates the Equal Protection Clause of the United States Constitution. The Motion is properly before the Court. Intervenor previously raised Constitutional Challenges to Utah Code Ann 78B-15-607, but the Court denied to address the Constitutional Challenges based upon Intervenor's failure to notify the State of Utah. Pursuant to Utah Rule of Civil Procedure 24(d)(3), "Failure of a party to provide notice as required by this rule is not a waiver of any constitutional challenge otherwise timely asserted." Based upon the foregoing, the Intervenor's Motion to set Aside is proper and should be addressed by the Court.

ARGUMENT

Respondent in his Memorandum in Opposition fails to address any of the Intervenor's arguments as to whether 78B-15-607 is unconstitutional. The Statute violates the Equal Protective Clause of the United States Constitution as addressed by the United States Supreme Court in Sessions v. Morales-Santana, June 12, 2017. The standard for analyzing whether a gender-discriminatory statute violates the Equal Protective Clause of the Constitution is settled: it is subject to "heightened scrutiny." This means that "the defender of legislation that differentiates on the basis of gender must show at least that the challenged classification serves important governmental objectives and that the discriminatory means employed are substantially related to the achievement of those objectives," (quoting United States v. Virginia 1996). The Respondent fails to address that the Statute does not serve an "important governmental objective." Therefore, the Court should find that Utah Code violates the Equal Protective Clause of the US Constitution.

CONCLUSION

The Statute discriminates based on gender because, when a child is born to a married mother, it permits every mother - but only some fathers - to establish the paternity of the child. Gender-based discrimination is subject to heightened scrutiny. The Statute fails the first prong of the heightened scrutiny inquiry because its judicially determined purpose of preserving the marriage is frustrated because Kelly H and Kirk J are divorced. Moreover, even if the State establishes an alternative important state objective for the Statute, the Statute's discriminatory means cannot be substantially related to that objective because Intervenor and Kelly H are similarly situated in that they both have an established relationship with PR. As applied to Intervenor here, the Statute violates the Equal Protection Clause and the Court's Memorandum Decision entered on November 14, 2017, should be set aside as it is unconstitutional.

JANUARY 3RD, 2018:   MOTION TO SET ASIDE MEMORANDUM DECISION ENTERED ON NOVEMBER 14, 2017, CONSTITUTIONAL CHALLENGE PURSUANT TO RULE 24(d), submitted by Danny P, Judge Stanley presiding

Intervenor, Jody Rhorer, by and through counsel of record, hereby files this Notice to Submit Motion to Set Aside memorandum Decision entered on November 14, 2017, and Constitutional Challenge pursuant to Rule 24(d). Intervenor filed his motion on December 11, 2017. Respondent filed his Memorandum in Opposition on December 13, 2017. Petitioner failed to file an Opposition to the Motion. The State of Utah failed to intervene after being served by US Mail. Intervenor filed his reply on January 3, 2018. Pursuant to Utah Rules of Civil Procedure 7 and 24, the Intervenor's Motion is ready to be submitted for decision.

JANUARY 25TH, 2018: EMAIL from Danny P

Here is the ruling, he refused to even address the Constitutional arguments. Let me know if you want me to file an appeal. Danny P, PPLC

FEBRUARY 3RD, 2018: RULING by Judge Stanley

The Court has before it a request for decision filed by the Intervenor, Jody Rhorer, seeking a ruling on his Motion to Set Aside Memorandum Decision Entered on November 14, 2017, and Constitutional Challenge Pursuant to Rule 24(d). Also pending is a Motion for Attorney's Fees filed by Connie, counsel for the respondent. This Motion has been fully briefed and has been considered by the Court. The Court ruled on both the Motion to Set Aside and the Motion for Attorney's Fees as stated herein.

Mr. Rhorer's Motion to Set Aside invokes Rule 60(b)(6) of the Utah Rules of Civil Procedure in seeking to set aside this Court's Memorandum Decision dated November 14, 2017. However, other than referencing Rule 60(b)(6), Mr. Rhorer does not provide any legal or factual basis for relief under the residuary clause of Rule 60(b). Specifically, in Laub v. South Central Utah Tel. Ass'n, 657 P.2d 1304, 1306-07 (Utah 1982), the Utah Supreme Court indicated that Subparagraph (6) has three requirements: "First, that the reason be one other than those listed in sub[paragraph] (1) through (5); second that the reason justify relief; and third, that the motion be made within a reasonable time." The court also reiterated that Rule 60(b)(6), "should be very cautiously and sparingly invoked by the Court only in unusual and exceptional circumstances."

Mr. Rhorer's Motion ignores the structure of Rule 60(b), fails to identify a reason justifying relief other than those listed in the remaining subparagraphs of Rule 60(b)(6) and, in general, fails to articulate the specific circumstances, let alone the exceptional circumstances, required to justify relief under Rule 60(b)(6). Rather, it appears that Mr. Rhorer is seeking Rule 60(b)(6) relief simply to advance an entirely new legal argument, one that could have been raised and preserved during the multiple instances when the Court and the Commissioners considered the issue of who has standing to challenge a presumed father's paternity under the UUPA.

Further, in order for Mr. Rhorer's present Motion to be placed in its proper procedural context, it is useful to revisit the recent procedural history of this case. Following the December 21, 2016, entry of the Order on Standing of Intervenor and Denying Motion for Orders, Mr. Rhorer, through his then-counsel Devin C, filed a series of Motions premised on Rule 59 and Rule 60 seeking to set aside, amend or otherwise modify rulings and recommendations determining that he didn't have standing to assert a claim of parentage contrary to the provisions of Utah Code 78B-15-607. During this time period, he also filed an Objection to Commissioner's Recommendations, which the court accepted and heard on May 10, 2017. The Court issued a Memorandum on June 1, 2017, denying Mr. Rhorer's Objection and confirming that he did not have standing to challenge the respondent's status as presumed father.

Following the entry of the Court's June 1, 2017, Memorandum Decision, Devin C withdrew as Mr. Rhorer's counsel and Danny P entered his appearance. Shortly thereafter, Danny P filed a Motion for Amended Findings and for a New Trial. This Motion came before the Court for hearing on November 6, 2017, and resulted in the entry of the Court's Memorandum Decision on November 14, 2017. Once again, in this Memorandum Decision, the Court confirmed that Mr. Rhorer didn't have standing to rebut the presumption of the respondent's paternity. On Dec. 12, 2017, Rhorer filed his presently pending Motion to Set Aside Memorandum Decision.

The procedural history paints a picture of Mr. Rhorer filing recurring motions seeking to set aside or reconsider rulings and re-litigate issues which have been decided. A dissatisfied litigant employing the continual tactic of filing successive post-judgement motions, through different counsel, can be viewed as an abuse of the judicial process and resulted in the Court cautioning Mr. Rhorer that attorney's fees may be awarded if the Court were to find repeated efforts to advance a meritless position.

In his most recent Motion, Mr. Rhorer once again seeks to set aside this Court's ruling, this time based on the argument that the UUPA violates the Equal Protection Clause of the United States Constitution. Yet, this is an argument which he clearly could have asserted when he appeared before Commissioner Bloom in requesting that the Court adjudicates him the natural and biological father of PR. He could have also raised this argument when he appeared before Commissioner Kase in seeking standing to pursue reunification with PR. During each of these proceedings and when he ultimately came before the undersigned Judge, he could have, but failed, to assert this position.

Indeed, in its June 1, 2017, Memorandum Decision, this Court analyzed the statutory framework of the UUPA and noted that while Mr. Rhorer argued in passing that Utah Code Annotated 78B-15-607 was unconstitutional, he failed to brief his theories and failed to give the Attorney General notice of any constitutional challenge. In his current Motion, Mr. Rhorer does not explain these prior lapses or provide any justification for reexamining standing based on a newly formulated equal protection theory. Ultimately, Mr. Rhorer has not adequately shown a basis for relief under Rule 60(b)(6).

Accordingly, the Court determines that Mr. Rhorer's Motion to Set Aside is not well-taken and is therefore denied. Further, given the procedural history outlined above, the Court has given serious consideration to Connie's request for attorney's fees. However, Connie does not invoke Utah's bad faith attorney fee statute, Utah Code Annotated 78B-5-825, nor is she seeking Rule 11 sanctions. While referencing "bad faith" and "vexatious litigation," Connie's Motion for Attorney's Fees does not identify the precise legal grounds pursuant to which the Court could award fees. Further, the Court's own legal analysis of the attorney's fee issue indicates that 78B-5-825 does not provide a basis for awarding attorney's fees based on a frivolous motion. The plain language expressly limits the award of attorney fees to situations where a party prevails with regard to an 'action' which by its plain language applies to 'actions' does not authorize the court's award of attorney fees based on a motion. Further, since Connie did not comply with the requirements of Rule 11, the Court cannot award fees under this Rule.

Finally, the Court could find no specific legal authority for awarding fees as a sanction for vexatious litigation. In addition, where Rule 11 would appear to be the more appropriate vehicle for evaluating whether fees should be imposed, it is not clear that the principles of vexatious litigation would even come into play. Nevertheless, since the Court has previously cautioned Mr. Rhorer, further filings akin to those identified above, could result in the imposition of Rule 11 sanctions, presuming that the requirements of the Rule were met. At this juncture, however, the Court denies Connie's Motion for Attorney's Fees.

All the winking must have resulted from the judge having something in his eye - like a beam, or a stye, or a mote. Is there some silent rule amongst the commissioner and judges that no matter what, they will uphold what the underlings decide at all costs? Or that they just don't want to stir the pot, change what has transpired, make ripples? As Commissioner Kase eluded to, "It's been so long we should just leave it the way it is." Every step, every effort, all hopes, squashed again.

FEBRUARY 13TH, 2018: NOTICE OF APPEAL Submitted by Danny P

Notice is hereby given that Intervenor and Appellant, Jody Rhorer, appeals to the Utah Court of Appeals the Minute Entry entered on January 25, 2018, Memorandum Decision entered on November 14, 2017, Memorandum Decision entered on June 1, 2017, and Order on Standing of Intervenor and Denying Motion for Orders entered on December 21, 2017.

Utah Court of Appeals

February 20, 2018   RE: Kelly H v. Kirk J
Dear Danny P:
Please be advised that the notice of appeal in this case has been filed with the Utah Court of Appeals. The case number has been assigned and should be indicated on any future filings or correspondence.

Contrary to the court's current practice, briefing set on cases after January 1, 2018, third extensions for the filing of briefs will ordinarily not be granted. And in all cases when a brief is filed beyond the time permitted by the court, the court, on its own motion, will not hear oral argument from that party.

The trial court has advised this court that the notice of appeal was filed without the payment of the posting of the $300.00 cost bond. Please be advised that the cost bond must be paid to the trial court, and a copy of the trial court receipt evidencing the payment, must be submitted to this court **within ten days of the date of this letter. If evidence of payment of the filing fee and cost bond is not received by this court within such time period, the appeal will be submitted for dismissal.**

Rule 11(e)(1) of the Utah Rules of Appellate Procedure requires that, within ten days of the filing of the notice of appeal, appellant must submit a transcript request for such parts of the proceedings as the appellant deems necessary.

Please be aware that the court resolves appeals, including in domestic cases, in published decisions that are widely disseminated and available on the internet. If resolution of your appeal requires the court's consideration of sensitive information, that information may have to be included in the court's opinion in the course of explaining its decision. Please note, failure to perfect an appeal at any time during the appeal process may result in dismissal of the appeal.

Sincerely,
NB, Judicial Assistant, Utah Court of Appeals

So, we come to the end of all we can do at the District level of the court system. Five and a half years and over three thousand court documents, tens of thousands of dollars, and we are no closer to where we were when we started. We are told the appellate process can easily take another three to five years.

When Jody tries to explain what happened with the taking of Payshence to people, he often gets the response, "If it were my child, I would have gone and gotten her." There has never been a day when he hasn't wanted to get in his truck, drive to Kearns, Utah, and take back his baby. He has contemplated so many scenarios of what would happen if he was to take matters into his own hands instead of leaving it to the worthless court system, but all those roads lead to incarceration charges against him and he figured it would be best for everyone if he stayed on the outside because one day, Payshence will be with us. Eventually her heart will lead her back to her family as she will come to an age that nothing can come between them.

CHAPTER 19
TENDER MERCIES

MARCH 12TH, 2018: THE UTAH COURT OF APPEALS

Pursuant to Utah Code Ann. 78A-4-103(3) and rule 43 of the Utah Rules of Appellate Procedure, the Utah Court of Appeals, on its own motion and by the vote of four judges of the court, hereby certifies this matter over which the Court of Appeals has original appellate jurisdiction to the Utah Supreme Court for original appellate review and determination.

The appeal presented important questions of law that have not been, but should be, settled by the Utah Supreme Court, specifically (1) whether Utah Code section 78B-15-607(1) violated the Equal Protection Clause of the United States Constitution by limiting standing to challenge paternity of a child born during a marriage to the presumed father and the mother, and (2) whether the standing limitation in section 78B-15-607(1) apples where the mother and the presumed father are seeking a divorce.

IT IS HEREBY ORDERED *that this is certified to the Utah Supreme Court for original review and determination.*

I can hardly breathe. I thought this book was done as it would be years before we would move forward in the case, but not even a month and a half after Danny submitted our request to the Appellate Court, they rendered a decision in our favor on not just the constitutional factor, but the fact that Kirk and Kelly are divorced and the law should not apply in our case to exclude Jody in order to preserve their marriage.

Now we move on to the highest court in the state - the Utah Supreme Court. I cannot imagine that we will lose. There will be four judges hearing our case and there are several other cases that have the same subject matter that are in front of the Supreme Court right now as well. It has not been determined if they will hear all of them and then render a decision or render a decision on each as it comes in front of them.

Danny has said multiple times that this is most likely his only chance to go all the way to the United States Supreme Court, in the event we don't win at the State level, in the course of his career. None of us are expecting that to happen, however, as our case is so strong.

There is the very minuscule chance that Connie would appeal to the US Supreme Court but that would mean she would have to front all of the expenses of doing so and that is highly unlikely. I imagine she has been paying every court filing fee and any other court expense thus far as I'm certain Kirk refuses to put one dime of his money into this fight - he hasn't even shown up in the past two years of proceedings. Kelly, on the other hand, is often being spoken for by Connie in court, even though she doesn't represent her. Maybe she is pitching in in some way.

Danny's submission to the Supreme Court is 121 pages long. 51 pages are his brief and the remainder are exhibits from past hearings. While much of the brief contains material that has already been presented and is in this book multiple times over, there is a section regarding the UUPA that is extremely profound and I wish so much it would have been brought up earlier in the process. Perhaps if Nancy has spent more time studying the law instead of coming up with conspiracy theories, she would have discovered how grossly unjust the UUPA is in comparison with the rest of the United States.

UTAH Supreme Court SUMMARY OF ARGUMENT

The Utah Legislature adopted the Uniform Parentage Act in 2005 with several modifications that effectively rendered the enactment of the Utah Uniform Parentage Act as unconstitutional. Specifically, the Utah Legislature eliminated an unwed natural father's standing to challenge paternity of a child that was conceived and/or born during the marriage of a mother with another man.

1. THE UTAH LEGISLATURE'S DEVIATIONS FROM THE UNIFORM PARENTAGE ACT CREATED UNCONSTITUTIONAL PROVISIONS IN UTAH CODE ANN. 78B-15-202 and 78B-15-607

A. Utah's adoption of the Utah Uniform Parentage Act.

In 2005, the Utah Legislature adopted the (federal) Uniform Parentage Act (2002) as the Utah Uniform Parentage Act (UUPA). The UUPA was intended to establish procedures and limitations on who and when can file to establish parentage of a minor chid. The UUPA deviated from the Uniform Parentage Act specifically as it relates to this case in Utah Code Ann. 79B-15-202 and 78B-15-607.

1. Utah Code Ann. 78B-15-202.

As part of the UUPA, the Utah Legislature enacted Utah Code Ann. 78B-15-202(2008)78B-15-202. No discrimination based on marital status. A child born to parents who are not married to each other whose paternity has been determined under this chapter has the same rights under the law as a child born to parents who are married to each other.

Utah Code Ann. 78B-15-202 deviates significantly from the 2002 Uniform Parentage Act Section 202:

The 2017 revision to the Uniform Parentage Act essentially eliminates gender in defining a parent as illustrated in Section 202:

SECTION 202. NO DISCRIMINATION BASED ON MARITAL STATUS OF PARENT.

A parent-child relationship extends equally to every child and parent, regardless of the marital status of the parent.

The 2017 revision of the Uniform Parentage Act eliminates all gender-based classifications after the United States Supreme Court landmark ruling of Obergefell v. Hodges that overturned laws illegalizing same sex marriages violated the Equal Protection Clause of the Fourteenth Amendment. The Obergefell Court redefined heightened scrutiny in determining the constitutionality of statues that rely upon gender-based classification. Utah Code Ann. 78B-15-202 is subject to heightened scrutiny as the statute relies on gender-based classifications and outdated over-broad generalizations regarding an unwed father that have been deemed unconstitutional.

2. Utah Code Ann. 78B-15-607

As part of the Utah Legislature adoption of the UUPA, the Legislature enacted Utah Code Ann. 78B-15-607(1) (originally 78-45g-607).

(1) Paternity of a child conceived or born during a marriage with a presumed father   as in Subsection 78-45g-204(1)(a), (b), or (c), may be raised by the presumed father or the mother at any time prior to filing an action for divorce or in the pleadings at any time prior to filing an action for divorce or in the pleadings at the divorce of the parents.

In Comparison, Section 607 of Uniform Parentage Act (2002):

(a) Except as otherwise provided in subsection (b), a proceeding brought by a Presumed father, the mother, or another individual to adjudicate the parentage of a child having a presumed father must be commenced not later than two years after the birth of the child.

The Utah Legislature eliminated the language of "or another individual." Based upon the enactment of Utah Code Ann. 78B-15-607(1), Utah Courts have since ruled that natural fathers have no standing to challenge paternity if the child is conceived and/or born during the marriage of the mother to another man. In 2017, Code 78B-15-607 was amended to include "or a support enforcement agency" but failed to allow the natural father to challenge paternity.

The UUPA deviates from the Uniform Parentage Act by removing the languages included in the uniform act's framework that allowed "another individual" to challenge paternity with in the first two years of life thus limiting the ability of an unwed father to file a parentage action within the state of Utah even when it is undisputed, as in the present case, that the husband is not the father of the minor child. The removal of the procedure allowing "another individual" standing to file a parentage action discriminates unconstitutionally against unwed fathers simply based upon gender.

What is even more interesting, which reflects the nations reexamination of gender-based classifications and distinction, the 2017 Uniform Parentage Act completely revised Section 607 as follows:

(a) A proceeding to determine whether an alleged genetic parent who is not a presumed parent is a parent of a child may be commenced: (1) before the child becomes an adult; or (2) after the child becomes an adult, but only if the child initiates the proceeding.

Thus, the 2017 revision of the Uniform Parentage Act eliminates any constitutional arguments and any outdated over-broad generalizations regarding an unwed father. The revised Uniform Parentage Act allows a "genetic" parent to rebut the parental presumption at any time before the child turns 18.

B.   The Colorado Supreme Court found similar provisions contained in Utah Code Ann 78B-150607 to be unconstitutional.

In 1980, the Colorado Supreme Court in *R.McG v. JW*, found Colorado's Uniform Parentage Act that contained similar provisions in Utah Code Ann. 78B-15-607 violated equal protection. The issue on appeal in *R.McG* was whether Colorado's Uniform Parentage Act, "by not expressly granting a claiming natural father the right to bring an action for a determination of his paternity of a child born during the marriage of the natural mother to another, violates equal protection of the laws "under the federal and state constitutions."

The language of the statute in question is almost identical to the language used in 204 and 607. Section 19-6-107 of the Colorado UPA existing at the time, read as follows, "(1) a child, his natural mother, or a man presumed to be his father under section 19-6-105(1)(a) may bring an action: (a) At any time for the purpose of declaring the existence of the father and child relationship presumed under section 19-6-105(1)(a)."

Furthermore, a man is presumed to be the natural father of a child if he and the child's natural mother are to have been married to each other and the child is born during the marriage. The Colorado court ultimately concluded that the statute impermissibly denied *R.McG* the statutory capacity of standing on his gender and that it violated the Equal Protection Clause. The statute established an impermissible standard denying the unwed father the ability to pursue a declaration of paternity while allowing "the natural mother to undo the state's interest in preserving family stability" by filing a parentage action at any time during the marriage. "The statutory scheme denies the claiming natural father judicial access to establish a constitutionally significant relationship while simultaneously granting the natural mother practically unencumbered access to establish that same relationship if she so desires." The strict application of the Colorado statute, similar to 204 and 608, would result in cases where an unwed father who cared for the children for years would be unable to challenge the married mother or presumptive father for custody even if they had no relationship with the children.

C. Utah may be the only state that denies a natural father standing to parent his child when the child is born during the marriage of the mother to another person.

A careful review of the Uniform Parentage Act begs the question as to how many other states have enacted similar laws to Utah Code. Appellant has attempted to review most state's statutes regarding standing of an unwed natural father. Appellant is unable to find another state that denies a natural father standing when the child is born during the marriage of the mother to another person.

In **Arizona**, Appellant would be the presumed father. "A man is presumed to be the father of the child if...Genetic testing affirms at least a ninety-five percent probability of paternity."

Colorado allows "any interested party" the right to raise paternity. **Idaho** allows for the presumption of paternity to be overcome simply by genetic testing that shows husband is not the father. In **Montana**, Appellant would be the presumed father. "A person is presumed to be the natural father of a child if any of the following occur...the scientific evidence resulting from a blood test, whether ordered by a court or administrative agency of competent jurisdiction or agreed to by the parties, shows a 95% or higher statistical probability of paternity.

In **New Mexico**, Appellant would be the presumed father. "A man is presumed to be the father of a child if...for the first two years of the child's life, he resided in the same household with the child and openly held out the child as his own.

In **Nevada**, "an interested third party" may bring an action to establish paternity. Furthermore, Appellant would be the presumed father. "A man is presumed to be the natural father of a child if...He and the child's natural mother were cohabiting for at least 6 months before the period of conception and continued to cohabit during the period of conception."

Oklahoma allows "a proceeding brought by a presumed father, the mother, or another individual to adjudicate the parentage of a child having a presumed father shall be commenced not later than two years after the birth of the child." **Wyoming** allows "another individual" to challenge paternity.

While this is just a sampling of the surrounding states, Utah may be the only state that denies a natural father standing to challenge paternity of a child that is born during the marriage of the mother to another person. By the Utah Legislature denying standing to a natural father similarly situated as the Appellant, the Legislature has denied the natural father's their Fourteenth Amendment rights of Due Process and Equal Protection.

JUNE 20TH, 2018: JOURNAL ENTRY

Today I was in Salt Lake City showing homes and stopped at the Holiday gas station on 5600 South. As I came out of the restroom, I recognized the person standing in line at the cash register. It took me a minute before I realized that is was Kelly.

Approaching me on the left was Payshence. She was walking towards the soda machine - which I was standing in front of. I didn't know what to do. This was the first time I had seen her in person. It was as if I were looking into her Dad's blue eyes. She had Jody's flawless, tan skin. Her hair had been cut to her shoulders and she was wearing shorts and flip flops.

When she got within two feet of me, I simply said, "Hi Payshence."

She stopped abruptly and looked at me. She didn't speak or move she just starred with a look on her face that said - I know you, I'm not supposed to know you, but I know you.

I wanted to cry. I wanted to hug her and tell her how long I had been waiting for this moment and to take her hand and run to my car with her so I could take her home to her Daddy where she belongs. But that would be kidnapping, and only the State was allowed to legally kidnap a child from her real family.

"I'm your Dad's wife," I continued. She still didn't move or blink. She didn't know what to do as much as I didn't know what to do.

Our moment was broken by the scream of Kelly, "Payshence, get over here! Get over here!" She had seen me and she was in a panic.

Payshence didn't argue. She didn't say, "But mom, I didn't get my soda yet," like a typical ten-year-old would have done in a normal situation. She knew something profound had taken place. She turned her body slowly towards her mom, but her gaze stayed on me.

"You're Daddy loves you, Payshence," I said. She said nothing but kept walking towards her mom. We never broke eye contact until Kelly grabbed her by the arm and pulled her hastily outside.

I found it interesting that Kelly did not move away from the convenient mart door, but instead waited for Payshence to come to her. Was she afraid to acknowledge me? Would she have to answer Payshence's questions if there were a confrontation? I happened to be parked right in front of the store and Kelly was parked at the gas pump directly behind me.

I was shaking so hard when I exited the mini mart that I hit the panic button on my car and set off the alarm. Payshence was standing near the gas pump, her gaze still locked on me. Kelly was fumbling with her phone and filling her car with fuel and not paying attention to what was going on around her. My car is a moving advertisement for my company. My company name, logo, and phone number are prevalent. I drove slowly past Payshence, hoping she would take note of my unforgettable vehicle (a Toyota FJ cruiser that looked like a giant bumble bee).

I watched her watch me for as long as I could before driving out of the parking lot.

GLOSSARY OF TERMS

- **Adjudicated:** Make a formal judgment or decision about a problem or disputed matter

- **AG:** Attorney General

- **AP:** Alleged Perpetrator

- **Bifurcated Divorce:** Divide into two

- **CJC:** Child Juvenile Center

- **CPS:** Child Protective Services

- **DCFS:** Department of Child and Family Services

- **DV:** Domestic Violence

- **Indigent:** Poor, destitute, needy person

- **ORS:** Office of Recovery Services

- **PGAL:** Private Guardian ad Litem

- **PO:** Probation Officer

- **Petitioner:** A person who makes a formal application to a court for a judicial action in a suite

- **Pro Se**: Representing oneself in court

- **Paternity:** The state or condition of being a father; the relationship of a father

- **Pro Bono:** Denoting work undertaken without charge; especially legal work for a client with a low income.

- **Respondent:** A defendant in a law suite

- **Res Judicata:** A matter that has been adjudicated by a competent court and may not be pursued further by the same parties

- **Acknowledged father:** A man who has established a father-child relationship.

- **Adjudicated father:** A man who has been adjudicated by a court of competent jurisdiction to be the father of a child.

- **Alleged father:** A man who alleges himself to be or is alleged to be the genetic father or a possible genetic father of a child, but whose paternity has not been determined.

- **Presumed father:** A man, who by operation of law under Section 204 of UPA (2000), is recognized as the father of the child until that status is rebutted or confirmed in a judicial proceeding.

- **Putative father:** The alleged or reputed father of a child born out of wedlock.

- **Uniform Parentage Act:** A landmark Act that was originally promulgated in 1973 and adopted by 19 states in full and in part by other states (most recent version was revised in 2000 and amended in 2002) by the National Conference of Commissioners on Uniform State Laws. One of its functions was to declare equality for parents and children regardless of the marital status of their parents.

UTAH CODE 78B-15-607:

(1) Paternity of a child conceived or born during a marriage with a presumed father, as described in Subsection 78B-15-204(1)(a), (b), or (c), may be raised by the presumed father, the mother, or a support enforcement agency at any time before filing an action for divorce or in the pleadings at the time of the divorce of the parents.

(a) If the issue is raised prior to the adjudication, genetic testing may be ordered by the tribunal in accordance with Section 78B-15-608. Failure of the mother of the child to appear for testing may result in an order allowing a motherless calculation of paternity. Failure of the mother to make the child available may not result in a determination that the presumed father is not the father, but shall allow for appropriate proceedings to compel the cooperation of the mother. If the question of paternity has been raised in the pleadings in a divorce and the tribunal addresses the issue and enters an order, the parties are estopped from raising the issue again, and the order of the tribunal may not be challenged on the basis of material mistake of fact.

(b) If the presumed father seeks to rebut the presumption of paternity, then denial of a motion seeking an order for genetic testing or a decision to disregard genetic testing results shall be based on a preponderance of the evidence.

(c) If the mother seeks to rebut the presumption of paternity, the mother has the burden to show by a preponderance of the evidence that it would be in the best interest of the child to disestablish the parent-child relationship.

(d) If a support enforcement agency seeks to rebut the presumption of parentage and the presumptive parent opposes the rebuttal, the agency's request shall be denied. Otherwise, the denial of the agency's motion seeking an order for genetic testing or a decision to disregard genetic test results shall be based on a preponderance of the evidence, taking into account the best interests of the child.

(2) For the presumption outside of marriage described in Subsection 78B-15-204(1)(d), the presumption may be rebutted at any time if the tribunal determines that the presumed father and the mother of the child neither cohabited nor engaged in sexual intercourse with each other during the probable time of conception.

(3) The presumption may be rebutted by: (a) genetic test results that exclude the presumed father;

(b) genetic test results that refutably identify another man as the father in accordance with Section 78B-15-505;

(c) evidence that the presumed father and the mother of the child neither cohabited nor engaged in sexual intercourse with each other during the probable time of conception; or (d) an adjudication under this part.

(4) There is no presumption to rebut if the presumed father was properly served and there has been a final adjudication of the issue.

UTAH CODE 78B-15-608: Authority to deny motion for genetic testing or disregard test results.

(1) In a proceeding to adjudicate the parentage of a child having a presumed father or to challenge the paternity of a child having a declarant father, the tribunal may deny a motion seeking an order for genetic testing of the mother, the child, and the presumed or declarant father, or if testing has been completed, the tribunal may disregard genetic test results that exclude the presumed or declarant father if the tribunal determines that:

(a) the conduct of the mother or the presumed or declarant father estops that party from denying parentage; and

(b) it would be inequitable to disrupt the father-child relationship between the child and the presumed or declarant father.

(2) In determining whether to deny a motion seeking an order for genetic testing or to disregard genetic test results under this section, the tribunal shall consider the best interest of the child, including the following factors;

(a) the length of time between the proceeding to adjudicate the parentage and the time that the presumed or declarant father was placed on notice that he might not be the genetic father;

b) the length of time during which the presumed or declarant father has assumed the role of father of the child;

(c) the facts surrounding the presumed or declarant father's discovery of his possible non paternity;

(d) the nature of the relationship between the child and the presumed or declarant father; (e) the age of the child;

(f) the harm that may result to the child if presumed or declared paternity is successfully disestablished;

(g) the nature of the relationship between the child and any alleged father; (h) the extent to which the passage of time reduces the chances of establishing the paternity of another man and a child-support obligation in favor of the child; and (i) other factors that may affect the equities arising from the disruption of the father-child relationship between the child and the presumed or declarant father or the chance of other harm to the child.

(3) If the tribunal denies a motion seeking an order for genetic testing or disregards genetic test results that exclude the presumed or declarant father, it shall issue an order adjudicating the presumed or declarant father to be the father of the child

7. Each party shall provide a hair follicle drug test to the new PGAL within two weeks.
has assumed the
 role of father of the child;
(c) the facts surrounding the presumed or declarant father's discovery of his possible non paternity;
(d) the nature of the relationship between the child and the presumed or declarant father;
(e) the age of the child;
(f) the harm that may result to the child if presumed or declared paternity is successfully disestablished;
(g) the nature of the relationship between the child and any alleged father;
(h) the extent to which the passage of time reduces the chances of establishing the paternity of another man and a child-support obligation in favor of the child; and
(i) other factors that may affect the equities arising from the disruption of the father-child relationship between the child and the presumed or declarant father or the chance
 of other harm to the child.
(3) If the tribunal denies a motion seeking an order for genetic testing or disregards genetic test results that exclude the presumed or declarant father, it shall issue an order adjudicating the presumed or declarant father to be the father of the child.